Stephen Dorril is a widely respected authority on the security and intelligence services. He has been a consultant for and appeared on a number of major television documentaries in Britain, France, Canada and Hungary. He is the author of several highly acclaimed books covering the activities of British Intelligence, most recently *MI6: Fifty Years of Special Operations*. He is a senior lecturer at Huddersfield University and lives in nearby Holmfirth with his wife and his dog, Roger.

STEPHEN DORRIL

Blackshirt

Sir Oswald Mosley and British Fascism

PENGUIN BOOKS

PENGUIN BOOKS

Published by the Penguin Group
Penguin Books Ltd, 80 Strand, London WC2R 0RL, England
Penguin Group (USA) Inc., 375 Hudson Street, New York, New York 10014, USA
Penguin Group (Canada), 90 Eglinton Avenue East, Suite 700, Toronto, Ontario, Canada M4P 2Y3
(a division of Pearson Penguin Canada Inc.)
Penguin Ireland, 25 St Stephen's Green, Dublin 2, Ireland
(a division of Penguin Books Ltd)
Penguin Group (Australia), 250 Camberwell Road, Camberwell, Victoria 3124, Australia
(a division of Pearson Australia Group Pty Ltd)
Penguin Books India Pvt Ltd, 11 Community Centre, Panchsheel Park, New Delhi – 110 017, India
Penguin Group (NZ), 67 Apollo Drive, Mairangi Bay, Auckland 1310, New Zealand
(a division of Pearson New Zealand Ltd)
Penguin Books (South Africa) (Pty) Ltd, 24 Sturdee Avenue, Rosebank, Johannesburg 2196, South Africa

Penguin Books Ltd, Registered Offices: 80 Strand, London WC2R 0RL, England

www.penguin.com

First published by Viking 2006
Published in Penguin Books 2007
2

Copyright © Stephen Dorril, 2006
All rights reserved

The moral right of the author has been asserted

Typeset by Rowland Phototypesetting Ltd, Bury St Edmunds, Suffolk
Printed in England by Clays Ltd, St Ives plc

ISBN: 978-0-140-25821-9

Contents

List of Illustrations

Section One
1. The Mosley family home, Rolleston Hall
2. Mosley's mother, Katherine Maud
3. Mosley's grandfather, Oswald
4. The seventeen-year-old Mosley joined the 16th Lancers on 1 October 1914
5. Ruins of the Cathedral and medieval Cloth Hall, Ypres, April 1915
6. Mosley in 1918
7. Mosley married Lord Curzon's daughter, Cynthia 'Cimmie' Curzon, on 11 May 1920 in the Chapel Royal, St James's Palace
8. The Mosleys on honeymoon at Portofino, near Genoa, 1920
9. In 1925 Cimmie's younger sister, 'Baba' (Lady Alexandra Curzon) married 'Fruity' Metcalfe, equerry to Edward, Prince of Wales
10. Cimmie's other sister, Lady Irene Curzon, 1923
11. Irene, Mosley's brother Ted and Mosley's father, Sir Oswald, at brother John's wedding in April 1924
12. Cimmie with Lionel Gable and Stewart Menzies, 1919
13. Mosley with Mrs Cole Porter, Venice, 1923
14. Mosley, Cimmie and his brother John at Antibes, 1927
15. Mosley's close friend, Bob Boothby, Isle de Marguerite, 1927
16. Mosley aquaplaning, 1927
17. Independent Labour Party school, 1926. Mosley with John Strachey and Fenner Brockway
18. Mosley and Cimmie at the Labour Party Conference, Blackpool, 1927
19. Savehay Farm in the village of Denham, Buckinghamshire
20. Labour Party leader Ramsay MacDonald at Savehay
21. Mosley canvassing for his wife in Stoke-on-Trent during the General Election, 1929
22. The New Party summer school at Denham, June 1931
23. New Party Chiefs, Denham, June 1931. *Left to right*, W.E.D. 'Bill' Allen, Robert Forgan, Cimmie, Mosley, John Strachey
24. Mosley, Venice, 1923

Illustration Acknowledgements

The author and publishers are most grateful to Nicholas Mosley for the use of his family photographs. Unless otherwise credited all the photographs are from the Mosley collection.

5, 34, 70, 71, Imperial War Museum; 38, 42, 45, 56, 57, 72, 73, 75, 79, Corbis; 46, 77, 78, 81; Popperfoto; 69, National Archives, Kew; 49, 50, 51, 61 from David Pryce-Jones: *Unity Mitford, A Quest*; 29 from Lewis Morton, *Ted Kid Lewis, his Life and Times*; 79, from F. P. Yockey, *The Enemy of Europe*; 62, Myles Eckersley; 68, McGuirk Hughes family; 52, Louise Gordon-Canning; 30, 39–41, 43–4, 47–8, 53–4, 58–9, 76 are from a BUF political pamphlet

Acknowledgements

I have a vivid memory of my first visit to London with my parents as an eight-year-old, during the summer of 1963. It was dark as we came out of Notting Hill tube station; here I saw two men in long trenchcoats selling a newspaper. For some reason I found them sinister and asked my mother who they were. She said, 'They are Mosley's men.' It meant little to me until the seventies when, undertaking independent research into the extreme right in Huddersfield, I came across the presence of Mosleyites in the area. In the small village where I live, just before the Second World War a member of the British Union of Fascists (BUF) used to run up the Union Jack in front of his house and march up and down the road in his jackboots and Blackshirt uniform. A neighbour told me that it seemed funny at the time, at least until the war came.

The tale of Mosley shows how thin is the line that exists between legitimate and respectable vote seeking, and what Ben Pimlott termed 'psychopathic rabble-rousing'. Mosley had been for much of his career 'very much part of the mainstream, the friend and ally of famous statesmen, and came perilously close to holding power'. Over the years, the image of Mosley, the Fascist leader attacking Jews in violent clashes, has softened and the idea of a new biography grew out of an awareness that a considerable volume of new material was being released to the National Archives in London, Belfast and Edinburgh. For the first time, use is made of files on Mosley from Germany, Italy and France, along with Freedom of Information Act records from the United States, Australia, Japan and Ireland.

When I read Robert Skidelsky's biography, published in 1975, I was deeply shocked by its sympathetic view of its subject and quite astonishing defence of Mosley's turn to Fascism and anti-Semitism. Nicholas Mosley's family-orientated account (1982–3) was published before the release of the Home Office's 'Mosley File'. Both books failed to shed light on the more mysterious and hidden aspects of Mosley's career: the attempts to influence the political establishment, the covert ties to both Fascist Italy and Nazi Germany, the radio project, the 'secret meetings' with Fascist fringe groups in 1939–40 and the creation of international neo-Fascist networks after 1945. Added to the role of the security services in the 1930s, Mosley's 'murky subterranean methods' represented an important aspect of his activities, which deserve attention.

This book grew out of a joint project with John Hope. My research, and studies in general of British Fascism, owe a great deal to John, whose ability to find sources outside the normal range of academic research opened up new channels of enquiry; he has not always been credited for his endeavours. I have benefited from long conversations with Bryan Clough, generous in sharing his own research, Kevin Coogan, Kirn Rattan (for access to his unpublished biography of John Amery), and Julian Putkowski and David Turner; both are models for other researchers with their attention to detail and ability to overturn accepted versions of history.

I would like to acknowledge the role of the leading expert on inter-war British Fascism, Richard Thurlow, at Sheffield University, in paving the way for studies in this field. The staff at the University's Special Collections archive on Fascism have been extremely helpful; research for this book will be placed with this archive. Academics specializing in this competitive area, including Dr G. T. Waddington, Colin Holmes, Professor David Marquand, Roger Griffin, Nick Hodson, Dr Alexander Prokopov (author of a Russian book on Mosley), Dr Eunan O'Halpin (for pointers to Irish documents), Peter Liddell (for access to an interview with Mosley) and in Australia, Barbara Pomienes-reski and Dr Andrew Moore, have been very co-operative. Dr David Rees provided many documents and his bibliography of British Fascism was invaluable. For reasons best known to themselves, two academics were deliberately uncooperative. In contrast, Dr Philip Coupland and Dr Graham Macklin were always enthusiastic about swapping information and discussing Mosley. I am grateful to Dr Keith Laybourn for reading sections dealing with the 1920s.

Some researchers in this field are wary of dealing with the Mosleyites, fearing 'contamination'. One or two have fallen for the Mosley line but not talking to such witnesses is disgraceful. The Friends of Mosley is split between those who want to keep Mosley's name alive and those who only deal with people sympathetic to his view. The late John Warburton was unfailingly co-operative in answering my enquiries, even though we disagreed on almost everything. I acknowledge David Irving's contribution in bringing to light a number of Italian documents. I would like to thank Michael Quill and John Wallader (for the loan of photographs), and two anonymous 'insiders' who knew Mosley in the fifties and sixties.

I would like to thank for their help Mrs Ian Hope-Dundas, Malcolm Fare, David Sylvester, David Pryce-Jones, Sally Lescher, John Pearson and his wife, Benjamin Wegg-Prosser, P. M. Luttman-Johnson, Michael Beaumont, Anne Wolrige Gordon, David Metcalfe, Sir Dudley Forwood, Peter Huxley-Blythe, Richard Cohen, Louise Gordon-Canning, Francis Beckett, Myles Eckersley, James Clark (for use of a photograph of Peter Eckersley), Michael Neal, A.

Baron, Nick Toczek, Larry O'Hara, Gerry Gable, J. Hancock, Nick Crowson and Daniel Hodson.

The federal archives in Germany were exceptionally efficient in dealing with requests for documents. I retrieved numerous files dealing with Mosley for the period 1933–6, but those for 1937–9 were taken to Moscow at the end of the war and have not been seen since. I received help from the Information Centre at the German embassy in London, Dr Ansgar at the Rundfunkarchiv, Dr Ritter and Herr Moser at the Bundesarchiv, Berlin, Karin Popp at the Institut für Zeitgeschichte, Munich, the Forschungsstelle für Zeitgeschichte, Hamburg, and Dr Grupp at the Auswartiges Amt in Bonn. Of particular importance was the translation work carried out by Alan Carey (German), Kazuo Ikegaya (Japanese) and Alfio Bernabei (Italian).

I am grateful for the help given by the staff at the Liddell Hart Centre at the London School of Economics, the Imperial War Museum, the National Archives at Kew, the National and the Military Archives, Dublin, the Public Record Office, Belfast, the Australian National Archives, the Franklin D. Roosevelt Library in Washington, the Military Intelligence Archives at Maryland, the Hoover Institute, California, Hull University Special Collections and the BBC archives. Help came from retired CIA officer Thomas T. Troy, who forced the release of documents from the National Archives, Washington, blocked by the British government, and Charles Higham and the Doheny Library at the USC Cinema-Television Library, Los Angeles. The Wiener Library in London, with its unique collection of anti-Fascist material, was a wonderful trip back into a pre-war Eric Ambler-style world. There was exceptional service from staff of Huddersfield Library. Formerly one of Britain's treasures, the library system is now falling apart due to lack of funds.

Nicholas Mosley (Lord Ravensdale) was wonderfully generous in allowing me to use many photographs that have never been seen before. I thank him for interviews and use of the Irene Ravensdale diaries.

There was only one moment of doubt. When shown German documents which made it plain that his father had planned an anti-Semitic campaign some years before previously thought, Nicholas said, 'Oh, I thought you would leave me something of my father.' He temporarily wavered in his co-operation but then allowed me to see the Diana/Sir Oswald Mosley archive at the Special Collections archive at Birmingham University before it was catalogued.

Unfortunately, almost all internal BUF documents have disappeared. Many records were hidden in a railway arch during the war and were lost when it was bombed. Others vanished, never to surface again when BUF members were arrested in 1940. Diana Mosley said that at Crowood there had been 'a lot of BUF records but I am unsure what happened to them. Some were lost with a fire at the house in Ireland after the war.'

Blackshirt finally reached the printed page with the enormous help of my agent Andrew Lownie, my long-suffering editor Eleo Gordon, my 'secretary' Linda Hamer, and my wife and sub-editor Stephanie. They have put up with so much.

Stephen Dorril
Netherthong, September 2005

Introduction

> to stand
> *As if a man were author of himself*
> *And I knew no other kin*
> William Shakespeare, *Coriolanus*

In the early 1970s, Sir Oswald Mosley asked his youngest brother, John, for the diaries of their mother, Lady Mosley. She had kept a diary for over fifty years and when she died in 1948 she left these to John. Mosley's second wife, Diana, recalled that John did not mind him taking the diaries which, initially, were 'hidden in a cupboard and forgotten about'. Then, seemingly on impulse, Mosley decided to dispose of them. They were taken out and burnt in the garden of their Paris home. Jerry, their chauffeur, 'did the deed. It wasn't a very brilliant idea,' recalled Diana. 'I begged and implored him not to. I thought it terrible of him. John had no idea that he intended to destroy them.'

According to Diana, the reason Mosley gave for their destruction was that 'books were becoming more and more personal. He believed investigative writers might use the diaries against him and his mother. OM thought that writers might regard his mother, whom he adored, as trivial. She was very devoted. She wasn't a brilliant person. Completely a country woman, not interested in ideas.' He felt protective towards her, as 'she wasn't as strong as she looked'.

Not all the diaries were burnt. Mosley kept back those to do with the first four years of his life, and one of a slightly later date which survived half scorched. He also tore out, and preserved, each entry for 2 January, his mother's birthday. According to Mosley's son, Nicholas, the remaining pages are testament to the emotional turmoil that beset this family – the 'quarrels, the separations, the lawsuits, the punch-ups'. Diana, however, challenged this version. She described the diaries as merely dull and domestic. In them were, however, details of the letters Mosley had written from school to his mother and from the front line during the First World War.

When interviewed in her Paris home, Diana said her husband, who was 'action-orientated', was 'always looking to the future and claimed not to be interested in the past. Not nostalgic, but – when it came to his memoirs he remembered it all very well.' She admitted that by burning the diaries he had hoped to cauterize certain memories. Diana agreed that Mosley was a secretive person. 'Not about his policies about which he was completely open. Nor his politics.' She admitted, however, there were areas which he considered closed and about which he refused to talk.

I

'Tommy'

Oswald Ernald Mosley was born in London on 16 November 1896. It was a difficult birth. His mother, twenty-one-year-old Katherine 'Maud' Heathcote, second in a family of three sisters and two brothers, had married the heir of Rolleston, Oswald Mosley, the year before. She wrote in her diary: 'infant Tommy began to arrive at 6.00 am and finished up after an awful 18 hours at 11.40 (nearly midnight).' Her own mother stayed all day and the family doctor, Sir John Williams, 'kept coming at intervals till 10.00 o'clock pm when he gave me chloroform and saw me through with it'. Aware the priority was to produce an heir, she underlined the entry: '*Thankful*. It's a boy.'

Maud's husband 'Waldie', a rake, gambler and heavy drinker, wrote 'endless wires' informing relatives of the grand event. On the following day he celebrated at the Derby. Maud was in a weak condition; Sir John ordered that she not see anyone except her mother. This suited a mostly absent Waldie. A month later Maud noted 'Tommy weighed 12 lb 2 oz' and, despite his size, added that the child was 'seemingly ill a lot'.

With a note of ambivalence, Mosley wrote in his autobiography that he was 'glad to know that I come from an old English and British family'. He added, 'there my interest ends.' He was always keen to have it known that he had achieved success through his own efforts, by his own creation. And yet, Mosley's account of his life is littered with references to his upbringing and positive images of his family heritage.

The Mosleys were never one of the great families of England but this was not through lack of money. Nicholas Mosley (1527–1612) was a prosperous merchant, with interests in woollen manufacture. At the end of the sixteenth century, he had been one of the 'swindling sheep farmers' who at that time were expropriating the commonlands of the English people. In 1596 he paid £3,500 for the manor, lordship and seigniory of Manchester, with 'all its appurtenances . . .' Manchester was an unimportant market town with an annual fair but it soon developed a monopoly of the woollen trade. With his new-found wealth, Nicholas commissioned Inigo Jones to design his house, Hough End Hall. He was also instrumental in raising soldiers and money to finance the building of warships for the navy to defend England against the Spanish Armada.

In 1599, with a reputation for shrewd business, Nicholas became Lord Mayor of London. His enthusiastic taxing of the London business community, together with his financial success at what was organized piracy against the Spaniards, earned him royal favour. Elizabeth I granted him a baronetcy and a family motto, 'Our Custom is above the Law'. Great wealth was created in Manchester before the industrial revolution and different branches of the Mosley family were able to add to an estate, which by the beginning of the eighteenth century included properties in Staffordshire and Derbyshire – among these was Rolleston-on-Dove in Staffordshire.

There developed two distinct divisions in the Mosley family – the Lancashire branch on the one side and the migrants to Rolleston on the other. The eccentric latter branch developed a farming tradition, deriving most of their income from the land on which Manchester was built. The Lancashire Mosleys farmed in Didsbury and Chorley, and were engaged in the burgeoning cotton trade. In 1729 Sir Oswald Mosley built the Cotton Exchange, which signalled Manchester had arrived. With the expansion of Manchester as an urban centre, new problems arose. The Mosleys played a 'rough part' in suppressing the 1819 Peterloo Massacre and the Chartist riots. Mosley was often reproached for his family's role but understandably was 'never able to understand why I should be held responsible for events so many years before I was born'.

In the early nineteenth century, Manchester's industrialists and traders took exception to the manorial rights exercised by the Mosleys. These included a 'tollage' tax on all goods entering the market and 'stallage' on the rental of market stalls. Municipal reformers clamoured for control of a town governed by the ancient Court Leet. Reformers sought 'incorporation' and elected local government, and after a fierce fight, in 1838 the reforms were conceded by the Privy Council. Effective family influence in Manchester ceased in 1846 with the sale to the Corporation of the Lord of the Manor rights. The demise of the Mosleys' Court Leet suggests the normal process of modernization, as the middle class replaced the aristocracy and 'assumed the political power appropriate to its economic position after decades of industrialization'. Manchester, however, was almost devoid of aristocratic influence. The Mosleys belonged to the squirearchy and as county gentry took little interest in a town unrepresented in Parliament.

The Mosleys remained attached to traditional values, cut off from industrial England and suspicious of their aristocratic leaders at Westminster. In 300 years as a leading county family, only two Mosleys were elected to Parliament. They were uninterested in academia, the arts and liberalism – 'processes that helped change and modernize sections of the aristocracy in the 19th century'.

The family's sphere remained resolutely local and their influence limited to that of parsons and soldiers.

The major part of the Mosleys' private property in Manchester was leased out, with the family continuing to draw ground rents. Mosley's great-grandfather, Sir Oswald, received from the sale of manor rights an annual income of £9,114, on a capital sum of £200,000. It was seen as a shrewd bargain, which was resented. According to one account, the family had a long-standing quarrel with Manchester's Jewish businessmen. In the 1880s, although Jews played only a minor role in money-lending, Walter Tomlinson, a local journalist, noted that the identification of Jews with extortionate usury was 'extensively believed in'. Mosley's grandfather was at the forefront of the campaign against Jewish emancipation.

It was not long before merchants took up the Mosley seats at Ancoats and Hulme. While bringing immediate financial reward, the sale of rights was in the long term a disastrous error – the leaseholds were for 999 years instead of the traditional 99. The family retired to 4,000 acres of farmland in Stafford-shire, a feudal enclave that survived into the twentieth century. The Mosleys simply ignored the nineteenth century.

Mosley's mother's family, the Heathcotes of Market Drayton, were Stafford-shire gentry, though on a less grand scale than the Mosleys. Her father, Justinian Heathcote, was a Tory squire and MP for Stoke-on-Trent. He enthralled his grandson with tales of parliamentary life. Mosley considered his grandfather a shrewd observer of politics. Justinian's brother was created Lord Anslow by the Liberal Party. The family had coal and steel interests around Stoke and centuries-long roots in the country. This, Mosley suggested, 'gave a certain vitality and resolution for very different purposes'.

For Mosley, it was 'an abrupt transition in childhood from a wayside house with a few rooms, a patch of garden, and one maidservant' to the massive edifice of Victorian comfort of Rolleston Hall. Situated in the picturesque village of Rolleston-on-Dove, near Burton-upon-Trent, the Hall was a large, rambling, Italianate, ivy-clad mansion built on to the shell of the original hall, which had burnt down in the 1870s. It had been inherited in 1879 by Mosley's grandfather, the fourth baronet, and was described by Mosley's second wife as 'fairly ugly without and hideous within'.

The 'chiming clocks inside, sweeping lawns outside' were the sounds and images Mosley remembered. Set in parkland, amid lakes and gardens, Rolles-ton was maintained by over forty gardeners and menservants, along with housemaids and cooks, and two still-room maids exclusively engaged in the making of cakes. At Rolleston everything was managed with a stately ritual, no more so than on Sunday when the well-ordered parade to church was followed by luncheon where the roast was ceremoniously set down before Mosley's grandfather.

Rolleston had a self-contained agricultural economy. There was, Mosley recalled, 'little need to go outside the closed and charmed circle, and we children never did. Our time was divided between farms, gardens and carpenter's shop, where the bearded Pritchard presided over a corps of experts who kept all things going as their forebears had done for generations. We were very close to nature.' He was convinced his roots in the soil were 'a very fine start to life'. The pursuit of good stockbreeding, and the farm's success in a declining agricultural market, required estate workers to accept their allotted place, with little scope for change. This social hierarchy deeply impressed itself upon Mosley's thinking.

Mosley's misty-eyed childhood memories were overloaded with positive images which ignored the experience of estate workers who made life at Rolleston so pleasurable for his family. The squirearchy rejected the class divisions of the city, which were only visible at church where the seating reflected the true position of the lord of the manor and the villagers, but life centred on a structured social hierarchy in which each person knew his place and function. Women 'curtsied, men doffed their caps and the curate made obeisance'. It was to be the same in Mosley's 'classless' Fascist movement.

Mosley described his mother as 'extremely beautiful'; but most mothers are beautiful to their sons. She had strong features and was tall at five feet ten inches. Strictly religious, with an interest in spiritualism, she had, Mosley recalled, 'a robust, realistic attitude to life. I never observed any male influence in her life other than her family and an occasional preacher of exceptional gifts. She was a paragon of virtue, but as loyal and vigorous as a lionness in defence of her own.' Friends remembered a good-natured woman of high spirits.

To Maud, 'Tom was God'. She treated him as an exclusive possession and this intense emotional environment gave Mosley an unshakeable self-assurance. He grew up knowing he was adored, that he was special, and that 'anything he did must therefore be justified – the barbs and criticisms of lesser mortals could never touch him'. Maud lavished suffocating yet emotionally distant attentions on her son, and it was the lack of boundaries and the setting of limits that distinguished his upbringing. Mosley's sense of self and boundary limits, however, developed not only in relation to his mother.

Mosley's father, Waldie, was a slim-built young man who reached the feather-weight semi-finals of the Amateur Boxing Association. He was 'a hard-riding, hard-drinking, hard-living Tory squire, much given to expletives'. He had an almost complete freedom of inhibitions – a trait derived from his own father – and was a typical aristocratic playboy. Waldie was a cad, who preferred racing to farming and amused himself with gambling and womanizing. His exploits included shooting out lights in Piccadilly with a pistol from a hansom cab before returning to the scene of his triumph to play a game of golf down the street. Such hooliganism was classed as 'high spirits' among the upper orders.

Unlike his own father, Waldie had little regard for the family's reputation and his betrayals greatly distressed his wife. He was described as a gloomy blackguard but Mosley thought such a description 'inappropriate, for my father in my experience was the very reverse'. But not always. His mother's remaining diary reveals an instance of Tommy being bullied: 'Had a miserable time W[aldie] teasing Tom and I trying to defend him; and finally W caught hold of my wrist hurting it badly.' Fearing his father's aggression, Mosley idealized his mother, as the good parent who came to the rescue.

The Mosley marriage had been under strain and during 1901, when Tommy was five, his mother found the quarrelling intolerable. Pregnant with a third son – a second son, Edward, had been born two years previously – Maud left her husband on account of his promiscuous sexual habits. This followed a family trait, in that Waldie's own father had pursued numerous extramarital affairs and he, too, had separated from his wife. Tommy's father's sexual habits contrasted strikingly with the Christian ethics and common sense exemplified by his mother. For Maud, it was not just the infidelities, but the discovery of a bundle of letters from his mistresses, which revealed he was saying the same things to them, and giving them the same presents, as he was to her. Waldie's father, Mosley recalled, 'felt strongly that affairs of this nature should be conducted with the utmost discretion and dignity'.

W. F. Mandle points out, in the only psychological study of Mosley, that his father disappeared at the height of the critical Oedipal phase when a boy discovers desires for his mother and a sense of rivalry with his father. The resolution of the conflict in Tommy's case was a dramatic one in psychological terms, in that 'the father left'.

A judicial separation followed, with Maud gaining custody of the three boys and taking them to Belton Hall, on the borders of Market Drayton, near her family's country houses. However, she had received a meagre alimony and they found themselves in relatively straitened circumstances, though that was in relation to other members of their own family and class, and not in comparison with the general poverty of the countryside. Her chief anxiety, recalled Mosley, was 'to enable her sons to take part in the sports of the field . . . the only possible training for a man, and to which almost from infancy we were ardently addicted'. Mosley now saw his father only rarely and regarded him as 'something of an ogre'.

With his father absent, Tommy occupied a special position in his mother's affections, being treated almost as a substitute for her husband. Maud did not remarry; she showered Tommy with praise, referring to him as 'my man-child'. Mosley wrote of how he had always been devoted to his mother: how, as a child, he had repaid her devotion to him by 'gratuitous advice and virile assertion on every subject under the sun. I had no father in the house to chase me around, to make me do little things for myself and keep my mouth shut until my contribution was opportune.' With no father to frustrate mother-fixated desires, such feelings can develop into a rejection of feminine values. The adult Mosley sought out non-threatening, undemanding, dependent, even infantile women.

Mosley saw women as symbolizing passivity, but rather than accept the reality of interdependence, denied the need for others. He had an inflated estimate of his own ability and his most secret desire – the one that inspires all deeds and designs – was the need to be praised. Few would confess to this but his autobiography comes close. That he suffered from overweening pride was well testified by his friends.

In Maud's attempts to compensate for his father's desertion, she paid Tommy overbearing attention in an attempt to make him stand out. She supervised her son's development, and conveyed to him her social and moral standards. However, even though he was absent, it was his father who determined his attitudes as he began to resent his mother's all-encompassing attentions. Mosley carried from his background an attitude to manhood which displayed a combination of sado-masochistic drives that were both aggressive and passive – he both inflicted pain and experienced it. Interestingly, George Orwell confided in his journal (August 1939) that he had 'reliable information' that Mosley – who was aggressively heterosexual – was 'a masochist of the extreme type in his sexual life'.

Mosley conformed to social rules more out of fear of punishment than from a sense of guilt. This made it impossible for him to experience concern for others. Narcissists such as Mosley function perfectly happily in the world with a mask of charm, although this may be no more than 'the aristocrat's frequent indifference to the existence or feelings of anything outside his own charmed world'. Many noted Mosley's immense charm and perfect manners.

Nicholas wrote that his own father had 'no father to instil in him knowledge of limits imposed by morals and tradition'. But that is not the case. Tommy's grandfather assumed the role of substitute male parent, albeit from an emotional distance. The 'company of one or the other grandfather,' Mosley recalled, 'was constant, and no one could have been more male than these two'. Tommy associated his grandfather with idealized virtues. Maud often took her sons to their paternal grandfather's Staffordshire home. Victorian English country-house life was 'dominated by a sort of philistine masculinity' and little had changed at Rolleston, where sport remained the chief subject of activity by day and discussion by night.

Mosley's grandfather was a national figure – he was the model for the traditional John Bull. The cartoons of Sir John Tenniel, published in *Punch* during the nineteenth century, had made the honest, solid farmer, John Bull, into a popular figure, with his Union flag waistcoat and accompanying bulldog. A judge at agricultural shows, he was well known in those circles for his knowledge of the breeding of shorthorns and shire horses. Sir Dudley Forwood, later the Duke of Windsor's equerry, was related to Tommy on both his parents' side. 'My father and mother constantly stayed with Tommy's grandfather at Rolleston. They told me that Sir Oswald would discuss the breeding of the Beef, Mutton, Pork or Poultry.'

Mosley considered his grandfather 'a man in every sense'. In his youth he had been runner-up in the British amateur middle-weight boxing championship. He was, Mosley wrote, 'a child of nature with a simple and generous nature'. He evoked 'almost universal affection from all who met him in his small world or in wider circles, where he moved with the same unaffected friendship as he did among his tenants, work people, country'. Although not part of the cosmopolitan aristocractic elite, Sir Oswald's contacts with the world outside included Bertie, the Prince of Wales (Edward VII), and the newspaper proprietor Lord Northcliffe, for whom he originated the Standard Bread campaign in 1911. Sir Oswald had written to the *Daily Mail* offering to anyone who sent a postcard a small specimen loaf made from wheat milled in the traditional way between stones. *Mail* journalist Hamilton Fyfe recalled that Standard Bread was pushed by Northcliffe until 'everyone was sick of it'.

There was an atmosphere of strife between the preceding generations and Mosley was aware his grandfather had a robust dislike for his son. Grandfather Mosley saw Tommy as a substitute son with the result that Waldie resented the understanding which existed between his own father and Tommy. Mosley knew that 'psychological wiseacres will at once draw their conclusions with the estrangement between father and grandfather' but questioned their pretensions.

There is no doubt that Mosley's childhood was action-orientated and fulfilled his view that 'the development or atrophy of the constitution depends on continual exertion of the will'. Tommy underwent his 'training to be a man' in the absence of his father and largely developed his masculinity through identification with popular cultural images and via the role model of his grandfather. He thus idealized the male role and appropriated those components of masculinity he feared would otherwise be used against him.

It was tradition that family quarrels should be aired publicly and each father challenged his son to a boxing match in front of assembled servants. Boxing, fencing and hunting were part of an aggressive upbringing in which being the winner was all important. The combination of this hyper-masculinity, which was a defence against feelings of dependence, and the lack of boundaries, which gave little consideration to others' feelings, ensured that Mosley was 'always in too much of a hurry. I rushed towards life with arms outstretched to embrace . . . every varied enchantment of a glittering, wonderful world; a life rush, to be consummated.'

Recalling his childhood, Mosley said his mother's main problem was how to pay the boys' public school fees. Although their father contributed nothing, it was 'out of the question to my mother's reserved pride to ask either family for help'. However, if the family looked enviously at the 'ample comforts' of his grandfather's estate, it was with the knowledge that Tommy would eventually inherit it.

In 1906, Mosley went to West Downs, Winchester, at the age of nine as a solitary, imaginative boy, prone to daydreaming. He was later joined by his brother Edward. Under its first headmaster, Lionel Helbert, West Downs achieved pre-eminence as the best English prep school. With its swimming bath and electric light, the school was considered very modern. Among Mosley's contemporaries were members of the Tennant family and the sons of military families, including John Sinclair, who went on to become Chief of MI6. Mosley was bright but did not shine, which he put down to the 'stress of growth'. Though regarded by some as rather stupid, essays of the period show he had 'developed the art of self-expression'. He did establish a reputation among fellow pupils as a debater.

The school's character was set by Helbert, who instilled in pupils a strong tradition of community service. A contemporary of Mosley, Rolf Gardiner, who became a 'blood-and-soil' National Socialist in the thirties, recalled that Helbert wanted every human being to succeed according to the laws of his own destiny and character, and 'sought to endow small boys with an inner fund of inextinguishable faith and fervour'. Mosley appears to have developed his love of pranks from the headmaster, who used them to keep pupils on their toes.

Helbert admired men of action: there was a custom for boys with grudges to challenge others to a boxing match before their equals in the gym. Mosley was in the Cricket First Eleven and succeeded at swimming, his favourite pastime. He was cast in a French play, *l'Avare*, wearing a female dress. He was later venerated at the school as a rising political star but there developed, old boy Daniel Hodson noted, 'a sort of conspiracy not to mention Mosley, once he had put himself beyond the pale by his activities in the 1930s'. In a school play, *The Venture*, written in the thirties by headmaster Kenneth Tindall, the name Mosley was featured as a swearword.

By now Mosley's father had obtained a court order for his three sons to visit him in the holidays. During one stay, when Mosley was twelve, their father told tales of actresses of his acquaintance and urged them to kiss the parlourmaid in front of the cook. Mosley's memory of his father, who was installed at Rolleston while his grandfather retired to a more modest house, was inconsistent. He claimed his father was a 'jolly fellow' with whom he established a happy relationship through their mutual love of horses. However, he also recalled that when the three boys visited their father, they 'sat around the house in postures of gloom and despair until he could bear it no longer and sent us back to my mother'.

Mosley's next school, Winchester, England's oldest, had been founded in 1382 by William of Wykeham as a monastic institution. By the beginning of the twentieth century, public schools had come to represent a revered ideal in the popular imagination. 'Eton, Harrow and Winchester are three schools of which all Englishmen are proud,' claimed the *Sphere*. They educate in a 'gentlemanly tradition of loyalty, honour, chivalry, Christianity, patriotism, sportsmanship and leadership'. These were the qualities deemed suitable for an officer class intent on entering the army.

Mosley entered Winchester in September 1909 at the age of twelve. He found the experience tougher than usual and admitted that entering a year early was 'one of the errors of my perpetual sense of haste'. He lacked a 'calm, male influence to say: what is the hurry?'. He hated the dreary waste of public school life, which was 'only relieved by learning and homosexuality', though he admitted that he had no capacity for the former and never had any taste for the latter. His dandified appearance, being very tall – by the age of fourteen he had already reached his full height of six feet two – with 'striking, dark, good looks' and his suits from Savile Row, made him subject to male attention. He was very conscious of his appearance; he wore his thick black hair parted down the middle, as was the custom of fellow Wykehamists. His peers noticed a certain theatricality about his appearance with its suggestion of 'a stage villain'.

To most boys, Mosley came over as being uninterested in work and aloof. He neither socialized nor, he admitted, was he a rebel, but kept himself to himself, sustained by daily letters from his mother. During the holidays he spent his happiest moments with horse, dog and gun, ferreting with one of his Heathcote cousins. Hunting was almost a religious observance. There was rough shooting at his maternal grandfather's and coarse fishing at Rolleston. Over the winter of 1909–10 Mosley's annotated game register recorded him shooting fifty partridges, eighteen pheasants, eleven rabbits and ten hares. 'These were the happy crumbs,' he recalled, 'which fell from the well-laden tables of two grandfathers.'

At home Mosley came across the social anti-Semitism prevalent in English society, though there is no trace of anti-Semitism in his own private life. During his interrogation before the Advisory Committee on Internment during the Second World War, Mosley told his inquisitors he had first come across anti-Semitism 'in my youth where most of one's friends and relations would not have Jews in their houses'. It was part of 'an old English growth' – a kind of 'whimsical brutality' but 'kinder' than that expressed by the Germans.

Just before his fourteenth birthday, Mosley underwent, as a typically sensitive adolescent, a spiritual experience. It did not provide any sense of revelation but he claimed to have become 'immensely impressed by the doctrine of love'. Mosley was a Christian and believed in God, but also admitted he was intrigued by the pagan world, which lingered on at Rolleston, and by his mother's spiritualism. He skipped over these areas in his autobiography, even though his spiritual experience coincided with him developing a sense of destiny, which he submerged in the 'first exuberance of physical vitality'.

Mosley's mother found it a struggle to meet the school fees and his grandfather helped by setting up in 1910 a trust fund for the boys. Mosley escaped from his dull existence at Winchester to the gymnasium. Lithe and quick on his feet, by fifteen he had developed into a formidable pugilist in advance of his years. The most potent influence was the boxing coach, Sergeant Ryan. Mosley won the light-weight championship and 'experienced for the first time incredulity that I could be winning'. He noted that his 'tendency to be doubtful of success until it was proven carried me to remarkable lengths in this first athletic encounter'. This is the first instance of the hesitancy which was a part of Mosley's personality. Although his mother instilled in him that he was destined for success, the bullying which he received in childhood from his father, and which continued at Winchester, seemed to stunt his natural self-assurance. It is perceived that Mosley – and he himself added to this perception – was always decisive. In fact, he was often unsure of his position and failure resulted from him choosing the wrong moment to jump.

When Mosley announced his intention of entering the Public Schools' boxing championship, headmaster Dr Rendell, who regarded the noble art with distaste, forbade his participation. Mosley subsequently discarded his gloves in favour of the sword and came under the charge of the fencing master, Sergeant Major Adam. Mosley said he and the boxing coach Sergeant Ryan had more influence on him than any schoolmaster.

Military training in schools had been regarded as a foreign concept but following the army reforms of 1906, the Officer Training Corps (OTC) at Winchester had been set up with the support of the War Office. Membership was not compulsory, but neither was it voluntary, since war was considered a probability. Those who took the corps seriously were often 'a lonely, earnest soul who appeared to see cadetship rather as a form of moral callisthenics fitting the individual for citizenship than a training in field combat'. This expression of militarism was derived from the late Victorian period romantic revival of chivalry; 'a conscious anachronism in which art, literature and fancy dress played a large part'. At Winchester chivalrous ideals were celebrated with the decorative figures of King Arthur and his knights.

An important part of the OTC ritual was 24 May, Empire Day, originally a commemoration of Queen Victoria's birthday. It came to represent 'something every bit as atavistic and fundamental as even Kipling could have wished'. Amid much flag waving, OTC members paraded and were encouraged to be aware of their duties as citizens of the world's greatest empire. These rituals were remembered by Mosley when he set up his paramilitary Fascist movement.

Fencing dominated Mosley's life and he won his school's foils competition against boys several years older. On 14 March 1912, aged fifteen, he represented Winchester in the Public Schools' competition, in both foil and sabre. The championship – once won by Winston Churchill – was organized by the army; an illustration of militarism's growing influence. Mosley captained the fencing team against Eton and gained fifteen points without letting his opponents touch him. He was the first boy to win both foil and sabre, and the youngest winner of the two events. Peter Portal (later Viscount Portal, Marshal of the RAF) was a team member. 'We were rather good at fencing as schoolboys go and easily defeated the Eton team.' Fellow pupils remembered their 'extreme surprise' when news of Mosley's victory was read out by the housemaster: they had not even known that he had taken up fencing. One contemporary wrote that he was 'precocious, impatient, full of contempt for most boys of his own age, and a complete hedonist'.

In his last year of school, Mosley applied himself to academic work but was let down by indecipherable handwriting. It was strange, a schoolmaster noted, that 'this hand can do anything with a sword, and nothing with a pen'. Mosley said the problem was due to his mind moving too fast for his hand. In such cases, graphologist Ellen Cameron notes, there is a common factor – lack of consideration for the recipient. Diana Mosley, too, ascribed his poor writing to his 'impoliteness and indifference'.

Mosley's style of writing generally indicates a person given to excessive rationalization, a characteristic of which he was guilty. His writing was typical of people who are self-indulgent and not well disciplined, but well adjusted emotionally to everyday life. His large signature displayed a wish to impress as someone of considerable importance. Mosley also had a tendency to enlarge his writing, a trait shared with people in the public eye. Such people are enthusiastic and self-confident, but unwilling to be confined or restricted in any way. Mosley's handwriting portrayed intelligence, will-power and the desire to achieve great things. However, given his tendency to pose, the writer's wish for success 'may not materialise but rather turn in on the writer who would possibly become boastful and swollen-headed'.

Mosley left Winchester at the end of 1912. Fellow Wykehamist and Labour Cabinet Minister Richard Crossman recalled that there were a few schoolboys in 'mental struggle with the tradition and in lifelong reaction against it'. These 'radical throw-outs' often became traitors to their class. Certainly, Mosley hated his time there with an intensity that went on into old age. In the late summer of 1913 he sojourned in Brest, France, learning the language and taking the opportunity to compete with experienced fencers. On his return to England, seventeen-year-old Tommy listed his occupation as 'private gentleman' and was intent on joining the army.

Maud was finding it difficult to fund the boys' education. In early 1914 she was forced to sell her jewellery, an action resented by the younger brothers, since the lion's share of the trust had been spent on Tommy. Fourteen-year-old Ted was destined to pursue a career in the army, while twelve-year-old John attended naval college before going on to Eton. The three brothers only saw each other during the holidays. According to John's son, Simon, on reaching adulthood their relationship became 'so sketchy as to be virtually non-existent'. The three brothers were all tremendously egocentric, but Tommy was in 'more of a state of megalomania'.

In January 1914, after a spell of cramming for the exam, Mosley entered the Royal Military College, Sandhurst. His short nine months as a cadet were 'one of the happiest times of my entire life'. The rather isolated boy came out of his shell and developed into a boisterous, rebellious young man. He returned to his first love, horse riding, and took up polo, though he had 'nothing like the capacity for handling horses' of his brother; Ted later entered the 1st Royal Dragoons and became an instructor at Weedon Cavalry School. Mosley lost out as a polo cup winner because a practical joker sent his favourite horse to the wrong college. He later dealt with this senior cadet with a knockout punch. His own love of practical joking gave him a frivolous image but contemporaries noted a streak of cruelty in his character.

Sandhurst's history was punctuated by rowdiness and violence. It taught its upper-class trainees 'impeccability on parade and hooliganism off-duty'. Mosley admitted cadets broke every rule and off parade had no regard for discipline. They spent free time in London provoking 'fights with the chuckers-out at places like the Empire'; the fights being more important than pursuing women. Back at barracks, they were helped to bed 'as if by nannies by the same sergeants who, the next day, would revile them for any indecorum on the parade ground'. This was all part of a so-called Corinthian tradition.

Older cadets decided that an arrogant Mosley needed to be taken down a peg or two and went to his room to punish him for his insolence. John Masters, in *Bugle and Tiger*, created the legend that Mosley, 'detested by his brother officer cadets, was thrown out of a window'. In fact, in seeking recruits for retaliatory action, he slipped on a ledge and fell, slightly injuring a leg. Skirmishing continued all weekend, as a result of which fifteen cadets, including Mosley, were packed off to reflect on their ill behaviour. His friend Robert Bruce Lockhart believed Mosley 'bore a grudge against society' because of this incident.

Mosley was at home when war was declared in August 1914 and was ordered back to Sandhurst. He recalled 'returning through London and walking past Buckingham Palace, the enormous crowds cheering in immense enthusiasm ... there was a tremendous excitement'. Passed fit for active service, Mosley was back in E Company for the final weeks of arduous training. He rushed through the course, though his essays were cited as models of precision and clarity, and he was marked fifth of the cavalry entrants. 'The change between peace and war was one of the most dramatic moments of my life. The playboy of the summer became the dedicated soldier of autumn.'

Most of Mosley's friends were cavalrymen and his fellow cadets – Mike Wardell, John Gray and Bruce Ogilvie – 'all had this mania to get into it because we were very much afraid the war would be over before we got there'. He recalled a *Punch* cartoon showing a cavalry subaltern's mess with the line – 'We've just time to beat them between the Polo and the Grouse.' The cadets regarded war as a tremendous adventure in which they were eager to participate. It was, Mosley recalled, 'almost a sporting event'.

2

The First World War

On the outbreak of war in August 1914, at Sandhurst Mosley's school-age volunteers grew impatient, worried they might 'miss the adventure of a lifetime'. They were gripped with a condition approaching despair in their desire to transfer to the battlefield. Their main fear was that the war would end before they arrived at the front. Mosley wrote: 'Never had men appeared more eager to be killed.'

Mosley had originally intended to join the 17th Lancers. Their commander, Vivyan Lockett, was a cousin and a leading polo player for England. It was such family connections, he knew, which took one into regiments. In the end, however, Mosley was persuaded to make the switch to a sister regiment, the 16th Queens Light Dragoons, by 'a grand old figure', Major Sir Lovelace Stamer, a friend of his mother's family.

The seventeen-year-old was gazetted to the 16th Lancers on 1 October 1914. In receipt of his commission, Second Lieutenant Mosley reported to the Curragh in County Kildare. Twenty miles south of Dublin, the Curragh was the depot for the Lancers. As part of the 3rd Cavalry Brigade, the 16th had been sent to Ireland in the expectation of trouble from the Ulster Volunteer Association in the wake of Prime Minister Asquith's Home Rule Act. In organizing the Volunteers, the eminent lawyer and leading Unionist MP Sir Edward Carson acted in a reckless manner, conveying the impression, which turned out to be false, that he was about to organize a military coup in Ulster. At the Curragh there was a fear Ulster-born officers might disappear and that others would resign if ordered north. The 16th moved out of Dublin just before Mosley arrived. The regiment's historian noted the reluctance to 'slaughter loyal Ulstermen for the benefit of disloyal Dublin'.

Mosley was the youngest member of his regiment which, just before Christmas, embarked for France. Expecting to be sent into action, Mosley discovered there was no need for cavalry; instead, he found himself engaged in routine drill. Eager to join the fray, he responded to an appeal for aerial observers and transferred to the Royal Flying Corps (RFC).

Established in 1912, the RFC quickly developed a high profile and dynamic image through the propaganda efforts of Northcliffe's *Daily Mail*. The newspaper had been at the forefront of publicizing the achievements of air heroes, whose autographs were eagerly sought by schoolboys. The aeroplane caught the spirit of the time. There was a widespread belief that it would 'usher in a new age in human development', arriving, as it did, 'on the heels of an apparently never-ending series of technological innovations'. Popular attitudes towards aviation were tied to feelings of patriotism and nationalism, and fear that an air war would be more devastating than anything that had gone before. However, the eagerness of young men to take to the air was seen as a sign of national vitality and an indication that they were willing 'to give up their lives for the sake of higher values'. In this romantic vision of a new frontier, the sky became a metaphor for 'a bright and shining future'. A decade later, aviators became a strong faction inside British Fascism.

The RFC was made up of two wings and comprised just sixty-four aircraft and fewer than 900 men. No. 1 Wing was commanded by Hugh Trenchard. On 24 January 1915 Mosley was posted to the 2nd Wing headquarters at St Omer as an observer. Two weeks later he joined No. 6 Squadron, recently formed at Farnborough. Led by Lieutenant-Colonel Burke, 6 Squadron was established on the coast near Dunkirk to assist the projected relief of Antwerp. Mosley was originally stationed with B Flight at Bailleul, midway between Poperinge and Armentières.

Mosley took his inaugural flight the morning after arrival at Bailleul with Burke: 'We flew along the lines not knowing if I was on my head or my heels.' It was a bumpy day, but he soon picked it up. His commander, Captain 'Johnny' Hawker, wrote that flying set you 'free from the clogging clamour of this world' and into the 'pure beauty of the skies above the cloud-damped earth'. According to the squadron's history, he inspired his men and was loved by all who served under him. His 'chicks', Hawker wrote home, 'are all bachelors and confirmed women-haters of 20 years experience or thereabouts and therefore very amusing'. He ran 'a school and not a Squadron – there is only one older than myself and the majority are not yet of age. They are a splendid lot tho'.'

Hawker was 'nervous as a cat on hot bricks before he flew' and would not eat. This worried his young, inexperienced observer. There was a belief that a pilot might faint in the air if he flew on an empty stomach. But the moment the plane left the ground, Mosley found that Hawker was transformed and became the 'boldest, perhaps the most reckless, certainly the most utterly indifferent to personal safety when a sense of duty was involved. He'd turn around 50 miles behind German lines to fight half-a-dozen people if he got the chance.'

As an observer on the three-hour reconnaissance flights which flew up to seventy miles behind enemy lines, Mosley had to survey sitings of German defences, changes of gun placements and troop dispositions. He admitted he was never handy with compasses and map, but then little attention was paid to the reports. Cloud and mist proved to be a major limitation and there was no effective co-operation with ground units.

Flying at only seventy to eighty miles an hour, which might drop to thirty in a stiff wind in the reliable BE2Cs (known as 'Stability Janes') and at a maximum ceiling of 6,000 feet, pilots and observers ran a considerable risk from heavy ground fire. On 5 March 1915 Hawker was sent out with Mosley on a wild scheme flying low over the lines to spot gun flashes. Hawker wrote home that they had to 'crash up and down between 500 and 800 feet just our side of the line. Occasionally we got rather near the Huns and were potted at but our people were very good and left us alone so we were all right. Quite the most amusing joy-ride I've had, flung about all over the place in a gale, and results quite successful, in fact it established a precedent.' Mosley recalled that 'no machine ever came back without being plastered by fire with holes through the wing'. A fellow observer told Mosley: 'You know, we're much too young to be killed.' Three weeks later he was dead.

There were few opportunities for dogfights, which were regarded as too dangerous. Nevertheless, public imagination was captured by the idea of the air ace, even if they built up their scores by attacking inexperienced pilots and defenceless reconnaissance aircraft. Firing through the propellers would often bring a German machine down. British air losses during 1915 were serious, particularly when the Germans began placing their accurate guns eight to each corner of a square, producing a blanket air barrage of thirty-two shells.

Mosley wrote asking his mother not to grieve if he should be killed, as he was sure he would find death 'a most interesting experience'. He had just endured the common sensation of a great exhilaration at coming under fire for the first time, but it was 'a peculiar ecstasy which soon wore off'. Mosley saw his share of death. When hit, men stayed with their machines until they crashed; there were no parachutes. He recalled that the 'flimsy contraption of wood and canvas would then almost invariably catch fire as the petrol exploded from the burst tank. The most fortunate were those killed instantly in the crash, or first shot dead.' Mosley's roommate was shot down. He saw his shattered skull amid the wreckage of the plane, though the image which stuck in his mind was his smiling face of a few hours earlier.

On 14 March the squadron was transferred inside the Belgian border to Poperinge, six miles west of Ypres. Captain Louis Strange took over B Flight. Mosley flew regularly with Strange who, in contrast to Hawker, was 'completely calm, cold and resolute'. Poperinge was regarded as 'a rotten aerodrome ... no sheds, no good billets', though the resident French pilots received the 6th with great hospitality.

While soldiers viewed the airmen with admiration, this was also mixed with a certain bitterness and the suspicion that they had 'somehow managed to escape from the degradation and daily torment of the trenches'. The fact that the airmen were only ever a small proportion of the total Expeditionary Force contributed to the myth of airmen as 'an elite of a *corps d'élite*'. Peter Liddle suggests in his study of the airmen that the technology of the air war 'preserved an individuality which was so swamped by sheer numbers and the nature of the work of the Army'. Mosley enjoyed good living conditions and there was a relaxed informality about billet life which was absent in the army, though RFC officers still expected to be waited upon at dinner. Food and drink were plentiful. There was a distinctive sense of liberation among the aircrews, which exhibited itself in an 'extreme gaiety', living, as they did, in the shadow of a short life expectancy.

Mosley knew that trench casualties were very heavy but thought 'death was more natural in those bleak surroundings. We were like men having dinner together in a country house-party, knowing that some must soon leave us for ever; in the end, nearly all.' He flew with a number of famous pilots, including A. J. Capel (later Air Vice-Marshal), Lieutenant Hereward de Havilland, whose brother was the aircraft designer Sir Geoffrey, and Captain John Liddell, awarded the VC posthumously. Liddell died of his wounds soon after landing, having flown back his damaged aircraft a considerable distance. 'It seemed,' Mosley wrote, 'that the will alone held the spark of life until the task was done; it was extinguished as will relaxed.' On a previous occasion at Poperinge, when Liddell landed in a pond, Mosley escaped with a minor leg injury.

With clearing skies at the end of March 1915, reconnaissance missions took place daily. Cameras recorded enemy positions, with photographs developed by a new Photographic Section whose head, Lieutenant J. T. C. Brabazon, was one of Mosley's most enduring friends. An international racing driver, in 1909 'Ivan' became the first Englishman to make a powered flight in the United Kingdom and later won the £1,000 prize offered by the *Mail* for the first English aircraft to fly one mile. He was holder of Pilot's Certificate No. 1 of the Royal Aero Club and pioneered the use of aerial photography. A witty, genial character, Mosley thought Ivan combined 'the most indolent demeanour with an exceptional capacity for action'.

In April Mosley's squadron turned to bombing, using hand grenades dropped from 2,000 feet. Hawker was the first to drop a 100 lb bomb which he strapped to the plane. On the 18th he dropped bombs on a Zeppelin shed at Cognelée, outside Ghent. This earned him a DSO, even though the Zeppelin LZ-35 which was supposed to be inside had crashed five days earlier.

The Western Front could not be described as heroic or chivalrous, but politicians sought inspiration from the airmen, whose war could be portrayed in romantic terms. David Lloyd George lauded the 'Young Heroes of the Flying Corps' and considered 'every aeroplane flight a romance, every record an epic'. Pilots were looked on as aristocrats of the air but the contribution by real aristocrats was meagre. A few patricians did fly and among the earliest were Lord Hugh Cecil (after the war a political colleague of Mosley and Brabazon), Lord George Wellesley (later Duke of Wellington) and the Master of Semphill, who both turned to the extreme right.

The air war offered an heroic alternative to the squalid and anonymous war in the trenches. Much was made of the custom of giving the downed enemy a decent burial and ensuring news of their fate went back to their squadrons. Mosley recalled that airmen on each side 'sometimes dropped wreaths to mourn the death of a great opponent held in honour for his courage and chivalry'; a practice which faltered later in the war, when there was, *Times* correspondent Aubrey Leo Kennedy agreed, 'little of the spirit of 1914–15 left, of great adventure, almost of a crusade'. When Mosley rushed to aid a German pilot who had crashed in a nearby field, he was appalled to discover that villagers had already put him to death.

While Mosley was on leave, he learned of his grandfather's death. Dogged by diabetes, he died aged sixty-seven. Mosley's father nominally inherited Rolleston but his grandfather had arranged that much of his legacy bypassed his son and went straight to his grandson. Mosley was now, on paper, a wealthy man, inheriting £60,000 (£3 m) and, eventually, the lion's share of land then worth £274,000 (£13 m).

By mid April 1915, Mosley was in France for the second Battle of Ypres. The Germans sought to break the deadlock in Flanders by mounting mass attacks on the British lines. They failed and a seventeen-mile salient was created around the Flemish town of Ypres. Not far away, in the trenches, was a German soldier, Adolf Hitler. His impression of Ypres was of towers 'so near that I could all but touch them'. Encircled by a medieval moat, the town was dominated by the towers of St Martin's Cathedral and the architectural glory of the Cloth Hall. The Ypres Salient took on 'an emotional significance which its strategic value never for a moment warranted'. On 20 April the Germans subjected Ypres to heavy bombardment. The Cloth Hall was utterly destroyed. 'The work of centuries of genius took only hours to destroy,' lamented Mosley.

Mosley had been ordered to help with the communications of the 2nd Canadian Infantry Brigade, which was holding dugouts on the Salient's eastern fringe. Royal Engineers had been experimenting with No. 6 Squadron on wireless signalling from aircraft to the artillery. Mosley helped set up a transmitter to radio back to base the location of gun placements. During his secondment, he witnessed the first gas attack of the war.

The 22nd of April was a warm spring day. At 5 p.m. Strange was on reconnaissance over German lines when he saw a burst of flares, which signalled the release of chlorine gas. His attention was attracted by what appeared to be streams of yellowish-green smoke coming from the German trenches.

The smoke swept towards the French lines, occupied by an African battalion, the 'Turcos'. Mosley and the Canadians heard the outbreaks of violent coughing as the Turcos fled to escape the gas. Mosley became aware of a 'curious acrid smell and a feeling of nausea'. The Canadians advised them to 'urinate on our handkerchiefs and place them over our mouths and noses; above all we must make no movement which required deep breathing'. Mosley suffered no consequences from the gas but hundreds of troops were poisoned, though only a few died. The gas had been effective more as a psychological weapon: it was the panic which caused the greatest damage.

'It was an unforgettable spectacle,' Mosley recalled. 'As dusk descended there appeared to our left the blue-grey masses of the Germans advancing steadily behind their lifting curtain of fire. It appeared there was nothing to stop them.' When Strange flew above the Salient he discovered a new front line close to Ypres. The ground lost had no strategic value but British C.-in-C. Sir John French insisted on defending it, with appalling consequences. War correspondent Philip Gibbs wrote that 'bits of bodies, and clots of blood, and green, metallic-looking slime made by the explosive gases, were floating on the surface of that water below the crater banks. Our men lived there and died there ... Scraps of flesh, booted legs, blackened heads, eyeless heads, came falling over them when the enemy trench-mortared their position.'

Making his way back to his squadron, Mosley passed through Ypres and had the extraordinary experience of finding himself alone in its great square under tremendous bombardment. It was the most poignant memory of his life. He was spellbound by the 'enduring vision as noble buildings collapsed in a sad fatigue born not of centuries but of a moment of bitterness, like a child's house of cards under a wanton hand, as heavy shells descended in direct hits'. He suddenly realized 'what the Europeans were capable of doing to each other; the waste, the tragic absurdity'. The Germans failed to launch a mass assault to capture Ypres but the British still suffered 60,000 casualties. This, combined with lack of ammunition, scuppered any chance of a successful counter-attack. Sir John French blamed the failure on the shortage of shells. The subsequent Shells Scandal had important repercussions at home.

On 23 April Poperinge's aerodrome came under German shellfire, forcing the squadron to retire to Abeele. On the following day, Mosley was ordered home for medical treatment. During a flight a piece of shell hit his head and knocked him unconscious, leaving him with slight concussion. On another occasion he crash-landed and damaged his knee when thrown forward in the cockpit. In London, he visited a bone setter who treated the knee. Although ordered to rest, Mosley indulged in high spirits in Brighton with an aspiring airman, Geoffrey Dorman (later a leading Fascist). He also had his first love affair with an older woman, Lady Wodehouse, 'a wax doll with her white fluffy hair and fur cap and muffs'.

In early May Mosley trained as a pilot at the Shoreham Flying School, near Brighton. The instructor was French pioneer aviator Maurice Farman, whose outdated Longhorn aircraft was used for training. Many pupils were rushed through their solo flight before they were ready. 'At the sight of the craft before us,' one of Mosley's contemporaries recalled, 'we put our heads on one side like puzzled terriers.' Mosley was more experienced than most but the solo flight was still 'a terrifying mixture of exhilaration, terror, panic and desperate concentration'. In fact, he was overconfident and, with his mother watching, crashed his plane.

Touching down too fast, Mosley's machine hit the ground with a bang before bouncing back into the sky. Swept up by a changing wind, he found himself flying at 70 mph towards a hangar. He managed to open the throttle and miss the hangar by a hair's breadth. His mother was impressed by his antics but Farman had made ready for a disaster. With difficulty, he made a pancake landing, smashing the aircraft's undercarriage in a heavy crash. His legs were driven hard into the floor of the cockpit and injured, one of them severely. Mosley scrambled out and, 'as sometimes happens with severe shock, I felt nothing much at the time as I was completely numb'. He was sent back to the bone setter and, though the injury was serious, his leg was patched up and he was declared fit for duty. A consolation was that he was awarded his pilot's certificate (No. 1293) on 2 June 1915.

Back in France, on 25 July Hawker won a VC for a solo attack on three German aircraft. It was typical of his fearless approach but in his letters he was anything but gung-ho. The air war 'will leave a world in mourning, for few will escape', though he recognized it would 'revolutionise thought'.

In Italy, syndicalist journalist Benito Mussolini realized aviation's 'symbolic implications went far beyond its technological significance'. Flight was a 'metaphor for the new Nietzschean age that was dawning'. The airman myth – a key component of Fascist thought – incorporated 'idealised visions of war and youth with futurist revolutionary ideas'. Writers such as the editor of *The Aeroplane*, C. G. Grey (later a Fascist and colleague of Dorman), put an optimistic spin on the war. He argued there had been comparatively little damage, due to the success of 'aerial reconnaissance detecting otherwise covert troop movements'. In reality, troops on the ground were dying in ever greater numbers.

A shortage of officers led to the recall to the front of those who had been seconded to duties elsewhere. On 21 February 1915 the Ypres Salient had seen the worst day in the 16th Regiment's war; ten officers and forty-seven men undertaking dismounted service in the line were lost to German mines. Although awarded his pilot's certificate, Mosley decided his first duty was to his regiment: 'It was not an order but a choice.'

Mosley's experience of the air war had a profound effect on him, but it had been brief. Wartime records reveal that he spent no more than seventy-five days in the RFC in France. He had seen action but it was typical of his manipulation of his past, that he would make more of his record than was warranted.

In autumn 1915, Mosley was on a troopship back to France at the head of a draft which he had collected from the Curragh. His regiment had seen little action and had remained billeted at St Marie Capel. Lieutenant-Colonel Eccles joined the regiment as Commander on 1 October, when the 16th was dismounted and served as infantry digging trenches around Ypres. After the Battle of Loos, Mosley reported to headquarters and, for a time, life was agreeable. 'I was put in charge of the squadron mess, but soon sacked for doing us too well; the fare was appreciated but the bills were not . . . These tranquil and happy days did not last long.' On 19 October Mosley was posted to Rouen for tunnel duty, digging placements for mines. It was 'the most unpleasant part of the war' because there was always the possibility of being buried alive.

The elite cavalry disapproved of being converted into infantry. Officers had their own made-to-measure uniforms with neatly pressed jodhpurs tucked into high leather riding boots and tended to look more impressive than the working-class recruits, who were on average five inches shorter than the men of the officer class. Despite a better diet and more robust health, like other troops the cavalrymen succumbed to 'trench foot', a form of frostbite aggravated by standing too long in cold water. Over 200,000 soldiers were invalided out because of it in the first three months of 1915. Colonel Henry Graham, in his history of the 16th, recalled 'crouching in shallow trenches, waist deep in mud and water, in some of the most detestable countries of violent climate in Europe'. The 16th came under 'an incessant rain of shells to which it was impossible to make any effective reply on account of the salvo of shells, of which the enemy had an apparently inexhaustible supply'. There was within the regiment a deep sense of suppressed anger and frustration at the lack of shells.

Following the publication of Sir John French's dispatch exposing the shell shortage, the press-led Shells Scandal caused outrage in Parliament. It undermined Asquith's government and led, in May, to the formation of a Coalition. The munitions crisis forced politicians 'towards positive collectivist action' and the setting up in June of the Ministry of Munitions (MoM) under Lloyd George.

The creation of MoM, vital for the mobilization of the engineering industries, provided a role to which Lloyd George was peculiarly suited. He was 'nothing of a theorist, very little of a planner', but justified Winston Churchill's assertion that 'at getting things done Lloyd George was incomparable'. It was a quality which made him a hero in the armed forces and, in particular, to Mosley. In

September, Lloyd George took over responsibility for all war materials and the supply of shells began to grow to thirty times more than it had been six months previously. Colonel Graham noted that there was great support for Lloyd George within the regiment but not for the 'amateur strategist' Churchill.

From 23 November Mosley was attached to the headquarters of the 3rd Infantry Brigade. His regiment had various billets until 2 January 1916, when it settled in Wavre. He reported to a Welsh battalion, composed of ex-miners: 'good troops suffering heavy losses'. He returned all the better for his sojourn with the infantry to the 16th, which remained in the trenches until 9 February. There was, Mosley recalled, 'a certain exhilaration in going up over the top at night'. Henry Williamson in the London Rifle Brigade (and a thirties Mosleyite) shared the experience of 'the night turning into a total brilliance as a battery of howitzers opened upon our left and 2,000 guns fired at once . . . as soon as the barrage began, all the nightingales came out, you could hear them singing like hell'. For Mosley, there was a 'tragic loveliness in that unearthly desolation, the ultimate nihilism of man's failed spirit', but the 'grinding shock of noise wore men down'. Surrounded by such horrors, a wound was a release, and death, peace. On 13 February, Mosley came upon the dead body of a friend in the Royal Scots Greys, Lord Weymouth.

The worst part for Mosley was navigating the trenches where the boards' large holes could not be seen in the dark. His injured leg went through them with 'a result not only painful but temporarily disabling'. The leg had swollen badly and each movement hurt. Standing for long periods up to his knees in water did little to prevent the injured bones, which had not entirely set, from becoming infected. Mosley was incapacitated and, although he refused to leave his men, he was ordered to hospital and left on a stretcher.

On 15 February Mosley returned to England to see a specialist. He wanted a well-known surgeon, Sir William Watson-Cheyne, to operate on his leg but he was about to retire. Fortunately, Sir William's son was a 16th Lancer and he persuaded his father to operate. There was a fear Mosley's leg might have to be amputated but the surgeon's skill in replacing the infected parts with other pieces of bone saved it.

The regiment remained billeted until 19 June, when it joined with the 3rd Brigade at Sec Bois. Recovering from surgery, on 17 July Mosley was promoted to lieutenant. It is unclear what he was doing during the autumn of 1916. Indeed, the army was unaware of his whereabouts and believed he was shirking his responsibilities. The army Director of Personnel noted his 'large amount of sick leave' – on two occasions he failed to show up for medicals. The army made strenuous efforts to track him down and consideration was given to disciplinary action. Towards the end of the year, he underwent a second successful operation, which left his leg an inch and a half shorter. In his absence, his regiment was posted to the Somme.

After four months away from the front, Mosley's war had effectively ended. National Archives military specialist William Spencer said on release of Mosley's War Office file that 'his war record hardly reflects the dynamic image he later tried to portray'. Nicholas said his father 'did not talk much about the trenches. He had seen little active combat, and this played on his mind.' Mosley recognized his record was not all he had hoped it to be. 'He had no personal fulfilment from his own role in the war.'

Mosley admitted that he owed 'my whole education to hospital in the first war'. He remained conscious of his lack of an academic education. He spent his time in hospital making the most of the opportunity for self-education. As is often the case in such circumstances, this learning had a longer-standing influence on him than a formal education might have achieved. His reading was voracious and influenced the strands of thought which made up his personal brand of Fascism.

Mosley began reading biographies of famous politicians – Pitt the Elder, Gladstone, Disraeli and Lord Randolph Churchill – in order 'to train himself for what he wanted to become'. He seemed more likely to become a soldier than a politician, though his great-great-grandfather had been a Whig MP at the time of the electoral reform of 1832 and, as a child, he listened to his maternal grandfather's stories of his own term in Parliament in the late 1880s. Mosley's hero was Pitt (Earl Chatham, 1708–78) and it is not hard to see why he modelled himself on a leader who had such an electrifying presence in Parliament. His speeches were regarded as great artistic performances, though his disdainful self-confidence won him few friends. Pitt was the Empire's true visionary and, as the authentic voice of patriotism, considered himself 'the only saviour of England'. Mosley aspired to be of the same stature and expected his aspirations to be achieved.

Mosley studied Benjamin Disraeli, whose speeches could floor them all. Like Mosley, he had been 'discontented, fascinated by new and esoteric ideas' and unwilling to play the 'docile party man awaiting his turn for promotion'. A dandified young bounder, Disraeli's Young England movement created a splash out of all proportion to their weight in the attempt to resuscitate a 'mythical benevolent feudal system'. The 1938 book, *Young England*, linked Mosley's Blackshirts to Disraeli's feudal socialism and his attempt to crush the bourgeoisie. The connection was made between Young England and Mosley's background in the squirearchy. The Tories stood for 'the sort of firm government which his ancestors enjoyed administering on their estates'. They had 'always preserved intuition based on tradition, and the Fascists have managed to preserve this in very good measure'.

Mosley saw in Chatham and Disraeli a tale of romance, in which 'great passions raise the soul to great things'. During convalescence, he read and learnt off by heart whole chunks of romantic poetry, which he later recited to his children. He was introduced to the romantics by Harold Nicolson, who knew him from when he was 'thrashed' at Sandhurst. Employed by the Foreign Office, Nicolson was, recalled Mosley, 'completely at home in that world. His *métier* was diplomacy and the writing of belles-lettres.' He wrote biographies of Alfred Tennyson (1923), Lord Byron (1924) and Mosley's favourite, the late romantic Algernon Swinburne (1926).

The *enfant terrible* of Victorian poetry came from an aristocratic family related to the Redesdales. He produced intoxicating works marked by an idiosyncratic brand of vitalism, mysticism, Hellenism, sadomasochism and political radicalism. Swinburne influenced modernists such as T. S. Eliot and Ezra Pound. A High Church Anglican who made elaborate use of biblical imagery in his poetry, at Oxford – where he was a member of the Pre-Raphaelite Brotherhood – Swinburne formed a club of religious sceptics and political radicals.

Mosley's favourite Swinburne poem was 'Atalanta in Calydon', a dark vision in the spirit of Greek tragedy. He was attracted to the poet's lyric powers, displaying insistent alliteration, rhythmic energy and evocative imagery. He was also drawn to the private world of 'masochistic and insatiable love and passions'. Beneath it all, Pound wrote, was a 'passion not merely for political, but also for personal liberty', with heroes 'enobled in dying for causes they exalt'.

Swinburne believed – as did Mosley – in intentionalism (a belief in the supremacy of individual historical actors). It was Thomas Carlyle (1795–1881) who initiated leadership theory with his biographies of 'Great Men'. He introduced German Romanticism into British culture, ridiculing the work of purist historians, whose work left the soul 'wearied and bewildered'. His writings left a deep impression on British Fascists, especially William Joyce. He was an impassioned political critic dismayed by the social breakdown of industrial Britain; the wealthiest country in the world was a country riven with 'poverty, misery and discontent among the working classes'. In proto-socialist language, he condemned laissez-faire and adopted the Chartist slogan 'a fair day's pay for a fair day's work'.

Carlyle argued that social balance required reverence towards those with heroic qualities to be encouraged, for they alone were 'capable of bringing society back into line with religious principles'. He became a bigoted reaction-ary and his epic studies of the French Revolution, Cromwell and particularly *On Heroes and Hero Worship* (1841) were censured for fostering militarism and totalitarianism. This great-man theory of history led to the belief – which Mosley signed up to – 'in the magically gifted individual who transforms his era and people'.

The mystical element in Swinburne influenced the occultist Aleister Crowley. Although Mosley's politics could not be regarded as 'illuminated' – i.e. he did not embrace the irrational – there was, Richard Thurlow noted, an element of magical thinking in wanting to control the actions of the universe. Influenced by his mother, Mosley read the theosophical works of Helena Blavatsky and Annie Besant.

A former circus bareback rider, Madame Blavatsky founded in 1874 the Theosophical Society, which fused ideas of International Brotherhood with research into comparative religion and the occult. A religious fraudster, she claimed to be in psychic rapport with ancient masters residing in the Himalayas, whose successors were the Aryans. It was a doctrine that appealed to the late Romantics. Mrs Besant was an anti-vivisectionist, friend of George Bernard Shaw and member of the Fabian Society. Theosophy, Mosley acknowledged, 'appeared to be a quite logical religious theory but it was, of course, entirely lacking in proof for anyone who had not enjoyed these strange and felicitous experiences in dream journeys'.

Theosophy was part of the cultural rebellion and quest of the late Victorian period against decadence. It was another modern movement concerned with achieving 'ecstasy' and acting as a catalyst for the 'rebirth' of a spiritually decaying West. Mosley was an intrigued non-believer but there was a marked similarity between his romanticism and the traits of the magician – 'the force of mind, the will to achievement, the striving to transcend human limitations, a dialectical view of the universe and the union of intellect and emotion'.

Proof that European civilization was in decay was to be found on the Western Front where, from the end of 1916 to mid 1917, Britain lost men at a higher rate than at any period of the war. However, Mosley remembered these days as 'magical'. He was not confined to hospital for the whole of the fifteen months between surgery and his return to his regiment. Until the end of the war, he engaged in a hectic social life, 'in an almost frenzied desire to swallow all beauty in one gulp. I was plunged into it even before I left hospital, as I was permitted to go out on my crutches to luncheon.' It has been suggested that 'in the sensitive survivor hedonism and nihilism struggled for mastery with idealism'. However, it was not a great struggle – hedonism won out. Mosley admitted he had 'an unlimited capacity for enjoyment, and fortune had given me the means to indulge it'.

Mosley was able to partake of his favourite pastime – hunting – despite riding in leg-irons. The sport transported him back to 'the life and spirit of the early 19th century, without crowds, only horses, hounds and the beautiful, sweeping scenery'. It was during these escapes from treatment that he became the lover of Margaret Montagu, a hostess in Leicester, where he was joined by Harold Nicolson.

Mosley took a flat in Grosvenor Square and sallied forth to houses of the famous hostesses – Mrs Ronnie Greville, who inherited a brewer's fortune and lived in Charles Street, and Lady (Sibyl) Colefax, a kindly woman with a charming house in King's Road, Chelsea, to which 'everyone of interest' in London life went. Lady Colefax presented a contrast to the sparkling Americans who dominated the capital's social scene. These included the dynamic Nancy, Lady Astor and the witty Lady (Maud) Cunard, who had 'limitless effrontery'. Lady Cunard, wrote Mosley, understood society 'should consist of conversation by brilliant men against a background of lovely and appreciative women, a process well calculated continually to increase the supply of such men'. Although aged only twenty, Mosley regarded himself as one of the 'brilliant men'.

Sporting a clipped moustache, suave, with a slight but suitably heroic limp from his 'aviator's ankle', Mosley appeared as a war veteran. He had the look, presence and manners to succeed, and already had a reputation as a seducer of women. Besides Margaret Montagu, he became the lover of Catherine D'Erlanger. The parties held by the hostesses were ideal for these assignations. They comprised largely the same group of people, with a similar morality with regard to affairs. It was a convention in this free-living, immoral set that young men had affairs 'only with married women of their social background who would know what the rules were'. They kept to a code in which 'no confidence is ever betrayed'.

Mosley had no burning desire to hurry back to the front line, though the army was agitated by his absence. He was declared fit and, on 22 June 1917, reported for duty to the Curragh in Ireland. The regiment had experienced the '16th' and the Easter Rising, which he saw as the beginning of guerrilla fighting. 'Soldiers moved about in military formation, point out flankers. You came into a village – point shot dead. We'd pan out and encircle the village . . . Every woman knitting, every man digging the garden. What was that shot? Never heard a shot. Who did that? And we leave completely baffled.' Mosley recognized guerrilla tactics were one reason why C.-in-C. Henry Wilson later withdrew the army and substituted the hated 'Black and Tans'. He realized, however, that Republicans had little choice except 'to fight us in that way' and that it was a very effective strategy.

Mosley was not in Ireland for long but enjoyed Dublin society and the hunting. But while their Irish hosts were 'giving us drinks and smiling at us', they were 'quite capable of putting a bullet in our backs'. On 2 July Mosley received orders to proceed to the Army Training Centre at the Eastern Command Cavalry Depot at Eastbourne, to instruct wounded officers. However, owing to his 'inability to march', he was categorized C3 – fit for office work only. 'I was out of the war for good with one leg an inch and a half shorter than the other.'

Mosley's army experience played a large part in the character of his later Fascist movement, with its paramilitarism. It is ironic, therefore, given the circumstances of his final assessment, that he had such a high regard for marching. On parade 'discipline was absolute, with the most meticulous regard for time-honoured rules vigorously enforced in a fashion quite adequately rough'. But in the mess, relaxing with intimate friends, the idea of a large family of arms looking after its members came to the fore.

Mosley's view of military life had echoes of his Rolleston childhood, with its blindness to notions of class and the idea of a natural order born of the soil. One of his cherished memories was of army athletics where 'an absolute equality prevailed between all ranks'. But this was not a matter of equality: notions of hierarchy remained intact, though in a more subtle fashion. Regiments, he believed, had a collective character, whose 'intimate relationship between ranks and practical working methods had slowly evolved under men with a pride in their ways and traditions in the manner of a natural and true aristocracy'. They sensed they belonged to an elite of service and achievement. Despite his admiration of the rank and file, Mosley argued that the army's collective spirit depended on 'something unique', namely leadership.

Mosley's romantic reminiscences of trench solidarity – 'fired by struggle and suffering' – were shared across Europe by the 'Front Generation' of socialists who turned to Fascism. French literary Fascist Pierre Drieu la Rochelle, whose own military service was a crucial formative experience, was already writing about how his generation had been transformed by the experience: 'There would soon come a time for these returning warriors to emit their cry of revolution. When peace comes the uneasy time will not be over.' The Front Generation hoped to release the war's 'noble inspirations' for creative purposes, even if this set them at odds with the traditional socialist movement. In contrast to trench solidarity, orthodox Marxist notions of class consciousness appeared 'pallid and theoretical'. The notion of 'war socialism' would not, however, extend further than putting the interests of society as a collective before the ambitions of the individual.

Mosley had yet to develop his ideas. He was still immersed in his social life and, using his friends, arranged a transfer to an administrative post in London, where he resumed his affairs. A renowed lover was the exotic American actress Maxine Elliott, who lived at Hartsbourne Manor, just outside London. A classic beauty, Elliott 'looked like a Roman Empress should have looked', wrote Mosley. She later migrated to the Château de l'Horizon in Antibes, where he continued to visit her. It was through such society that he came to know a diversity of gifted people and met eminent politicians, including Minister of Munitions Lloyd George, Minister of War Winston Churchill and Attorney-General F. E. Smith, who sat up 'till three or four in the morning talking in fashion entrancing or combative according to the company'. Smith advised him that 'if you were a Frenchman or a German your profession would clearly be the army, because in those countries it is the great profession. In England it must, of course, be politics or the Bar, or both.'

On 25 February 1918 Mosley was seconded to the Ministry of Munitions (MoM), where he was able to study the administrative machine. He was particularly impressed by wartime intervention and planning, and the possibilities for the peace.

Lloyd George was Mosley's first hero. The New Liberalism of the 1890s had changed the ideological background to British politics. 'A body of theorists had seen the collectivist successes of German social reform and worried about the onset of Britain's economic decline. Lloyd George emerged from that landscape of mind.' He was a hero to soldiers because of his actions over the Shells Scandal. He understood his enemies and, although intensely disliked by the aristocracy, many admired him because in power 'he knew what he wanted to do and why he wanted to do it'. As Minister, Lloyd George had appointed his own staff from outside the Civil Service, and reorganized without regard for the orthodoxies which slowed reform. These pioneers proved an inspiration to Mosley, who was particularly impressed by the 'brains behind the throne', E. M. H. Lloyd, responsible for army contracts, and E. F. Wise, director of offensive and defensive operations.

'The idea that industry would have to be deliberately organised for war production', Lloyd wrote, 'encountered subconscious resistance in a Government committed to the doctrines of free trade.' However, the sacrifices demanded by the war, combined with Lloyd George's populist instincts, encouraged collectivist elements. The experience of state intervention led to talk of social reform and reconstruction, and re-stimulated ideas of 'social imperialism'.

Mosley was part of the metropolitan elite which constituted the readership of *The Times*. It is almost inevitable, therefore, that he read the articles on post-war industrial organization which *The Times* published during July and August 1916, republished as *The Elements of Reconstruction*, with an introduction by Lord Milner, right-wing diehard and enthusiastic social imperialist.

The anonymous authors – 'men of high intelligence and right-wing sympathies' – argued wartime experience should be joined to the lessons of 'German State socialism tempered by elements of British guild socialism'. They wanted a national plan to counter the 'chaotic world of individualistic business run for unchecked private profit'. Prefiguring Mosley's later ideas, the authors acknowledged their approach was a development towards nationalization; not by socialist 'appropriation', but by 'co-ordination and co-operation, and by bringing the State into partnership by developing the crude beginnings of the "controlled establishment"'. Against class warfare, like Mosley, they supported guild socialism, which had prepared the minds of workers for industries upon a national scale. Observers later said there was about the programme, 'faint shades of an incipient fascism'.

In December 1916 a press campaign against Prime Minister Asquith over the shells shortage had been launched with the energetic assistance of Max Aitken (Lord Beaverbrook), and *The Times* and *Mail*, owned by Northcliffe, 'a more megalomaniac and less likeable newspaper proprietor than Beaverbrook'. Lloyd George cultivated self-made men and constantly intrigued with Northcliffe, while parliamentary machinations were initiated by W. A. S. Hewins, a leading social imperialist and former secretary of Joseph Chamberlain's Tariff Commission. The moves led to Lloyd George replacing Asquith.

The new Prime Minister bypassed the Treasury in authorizing military expenditure and an aggressive MoM expanded its spheres of interest with a multiplying of controls. It added up to a system of economic planning of a kind never before possessed by government. Lloyd George introduced a five-man War Cabinet and departments headed by 'Controllers' dealing with labour and food production. Imports were negotiated by government contractors, while prices were fixed and the channels of distribution controlled. Technocratically run, businessmen exercised wide powers, even if they declined to draw fully upon the extensive powers conferred on them by the State.

MoM became a key player in the conduct of air policy. It liaised with the Air Board, which had been created in 1916 under the presidency of the Lord Privy Seal, Lord Curzon. Like his two successors, he was to play a significant role in Mosley's life. Curzon resigned in December and was replaced by the industrialist Lord Cowdray, who in turn was succeeded by the newspaper proprietor Lord Rothermere. The Air Board's responsibility for overseeing aircraft procurement was a success and, during 1917, aircraft production increased by 74 per cent and helped strengthen the RFC.

Increased production resulted from a crackdown on labour unrest (strikes were declared illegal) and the introduction of compulsory arbitration. It was in the industrial relations area that Mosley was employed and where he had his 'first insight into industrial conditions and the negotiations with trade unions'. There has been speculation that he had contact with the security services. The MoM developed its own security agency, PM2, to counter industrial militancy. Mosley did deal with the captains of industry who staffed MoM's upper echelons. They had previously been denied access to the 'secret councils' of government by the alliance of landed and commercial wealth that largely controlled the State.

The MoM experiment in State intervention undoubtedly contributed to the winning of the war. Modernizers looking to the future contemplated the possibility of continuing the model for peacetime reconstruction. They did not, however, anticipate the determined effort to revert to pre-war laissez-faire. The 'Official History of the Ministry of Munitions' insisted there had been 'no definite plan' and argued that the experience of wartime State control 'retarded rather than hastened the spread of State socialism'. No one at this time presented the theoretical case for State intervention, but Mosley did not forget this example of national planning. Faith in a technocratic approach was to find full expression in the enthusiasm for planning which emerged in the 1930s; in particular in Mosley's ideas. Revolted by the slaughter in the trenches, but encouraged by the sense of community engendered by the need for co-ordinated national effort, the war provided him with a model for national planning and a stimulus for Fascism's more socialist origins.

On 8 July 1918 Mosley was declared 'permanently unfit' by the army and twelve days later Nicolson found him a job in the Foreign Office, as a military adviser, though he knew little about foreign affairs. He became an administrator in the War Department, providing quick answers to letters. The 'rigmarole was absurd' but he came to realize the importance of regulation. His colleagues became key figures in his early political career. Lord (Robert) Cecil headed his department, which consisted of 'one soldier and myself, three professional diplomats, Nicolson and two others', while a number of young Conservatives drifted in and out. Both Mark Sykes and Aubrey Herbert displayed 'charm and intelligence', while Henry Bentinck, brother of the Duke of Portland, and Godfrey Locker-Lampson, the elder of two MP brothers, were known to detest the 'goat', Lloyd George. Mosley combined shooting with speaking for Herbert in his Yeovil constituency.

A visitor to Maxine Elliott's salon was Freddie Guest, Chief Whip of the Lloyd George Liberals in the Coalition government, and cousin and crony of Churchill. He played a dubious role as 'evil genius' in raising funds for the PM's notorious slush fund. He suggested to Mosley he enter Parliament under the Liberal banner; but he already had an arrangement with the Conservative Whip Sir George Younger. Knowing 'little of Conservative sentiment' but 'propelled by a sense of patriotism', Mosley became an MP in order to represent the war generation or, as his son suggests, himself. Brooding in Whitehall, Colin Cross wrote, he 'acquired a sense of personal destiny which was never to leave him'.

On 23 July 1918 Mosley was adopted by the Harrow constituency, despite complaints that his wealth had bought him the nomination. Under the nomenclature 'Omega' in the *Harrow Observer*, he suggested 'the electorate will turn with relief from the last throes of these legal intriguers to the original and vigorous reconstruction programmes of the young soldiers who are now appearing in every constituency'. Like a number of aristocratic friends, he combined 'an uninhibited private world with a sense of social responsibility', though he took the opportunity to pander to voters' anti-German sentiments. He said Germany's chief war aim was the 'creation of an empire in eastern Europe, self-sufficient in raw materials, moulding primitive Balkan and Russian peasantry into a slave labour force capable of under-selling Britain's traditional exports, in a colossal economic war that would decide the fate of the Western world'. He wanted to 'bind our colonies to us with bonds that no strain can ever burst asunder'.

On 26 September the Foreign Office informed the War Office it was dispensing with Mosley's services 'owing to reorganisation of political departments'. He requested he 'be placed on half-pay in order to devote himself to his business and political activities. I feel that I could render more service to the country in that capacity.' Pay was a matter of indifference to him and he no longer required his army pay of £91. He was released by the Foreign Office on 1 October 1918, by which time the Germans were on the point of collapse, the war's end was in sight, and with it would come a general election.

In the year 1918 teenage conscripts took their place in ranks depleted by huge losses. At the front there was no longer the enthusiasm of 1914. Morale, one officer wrote, had 'settled on to a rock-bottom of fatalistic despair, in which the majority carried on mechanically, waiting for their next wound'. The end of the war delivered a tremendous outburst of emotion, tinged with despair at the scale of human sacrifice that the carnage had wrought. Just after 5 a.m. on 11 November the instrument of armistice was signed. Wireless signals were dispatched proclaiming a ceasefire for 11 a.m.

The Times reported unceasing drizzle during the day. This did not dampen people's 'intoxicating spirit of joy'. The crowds in Parliament Square, cheering and weeping, heard Big Ben strike for the first time since the start of the war. At twelve noon Henry Williamson 'mourned alone, possessed by a vacancy that soon the faces of the living world would join those of the dead, and be known no more'. And then a great terror came over him, 'that the whole world that I had known for so long had come to an end . . . It must NEVER HAPPEN AGAIN.'

Just six days short of his twenty-second birthday, Mosley entered the Ritz interested by the 'sounds of revelry which echoed from it. Smooth, smug people, who had never fought or suffered, seemed to the eyes of youth – at that moment age-old with sadness, weariness and bitterness – to be eating, drinking, laughing on the graves of our companions.' On that same night he saw his future wife, Cimmie Curzon, draped in a Union Jack, singing patriotic songs. Later, she 'tore round Trafalgar Square with the great crowd setting light to old cars'.

In the square Osbert Sitwell, a Grenadier Guards officer, later a Mosleyite, found the crowd dancing 'so thickly that the heads, the faces were like a field of golden corn moving in a dark wind'. But his joy that the nightmare was over was tinged with melancholy. He had seen the crowd when it 'cheered for its own death outside Buckingham Palace on the evening of the 4th of August 1914; most of the men who had composed it were now dead. Their heirs were dancing because life had been given back to them.' Mosley 'stood aside from the delirious throng, silent and alone, ravaged by memory'. From a regular strength of 400, his own regiment had been reduced to fifty-three men. 'There must be no more war,' he vowed. 'Through and beyond the failure of men and of parties, we of the war generation are marching on and we shall march on until our end is achieved and our sacrifice atoned.'

Whether Mosley had those thoughts at the time or embroidered his memory is unclear, but he certainly came to regard himself as the spokesman of the trench soldiers – a society of men bound together in a special brotherhood. The *Manchester Guardian*'s drama critic, C. E. M. Montague, published *Disenchantment*, in which he suggested people would 'find it hard to understand the simplicity and intensity of faith' with which phrases such as 'the war to end war' were 'taken among our troops, or the certitude felt by hundreds of thousands of men who are now dead that if they died their monument would be a new Europe, not soured and soiled with the hates and greeds of old'.

Nicholas recalled that his father 'talked with genuine horror about the war'. Friends remarked that tears would well up in his eyes. The enormity of the war induced Mosley to re-examine his life and became the recurring memory that forced itself to the surface at moments of doubt. Its lesson was simply 'the necessity to keep faith with those who had paid the ultimate price'. He now devoted his life to politics 'to ensure that the useless slaughter of the war was not repeated, and that the survivors of that horrific experience should live in a better world.' These were not ignoble aims.

There was nothing inevitable about Mosley's conversion to Fascism. Many who shared similar experiences turned to the left and to Communism, or reverted to their pre-1914 world and conventional party politics. But Fascism was a phenomenon tied to the First World War. Without it, a similar creed might have developed but its character would have been very different. Richard Bellamy, author of a semi-official history of the British Union of Fascists, *We March with Mosley*, believed Fascism was conceived 'in the mud and blood, and brotherhood of the frontlines'. The shattering experience of war shaped Mosley's particular form of socialism and nationalism, as it did for others of the Front Generation.

In *The Birth of Fascist Ideology* Zeev Sternhell suggests the war 'offered proof of the mobilising capacities of nationalism [and] revealed the tremendous power of the modern state'. It demonstrated the 'capacity for sacrifice, the superficiality of the idea of internationalism, and the facility with which all strata of society could be mobilised in the service of the collectivity'. Besides displaying the importance of authority, leadership and propaganda, the war had shown, above all, 'the ease with which democratic liberties could be suspended and a quasi-dictatorship accepted'.

Mosley claimed the 'horror of Europe simply committing suicide' was his impulse in politics. He admitted, however, that he 'hadn't the faintest idea whether I could do it or not'. In a German military hospital, Adolf Hitler was recovering from a gas attack, which had left him temporarily blind. 'So it had all been in vain the death of two millions . . . In these nights hatred grew in me, hatred for those responsible for this deed. That night I resolved I would enter politics.'

3

The Patriotic Peace

Three days after the armistice was signed, Prime Minister Lloyd George went to the country as head of the Coalition. His appeal was basic: trust the man who had produced the shells to build the houses. In a speech nine days later he said: 'There are many things that are wrong and which ought not to be – poverty, wretchedness, and squalor. Let us cleanse this noble land. Let us cleanse it and make it a temple worthy of the sacrifice which has been made for its honour.'

Candidates acceptable to the Conservative Bonar Law and Liberal Lloyd George received an official letter signed by both leaders (described by Asquith as a 'coupon'), which ensured the electors of the two parties would not vote against approved Coalition candidates. As a Coalition-Unionist, Mosley was an enthusiastic supporter of Lloyd George and, as a representative of the young soldiers who had perished, shared the yearning for unity that the Coalition expressed.

In his election addresses, like other politicians who had served in the State machinery during the war, Mosley saw no reason why the same policies could not continue in peacetime as part of the reconstruction. Mosley looked to the State to create the 'land fit for heroes' by taking a directing role with the 'State as Leader'. 'Munitions were produced like that in war, so why not houses in times of peace?'

Mosley wanted education from the cradle to university and schemes for health and child welfare. Power and transport would come under public control, though the debate between public and private ownership seemed to him irrelevant. Many of his later ideas were here in elementary form with essential industries shielded, and unfair competition and foreign dumping curtailed. A prosperous home market would be sustained by a minimum and high wage system. He argued the 'cost of production depended not so much on the rate of wage as on the rate of production in mass-producing industries'. It would be achieved by 'increased efficiency and organisation'.

Mosley was blessed by the support of Field Marshal Edmund Ironside, C.-in-C. Allied Troops Archangel, northern Russia, who appeared on his election platform. Mosley espoused standard patriotic sentiment but also anticipated his later politics, with the call for immediate legislation 'to prevent undesirable aliens from landing; and for the repatriation of those who are now resident in this country'. He supported the xenophobic attitudes towards the Germans in language which paralleled his later attack on the Jews. They had 'brought disease amongst them, reduced Englishmen's wages, undersold English goods, and ruined social life'. But he refused to follow the 'old men who had never fought', in demanding 'reparations and revenge'.

When asked on 26 November 1918 to summarize his own policy, Mosley, reported the *Harrow Observer*, said it was socialistic imperialism. 'It was an ugly phrase, but it was pregnant with the future' as a policy designed to evoke action from the whole nation. He countered criticism that the combination of nationalist and socialist ideas was a foreign invention with the claim that such ideas were 'in the very air of Europe, thrown high by the explosion of the war', but the combination emerged in 'completely different forms' in each country.

Mosley argued that the seeming paradox of nationalism and socialism was the 'first crude expression of political synthesis', which he saw as 'the solution to many of the false dilemmas of our time'. His socialism was the socialism of the trenches and referred to a sense of comradeship and the (imagined) dissolving of class barriers of the 'Greatest National Party that the country has ever known'. In peace, the military ideal was the model for the social ideal.

Mosley insisted that the roots of his ideas were already in English soil, in the combination of radicalism and imperialism of the pre-war Birmingham school of Joseph Chamberlain. His turn-of-the-century social imperialist movement had been a major attempt to change the direction of official economic and political policy. In his study of social imperialism Bernard Semmel argues Mosley 'combined virtually all of the salient views of virtually all of the social imperialists and to have welded them into a British fascism'. Indeed, many of his early political statements consisted of paraphrasings from their writings and speeches.

The social imperialists proposed to defend Britain's position by consolidating its Empire within the world economy, thus making the country self-sufficient. It embraced a tariff reform programme which was designed to maintain prosperity, but also to meet the military challenge of other states. Internally, they aimed to increase industrial efficiency by granting concessions to secure working-class loyalty and hoped to stabilize class relations through appeals to patriotism and collective national goals. Social imperialism embraced the Fabian–Liberal imperialist strategy of 'national efficiency' associated with Sidney and Beatrice Webb; the 'constructive imperialists' such as the economist, W. A. S. Hewins; the 'nobler socialism' of the idealist High Commissioner in South Africa, Lord Milner; and naval imperialist and MP Carlyon Bellairs, who later supported Mosley's Fascist movement.

National efficiency was an outgrowth of the Boer War (1899–1902), which raised questions about the capacity of the State to organize for war. In its aftermath, Conservative diehards emphasized the need to modernize Britain to meet the German challenge. Upper-class Liberal imperialists such as Milner, who thought the democratic system 'rotten', emphasized technocratic solutions with the 'higher types' of George Bernard Shaw's plays, organizing the Empire. From 1903 a core of constructive imperialists – Hewins, Leo Amery and J. L. Garvin, editor of the *Observer* – supported an alternative strategy of tariff reform identified with Colonial Secretary Chamberlain, who was convinced the working class wanted 'imperialism and social reform'.

Following in the footsteps of Disraeli's Young England, which had unsuccessfully pushed a similar agenda, Chamberlain determined to transform the Empire into an integrated unit large enough to sustain Britain as a great power. A key influence was London School of Economics economist H. J. Mackinder whose book, *The Geographical Pivot of History* (1904), argued that in order to defend itself against Germany, Britain had to be transformed. He wanted investment in the lower classes' productive potential; attacked the slums as the 'scrap-heaps of abandoned and disused portions of our national man-power'; and promoted a minimum wage.

Mackinder's enduring influence was on the concept of 'geopolitics'. He shared the view of historian Sir John Seeley that the Empire was 'not an Empire at all in the ordinary sense of the word but a supernation'. The two argued, as did Mosley later, that in order to protect its industrial position, Britain needed to adopt imperial federalism so as to integrate the scattered British 'white settler colonies' of the Empire into a 'Greater Britain', economically integrated by means of a system of tariff protection.

However, Chamberlain's plan for an Imperial Zollverein failed to carry the Conservative Cabinet and in 1903 he resigned to campaign for the Tariff Reform League (TRL), chaired by the Duke of Westminster. He mobilized support through a campaign directed by the editor of the *Express*, Ralph Blumenfeld, a Mosleyite in the thirties. He promoted a 'producers' alliance of industry and labour', and introduced the idea of a patriotic 'national community' as a defence against free-trade internationalism and working-class militancy. But he also emphasized the dangers of foreign competition and the threat posed by alien immigrants employed as sweated labour. In the same East End Limehouse district – the centre of Jewish immigration from Eastern Europe – in which Mosley would launch his own anti-Semitic campaign, Chamberlain attacked the 'only one race which I despise – the Jews'.

The campaign descended into stereotypical racial caricatures of the banker as a 'sly, ill-shaven East End huckster'. The racial arguments would be deployed in the same manner by Mosley. However, although anti-Semitism was common, there were few prominent figures who would openly support the campaign. Mosley would discover the same reticence.

Chamberlain was forced to abandon the Zollverein plan because white colonies feared exploitation by Britain. It was never a coherent policy since the majority of exports went to countries outside the Empire and, within it, there was comparatively little trade with Britain. H. G. Wells's criticism that such a policy would bring Britain 'into conflict with every people under the sun' was as valid then as when Mosley promoted the idea in the 1930s.

Protectionism was adopted to broaden support into a mass movement. Diehard MPs and manufacturers in the West Midlands and North demanded protection from increased foreign competition in a self-contained empire, sheltered by high tariff walls, in a version of economics based upon scientific Social-Darwinism. Like Mosley's hero, Chatham, they regarded trade as war in 'an unending duel for raw materials and markets'. In the view of free trade economist J. A. Schumpeter, they had joined with 'the dark forces of the feudal past'. The most interesting diehard was Henry Page Croft. From a family of landed baronets, Croft saw himself as another Chatham, saving the State from parliamentary stalemate by promoting the nation and empire. He advocated an aggressive State activism to facilitate co-operation between the classes in order to end class conflict. Like Mosley, Croft merged '20th century expectations with a degree of 19th century paternalism'. There was something 'almost Elizabethan' about Croft. Again like Mosley, he saw himself as 'a man of action', who wanted to translate ideas into action.

Also a man of action was Robert Blatchford, editor of the socialist *Clarion*. A spokesman for the rank and file, he criticized the Labour Party leadership for being 'totally subservient to anti-patriotic, cosmopolitan Liberalism'. His socialism was characterized by economic nationalism, imperialism and patriotism. Blatchford rejected parties as purposeless factions, politicians as frauds and parliament as undemocratic. There were many similarities between his ideas and Mosley's, and a number of his 'Merrie England' socialists, including his own family, joined the BUF.

Chamberlain's stroke in 1906 left the tariff reformers bereft of their source of inspiration. In truth, the country's democratic tradition ran too deep for social imperialists to challenge parliamentary institutions. Also rejected was Corporatism which, for continental syndicalists, was the 'embodiment of the concept of identity of interest of all producers – worker and capitalist'. Social imperialists accepted the observation of Charles Maurras of Action Française that socialism could be made to fit nationalism 'as a well-made hand fits a beautiful glove', and he foreshadowed Mosley's own National Socialism.

Mass support had been expected but the many-faceted nature of the tariff left many baffled. In addition, a widespread belief – fuelled by Treasury reports

– which insisted tariffs would increase bread prices and reduce wages was a major obstacle to working-class support. Tariff reformers suspected newspaper support was censored by threats of an advertising boycott – the same explanation Mosley later used to account for his poor press coverage in the 1930s.

The Tariff Reform League represented a serious challenge to the liberal economic system and drew formidable opponents. It threatened to mobilize forces of discontent into a political movement drawing support from both the right and the left. Industrial modernization required drastic institutional restructuring, which implied – and Mosley concurred – planning, protection and monetary policies to meet the needs of production. Chamberlain, however, had been unable to usurp the stability of the 'institutionalised network of the City, Bank and Treasury which stood for economic orthodoxy' and the required State intervention was out of the question in Edwardian times. Chamberlain's plan never 'moved beyond the conception of a protected system to the idea of an organised or managed one'. This was to be Mosley's contribution.

Some of Mosley's ideas, A. P. Thornton noted, 'came from Milner, who for long inveighed against the waste of human power through bad social and industrial arrangements in England'. The imperialist Leo Amery agreed that Mosley had drawn on the ideas of Milner, who advocated a Parliament of Industry, producer co-operatives uniting workers and managers, and a National Industrial Council to co-ordinate trade corporations. From social imperialism came the notion of the nation above class, social efficiency, militant nationalism, centralized state power, controlled economy and anti-Semitism. However, the fact that during the Edwardian era, unlike on the Continent, there had not been a populist nationalist movement nor significant influence from romantic nationalism helps explain, suggests Thurlow, the uphill task which Mosley later faced in his attempt 'to revolutionise society'.

The general election of 14 December 1918 was a sober affair. It had been called in haste; most troops were still abroad and only one in four soldiers voted. The election was favourable to young soldiers: 'old enough for Flanders, old enough for Westminster'. On the wave of post-war enthusiasm, the twenty-two-year-old Conservative Unionist Mosley was swept on the Coalition coupon to Parliament as the youngest MP. 'The astonishing thing', wrote a reporter in Harrow, 'was the almost unanimous support for Lieutenant Mosley. From every other window his face looked out; his red favours met the eye of men, women, and children; his supporters harangued the crowds at street corners; and Mr Mosley himself was here, there and everywhere.' With the receipt of the postal military vote, the final figures gave Mosley 13,950 and his opponent 3,007.

More than half of the electorate voted for the Coalition, giving it 484 MPs. The Labour Party became the largest opposition party, with fifty-nine members, while the Asquith Liberals secured only twenty-six seats. About a hundred of those elected were of the war generation. It appeared, Mosley wrote, that the 'young men, the new men, the men of the war, were in charge'. In fact, of the 168 newly elected Unionist members, fewer than forty-five were under forty years of age, while only sixty-eight had been in uniform during the war. Traditional Tories queried the new intake's quality. Stanley Baldwin considered them 'a lot of hard-nosed men who look as if they had done well out of the war'. J. C. C. Davidson was surprised that 'the old-fashioned country gentlemen are scarcely represented at all'.

Lloyd George's Cabinet was fired by 'a conviction that party controversy was out-moded and that the government's programmes, seeking for a middle way between socialists and die-hards, represented a viable and valid consensus acceptable to men and women of goodwill'. For younger MPs the idea of 'centre' politics was taken exceptionally seriously and was inextricably tied to the fortunes of the Coalition, which symbolized for them the 'mass urge for social improvement'. In reality, the Coalition lacked a coherent policy or effective machinery of co-ordination. It remained on the level of rhetoric. The election destroyed old-style Liberalism and, despite the advances of Labour, established the supremacy of Conservatism for two decades. Lloyd George accepted he was the 'captive rather than the leader of a majority' which preferred Conservatism to reconstruction.

Mosley entered Parliament intoxicated by the idea of renewal but recognized he was beginning his political career 'without the benefit of a modern political apprenticeship'. He was 'an émigré from a dying enclave of old England, with something of the attitude of a professional soldier', who believed the nation was 'an ideal homeland of democracy and social justice'. He wanted to build a better and more modern nation, constantly adapting to the developments of the age. It was no surprise, therefore, that he chose for his maiden speech on 17 February 1919 the 'Aerial Navigation Bill', which aimed to develop civil aviation.

Mosley had made few set speeches and recognized he was 'shockingly bad' in delivery, though he had a talent for vituperation. He consciously worked on becoming a great parliamentary speaker and studied past orators. He took voice lessons and practised by replying to points made in *The Times* leader. He studied 'every nuance of gesture and expression in front of a mirror' in an effort to perfect his act.

Mosley's speech was described by C. C. Grey in *The Aeroplane* as 'somewhat flowery and needlessly polysyllabic'. Apologizing, in the words of Chatham for the 'atrocious crime of being a young man', he claimed 'British air supremacy was threatened' by a Bill which would stifle the one remaining realm of heroic activity where the fruits of science and modern production were incorporated. He opposed control by 'anonymous bureaucrats in Whitehall who had hindered rather than brought an end to the War', and supported a shift of responsibility to those who understood flying, such as the 'private exploiter of aviation'. He wanted control of aviation by aircraft makers and airmen. In a theme central to his thinking, Mosley argued against officialdom stifling 'entrepreneurial spirit'.

In a second speech on aviation, Mosley called for a single air chief instead of control by the Secretary of State for War and Air, Winston Churchill (whose parliamentary private secretary was Mosley's friend Ivan Moore-Brabazon). 'The innovative nature of aviation technology and the role it played in national identity and defence demanded the full, undivided attention of one man and should not be allowed to drift into the control of bureaucrats.' Mosley doubted whether Churchill was suited to the 'less exacting pursuits of peace' or had the capacity to do both posts. He declared they were 'living in a period which is seeing what I may call the passing of the superman or the "twilight of the gods"'. He reminded Churchill that 'the first Napoleon excelled, not merely in the realms of martial display and military achievements, but also in the gentler sphere of peaceful administration'.

Mosley's espousal of aviation revealed, noted Colin Cook, an early sight of his corporatist ideas and his proposed Fascist society where individuals would only vote on issues based on their occupation, and with direct experience essential for the 'true expression of the nation'. It also reflected his love of the Elizabethan buccaneers, whom he regarded as the true spirit of Britain, which was now embodied in the airmen.

After his maiden speech, Mosley celebrated with dinner at the house of Margot Asquith, the former PM's wife. She had an original way with phrases which amused Mosley. He recalled that 'Margo seized his hand with a claw-like grip' and said his speech 'reminded me in some ways of my old friend Lord Randolph Churchill. But, dear boy, do not share his vices, never live with six women at once, it is so weakening.'

During these first months of parliamentary life, a colleague remembered a lonely Mosley 'wandering unhappily about the lobbies of the House, uncertain of his mind'. The war had 'planted the seeds of doubt; parties were changing, new political creeds running molten from the crucibles of old faiths, and he did not know which to make his own'. On unknown ground Mosley could be awkward and shy, and found it difficult working with others. One cause he did take up was promoting the embryonic League of Nations. 'If we allow these miniature Napoleons, who exist in every country, to continue to strut the European stage with these weapons in their hands, there will never be peace.'

During a by-election at Plymouth in March 1919, Mosley spoke on behalf of Lady Astor. It is obvious from her adoption speech why Mosley supported her campaign. 'If you want a party hack don't elect me. Surely we have outgrown party ties. I have. The war has taught us that there is a greater thing than parties and that is the State.' Mosley liked her 'unlimited effrontery' and felt she was 'much better when she was interrupted' and dealt with hecklers. Nancy's hectoring style, however, antagonized male voters and she had to temper her 'assertiveness with humility, presenting herself as a wife doing her duty for her husband'.

Mosley knew Nancy through her sister, Phyllis Brand, who was 'immensely' attracted to the young MP and invited him to help with the election. Unfortunately for Phyllis, he only had eyes for another young canvasser, Cynthia 'Cimmie' Curzon, daughter of Lord Curzon, one of the most glamorous figures of the Imperial age. A Cliveden habituée and favourite of Lady Astor, Cimmie had briefly met Mosley at Trent Park, home of the rich socialite Sir Philip Sassoon. Here in Devon they met by arrangement early each morning on Plymouth Hoe.

Curzon had been appointed Viceroy of India at the young age of thirty-nine. The family lived in great splendour at Hackwood Park, Hampshire, and later at Kedleston, Derbyshire, the home of Curzon's father Lord Scarsdale. Cimmie's mother, Mary, was the daughter of Levi Leiter, a Chicago millionaire, whose family originated from Leitersburg in Maryland. The Leiters were thought to be Jewish, but – despite many Semitic first names among the family – they were, in fact, Mennonites, a Protestant sect from Switzerland.

Curzon disliked Americans with 'Jewish-sounding origins' who lacked distinction. On the other hand he was obsessed with the spectacle of wealth; money, and lots of it, helped to assuage his prejudices. His father owned 10,000 acres and on his death left an estate of £450,000 (£22.5 m). Curzon was also happy that Levi Leiter settled £250,000 (£12 m) on Mary, and provided an annual income for his daughter of £6,000 (£300,000). Out of the marriage settlement, Curzon received an income of £4,000 plus his daughters' shares, amounting to £10,000 per year until they came of age. Leiter left the money for his granddaughters in a trust controlled by their father, who was officially designated their guardian but had to appear before a judge each year for permission to use it.

Curzon had three daughters, Irene (born 1896), Cimmie (August 1898) and Alexandra or 'Baba' as she was known to her family (1904). Cimmie inherited her father's congenital malformation of the spine, though months of treatment ultimately proved successful. As upper-class Edwardian children born into wealth and privilege, the girls viewed their father as loving but distant, 'an Olympian figure whose letters expressed the affection he was too busy to show by companionship'. Their father would occasionally join them in summer at the family villa, Naldera, in Broadstairs.

When Levi Leiter died in 1904, £10,000 per annum was left in trust to each daughter, though Curzon used the income to pay for houses at 1 Carlton

House Terrace in London, and Hackwood Park. Hopes for a male heir were dashed when Mary suffered a miscarriage. Cimmie was only seven when her mother died of a heart attack in 1906, aged thirty-six.

The war meant that Cimmie, who reached eighteen in 1914, did not have a coming-out season and ball. She was sent to a boarding school at Eastbourne where she was the centre of a rather tomboyish, dashing circle of girls. Cimmie enjoyed a certain degree of freedom, which was not to her father's liking (he was President of the Anti-Suffrage League). In 1917 he married an Argentinian divorcee, Grace Duggan, who enjoyed an amorous life; her wealth allowed him to maintain the grandeur of his way of life. Like the rest of his circle, Curzon viewed his friends' liaisons with sympathy and pursued his own affairs wholeheartedly but discreetly.

Over the winter of 1917–18 Cimmie set up house in a Mayfair maisonette with her sister Irene, and worked as a clerk in the War Office. During the summer she was a landgirl on a farm and undertook a social welfare course at the London School of Economics, which included working in the East End. This was regarded as daring. Cimmie had a reputation for being 'wild: a rebel with a conscience'. She remained, however, as a rich, privileged woman, part of London society. She was tall, with strong features, and had great charm which, those who knew her agreed, 'came from a genuinely sincere and lovable personality'. By the end of the war many of her male friends had been killed. Those who survived and came to call were treated by her father, who regarded Cimmie as the 'most Curzon' of his three daughters, as assailants. Mosley was more discreet than others and the couple continued to see each other during the spring.

In Parliament, Mosley maintained his verbal attacks on opponents. Yet he also thought it 'much better to hold great principles without personal animosity than to have no principles and yet to feel enmity'. He attracted attention from older politicians, who 'gave me the sense of being eternal contemporaries'. He felt an affinity with Lloyd George, with his passionate appeal for reform. This was partly because Mosley saw himself as a potential member of this select group of 'great men'. 'What is wrong with our civilisation is that the best men are often either excluded altogether until they are needed in some catastrophe or kept waiting for their chance too long, which wastes not only their time but the vital assets of the nation.'

Churchill developed a 'kindly flattery' by seeking Mosley's opinion as typical of the new generation. He helped promote the political careers of a number of 'suspect patrician lightweights' but it was Churchill's great friend, F. E. Smith, who exerted the most influence. The Lord Chancellor regarded himself as a 'progressive Unionist, social reformer and friend of the ordinary un-unionised working man: a Tory Democrat'. Described by Beaverbrook as the 'cleverest man in the kingdom', Smith dispensed lavish hospitality to young men at his house, Carlton, in the Cotswolds. He spurred them on by referring to the glittering prizes that life had to award. He was, David Clark observed, 'a walking illustration that there is such a phenomenon as an over-endowment of charisma. No one trusted FE, though many loved his company.'

In his study of Mosley's contemporaries, *Children of the Sun*, Michael Green identifies Smith as an uncle to such young men, conveying an attitude of 'unscrupulous roguery' about the rules of life. Like the other 'wicked bachelor uncles' to the '*Sonnenkinder*' of the twenties – Churchill, Beaverbrook and Lloyd George – he was the enemy of pious father figures such as Stanley Baldwin. Mosley had seen Smith's character traits in his father: the lack of boundary setting and the willingness to gamble. A great drinker, Smith attempted 'to burn the candle at both ends without ill-effect on his physical or intellectual powers'. Mosley, who drank little, wrote that 'while the performance of youth could be indefinitely repeated, with almost greater effect in age, it was not so easy with such a habit of life to absorb new knowledge or to learn new tricks, equally difficult for old dogs and old drunks'. He noted that 'the wayside became strewn with young men who thought that to be brilliant it was necessary to adopt his fashion. What was the secret of his Pied Piper appeal to the young? Wit and irreverence.'

Another Smith acolyte was Robert Boothby, a rebellious quasi-Tory supporter of the Coalition. He became part of Mosley's circle, which included Harold Nicolson, Leslie Hore-Belisha (MP), newspaper publisher Esmond Harmsworth, the young Irish journalist-adventurer and Churchill devotee Brendan Bracken, Walter Elliott (who was regarded as a future prime minister), Moore-Brabazon, Cecil L'Estrange and journalist Colin Coote, a Coalition Liberal fresh from the trenches, where he had suffered gassing. Mosley's circle deferred to experienced politicians but it was not long before disillusionment crept in and suspicion tempered their deference.

The old games soon resumed and the old men again took a firm hold of the reins. 'The young men were in a minority,' Mosley recalled, 'and the "hardfaced men" were in a great majority. The profiteer outnumbered the fighter.' Fired with the ideals of wartime unity, new members wanted 'to teach the old fogeys their business'. Dubbed 'the Babes' by the press, they attempted to build a base in Parliament and, on 7 April, a forty-strong New Members group was formed, consisting of Unionists (though the Coalition Liberal Oscar Guest was elected chairman). Mosley joined Coote as a secretary.

New Members, Coote recalled, were determined 'to see that our generation had not died in vain' and took their election programmes seriously. They backed Lloyd George's crusade to 'force through the great measures of our programme against the resistance of the reactionaries within the Coalition'. Mosley already regarded himself as 'a man not of the parties but of the centre'.

By and large, it was the able Clydeside Unionist Walter Elliott, a firm supporter of Colin Addison's policies on health and housing, who advocated a permanent Coalition Party. In their ambitious dreams, young Coalitionists envisioned a centre party under Lloyd George reaching out to the moderate wing of the Labour movement, though they regarded the Labour Party itself as irrelevant.

Mosley became the rising star. 'Bursting with energy and ideas', he stood in 'glamorous contrast to the old gangs'. He received universal praise for his early speeches, which upheld the free trade system. Coote testified to the genuineness of 'his contempt for the old fuddy-duddies' bafflement with unemployment'. Mosley regarded his early speeches as immature, but acknowledged that their positive reception meant that it was 'impossible to call me just a crank'.

Coote thought Mosley displayed enormous talent. 'He could absolutely flay the skin off anybody inefficent in debate. He was no admirer of persons.' But he also suffered from 'a persecution complex which caused him to be much more rude than he need be'. He was not popular, since he 'always exuded an air of too gracious condescension'. Coote recalled the way he played on his limp, 'and that curious curl of the upper lip which made him always look as if he had a bad smell under his nose'. Observers suspicious of his sudden reputation for brilliance and wit marked him down as arrogant.

In the months following the conclusion of the Versailles peace treaty of July 1919, the PM was determined to fuse the Coalition government into a centre party. 'National unity alone can save Britain, can save Europe, can save the world,' Lloyd George declared. The Cabinet, however, was sceptical of fusion's merits and was 'inclined to reflect on the sad fate of Joseph Chamberlain'.

Churchill had become a 'reactionary of the deepest dye', and wholly without sympathy for the 'foreign and fallacious creeds of socialism'. Like many disaffected patricians, he supported Lloyd George's claim that Labour's success had opened the door to Bolshevism. In the *Weekly Despatch*, Smith proclaimed the need for a National Party to fight a crusade against this evil. The three senior politicians encouraged co-operation with businessmen on a common programme to fight by-election Labour candidates in industrial constituencies.

In a speech to a hundred MPs at the Criterion Restaurant on 15 July 1919, the New Members heard Smith argue 'modern problems were technical rather than ideological, calling for managerial skills rather than grand debates on principle'. The young men applauded his call for 'a great National Party'. Primed by Chief Whip Freddy Guest with Lloyd George's approval, the press reported on a 'political sensation' but the enthusiasm quickly evaporated. 'We met and we discussed,' Mosley recalled, 'but not much more happened.' The limitation was 'the power of the party machine, which in the absence of grave crisis is always overwhelming in British politics'.

Also addressing the New Members was Lord Robert Cecil, a rigid free trader who headed a 'group of high-minded centrists whose effectiveness rose and fell with the fortunes of their eccentric leader'. The son of former Prime Minister, Lord Salisbury, the aristocratic Cecil had been removed as foreign minister at the peace conference. Thereafter, he attacked Lloyd George's foreign policy 'hip and thigh'. A passionate evangelist for the League of Nations, Cecil criticized the PM's cynical circumvention of his beloved League as an 'instance of old-style nationalism rejecting the glowing opportunities present for creating a new international law and international morality'. His solution to domestic troubles was profit sharing and industrial co-partnership, which he hoped would create a bulwark against socialism. These ideas attracted Mosley, though he realized it was naive to believe conflicts between labour and capital could be resolved by restoring Christian fellowship within industry.

A combination of support for the League of Nations and the Anti-Waste League of Rothermere was the programme Cecil wanted to push in by-elections. What he sought above all was 'a union of landowners and labour against the intervening classes'. It was Young England in a more appropriate setting. Cecil enlisted aristocrats of conscience against the 'money-grubbing Coalitionists'. This dream of a non-ideological party of the centre made up of moral Conservatives and patriotic Labour was shared by Mosley. The Tories, he told Cecil, had sold out to the 'bourgeois profiteer', while the socialists were too concerned with 'ultimate issues'.

The hope that a 'backstairs fronde of big politicians and press magnates could shake the system' was out of date but Rothermere continued to play the kingmaker. He campaigned against wasteful public spending (squandermania) and helped create a public demand for 'efficiency'. His newspapers praised anti-waste MPs such as Mosley. For once his propaganda exercise did chime with the Treasury, which wanted to return to the pre-war system of free trade based on the gold standard as a necessary means of continuing its dominance of the State system and control of expenditure.

Rothermere's papers warned the country faced economic ruin unless there was remorseless economy. A link was made between squandermania and 'bungling officialdom', as his propaganda, sparked by the 1917 Russian Revolution, attacked all forms of government control. Advocates of State control were labelled crypto-Communists and were excluded from major participation in national affairs. The three-way relationship between the State, capital and labour, which had been fostered during the war, was allowed to collapse and few of the changes endured. Trade soon converted back to private hands, the government abandoned reconstruction and withdrew from intervention in the economy, as the control apparatus was dismantled in an effort to restore the pre-war status quo.

Mosley was persuaded by Lord Salisbury to become Secretary of his People's League for Economy, an upmarket version of the Anti-Waste League. He considered its dashing and amusing president, Leslie Hore-Belisha, to be an 'outstanding Jew'. Mosley supported the Rothermere-backed League's attacks on the 'profligacy of the Coalition Government, both in the wild expenditure of public money and the sale of public assets at knock-down prices, often to dubious political characters'. Salisbury used the League to strengthen the diehard position and to persuade Bonar Law to stand as leader.

In October 1919 Mosley became President of the League of Youth and Social Progress, in which role he achieved notoriety for exploiting the youth racket. In his inaugural address he spoke of the two mentalities – 'the mind of 1914 and the mind of today'. He warned of the old men creeping back 'to dominate your new age, cleansed of their mistakes in the blood of your generation'. Mosley discovered that the League was run by a 'smooth and smug little Liberal typical of the middle-aged politicians who in each generation exploit youth'.

In supporting the entrepreneur and attacking bureaucracy there was a glimpse of the future Mosley, with his commitment to efficiency and free markets, but there was little evidence of his later radicalism. He associated with dyed-in-the-wool Tories whose commitment to reform was wafer thin. What they proposed was an attempt to stave off socialism with minimal change to institutions and the political system. The diehards' whole stance was paternalistic and tied to outdated values derived from their aristocratic backgrounds. They veered from an incipient modernism to nostalgia for a feudal past.

During the peace conference Cimmie Curzon had stayed in Paris with Elinor Glyn, who reported on the treaty negotiations for the Hearst newspapers. Until he married for a second time, Lord Curzon had an affair with Elinor, who was known as a great courtesan. They talked about Mosley and Elinor told Cimmie 'there is a reason for knowing your Tom very thoroughly'. She had heard something of his reputation. Cimmie subsequently rebuffed Mosley's advances and a proposal of marriage; an unusual outcome for Mosley, who regarded himself as irresistible. She had an inkling that her father and Mosley were two of a kind. Elinor warned her Mosley was a type of man with whom she was all too familiar and that she was about to make a serious mistake.

Elinor wrote a memoir about her relationship with Curzon in which she said he had 'always been loved by women, but he has never allowed any individual woman to have the slightest influence upon his life'. She believed he had 'never paid real homage to a woman in his life; it is women who pay homage to him'. Mary Curzon's biographer noted her unhappiness derived from her husband's failure 'to nourish her intelligence and to notice her loneliness'. Elinor added that 'all his concern for her when she was ill, did not compensate for his neglect of her other needs'. Cimmie's father had wanted a wife who was 'like a daughter, presumably busy with her feminine occupations, while he was busy with his'. The husband must be free and unhampered. Unconsciously, the man Cimmie was rejecting was a version of her father.

On her return from Paris, Mosley wrote to his 'darling' that he had been told his writing 'could only mean genius or lunacy: in my youthful arrogance I welcomed the former conclusion, but since the present obsession I am driven to believe that the latter alternative is true'. He believed 'the will of men could conquer all emotion or pain whether spiritual or physical and mould the world to be just a reflection of its own personality'. But he had discovered 'an emotion which is more powerful than even the human spirit'. He again proposed marriage but Cimmie was unmoved. 'And now Dear about your lunacy,' she teased him, 'don't let it be a disease . . . I can't love you as you love me . . . I should adore to be the really glorious friends we could be: please be satisfied with that, I know it's a rotten poor return.'

Mosley returned to the offensive, but again Cimmie dismissed him: 'Let me know that my being unable to love you in the way you want isn't going to spoil things for you between us . . .' He persuaded her to go hunting in Leicestershire, where she was finally worn down and gave in. He declared he had never given his love to any other woman but warned of his vital side, which was necessary for 'a life of struggle'. However, he assured her that his real love would 'always prevent the original wild animal hurting or distressing you'. Unhappily for Cimmie, she would discover that Mosley's vital side was the stronger.

Lord Curzon's expectation that Cimmie would marry a peer or statesman was rudely shattered by Mosley's proposal. On 21 March 1920 he informed his wife he had known the Mosleys in the old days in Derbyshire and noted that Rolleston was advertised in *Country Life* as to be sold. He added that Mosley had admitted to Cimmie 'flirting a bit with married women but had now, at the age of 23, given that up and was full of ambition and devoted to a political career where every sort of prize awaited him'. The Salisbury–Astor set 'looks upon the young man as rather a hero and that he is really promising'. Cimmie had no idea if he had money and her father feared that 'financially it will hit me rather hard'.

It was a daunting experience for a young suitor to meet a man from whom Stanley Baldwin received 'the sort of greeting a corpse would give to an undertaker'. Following the meeting, Curzon wrote to his wife that their prospective son-in-law had 'rather a big nose' and was Jewish in appearance. He had discovered he was 'quite independent and has practically severed himself from his father who is a spendthrift and a ne'er-do-well'. The estate was run by trustees who 'will give him £8,000–£10,000 a year straight away and he will ultimately have a clear £20,000 [£1 m] per annum. He did not know that Cim was an heiress.' After Cecil described Mosley as an 'able and promising warrior, not in the first flight, but with a good future before him', Curzon gave his consent to marriage.

Mosley dispatched a proposal of marriage to Cimmie, who finally relented. Their engagement was announced on 26 March. 'They were going to have a great career together,' Cimmie told her father. 'He was destined to climb to the very top – with her aid.' Nancy Astor wrote to her that she would be 'just the kind of wife he needs and wants. I feel he must have a great soul, or he would never have asked you to share it.'

Lydia Allen, a housemaid at Rolleston, remembered the newly engaged couple staying at the Hall. Mosley was 'not half so nice as his father. He was more of a snob. He would never even say "good morning" to you. She was very nice. We had champagne.' Lydia recorded in her diary that when the couple left, Mosley 'did not tip any of the staff. Sir Oswald tipped us all, saying his son had no change, which he knew was a lie.' The family's nanny recalled his 'terrible rudeness to servants'. Nicholas Mosley admitted his father 'was sometimes frightening. He had a way of suddenly switching from being the benign joker to someone with his chin up, roaring, as if he was being strangled. He would usually roar when he was not getting what he wanted from servants.'

Lydia would not have a bad word said against the Mosley family. 'They did a lot for the village. They used to hold benefit cricket matches for the soldiers returning from the War. They employed most of the village. The farmers on the Rolleston estate belonged to them.' Their self-enclosed, almost feudal world, however, was about to collapse. They were badly affected by the inflation crisis of 1920.

In the immediate post-war period there had been an economic boom, characterized not only by low unemployment but also by rapid inflation. Rothermere's newspapers were full of tales of boom-time speculators who flourished because of government waste, and helped forge a coalition of savers and middle-class consumers, who supported deflationary policies. With support from Salisbury and Cecil, Anti-Waste independent Conservative candidates at several by-elections, including the successful election of Rothermere's nephew and Mosley's friend, Harold Harmsworth, put pressure on the government. In April, Chancellor of the Exchequer Austen Chamberlain delivered a deflationary budget which 'slammed on the brakes', ended the boom and signalled the return to 'sound finance'.

Largely indifferent to economic issues, Mosley was unconcerned by the reassertion of traditional institutional control, even though deflationary measures were incompatible with ideas of reconstruction. The economic collapse put paid to hopes of a land fit for heroes and ushered in a decade of mass unemployment and inter-war depression. Politically ambitious, Mosley was preoccupied with seeking advancement. He liquidated all his 'outside interests and distractions', selling off his hunting horses and polo ponies, and because the war had made it unviable, put Rolleston up for auction.

Inflation, taxation, death duties and the decline of incomes destroyed the wealth of many landed gentry. It led to the sale of country houses and farms in a 'most fearful and prolonged haemorrhage'. During the twenties, 29,000 small country estates were put on the market. The effect on middle-class society in rural areas was profoundly disturbing. 'With rupture of continuity came loss of faith.' Rolleston was sold to a speculator, the estate divided into separate farms and the Hall pulled down in 1928. Mosley said it was a 'terrible uprooting causing me much sorrow at the time. An established institution of old England had come to an end.'

Mosley was rich, but taxation and inflation ate into his wealth. In 1914, with an annual income of £10,000 (£540,000), he would have retained 92 per cent of it; by 1920 this fell to 57 per cent. Taking into account inflation, by 1925 Mosley would have required £18,000 (£1 m) per annum to preserve the real value and, because of taxation changes, he would have actually needed a gross income of £30,000 (£1.6 m).

Seven weeks after the announcement of their engagement, Mosley and Cimmie were married on 11 May in the Chapel Royal, St James's Palace. Newspapers reported the chapel was 'so small that the guests scarcely have room even to study one another's gowns – but the privilege of being married in this building is a highly prized favour'. Best man was Mosley's Sandhurst friend Bruce Ogilvy, brother of the Earl of Airlie, and his guests included Robert Boothby and Harold Nicolson. Cimmie had wanted a quiet wedding but her father was intent on planning the social event of the year. The cream of high society were invited, along with the highest ranks of Europe's royal families. King George and Queen Mary were present, as were the King and Queen of Belgium who had flown across the channel in a two-seater aeroplane especially for the occasion. In addition to the select hundred guests inside, several hundred more were invited to a glittering reception at the Foreign Secretary's residence at 1 Carlton House Terrace.

Outside, the crowds were twelve deep and had to be held back by the police. The King acknowledged the cheers, as did Mosley, who looked stiff, like an actor unsuccessfully taking off Douglas Fairbanks. The other Curzon daughters were in attendance: Irene noted that sixteen-year-old Baba seemed 'even more in love with Tom than Cimmie is'. The bride was showered with gifts of pearls, diamonds and sables. Mosley gave his wife a diamond tiara, a silver wristwatch and a sapphire ring. The newspapers proclaimed Cimmie the 'Bride of the Year'.

The honeymoon was spent near Genoa, at Portofino, then a small fishing village. The Mosleys stayed in the Castello Brown, which belonged to the family of Francis Yeats-Brown, later author of *The Bengal Lancer* and Fascist sympathizer. 'Across the lovely bay', wrote Mosley, 'you could see at Spezia the tragic water, wine-dark with Shelley's drowning; along the heights which linked Portofino with Rapallo strode Nietzsche in the ecstasy of writing *Zarathustra*.'

Newspapers described Cimmie as the 'personification of the society girl, tall, willowy, with a slightly bored expression, lovely complexion, and expressive blue eyes. She dresses in the most exquisite taste, and is a fine set-off to her handsome husband in whose company she almost invariably appears.' Mosley emerged as one of the leaders of the new beau monde and every week he and Cimmie were seen in attendance at society events. The Prince of Wales was a frequent guest at Carlton Gardens where Cimmie's stepmother held 'frivolous parties' for her. The Mosleys were photographed at Ascot, Henley and countless charitable functions before they flew off to chic foreign resorts such as Venice and Deauville. The society columns gushed about her beauty, though the photographs reveal a very tall (compared with her contemporaries), stout, average-looking woman with a pleasant smile.

Mosley's descriptions of his wife are endearing but not passionate. Most relationships are repetitions to a greater or lesser degree of the original relationship with our parents. Elinor Glyn's memoir suggests Cimmie simply ended up colluding in a replay of her own parents' marriage. His relationship with Cimmie was a mirror image of the one with his mother.

'Like most people,' Mosley wrote, 'I have a great appreciation of real goodness of character, and I have never seen that finest of qualities in higher degree in any human being. She was a good woman in the true, natural sense of the word.' Cimmie was a champion of the underprivileged, at least in theory. Mosley described her as having advanced liberal views, though she considered herself to have 'Bolshevist' sentiments. Cimmie, in fact, was 'in the well-known tradition of the warm-hearted, emotional person with an instinctive sympathy for the underdog'. She rebelled against her father and for that reason reacted strongly against Conservatism. It did not go much further, however. Her intellectual understanding of socialism was limited. Nicolson unkindly thought her 'stupid'.

People reacted to Cimmie in a very different manner from the way they did to her husband, who was seen as remote and lacking warmth. He gave the impression of using people for his own ends. That was never said of Cimmie, who was transparently sincere. She had many admirers but there was never any hint of a sexual charge in their devotion to a mother-like figure. After the marriage, Elinor Glyn emphasized to her the importance of loyalty and the need to be her husband's 'Chief of Staff always'. There is little doubt that

Cimmie adored her husband but she did not appreciate until near the end that he wanted a mother substitute who would set no boundaries but would support him at whatever cost to her own feelings. Mosley loved her after his fashion but it was not a mature love. The fact that he idealized her, while at the same time abused her trust, is indicative of narcissism.

Everything seemed to be going Mosley's way. He combined the 'attributes of the old school – a baronetcy and huntin', shootin' and fishin' in the shires – with the preoccupations of the new, post-war world'. He had the background, war record, marriage and burgeoning career for a successful future as an MP. The couple acquired a Queen Anne town house, a few minutes' walk from Parliament, at 8 Smith Square, from where Mosley conducted a hectic social life, which he claimed was a necessary balance to the obsessions of politics. However, he spoiled an entirely reasonable defence with his gift for self-dramatization. To become the complete man, what was required, Mosley argued, was '*Ganzheit*' (wholeness). Perhaps, but he was also simply having a good time.

The gossip columns were busy with accounts of Mosley's 'jazzy' private life. He continued to be an habitué with Boothby of the salons of Mrs Ronald Greville, and Ladies Astor, Cunard, Londonderry and Colefax. Boothby thought he was in paradise, amid the luxury and generous hospitality of these wealthy hedonists. Leaving Parliament after late sittings, Mosley would frequent fashionable nightclubs where it was observed he was not in the company of his wife. It is not clear how long it was before he betrayed Cimmie; her sisters imagined a few years. More likely is Mosley's second wife's suggestion of a few months. He was accustomed to using the salons for 'flushing the covers' (a reference to pheasant shooting) of married women. Romantic novelist Barbara Cartland often saw him at the Café de Paris, where he presented a 'rather frightening figure – tall, dark, with almost black eyes which never seemed to smile'. But he kept a smile for Cartland's friend Hilary Charles who, with her sister, resembled 'pretty, fragile butterflies'.

The social scene also extended abroad when the Mosley circle travelled to Italy and France. In Rome, the widowed Princess Jane di San Faustino presided over a cosmopolitan crowd. Mosley found Rome a 'university of charm, where a young man could encounter a refinement of sophistication whose acquisition could be some permanent passport in a varied and variable world'. In Paris, the house of Elsie de Wolfe, who had made a fortune as an interior decorator, had 'one of the most voluptuous settings it was possible to encounter'. With the latest fad, a floodlit garden and swimming pool, Sunday was a 'delicate scene of beautiful women and young men'. Mosley had been introduced to Paris society through Elsie's English and half-Jewish husband Charles Mendl. Late in the war he served as an intelligence officer in Paris, where he was responsible for handling the press at the embassy. Rumours which circulated suggesting he had ample funds with which to bribe the foreign press were dismissed by Mosley, but he did have a long-standing relationship with MI6.

Mosley had many admirers. After reporting on one of his appearances on the polo field, the *Tatler* ran the caption, 'Is it true that he is future Prime Minister of England?' This was not taken seriously but when the old Speaker of the House, Lowther, heard Mosley make a speech, he remarked to Edward Wood (Lord Halifax): 'Watch that young man. He will probably be Prime Minister.' There were, however, those who wondered if the whole edifice was 'almost too good to be true'.

4

'The Vision Splendid'

Mosley said his political life was predetermined by an 'almost religious conviction to prevent a recurrence of war'. His allegiance now swung towards the leading advocate of the League of Nations (LoN), Lord Robert Cecil. On his return from honeymoon he became secretary to the Lord Cowdray-funded League of Nations Union. Whereas the League represented to Cecil a forum of moral opinion, for Mosley it meant the willingness to use power to settle international disputes. However, with the United States' withdrawal, the League became in practical terms a European organization for the maintenance of peace. Despite differences, Mosley admired Cecil's 'experienced and traditional wisdom of statesmanship'.

By the summer of 1920 Cecil established himself as a leading critic of the government not only on foreign policy but also on industrial questions. Against a background of ongoing industrial unrest, Cecil discussed with newspaper proprietors Rothermere and Cowdray the idea of a centre party to promote high wages and productivity, and oppose reactionary employers and militant workers, in opposition to both Labour and Lloyd George. They would advocate 'conciliation and union of Classes at home, peace in Ireland, L of N foreign policy and above all economic sanity and retrenchment'. It would overcome the Lloyd George Coalition by 'innate moral superiority'.

Mosley recognized that the 'intoxication of the early days had fizzled out' and now felt betrayed. No attempt had been made to use the 'great machine of war for greater purposes of peace. Despite every protest, the productive machine so painfully and laboriously erected was scrapped or sold at knock-down prices to the profiteers ... Everything for which we fought – peace abroad and reconstruction at home – was thrown to the wolves of the great vested interests.'

Ireland was the issue around which disillusioned Tories joined in opposition to the Coalition. During the autumn, Mosley and his young Unionists – Robert and Hugh Cecil, Henry Cavendish-Bentinck, Godfrey Locker-Lampson, Aubrey Herbert and Mark Sykes – advocated granting Home Rule to Ireland with dominion status. In the *Harrow Gazette* on 15 October 1920 Mosley said, 'The answer is not reprisal and counter-violence but a separate Ulster, naval and military safeguards for Britain, a limited right of manoeuvre in foreign policy for Ireland, but a basically independent nation.'

The diehards pressed Lloyd George to introduce tough measures in Ireland. Sinn Fein and the Dáil had been declared illegal. The government had pushed through the Government of Ireland Act, 1920, providing for Irish Home Rule, with two Irish Parliaments, one for the South in Dublin and the other for the six Protestant counties of the historic province of Ulster in Belfast. The unwillingness of hardliners to grant concessions led to the use of counter-terror against Irish nationalists. Ulsterman Sir Henry Wilson, C.-in-C. of the army in Ireland, acknowledged his troops were acting rough, but since they were being constantly sniped at, thought it acceptable to hit back. Even though they offered no alternative, Tory MPs Samuel Hoare and Edward Wood warned, in August, that 'coercion alone will not re-establish law and order in Ireland'.

Faced both with backbench pressure and limited available forces, the government decided to employ 'irregulars'. Mosley subsequently received evidence from a neighbour of the Curzons that torture was being used in Ireland. This was confirmed by information he received from the Irish poet and economist A. E. Russell, and a country lawyer in Tralee, J. D. Connor.

Hardened ex-officers and disillusioned demobilized veterans were recruited into auxiliary police units known, because of their black belts and khaki uniforms, as the 'Black and Tans'. Recruited to maintain order, these 'gentlemen adventurers' brought their knowledge of brutality to the task. Their 'habit of charging round wildly in open lorries' also led to many casualties; in six months 600 auxiliaries were killed. 'The rage of men without discipline who feel unable to hit back while suffering heavy losses', noted Mosley, 'produced the stupid and brutal acts of individual violence which could have no effect except to swing opinion against them.' He said the name of Britain was 'being disgraced, every rule of good soldierly conduct disregarded, and every decent instinct of humanity outraged'. He had no problem with hitting back at the IRA but the reprisals were an 'inefficient way of going about things'. For Mosley, the policy was 'symptomatic of a fundamental weakness brought about by a failure of leadership', which undermined Britain's greatness.

By attacking their Irish policy, Conservatives claimed Mosley was 'badly letting down the side, adding disloyalty to impudence'. It was impossible for him to get a hearing in the Commons and he decided, on 3 November, to cross the floor and face his critics as an Independent. 'It was better to confront what appeared to me as a charge of howling dervishes than to stand in the middle of it.' Lord Henry Bentinck and Aubrey Herbert also crossed over in a gesture against government policy. At the time, changing sides was not considered an event of significance. Mosley thought Herbert, who had a passion for the League of Nations and Albania – as head of the wartime

Adriatic Mission he had been offered its Crown – charmingly vague but blessed with 'very acute intelligence'. Thereafter, Herbert's energies were exercised in forming a centre party.

Suddenly, the storm burst as the Conservatives tried to prevent other rebellious 'class traitors' crossing over to the opposition benches. The backlash surprised Mosley and he had speedily to develop a 'certain ferocity in debating method'. He acknowledged it was a 'wicked animal which defends itself when attacked', but it was only 'by assailing with personal ridicule the noisiest of my assailants that I could get a hearing'. He admitted it was several years before he advanced an argument 'without first beating down interrupters'.

Time and again, Mosley and the small group of cross-party dissidents spoke out against the terror in Ireland. His energy and the ferocity of his attacks on the government marked him out as a potential leader. There were those who had reservations, especially when it became apparent he believed he had 'a special role to fulfil and was somehow marked out for greatness'. David Cecil disparagingly told Herbert that the twenty-four-year-old Mosley 'had got hair that is too new and an unused face'. Herbert noted that Mosley had the 'elements of great success in him but will be a lost leader one day'.

Early in November a Peace with Ireland Council was formed to campaign against attempts to solve the Irish problem by force and for a just and lasting settlement between the two countries. The Council's strength lay in its non-party and mainly English membership, which could not be dismissed as a 'fifth column' of Sinn Fein. Lord Henry Cavendish-Bentinck was appointed Chairman, with Mosley as Honorary Secretary. In the Commons on 11 November Mosley asked MPs to recognize 'that we have lost in the catastrophic competition (of fighting terrorism with terrorism), and must start again on a new basis, to rebuild the efficiency of civil administration, and restore our discipline'.

Large meetings against the policy of reprisals were addressed over the winter of 1920–21 by a galaxy of eminent supporters, including the Tory Sir John Simon; Labour's J. R. Clynes, Margaret Bondfield and Ramsay MacDonald; Mosley's friends, Lady (Mark) Sykes and Lady Bonham Carter; and leading writers G. K. Chesterton and Hilaire Belloc. Chesterton's pamphlet, 'What are reprisals?', argued that 'to burn down a factory and a row of shops because a comrade has been murdered is not self-defence – it is senseless revenge'. The Council attracted Englishmen whose 'sense of justice and fair play had been wounded' and pride in their country damaged by the actions of the Black and Tans. Council member Aubrey Herbert apologized for his youthful folly in supporting Sir Edward Carson's call for Ulster resistance 'as he now feared that such support would lead to problems in the empire'. Such opposition represented real unease inside Coalition ranks.

The Irish troubles became a conflict of terrorisms, symbolized for both sides by 'Bloody Sunday'. On 21 November Michael Collins's IRA volunteers assassinated eleven suspected British intelligence agents and, in revenge, the Black and Tans fired on an Irish football crowd killing twelve people. Lord Robert Cecil called for an inquiry and three days later along with Mosley voted against his own front bench. Mosley's speech won high praise for its 'cogency of argument and the loftiness of its tone'. He was shocked at the government's defence of reprisals which 'slurred over entirely the difference between the right of a man to hit back and to defend himself against cowardly and dastardly attacks, and the right of men to revenge themselves for the sins of the guilty upon the heads of the innocent population of Ireland'.

In *Common Sense*, 'Socraticus' wrote that Mosley's stand had been taken 'not out of a desire for notoriety – no one who has had half an hour's talk with Mr Mosley could entertain that suspicion for a moment – but from obedience to strong conviction'. Mosley said that 'if the Government could only prevent the murders, or catch and punish the men who commit them, there would be no demand for reprisals'. He blamed the failure on the inefficiency of the security police and called for a 'well-organised Intelligence Service'. Mosley described the Irish policy as a 'competition in terrorism' in which there was a 'struggle between the Government and the murderers to see which can intimidate the community more successfully'. The government wanted 'to burn villagers out of their houses but it would be to no avail since such action gives them precisely what they want – a propaganda case against us all over the world, which brings them in fresh funds'. Affairs in Ireland, Mosley regretted, had developed into war. The only solution was a withdrawal of British forces to the coast, where ports could be held as strategic posts.

Ireland was one more issue with which Lloyd George had to deal as the Coalition struggled. The boom had collapsed, two million were unemployed and organized labour was increasingly militant with eighty-six million working days lost in strikes. Housing was cut as part of the Treasury's deflationary strategy.

Mosley's orthodox solution to the economic crisis emphasized that free trade was the only way to maximize prosperity. 'Half the world is unable to buy the goods which this country is in a position to offer.' He shared the views of the centrists who opposed protectionism and, as a fully fledged internationalist, championed League of Nations reconstruction loans, currency stabilization and lower tariff barriers. He did not criticize policies of economy, which he advocated 'with all the fervour of a Gladstone', and deflation, because he 'did not as yet see the connection between the two'. It was another two years before he perceived the contradiction between sound finance and the dream of a land fit for heroes.

With the new year, the Wilsonian vision of a new international order lay crippled. In its place stood the Versailles treaty, which split Europe into those states it had benefited and those it punished. Convinced Germany would inevitably revive, Lloyd George warned his fellow peacemakers against the treaty conditions. A. L. Kennedy wrote (27 January 1921) that the assumed 'perpetuity of arrangements made for Germany by her victors . . . raised the perplexing question of how the provisions of the treaties could be maintained: "Who is going to prevent her maintaining or assembling armed forces?"' Mosley was the most energetic advocate in the Commons of the LoN, but realized it was floundering and with it the hopes of a new politics of co-operation.

Mosley wanted to unite all the anti-Coalition forces – Liberals, 'patriotic' Labour and Cecilian Tories – in partnership. Its nucleus would comprise political friends such as Herbert, Cavendish-Bentinck, the two Cecils, Locker-Lampson, Walter Guinness, Billy Ormsby Gore, Sam Hoare and Edward Wood, who combined 'high-mindedness with wit, and polemics with laughter'. During February Lord Robert Cecil announced he would sit among the opposition MPs, fuelling speculation that he might support the Labour Party. He acted as a 'vital catalyst' in Mosley's progression from Coalition Unionism to the Independent Labour Pary, but he proved a reluctant leader, being neither ambitious nor decisive.

Mosley continued to bully the PM into replying to questions about government approval of reprisals. On 25 February, while her husband was busy campaigning with the Peace with Ireland Council, Cimmie gave birth to their first child, Vivien. The first to congratulate the Mosleys was Margot Asquith, who was aware of the dangers of childbirth as a result of her own tragedies; she had experienced three stillbirths. She impressed upon Cimmie the 'importance of avoiding pregnancy for a long period'. She knew how this was to be done: 'Henry always withdrew in time, such a noble man.'

On 7 March Mosley taunted the government as having 'denials on its lips and blood on its hands'. He was not surprised Lloyd George was committed to 'a wicked policy, but I am astonished to find them committed to a thoroughly stupid policy'. He then trapped the PM into a damaging exchange by asking if 'any proposals for the initiation or continuance of the policy of reprisals in Ireland were laid before the Cabinet'. Lloyd George refused to answer. Mosley's retort, 'Does the Right Hon. Gentleman admit official sanction?', was met with opposition cheers. Mosley had private information and had framed his questions accordingly. A week later the Council adopted a peace policy calling for the withdrawal of the Black and Tans, talks with Sinn Fein and a military truce.

Mosley tried to persuade Cecil to assume the leadership, as he was convinced that it lay within his power 'to change the whole course of the history of the decade'. As to his own position, he thought it 'no use chopping and changing, and until I see a very clear advantage in moving again I think it would be better to stick where I am'. He had, however, dropped the label 'conservative'. On 17 April Mosley wrote again: 'The hour lends itself entirely to our purpose and especially to the reappearance of Grey [Liberal Foreign Secretary at the outbreak of war who supported the LoN].' There was an opportunity 'for a confederation of reasonable men to advance with a definite proposal for the reorganisation of our industrial system . . . We are anathema to the bourgeois profiteer who really is the present Government and no true reconciliation could ever take place while that element predominates on the other side.'

Mosley observed to Cecil that they were 'so immersed in the detail of every day existence that . . . one loses entirely the vision splendid of politics within the four walls of the H. of C.'. He had not, however, lost the ability to spot a political opportunity. 'The yearning of the electorate for any escape . . . might be lashed to a white heat by a timely exposure of the Irish atrocities to crown the present disgust.' Further indiscipline on the part of the auxiliaries was duly exposed. On 21 April Lloyd George was compelled to admit there had been 'deplorable excesses'. Cecil argued the law had been brought into disrepute because the reprisals had never been placed on a constitutional basis.

When Cecil declined to take the lead, Mosley turned to Lord Grey as the 'best hope of an effective rallying together of all the stable progressive elements in the country'. Grey was seen as the one public figure 'unsullied by the war and the internecine political strife that followed it', though some considered him an authoritarian figure hovering in the wings for his chance at power. Cecil inaugurated a conspiracy to project Grey as head of a centrist movement. Impatient for results, Mosley's own intrigues became 'quite febrile'. He appealed to Lord Cowdray for financial backing and arranged a secret meeting between Cecil and Labour's Arthur Henderson to discuss an anti-Coalition alliance. News of the manoeuvres leaked and was splashed on the front pages under the headline GREY WHIGS ON THE GREEN BENCHES. The high-minded intrigue was stillborn. The aristocratic call for unity on a radical non-party basis was nothing more than anti-socialism and its non-partisanship a mask for old-style paternalism. The quest failed because there was no consensus on 'what unity was composed of and where the centre was to be located'.

By spring 1921 Northcliffe's newspapers and the liberal dailies were hostile to the government's Irish policy, which was discredited even among those who had advocated it. Ardent Unionists such as Sir Henry Wilson insisted that 'unless the Government used the regular army in a properly conducted military campaign, it should abandon repression altogether'. Organized ex-servicemen, however, considered such criticism an attack on the army and took the opportunity to break up meetings of the Peace with Ireland Council. Mosley wrote on 7 May to the writer J. L. Hammond that Lord Bryce, who had chaired an inquiry into alleged German atrocities in Belgium, had agreed to be president of a commission which would 'delegate certain persons armed with legal assistance to go to Ireland and secure evidence in to the reprisals'. It was not required as, after months of bloodshed, the Cabinet suddenly reversed policy and in June ended the reprisals.

On 11 July, government negotiations with Sinn Fein produced an autumn truce. Mosley wanted Irish leader Eamon de Valera to 'accept Lloyd George's invitation right off, without any conditions'. If 'he took this course he would have the whole of the English public opinion at the back of him'. In December, a peace treaty was signed in which Collins and James Griffith surrendered the North and accepted both membership of the Commonwealth and an oath of allegiance to the Crown. They also allowed Britain use of certain ports.

While the treaty was a potential disaster for the Irish, for Conservatives it shattered the unity of their party and for this they never forgave Lloyd George. Mosley felt the PM had forfeited his claim to speak on behalf of the Liberal ethic because of his morally repugnant policy. Mosley later compared his stance to the revulsion felt by the young during the sixties to US policy in Vietnam. Irish policy, concludes Kenneth Morgan, was a 'monument to ignorance, racial and religious prejudice, and ineptitude'. It 'tore the heart out of the Unionist Party, leaving it without a cause to defend', and was the beginning of the end of Lloyd George. By contrast, Mosley's stance made his name both in Parliament and among Catholics. Nationalist MP T. P. O'Connor honoured Mosley as 'the man who really began the break-up of the Black and Tan savagery'. He would 'always be regarded by every good Irishman with appreciation and gratitude'.

Mosley's actions brought down Conservative wrath and led to sustained criticism from his local newspaper, the *Harrow Observer*. In riposte he bought its rival, the *Gazette*, and launched a broadside against the 'budding Napoleons of the press world who purposely dedicate their pens to the power of evil'. Although political parties no longer owned newspapers, they exercised considerable influence through their patronage of proprietors and channelling of information to editors. A modern politician, Mosley grasped the necessity of access to the media. He also knew that money was at the heart of politics. Without it, politicians were doomed to failure. He funded his local Unionist Association and by doing so 'retained the organisation in his own hands'.

Mosley's time as a press lord was brief and in July 1921 he was forced to sell the loss-making *Gazette* to its rival. His habit of printing his own speeches verbatim contributed to the paper's declining circulation. He was in difficulty over the settlement of his estate and had incurred debts through buying unsuitable houses. He turned for help to Cimmie, whose father still had access to her allowance. On her twenty-first birthday she was awarded Leiter Trust money of £150,000 (£7.5 m) and an annual income of £9,000 (£450,000). In addition, she was left £20,000 by her grandmother.

When Cimmie married, her father consulted Mosley's lawyer 'as to the propriety of asking her to leave a portion of the entire fortune now hers to assist her father'. Arrangements had been made for her to leave with him the income which accrued from the Marriage Settlement, estimated to be about £3,000 (£150,000) a year. He was, however, embarrassed by the sudden withdrawal of the income of his eldest daughter, Irene, and Cimmie's request for her rightful share. Curzon's art collection had been purchased with money from his daughters' account. 'It was therefore a difficult moment when Cimmie decided,' Mosley recalled, 'with my support, to take the rest of her own. I insisted, and she agreed, that no detailed rejoinder should be made to his reproaches.'

Curzon complained to his wife that he had received (21 September) the 'most outrageous letter from a daughter to her father'. Cimmie described his attitude as 'unwarrantable, unaccountable and incomprehensible'. Leiter Trust cheques had gone to her and she had passed them on, but she gave warning that this would no longer be the case. A despairing Curzon pondered whether he would have to sell Broadstairs. 'What a fool Tom Mosley is making of himself,' Grace wrote back. Curzon, angered by his 'sinister' son-in-law's role in the quarrel, replied that the Mosleys 'mean to take the whole money. The best thing to do is to say Take it. I cannot stand the perpetual torrent of threats and abuse.' On 1 November he informed Grace that Cimmie had offered him an allowance but he would 'sooner not accept it at all than know it is found grudgingly and with obvious regret'. It ended his relationship with his two eldest daughters and the estrangement lasted till his death in 1926. Beaverbrook later revealed that Curzon died owing £80,000 (£4 m) in unpaid taxes.

Hunting was Irene's ruling passion and she devoted most of her time to the Craven Lodge, a noted hunting box at Melton, Leicestershire. In 1922 the Lodge was bought by Mosley's close sporting friend Michael Wardell, who converted it into an exclusive hunting club for weekend visitors from London. They included Curzon's third daughter, Lady Alexandra, dubbed the 'most beautiful brunette in London' during the 1922 Season. The chic Baba had been the girlfriend of Prince George, the younger brother of the Prince of Wales. She soon threw the Prince over for a dashing Indian Cavalry officer, Captain Dudley 'Fruity' Metcalfe, son of the head of Industries in the Irish prison service. High-spirited and a superb horseman, Fruity was on the Prince of Wales's staff to look after polo ponies. Royal staff thought him an 'excellent fellow' but 'weak and irresponsible'. Baba had also taken an interest in Cimmie's husband, though the feeling had yet to be reciprocated.

In Parliament, Mosley was one of the few MPs capable of delivering a major speech without notes. He could dominate an audience with a mastery of voice and technique, though he admitted the 'weapons of sarcasm and invective' took precedence over 'more reasoned passages'. This, however, was necessary since he had been educated 'in a tough school of debate'. He attacked Lloyd George over his partiality to being treated as a 'Roman emperor' at soirées at the villa of Sir Philip Sassoon, the PM's millionaire Parliamentary Secretary, who was regarded as a joke by younger MPs. Mosley said the PM would be 'regaled in the evening with the frankincense of admiring friends and the abrasions of controversy', and then soothed by a 'liberal application of precious ointment from the voluptuous Orient'. When he attacked Churchill, Clementine wrote to her husband, on 13 February 1922, that 'Master Oswald is a very cheeky young Cub and needs keeping in his place, but of course it is rather an honour to have one of the leading figures in the Country holding you down to it'.

Throughout the spring, negotiations took place between Harrow's Unionist Association president and Mosley over his status. A. K. Carlyon found it 'extraordinarily difficult' to bring him to the point. He could never give a straight answer and developed 'an unrivalled skill in qualifying any written or spoken statement he could be induced to make with some loophole, by which, if convenient, he could escape from the obvious meaning of his words'. Patience wore thin for an MP who was the master of 'procrastinating devices'.

An explanatory document from Mosley on 24 May, Carlyon claimed, 'would make it extremely difficult, if not impossible, for us to put him forward as a Unionist candidate'. Mosley would accept the label of Progressive Conservative but would not enter Parliament unless he was 'free to take any action compatible' with his principles. His first consideration 'must always be the triumph of the causes for which I stand'. When asked if he would take the Conservative whip, he replied that 'a gramophone would be more suitable to these requirements than a human being'. Typically, he bypassed the local Association by circulating a letter to its 4,000 members, proclaiming that he had 'no intention of becoming a spokesman for lost causes on the Government backbenches'. The break with Harrow Unionism was inevitable.

The Coalition had substantial achievements to its credit in the field of housing policy and the relief of poverty. They were, however, judged to be little more than 'cunning devices, mean expedients, crafty compromises and shoddy betrayals'. When the PM announced, in October, that the Coalition would call an election to renew its remit, Conservatives rebelled. On the 19th Bonar Law, who had announced his withdrawal from politics, was persuaded to lead the rebellion at the Carlton Club, where a decision was taken to withdraw from the Coalition. A week later, Parliament was dissolved. The Conservatives were divided between a Bonar Law majority and an influential minority who wanted to maintain the Coalition; the Liberals were split into rival factions led by Asquith and Lloyd George; and Labour hardly seemed a party.

In his election address, Mosley said the war had 'destroyed the old party issues, and with them the old parties. The great new issues will shortly create new Party alignments.' Only then would he be prepared to state his party allegiance. He was convinced 'some new political force was on the point of being born' and, in a powerful Commons speech, urged the creation of a 'third force' between Bolshevism and reaction. He was prepared to work with men who held similar opinions, but colleagues considered him too much of a maverick ever to be restrained within the confines of a traditional party.

At the age of twenty-six, Mosley stood at the general election as an Independent. Crucially, the Liberals and Labour decided not to run candidates against him, and many party workers canvassed on his behalf. Funding his campaign was eased when, on Cecil's advice, he secured from Cowdray £10,000 (£500,000) to fund Independent candidates, including leading feminist and LoN campaigner Mrs Ray Strachey. His endorsement of Mrs Strachey dismayed Conservatives. Mosley's own election address ran to 5,000 words and was liberally sprinkled with tributes from the eminent – an early example of what was to become a characteristic practice. He always felt himself to be unjustly maligned and the frequent quotation of statements of praise was his method of redressing the balance.

The result in the November election surprised even Mosley's most optimistic supporters. He polled 15,290 votes to his Conservative opponent's 7,868. In the *Nation*, H. W. Massingham said he was the 'most attractive personal element in the election. He is a figure of individual strength and purpose, a young man of genius, perhaps the most interesting in the late parliament. If character, a brilliant and searching mind, and a repugnance for mean and cruel dealings fit men for the service of the State, Mr Mosley should rise high in it.' He is 'something of a star, and of no common brightness'.

The election gave Bonar Law's Conservatives, with 347 seats, a majority of eighty-eight over the combined seats of Asquith's Liberals (sixty), Lloyd George's Liberals (fifty-seven) and Labour (142). The election's significance was that the Tories were back in the saddle and were to remain so for most of the century. It also signalled the demise of the Liberals. Lloyd George never regained power and few of his colleagues worked willingly with him again. Ironically, it was the negatives which made him an attractive figure for Mosley. There was the brilliant oratory, contempt for traditional parties and the capacity 'to secure the loyalty of men of ability, who nevertheless recognised that he was a vulgar upstart'. Mosley admired his capacity for action which 'many Englishmen later regarded as a sufficient justification for the continental dictators'.

Aubrey Herbert realized the centre party experiment was over: 'It was obvious that we were broken up.' Cecil entered the Conservative government and offered Mosley a post, but he declined. 'Tom', Herbert wrote, 'is a fox who has lost his tail and wants the rest of us to do the same.' The rift with the Tories had grown too wide and he wanted 'far more positive action than it then presented'. He was courted by the Liberals but they were a lost cause. It seemed only the Labour Party could offer opposition to the Tories.

Mosley was still largely known for his speeches on foreign affairs and the British Empire, which 'could supply all our needs'. He advocated a return to the Salisbury days of 'splendid isolation', which expressed the 'deeper wishes of the nation at large'. For Mosley foreign and domestic affairs were intricately connected, since foreign adventurers wasted resources which should be directed to domestic concerns.

Following the Balfour Declaration of Britain's intention to work for the establishment of a national home for Jewish people in Palestine, violence spread throughout the Middle East. The British managed to ride out the storm and Churchill, the Minister responsible for the region, forged an 'ingenious compromise' for Mesopotamia (now Iraq) to become a nation, with Feisal as its King. Mosley, who was known to the Zionist office in London as an opponent, spoke out against Churchill's adventure. Expressing a view that he retained all his life, he told MPs he was 'strongly opposed to the sacrifice of British lives in any but a British quarrel'. He charged the government with 'running round the world looking after the business of every people except their own'.

The slump and long-term unemployment brought poverty to many ex-servicemen and Mosley began to take an interest in their plight. If his solution still revolved around traditional control of finance and reduced taxation to stimulate free enterprise and efficiency, he also favoured discrimination in favour of ex-servicemen and urged that capital projects 'contribute in some degree to the solution of the national question of unemployment'. He viewed unemployment as a symptom of a country in decline and saw its cure in a social imperialist vision of a greater Britain. British Fascism's own chronicler, Richard Bellamy, wrote that if Fascism was conceived in the war, it was 'born out of the hopeless misery and squalor of the post-war slump'. For the moment, however, Mosley remained 'the very independent Member for Harrow'.

Sometime during the winter of 1922–3, while pregnant with their second child, Cimmie learnt of her husband's affair with a mutual friend with whom they had spent time in Venice the previous summer. Cimmie remained unaware, however, of another illicit relationship. On a hunting weekend in Melton Mowbray, Mosley had slept with her sister Irene. On another occasion in St Moritz, unable to ski because of his leg, Mosley had a fling with her stepmother Grace. He only managed to escape scandal because it was confined to a 'charmed circle', who were 'clued-up about contraception'.

Despite their brief encounter, Irene was 'heavily censorious' of Mosley's affairs and especially of the pain caused to his wife. Cimmie was distressed but it was always she who ended up apologizing: 'I am so sorry for the way I harry you – have made too high a mountain out of the molehills of your faults . . . No one has ever had a sweeter man.' There were, however, terrible rows. He had a frightening temper and was known to abuse her verbally, sometimes publicly. Cimmie forgave his philandering and acted the dutiful wife, playing hostess at their home in Sloane Square where politicians such as F. E. Smith, now Lord Birkenhead, were regular visitors. Birkenhead described Mosley – a welcome guest at the inter-war salons, where both politicians pursued women – as the 'perfumed popinjay of scented boudoirs'.

When Bonar Law's Cabinet first met, Birkenhead sneeringly referred to its 'second-class intellects'. Cecil drew huge cheers at a meeting when he replied that 'England preferred to be governed by second-class intellects than by second-class characters'. A few months later the PM was struck down by an illness and he was to succumb to it during the autumn of 1923. Throughout Bonar Law's illness, Foreign Secretary Lord Curzon presided over Cabinet meetings. Over the short term of the 1922–3 Parliament, during which Curzon did not quite become PM, Mosley honed his political skills.

The *Westminster Gazette* said Mosley had 'courage and coolness, an excellent command of English and a quick wit'. His voice, however, was betrayed by a 'high-pitched note'. Determined to eradicate it, he took voice lessons, which eliminated the falsetto. He acquired a measured rhythm of speech with his 'calculated changes in pitch sounding like a car changing gear'. The *Gazette* now wrote that he was 'spoken of by old and experienced parliamentary hands as composed of the stuff of which Prime Ministers are made. The most polished literary speaker in the Commons, words flow from him in graceful, epigrammatic phrases that have a sting in them for the Government and the Conservatives.' He told Archie Sinclair he was determined to be PM in twelve years' time.

Mosley's support of the LoN wavered as he veered away from policies of intervention. When, in January 1923, French troops occupied the Ruhr in pursuit of reparations, he suggested that if the League policy failed, then Britain should withdraw into isolation. He did not think the 'generation which bore the brunt of the last war . . . are going to lift another finger to cleanse the Augean stables of European diplomacy. I do not believe they will consent to the pouring of another drop of British blood down the gaping drains of its seething animosities, its racial hatreds, its atavistic prejudices . . . it is perfectly useless for any Government to appeal for an armed intervention in European affairs.' However, on 15 February he admitted if the French matter was allowed 'to drift on we should be faced with the alternative of fighting a disastrous war, entailing immense expenditure in lives and money, or of withdrawing with grave loss of prestige'.

Curzon worried that his son-in-law might 'become a good debater in the wilderness, a brilliant lone-wolf'. Mosley, however, had calculated that the Labour Party was the logical vehicle for his ambition. 'I shall not blame you if you join Labour,' Curzon wrote, 'but do not remain in ineffective isolation.' For the Front Generation, an institutional base in politics was a necessity but locating one was not easy and to an extent 'circumstances dictated individual choices'. Mosley was uncertain of the Labour leadership and wished 'they would abandon their habit of discussing ultimate issues and advance in a concrete and concise form an immediate programme to deal with immediate issues'. A *Morning Post* reporter was reminded of 'Disraeli before he had taken his political bearings'.

On 25 June 1923 Cimmie gave birth to their first son, Nicholas. Mosley believed his wife's distress over his adultery upset the child, but it did not alter his behaviour, nor her total allegiance to him. He believed the upbringing of children should be left to professionals, such as Nanny Hyslop, Cimmie's nursery maid. Mosley venerated motherhood; it reinforced his image of Cimmie as 'a paragon of virtue'. Ever the dutiful wife, she entertained Labour leader Ramsay MacDonald and even invited him to join them on holiday in Venice. MacDonald politely declined but, susceptible to the aristocratic embrace, soon became part of the Mosleys' social circle, which now included Fabians Sidney and Beatrice Webb. The daughter of a liberal industrial magnate, Beatrice had led a conventional upper-class life until her friendship with Herbert Spencer made her aware of social injustices.

Tall and handsome, 'Gentleman Mac' had the bearing of an aristocrat but his unmarried parents had been a ploughman and a Scottish servant girl. Because of his illegitimacy and the social stigma, MacDonald was insecure and 'intolerant of all who questioned his omniscience'. Beatrice Webb considered him 'an egotist, a poseur and a snob, and worst of all he does not believe in the creed we have always preached – he is not a socialist'. MacDonald was a champion of moderation, who instilled confidence, even in his political opponents.

Mosley, Beatrice noted in June 1923, is 'the most brilliant man' in the Commons. 'He would make his way in the world without his adventitious advantages, which are many – birth, wealth and a beautiful aristocratic wife. He is also an assiduous worker in the modern manner – keeps two secretaries at work supplying him with information but realises that he himself has to do the thinking!' She added: 'So much perfection argues rottenness somewhere. Is there in him some weak spot which will be revealed in a time of stress by letting you or your cause down or sweeping it out of the way?'

Mosley said Beatrice 'bestowed angels' wings or a tail and horns entirely according to her agreement or disagreement with the views of the person in question'. She had nevertheless pinpointed a flaw in Mosley's otherwise perfect front – his loyalty was not to any party or faction but only to himself. MacDonald, she added, was 'much taken with him, and he with MacDonald'. The editor of the Independent Labour Party's journal *Forward*, Thomas Johnston MP, told her that there were three men – Sidney Webb, Patrick Hastings and Mosley – who were detested by the Tories because they were traitors to their class. This accounted for, she realized, 'the growing popularity among the extremists of the two very "bourgeois" figures and the one super-aristocrat'.

A week later Beatrice wrote to Harold Laski at the London School of Economics that Cimmie was 'ready that her husband should join the Labour Party'. He was asked to help expedite the move. The young don was fascinated by the aristocracy and eager to help the 'clever and eloquent' Mosley. He organized a debate with the Duke of Northumberland on whether man's aggressive instincts could be permanently curbed. Mosley quoted from Tennyson's *In Memoriam*: 'Will the ape and tiger ever die?' He opposed the Duke's arguments against the League of Nations with a call for effective machinery to settle international disputes.

At the end of August Mussolini's Italian army occupied the Greek island of Corfu. Mosley wanted Britain to invoke the League's Article 16, which provided for economic sanctions against an aggressor. Curzon consulted the Treasury about the possibility of enforcing sanctions but this was not pursued. Mosley felt his father-in-law had done little and attacked Prime Minister Stanley Baldwin's lack of interest. The diehards, however, were sympathetic to the anti-Communist dictator and their mouthpiece, the *Morning Post*, treated the matter as a simple case of 'Mussolini versus Lenin'.

Cecil worried that Mussolini's successful defiance of the League might lead to chaos in Europe. 'A powerful member of the League has refused to carry out its treaty obligations and has succeeded in doing so with impunity, some might even say with an increase of prestige.' Following an Italian assault on Malta, Mosley claimed the 'essential ingredient of will in statesmanship was lacking from the League', which had been wrecked by the dictator. He made 'a most offensive speech about him to the effect that he had triumphed like a drunken motor-car driver, not by reason of his own skill but because all sober people had been concerned to get out of his way'. Mosley subsequently developed a sneaking admiration for Mussolini for upholding the interests of his country 'much more vigorously than Baldwin and Curzon'. He saw the failure to intervene, however, as the end of the League. Isolationism, and the desire not to become entangled in Europe, was the central plank of his thinking. He attacked Churchill for his reckless campaigns, which deprived Britain of 'essential air squadrons' for home defence.

For their summer vacation the Mosleys visited Venice where their hostess,

Olga Lynn, a popular opera singer, gave glamorous dinner parties at the Restaurant Cappello for her exotic 'Oggie's circle'. This included Cecil Beaton, Tallulah Bankhead, Diana Cooper and, occasionally, the Prince of Wales. A recent addition was Mosley's friend, Foreign Office diplomat Josslyn Hay (later the Earl of Erroll). Hay announced his engagement in the *Tatler*, on 23 September, to Lady Idina Gordon. She was hardly the ideal diplomat's wife as she did not give a damn what other people thought. Idina's dictum was 'to Hell with husbands', and Mosley took due advantage.

In late October the Mosleys travelled to Paris to spend a few days with their friends the Mendls. They met up with 'Jimmy', Duke of Alba, Diana Cooper and her husband Duff (a diplomat at the Paris embassy), the wealthy Murphys, and songwriter Cole Porter and his new wife. Porter was showcasing his futuristic jazz ballet, *Within the Quota*, written by Gerald Murphy, the man Scott Fitzgerald drew upon for Dick Driver in *Tender Is the Night*. Murphy was the centre of the American movement of *Sonnenkinder* in exile.

Revered as the most beautiful woman in the world, Porter's wife, Linda Thomas, was aware her husband – described by Mosley as 'a little dark elfin creature' – was homosexual but was prepared to maintain the façade of a heterosexual marriage. There were rumours she was a lesbian. She was a close friend of Charles Mendl's wife, a member of an international sapphic set. Duff Cooper wrote to his wife that Mosley 'got into trouble in Paris owing to his excessive attentions to Mrs Cole Porter. He went to her bedroom uninvited so that she had to complain to Cole. Adulterous, canting, slobbering Bolshie – I don't like him.' Cooper never altered that view. Such behaviour was typical of Mosley. Lady Rosebery told Robert Rhodes James that she had had 'one of her best ball-gowns torn and ruined when escaping from his amorous clutches!'

Barbara Cartland, who had just published her first novel, considered Mosley to be a cad – defined by Charles Mendl as 'someone who makes you go all crinkly-toes'. He was, she told a friend, 'sinister and aggressively masculine'. He was 'a seething volcano and I am sure when he stood at the crossroads he took the downward path to hell. He seldom smiled and when he talked he would stand, staring with black eyes as if he looked into a fathomless future.' She asked him once if he was 'doing anything exciting'. Mosley replied he was, but 'the people who are exciting are very difficult to excite. They are quite content with everything as it was yesterday.'

Mosley had not previously expressed interest in economics but during 1923 he switched his interest from foreign to domestic affairs. The fight for such ideals as renewal 'would have to go on, and that the field on which it must be waged was home ground'. He studied contemporary theorists and subscribed to, and even considered buying, A. R. Orage's *New Age* – an 'Independent Socialist Review' – which championed economists from what Keynes dubbed

the 'underworld of rejected knowledge'. He was convinced government policies, 'far from ensuring a return to prosperity, were actively discouraging it
through deflationary policies and an obsession with the return to the gold
standard at pre-war parity'. He had moved a considerable distance from being
a Cecil acolyte and was not tied to the intellectual baggage of orthodox
economics. Free trade, budgetary balance and the gold standard were no
longer seen as permanent fixtures of the institutional system.

An election was due in 1923 and Prime Minister Baldwin decided to make
protectionism the issue upon which it was to be fought. The mounting
unemployment figures strengthened the argument for protectionism and the
government proposed a number of mild measures which would largely leave
free trade unaffected. Mosley was not infected by the sudden enthusiasm for
protection, since he believed 'fluctuations in the exchange rate of foreign
countries made nonsense of any tariff barrier'. He had, he wrote, 'foreseen
the era of competitive devaluation to gain an advantage in the export trade'.

Baldwin's dissolution of Parliament on 13 November gave Mosley his third
fight for the Harrow seat. 'Almost alone among candidates', noted the *Sunday
Express*, he pointed out that the government's 'insanely exaggerated
deflationist policy was one of the principal causes of unemployment'. He
opposed protectionism, since it would prove to be beneficial mainly to the
profiteers. 'Is there any chance', he asked, 'that wages will rise to correspond
to prices? They will be kept down, there will be more unemployment and the
wage-earning classes will be at the mercy of monopolistic industrialists.' He
insisted he was not a free trader, it was simply that protection which relied on
half measures would be undermined by a lack of control and organization.
He wanted more attention paid to Empire development through organized
transport and credit facilities.

At the general election on 6 December the Independent Mosley polled
14,079 votes, his opponent only 9,433. That he held the seat with a substantial,
though reduced, majority in the face of local protectionist tradition was a
triumph. His refusal to stand as a Conservative and his avowal as 'an unremit-
ting opponent of any Conservative administration' in a Tory district, where
he was routinely denounced in the press, lost him many votes. The country
decisively rejected protectionism. The Conservatives lost eighty-six seats and
found themselves in a minority of almost a hundred. The reunited Liberal
Party, with Lloyd George campaigning under Asquith's free trade banner,
secured 159 seats, an increase of forty, but it would never again win as many
seats. Labour, which denounced protectionism as a cause of higher prices, had
a total of 191 MPs. It did not escape Mosley's attention that the up-and-
coming party was Labour, which had seen a dramatic rise in its vote, doubling
it to four and a half million.

Baldwin did not resign, but held on until January 1924, when his government was defeated on a vote of confidence. Speaking from the opposition benches, Mosley said he was voting against the Conservatives because

administrative blundering has added to our miseries of unemployment, a policy which leaves us a ghastly heritage of slums, starvation and suffering in our midst. The handiwork of this Government is written all over the map of our country in the characters of human anguish. For my part, if I gave one vote to keep in power for one night such a Government, I should feel that I deserved to be drummed out with ignominy from the great army of progress.

On 18 January Ramsay MacDonald became the first Labour Prime Minister. He hailed Labour as a progressive party, which appealed to a broad range of voters. On the eve of taking office he told constituents he did not care to be called a Socialist and preferred to be looked on as 'a sort of non-party Party leader'. The party was a loose alliance representing a variety of semi-socialist ideas. Socialist rhetoric was acceptable as long as commitments did not disturb working-class interests.

Mosley had for months hovered on the edge of joining Labour but was unconvinced it represented the new political alignment he was seeking. His friends likened him to 'a Victorian Tractarian clergyman trembling on the brink of Rome'. His talks with the Webbs and Harold Laski finally persuaded him of the party's technical competence. Despite the huge social divide that separated potential middle-class and aristocratic recruits from the grass roots, he recognized his path now led inevitably to Labour. Celebrating the formation of a new government, Mosley said 'the army of progress has struck its tents and is on the move'.

Mosley's mother congratulated him. 'How enormously I admire your amazing courage and self-sacrifice of most things that appeal to men of your age and up-bringing; and how I pray with all my heart that your dreams for the benefit of struggling humanity may come true, and that I may live to see your present attitude justified by results and the world appreciate that far from being a pushing self-seeking politician you were in fact willing to be a martyr for your Religion – for it seems to me that is what your Politics are.' She also issued a note of warning. If Labour 'meant what you and some of those in the party are striving to make it every one of us would back you. But to my mind the tragedy of it all is that the vast mass of your often very ignorant supporters do not mean what you mean by Socialism.' It was 'an old story – as old as the Bible. When the Jews found following Christ meant the cross and not an earthly sovereignty and defeat of the Romans they turned on him and crucified their Lord.'

Was Mosley a pushing, self-seeking politician as his critics alleged? An ambitious young man seeking a quick route to the top of the greasy pole? Many of his contemporaries believed so, but the Tory press also referred to his socialistic leanings while a Labour paper described him as a guild socialist. Amabel Williams-Ellis, sister of John Strachey, wrote a novel, *The Walls of Glass* (1927), which referred to Mosley at this time. ' "And then he suddenly went over to Labour. To Labour!" repeated the girl, mildy surprised. "Why?" "Vanity", answered Lady St Aubrey succinctly. "He thought there would be less competition." ' He hoped Labour would provide a receptive political vehicle for his ambitions but he was doing so at a moment when the great divide was not between a Conservative Party which abhorred activism and a Labour Party calling for change, but between 'the economic conservatives and economic radicals across the political spectrum'. Mosley would find it as hard to fulfil his ambitions in Labour as he had in the Conservative Party.

5

The Underworld of Rejected Knowledge

'My path now led inevitably to the Labour Party,' Mosley recalled. It seemed clear that 'the only hope now lay in the party which had been thrown up by the mass of the people to right their wrongs. Through and beyond the failure of men and of parties, we of the war generation are marching on.' On 27 March 1924 he joined the Independent Labour Party (ILP), the means of entry for middle- and upper-class recruits.

He had been busy reading 'socialist' sources, in particular the pre-First World War guild socialists G. D. H. Cole, S. G. Hobson and A. R. Orage. Commentators later ascribed his Fascism to a number of writers from whom he drew little of interest. 'The tradition of the medieval guilds in England, of the Hanseatic League and the syndicalism of the Latin countries', he admitted, 'was much nearer to my thinking.'

Guild socialism was a fusion of the co-operative movement and the English medievalist reaction against the nineteenth century. The latter strand was evident in Arthur J. Penty's *The Restoration of the Gild System* (1906). A disciple of William Morris, he believed trade unions could restore workers' control through industrial guilds based on workshop methods of production. From Robert Owen was derived the idea that self-governing workmen would develop higher moral characters and a desire to serve the community. Penty's Utopian plan for social reconstruction struck a chord in Edwardian radical thought, but he failed to make a breakthrough and it was left to Alfred Richard Orage to promote guild socialism.

Like many spiritualists, Orage was dismayed by the suppression of individuality envisaged by socialist collectivism and wanted a socialist party 'untainted by the gross material demands of the working man'. Inspired by nationalism's ability to rouse the people, he applauded the 'imagination, wholeness and sanity' of what Tom Steele identifies as a National Socialism, which envisioned an aristocratic elite ruling a democracy subordinate to 'beautiful' ideas. Influenced by G. B. Shaw – the 'leader of a new patriotism' – and German romanticism, during 1906–7 Orage introduced Friedrich Nietzsche's ideas to Britain. He was intrigued by the galvanizing myth of the 'superman'. His was a dynamic ideology linked to Carlyle's hero-worship with a belief in the 'evolution of a higher type through achieved states of consciousness'. Nietzsche reaffirmed Orage's belief that society was 'decadent and in need of regeneration'. This was all close to Mosley's own thinking.

In 1907 Orage became co-owner-editor of the *New Age*, which served as a clearing house for new ideas. With a circulation of 25,000, its contributors included G. D. H. Cole, T. E. Hulme, Wyndham Lewis, Ezra Pound, H. G. Wells, Hilaire Belloc and G. K. Chesterton. There were strands of thought within *New Age* thinking which led to Fascism, though most contributors finally opted for 'something closer to the neo-feudalistic corporatism of T. S. Eliot's thirties Christian clerisy'.

The outburst of pre-war industrial protest seemed to vindicate Orage's anti-parliamentarianism. A section of the labour unrest was led by syndicalists, who advocated open industrial warfare, culminating in a general strike that would destroy capitalism. Orage interpreted syndicalism in Nietzschean terms as 'a contribution towards the revaluation of values'.

A key contributor to the *New Age* was philosopher and art critic Thomas Ernest Hulme, who acted as a transmitter of proto-Fascist ideas. In the 1930s, H. W. J. Edwards noted that before Hulme died in the Great War, 'he wrote about the arrival of a new age, which neither he nor his generation would live to see. It is beginning to arrive now.' Hulme promoted the vitalist philosophy of Henri Bergson and adopted the position of French Catholic intellectual Charles Maurras and his anti-Semitic Action Française, with its support of a revolutionary conservatism of hierarchical values, authority, nationalism and obedience to the State. Unsurprisingly, this has been portrayed as being synonymous with Fascism.

Hulme was the intellectual mentor to the American émigrés – painter Wyndham Lewis, poets Ezra Pound and T. S. Eliot. 'Who today', asks Zeev Sternhell, 'could deny the importance' of these writers 'in the culture of the twentieth century?' Sternhell argues the cultural revolt preceded the political and, in effect, Mosley's modern movement would not have developed in the way it did without this cultural revolt. Eliot, who admired Action Française, acknowledged Hulme as the 'great precursor of a new state of mind'.

During 1912 *New Age* opened its columns to social movements hostile to parliamentary democracy, including syndicalism and guild socialism, sections of women's suffrage and the distributists of Belloc and Chesterton. Through Odon Por, *Avanti*'s London correspondent, contributors were introduced to a radical mix of socialism and syndicalism. British syndicalism had none of the radicalism or violence of the Continental version, partly because there was no ingrained hostility to the State. Its influence waned as the wave of industrial unrest abated. However, it was not insignificant, particularly with its masculine work-centred ideology, espousal of direct action and appeal to a movement instead of a party. In its attack on Labour leaders seduced by the trappings of power and refusal to treat the State as 'neutral', it offered an alternative Labourism. Mosley took this alternative vision into the Labour Party.

As his imperialist sentiments came to the fore, Orage sought a patriotic theory of the State and found in guild socialism a movement better suited to Britain. Power would be transferred from employers to the unions by means of encroaching workers' control. *New Age* ran articles by Quaker and ILPer Sidney G. Hobson, who wanted a spiritual revolution to reunite the community under a national culture. A government of industry would embrace all workers, while economic policy would be controlled on behalf of the whole community and not, as the syndicalists intended, by a section of it. Guild socialism sought a third way between syndicalism and orthodox socialism, but in Hobson's authoritarian vision the individual would be subordinate to the State. Observers made the connection between his ideas and Mosley's corporate Fascism.

Bloomsbury artist Quentin Bell remembered Wyndham Lewis as 'a brutal Fascist before the Fascists existed'. Lewis had been introduced to Nietzschean ideas in Paris, where he attended lectures by Bergson, encountered Maurras and Georges Sorel's anti-materialist revision of Marxism. With Hulme as its chief propagandist, Lewis's and Pound's vorticist wartime art project aimed to revitalize the 'sick sensibility of an apathetic generation'. There was an affinity between vorticism and Fascism in its synthesis of the Fascist style of aggression with Sorel's ideas.

In 1916 Hulme translated Sorel's *Réflexions sur la Violence*, which proclaimed the highest good is heroic action enacted by an exclusive group 'bound together in fervent solidarity and impelled by a passionate confidence in its ultimate triumph'. Sorelians were sympathetic to capitalism because it encouraged technological and social progress. They refused to question private property and profit, and were hostile to plutocracy and high finance. This was the origin of the 'intermediate regime' idea put forward by Front Generation neo-socialists such as Mosley. In this form of National Socialism the masses would be inspired to overthrow the bourgeois order by social myths which would centre on a 'strict morality and expectation of apocalyptic success'. Sorel's ethic was of the political sect 'living in the midst of a continuous crisis, with all the stress on purity and all the fear of contamination'. Mosley based his political philosophy on the inevitability of 'crisis' and the transformation of society by what was, in essence, a millennial cult. An aristocracy of producers joined to a youth avid for action would rule in the new society.

These ideas were promoted in *New Age* by Ramiro de Maeztu, a Basque philosopher, who argued wartime solidarity had a 'permanent value which will make it survive the necessity that has brought it forth'. Influenced by Hulme, he claimed the army was organized like a guild, with every member having a function, and hoped, like Mosley, that this social organization would spill over into civilian life.

The architect of the new phase of guild socialism was Oxford don George Cole. He extended Hobson's ideas on national organization to a congress of guild delegates and consumers' bodies, which would serve as a court of appeal, with supreme power resting with a 'national commune', but rejected his mystical view of the State. There were ideological divisions between his vision of decentralized socialism and Penty's medievalism. Penty called himself a nationalist and drifted off into the preservation of rural England, helping establish the Rural Reconstruction Association. He finally joined the BUF which recognized him as one of its inspirations.

With the war exposing the gulf between the financial and the industrial spheres, the *New Age* became a vehicle for monetary reformers and much 'funny money' theory was run through its pages. Out of frustration that they were not taken seriously, almost all these 'currency cranks' turned to the right.

A prolific inventor, Arthur Kitson, made a fortune from his Birmingham engineering firm but was lost in financial crashes. His critique of banking derived from his failure to finance his own patents. A devotee of the 'quantity theory' of money (the larger the supply of money, the higher the price level), he opposed the gold standard, because it 'was what was produced and not the amount of gold bullion, which defined the wealth of the nation'. He argued that the possibility for plenty was thwarted by the monetary system and the manipulation of financiers. Kitson wanted the Bank of England nationalized, a managed currency and a policy of high wages. His ideas were derided by economists but he did influence radicals, including Mosley, who developed them into a more coherent vision.

Orage was a convert to the 'social credit' theories of former RFC pilot Major Clifford Douglas, who was convinced economic depressions stemmed from the inability of demand to absorb current production. This was because money represented by the wages paid to the producers had already been spent on consumption before goods had reached the retailer. He argued people could not consume the full product of their labours because of intricate accounting, which created costs faster than purchasing power was distributed. If technology increased productivity, then the State must increase proportionately the ability to pay for such goods. This could be done through a 'national dividend' for those on low incomes and the fixing of a 'just price' at the retail end.

Building on the ideas of de Maeztu, Douglas argued for the continuation of wartime price controls and credit changes to increase production. He believed industry, financed by interest-free credits, could institute rapid technological development and create a 'leisure state'. However, New Agers realized the working classes were not sharing 'in the benefits of this new age of plenty and that what was transpiring was increasing poverty in the midst of plenty'. Mosley shared this view and came to see social credit ideas on 'underconsumption' as a possible solution to unemployment.

Douglas's national dividend was the precursor of Mosley's advocacy of consumer credits, which would be 'scientifically' directed to the working class to increase consumption. But, whereas Douglas viewed it as a citizenship right, Mosley saw credits as a reward for work effort. The New Age supported social credit's reduction of economic injustice to a single cause: the lack of sufficient purchasing power on the part of the consumer. It expressed popular resentment against capitalism and promised the resolution of economic problems but without any major alteration of political structures. Douglas believed that the battle was now between 'Finance, on the one side, and Capital and Labour on the other'.

Wyndham Lewis and Ezra Pound embraced social credit. Orage taught them that without economic change, political reform was useless. Through the New Age, they converted to social credit and, more particularly, to anti-Semitism. Douglas talked of 'international money-power' and a 'hidden government'. Kitson's interest in the Jewish bankers' conspiracy was inspired by his friend, Henry Hamilton Beamish, Chairman of the anti-Semitic Britons group, and his reading of the Protocols of the Elders of Zion. 'The world's rulers', Kitson wrote, 'are men mainly conspicuous by their noses, who occupy quiet offices at the backs of the great banking houses of London.'

Guild socialism was not haunted by the cesspit of anti-Semitism, but it was torn apart by the Bolshevik Revolution and, in 1920, militants split off to form the Communist Party of Great Britain. Cole worried that Austrian interest in guilds as a 'third force' attempt at direct democracy 'will show itself hostile not only to the old political Socialism but also to Communism, and even that it may become the rallying-point of the much-despised "Centrist" elements'. This reactionary faction was 'trekking at its best speed for the land of spiritual values, in which gross material things can be forgotten'. It derived its inspiration from an idealized past rather than a future vision. In its ranks were not only theosophists but also advocates of the return to the land and social credit theories.

Mosley was influenced by this form of national guild socialism when forming his modern movement. Some guild socialists found their spiritual home in the BUF, attracted by his economic ideas and his synthesis of social imperialism, syndicalism, guild socialism and the New Age philosophy.

Guild socialism was accepted at the 1922 ILP conference – at the moment when it collapsed as an effective doctrine. The post-war economic slump exposed that this bureaucratic form of decentralized socialism, where decisions were made on the basis of 'instantaneous, direct and complete knowledge of decision-making throughout the economy', had no practical policy to deal with it. The solution was 'planning', with each industry regulating its own affairs subject to co-ordination at the centre. This was attractive to proto-corporatists such as Mosley, who believed 'self-government for industry' might be 'an enticing slogan for the capitalist class'.

Clifford Allen was the driving force behind the recruitment of middle-class and radical intellectuals whose contributions reinvigorated the ILP. From 1923, greater attention was paid to measures for dealing with unemployment and included debates on 'funny money' theories and state intervention led by E. H. Lloyd, J. A. Hobson, Frank Wise and H. N. Brailsford. These were not true socialists but reformers who wanted a more equitable capitalism. Author of *Stabilisation: An Economic Policy for Consumers and Producers* (1923) and *Experiments in State Control* (1924), Lloyd said monetary policy should aim to stabilize internal prices – by centralized purchase of food and raw materials on long-term contracts – rather than the exchange rate, and argued for state intervention in funding investment. As Principal Assistant Secretary at the Ministry of Food, the economist and MP Frank Wise understood planning issues 'in a way which was denied to his purely political colleagues'. He popularized the writings of John Atkinson Hobson, an economist in the Ministry of Reconstruction, who tried to reconcile liberal and socialist principles.

Hobson's recognition came by way of his seminal study *Imperialism*, written against the background of the shambles of the Boer War. Arguing that imperialism did not pay, he put forward a conspiracy theory of 'sinister interests'. To Hobson, Jews were international financiers, who took their gains 'out of the financial manipulation of companies'. The war had been planned by 'organised international Jewish power' with support from 'Jew press' magnates, who had brainwashed the public into supporting their piratical imperialism. Hobson eventually revised his views but his analysis of 'Jew power' was accepted by many ILPers, who propagated a rich Jew anti-Semitism as part of their anti-capitalism rhetoric. It served as the basis for Mosley's own 'rationalist' anti-Semitism.

Fortunately, it is *The Economics of Unemployment* (1922) for which Hobson is best remembered. Hobson argued lack of consumer demand was the reason for unemployment. There was 'insufficient effective demand in the economy because the rich could not buy more than a limited amount of the goods produced, as their needs were sated, while the poor could not do so because they lacked the necessary purchasing power'. Redistribution – the key to eradicating the oversaving surplus of the rich and raising demand – would enable industry to produce at full capacity, and thereby increase the demand for labour and cure the unemployment problem. Hobson suggested unemployment was exacerbated by high interest rates and argued for the 'scientific control of credit in the public interest' with the bank rate varied with the volume of industrial activity. Mosley drew heavily upon these ideas for his own economic thinking.

Hobson's under-consumptionist thesis was only seriously scrutinized by J. M. Keynes, who made his name with his controversial book *The Economic Consequences of the Peace*, published in 1919, the year he resigned from the Treasury and returned to Cambridge to teach economics. A free trade Liberal, who dismissed nationalization and rejected class division, he argued for pragmatic State intervention, a managed currency system and the stabilization of domestic prices at the expense of the exchange rate. Although he accepted Hobson's thesis that over-saving depressed effective demand, they disagreed on the consequences. Hobson argued it resulted in underspending, whereas Keynes held it led to under-investment. The solution was either an increase in consumption or investment. Keynes's preferred remedy was a small public works programme financed by borrowing to increase jobs and help restore a cycle of cumulative prosperity. Hobson's was to promote spending by raising working-class incomes by means of higher wages.

Hobson sympathized with the social credit hypothesis with its under-consumptionist element. The idea of a national dividend to increase spending won the support of activist Clydeside MPs, within whose ranks the guild socialists had been active. They were led by John Wheatley, an ex-miner of Catholic Irish descent. 'Dumpy, unprepossessing, peering myopically through thick round spectacles', he did not look like a working-class hero but to Glasgow slum dwellers there was no greater figure. Wheatley kept alive Labour's 'aspirations to social justice while offering it the means, in office, to lift the economy out of recession'. In sanctioning the building of thousands of new houses he became acutely aware of the crippling effect of high interest rates. He rejected free trade and simple protectionism in favour of planning. If there was one Labour person whom Mosley admired it was Wheatley.

Wheatley detested the internationalism of Shadow Chancellor Philip Snowden and Labour leader Ramsay MacDonald. He believed a socialist 'had done his duty when he had seen British workers all right'. Echoing later criticism of Mosley's own thinking, *New Leader* editor H. N. Brailsford dismissed this statement as 'socialist nationalism'. Wheatley denied his solution would 'degenerate into socialist imperialism' and countered that 'to advocate an economy based on exports was to be forced into a position of capitalist imperialism'.

Hobson's under-consumptionist thesis informed the ILP's 1923 'Socialist Programme', which aimed to distribute wealth by way of a 'living wage'. Credit would be scientifically controlled to expand purchasing power. A Committee on Production would 'consider the needs of the nation, and the labour, agriculture and industrial resources available to meet them'. Industrial and Import Boards, based on the ideas of Lloyd and Wise, would purchase and distribute raw materials. Finally, a National Industrial Authority would be charged with administering a military-style 'common plan'.

Interest in monetary policy was awakened within the ILP by the editor of *Forward*, Tom Johnston. When Keynes published *A Tract on Monetary Reform* and pointed out the connection between inflation and employment, Wheatley took note: 'When the first symptoms of a boom occur, credit should be instantly restricted, and the bank rate raised. At the first suspicion of a slump credit should be expanded in volume and cheapened by lowering the bank rate.' The ILP wanted to nationalize the Bank of England in order to control the banking system and credit. Johnston, who had a populist approach in his sympathy for the Empire, relentlessly attacked finance capital, which he associated with a 'cosmopolitan and parasitic rentier class', and was not above descending into anti-Semitic innuendo with his remarks about bankers. The similarities with Mosley's later rhetoric are apparent.

The ILP's strategy was laid out at its 1924 conference. The economic 'chaos and suffering cannot be remedied unless we reorganise our national resources by means of . . . national planning'. Crucially, just as he was about to join the Labour Party, it was planning which came to dominate Mosley's thinking, not Keynesian monetary policy.

6

The Labour Party

Following his entry in April 1924 into the Labour Party, Mosley wrote to Labour's first Prime Minister, Ramsay MacDonald: 'You stand forth as the leader of the forces of progress in their assault upon the powers of reaction. In this grave struggle I ask leave to range myself beneath your standard.' MacDonald replied how pleased he was that he had joined Labour and expressed 'the hope that you will find comfort in our ranks and a wide field in which you can show your usefulness'. He was 'very sorry to observe in some newspapers that you are being subjected to the kind of personal attack with which we are all very familiar'.

Mosley's motives were questioned in attack after attack by the press, which accused him of betraying his class. The *Evening Standard* described him as a 'political renegade' and his career as a political rake's progress. In the Commons, Tory MPs intensified their barrage of 'snarls and jeers' at this 'irresponsible careerist and adventurer'. When his father joined in, Mosley said it was unsurprising that 'our tranquil relations exploded when in his view I entered the devil's service by becoming a socialist'. A move to expel Mosley from White's Club was quashed by Ivan Moore-Brabazon.

Cimmie supported her husband's decision and also joined Labour. He said she was 'someone with whom in partnership he might set out to alter the world'. She claimed humanitarianism directed her towards the Left. She advocated protection of the countryside and preached a variant of Christian socialism.

MacDonald predicted that the more Mosley was attacked, the 'greater the enthusiasm of the Left'. His reception on a speaking tour was ecstatic. Observing the reaction, the ILP's John Scanlon wrote that 'stories of his fabulous wealth had spread all over the country ... The press lost no point in this human story, and those of us who had visions of a dignified working class steadily gaining confidence in itself as the future owners of Britain had our first shock of disillusionment.'

Mosley's debut at a rally organized by London Party Secretary Herbert Morrison was reviewed by Egon Wertheimer, German correspondent of the socialist newspaper *Vorwärts*. He thought Mosley had found his true constituency. 'Suddenly a young man with the face of the ruling class of Great Britain but with the gait of a Douglas Fairbanks thrust himself forward through the throng to the platform followed by a lady in heavy, costly furs.' Greeted by 'For he's a jolly good fellow', his speech was 'a hymn, an emotional appeal directed not to the intellect, but to the Socialist idea, which obviously was still a subject of wonder to the orator. No speaker at such a meeting in Germany would have dared to have worked so unrestrainedly on the feelings without running the risk of losing for ever his standing in the party movement.'

'But then came something unexpected,' Wertheimer observed. 'Suddenly the elegant lady in furs got up from her seat and said a few sympathetic words. She said that she had never before attended a workers' meeting, and how deeply the warmth of this reception touched her. She said this simply and almost shyly, yet like one who is accustomed to be acclaimed and, without stage fright, to open a meeting for charitable purposes.' An excited steward whispered in Wertheimer's ear that it was 'Lady Cynthia Mosley'; and later 'as though thinking he had not sufficiently impressed me, he added "Lord Curzon's daughter". His whole face beamed proudly.'

Scanlon was taken aback by the response. 'They still had the superstitious notion prevalent in all simple minds that salvation would come from above . . . Heaven to them was a place where only rich people congregated and where was an abundance of rich food, rich drink and rich raiment . . . To most of them it was quite unattainable, and therefore when anyone chose to leave this perpetual nightclub in order to mix with the workers, their love and admiration knew no bounds.' Then there began the 'heartbreaking spectacle of local Labour Parties stumbling over themselves to secure him as their candidate', even though, there was 'not a particle of evidence to show that he understood one of the problems in their lives'. Although Mosley's wealth engendered mistrust, party members were welcoming. In Germany, he would 'have been mistrustfully watched to see whether he was genuine and no careerist'.

Mosley was one of a group of wealthy socialists who helped the Labour leader, whose wife had tragically died early. Mosley subscribed to the running costs of his car and Cimmie saw to his every need on trains and in hotels. Chancellor of the Exchequer Philip Snowden observed that an intimate social relationship was established 'such as never existed between MacDonald' and Labour's 'plebeian members'. It was difficult to determine whether Mosley was courting MacDonald, or vice versa. To other social superiors MacDonald was infinitely more ingratiating. The Labour hierarchy 'wore evening dress, hobnobbed with the rich, hankered after knighthoods and kowtowed to royalty'. Beatrice Webb thought it shocking that its leaders were entranced by London society and royalty.

Mosley claimed he associated with MacDonald as an intermediary in the interests of party unity, as he was – except for the sickly Clifford Allen, who was doomed to early death – one of the few people on speaking terms with both wings of the party. Mosley was on amicable terms with the party's chief organizer, 'Uncle Arthur' Henderson, who was anxious to attract intellectuals to Labour. MacDonald, however, considered the 'aristocrats of the Ponsonby–Trevelyan–Buxton type' to be a 'big disappointment' because they joined the Left. Mosley formed a close relationship with Charles Trevelyan, brother of the historian, whose pacifist sympathies had led him to resign from the Liberal government. Although no one questioned his idealism, Trevelyan proved to be uncritically enthusiastic about the Soviet Union. He was appointed president of the Board of Education and became Mosley's 'most intelligent supporter in the Cabinet when it came to the crunch'.

Mosley's great enemy within the party would be Philip Snowden, whose voice was the only one to be heard when it came to economic policy. Just before he joined, and had already expressed an interest in Keynes, Mosley asked Snowden 'whether, in view of the recent researches of leading economists into the possible effects of a reform in the monetary policy upon employment, an authoritive committee to enquire into this subject will be constructed by His Majesty's Government'. Snowden dismissed the idea as irrelevant.

Snowden advocated thrift and hard work as the cornerstones of his economic policy, and zealously advocated free trade and deflation as the essential road back to normality. On taking office, he was visited by Bank of England governor Montagu Norman, who was taken aback by his desire to rebuild the gold standard, which was Norman's singular obsession. Snowden was in awe of Norman, who embarrassed himself by his 'ineptness in front of academic terriers' such as Keynes, with his readiness to 'sacrifice the investment needs of British industry on the altar of restricted credit'.

Snowden was a bitter man who seemed to 'loathe his fellow human beings'. Son of a Yorkshire weaver, he had contracted spinal TB and walked with some difficulty. Encouraged by an ambitious wife, Snowden preferred to move in society circles rather than among ordinary members. Mrs Snowden had no compunction in accepting some diamonds from Lady Rothschild. James Maxton said her 'sole ambition in life was to occupy the position in society which Lady Cynthia Mosley had recently vacated'.

ILP members were impressed by Mosley's speech to their April 1924 conference and Beatrice Webb was already suggesting the time had come for a new generation of Labour leaders – 'Frank Wise–Wheatley–Greenwood–Shinwell–Alexander–Mosley' – who would be 'free alike from the cold timidities of the old trade unions and the hot-air conditions of the ILP leaders'. She expected this younger left wing would become disillusioned with MacDonald, but would have 'a tussle to remove him'.

When Mosley visited some Liverpool slums, he told a journalist it was 'damnable. The rehousing of the working classes ought in itself to find work for the whole of the unemployed for the next ten years.' It was the Clydesiders, Maxton and Wheatley, with their 'real impulse of vital feeling' and determination to carry out rank-and-file wishes, which attracted Mosley. Wheatley's Housing Act was regarded as the government's only achievement. He pushed through radical measures to alleviate overcrowding and high rents by constructing 500,000 council houses over the following decade and demonstrated that Labour 'could do more than tinker with the capitalist system'.

Wheatley, said Mosley, was 'the only man of Lenin quality the English Left ever produced'. In debate, he was a master of fact and figure, a quality which appealed to Mosley, who, too, adopted the 'lawyer's ability to master a complicated brief rapidly'. Wheatley attacked free trade as anti-socialist and argued for non-tariff protection, national import boards for stabilizing prices and eliminating profiteering by middlemen, and nationalization of key industries. It was a set of policies which Mosley largely appropriated for his own.

Seventy constituencies, including highly winnable ones, offered Mosley a seat in place of Harrow, which would be difficult to hold as a socialist. Glasgow leader Patrick Dollan persuaded the ILP to waive the rule that no one could be a candidate until he had completed a year's membership. In July, Mosley chose the Birmingham Ladywood constituency, whose previous candidate had been expelled for joint membership of the Communist Party. The *Daily Worker* accused Mosley of turning to Labour only when he was 'seated in the saddle' and the seat had been worked 'up to within sight of victory'.

The bait for taking on Ladywood was the sitting MP, Neville Chamberlain. Mosley had fought clause by clause his Rent Act, which removed rent controls, claiming it was the 'most monstrous piece of class legislation that ever disgraced the Statute Book'. Mosley told reporters in Birmingham that he aimed 'to win a victory that would not merely give him a hardly-won seat, but would entitle him to his spurs in the movement to which he is a recent convert'.

Mosley asked Birmingham to 'overthrow the false gods of reaction which have dominated the city for the last generation at the cost of so much suffering'. The city was a Chamberlain family stronghold, but Neville had just a 1,500-vote majority and was vulnerable. Mosley employed two ILP organizers, Allan Young, a young Clydesider who was agent for the Borough party, and Bill Risdon, a miner from South Wales, as full-time propagandists. Another key figure was Frank Horrabin, an ILPer with a guild socialist background. Local official J. Johnson said Young was 'forever building schemes of organisation that were splendid if only they could have been carried through!' An astute economist, he acted as Mosley's political secretary and provided research assistance. As close to Mosley as anyone, Young was, like many Mosley acolytes, smitten with Cimmie. She helped 'make life less lonely because of your capacity to "feel". Ideas and actions are the playgrounds of life – but to feel is to live greatly.' Young and Risdon were excellent organizers, and by September Chamberlain was acknowledging 'that viper' as a credible threat.

Mosley contributed substantial sums to the ILP and was soon elected to its National Administrative Council and Financial Committee. The latter was chaired by J. A. Hobson, and committee members included Wise, Brailsford and a middle-class academic recruit, Hugh Dalton, a fierce rival of Mosley. Dalton was an admirer of the libertarian, anti-socialist economist, Friedrich von Hayek, and a believer in free trade.

ILP Secretary Fenner Brockway recalled the powerful presence on the committee of the 'arrogant and compelling' Mosley, and the 'extrovert and confident' Dalton. Both men came from Tory family backgrounds, were ambitious and aggressive, and treated politics as 'a battleground, without regard for injuries inflicted or received'. Dalton, however, disliked his rival more intensely than anyone else in his entire political career, while Mosley was unimpressed with the 'third-rate don', especially since Labour seemed to love a don 'like the Tories loved a lord'.

That September, at the Webbs' house, Mosley met his most important collaborator. Mosley thought the twenty-three-year-old Evelyn Strachey – he used the name John from the late twenties – had 'the right blend for action'. Both were well-off socialist converts and refugees from the upper class. As Strachey's biographer suggested, the relationship was based on mutual needs: 'if Strachey welcomed a leader – perhaps had often looked for one – Mosley needed a man of ideas.'

Strachey's father, St Loe Strachey, was the free trade editor of the *Spectator*, mouthpiece of the radical Right. St Loe's cousins included historian Lytton Strachey and James Strachey, psychoanalyst and translator of Freud. Deeply affected by the death of his elder brother, Strachey hated his father and his public school. He showed respect for authority but constantly rebelled against it. At Oxford he was something of a dandy and edited a Conservative journal with his friend Robert Boothby. Strachey left without graduating, having become conscious of a 'sudden and bewildering loss of faith in the whole moral, religious and social ideology which we had inherited'. He became intoxicated with the sexual freedom he found in the bohemian milieu in which he lived his disordered life. One observer said he was only ever a 'potential' personality, always 'in subjection to some idea outside of himself'. Sister Amabel thought him cold-hearted and there was an element of the cynic in him, as there was in Boothby.

Strachey spent his holidays at Lake Como, where Boothby educated him in monetary policy. By early January 1924 he was arguing against free trade and a return to the gold standard, which his father thought was 'a conspiracy to enslave Britain by the Jews of the City'. Strachey had an affair with Elizabeth Ponsonby, daughter of Labour Minister Arthur Ponsonby, who introduced him to Fenner Brockway. Strachey was offered a winnable seat in Birmingham's Aston area, which encompassed 'some of the worst slums of the city'.

Although he later attracted the label Communist, Strachey feared 'social regression and catastrophe – a dark age of unreason'. Capitalism's decadence and the development of a militant working class created the danger of a 'blind head-on collision between the two contending forces'. He agreed with Mosley that the 'wrongs of life are not righted simply by turning the world upside down and putting what is underneath on top; in effect, just replacing the gentle tyranny of an old order with the harsher tyranny of communism'. He wanted a socialism of reason as a defence against barbarism but, paradoxically, raised reason to 'the level of a faith'.

Mosley considered Strachey had 'one of the best analytical and critical intelligences' he had known, but not a particularly creative one. He claimed Strachey's earlier work described his thinking but had added no 'substantial invention'. Mosley probably underrated Strachey's abilities, just as he overrated his own. It is largely true that Strachey was the 'thinker' and Mosley the 'interpreter'. One observer said Mosley's speeches were 'brilliant, political creations, though not very philosophical'. ILPer Jon Paton confirmed from staff members that Mosley's effectiveness 'largely depended on the quality of his briefs. His knowledge of the matters we were discussing seemed to me always to have a superficial quality, and more than once I thought I detected him floundering when some of the more technical aspects emerged.'

Mosley was a magpie political operator who stole ideas from wherever he found them. He discussed monetary matters with Strachey, and with Young and Sydney Potter, who kept abreast of current economic thinking and were close to Frank Wise. Mosley was a consummate politician, putting forward clear-sighted policies based on coherent research. He put an intellectual gloss on what he was doing by referring to the need for synthesis but often the process was crude. Sometimes it worked, at other times the contradictions were apparent. His great ability was to adapt quickly to new ideas.

After 'scandal and mismanagement' wrecked the government's reputation, the Liberals joined the Conservatives in a temporary alliance. On 8 October 1924 the two parties voted MacDonald's minority Labour administration out of office. Mosley threw all his oratorical energies into the general election, speaking from dawn to dusk in Ladywood. 'None of us who went through that fight with him will ever forget it,' reported the *Town Crier*. 'His power over his audience was amazing, and his eloquence made even hardened Pressmen gasp in astonishment.' Mosley's vigorous campaigning had an effect. 'It was a joyous day when in the courtyards running back from the streets in the Birmingham slums we saw the blue window cards coming down and the red going up.' Mosley wanted Birmingham 'to lead England in the march of Labour'.

Chamberlain alleged the government had been under the thumb of Communists and reminded constituents that it had lent Russia millions. The Conservatives built up the 'Red Bogey' threat to devastating effect. On 25 October, four days before polling, came the 'Zinoviev Letter' bombshell. In itself, the *Mail*'s use of the forged letter was not decisive, but the cumulative effect of such smearing did have an impact. A tired MacDonald addressed numerous meetings with increasing anger – he referred to opponents as 'mangy dogs sniffing round a garbage heap' – but voters deserted the Liberals and supported the Tories. Labour's failure was one reason Mosley did not manage to pull off an election coup. The second was his presence on a 'White list' of candidates who endorsed women campaigners. Anti-feminist feeling ensured that he lost votes.

There were two recounts. First, Chamberlain was in by seven; then Mosley in by two. Mosley, a counter recalled, was an 'agitated man', while Chamberlain was as 'calm as you like it'. Chamberlain asked for a recount, in which sixty votes for Mosley suddenly vanished. A Tory teller was allegedly seen 'disappearing towards the lavatories with a pile of votes in his pocket'. The final count was not concluded until 4.20 a.m., when the 'wretched members of the counting staff were completely exhausted'. The final figures were Chamberlain, 13,374, and Mosley 13,297. Labour officials agreed the final figures did not tally with the total votes cast.

The election returned 415 Conservatives to Westminster, 152 Labour MPs (a loss of fifty seats) and forty-two Liberals. The Tory vote rose by two and a half million and the Labour vote by just over a million, whereas the Liberal vote fell by 30 per cent. Stanley Baldwin returned to form his second administration.

The closeness of the Ladywood result seemed a victory to Mosley's supporters who left the town hall to find a massive crowd in the square singing the 'Red Flag'. For Mosley it was 'a defeat of far more benefit than an easy victory in some safe district'. To his followers he was a hero denied, who had earned his socialist credentials. The result heralded the crumbling of the Tory hold on the West Midlands.

Mosley's continuing attacks on Chamberlain – 'once more we have got the old dud back at the Ministry of Health' – infuriated the Tories, who accused him of being unscrupulous. To Edward Wood he was 'that swine'. The PM's wife considered Mosley the 'most objectionable candidate standing in the whole country'. It seemed that if Mosley cultivated Ladywood, he would win the seat at the next election. The *Birmingham Mail*, however, revealed that 'despite the protestations of undying love for Ladywood and his great mission to fight for the soul of Birmingham, he has decided to cross the city boundary. Now the soul of Birmingham can go hang for all Mosley cares.'

Mosley was free of the parliamentary calendar and engaged in intensive reading and reflection, in an effort to outline his own position. Over the winter the Mosleys travelled to India and he took with him Keynes's *Tract on Monetary Reform*, which said economics was 'about choices and the need to make choices'. The bankers had chosen to cut costs and deflate, which could only lead to a 'transfer of wealth from the rest of the community to the rentier class . . . from the active to the inactive'. He said governments, by directing the money supply, could affect the economy in areas which previously had been thought to be at the whim of the market.

Keynes was unconcerned with class struggle and promoted 'an identity of interest between workers and manufacturers against their common enemies – the rentier and banker'. It was a position to which Mosley subscribed. Was Mosley, therefore, a proto-Keynesian? Skidelsky championed the view that he was and had been among the first to perceive Keynes's importance and translate his ideas into practical policy. It is easy to see why Mosley, eager to seize an opportunity for rehabilitation, willingly accepted this argument and, indeed, helped promote it. What better than to be presented as the lost prophet of his generation who had presented the economic solution to the problem of unemployment, while his mentor's economic theories had shaped the post-Second World War world.

That Mosley appropriated certain of Keynes's ideas is beyond doubt, but for the notion that Mosley was foremost a Keynesian the evidence is slim. Whether he actually read all of the *Tract* is unclear; by his own admission, he did not read his later works. His knowledge appears to have been derived from a series of articles Keynes published in the press during 1924. The main input came from discussions between Boothby and Strachey; the latter transmitted the ideas to Mosley, as did Young. This was only part of 'an eclectic blend of many different, often contradictory, elements which he combined into a mixture peculiarly his own'.

Central to Mosley's thinking were the ideas he encountered within the ILP. He subsequently argued that Fascism 'simply added ideology to the economics of my Labour Party days'. Keynes was the intellectual icing which Mosley applied to his synthesis, in order to appease critics who considered his original sources of inspiration 'cranks'. Keynes stated that Mosley was first and foremost an ideological planner, which Keynes was most definitely not.

At Port Said, Mosley picked up a copy of G. B. Shaw's *The Perfect Wagnerite*, an interpretation of the allegory in Wagner's *Ring* cycle of operas. Shaw portrays it as a 'parable about the collapse of capitalism and the emergence of a classless type of man to lead the proletariat'. Mosley admired Shavian vitalism with its belief in the power of ideas as the decisive motive force in human history. Shaw was supreme 'in his understanding of the great men of action and in his adumbration of what men might one day become'. Like Carlyle, he was convinced that government must be carried on, 'liberty or no liberty, with a conviction that only the superior individual can enforce the necessary discipline'.

Mosley saw himself acting out in life the central drama of Shaw's plays: 'the vital man, with ideas and impulses, confronting the inert creature of ideology and habits'. In 1925 he saw *Caesar and Cleopatra* at the Royal Court, paying particular attention to the unconventional heroic portrayal of Caesar, 'the supreme example of the great masters of action'. Mosley recognized Shaw's insight into a hero who is absent of 'passion in serving his overriding purpose'. He recalled with delight 'the scene when Caesar takes Cleopatra's arm to escort her into dinner, whispering that it was time to get down to business for he had despatched her assassin with one of his own a few hours before. This was Julius to a "T".'

The drama critic Desmond MacCarthy wrote, after seeing the same production, that Shaw's Caesar was 'a man in whom the black passion of personal domination was at least as marked as practical reason'. His driving force was 'the desire of the unscrupulous adventurer for glory in the Roman sense – the desire to make or destroy something great'. MacCarthy argued that 'great men have been of all shapes and sizes, and the plungers, the colossal egotists, who go so far because they do not know where they are going, seem to me to have drawn even more men irresistibly after them. If that is true, it is a reason for being a republican rather than a Caesarean, in the past, now, and for ever.' Given our knowledge of the twentieth century, MacCarthy was surely right.

Mosleyites believed Shaw had sympathy for Fascism and considered him a seminal figure in its development, pointing to his authoritarianism. His goal was the social organization of the Empire, and 'its rescue from the strife of classes and private interest'. He had belonged to a group of imperial Fabians, the Coefficients, who called for national efficiency and fused together national and socialist aspirations into a pre-Fascist ideology. It was left to Mosley to channel 'the immense volume of intellectual national socialism into a fascist party'. Shaw considered Mosley's 'air of certainty, driving perhaps from maternal adoration unchecked by any paternal competition, and furthered by his wealth, social privilege and prominent looks, was marvellously appealing in a world of danger and confusion' – could he be the superman whose advent Shaw had been prophesying? All Ramsay MacDonald had to offer was muddle, whereas people would 'hear something more of Sir Oswald before you are through with him'.

When the Mosleys reached India they visited Madras, where they entered the strange circle of Mrs Besant. A non-believer in theosophy, Mosley pointed to the effect of the war 'on the spiritual needs of people and the rise of bogus mediums'. Besant explained 'man's rise from bestiality was accomplished with the help of visitors from Venus' but Mosley found that 'any request for evidence would be regarded as philistinism'. He believed 'highly rational people often lose the faculty of reason when confronted by occult powers'. Initiates such as J. F. C. Fuller (admirer of Aleister Crowley and Mosleyite) were seekers after truth, which was 'an end in itself; truth may not be found but the search was worthwhile'.

Besant was a champion of Indian independence: Mosley was not, even though he could not help but notice the suffering of the masses in the slums of Bombay. He developed a deep affection for India, which was enhanced by his introduction to Gandhi. He subsequently wrote a report on India, which he circulated among British politicians. He suggested 'we could stay in India as long as we wished without so much trouble as some anticipated' but 'if we did go, there would be bloodshed on a great scale'. He studied the country's agriculture and concluded what was required was 'a mogul with a tractor and a deep plough'. Typically it would require someone of 'an extraordinary genius of thought and action of the supreme Caesarean category'.

On his return from India, Mosley declared that Birmingham, home of Chamberlain's unauthorized programme, 'must be to the Labour movement what Manchester has been to Liberalism'. By March, Mosley had put together an ambitious second programme to deal with unemployment. Allan Young had helped shape the ideas and instilled in them the Hobson and Wise doctrine. Strachey was chief assistant in working out the 'Birmingham proposals', though Mosley was certain his own contribution made it decisive, though they had largely originated in discussion circles before he finally synthesized them.

Input came from Boothby, who made his successful Commons maiden speech on unemployment on 25 March 1925. From the beginning of the year the Conservatives had engaged in a deflationary drive to put the pound back on the gold standard. The speedy restoration of pre-war normalcy and deflationary policies, however, only served to increase unemployment, which Boothby regarded as an 'unnecessary evil'. He called for new industrial confidence, taxation cuts and an end to the class war. Boothby was already immersed in Keynesian thinking.

It has been suggested that it was Mosley who moved the ILP towards an interest in monetary policy as a means of expanding demand but, as he himself admitted, discussion along these lines had already taken place. Clifford Allen argued in the Socialist Programme for 'an expansion of purchasing power brought about by an increase of bank advances' as a remedy for unemployment. *New Leader* editor H. N. Brailsford acknowledged his debt to Hobson, Wise and, more specifically, to the credit policy ideas of Lloyd and Keynes, and wrote articles ('Socialism for Today') on the lack of 'effective demand' and the need for the stabilization of prices to counter potential inflation. It was Brailsford not Mosley who won over the ILP to the necessity of controlling banking since 'one could not impose on industry the obligation to pay a true living wage, without at the same time facing the regulation of credit, the control of prices through the importation, by a National Board, of food and raw materials, and the reorganization of the more depressed industries'. Brailsford and Mosley often worked in parallel, and the latter's own credit theory was derived from the ILP's under-consumptionist thinking.

In April 1925 Britain returned to the gold standard at the pre-war rate of exchange of $4.86. With free trade reaffirmed, the 'holy trinity of liberal financial orthodoxy was completed by the Treasury's sustained pursuit of the balanced budget', which only served to deepen the slump. Mosley attacked the Chancellor, Winston Churchill, who 'faced with the alternative of saying good-bye to the gold standard and therefore to his own employment, or good-bye to other people's employment, characteristically selected the latter course'. Following Kitson's line, Mosley charged that Britain clung to free trade 'for the sole reason that the process is a means of collecting the usury of the City'. Transport and General Workers' Union leader Ernest Bevin declined to join the attack because he regarded Mosley as 'the kind of unreliable intellectual who might at any moment stab him in the back'.

At an April ILP conference in Gloucester, Mosley presented the Birmingham proposals: an incomes policy, control of credit, abandonment of the gold standard and a national corporation to plan output in key industries. He moved a resolution for a 'public banking system capable of giving such accommodation to industry as will enable it to increase the purchasing power of the workers, so that new home markets can absorb industry's real productive capacity'. His chief contribution was the 'requirement of consumer credits in addition to producer credits and their combination with national planning'. Banking and credit, he added, were the economy's key points and their control was essential to any effective planning. A floating exchange rate coupled with the bulk purchase of foodstuffs and raw materials would protect external trade.

Mosley outlined his proposals in *The Times* ('Socialisation of Banking') on 15 April. They were criticized by the economist Robert Brand, who said they would lead to inflation and render exports uncompetitive. Mosley replied that 'an increase in the supply of money accompanied by a corresponding increase in the supply of goods available for purchase is not inflation'. Manufacturers would increase production if markets were provided, so that inflation would only arise when unemployment had declined to a point 'at which the maximum productivity of the nation had been nearly reached'. Given that real demand existed 'in the shape of underpaid poverty but not effective demand in the shape of purchasing power', an increase in the purchasing power would engage the services of 'men and machines now idle' and result in a 'substantial increase in real wealth'. Mosley had anticipated the Keynesian position that in conditions of idle capacity, an increase in production would not necessarily lead to a rise in price.

Mosley's inability to supply a satisfactory answer to Brand's question of how an increase in purchasing power could help exports raised the question of his real knowledge. Strachey's answer that an increase in demand would lead to an increase in demand for foreign goods and, in turn, expand foreign trade, supports the idea that he was the thinker, not Mosley.

There were fundamental differences between Mosley and Keynes. Whereas Mosley proposed a supply of credit to increase demand and stimulate extra production, the latter believed credit should be expanded to meet an increase in production. For Mosley, the danger of inflation resulting from the injection of new money would be met by socialist planning by way of an Economic Council to co-ordinate productive capacity. In this way he 'welded together the socialist case with modern monetary theory'. To appease ILP fears, the Council would not have legislative powers, so there would be 'no possibility of a thinly disguised state tyranny operating through such a board'. The proposals were well received by John Wheatley, though he criticized the absence of any commitment to redistribution through taxation.

Hugh Dalton attacked Mosley's 'half-baked schemes' and his willingness 'to seize any panacea that might offer a political advantage'. However, Daniel Ritschell notes, it is 'the job of politicians out of power to have bold opinion. It is not to Mosley's discredit that he should have taken up and embellished with socialist rhetoric the boldest opinions around.' He sought intellectual guides who would take him 'beyond Marxism'. He discovered them among the most progressive of liberal thinkers but he believed he needed to go 'beyond Keynes'. The search for radical ideas to synthesize with progressive economics led him into areas which were distinctly non-socialist.

Strachey was all but a social creditor and, with Mosley's help, attempted to move the ILP in the direction of Major Douglas. Unfortunately, Douglas had shortcomings as a leader and a minority faction, led by H. E. B. Ludlam, a Coventry printer who headed the Economic Freedom League and edited its journal, the *Age of Plenty*, demanded a more action-orientated movement. Under Strachey's direction, Ludlam organized support in the *New Age*. A League member was the youth leader and theosophist John Hargreave. After coming under the influence of Rolf Gardiner, Cambridge social creditor and student of German youth movements, he initiated a brand of anti-war, outdoor philosophy known as the Kibbo Kift, an 'instrument of social regeneration and pure action'. Strachey urged the League to concentrate on those the *New Age* ignored – the unemployed masses.

In mid 1925 the ILP reviewed its 'living wage' policy as a piece of political propaganda. It was, for Wheatley, 'no longer a question of the plan's being logically practicable, politically expedient, but of its advocates' success in hammering the symbol so deeply into the consciousness of millions of people that they are ready to march for it'. This was a Sorelian, syndicalist appeal for a single challenge by the industrial and political movements acting together. 'With our eyes open we are asking for the impossible.'

A pragmatic Mosley was interested 'neither in the ILP's dreamy vision of a socialist world nor in nineteenth-century capitalism, which was breaking down before our eyes'. He wanted Labour to meet the challenge of unemployment 'here and now'. He rejected his collegues' preoccupation with ultimate issues and lectured them on the need for realism. Within the ILP, critics charged that he aimed merely to bolster capitalism. However, he had the support of Wheatley and George Lansbury, who explained that as socialists they had to take the world as it was. They departed from ILP policy in adopting 'a progressive policy towards the Empire'. Internationalists such as Brailsford and Brockway regarded this as heresy, and dismissed them and Mosley as the 'new school of Socialist-Imperialism'.

Mosley's proposals were completed in August and detailed in his pamphlet, 'Revolution by Reason'. On the 7th he outlined the content at the ILP summer school at Dunmow, Essex, where he urged socialists to recognize that monetary policy was 'a factor upon which prices, employment and everything else depended. A gold standard socialist is a contradiction in terms.' He wanted to expand credit in a scientific manner by way of consumers' credits. Producers' credits would also be necessary for 'the production of the goods for which consumers' credits create the demand now lacking'.

This was 'sweet to the ears of social creditors' who agreed that demand must precede supply and that absence of purchasing power was the central problem. The idea of selective credit expansion had been dismissed by the ILP as dangerously inflationary but Mosley argued the 'costs of production depended primarily on the rate of production rather than the rate of wages'. He maintained that wages could be increased almost indefinitely to the limits of 'maximum productivity'. Defending what became Keynes's post-General Theory position, Mosley recognized that 'when the maximum production of the nation is nearly reached, no new money must be created or inflation will follow'.

The quantity theory of money which underpinned Mosley's monetary policy prescriptions was derived from Kitson. The concept of the creation of purchasing power to evoke production, Mosley noted, was rejected out of hand; 'even Keynes went no further than urging on quantity-theory lines an adequate supply of credit to prevent a fall in the price-level, credit which would only be available to producers and general borrowers through the ordinary banking mechanism'. His long-standing unwillingness to abandon the quantity theory reinforced the impression that he 'never read, or never properly understood Keynes's later General Theory'.

Credit expansion, Mosley argued, would be an emergency measure and, once the economy recovered, new demand would allow industry to pay higher wages through rising productivity. It was, Daniel Ritschell suggests, 'an economy of high wages, rather than either Keynesian credit expansion or the socialist option of redistribution of wealth, that was his distinctive remedy for the slump'. But because 'capitalism lacked a co-ordinating intelligence', such a remedy, Mosley argued, required socialist planning. Otherwise it would lead to inflation with higher prices and not increased production. He embraced ILP planning and wanted an Economic Council – an idea welcomed by social creditors as their own – with statutory powers 'to estimate the difference between the actual and potential production of the country and to plan the stages by which that potential production can be evoked through the instrument of working-class demand'. It would ensure that demand did not outstrip supply and cause a price rise.

To stimulate consumption, wages would be fixed at generous levels and financed by forcing companies to accept overdrafts from nationalized banks. Credits would be earmarked as assistance to wages but would not subsidize industry, though producer credits would be given to socially useful industries to raise output and lower prices. Taking ideas from Frank Wise and E. M. H. Lloyd, he proposed that Import Boards would replace some imports with domestic production and bulk purchase food and raw material on favourable contracts.

Mosley depicted 'Revolution by Reason' as a practical alternative to the nationalization of industry in which the central position of the City and its restrictive financial policy would be replaced by a producers' alliance. The document was impressive. It identified the major constraints to expansionist policies – 'sound' money and the high exchange rate – and proposed workable policies on both counts. He received, however, only a respectful hearing as the content drifted above the heads of the ILP rank and file. Few could grasp that 'the value of money itself could be, and was, manipulated'. The high-wage thesis was anathema to Snowden, who argued 'it was for wages to adjust to whatever monetary policy was deemed best by Montagu Norman'. ILPers did not believe industrialists and workers had common interests and dismissed Mosley's policies as reformist. The impact within the Labour Party and trade unions was minimal.

In the *Daily Herald* (24 April 1925) Mosley insisted that socialism's core was 'not so much a political spirit as a religious one'. He took his lead from Lassalle, who spoke of love and reconciliation in opposition to class conflict. He saw modern problems in terms of 'the struggle between the Christian and the Nietzschean conceptions of man'. He took from Christianity 'the immense vision of service, self-abnegation and self-sacrifice', and from Nietzschean thought 'the virility, the challenge to all existing things which impede the march of mankind, the absolute abnegation of the doctrine of surrender'.

Despite the title of his pamphlet, the substance of Mosley's rhetoric was permeated by a concern that had nothing to do with reason. His vision at the end of 'Revolution by Reason' was apocalyptic. 'Crisis after crisis sends capitalist society staggering ever nearer to abysses of inconceivable catastrophe for suffering millions.' Therefore 'we must recapture the spirit of rapturous sacrifice. In our hands is the awakening trumpet of reality. Labour alone holds the magic of sacrifice. Dissolved are all other creeds of baser metal beneath ordeal by fire.' Such talk was reminiscent of millenarianism and bore resemblance to the 'illuminates' and the emerging Fascist movements, characterized by similar demands for guilds and assaults on international finance. The shared enemy was the banker. Mosley told ILPers that by controlling banking they could 'dominate the whole field of capitalism and capture its innermost fortress'. It naturally followed that projected on to the bankers was a hatred of Jews.

Within the plan of 'Revolution by Reason' to avoid the 'middleman', Stuart Rawnsley spotted evidence of Mosley's later attacks on Jewish financiers.

Purchasing power is transferred from the pockets of the workers to the pockets of the idle rentier and owner of fixed interest-bearing securities . . . By *the obscure and secret working of the hidden bankers' hands*, wealth is thus filched from the poor and poured into the coffers of the idle rich. When we regard the present condition of the anguished masses, may we not ask whether history itself holds evidence of a more *sinister and heartless villainy*?

For those ILP members reared on Hobson's anti-Semitism, there was no need to decipher its coded meanings.

At the summer school, responding to a talk by Communist Willie Gallacher, Mosley said he would 'use every means to crush' any attempt by Communists to overthrow the government. This would not, however, involve Fascist means. He warned that Fascist Italy was the greatest danger to peace. Ministers had shown their true intention by praising Mussolini. They 'would like to be Fascists but have not the courage; they have not the courage to wear their black shirts'. The Conservatives wanted to use Fascism to overthrow Russia.

Ten days later Beatrice Webb observed that 'the ILP and their middle-class friends, fearing to be superseded, as the left-wing, by the Communistic trade union leaders are plunging head-over-ears into grandiose schemes of revolutionary change'. She singled out Mosley's state organization of credit as mischievous. He had warned ILPers that 'evolutionary socialism was not enough' and that measures of a 'drastic and socialist character' were required. However, his socialism was simply defined as the 'conscious control and direction of human resources for human needs'. It differed little from Labour's 'sentimentalised cult of human brotherhood'. He later admitted it was 'an error to use the term socialism'.

*

In July 1925, before leaving for their annual holiday in Italy, the Mosleys celebrated the wedding of Cimmie's sister, Baba, to 'Fruity' Metcalfe, who had just joined the British Fascisti. For a wedding present they gave Baba ruby-and-diamond earrings. On the journey through France they were joined by Strachey, who aided the slow evolution of a book version of 'Revolution by Reason'. Boothby appeared in Venice, where he joined in discussions with his two friends as they wrote together, which he thought the 'height of political audacity'. Oxford academic C. M. Bowra recalled having dinner with the pair in a palazzo on the Grand Canal. Mosley 'put forward bold and constructive ideas. He was a forcible talker, who set out to be magnetic and tried to win my support by saying that he wished Britain to resemble ancient Athens.' Bowra found his manner disturbing but was enchanted by Cimmie's 'genius for healing the wounds which her husband inflicted on all kinds of people'.

Another observer, Celia Simpson, thought Strachey was unwisely under Mosley's influence and despite his extreme socialism was 'snobbish and imma-ture'. His sister Amabel, a literary figure and wife of Clough Williams-Ellis, creator of Portmeirion in Wales, recalled that Mosley and her brother were, like Boothby, 'apt to enjoy themselves, but they were less thorough about it. Pleasure was only pursued between anxious moments.'

'This was the period', Boothby recalled, 'when Mosley saw himself as Byron rather than Mussolini' and self-consciously tried to match the poet's feats. He was 'certainly a powerful swimmer and used to disappear at intervals into the lagoon to commune with himself'. On one occasion he set out to swim to the Lido because Byron had done it. The press had no interest in his ideas but was interested in him as a celebrity. 'We were pursued throughout our holiday,' Mosley recalled. It was felt scandalous 'for moneyed people to pretend to be Socialists'.

Friends had 'seldom contemplated a more whimsical turn of the social and political wheel' than when, on 21 September, Cimmie was adopted as a Labour candidate for Stoke-on-Trent. She was, however, revered by Boothby, who praised her legendary 'valour and devotion', and predicted that 'your husband (damned Socialist though he is by God) will be Prime Minister for a very very long time, because he has the Divine Spark which is almost lost nowadays'.

In September 1925 Strachey published his extended *Revolution by Reason*, dedicated to 'OM' – 'who may some day do the things of which we dream'. It was more urbane than Mosley's version. Strachey said capitalism was 'in a blind alley' and argued, as did the social creditors, that 'the only way capitalism had of saving itself was to engage in cut-throat, and eventually ruinous, competition, or in imperialism, or in what was perhaps the worst evil of all, a state tyranny working through gigantic combinations'. Social credit hopes were encouraged by his acknowledgement that the 'whole scheme would depend upon the National Credit, which was "directly proportionate to the national capacity to produce wealth" '. He was, however, more directly influenced by Keynes, that there was a close relationship between the amount of money in circulation and price levels. He accepted money supply had to be related to the needs of production and not to gold reserves. A general theme was his belief that capitalism's crisis would lead to violent revolution. It was imperative to find an alternative to the 'blind, head-on collision' between workers and capitalists. A revolution by reason was needed to prevent class conflict bringing about a dark age of unreason.

ILP response was positive but Labour intellectuals were hostile. They highlighted the 'vast practical problems in co-ordinating the money supply, production and demand as he envisaged'. Dalton, appointed Reader in Economics at the London School of Economics, said that 'to go off gold again isn't practical'. He criticized the proposed Economic Council and its many tasks because he could not 'see the necessary supermen on the horizon who could tackle them all'.

Keynes liked the book. However, he could not appreciate Mosley's 'flash of intuition about a "lack of effective demand" '. Had Mosley been able to explain properly how it could occur, noted Skidelsky, 'he, and not Keynes, would have been the author of the new economics'. The economist considered the proposals failed to 'face the fact that it is precisely the industries which cater for foreign trade [coal, steel and textiles] which are underemployed and not those which produce for working-class consumption'. Even so, Keynes said 'it is scarcely to be expected that we should agree on all the very complicated monetary points which arise, about which no one has ever written clearly. I am still too confused in my own mind to know exactly what I want to do.'

Even Dalton considered the book a remarkable achievement for a 'twenty-four-year-old, untrained in economics to explain and synthesise differing theories'. Strachey's and Mosley's attempt to understand the relationship between banking and the economy as a whole was unusual on the Left. Their measures were not socialism but were an advance on Labour policy and more relevant than their critics' efforts, which reiterated 'existing orthodoxies camouflaged with socialist rhetoric'. Their problem was that as critics of the Bank of England–Treasury–City nexus, they were on their own. Their proposals were not seriously considered because they 'clashed with the City's most cherished tenets'. And at no point did Labour display a willingness to challenge this consensus.

Mosley lamented that it was 'impossible to get serious discussion of any subject except at the mass meetings'. The *New Leader* (20 November) noted his visit to Glasgow and the huge crowds singing the 'Red Flag'. But even if he attracted the largest meetings, his speeches were not reported in the press. He developed a conspiratorial view that 'dominant forces' – 'King Bank and

King Bunk' – were determined to prevent change. The press lords were 'masters of certain aspects of business and finance but almost entirely ignorant of serious politics'. Their dream was to form governments of 'their cronies in the way that men form clubs, not serious parties supporting new ideas and clear courses'. He later recognized that he cronied himself 'with some result'.

The ILP suffered a blow with the resignation of an ailing Clifford Allen. Before he resigned, Allen appointed Mosley to a Living Wage commission under Brailsford, whose collection of articles, *Socialism for Today*, was published in October. In the following month the ILP issued its Industrial Policy which drew on guild socialism and wartime planning. The ILP now fell victim to hasty projects, with decisions determined by propaganda necessities. When supporters moved to the left, the ILP lost its influence with Labour leaders. This explains why Mosley began to snuggle up to MacDonald. Dalton watched with a 'special loathing' as he turned the 'lonely susceptible old man into an intimate friend'. When Mosley invited MacDonald and Dalton to his country house, the latter refused, irritated that the Labour leader had swallowed the bait.

Mosley's distancing from the ILP coincided with his trip to the US over the winter of 1925–6, when he claimed he changed his thinking, having discovered the secret of American economic success. The striking feature is the large number of other politicians who made the discovery. During his own visit, Boothby wrote that the 'era of mass production is upon us. And mass production involves large economic units.' Vernon Willey, President of the Federation of British Industries, noted that, despite high wages, 'prices were actually falling because the huge home market enabled industry to make rapid technical progress and pass on the economies to the customer'.

In the US, the Mosleys were stalked by journalists and were treated like celebrities. They were interested in Cimmie's own turn to the left. She explained that she and her father were 'two very typical figures, and that the same drama has been enacted in many homes; only I do not know another man who was so splendidly, so utterly symbolic of the old world, the pre-war world, as was my father. I should like to think that I am as typical of the new world, the post-war world.'

In Washington, Cimmie visited her Leiter relatives, who were involved in a lawsuit with an English branch of the family, the Suffolks (Mary Curzon's younger sister had married the Earl of Suffolk), over misappropriation of trustee funds. Mosley was surprised by the strong anti-Semitism prevalent among the Leiters, particularly since it was assumed, wrongly, that they were Jews. In New York, he observed the slums and the segregation of communities. He wrote to Strachey on 15 January 1926 that the slums were 'not so bad as our worst. The interesting thing from our point of view was that the rents have all increased in proportion to wages ... it seems as long as rent and interest survive, the proportionate toll is taken of the workers whatever wages they may draw.'

The ultimate destination of those interested in American industrial success was the Ford Motor Company's vast River Rouge plant in Detroit. Front Generation socialists were interested in the new phenomenon of scientific management known, firstly, as Taylorism and then as Fordism. Frederick 'speedy' Taylor, father of the stop-watch-and-clipboard approach, popularized a process of labour discipline and workshop organization based upon studies of human efficiency and incentive systems. It became the basis of all time and motion studies, and the norm in Detroit factories.

Americanism, suggests Charles Maier, reflected the 'powerful demand for technocratic expertise that had been encouraged by the First World War'. Technocratic management appealed to proto-Fascists because it promised a 'non-zero-sum' world in which expanded production would make socialist redistribution irrelevant. It would eliminate scarcity and offer a revolution in the nature of authority, with the neutrality of scientific managers ending class confrontation. This change from 'power over men to the administration of things' undermined notions of class and, as such, there was 'an element of elitist proto-syndicalism about the model'.

In Britain Mary Follett, a scientific management theorist, published at the end of the war *The New State*. Influenced by guild socialism, she argued that 'scientific government by experts and schemes for the self-regulation of industry' aimed at increased production, reflected a 'quest for a new concept of authority that would transform the economic interests now smothering the public welfare into the very bearers of the community's advance into abundance'. The quest for a 'public syndicalism of the producers' was promoted in Germany by Walter Rathenau. It went beyond the old guild system by appealing to a community of production in which 'all members are organically interwoven'. The social creditors opposed this planned approach precisely because it was in essence syndicalist and did not differ widely from Fascism.

At the Ford factory Mosley found 'striking confirmation' of his thinking. Fordism looked at production as a whole and its results were spectacular in reducing costs, lowering prices and increasing sales and profits. Ford produced 'the cheapest article and paid the highest wage in the world [five dollars for an eight-hour day]; in terms of money value, nothing on earth could compare with that original Tin Lizzie'. However, the speeded-up assembly line left workers struggling to keep pace. Mosley thought them 'primitive types ... ideal for the job because normal labour was apt to find it too monotonous'. Ford's de-skilled workers hated the regime and even high wages could not mask the rapid turnover of labour.

Henry Ford hoped high wages would turn workers into 'partners and accomplices' in a producers' alliance against finance capital. He attacked the bankers for their unwillingness to invest in manufacturing and, like Britain's self-financing Morris Cars, was forced to plough his own money into the business. He was a currency 'crank', opposed the gold standard and, inevitably, turned to anti-Semitism. His own newspaper, the *Dearborn Independent*, attacked Jewish influence on American politics. Such propaganda was admired by Hitler, who kept a life-size portrait of Ford next to his desk.

Mosley saw the 'birth of a new world' at a Pittsburgh steel works where a few men were 'manipulating masses of machines'. In this technological vision, Mosley realized there would be chaos as economies adapted to new realities. Automated machinery and unskilled labour would threaten British industry by enabling undeveloped countries – 'Oriental and African labour does not mind monotony as much as the Europeans do' – to compete against it. In fact, this was decades off but Lancashire cotton was already being undermined by low-wage competition. Mosley believed this could be countered by the State aiding private enterprise to conduct business freely. There was not much socialism here.

On his return from the US, Vernon Willey urged on the FBI the need for 'collectivism, amalgamation and cartel agreements'. Fordism was accompanied with a shift to protectionism, but despite the promises of social revolution, its ideological implications were conservative and firmly pro-capitalist.

Britain's most successful mass car producer, William Morris, had a hand-powered assembly line with craftsmen on piecework rather than a daily wage. Productivity was modest and because of lack of investment, weak demand and ruthless price cutting, car makers faced a constant cash crisis. The problem was the small domestic market, which industrialists argued required low wages in order to be competitive with exports. For Mosley, mass production for a large home market held the industrial key and it was 'not so much the rate of wage as the rate of production which determined the cost of production'.

Out of the blue, the Mosleys received an invitation to meet Franklin D. Roosevelt, Governor of New York and a likely presidential candidate. They were invited to Florida to meet Roosevelt on his houseboat, the *Larocco*, for a fishing trip. 'We had a great mutual sympathy,' Mosley recalled. 'He had a tremendous sense of compassion – a feeling that the suffering to which the mass of people in unemployment, in bad housing and the rest of it were being subjected at the time was unnecessary and should be remedied. He was therefore a radical in politics.' FDR wrote that they were 'a most delightful couple and we shall miss them much'.

Mosley was not entirely impressed by their host. 'Here was this man para-lysed below the waist, a superb-looking man, a kind man, a man whom you couldn't help but liking but at the same time seemed to me largely without the mental capacity to be President of the United States.' He had 'scarcely an inkling of the turmoil of creative thinking then beginning in America, in the technical sphere of money, and in the industrial regions with the vastly paid technicians of the mass-producing plants who already foresaw a productive potential which would eventually confront statesmanship with a problem to overwhelm all previous economic thinking'.

On 15 February Mosley wrote to Strachey that he had conversed with Federal Reserve Board economists, who were 'fully abreast of the thinking of Keynes'. On his return, Mosley described the Federal Reserve as a 'semi-socialist banking system'. He was interested in hire-purchase – then almost unknown in Britain – but saw it as a 'haphazard form of his own more scientific consumer-credit proposals'. What was required was national planning, not the piecemeal way in which the Americans applied these new ideas.

In April 1926 Mosley's article, 'Is America a Capitalist Triumph?', praised the 'amazing feats of mass production' and claimed high wages was the 'thinking medicine with which we must dose British industry'. The ILP welcomed the concept of high wages and recognized the necessity of a large home market in developing in full the possibilities of mass production. Brailsford's *Can Capitalism Save Itself?* accepted that American technique held out the promise of eliminating poverty. He presented it as an alternative to Communism: Henry Fordism, not Marxism, was the future that worked.

Mosley argued that Britain needed to be part of a larger economic unit 'insulated' from those external factors that caused economic failure. He retreated to social imperialism but not the 'old, crude Conservative protection of industrial inefficiency'. Protection 'in a small island which contains a few of the necessary foodstuffs and hardly any of its industrial raw materials is a very different thing from an empire containing nearly all of these requisites'.

In April 'Socialism in Our Time' was adopted at the ILP's Easter conference. An ambitious vision of socialism, it proposed redistribution to alleviate under-consumption. State-imposed wage levels would redistribute income towards the poverty-striken working class as a way of generating new consumer demand and thus eliminating unemployment.

Mosley claimed the new ILP policy was largely set out in *Revolution by Reason* and, therefore, the debate 'solely concerned the best method of putting into practice the great conception of a Living Wage'. He thought it 'useless to undergo the great struggle to nationalise the banks if, in the end, we employ them exactly as our enemies would employ them'. He criticized plans to nationalize weak industries with the result that they would be left to 'hold the baby'. Whereas Brailsford wanted to persuade industries to reorganize themselves, Mosley argued capitalism had 'never responded to anything except the stern use of economic power in the hands of the workers'.

Mosley's militant urge to action was the 'common spark' of the Front

Generation's dissatisfaction with orthodoxy. They recognized that progress towards socialist goals did not have to wait until capitalism had collapsed. Geoffrey Elton belonged to a group of parliamentary candidates who met regularly with Mosley and Strachey to discuss a 'party of the classes motivated against the profiteer'. A 'ruthless' Strachey was also demanding action. They would experience direct action during the General Strike of May 1926.

' "All the workers of this country have got to face a reduction of wages," murmurs Mr Baldwin between a sermon and a subsidy,' Mosley said in a speech. When mine owners demanded a 10 per cent wage cut from their workforce and the TUC warned this would mean a general strike, Baldwin offered a compromise. The miners were supported by railwaymen and transport workers, who persuaded the government to buy off a strike with a temporary subsidy to the coal industry. The subsidy was due to expire on 30 April and the unions prepared to resist. The time bought allowed the Chancellor, Winston Churchill, and the reactionary Home Secretary, Sir William Joynson-Hicks, known as 'Mussolini Minor', to stiffen the PM's resistance. The government broke off negotiations and the General Strike began.

Mosley had a core of followers and an operating base in Birmingham. However, he did not establish lasting support in the West Midlands, where not all Labour members endorsed his leadership. They did, however, praise his role in the strike – he made up to twenty speeches a day – which included buying an interest in the *Town Crier* and funding a strike bulletin, edited by Strachey. Mosley narrowly escaped arrest – he was out of town at the time – when the Birmingham Strike Committee was rounded up on charges of stirring up disaffection.

Mosley established close relations with Arthur Cook, the Miners' Federation's fiery secretary. He admired the Leninist Cook as a 'true product of England if ever there was one'. The friendship developed under the influence of Strachey who edited the Federation's journal, the *Miner*. Cook resigned from the Communist Party in 1921, but he had few political differences with the Communists. Arthur Horner recalled that to the miners Cook 'was magnificent, utterly inspiring; the man who always raised them to the furthest heights of their determination to end the injustices and miseries from which they suffered'. Beatrice Webb, however, considered him a man with 'no intellect and not much intelligence – drunk with his own words, dominated by his own slogans'.

When the strike dragged on into the autumn, Mosley spoke in mining areas and helped starving miners with a donation of £500 (£15,000). He saw in the miners' solidarity the comradeship of the war years and became a regular speaker at the Durham miners' gala, where he was given a tumultuous reception from the 100,000-strong crowd. He said watching the miners marching with bands and banners convinced him 'colourful methods were not so inappropriate to British politics as some supposed' and inspired his later Fascist marches. The strike's end, however, was a disillusioning experience for those of the war generation who hoped returning soldiers 'would be a political force for peace; 1926 showed that no such force, no such unity existed'.

During the summer, Mosley attended the ILP's annual school at Lady Warwick's ancestral Easton Lodge in Norfolk. Its grounds were then as freely available to socialism as her previous favours to her royal lover, Edward VII. Jon Paton recalled that the lecturers included the 'famous or near-famous', such as H. G. Wells, Major-General J. F. C. Fuller and Basil Liddell Hart, 'whose lectures were certain to be given space in the newspapers'. Included among the acknowledged experts in their field were Keynes, Lord Lothian, Walter Elliott and Beaverbrook, a defender of a lost cause.

Mosley arrived, Amabel Williams-Ellis noted, with 'a pigskin suitcase and golf clubs as well as a tennis racquet. In Labour gatherings he was apt to walk through the life of the place, but this was seldom if ever resented. After all, he genuinely wanted to know other people's views.' However, Fenner Brockway felt he displayed 'intolerance and a growing impatience of public opinion'. When Wells intervened in a discussion and insisted on the need for technicians in the transformation to socialism, Mosley 'attacked him demagogically as a paternalist, intellectual'. It angered Brockway who went for him 'in what was perhaps our first conflict'. Cimmie soothed any bad feelings by singing Negro spirituals!

During 1926 the Mosleys bought Savehay Farm, a red-brick, half-timbered Tudor house, near Denham, in Buckinghamshire, for £5,000 (£150,000). The house was redesigned by Clough Williams-Ellis who, a few months previously, had entertained strike-breaking bus drivers. Leading ILP figures were invited to Denham, in what were 'less like practical experiments in socialism than lavish exercises in feudal patronage'. Allan Young was overcome by the experience. He wrote to Cimmie: 'You gave me beauty – pictures that will live for ever: space – in the sense that I was separated from the vortex of petty problems: privacy – in the sense that your fine culture (which is feeling) enables you to refrain from interference . . .'

In September the ILP's commission, chaired by Hobson and among whose members was Mosley, reported on the viability of the living wage. It argued for redistribution and increased consumption by way of a family allowance scheme and a minimum wage. The living wage's initial cost would be achieved by printing new money. Industries which refused to co-operate by raising wages would be summarily nationalized. This led inexorably to the adoption of full-scale planning, based on the guild socialist notion of encroaching control. As the planning centre of the nation's industrial life, an Industrial Commission would be able to enforce the amalgamation of businesses in the interests of efficiency. Joint-stock banks would direct the flow of credit and a National Industry bank would foster staple industries. It has been suggested that planning owed its presence to the publicity given it by Mosley but ILPers were already discussing a socialist model.

Neither Mosley's 'Revolution by Reason' nor 'The Living Wage' was accorded the attention they deserved. Ramsay MacDonald did not bother to read ILP documents and senior figures rejected the policy. It was remitted to a Committee of Inquiry and quietly forgotten. However, these were 'incisive, coherent programmes with greater realism than anything produced by contemporary academic economists'. They recognized the economy was not a self-righting mechanism, implicitly assumed the multiplier effect of putting money into the economy and the importance of monetary demand in determining the level of employment. Keynes was sympathetic, on the basis that it was worth trying new ways to increase demand, but was wary of the credit expansion, because of the threat of inflation.

Mosley made no attempt to align himself with any faction within the Labour Party but retained good relations with the Labour leader. MacDonald, noted Beatrice Webb, 'consorts with the de la Warrs, Mosley and J. H. Thomas and one or two smart ladies, whilst he is constantly in the company of the great who emphatically can't belong to the Labour party'. He associated with a circle distinguished by 'its aristocratic flavour – leaders of fashion or ladies of the stage attended by six-feet-tall and well-groomed men [Mosley]'.

Neville Chamberlain decided not to seek re-election at Ladywood. He explained to his agent that there was 'such a large mass of uneducated and credulous people, ready to be influenced by the sort of opponents I have had in the past, that my position must be precarious'. Conservatives believed they might succeed with a new candidate, on the basis that Mosley's 'perpetual abuse aroused more criticism than sympathy'. However, when Chamberlain abandoned the seat, Mosley felt free to seek a by-election opportunity, rather than wait for the next general election.

Mosley had been selected for the Forest of Dean, but was forced to withdraw because of protests from the Birmingham Labour Party. Herbert Morrison, a former critic of the parliamentary party who had become 'the prudent defender of the party establishment', had been outraged by this 'disdain for the party's constitution' and Mosley had had to appear before the National Executive Committee (NEC). He was reprimanded but then, on 26 November, the sitting MP for the Smethwick constituency announced his retirement.

Mosley was adopted for the seat on 4 December, but without consultation with head office, which was entitled to select a candidate for a by-election. Morrison regarded this as a serious irregularity. Mosley was accused of 'having bribed the previous Member of Parliament to retire' (he was ill and died three months later). Snowden warned the party not to 'degenerate into an instrument for the ambitions of wealthy men' and referred to candidatures being 'put up to auction and sold to the highest bidder'. Mosley's avowal of socialism gave him 'feelings of nausea'. Newspaper cartoons portrayed Mosley as a 'Jewish-looking money-lender bribing the poor with bags of gold'. At first he was refused endorsement but the NEC eventually relented. However, relations between Morrison and Mosley were permanently embittered.

Following his decision to leave Ladywood, Labour members suspected Mosley of putting his own ambitions before the good of the party. They said there was 'not much difference between Chamberlain leaving Ladywood in order to be sure of keeping in parliament, and Mosley leaving Ladywood in order to be sure of getting into parliament'.

There was little doubt that Mosley would win as Labour had taken the seat in 1924. However, the campaign turned vicious very quickly with a press onslaught from Beaverbrook and Rothermere. His opponents were portrayed as genuine working-class candidates in contrast to 'the aristocratic poseur fighting them on behalf of the working class'. Rumours about Mosley's luxurious lifestyle circulated. He allegedly left his Rolls-Royce (he did not have one) on the outskirts of town and transferred to a lowly Ford, while Cimmie had changed her dress embroidered with diamonds for more modest attire.

The *Mail* persuaded Mosley's alcoholic father to pour out his grievances against his son. On 13 December he said 'more valuable help would be rendered to the country by my Socialist son and daughter-in-law if, instead of achieving cheap publicity about relinquishing titles [Mosley said he would not accept the baronetcy he would inherit from his father], they would take more material action and relinquish some of their wealth and so help to make easier the plight of some of their more unfortunate followers'. In the *Express*, Sir Oswald said his son was 'born with a gold spoon in his mouth – it cost £100 in doctor's fees to bring him into the world. He lived on the fat of the land and never did a day's labour in his life. If he and his wife want to go in for Labour, why don't they do a bit of work themselves, or why doesn't Lady Cynthia sell her pearls for the good of the Smethwick poor?'

Mosley replied that 'my father knows nothing of my life and has very seldom seen me. So far as I am aware, he contributed nothing to my education or upbringing, except in the form of alimony which he was compelled to contribute in a court of law.' The *Town Crier* remarked that the press lords had 'created such a position in Smethwick that if on the eve of poll Mosley had committed bigamy or murdered his wife, nobody in Smethwick would have believed the story'. Wheatley supported his colleague and told the *Herald* that he was 'one of the most brilliant and hopeful figures thrown up by the Socialist movement during the last thirty years'.

At the by-election of 21 December 1926 Mosley received 16,077 votes, a majority of 6,582 over his Conservative and Liberal opponents. Mosley told

8,000 triumphant supporters outside Smethwick town hall that his election was a 'great victory over Pressocracy'. His success, however, earned him a reputation for extremism. Tories said he was an 'unscrupulous demagogue playing shamelessly on the passions and cupidity of a moronic electorate'. The *Morning Post* warned that his electioneering was 'an experiment in mob psychology of a kind that has never been attempted before'. *The Times* suggested Mosley was seeking 'the readiest way to power'.

The Mosleys celebrated Christmas at Nancy Astor's. She had 'greatly disapproved of what she thought of as Tom's defection to Labour' but Cimmie's sister, Irene, noted that 'everyone was very decent to him'. He did, however, look 'lonely and lost for once'.

Labour leaders were wary of Mosley but activists talked about him as a future leader. They understood he wanted to create policies and a broad consensus to deal with unemployment and had soft-pedalled on some issues in order to attract neutral minds. However, on his return to Westminster in January 1927, he learned, as his Front Generation counterparts discovered on the Continent, that 'in the eyes of party elders, new men on the move might easily appear to be young men in too much of a hurry'.

7

'The Coming Figure'

When Mosley returned to Parliament in the new year of 1927, MPs speculated about his motives. He seemed to be someone with 'a great soul, but little heart' and no deep attachments. Beatrice Webb thought him 'brilliant but without weight'. Philip Snowden dismissed him as 'a man on the make', while Michael Foot later argued that he used the party as 'a vehicle for his ideas and ambitions'.

Labour MP Ellen Wilkinson was questioned continually about Mosley's sincerity. Colleagues considered him 'all artifice, a series of roles carefully put on for different occasions'. They observed his stylized performance with his studied movements of hands and body, the polished phrases, the elaborate courtesy. Leslie Hore-Belisha thought his friend's persona was an act and noted his resemblence to Chatham, who was 'an actor. Natural only in his unnaturalness, he cannot be imagined off-stage. Nor can Mr Mosley. Dark, aquiline, flashing; tall, thin, assured; defiance in his eye, contempt in his forward chin, his features are cast in a mould of disdain. His very smile is a shrug. His voice is pitched in a tragedian's key. His sentences are trailed away. He is the only man in the House who has made an Art of himself.'

Analyst James Glass argues the narcissist is the ideal type of Hobbesian natural man who forsakes internal dialogue for the restless pursuit of power. Cold and ruthless, he moves through the world 'without any inner feeling of constraint, without any sense of principle or commitment to anything other than self-gratification'. Mosley learnt from Shaw the doctrine that for a man of action, 'people and ideas are not right or wrong, good or evil, but useful or useless'. Mosley remarked that 'the ability to assume as many shapes as Proteus is an indispensable requirement for political leadership in the modern age'. He was a perfect politician for a mass society. ILP colleague Sydney Potter admired his 'extraordinary maturity of mind' but knew him as 'an arch-flatterer'. He 'grasped my hand between both of his and said: "Sydney, old boy, they tell me you were superb." But when he said this, he wasn't looking at me at all, he was looking over my shoulder at the hungry mob longing to see him.'

Amabel Williams-Ellis described Mosley as a swashbuckler. His 'unparliamentary good looks' were suggestive of the 'dark, passionate, Byronic gentleman-villain of the melodrama, in whose presence young ladies develop unaccountable palpitations and sedate husbands itch for their riding-whips'. When Mosley lunched with Keynes, they were joined by his wife, Lydia Lopokova, a brilliant demicaractère ballerina in the Diaghilev company. She confessed to her husband that 'she dreamt of kissing him'. Keynes described him as 'a rake, a seducer of both crowds and women'. To Ellen Wilkinson he was 'The Sheikh' – not the 'nice kind hero who rescues the girl at the point of torture, but the one who hisses "At last . . . we meet" '.

Mosley defended his public artifice as an elaborate defence of his privacy. His infidelities were the subject of comment, though the gossip was not taken seriously, either by those who peddled it or by his conquests. Such episodes were 'tacitly forgotten by all parties the next morning'. Irene and Baba knew he had a mistress in Paris, called Maria. He was also pursuing a Hungarian beauty, Blanche, actress wife of the American star John Barrymore. Mosley confessed that she had 'extraordinary qualities'. She would have 'felt at home with the men and women of the Renaissance, perhaps, in their less extreme moments, even with the Borgias; in some moods she might even have been equal to their extremities'.

If he allowed himself introspection, Nicholas thought his father 'might have seen that within the area of his own short-term drives and obsessions there were possibly seeds of self-destruction: he had a gambler's love of challenge and risk'. Mosley's priorities were clear: 'Vote Labour; sleep Tory'. He felt no guilt about his infidelities and protested his undying love for Cimmie, who was humiliated by his philandering but still forgave him. Theirs was a typical upper-class inter-war marriage in which it was perfectly acceptable to play the field in private as long as the public face was straightforward and virtuous. Mosley's was neither.

Zita Jungman, wife of painter Nico Jungman, first met the Mosleys in August 1927 at Cannes. Aware of the popular view of Mosley as the 'dashing, debonair buccaneer', Zita had not expected to like him. She found, however, that he was 'gentle and attentive'. Others had noted his charm and shyness. There was a staged vulnerability, apparent in the almost childlike ability to get what he wanted. Zita described Cimmie as 'pretty, rather fat, strong, and ruthlessly direct'. She was having a terrible time trying to please her husband. Cimmie wrote to him that she felt 'like a Mum as well as a Mistress (can one be the Whore as well as the Bore or vice versa?)'. She could not win. He had a fling with a married woman at an ILP conference and then with the wife of a Conservative MP, who obtained a photograph of a naked Mosley. During a speech in the House, Mosley became aware from the laughter that a photograph was being passed round the Tory benches. This was outside the rules of the game and he threatened a fight.

John Strachey's own life was an emotional wreck as his relationship with

Yvette continued to deteriorate. He wrote of his 'emotional failure and impotence towards the outside world'. When his father died, he fell into depression. He had made no progress in persuading Labour to take Mosley's ideas seriously. When Midland Bank Chairman Reginald McKenna made proposals for credit reform, Labour leaders greeted them with contemptuous silence. Strachey declared, 'such inactivity might almost lend itself to the interpretation that those who direct the financial policy of the Labour Party are even more Conservative than the bankers themselves!'

By September 1927 Mosley was openly criticizing Snowden for being wedded to sound finance, which meant restoring investors' confidence by paying off the national debt. He argued money should be spent on stimulating the home market, and 'not be passed on to wealthy bondholders who might save it or invest it abroad'. Mosley attacked the adherence to the gold standard, complaining that 'the expansion and contraction of credit is dependent on the discovery or exhaustion of far-away goldfields and the gold manipulation of foreign statesmen and financiers'. He also chided Snowden for being an ardent supporter of the City's 'reactionary elements', which were a 'fantastic negation of the purposes of our Party'.

Mosley was targeted as a dangerous socialist by the diehards and their allies in the British Fascists. A Cambridge meeting was broken up by hundreds of undergraduates, carrying Union Jacks and Fascist flags. Turning on them, Mosley retorted that they were no more than 'black-shirted buffoons, making a cheap imitation of ice-cream sellers'. Such robust rhetoric went down well with the ILP rank and file who, in October, elected him to Labour's National Executive Committee. The secret of his advance, observed Egon Wertheimer, was that he was 'a much harder worker than even his closest friends realise'. Dalton, who had been pushed off the NEC, considered Mosley's talk of creating markets by printing money as 'arrant nonsense, bad arithmetic and bad economics'. Keynes replied that Dalton lacked 'either subtlety or distinction'.

Mosley was absent from Parliament for long periods owing to illness. There may have been an element of hypochondria in his absences, which a Tory critic described as 'politically useful'. It was observed that he liked to trust glamorous doctors 'whether or not there was very much for them to cure', though there was the recurring problem of his leg. Long days of canvassing brought on a debilitating attack of phlebitis, which left him in pain. Cimmie was 'miserable at your being phlebitic, it really does seem that your troubles are unending and cumulative . . . always piling up'.

Mosley served on an NEC committee preparing a programme for the general election and sent MacDonald a memorandum – less radical than the ILP's policies – urging revision of monetary policy, children's allowances and an extra £1 a week pension for those aged sixty-five and over who retired. He advocated a tax on luxuries, an embargo on the export of capital, bulk purchase of foodstuffs and raw materials, and the setting up of a powerful Economic Council. MacDonald, however, wanted a general statement to appeal to middle opinion and rejected Mosley's desire for an unambiguous programme of action to deal with 'unemployment, wages, rents, squalor, the threat of war – all the issues which send Parliament to sleep'.

MacDonald acknowledged in January 1928 that 'someone who would put the trumpet more frequently to his lips would be a better leader, but would that be good for the Party?' There were many 'inflammatory influences in the Party to keep it hot', but 'confidence goes further than programmes'. Mosley submitted a shorter memo but when MacDonald dithered, he moved at the NEC on 28 March that the draft be considered immediately. This was defeated by only ten votes to eight. Even so, ministers from the first Labour government had undergone a psychological change, which expressed itself in a ridiculous fear of 'being identified with left-wing political sentiments of which but a few years before they had been the exponents'.

During spring 1928 relations between the ILP and Labour deteriorated sharply. Responding to increasing disillusionment among Clydesiders, Wheatley discussed with ILP leader James Maxton and Miners' leader Arthur Cook plans to unite the Left. In June, they prepared the 'Cook–Maxton Manifesto' for a mass propaganda campaign intended to overthrow Labour's compromising leadership. The campaign failed to generate support and was written off as a failure. It illustrated, Brockway recognized, 'that the rank and file, however dissatisfied with the leadership, will not countenance the destruction of unity'.

There was in Wheatley's failure a lesson to be learnt, but Mosley later failed to heed the warning, even if he now broke contact with the ILP and devoted himself wholly to the work of the Labour Party, in the belief that unity was necessary to win a majority at the next election. Even so, he was not re-elected to the NEC and appeared as something of a solitary force. In areas such as Lancashire he was unable to dispel the suspicion that he was a pampered, rich man.

In contrast, Irene viewed her sister's political development as 'astonishing'. On 13 May 1928 'Cim gave us a long socialist dissertation. She was so certain and heartwhole one could not argue with her.' When she was adopted as Labour candidate for Stoke, she was ostracized by former society friends, who turned 'a cold shoulder to the renegade'. Lady Astor was one of the few still willing to see her. The Mosleys were welcome in the international set centred on a handful of rich hostesses in the principal European cities, where they enjoyed a world of gossip and a rather cruel kind of fun. Nicolas has described his parents' circle as one in which 'personal relationships, even love, were matters of intrigue, conquest, possession, power; everyone was in the business of becoming one up on everyone else'. Adultery was accepted and while the participants 'knew everything about everybody, the papers knew nothing'.

During the summer of 1928, Denham was host to the Tennants, Sitwells, Cecil Beaton, William Walton, Oliver Messel and other 'Bright Young Things'. The writer and poet Osbert Sitwell was the inheritor of the baronetcy and the literary family's home, Renishaw, in Derbyshire. He served in the war, but became a pacifist and much of his early work was devoted to this cause. Sacheverell, youngest of the Sitwells, was an incurably romantic poet and writer, regarded as a cultural trail-blazer of twentieth-century taste. 'Sachie' and his wife Georgia, a banker's daughter, were regularly seen with the Mosleys in London or on weekends at Savehay.

A great friend of the Mosleys was Dick Wyndham, with whom Sachie had collaborated on *A Book of Towers*. Others included Idina Erroll, chic wife of the Earl of Erroll. After one party, Georgia wrote that Idina was 'hungry looking, spoilt and vicious'. She had been married four times and had numerous lovers, including Mosley. Georgia 'flung herself into this new, smart, party life, taking to its customs and values with almost frantic enthusiasm'. Flirting with Mosley was one custom. Sachie's biographer noted that the self-centred and dominant Mosley was the opposite of Sachie, which was part of his attraction for Georgia.

On 6 July the Sitwells spent a weekend at Savehay with Beaton, Wyndham, Strachey, Zita Jungman and Stephen Tennant as guests. Dressed up in old Edwardian clothes belonging to the first Lady Curzon (Mary Leiter), they made a cine-film with a script by the homosexual and transvestite Tennant, involving motor-car chases, seduction, abduction and attempted murder. Cimmie played the role of a prostitute, while Sachie, Georgia and Mosley were uncomfortably cast together as three detectives. Georgia thought the weekend hilarious, though she quarrelled with her husband about her plans to travel to Antibes to holiday with their hosts.

A pupil at West Downs and Winchester, Stephen Tennant was a neighbour to Mosley in Smith Square. His mother was Pamela Wyndham. Brother David ran Soho's Gargoyle Club, which by day was patronized by politicians and civil servants; by night, it was a bohemian club for a social, sexual and intellectual set, which included Mosley. The Tennants' eldest brother and their cousins were killed in the war. David subsequently developed a 'romantic death-wish, cloaked in the mystic cult of chivalry'. The Tennants were rich: the Wyndhams were aristocratic; both produced politicians and intellectuals.

'Dirty Dick' Wyndham had grown up in Wiltshire, at Clouds, a Victorian country house decorated with Pre-Raphaelite paintings. Wounded in the war, Dick remained in the army and was appointed ADC to Field Marshal Lord

French, Lord-Lieutenant of Ireland. In 1920 he married the daughter of French's mistress, Winifred Bennett. It took some days before the 'puzzled newly-weds, virgins both, managed to discover how "it" was done'. After divorce in 1925, Dick broke from his upper-class roots and 'sought to embrace a wider world where his muffled artistic talents might find expression'. He found a mentor in Wyndham Lewis. When in London, Dick stayed at the Hyde Park Hotel with one foot in White's (Mosley's Club) and the other in Bloomsbury. He always carried 'a battered black book containing short, cryptic notes – "small breasts, tight bottom, free on Wednesdays"'.

The Mosleys' circle found itself portrayed in Aldous Huxley's *Point Counter Point* (1928). The suitably named 'Everard Webley', leader of the 'Brotherhood of British Freemen', was Mosley, with all his 'bombast and pomposity'. Huxley was prophetic of his Fascism and incisive about his relations with women. He suggested a 'marriage between sexuality and violence in the Webley/Mosley mind, a sadistic streak in his character which aligned with the tradition of the strangely alluring Gothic villain'. In June, Nancy Mitford had wondered: 'How is one to find the perfect young man, either they seem to be half witted or half baked or absolute sinks of vice or else actively dirty like John Strachey.'

That year, 1928, the Mosleys spent their holiday at Cap d'Antibes, where their guests included Irene, Baba and her husband, Charles and Elsie Mendl, Douglas Fairbanks, the Benjamin Guinnesses and the Casa Maurys. Married to the Cuban racing driver Marquis de Casa Maury, Paula Gellibrand had posed for Beaton and was another conquest of Mosley. Educated in England and a Royal Flying Corps pilot, 'Bobby' de Casa Maury had founded Curzon Cinemas. Barbara Cartland recalled that Paula had 'an exoticism about her which makes her outstanding, even in a room filled with other beauties'. Mosley's circle also included what *The Times* called a 'summer club for socialist intelligentsia' of G. B. Shaw and Somerset Maugham. Cimmie, who 'queens it with the best' on the beaches, Shaw observed, was nervous of exposing herself to the waiting press photographers. Mosley had no such fears. He 'evidently fancies himself very much in bathing shorts and displays with pride a sunburnt, muscular torso', wrote Georgia Sitwell. At dinner, he flirted with Georgia. Shaw loved the landscape but hated the people, and left for Geneva.

Mosley was rude in public to Irene, who recalled with despair the rows between him and her sister. These usually ended with Cimmie sobbing and Mosley shouting. When he went to the casino, she talked to Cimmie, who was on the edge of a breakdown, 'over the misery of her present life and Tom's insulting behaviour to her'. It hurt Irene to hear her sister's 'rending loyalty to him saying he had never been unfaithful, she only wished he would not make a fool of her in public'. Despite the betrayals, Cimmie led the party-going activity. She was pathetically dependent upon him and there was something almost self-destructive about her obsession with her 'hero'. She would forgive her 'baby boy' almost any misbehaviour.

The fun was broken by news that Mosley's father, who was in France, was dying of sclerosis of the liver. When a telegram from his brother Ted, who was with their father at La Baule, reached him Mosley did not react. Ted wrote that he was 'disgusted to find that on the one occasion I have asked you to help me you have let me down ... I can assure you I should not have asked you to come here if I considered that your presence would disturb my father at this time.'

In October Mosley's father died aged fifty-four. Mosley recognized the 'final explosion' was due to his increasing drinking. He attended the funeral along with his mother and two brothers but was not mentioned in his father's will. He did, however, inherit the family estate worth £250,000 (£6 m) before death duties. Much of it was in the form of land in Manchester but, with 999-year leases, the income was fixed and, with inflation, its value quickly diminished. Mosley had an annual income from trustees of £8,000 (£200,000). He was rich but not extravagantly so. However, there was Cimmie's income from the Leiter Trust of a similar amount. Naturally, details of the inheritance 'started the Press hounds yelping'.

Mosley decided his father's baronetcy, which had not been 'worth taking up', was now 'not worth giving up'. When Georgia Sitwell remarked that a baronetcy was rather a false position, neither one thing nor another, Cimmie took care to point out her husband's exact rank. 'So different a point of view', she thought, 'to what one feels ... a socialist should have.' Arriving at the Mosleys' London home, she found them admiring the family diamonds. 'Tom actually says [Cimmie] will need the tiara one day, to wear – as Queen of the Communists I suppose!' Georgia's reaction did not affect her affair with Mosley and she continued to visit him at 22b Ebury Street, a bachelor-style flat that was just one huge bedroom, where 'at the press of a switch warm air wafted in'.

Mosley was becoming a force to be reckoned with in Labour. MacDonald saw in him a worthy successor, 'someone who might some day do the things which he himself had once dreamt of doing'. In October, he travelled with the Mosleys across Europe. In a passage deleted from his autobiography, Mosley described meeting in Austria 'a woman who as a type seemed to me something of an old Viennese tart: faded blonde, very sophisticated, very agreeable'. Frau Forster was MacDonald's mistress and was well known at socialist gatherings.

In Berlin, the Mosleys met Harold Nicolson at the British embassy. He was bored and under pressure from his wife, novelist Vita Sackville-West, who had a low opinion of creative people working in public service. An aristocrat by temperament whose world consisted of 'weekend parties, exclusive luncheons, Bloomsbury and the Travellers Club', he was looking for fresh horizons. He was well aware that he belonged to an elite. Witty, urbane and anti-Semitic, he was a colossal snob.

Nicolson acknowledged that there was an ambiguity about himself. He was regarded 'by the bohemians as conventional, and by the conventional as bohemian'. This was symbolized by his bisexuality and his marriage to Vita, a lesbian and more masculine character than her husband. They maintained a marriage which avoided 'all admission of sexual irregularity', including his trips to Berlin's homosexual bars. The clubs shocked Mosley and suggested a 'nation sunk so deep that it could never rise again'. The Friedrichstrasse was described by one visitor as the 'pornographic shop-window of Germany's shame' where sleazy clubs offered every vice. Mosley was revulsed that the 'sexes had simply exchanged clothes, make-up and the habits of Nature in crudest form'. Berlin was damned by the Nazis as the capital of 'cultural Bolshevism'. Nicolson had learnt from friends in Munich of Hitler's increasing influence but had been reassured by their protestations that the 'ex-corporal could never become a serious menace'.

On his return to London, Mosley encouraged Strachey to visit America to study industry but also to seek a rich wife. He found one in Esther Murphy, daughter of Patrick Murphy, owner of a New York department store. Part of the American bohemian literary scene, the Murphys had holidayed with the Mosleys in the south of France. Strachey's subsequent visit to the Soviet Union influenced his increasingly radical perspective, which was joined, through the encouragement of his cousin James, to an interest in psychoanalysis. First signs of this synthesis appeared in a series of articles ('The New Generation') in the *New Leader*. Strachey wanted a society of 'pure Communism' based on a new morality, which would see the abolition of private property – a view certainly not shared by Mosley.

Mosley had begun to attract interest from the other end of the political spectrum. Beaverbrook focused on him as a coming figure in socialist politics. On 1 October he informed US journalist Herbert Swope that Mosley's opponents 'stigmatize him as an adventurer and declare that as a consequence he has no future in politics' but this was 'premature and ill-informed'. Mosley was not 'any more of an opportunist than a good many other eminent politicians I could name'.

Hugh Dalton wrote in his diary (1 October) how Mosley 'stinks of money and insincerity . . . a huge gap existed between his public rhetoric and private values'. Mosley drew attention to the fact that aristocrats such as himself 'tended to be on the Left', while the middle-class newcomer Dalton was a reliable supporter of the Party hierarchy. Wertheimer observed that Dalton was 'not flashy like Mosley and in the Party his position is welded by closer bonds of affection and respect'. Intellectually he was made of 'incomparably better stuff' but on virtually every economic point he was simply wrong.

In October Labour's draft programme, 'Labour and the Nation', was agreed but Mosley regretted that progressive ideas made only a fleeting appearance. It consisted of a 'high-minded statement of the moral case for gradualist socialism, heavily flavoured with the scientific optimism of the day'.

Snowden told the annual conference that he had no intention of using the budget to create jobs. He warned that while an 'unprincipled Government in the absolute control of currency and credit' could reduce unemployment by a million, it would be at a 'terrible price which the country would have to pay sooner or later'. This was 'a power I am not prepared to put without reserve and control into the hands of any political government'. Members assumed unemployment was capitalism's fault and only a few believed it was possible to do something while the means of production were privately owned. However, the leadership had even less interest in fulfilling members' desires than dealing with unemployment.

Mosley despaired at Snowden's unwillingness to try solutions at hand. Lloyd George's Liberal Party's 'Britain's Industrial Future' was pioneering in advocating a Keynesian investment programme to tackle unemployment. It was pro free trade but Keynes concluded that loan-financed public works were required to deal with unemployment. He was suggesting state management of demand by means of varying public spending and investment. The *Yellow Book* included pragmatic proposals for industrial rationalization and portrayed corporatist self-government as an 'ideological compromise between state socialism and individualistic private enterprise'. The mixed-economy proposals were not radical but still had little impact. Labour moderates, who 'proved to be far from wedded to socialism', criticized the *Yellow Book* for its 'aversion to the socialist principles of public control and ownership'.

In Parliament in November Mosley suggested the Empire, as a market for British products and a source of raw materials, could be an economic unit which rivalled the US in self-sufficiency. Essentially a social imperialist, he saw the Empire as a means to a 'greater Britain' and the guarantee of peace. 'If the world was carved up between the great powers in such a way that their requirements for raw materials were satisfied, and so that they contained sufficient population to absorb the ever-increasing output of industry, then the chief cause of modern wars would be eliminated.' Like the Marxists, he interpreted great-power struggles 'almost exclusively in economic terms'.

Mosley's speech attracted Beaverbrook's attention as a potential recruit to his Empire Free Trade campaign. On 26 November he told former Canadian Prime Minister Sir Robert Bowden there were no young men to rescue Britain from its deep sleep, except Mosley. 'He is a careerist like Birkenhead and

Churchill. The type is familiar. Mosley has more character than Birkenhead but less personality than Churchill.' A few weeks later Beaverbrook wrote to Mosley about their 'personal relationship'. Mosley found himself confronted by two alternatives: either 'to serve the new world in a great attempt to bring order out of chaos and beauty out of squalor' or become a 'flunkey of the bourgeoisie'. He regretted that many of his class had chosen the latter course.

On Christmas Eve the Mosleys stayed with the Webbs. Cimmie told Beatrice that Labour people, 'especially the better sort and the intellectuals, are shy of us, except the few snobs among them who are subservient'. Beatrice thought Mosley was 'dead certain of Cabinet office, and possibly has a chance of eventual premiership'. Harold Laski had overcome his own fascination with Mosley, partly, he told Beatrice, because of his 'luxurious and fast life'. Despite reservations, she regarded Mosley, Dalton and Trevelyan as the most likely successors to MacDonald as party leader.

Published at the end of the year under the pseudonym 'Janitor' (J. G. Lockhart and Lady Craik), *The Feet of the Young Men* contained a prophetic and telling profile of Mosley. He was compared with Philippe Egalité, an aristocratic revolutionary featured in Thomas Carlyle's history of the French Revolution. Egalité had been 'disappointed in his early ambitions, turning against his own caste, sunning himself in the applause of the crowd'. This unpleasant fate had lost 'none of its attractions for the young politician of ample purse and elastic principles'. Mosley had 'cast himself for the same glittering part but lacked the power to play it'.

Mosley, Janitor observed, had been ragged at Sandhurst but 'not as frequently as was desirable'; his war service had been useful for 'receiving a severe wound which has not been without its political value'. His Smethwick campaign had been 'one of the most unpleasant contests that has taken place since the War'. Janitor noticed the 'atmosphere of violence and unrestrained personalities which surround Mr Mosley's political career is always someone else's fault'. It suggested a dog, whose appearance when taken for a walk was 'the signal for every dog within sight to set upon him. So far as I could see, he did nothing to provoke them; but I am bound to add that he seemed thoroughly to enjoy the succession of general action into which our progress invariably developed.'

Mosley was not a popular figure 'save for brief intervals and among men who do not know him. That his own class should dislike him is only natural, for it is not enough for Egalité to turn his own coat; he must also thoroughly dust the coats of his former friends.' His attack on banks was 'calculated to appeal to the more extreme of his colleagues'. The ILPers will

use him for just as long as he serves their purpose, but they will never make a friend of him. It is this sense of ostracism that is the secret of Mosley's truculent demeanour, for when a man of his years becomes embittered he becomes very bitter indeed, and the less sure he feels of himself, the more noisily will he confront the world. Yet truculence, bitterness, are likely to avail him little in the course he has set for himself. If he fails in it, his failure will be final.

It was a remarkably prescient commentary.

Although generally viewed as a playboy, during 1929 Mosley began to be seen as a 'serious politician who worked hard with big ideas – ideas he was desperately eager to see translated into action'. His 'scientific and practical creed' was influenced by Douglas Cole, whose *The Next Ten Years in British Social and Economic Policy* (1929) was a prophetic treatise, anticipating the next decade's socialist thinking on State planning. It envisioned the 'conscious development of national economic resources' by an Employment and National Investment Board and public corporations.

In March, Lloyd George produced a modified programme, the 'Orange Book – We Can Conquer Unemployment'. Drawn up by Keynes, it envisaged two years of emergency public investment paid for by government borrowing. Plans for road construction were on a scale of German efforts in the thirties. A house-building initiative would restore the Wheatley housing subsidy, which the Tories had cut. Altogether, 600,000 jobs would be created at a cost of £250 million. Keynes claimed there would be a 'cumulative effect' with 'greater trade activity making for further trade activity'. Labour's response was to delete from its own draft proposals for investment through deficits so that they could point the finger of irresponsibility at Lloyd George and his 'madcap finance'.

At the committee considering the manifesto, 'How to Conquer Unemployment', Mosley and Cole put forward constructive plans for the reconstruction of industry under the authority of a National Economic Council promoting the scientific planning of production. However, during the strenuous NEC debate, MacDonald objected to Mosley's draft, with its 'hectic rattle of machine-gun prose', and the inclusion of commitments he had no intention of implementing.

The arguments did not affect their personal relationship and MacDonald suggested to the Mosleys they 'all go down to Fowey in Cornwall, and named the party which he wanted to take'. She turned out to be the 'obvious vamp' from Vienna, Frau Forster, recalled Mosley. He believed MacDonald's 'conduct in private affairs was all too similar to his action in public affairs'. He was a model of 'public virtue and private decorum', and the product of the 'squalid curse of Puritanism'. Mosley suggested statesmen 'should either know much about love, or refrain from it'. Oddly, given his own proclivities, he said Ministers 'ought to live like athletes, not dine out, go to banquets and dinners, but only see people relevant to business'. What was required was a new kind of statesman (i.e. Mosley) – 'men of calm and balanced character, of freedom yet of self-control, of discriminating taste rather than of inhibition'.

Taking his lead from Shaw, Mosley said Caesar's experiences in early life 'certainly gave him more practice in handling all situations, both delicate and dangerous, than had the less fortunate MacDonald'. In Caesar, 'hysteria was excluded, all was ruled by purpose served by character. We need a return to character with neither the hysteria of repression nor of licence, in harmony with life, nature and purpose reaching ever higher.' Mosley quoted Nietzsche that such supermen appear 'immune from the glow and blast of the passions'.

Mosley displayed ineffable self-importance and an obnoxious, inflated sense of superiority. He adored himself. The key to the success of such people is often not their talent but an irrepressible desire for admiration. They crave opportunities for self-enhancement and believe they are entitled to special treatment because they are 'God's gift to the world'.

In April Mosley was best man at Strachey's marriage to Esther Murphy, a dandy wife, who was clever, dominant and a lesbian. Strachey was attracted to her bohemian world and her money. Within months he was confiding in Mosley that the marriage was 'awful'. He had difficulty in reconciling his politics with the turmoil and materialism of his private life.

On 10 May 1929 Parliament was dissolved. Stanley Baldwin went to the country against a backdrop of high unemployment with the slogan 'Safety First'. In his election address, Mosley said it was 'an offence against God and man that women should be imprisoned in the damp and disease ridden walls of a slum house and have to bring up children to share their misery'. Such problems 'can never be solved by a creed of indifference and despair. These pleasant, sleepy people are all very well in pleasant, sleepy times, but we live in a dynamic age of great and dynamic events. In such an age we summon all classes to a united effort of the whole nation in the war against poverty.' He also wrote of his fear 'not that the Labour Party will do more than a united nation demanded ten years ago' but that 'in the face of the terrific opposition they will encounter, they will not do as much'. He was determined that 'through and beyond the failure of men and parties, we of the war-generation are marching on and we shall march on until our end is achieved and our sacrifice atoned'.

There was suspicion of ruling-class recruits but Wertheimer observed that 'far from having weakened the Socialist character of the movement, it is they who have given new life and impulse to the Socialist side of the agitation'. Mosley lent glamour and respectability to the party, and could gain seats which 'must otherwise have fallen into enemy hands'. He intended to create his own Birmingham caucus and sponsored candidates, with up to £250 (£7,500), while four-page election sheets were distributed throughout the city. Standing in Erdington, Jim Simmons discovered 'money was no object'.

*

Cimmie had a difficult campaign in Stoke-on-Trent. Opponents derided her as a 'Dollar Princess' on account of her American inheritance. She insisted she had invested it in Britain and the Labour Party. She was also not forgiven by former friends for what was viewed as treachery. Irene had walked out of a party at Georgia Sitwell's because of 'all the filthy things' said about her sister's 'election in sables and pearls'. Wertheimer considered Cimmie the 'most eloquent and debonair figure in the Socialist world, whether here or abroad'.

A fortnight before election day, Irene was at Savehay when a row took place over the trivial matter of cars for the election. Mosley was ruthless and 'vilely rude' to Cimmie, despite her being 'exquisite and faithful in her love'. On top of this, Cimmie was pregnant. The majority of women candidates were single, or childless wives, or had grown-up children. She was the exception but she refused to be defensive. Articulate on the platform, Cimmie agreed a woman's place was in the home but that was the 'very reason why we should take an interest in politics' which was the 'bread and butter of life'. She recognized she was in a privileged position but was 'not satisfied with things as they are. Surely to goodness if I am not satisfied, then the millions who live in squalid and miserable conditions are not.' Working-class audiences took to her and, as the campaign wore on, 'it was her opponent who found himself struggling to cope with hostile heckling'.

In the general election on 30 May, Cimmie scored the most impressive victory by any woman between the wars. She doubled the Labour vote to 26,000 and achieved a majority of 7,850, despite facing a well-entrenched sitting member. The local newspaper speculated that 'many of the flappers were doubtless flattered by the opportunity of voting for a lady of title and wealth', though clearly many men were equally keen. To celebrate the success, Irene gave Cimmie a gold bracelet inset with diamonds forming the words 'Stoke 1929'.

Mosley's West Midlands colleagues enjoyed similar success, with eleven Labour gains. Strachey was elected for Aston. J. Johnson, President of the Birmingham Labour Party, recalled that when they won Erdington Mosley ran 'across Victoria Square easily outstripping the crows at his heels, with his huge strides, throwing his hat into the air and nearly breaking the back of our little four-seater car as he jumped upon it to congratulate us. Nobody present could have doubted the genuineness of his Socialism at that time.' In Smethwick Mosley secured a majority of 7,340 over his opponents. He told the cheering crowd, 'I am sure, now that it is all over, we can settle down together quite happily as members of one great nation.' He had earlier expressed the view that 'we might lift our national problems above the clamour of faction and party strife', which seemd to imply his willingness to sacrifice Labour for a non-party, nation-orientated movement.

Irene and Cimmie drove to Smethwick to a tremendous reception. 'Everyone murmured that Cim and Tom had broken the great Chamberlain backbone in Brum,' wrote Irene. 'Seldom have I taken part in such a frenzy of thrill and nervous tension.' Six days later an exhausted Cimmie had a miscarriage. Close friends believed Mosley had 'exploited his wife's willingness too freely, often persuading her to speak when she was exhausted'. Harold Nicolson observed that beneath his teasing of Cimmie lay 'a streak of cruelty'.

Outside the West Midlands there was no spectacular Labour advance, though the party emerged as the biggest single party with 287 MPs compared with 260 for the Conservatives. The Liberals trailed with fifty-nine seats. Also rejected were several progressive young Tories sympathetic to Keynes, and ideas of planning and industrial reorganization. Harold Macmillan took the defeat personally, as he saw himself as the guardian of Stockton's unemployed. However, he was regarded as being 'eccentric and without serious political prospects'.

The electorate had conspicuously failed to make up its mind and, without an overall majority, Ramsay MacDonald was forced to form a minority Labour government. For three years he and Mosley had been working together on the NEC's foreign affairs subcommittee. They were social friends and had toured Europe together. It seemed that Mosley was slated for a senior post.

8

'A Young Man in a Hurry'

Speculation within the Labour Party centred on whether Mosley might become Foreign Secretary in the new government. He had an inkling he was being considered for the Foreign Office and certainly Harold Nicolson hoped his friend would recall him to a post in London. In a letter dated 15 June 1929, Harold Laski reveals colleagues argued about the Foreign Office, which Prime Minister Ramsay MacDonald would have given to Mosley had not Arthur Henderson 'stood out to bursting point'.

As he went in to see the PM, A. V. Alexander passed a leaving Mosley. Accepting the post of First Lord of the Admiralty, Alexander said, 'I'll try anything you like to give me.' A pleased MacDonald replied, 'I see you're in a very submissive mood. Very different from our friend who has just gone out.'

The antipathy felt towards Mosley by Labour leaders meant there was little chance of him becoming Foreign Secretary. In the event, Henderson was appointed to the post. Mosley was appointed Chancellor of the Duchy of Lancaster, which was not a Cabinet post. He was furious at a snub that 'rankled'.

Mosley served under Jimmy Thomas, with responsibility for unemployment. The National Union of Railwaymen's chief was self-consciously aware of his working-class origins and lack of education, which found expression in an open scorn for intellectuals and distrust of economists. 'Go upstairs; see what the experts are doing; and tell them not to' was one of his sayings. He was corrupt; his drinking and gambling were a serious problem. From his vantage point in the City, Oliver Stanley remarked to Mosley that Thomas was 'finding it more difficult to move in and out of the market than previously, when he was selling a bear on railway stock before a strike he called or threatened himself'. Mosley commented that among his cronies Thomas claimed his dabbling on the market was a 'little perquisite of office which his abilities and services justified'. It eventually brought about his downfall.

Churchill described Mosley as a 'ginger assistant to the Lord Privy Seal and more ginger than assistant'. Further assistance came from the Under-Secretary for Scotland, Tom Johnston, and George Lansbury, who held the post of First Commissioner of Works. They were suspicious of the aristocratic Mosley with his 'metallic charm and Douglas Fairbanks smile', but accepted he was out to get something done. However, Thomas had no executive authority and they could only co-ordinate existing instruments in efforts to deal with unemployment. Realizing they were assisting a man out of his depth, they bypassed their boss, who spent his time travelling abroad, failing 'to unearth any new answers to British unemployment'.

Lansbury's appointment was compensation for the exclusion of John Wheatley, the one ministerial success in 1924. His reputation had been damaged by an unsuccessful libel action. However, he was still hero-worshipped by the grass roots. He warned colleagues against accepting office in a minority government because the country was entering a slump. He said Labour would become capitalism's instrument for implementing cuts. MacDonald dismissed the ILP's position – that it would prefer defeat as it would make socialism the dominant issue in politics – as romantic. Within days of Parliament reassembling, James Maxton proposed that the ILP's block of nineteen MPs consist only of those who agreed with Wheatley. Appointed secretary to this 'parliamentary suicide club' was the new MP for Peckham and future Mosleyite John Beckett.

Beckett's wartime experience turned him to the left. He became Chairman of the National Union of Ex-Servicemen, secretary of the No More War Movement and was then employed as Clement Attlee's agent. He helped formulate the ILP programme during the mid twenties and was elected to Gateshead as Labour's youngest MP. Despite these credentials, Fenner Brockway believed Beckett lacked a socialist philosophy and built up his following through rabble-rousing oratory. He had to be restrained 'from going to extremes in action and language'. He was particularly contemptuous of Chancellor of the Exchequer Philip Snowden.

Labour had pledged to deal with unemployment, but MacDonald interpreted the lack of a clear majority as the need for caution. However, even if Labour had received a decisive vote, it is unlikely that policy would have differed. Snowden, who did not waver in his commitment to long-held prejudices, had 'the mentality of a Poor Law Commissioner'. He was more reactionary than his Tory counterpart, Neville Chamberlain, who was in comparison 'urbane and humanitarian'. Snowden believed in balanced budgets, free trade and had no faith in public works to cut unemployment. On his appointment, Churchill said the 'Treasury mind and the Snowden mind embraced each other with the fervour of two long-separated kindred lizards'.

Snowden hated Mosley's advocacy of State intervention and despised his new economics. He chided him: 'You are a young man who cannot remember previous depressions; they have often recurred in my lifetime and have passed away.' In Cabinet, he insulted him with the aside that he was a 'presumptuous fool and an economic ignoramus'.

When Labour took office in June, unemployment stood at 1,164,000, just under 10 per cent of the insured population. Thomas, however, proved incapable of grasping the scope of the problem. Deputy Cabinet Secretary Thomas Jones thought the team around him 'ill-assorted and ill-qualified'. Johnston was lightweight, Lansbury's ideas were limited to a romantic ruralism, while Mosley had the 'disruptive quality of being a young man in a hurry'. It was inevitable that the relationship between the viceroy's son-in-law and the ex-railwayman would prove to be an unhappy one. Opposition leader Stanley Baldwin, who was resting at Sir Philip Sassoon's Trent Park after the election defeat, remarked that Mosley was 'a cad and a wrong 'un, and they will find it out'.

For the only time in his life, Mosley kept a diary – largely indecipherable – which ran for six weeks (11 June to 22 July). He discussed unemployment with civil servants, uncertain of the purpose of his department; economists, including Keynes, and the Midland Bank's Reginald McKenna, who agreed with a Treasury recommendation for 'expansion in small doses'. They were useful talks even if Thomas only had 'good railway projects and little else'. On 22 June Mosley invited the PM to Denham to 'a review of the entire unemployment situation – stressed that only speedy results could be obtained from three measures (1) lowering retirement age (2) raising school leaving age (3) in addition, discussed railways, roads, colonial expansion, in particular, Western Australia'. MacDonald's response was to utter 'Oh'. It was 'Party policy – Snowden must agree'. The PM agreed his Chancellor was an obstacle to efforts to tackle unemployment.

Four days later Snowden informed Cabinet he would permit increases in unemployment benefit and a relaxation of the means test, but refused to countenance job creation schemes which were not self-financing. He refused to believe that relief works could contribute to the export problem which lay behind unemployment. Thomas concurred and opposed the raising of loans. In late June, Douglas Cole said he hoped the reason why Thomas had not announced new employment schemes was because he was about to put forward a 'more comprehensive scheme'. The government, however, was committed to no more than launching inquiries. Stanley Baldwin summed up their approach as 'My Ministers are going to think'.

On 29 June Thomas created a committee of his junior ministers to study the proposals Mosley had raised with the PM. Four days later, during the King's Speech, Thomas unveiled a modest five-year £37½ m programme of road building and £25 m credit facilities for public utilities. Churchill complimented Thomas for 'not being hampered by foolish Socialist ideas' and expressed compassion for the ILP, who 'dreamed that they were clearing a pathway along which the toiling millions were to advance towards Utopia, but they wake to find that all they have been doing was to set up a ladder by which the hon. Baronet [Mosley] could climb into place and power'.

Anxiety deepened following a rise in US tariffs, which hit British exports and reduced commodity prices in the dominions. Seizing the opportunity to exploit Tory unease, Beaverbrook called on 30 June 1929 for an Empire Free Trade crusade. Under his proposals Empire trade would be protected by tariffs and an internal free trade area. On 9 July his editor-in-chief and former Tariff Reform Leaguer Ralph Blumenfeld met with Mosley, along with *Evening Standard* diarist Robert Bruce Lockhart. Mosley said Labour 'must do something for the underdogs and that if he could have another sixpence on to the income-tax he could keep Maxton and the Clydesiders quiet for ten years'. He also said he intended to be Prime Minister. On 15 July he announced a Colonial Development Bill, the handling of which, with 'good temper and grasp of detail', impressed the *Express* 'as the Minister responsible for the first Act laying down these important principles to protect native labour from exploitation'.

When Treasury opposition made the work of the Thomas committee ineffectual, members decided to develop their own proposals. Mosley moved into offices in the Treasury Chambers and brought in his Birmingham organizer, Allan Young, and Strachey as his Parliamentary Private Secretary. Lansbury sent his proposals to Thomas but 'only slowly did he realise that none of them would be tried'. On 28 July Beatrice Webb heard from Mosley and Lansbury that Thomas 'does not see them [and] is in the hands of that arch-reactionary, Horace Wilson [his Permanent Secretary], whom he obeys implicitly'. Thomas was rattled and when not drunk was in a state of panic.

In August the Mosleys began their vacation in Antibes with Irene and the Metcalfes. Guests included Strachey and his new wife, Dick Wyndham, American actor John Gilbert, and the de Casa Maurys. Mosley spent most of the time closeted with Paula de Casa Maury and at dinner they speculated about which of the Curzon sisters would succeed in attracting Gilbert – 'the heavyweight (Irene), the lightweight (Baba) or the middle (Cimmie)'. When Cimmie spoke, he cut her dead with sarcastic remarks and the evening ended in uproar, when he accused his wife of being drunk.

Following his return to London on 4 September, Mosley talked to Keynes, who said that 'exceptional conditions required exceptional measures'. Mosley studied any scheme – even if 'a little fantastic' – he thought might stimulate employment. He asked Air Minister Lord Thomson about the 'possibility of roofing over Termini on the South Side of London, such as Victoria Station, in order to make a central aerodrome'. He envisioned aeroplanes landing on its roof.

Labour MPs were disillusioned with the PM's indecisiveness but the rank and file idolized him. Working-class criticism of policy took the form of 'a vague feeling that aristocrats and intellectuals were gaining too much influence'. Mosley and Charles Trevelyan were voted off the NEC, despite being industrious members. Local authority deputations who met Mosley to discuss public works found him 'blazing with enthusiasm and returned to their towns with a high opinion of the young minister'. In September, he set off on a speaking tour to ginger up local authorities. He was annoyed that he could not order them to carry out national plans and, on 11 September, proposed that central government take over responsibility for road building. With an eye to the November municipal elections, he advised voters to return council-lors who are 'energetic and prepared to support large local plans for dealing with unemployment'. Henderson regarded him as a 'wealthy pusher' for openly expressing his irritation with the slow pace of government.

Mosley called for a body under the PM to consider proposals for long-term reconstruction. Civil servants who worked with him were enthusiastic but the Treasury believed money was best spent modernizing export industries. When he begged Ministers to decide on the amount of money they wished to spend on unemployment, he was ignored. Snowden's view that public works should be self-financing dominated proceedings and became an obstacle to road-building schemes. However, the rapid growth of unemployment convinced Mosley of the need for short-term measures though he faced opposition from a hostile Minister of Transport. 'Clearly Mosley suffers somewhat from Lloyd George's complaint: the road complex,' commented Herbert Morrison. 'A road is a means of transport; road works can assist, but cannot possibly be a principal cure of immediate unemployment.' Morrison reacted with shock to a Mosley memorandum of 24 September calling for a dozen 'speedways' traversing the country.

On 4 October, in the *New Leader*, Strachey noted the 'lack of action in overturning the obstacles' Ministers found in their way. Douglas Cole, too, was openly critical of the government and, like Mosley, believed industry's rejuvenation depended on extending the home market, since an upturn in overseas trade was unlikely. Social imperialism re-emerged as central to Mosley's thinking. The international system of trade placed the country at the 'mercy of international finance and exchange manipulations'. He worried about competition from developing countries with their sweated labour, and shared the social creditor fear that modern machinery would destroy rather than create employment, as deliberate dumping below production costs would lead to the collapse of world markets. He said imperial socialism had grown up and become 'adult in a greater sphere', even though it was a form of National Socialism.

Similar ideas were espoused by car manufacturer William Morris, ICI Chair-man Lord Melchett and Beaverbrook, who wanted to encourage imperial solidarity through economic links in the dominions, which provided British industry with an assured market. His Utopian Empire Crusade was a revival of tariff reform and again food taxes were the key issue, since it was questionable whether the public would accept them or whether the dominions would open their markets. Conservatives were also uneasy that the policy implied a system of planning.

A. L. Rowse said the clue to understanding Beaverbrook was that he took after his Irish mother. He was warm and generous but also 'vindictive and venomous', with no respect for truth. He was a good raconteur but was 'unreliable and irresponsible'. He was financially corrupt and corrupted others. It was his generous side which attracted left-wingers, such as new MP Aneurin Bevan, whose future wife, Jennie Lee, recalled Nye being 'quickly taken up and petted as an amusing bit of political rough trade by the Beaverbrook set'. Bevan was also susceptible to Mosley's charms and his closest ally was Strachey, who introduced him to his raffish circle and the Portmeirion home of Clough Williams-Ellis.

In developing his ideas, Beaverbrook turned for advice to Frank Wise. It was understood that Wise and Lee were a couple. A dark beauty, Lee was entirely at ease with her sexuality and capable of seducing anyone. Charles Trevelyan was her wealthy mentor, supplying money and advice. She, in turn, 'twisted him around her little finger'; and, given his promiscuous life, his wife had reason to worry. The two were lovers and there is reason to suspect that Lee may have been tempted by Mosley. Early on, he invited her to dinner where he introduced her to the delights of 'eating half a dozen slobbery grey oysters'. In an interview, she admitted Mosley had been her pin-up.

In Parliament, Lee was indignant at the failure to begin roadwork schemes. She wanted 'no more dilly-dallying' and was not appeased when Mosley 'looked down on me from his superior height and tried to calm me. His tone would have been quite all right for reciting poetry in the moonlight, but it simply added to my wrath on this occasion.' She was unaware that he was 'fighting his boss as hard as we left-wing ILPers were attacking openly on the floor of the House'.

The official report on retirement and school-leaving age, and Mosley's response, were sent on 22 October 1929 to the Treasury for assessment. On the following day, 'Black Thursday', Wall Street succumbed to panic when the US share index fell from 452 to 372. Thomas turned to drink for consolation. Two days later Lansbury told Mosley he was 'in despair about the whole business of unemployment. We all seem to be working in such an uncoordinated way.' Across the Atlantic, 'Black Tuesday', on 29 October, was catastrophic, with losses amounting to $10 billion. The Wall Street Crash reverberated all around the globe and was followed by a decline in world trade, which ushered in the worst depression of modern history. With a collapse of exports and upsurge in unemployment, it might have been expected that the stranglehold of orthodox economic management would be challenged by the economic radicalism of Mosley and Cole. Thomas, however, failed to push his Ministers' proposals and with an adverse Treasury report their positive merits were doomed. Thereafter, the Cabinet simply staggered into what MacDonald called 'an economic blizzard'.

Cimmie made her Commons maiden speech during the Old Age Pensions Bill. Described as the 'bright star of the debate', she demolished Neville Chamberlain's argument that people were demoralized by being given something for nothing. It was a 'ground on which I am very much at home. All my life I have got something for nothing . . . Of course, some people might say I showed great intelligence in the choice of my parents, but I put it down to luck.' Pointing to the Tory benches, she said, 'People on the opposite side of the House are also in that same position. They also have always got something for nothing. Now the question is: Are we demoralised?' Cimmie charmed the Commons and was more trusted than her husband. She had no great interest outside her home and children, but she had a good rapport with 'the common people and did her best, according to her lights, to assist them'. After her speech she was invited by the BBC's Hilda Matheson, whom she had known as Lady Astor's secretary, to talk on *The Week in Parliament*, explaining politics to women.

On 2 November Beatrice Webb talked to Mosley, who was 'contemptuous of Thomas's incapacity'. Thomas's defence in the Commons of his stewardship was a bitter disappointment for James Maxton: 'One of my enthusiastic colleagues on these benches said that Labour was in for twenty years. Well, I hope so. God knows that at the rate of progress indicated in the Lord Privy Seal's speech they will need every minute of it!' Thomas's failure inspired Ministry of Labour official H. B. Butler to put together a memorandum which argued that what was needed was for the PM to chair a policy-making economic general staff consisting of all Ministers connected with unemployment. Under its auspices, standing committees would advise on economic policy. Butler proposed a secretariat consisting of twelve higher civil servants, who would act as the research and collation body for the work of the economic staff and standing committees. It was to be an influential memo, to which Mosley clearly had access.

With Mosley disillusioned with senior Ministers, his Tory and business friends believed he might jump. In early November he presented to a ministerial conference a version of the Butler memo and called for a Cabinet of action on the lines of the War Cabinet, assisted by an economic general staff to coordinate policy. He also preached the 'productioneering' philosophy of a high-wage, high-productivity economy through labour co-operation and market stability. This had strong corporatist overtones and would have led to a radical departure in economic policy, as most fought shy of the kind of full-blooded approach that Mosley advocated.

In the face of strong foreign competition, older industries had contracted and Lancashire cotton, priced out of the India and Far East markets, only survived because of the forced adoption of short-time working. In contrast in the US, where the tariff on imports was raised to 40 per cent, the economy grew by an annual 7 per cent and exports by over 25 per cent. American merchandise increasingly replaced British goods in foreign markets. America's prosperity was explained, said Reginald McKenna, by 'the superior working of the American Federal Reserve System, which was far more responsive to industry's credit requirements than the Bank of England'. Since his trip to the US, Mosley had been expressing similar ideas and was applauded by industrialists such as British American Tobacco's Sir Hugo Cunliffe-Owen and Alfred Hacking, Secretary of the Society of Motor Manufacturers. They were crusaders for a self-contained 'United Economic Empire' and praised Mussolini's success in restoring order in Italy.

Protectionism in Britain was promoted by the Empire Industries Association (EIA), which campaigned for 'the Extension of Empire Preference and the Safeguarding of Home Industries', and whose leaders, Sir Henry Page Croft and British Fascist Patrick Hannon, were survivors of the Tariff Reform campaign. Members included agricultural protectionists, imperialists and captains of industries such as textiles, cars and chemicals, which faced technological change. They included those who later supported Mosley – Sir Felix Pole, closely aligned with William Morris, and social imperialist MP Carlyon Bellairs. Major funders were Sir Samuel Courtauld and stockbrokers J. and A. Scrimgeour, who later contributed to the BUF.

With Lancashire a hotbed of radicalism and farmers claiming they were being 'crucified on a cross of gold', protectionism, through the energetic efforts of the EIA, became a force within Conservative ranks. It was this constituency to which Beaverbook hoped to appeal as he broadened his Empire Free Trade campaign with the help of Rothermere, in a classic example of press barons attempting to wield power.

EIA adherents had been involved with the wartime Ministry of Munitions and supported Lord Milner's semi-corporatist and anti-socialist approach to industrial relations. When Milner died in 1925, his call for a new industrial framework based on the co-operation of labour and capital in industrial Joint Councils, and a national 'Parliament of Industry', was taken up by the middle-way 'young Tories' led by Robert Boothby, Oliver Stanley and Harold Macmillan. On 5 November 1929 Beaverbrook discussed with Boothby, Macmillan, newspaper publisher Edward Hulton and Walter Elliott the possibility of ditching Baldwin. Churchill suggested forming a 'Young Party'. They were, however, suspicious of him as he was 'bound hand and foot to Free Trade'. Among possible recruits were Mosley, Keynes and Labour MP William Jowitt, who was ready to jump. All the mavericks seemed to be contemplating setting up new political groupings. Shortly after, Beaverbrook and Rothermere formally launched their Empire Crusade.

On 22 November Mosley, Lansbury and Johnston proposed to a ministerial conference a scheme for pensions for those over sixty years of age, belonging to 'insured industries who can be regarded as effective competitors in the labour market'. Its Chairman, Arthur Greenwood, was sympathetic, but Thomas – at Snowden's bidding – forbade a vote on it. Mosley complained that the road programme was 'not good enough'. He castigated Morrison for believing money was saved 'if the Treasury contribution to schemes was low and the local authority share high'. Snowden resisted providing 100 per cent grants to local authorities for road building, because it would replace local authorities with 'state dictators'.

Morrison was the sort of Minister civil servants liked. Mosley thought him a 'bureaucrat, devoid of vision and incapable of movement beyond his office stool'. London's 'Mr Fix-it' was a popular figure among members and had been voted ahead of Mosley in the NEC elections. His biographers claim his arguments were those of 'an energetic minister who fought vigorously for policies he believed in'. He saw as well as Mosley that the existing policies were failing and worked hard to get money out of the Treasury. During December he proposed an annual increase of £17 million to the five-year programme, but it was still inadequate for the scale of the problem.

According to Henderson, Thomas was 'in such a state of panic, that he is bordering on lunacy'. Mosley wanted him sacked but MacDonald was dependent on Thomas's trade union power base and support in the party. Mosley worked on ideas, with research help from Strachey and Young. On 12 December the PM spoke to him and acknowledged Thomas had handled things badly, but was baffled on what to do – 'the cup has been put to my lips and it is empty'. On Christmas Eve he wondered 'if the sun was setting on the empire, worried about the rise of tariffs and the decline of trade, brooded on the backwardness of British industry, dreamed about the dearth of work'. Along the lines of the Butler plan, Henderson suggested the PM take charge of policy, set up a committee on unemployment, employ Cole as chief researcher and let Mosley carry out agreed plans.

On 30 December MacDonald informed Mosley he had received many letters 'warning against those who are sponging'. He had been looking into pensions at sixty to relieve the labour market but 'Malthus is right', the country was overpopulated. He wanted it tackled in a way other than by money. As he dimly saw the problem, the solution was to 'hang on to what we are doing but weed out the spongers all round'. In essence, he confirmed Wheatley's initial fears that Labour would do capitalism's bidding and reduce the standard of living of its own supporters.

In January 1930 the unemployment figure rose to 1,537,000. Cole, a member of the PM's Economic Advisory Council, said the unemployment situation constituted a national emergency and the government would be judged on its ability to tackle it. When Fenner Brockway took a memorandum on work schemes to the Thomas committee, Mosley and Lansbury admitted they were 'utterly disillusioned'. Mosley casually told Thomas he had 'jotted down a number of new proposals. Some you will agree with and some you'll probably turn down; but, in any case, Jim, I'd like you to see them.'

On 15 January Lady Curzon told Harold Nicolson that Mosley was 'anxious to leave the Labour Party and to reconcile himself with his old friends'. The fact that he had rented an office and taken on staff suggests he was organizing in case things did not work out. Political commentator Cecil Melville believed leaving was a foregone conclusion but 'without some form of powerful financial support his ambitions would just fizzle out. These considerations caused him to delay his resignation.' When, on 16 January, he asked for Lansbury's and Johnston's support, they hesitated since they suspected he was 'preparing his ammunition for a break-away movement'. ILPers agreed he 'prepared his scapegoats well in advance'. Four days later he informed Nicolson that 'big things are happening'. On 23 January 1930 he sent his memorandum to the PM.

Mosley admitted the memorandum was a synthesis of available plans. He had help from Boothby and Strachey had been a major influence on its direction, prefiguring much of it in the *New Leader*. Mosley's 'opening shot in his rebellion' within the government called for control of banking; bulk purchase of imports; credit to revive purchasing power; raising the school-leaving age and lowering the old age pension limit. A coherent package, it bore similarities to Cole's criticism of government policy, Ernest Bevin's ideas on pension and school-leaving schemes, and Lloyd George's road programme. There were sections on government machinery; reconstruction planning; credit policy; and short-term relief for workers displaced by rationalization. There were larger grants for road building – £200 million was expected to employ 300,000 men for three years, whereas Lloyd George wanted to employ 600,000 men over two years – but it was modest and designed to be executed with the 'maximum speed and minimum cost'.

Mosley's vision of a large domestic market with high wages and cheap money remained the central theme of his thinking. He supported this with a Keynesian argument about the multiplier effect of public works, which he argued would 'siphon off the surplus unemployed from the job market, create a "shortage of labour", and thereby lend substance to higher wage-demands'. Such a policy 'might well produce here conditions on which prolonged American prosperity has rested'. Having had 'to walk warily through a labyrinth of time-consecrated departments, and to deal amiably with many agreeable gentlemen at not much more than the pace they were accustomed to travel', he admitted public works could not be set in motion without organizational change. Following the Butler proposals, he wanted 'in supreme control a Minister who controls nearly all the major Departments of State', and was serviced by a committee of economists. He attacked the Treasury view as a 'white flag' policy in that 'nothing can ever be done by the Government . . . it is a policy of complete surrender'. His novel concept of deficit financing shocked Snowden.

The memorandum was less radical than 'Revolution by Reason'. It ditched nationalization of banking and consumer and producer credits in favour of public works as the means of increasing credit. What distinguished it was the proposed siege economy, with the State assuming responsibility for economic welfare. It was, David Marquand observes, 'a young man's memorandum – brash, perhaps lacking in a sense of administrative practicality, yet with an intellectual vitality and panache that still sparkle through its pages'. Despite this, he received lukewarm support from the PM, who considered it 'too complicated'. Home Secretary John Clynes viewed it as 'something approaching insanity'. Mosley had acted beyond his brief and it was not for a junior Minister 'to reorganise the nation's economy'. Snowden was provoked to fury: 'What would be the effect of a sudden reversal of our present policy and the announcement that we were going to embark on a campaign of unrestricted expenditure financed out of loans?' The effect 'might well be to create a very serious shock to confidence not only in this country but abroad'.

In attacking Mosley, on 13 January Morrison told Thomas that spending Ministers had 'as much duty to have proper regard to economy as Labour understands it as the Chancellor himself'. His dislike of Mosley was based on his experience in committee. When questioned by him, Morrison 'felt something of the superiority of the aristocrat in his attitude in relation to myself as a working class Minister. If he had asked him as a colleague, he would have complied but he acted like an aggressive Counsel in Court severely cross-examining and attacking a hostile witness.' In Cabinet, on 3 February, Thomas drew a melancholy picture of rising unemployment but Ministers refused to criticize him in the expectation that economies would eventually produce expansion. Mosley fine-tuned his proposals in an attempt to overcome their fears. He sought advice from Keynes on raising a loan of £200 million over three years for public works. Keynes, who had been almost wiped out financially with the crash, said the Treasury's objection to borrowing was a 'most desperate fallacy'.

On 8 February Mosley's memo was leaked to the *Telegraph* and Ministers thereafter spent more time discussing the propriety of Mosley's methods than his policies. On 19 February the Cabinet discussed the wide circulation of the memo, which had been left 'lying about quite openly' in Strachey's house. Thomas accused Mosley of leaking it, but since MacDonald wanted to ensure

Thomas was not upstaged by Mosley he took no action. Two days later Thomas offered his resignation but the PM declined to accept it – 'we must endure however hard the road may be'. In despair, MacDonald asked, 'Is the sum of my country sinking?' Mosley argued it was for critics of his proposals 'to present a reasoned alternative which offers a greater prospect of success'. He did not want further inaction. 'If the Cabinet wished to adopt his plan, well and good; if not, he would rather fight than talk.' MacDonald settled for the appearance of action by setting up expert inquiries, whose reports were destined to gather dust. Mosley's memo was assessed by a committee, chaired by his arch-enemy Snowden. On 22 February, after dining with Mosley, Georgia Sitwell wrote in her diary: 'Will Tom resign?'

The collapse of exports led to an interest in tariffs among economic interests hitherto opposed to them, and a retreat to Empire as a way of coping with the chaos into which the country had been plunged. As the *Manchester Guardian* reported friction inside government and possible resignations, Mosley made overtures to disillusioned Tories who talked of creating a 'New Party' and Beaverbrook, who launched a fighting fund for his own Empire Crusade. Its head, Sir Hugo Cunliffe-Owen, had been promised £70,000 (£2.1 m) from Beaverbrook's business colleague Sir James Dunn, the Duke of Westminster and Lord Rothermere. The Crusade attracted recruits from the Empire Industries Association and the young Tories' guarded support. The day after the launch, Mosley was at Oliver Stanley's house, with Ralph Blumenfeld, Boothby, Elliott and Ivan Moore-Brabazon, who ran the Conservative Candidates' Association with Macmillan. Nicolson recorded that the conversation turned to 'talk about the decay of democracy' and centred on 'whether it would be well to have a Fascist coup'.

The Empire Crusade was transformed into the United Empire Party (UEP) on 18 February 1930. Until then, Beaverbrook's concept had oscillated between a pressure group – which was spectacularly modern with aeroplanes bombarding the populace with leaflets – and a fully fledged political party. With a combined total of eight nationals and Rothermere's chain of provincial papers, the press barons were 'laying down a joint barrage scarcely paralleled in newspaper history'. The Crusade took off like wildfire in Tory areas in the south but it was not supported by a single senior politician of weight, though there were hopes of recruiting Mosley. The hostile response to the UEP's foundation shook the newspaper barons, who had misjudged the diehards' loyalty and willingness to break ranks. Beaverbook decided to withdraw and Rothermere used the UEP remnant to publicize his diehard manifesto.

By March, MacDonald felt his tiredness 'right to the centre of my being'. He was under considerable personal strain. Mosley was contacted by MacDonald's Viennese mistress who said the government would be in trouble if she were not helped. He went to see her in a flat in Horseferry Road. She said she had known MacDonald in Switzerland when he was an impoverished young man. She had been to Downing Street but an hysterical PM had thrown her out. She was demanding money for a number of lyrical but pornographic letters from MacDonald, which she threatened to publish in France. In a passage cut from his autobiography, Mosley said he called her bluff and told her if she tried to get them published, the Secret Service would make sure her life was 'not worth a moment's purchase'.

On 12 March Nicolson believed Mosley was about to resign: 'Even Ramsay who till now has been a pillar of strength to him is said to be looking at him with a cold eye.' Two days later Snowden's committee attacked Mosley for his 'confusion of mind'. State action to reduce unemployment was inherently suspect and 'the finance of these schemes would not stand a moment's consideration'. Mosley said he was not advocating 'wild-cat finance' and claimed the backing of Keynes, who thought it an illuminating document. Keynes, however, was discovering he was 'not quite as fashionable as he thought'. Snowden forbade his Committee on Economic Outlook from discussing State-aided schemes.

Nine days later Mosley's memo was leaked in the *Manchester Guardian*, which confirmed he had been 'muzzled' but said 'even the ILP has never produced anything more fantastic'. Labour MPs rejected it, either because it was too extreme or they simply could not understand it. Having consulted Keynes and Boothby, he issued a proposal for a State finance corporation to provide long-term credit for newer industries. Investment could not be left to banks, because they had never played 'a big and consciously formative part in the industrial development of the country'. There was support from the Federation of British Industries (FBI), which wanted trade flows and investment plans to be linked and, with the TUC, wanted the Empire developed as an economic unit. On 15 April the FBI presented to the Economic Advisory Council proposals for intra-imperial economic co-operation, with Britain keeping existing preferences, and industrial growth in the dominions. For once, the arguments were going Mosley's way.

To MacDonald, all solutions appeared unpromising. On 1 May Snowden's committee report condemned Mosley's memo. State-financed works were an illusion as they interfered with normal business and undermined the democratic system of local government and the Chancellor's special responsibility in the sphere of finance. His unyielding adherence to a balanced budget was the decisive obstacle.

When, on 8 May, Thomas accused his Ministers of leaking the memorandum, Lansbury lost his temper. Cabinet Secretary Maurice Hankey then 'put his pencil down, and took no notes'. Policy on unemployment was in ruins. Five days later the PM informed the Cabinet that the country would find itself with two million unemployed before the end of the year but was confident things would then get better. He acknowledged that 'owing to slowness of local authorities', only £10 million of the £95 million available for employment schemes had been used. Mosley pointed out that spending on roads was 'no greater than under the Conservatives'. When he argued local authorities should be bypassed, Arthur Greenwood said 'the result would be chaos'. Mosley was exasperated by the lack of urgency.

The Economic Advisory Council decided, on 16 May, against developing the Empire as an economic unit. Though Empire trade was important, foreign trade was more important still. It was 'absurd to compare the conditions prevailing in the United States – a self-supporting country, with vast internal resources and a high protective tariff – with the competitive conditions under which the population of these islands must live and work if the standard of living to which we are accustomed is not to be radically altered'. Only one worker in seven, however, was engaged in exports, which undermined arguments against concentrating on the domestic economy.

Mosley was finding himself increasingly isolated. He had the support of Cole, who had become less enthusiastic about his capacity to effect any change in policy and was closer to Mosley than his wife, Margaret, would concede. ILPers were sympathetic but many distrusted him. One critic said he looked far too much like 'a man in search of a party to lead'.

John Wheatley was still greatly admired by ILPers as the main hope for change. During spring 1930 he regularly met with John Beckett, the ILP's unofficial whip, who was 'lovable in his utter devotion' to Wheatley, and later to Mosley. In early May, Wheatley, Beckett and Maxton decided to transform the ILP into a new political party, and hoped to 'asset-strip' the Communist Party of its best people. But then tragedy struck. Already ill with a heart condition, Wheatley suffered a brain haemorrhage and died on 12 May 1930. Mosley was shocked by the death of the one ILP figure he unreservedly admired.

Mosley had lost patience with the Labour leadership. On 13 May he met with Bruce Lockhart, Empire Crusade factotum to Beaverbrook, and his friend Mike Waddell. Although they believed 'Tom will probably resign next week', he delayed his decision. Crusade fund-raiser Cunliffe-Owen said the mood in the City was 'apathetic and there was little chance of raising money'. The next day Mosley left for Wheatley's funeral, where he laid the biggest wreath. He walked along Glasgow's rain-swept streets, where thousands of constituents paid their respects to the last substantial voice of British socialism. Dalton smugly assumed that without Wheatley the Left 'will be like sheep without a shepherd'. Beckett wanted to fight on but Maxton had a 'queer philosophy' which made him 'an impossible leader'. The obvious candidate was Mosley but he was a 'spoiled young careerist, with more money and ego than sense . . . whom real socialists regarded with amused disdain'.

On his return to London Mosley had a letter from Boothby, who had contemplated the state of politics with 'a jaundiced but more or less unbiased mind'. It would be a great tragedy if he resigned. He was the 'ONLY ONE of my generation who is capable of translating into action any of the ideas in which I genuinely believe. If you stay where you are that opportunity is bound to come soon. Go, and where are you?' He cited the example of Lord Randolph Churchill, who resigned in 1886 over his thwarted spending plans. He never resurfaced, notes Graham Stewart, 'from the quicksand of political wilderness into which he plummeted. He had chosen the wrong issue upon which to resign and paid the penalty accordingly.'

Boothby pictured his resignation. 'You will make the case against the government – but nine-tenths of the audience will be hostile. All the pent-up fury which you have deliberately, and I think rightly, roused in so many breasts will simultaneously be released . . . The cumulative effect of so many hostile forces would overwhelm Napolean himself.' Among the young Tories 'there is not one of them with either the character or the courage to do anything big'. Walter Elliott would not 'take a step that might even remotely prejudice his political position'. The alternative was 'to remain within the official fold and by making yourself increasingly oppressive to the "Bright Old Things", strengthen your power. With every increase in the unemployment figures the position which you are known to have taken up becomes more impregnable and easier to justify.' He urged him not to 'chuck it away'.

On 19 May Mosley went to see the PM and informed him of his intention to resign. According to Melville's version, he said he was 'prepared to remain if the Government would give him an undertaking to include certain financial provisions in the next Budget'. This brought him into collision with Snowden, who warned MacDonald that in Mosley he had 'a more dangerous enemy than in any one in the other political parties'.

The Cabinet engaged in a heated debate. The PM thought the unemployment figures deplorable and required 'fundamental thinking' but Greenwood was 'not sure how to handle the problem'. A frustrated Mosley snarled that 'you must make a greater effort or throw up the sponge'. He called for a programme of £100 million to be raised by loan, but Lansbury retorted that 'you've got a £100 million and you have spent £15 million. Where are your schemes?' Mosley replied, 'money could not be spent if detailed inquiry had to precede the spending. A Napoleon could spend £200 million in three years.' Thomas warned it would bring local government to a standstill. To employ 300,000 on roads, added MacDonald, would mean 300,000 back where they were at the end of three years and was no permanent solution. But, asked Mosley, 'can we have 2 million unemployed?' He quoted the authority of Keynes against the Treasury but Thomas said 'business men riddle Keynes', to which Mosley replied, 'Keynes wipes the floor with them.'

'This country,' Mosley went on, 'if it is to survive at the present standard of life, has got to be isolated from other countries . . . The high purchasing power of home population is the only solution.' Ministers had little to offer. Morrison said it was 'still open to us to remember that Socialism is the only remedy'. Lansbury claimed 'there is no way out of the world situation, but by some form of international agreement'. MacDonald recorded that Mosley made a 'very bad impression' and had been 'on the verge of being offensively vain in himself'. Johnston, however, pleaded they should use his talents which had been 'trampled on and ignored'. Mosley refused to speak at that night's debate, since he no longer supported the government's position.

After the debate the Mosleys stayed with Beatrice Webb. 'Is he or is he not going to resign?' she wondered. He said the party was 'breaking up in the country', MacDonald was a 'great artist' and, strangely, that he respected Snowden, even though he had under his wife's influence become anti-socialist. Mrs Snowden said 'she needs no friends because she is so intimate with the royal family'. Beatrice wondered if Mosley had 'sufficient judgement and knowledge' to lead the party. He intended to head 'a new group who will vote solidly to keep the Labour government in office, but will be continually critical in the house and propagandists in the country'.

On the next morning, 20 May, Mosley handed the PM his letter of resignation as Chancellor of the Duchy of Lancaster. The PM noted it was written in a tone of 'graceless pompousness'. When Ministers met that afternoon, Thomas said, 'Let us play the game. No one wants to kill the ambitions of a young man.' The PM claimed the Cabinet had not accepted Snowden's report rejecting Mosley's memo but had referred it to the party conference and that credit would be considered by the Macmillan Committee. Mosley, however, could not wait: Were the Cabinet in favour of a £200 million scheme or not? Perhaps he had misunderstood them. 'All these thousands who trusted us should be given a chance of saying what they prefer. Only clean thing is to submit it to the test.'

'Are all these revelations today', asked the PM, 'reason for resignation? I say No, and I am very sorry.'

Mosley replied, 'I say Yes and am very sorry. Better for me to go. I'm a dissident Junior and a minority.'

MacDonald who, Mosley recalled, was 'superb in the injured role of the old queen suffering an attack of lèse majesté', claimed, 'It is I who am a dissident Senior in a minority and tired, and should go.' He begged Mosley to 'stand by the Government, the Movement, and the Party'.

An exasperated Mosley replied that for ten months he had warned them and 'stood the racket for principles in which I fundamentally disbelieved'. He had now decided to 'fight on principles and policy'.

According to Melville, Snowden dramatically accused Mosley of being 'a traitor to the cause of Labour, and one who was incapable of political loyalty; adding that the English people had no time for a "pocket-Mussolini" '. Mosley stormed out.

MacDonald thought the situation appalling. Ministers had to push local authorities to speed up their work and he wanted weekly meetings with heads of departments to 'speed up everywhere'. Which was close to what Mosley had demanded.

Johnston and Lansbury pleaded with Mosley to reconsider. MacDonald put forward a compromise formula, drafted to satisfy Foreign Secretary Henderson. Agriculture was offered to Mosley, who 'turned to his satellite moon (whom some would hold to have been his evil genius) John Strachey for advice'. His counsel was to refuse: 'What the people want is Action.' MacDonald thought the 'test of a man's personality is his behaviour in disagreement: in every test Mosley failed'.

Mosley slammed 'the door with a bang to resound through the political world'. Boothby was in the House and remembered his friend's relief and determination to 'bring these grave matters to the test'. That night, Mosley admitted to Bruce Lockhart that he had been 'meditating on this step for weeks': it would strengthen his position in the party. Irene thought he had committed a 'stupid egotistical error', but was thankful Cimmie wholeheartedly agreed with his stance.

Mosley sincerely wished to get things done, but his actions were rarely interpreted so generously. *The Times* said his ambitions were 'always stronger than his allegiance'. The *Herald*, however, declared it was the adherence to 'Treasury dogma' that caused the dispute. As J. R. Cline acknowledged, the weight of Mosley's criticism was directed 'specifically against Snowden who was a bitter critic of MacDonald'. 'To put the matter simply,' George Catlin admitted, 'by and large Mosley's policy was right and Snowden's wrong.'

Mosley's resignation was treated sympathetically by Birmingham newspapers and by the rank and file, which expected him to stay loyal to Labour. On 22 June there was almost a revolt in Cabinet when proposals were put forward for pensions at sixty, raising of the school-leaving age, expanding the road programme and an emergency council of Ministers. Clearly Mosley's resignation had an effect. Whether his proposals would be put into practice was another matter. That evening, Mosley appealed to MPs to support a motion expressing dissatisfaction with government unemployment policy.

At 8 p.m. Mosley rose to deliver his indictment. George Strauss, Morrison's Parliamentary Secretary, considered it 'one of the most dramatic meetings I have ever attended'. He made the speech with 'no bitterness, no recrimination' but with 'a very high note of emotion. It was a magnificent piece of rhetoric which I wouldn't have missed for worlds.' Strauss still considered the proposals weak, but others felt he 'must know what he was talking about and as something, obviously, had to be done to stem the rising tide of unemployment, his plan should, at least, be carefully considered, and, in view of the apparent failure of the Government to cope with the matter, they certainly deserved some censure'.

ILP Parliamentary Secretary W. J. Brown thought the speech a 'magnificent performance that moved the party deeply'. The platform was nervous as to the outcome, since MacDonald's 'vague phrases carried no conviction'. There was a dramatic moment when Mosley – who, if he had been smart, would have withdrawn his resolution – let his 'vanity overstep itself' and allowed Arthur Henderson to outmanoeuvre him. Brown considered Henderson's attitude to Mosley similar to those who said, 'He isn't really one of us! True, we have drunk his wine and smoked his cigars, and been flattered by an invitation to his house. But he doesn't really "belong". Got too good conceit of himself! – a bounder.' Despite Mosley's efforts to rouse them, trade union-backed MPs reacted, in Jennie Lee's phrase, 'like a load of damp cement'.

Henderson appealed to Mosley 'to take the noble line which would be consistent with the manner in which he had affected his resignation, to withdraw his motion, and allow his various proposals to be discussed in detail at Party meetings'. Everyone assumed Mosley would agree but after asking a henchman how many votes they had, and when told fifty, he insisted on putting it to the vote. Instantly, support deserted him. There were twenty-nine votes for Mosley and 210 for the government. Junior Minister Vernon Hartshorn remarked that it was 'a pity he didn't withdraw. He would have done himself a lot of good.' Whereupon, Cimmie indignantly said 'he didn't care for his own good, but only for his Party'.

Thanks to the tactical misjudgement, little damage was done to the government. Mosley had 'turned his supreme chance into defeat because he thought the rescinding of his vote of censure would show weakness on his part'. But he had decided 'in advance of the meeting, to bring the party to a decision or eventually to leave'. The *Herald* considered his decision courageous and predicted 'he will do big things'. The *Manchester Guardian* argued it would be good for the government to be harassed by a left-centre critic with his influence outside greater than inside it. *The Times*, however, considered his tactics a sign of 'petuousness'. Looking back, Irene thought that he always 'failed in his judgement of his fellow-men, and was inept at the vital crossroads in his political career'.

Strachey recalled the 'spectacle of Mosley sitting silent and alone, brooding with an indescribable bitterness, as the elderly, portly trade union officials and nervous pacifist intellectuals filed out'. A stab of premonition flashed through Strachey's mind. 'How had the Italian Social Democrats looked at the Congress of the Italian Socialist Party which expelled the Editor of *Avanti*? Had they not been sure that they had finished with that tiresome fellow Mussolini?'

9

'After Baldwin and
MacDonald Comes . . . ?'

On 28 May 1930, in the Commons, Mosley sat with folded arms, 'grand, gloomy, wrapped in the solitude of his own originality', as he prepared to defend his resignation. He rose, 'a sheet of paper in one hand, stabbing the air with his favourite gesture of a man throwing a dart'. He had begged the government 'to make up its mind how much it was prepared to spend on unemployment, how much money it could find, and then to allocate the money available according to the best objects we could discover. As it is, like bookmakers on the race course, the man who can . . . make most noise and get through the turnstile first, gets away with the money.'

Mosley argued it made no sense for capital to 'go overseas to equip factories to compete against us, to provide employment for people in those countries; while it is supposed to shake the whole basis of our financial strength if anyone dares to suggest the raising of money by the Government of this country to provide employment for the people of this country'. Described as 'Birmingshamism rampant', he was responding to a situation which left 'British producers vulnerable in an era of high tariffs and low prices'. He struck a unique note, notes Daniel Ritschell, 'in his willingness to combine the expansionary economics of high wages with the protectionist heresy usually associated with the Tories'. This would require, however, the reorganization of the whole basis of industrial life by a strategy of national planning.

Speaking without notes, Mosley's speech lasted over an hour. At the end, he became 'visibly exhausted and the pallor of his face in combination with a break in the voice' rendered the speech all the more effective. Building to a climax, he roared that 'if the great powers of this country are to be mobilized and rallied for a great national effort, then Government and Parliament must give a lead'. He begged MPs 'to give the vital forces of this country the chance that they await'.

Then the cheering broke out, 'loud and prolonged, from every section of the House'. His speech, the *Evening Standard* stated, was the 'triumph of an artist who has made his genius perfect by long hours of practice and devotion to his art. There is no politician who works harder or who takes more pains to master his problems.' Boothby considered it 'the greatest parliamentary tour de force this generation will hear'. In the gallery Lady Mosley was 'so full of pride and joy in my man-child it almost choked me . . . How I hope I may live to have the joy of seeing "all your dreams come true" for the good of the country and your own honour and glory.'

Speaking after Mosley, Lloyd George described his proposals as 'an injudicious mixture of Karl Marx and Lord Rothermere'. Churchill criticized both Lloyd George and Mosley with the jibe that there was little difference between the two, except that while the former had said 'we' could conquer unemployment, the latter had claimed, typically, that only 'he' could achieve it. Before the debate, MacDonald had feared the government might be defeated. In the end only five Labour Members abstained and it survived with a majority of twenty-nine.

Labour's Joseph Wedgwood observed a changed mood on the backbenches. 'Man after man was saying to himself: "That is our leader."' Ellen Wilkinson realized the speech had made Mosley 'a hero of all the young members in all parties who are impatiently demanding new ideas to meet a catastrophic situation'. The *Herald* reported that a 'sense of national emergency breaking down Party barriers seemed to sweep over the Members'. *The Times*, however, warned that 'parties cannot be expected to combine in nationalising the banks, in drenching the roads with money'. Mosley's approach to planning proved to be a stumbling block to any hoped-for coalition.

After the speech, Mosley celebrated at the Astors'. Frank Pakenham (Lord Longford) recalled Mosley staring at him with that 'odd look with which he seemed to transfix women'. He said, 'After Peel comes Disraeli. After Baldwin and MacDonald comes . . . ?' When Pakenham asked, 'Who comes next?' Mosley growled, 'Comes someone very different.' On the following day Beatrice Webb wondered whether MacDonald had found his successor in Mosley. He had a young man's zeal but she doubted whether he had the strength of character to succeed. He was loose with women and aroused suspicion because he was an intruder who was 'not easily assimilated'.

The debate was followed by news of another by-election defeat. When rumours of a ministerial revolt circulated, MacDonald worried that Mosley's supporters were 'buzzing in the lobby and signing petitions'. On 31 May the PM received a letter from sixty Labour MPs calling for the head of Thomas, who was subsequently shunted off to the Dominions Office. By taking charge of unemployment policy himself, MacDonald hoped 'to quell the disaffection which Mosley's resignation had brought to a head'. Mosley's post was downgraded and handed to Clement Attlee. That the future belonged to 'this small, quiet man and not at all to Mosley', noted Seaman, 'is a comforting illustration of history's unpredictability'.

Mosley's appraisal of the poor prospects for a revival of exports evoked a sympathetic response in the Board of Trade. Indeed, so sympathetic was its report that Snowden refused the PM a copy. Scribbled in its margin is the note: 'Written for the Chancellor alone.' A. J. P. Taylor commented that rejection of Mosley's memorandum was 'the moment when the British people resolved unwittingly to stand on the ancient ways'.

Mosley rented rooms off Ebury Street and put together a secretarial staff, and employed political scientist George Catlin – married to Vera Brittain – as chief researcher. When Catlin lunched with Mosley, he was impressed by the galaxy of talent which included Wedgwood Benn (later Lord Stansgate and father of left-wing Labour MP Tony Benn), Keynes and Douglas Cole. A parliamentary candidate for a West Midlands seat, Cole acknowledged that Mosley's memorandum was 'broadly on the right lines' and expressed his support in speeches, though it was conditional upon Mosley remaining loyal to the party.

Churchill had been rattled by Empire Crusade and feared a United Empire Party candidate might stand in his constituency. On 19 June he elaborated the case for an 'Economic Parliament' in his Romanes lecture at Oxford University. He wanted the issue of protectionism to go away and conceived the lecture as a way of distancing himself from the controversy. Churchill set out the classic doctrines of free trade, which had 'found their citadels in the Treasury and the Bank of England' but could see that 'they do not correspond to what is going on now'. Having championed Treasury orthodoxies, this was a remarkable admission. He further argued that economic issues should be dealt with by an economic sub-parliament 'free from party exigencies, and composed of persons possessing special qualifications in economic matters'.

Two days later in *The Times*, Mosley called for a twentieth-century parliament which would act like a shareholders' meeting, possessing the power to reject but not amend government motions and uninvolved in day-to-day administration. 'Here', suggests Skidelsky, 'was an outline sketch of the Corporate State. In time Mosley would fill in the details.' However, Churchill's lecture did not make him a closet Mosleyite. His economic sub-parliament had little to do with a corporatist, quasi-Fascist state, since he saw it as an advisory body wholly subservient to the will of Westminster. He soon abandoned such calls for intervention. That Mosley's ideas became 'progressively more interventionist', Graham Stewart notes, 'only made alliance with Churchill less likely'.

Catlin thought it significant that the walls of Mosley's offices carried large-scale maps of the Empire and the Soviet Union. The Soviet map was inspired by John Strachey, who promoted Russia as a market for British trade. His new paramour, Celia Simpson, had become increasingly interested in Communism and her strong character influenced the course of his political trajectory. During the summer he re-established ties with the ILP, willing as he was to vote against the government.

Mosley's advocacy of import controls, quotas and bulk purchasing, to get round the problems of food taxes posed by Empire Crusade, was very contemporary, Catlin thought. Mosley's article for the *Herald*, 'Empire Unity – But No to Food Taxes', was echoed by Ernest Bevin, who backed a TUC report issued on 26 June, which pressed for 'as full a development as possible of the economic relations between the constituent parts of the British Commonwealth'.

In the Commons on 16 July, Mosley proposed an insulated Commonwealth, containing 'nearly every resource, human and material, which industry requires'. Commodity Boards would restructure industries into a centralized organization for the home market, while Import Boards would be made up of consumer, employer and worker representatives. He realized opponents would dismiss 'your planning, your control, your import Board as all socialism and have none of it' but 'many useful things, from the pavements we walk on to the drainage system of our homes, are Socialism at present'. He expected a crisis but had faith people would know how to handle it; 'it clears their heads and steels their nerves'. However, he feared a 'long, slow, crumbling through the years until we sink to the level of a Spain, a gradual paralysis beneath which all the vigour and energy of this country will succumb'.

Beaverbrook congratulated Mosley for 'a very fine achievement' and was ready 'to make overtures in your direction in public, if you wish me to do so'. Mosley wrote in the *Express* that the modern man is a 'hard, realistic type, hammered into existence on the anvil of great ordeal'. Pre-war men were much nicer but the question was 'whether their ideas for the solution of the problems of our age are better than the ideas of those whom that age has produced'. He had 'always been painfully aware that our outlooks and methods' of party leaders were 'those of different planets'. This was his familiar theme of the 'young minds' against the 'old gangs'. A realignment of political forces was widely anticipated and Mosley was considering forging 'a national consensus of the most vital elements in the country'. He continued discussions with the young Tories and was surprised by the interest shown by the shy Harold Macmillan. Temporarily out of Parliament, Macmillan worked alongside Boothby, even though the latter was conducting an affair with his wife, Dorothy. The pair were irresponsibly indiscreet, but the affair never reached the papers.

Hugh Massingham remembered the hive of activity at Smith Square and the lively discussions with Nicolson, Stanley, Macmillan, Elliott, Boothby and two liberals, Leslie Hore-Belisha and Sir Archibald Sinclair (Churchill's adjutant during the war). Cyril Joad cowered in the corner 'occasionally letting out a squeak of protest whenever the necessity of violence was mentioned, as it usually was'. Macmillan warned that economic collapse would 'lead to a breakdown of the whole party system. No other single party will form a

Government and there will be a cabinet of young men', with Mosley as Prime Minister. Nicolson added that Macmillan was 'kind enough to include me in this Pitt-like Ministry'.

ILPers were angry over the lack of action on unemployment. On 18 July the fiery John Beckett seized the House of Commons Mace – the first person to touch it since Oliver Cromwell – shouting, 'Mr Speaker, these proceedings are a disgrace.' He stormed out of the Chamber to the toilets, planning 'to place its head in one of the magnificent porcelain receptacles which I believed would conveniently accommodate it'.

Although he had been forthright in criticizing the government, Mosley did not vote against it. He did not want to antagonize members because he still hoped to become leader. His message was spread within the ILP by Strachey and W. J. Brown, but many members were wary of his thinking, which Brockway thought leant towards 'Economic Imperialism'. Ellen Wilkinson noted that he was beginning 'to stray rather dangerously'. Harold Laski told Beatrice Webb that Mosley and Cole were co-operating. On 25 July Cole called for non-tariff protection and extended co-operation with the Empire. Laski thought Mosley 'ignorant' and that Cole was 'gambling with one proposal after another'; which said more about Laski than the proposals. The ILP became hostile because he was 'too close to the Tory position'. That was unfair since he added little to its 'own position on the subject of controlled trade with the empire'.

Mosley behaved with 'punctilious correctness, neither seeking the publicity of revelatory interviews, nor indulging in criticism of his colleagues'. His loyalty countered suspicions of ambition. His tragic flaw, however, was impatience, and his conviction that he was right. 'The one', suggests W. F. Mandle, 'fed on the other and Mosley's errors grew greater as time went on.' But as unemployment increased and the government failed to respond, a very sincere man might well have acted in the same way as a very ambitious one.

Attlee submitted on 30 July his own memorandum, 'The Problems of British Industry', which owed a great deal, with its call for industrial rationalization, to his secretary, Colin Clark, who had previously assisted Mosley. Attlee said Snowden's argument against a tariff was 'fatal to any project whereby a special position is given to any branch of British industry . . . and most Socialist proposals'. His conclusion was pure Mosley – 'the essential thing is the translation of ideas into action'. Inevitably, the Treasury ensured that the memorandum never reached the Cabinet and it sank without trace.

Alone at Lossiemouth, on 14 August the PM had 'private concerns, so unsettling that I have no peace here and must seek it in London'. MacDonald's former mistress had reappeared on the scene. It seems that his mental decline in the early thirties was due, in part, to this woman's blackmail attempt. Mosley found MacDonald 'quite unconscious of anything in this affair except his personal emotions; he ran true to the form of Puritanism relapsing into hysteria'.

The man chosen to buy off the woman and retrieve the letters was Jimmy Thomas. This was not wise, as he was corrupt. The £3,000 (£100,000) bribe came from Thomas's friend, Sir Abe Bailey, a South African mining millionaire involved in the 1926 General Strike negotiations. Thomas was sent to Paris, where he met the woman but came back without the money or the letters. When Mosley learnt that he had 'sidelined to Monte Carlo and lost the lot', he contacted Sir Charles Mendl, Press Attaché and MI6 agent at the Paris embassy, who paid her off with secret service funds sent by Sir Robert Vansittart, head of the Foreign Office and previously MacDonald's Principal Private Secretary. Mendl later told Mosley that all he remembered of the destroyed letters was a line from a poem – 'Porcupine through hairy bowers shall climb to paradise'.

Mosley gambled with his own private life. Cimmie knew he was conducting affairs with their friends but, despite the urging of her sisters, refused to stalk his Ebury Street bachelor flat. She did write that she was 'entirely bewildered and depressed' and did not understand why he was 'so horrid' or why her mere presence drove him 'demented'. She complained he left her to look after Nicholas, who had had an operation for appendicitis, and went away 'with another woman for the weekend'. He replied, 'You can be the sweetest most feminine one in all the world, or you can be a real old nagging harridan.'

During the summer, Wyndham Lewis published his satire *The Apes of God*, featuring the Mosley circle. Dick Wyndham (Dick Wittingdon) was portrayed as the 'Ape-Flagellant' with a taste for 'fast cars and whips' and the Sitwells were caricatured as 'baby-talking middle-aged infants'. However, the satire was blemished by undercurrents of anti-Semitism. Sachie's wife Georgia was described as a Jewish enchantress holding 'all the trumps in her neat kosher fist'. The woman whom Mosley went away with was probably Georgia, who later confided to his second wife that 'we all went to bed with him but afterwards we were rather ashamed'.

Mosley was increasingly aware of the sexual allure of Cimmie's sister Baba. Beautiful and exquisitely dressed, she delivered her 'witty remarks in a languid drawl'. Fruity was charming and loyal, but was considered 'too stupid' by Georgia. He did not notice the attention Baba was paying to Mosley because she was pregnant. The birth of twin daughters took place after a long labour, during which it was feared she might die.

The Mosleys went their separate ways after their usual summer break at Antibes. Cimmie travelled to Turkey accompanied by Zita James. On 5 September the women visited Leon Trotsky, who was charming but scathing about Labour. He later referred to Cimmie's husband as an 'aristocratic coxcomb who joined the Labour party as a short cut to a career'. He found the meeting 'banal in the extreme' and recorded that Cimmie referred contemptuously to MacDonald and spoke of her sympathies towards Soviet Russia. When the pair reached Russia, Cimmie noted 'all the nonsense talked about only wearing old clothes so as not to be conspicuous, typhoid, the frightful food shortages, no soap – bunk from beginning to end'.

Cimmie wrote home to her husband that 'even when I am hundreds of miles away your shadow falls on me'. She believed he was carrying on with Paula Casa Maury, who was now, in fact, with Bill Allen. 'All my talk about self sufficiency serenity peace etc – Balls Balls Balls.' She had 'never really in my heart of hearts trusted' him and her efforts 'to adjust myself to you so as not to be hurt result in the very symptoms that make you hurt me more'. If she appeared indifferent, he 'just got fiercer and fiercer and destroyed me more and more'. Cimmie noted that in the 'hols you play hard – with other people', but 'where does Mum come in?' She confided in Dick Wyndham how distressed she was. He said she had the misfortune of being a happy person and had to dampen her natural happiness 'in order to be immune from the misery of a miserable world'. If her husband did 'an occasional flit to Paris: they are annoying, but no more so than an occasional attack of flu'.

Mosley wrote to Cimmie in the rational manner he used for a ministerial brief. The problem was how to 'reconcile and to blend into a perfect life' their marriage (1) and their individual happiness and freedom which were 'essentials of the full personality' (2). They were afraid the 'small incidents of (2) may destroy (1): each of us consequently is inclined to snatch small bits of (2) for himself or herself while striving to thwart rather than to assist the other. That situation is commonplace in the marriage of all remarkable people – it is small, contemptible and atavistic – in our case it should be entirely lacking because (1) is so much stronger than in almost any other example of which one can think.' He might be more reasonable if he 'did not feel that you had severely restricted me'. It was all one-sided. He admitted he slept around, though there was no evidence that Cimmie had ever contemplated such an action, and was simply oblivious to the hurt he inflicted.

Mosley wanted her to have such confidence in their marriage that 'we should have no feeling of fear and regret of any kind if one of us enjoyed things apart from the other'. To lead 'what we believe to be a moral life in our immoral society some subterfuge is necessary if we are to retain our power to change that society'. In this 'triumph of the modern mind', freedom was possible if they ended 'all small jealousies and fears'. He believed in these statements, which indicated his incapacity for mature love. His rational manipulation of Cimmie, the demand to be admired and loved, and his ruthless behaviour to one the self perceived as necessary for his own interests was typical of a narcissist.

Just as crowds were swayed by the glorious words, so too was Cimmie, who replied that everything he said was true. She was 'tricky' because she was unsure of the marriage's permanence. The affairs had begun early; she lost confidence and developed an inferiority complex. She had not been 'persuaded you really really appreciated me, you were always finding fault, and liking people so utterly different to me'. She went through 'agonies . . . when you have got off with lovely ladies . . . it has very often nearly driven me dippy. I have always felt that you won on the swings and roundabouts.' She acknowledged that he wanted a mother figure for a wife and only stayed together because of their public position and 'not because we really do love and value each other'. And then, cravenly, she apologized and hoped 'this won't appear as a very one-sided sort of letter as yours was so fair'. Cimmie was cajoled into accepting a position which was immoral and dispiriting.

The exchanges illustrate the ways in which the personal and the political are intimately intertwined. The negatives of Mosley's character became positives in terms of leadership. The utter self-belief and the unwillingness to contemplate that he could ever be wrong added to the turning outwards of his internal rage, ensured that his gift of popular leadership was, as Catlin admitted, formidable. He could display 'courage, intelligence, originality and eloquence'.

Mosley adhered to the contingency theory that leaders are people whose qualities work in times of crisis. Barely concealed was the idea that when the crisis erupted it would require great men, such as himself, to save the nation. There was a sense of him willing the crisis. Not fearing failure, Mosley types 'respond brilliantly to crises because it gives them a chance to glorify themselves'. He was the Hobbesian predator, who engages in a restless pursuit of power and, in the process, searches for others to devour 'in the incessant motion that determines life in the natural condition'.

Harold Laski asked George Catlin whether he had 'penetrated beyond the periphery of Mosley's consciousness'. He replied that he was 'a great egotist but did not know the answer'. He had, John Beckett noted, the 'worst possible temperament for success at Westminster'. He suffered fools badly and had no time for the 'wearisome babblings of decrepit Trade Union leaders'. Beckett noted that, whereas Stafford Cripps and Hugh Dalton would 'spend hours walking from one simple Labour member to another . . . listening with charm to their reminiscences', Mosley had no time for such pleasantries. They suspected he was only interested in using colleagues. Beckett recalled Cimmie 'running to and fro in the lobby using her charm to undo the harm of Mosley's brusque manner. The poor lady fought a losing battle, seldom succeeding in securing more than two friends for three enemies made by her husband.' This explained his unpopularity.

Following victories in the September 1930 German election, Hitler increased his representation from twelve to 105 seats. The *Mail* published a celebratory article by Rothermere (written by his journalist mouthpiece George Ward Price). 'These young Germans have discovered, as the young men and women of England are discovering, that it is no good trusting to the old politicians. Accordingly they have formed, as I should like to see our British youth form, a Parliamentary party of their own. Under Herr Hitler's control the youth of Germany is effectively organised against the corruption of Communism.' He had for the same reason founded the United Empire Party, 'for it is clear that no strong anti-Socialist policy can be expected from a Conservative Party whose leaders are themselves tainted with semi-Socialist doctrines'.

Others took note of events in Germany and were also looking for leadership. On 19 September twenty-two businessmen signed a letter in *The Times* announcing the setting up of a National Council of Industry and Commerce (NCIC). Created by Sir William Morris because no party was prepared to champion big business, its backers included Lord Melchett, ICI's Sir Harry McGowan, Sir Felix Pole of AEI and the spokesman for the metal-bashing industries of the West Midlands, Sir Ernest Petter, who had previously advocated a National Industrial Party. Behind the scenes were figures such as Conservative MP Arthur Steel-Maitland, a life-long social imperialist. The NCIC claimed people were 'tired of the ... slavish adherence to economic theories which have lost all relation to the facts of modern business life'. Industry was 'going to the wall and normally peaceable, patriotic workmen were being driven to Bolshevism'. Government needed to be run on business lines, freed from 'the fog of party politics'. Morris said British workmen were 'screaming for a leader'.

Morris had successfully fought to retain the McKenna Duties, which imposed a tariff on motor imports, particularly against cheap US cars. Ill health prevented him running as a pro-protectionist MP but he used strong-arm squads from his workforce in rumbustious election campaigns. Morris was an enthusiast for the monetary theories of Arthur Kitson and subscribed to the diehard and anti-Semitic *Patriot*. He was a power in the land and saw himself as 'the Englishman's Ford', presenting the masses with a 'technological key to a new society'. Pro-rearmament, he manufactured aero engines because he feared economic weakness 'might be matched by a military weakness too'. By 1930 Morris believed the industrial system was collapsing and sought a benevolent dictatorship.

It is easy to see why Morris found Mosley's ideas attractive. Taking advantage of Imperial Preference, almost 90 per cent of car exports went to the Empire. The NCIC wanted to protect the home market and to advance the cause of inter-Empire trade. It hoped to push the Tories into adopting pro-tariff and imperial policies, and to persuade the public of the merits of protection and capital's case against Labour. Morris's link to Mosley was through Wyndham Portal, Chairman of Portal's, manufacturers of paper for the Bank of England.

On 25 September Mosley discussed with Bruce Lockhart 'the growth of feeling against Parliamentary government'. He was not in favour of Fascist methods. 'General opinion was that so far feeling is against the politicians, but not against Parliamentary traditions.' Beaverbrook was seen in the company of Mosley, Lloyd George and Morris, but despite his hostility to Baldwin, he had not given up hope of rejoining a reformed Tory Party. Exceptions were NCIC members 'whose disgust with the Conservative leaders was such that they no longer trusted in Tory support'. These manoeuvrings were frowned upon by Tory loyalist Sir Cuthbert Headlam, who considered Mosley an 'unpleasing type' who was willing 'to ally himself with any party or body of persons which would accept him as its leader. The eternal "ego" is the only thing that interests him.' What the politics of a Mosley party 'might be is quite immaterial so long as he is its big noise. He is no more a socialist than I am. He is in fact and always an "Oswald Mosleyite".'

In early October, fearing the country was on the edge of an abyss, Morris's circle called for the formation of a coalition government supporting an import tariff. The King sent the PM a message urging him to heed the warnings. MacDonald arranged through the King's friend Lord Mottistone a private dinner with Lloyd George and Churchill to discuss the possibility of a national government. No records were kept but 'all those present were dissatisfied with the existing party system and hankering after a new right-wing social democratic coalition'. MacDonald talked of his readiness to form such a coalition and was 'doing everything possible to telegraph his availability for a National Government to other party leaders'.

A Mosley ally in Birmingham, Jim Simmons, had complained in the *Town Crier* of Westminster's 'futile hopes and bitter disappointments; and the insurmountable barriers that burden progress'. The hopelessness was 'embittering our souls', and those 'crushed by the machine' were meeting in the corridors. Ernest Bevin's report on trade policy, which closely followed Mosley's own proposals, was accepted at the September TUC conference. However, his personal distrust of his colleague ensured that when it came to the party's Annual Conference in October at Llandudno, Mosley would not receive his, nor trade union, support. Mosley was not surprised, as he noted on a speaking tour a distancing between the unions and constituency parties. He would have to rely on the support of the grass roots for whom he shone as 'a beacon of hope'.

In the weeks leading up to Llandudno, several thousand copies of Mosley's memorandum were dispatched to local parties with requests for delegates' support. Mosley, however, had lost ground in his own territorial power base. It was Doncaster not Birmingham which moved his resolution at Conference. By going over the head of the government, he had 'thwarted any possible return to it in its present form'. Conference opened the day after the loss of the airship R.101, which had crashed near Beauvais. Among the forty-eight killed was Lord Thomson, Secretary of State for Air and the PM's closest political friend. The disaster was a tragic blow but MacDonald retained his oratorical skills and 'touched the heart' of delegates. On 7 October Doncaster moved that the Mosley memorandum be considered by the National Executive Committee and that it issue a report. George Catlin sat in the gallery with Cimmie, 'all taut with anticipation about Tom's speech'.

Mosley summarized to delegates the difference between his proposals and the government's public works programme costing £122 million. What had not been revealed was that it was spread over five years. As it had been estimated there would be 4,000 new jobs for every £1 million spent, the proposals only provided work for 100,000 men – 'one man in employment for every ten men out of employment since they came to office'. Mosley had grasped, David Marquand notes, 'the central point of the doctrine which Keynes was now beginning to hammer out – that what influences the level of unemployment is the effect of Government spending on demand, not the intrinsic value of the projects on which Government money is spent'.

The government's policy rested on rationalization, which Mosley agreed was necessary but would undoubtedly 'displace more labour than it employed fresh labour' and could not be considered a solution for unemployment. 'Force of words and that confident, arrogant, dominating personality', Catlin observed, 'were given body in argument by citation after citation of effective statistics at the expense of the platform's decisions.' One eyewitness was 'hypnotized by the man, by his audacity, as bang! bang! bang! he thundered directions'. He electrified them with his call for a policy of permanent reconstruction. He renewed his criticism of relying on a revival of exports; he supported the TUC's advocacy of closer ties to the Empire, which was 'the proper basis for developing the "American system" on an American scale'. He argued that 'the principle was to have an organism planning, allocating, regulating trade rather than leaving those great things to the blind forces of world capitalistic competition'. Such a policy was in direct conflict with Snowden's policy, but it was 'vitally necessary to adopt it'.

Mosley said if Labour's proposals were 'rejected then they too could be put before the country. At best, they would have their majority, at the worst they would go down fighting for the things they believe in. They would not die like an old woman in bed; they would die like a man on the field – a better fate, and, in politics, one with a more certain hope of resurrection.' As he ended, Brockway recalled, 'delegates rose en masse, cheering for minutes on end . . . Here was a potential leader, authoritative, courageous and passionate.'

Mosley's resolution was narrowly defeated by 1,251,000 votes to 1,046,000. The constituency parties voted ten to one in his favour but trade union leaders won for the executive. It was rumoured he would have won had not the miners' leader, A. J. Cook, been delayed by a late train. In fact, the miners' executive had decided to oppose the resolution. Constituencies had their revenge by removing Jimmy Thomas from the NEC and electing Mosley with 1,362,000 votes, fourth in the poll behind George Lansbury, Hugh Dalton and George Dallas, but ahead of Herbert Morrison. Initially, Mosley looked to be the victor, but it proved a miscalculation. He overestimated his position and underestimated the leadership's strength. Most politicians would have regarded the vote as a good campaigning base but Mosley did not take that view.

That night, Catlin found Mosley in the Grand Hotel's dining room in discussion with Allan Young. 'Suddenly, Mosley pulled himself up. "This means a dictatorship."' Catlin recalled 'the frisson when my singing ears heard the remark. A dictatorship in Britain?' A Continental journalist observed that the Labour movement might have found in Mosley its Hitler. The *Manchester Guardian* agreed that to compare the 'new Socialist Imperialism, subordinating Parliamentary institutions to its own imperative needs' with National Socialism was not so absurd. A few days later Snowden's PPS wrote to Churchill that he did not 'think this country will really follow Sir Oswald Hitler'.

Mosley remained popular in the constituencies and received rousing receptions to his speeches to the rank and file. He cultivated the Wolverhampton MP W. J. Brown, Secretary of the ILP MPs and founder of the Civil Service Clerical Association. He had a high reputation as a trade union negotiator and was personally charming. He had been on a spiritual journey since his youth, which led him to eastern mysticism. His time in Parliament, however, represented the 'greatest period of disillusionment of my life. I emerged from it disillusioned . . . with the whole political set-up.' Beckett said Brown had intense conviction and his 'fireworks in contact with Mosley's explosives were bound to cause trouble'.

Mosley assembled around him a parliamentary ginger New Labour group. Brown acted as its secretary and contact man with other dissident groupings, including the 'intelligentsia', which criticized the lethargy of trade union MPs who unquestioningly supported the government. He wanted Mosley to leave Labour and start a new movement with the ILP but Mosley resisted because of the incompatibility between his ideas and those of former colleagues. The New Labour inner core was Mosley, Cimmie, Strachey, Brown, Dr Robert Forgan and Aneurin Bevan, who had the ear of Beaverbrook.

Nicknamed the 'armchair revolutionary', former Welsh miner Bevan wrote to Strachey on 17 October that there was 'a tremendous mass of opinion on the OM lines and I am pretty anxious to have a hand in shaping what those lines should be'. Bevan acted as a bridge between Mosley and left-wing unionism, in particular A. J. Cook. Bevan's biographer notes that he had an overwhelming desire 'to do something or anything to tackle the nearly 50 per cent unemployment' among his constituents and only Mosley 'seemed to offer action'. Bevan was attracted to his fighting quality and the fact that he denounced the complacency of the Commons in the sort of apocalyptic terms which impressed Bevan. Mosley thought Bevan 'brilliant but frothy'.

Forgan was a charming but naive son of a Church of Scotland minister. An army medical officer, Vice-President of the Medical Society for the Study of Venereal Diseases and an international authority on sexually transmitted diseases, he became a socialist as a result of his experience in the public health services of Glasgow, where he developed a 'sincere enthusiasm for slum-clearance, better nutrition and preventative medicine'. Forgan was regarded by ILP colleagues as kindly and generous, and full of vitality.

Flirting with Mosley was Oliver Baldwin, wayward son of the Tory leader. He fell out with his family when they suggested he had invented his account of imprisonment by Bolsheviks and Turks during the 1921 Armeno–Russo war. The *Evening Standard* said he had 'absorbed something of the Russia in which he has lived and suffered', and had an arty appearance 'reminiscent of the William Morris–Rossetti days'. He displayed the 'classic symptoms of a demoralized and emotionally shattered youth', and it was only when he committed himself to Labour that his life regained a sense of purpose.

ILP journalist John Scanlon reported that talk centred on how long it would be before Mosley became party leader. Labour's old men could not stay in power long and 'even Socialists, who had no particular love for Sir Oswald, were saying nothing could stop it. The prophets, however, had overlooked the one man who could stop it – Sir Oswald himself.' If he had had a little humility, Jennie Lee wrote, 'many of us on the left could have come together and, in time, offered effective alternative leadership'. He had, however, 'an unshakeable conviction that he was born to rule'. She wrote to Frank Wise, 'The Mosley–Bevan group is young, vigorous, unscrupulous. They are to be reckoned with but I simply cannot conceive of myself working with them. There is something fundamentally unsound mentally and spiritually.'

A certain bitterness had entered Mosley. When MPs rejected his proposals and he angered them by saying that he would appeal to the wider movement, Brockway believed the 'dangers of his personality were becoming apparent' and his isolation within the party led him 'to take his first step to separate himself from it'. Mosley thought the moment had arrived to revive ideas of a centre party. However, it was not clear to what extent his collaborators would be committed. He knew that, privately, Ernest Bevin was critical of Snowden's negative attitude and MacDonald's vagueness, and it was on the basis of such feelings that he approached Arthur Henderson and 'urged him to lead a revolt against MacDonald in order to seize the prime ministership for himself'. Henderson despised MacDonald but recognized he was indispensable as national leader. He distrusted Mosley, as did Bevin, who would not compromise the unity of the party.

Fifty backbenchers attended Mosley's weekly meetings but he discovered that 'listening was one thing, and acting, quite another'. He cut a solitary figure on the NEC, supported only by Fred Jowett and C. P. Trevelyan. His efforts to rally MPs behind imperial insulation were rebuffed. Dalton, who regarded such ideas as 'pitiable', wrote derisively on 23 October that Mosley was 'much with Keynes at present but could only take in the cruder arguments'. Keynes's Economic Advisory Committee recommended changes to benefits, public works schemes and a temporary 10 per cent tariff on imports, but Snowden ensured the report was buried. He gave way to Transport Minister Morrison on the need to finance modest public works schemes but demanded cuts in benefits to balance the budget.

By October 1930, after fifteen months in power, unemployment stood at 2,319,000. On the 28th the King's speech set out Labour's programme, including raising of the school-leaving age and a Royal Commission on unemployment insurance. It was savagely attacked from all sides for its timidity. Mosley had come to the conclusion 'that in a real crisis Labour would always betray both its principles and the people who had trusted it'. He likened the government to a 'Salvation Army Band which turns out with banners flying for Judgement Day but when the first rumble of the approaching cataclysm is heard, turns in disarray and flees'.

The air was full of initiatives for coalitions and demands for a government of businessmen. These were encouraged by the *Observer* and *Week-End Review* (*WER*), which exposed the old gang's 'ineffectual ways of running the country'. The *WER* had been launched earlier in the year by staff of Beaverbrook's *Saturday Review*, following their resignation in protest against his Empire Free Trade Crusade. Through editor Gerald Barry, an RFC pilot and pacifist, and leader writer Max Nicholson, the *WER* established itself as a dissident Tory journal seeking 'leadership, industrial leadership, moral leadership'. They found it in Mosley.

Mosley's discussions with young Tories were led by Oliver Stanley, with contributions from Macmillan. Boothby was a regular with his friend W. E. D. 'Bill' Allen, Ulster MP for West Belfast and Chairman of David Allen & Sons, printers and advertisers in Northern Ireland. Allen believed in the need for action and decided Mosley was the man to provide it. Philosopher and adventurer, he was widely travelled, with a romantic political outlook. He had been a special correspondent for the *Morning Post* in the Balkan and Riff wars, and was fluent in Russian and Turkish. He visited Soviet Georgia in 1926 and produced histories of Georgia, Ukraine and the Caucasus, as well as papers on mountain warfare. 'Immaculate in appearance and unruffled manner', Allen had the 'qualities and some of the defects of the gentleman scholar'. He could afford, *The Times* noted, 'to indulge in hypotheses and idiosyncrasies which would make a professor's hair stand on end'. Allen has wrongly been profiled as an MI5 agent (possibly mischief making on Mosley's part), whereas his background is typical of an MI6 or Military Intelligence agent.

Allen was deeply affected by the death in 1927 of his elder brother Drennan, and beholden to his mother Cissy, who funded his excursion into politics. He inherited her 'adventurous cast of mind but lacked her tenacity'. John Beckett said he represented 'the spirit of modern chivalry'. In Parliament, he was the spokesman for a group of young Tories who 'took "noblesse oblige" in a practical form, and to whom patriotism and imperialism meant care for the British and Imperial peoples, rather than a careful network of financial intrigue cloaked by wild waving of the Union Jack'. The Allens had a Tudor-style mansion at Commonwood, Chipperfield, where they brought their guests, including Mosley. Close to Jennie Lee, his marriage to Lady Phyllis King, daughter of the Earl of Lovelace, was not a success and he later became intimate with Paula Casa Maury, Mosley's mistress.

Allen was among the disgruntled Tories who met on 26 October at Cliveden with Boothby, Macmillan, Elliott, William Ormsby-Gore, Brendan Bracken and Terence O'Connor. They differed little from Mosley on policy and could count on the support of half a dozen Liberals and twenty Mosleyites.

Agreement was reached between the young Tories and Mosley's supporters to make converging speeches in debates. On 29 October he claimed sweated labour, cartels and commodity price falls required an insulated Empire, behind a 'wall of modern design, of varying type and size of brick and of device'. Its size would 'give us power to exact concessions from foreign countries'. He agreed decision making would be complex but 'every modern process is complicated'. He appealed for a cross-party coalition 'to lift this great national emergency far above the turmoil of party clamour'. Strachey admitted this ran counter to Labour principles but 'in a world such as it is today we must face the fact that something of the sort is necessary'. He was aware they were arguing for National Socialism. Oliver Stanley accepted 'nationalization' of the Empire. There followed the spectacle of W. J. Brown expressing his admiration for Stanley and, in turn, receiving praise from John Buchan, who called for 'an emergency Government to deal with an emergency situation'.

Distrust of Baldwin led rebels to flirt with figures such as Beaverbrook, to whom they were not normally attracted. Mosley acted as their representative at dinners given by Lloyd George, the moving spirit in the group of 'brilliant old men', or by Rothermere, who loathed weak leadership, which was an 'unhealthy inclination in the decade of dictatorship'. Rothermere proposed Mosley for membership of the influential Other Club, founded by Churchill and Lord Birkenhead as a political dining club. Support in the constituencies for protectionism alarmed the leadership, which feared losing seats to the

United Empire Party. On 30 October its candidate at the South Paddington by-election romped home to victory.

'Prospects for the break-up of old party alliances seemed good,' said the *Observer*. 'No one remembers a time when discontents were so rife in all parties together and when movements were so kaleidoscopic.' On 3 November Harold Nicolson, now working on the *Evening Standard*'s 'Londoner's Diary', met *Mail* Chairman Esmond Harmsworth and Beaverbrook, who said Mosley would form a new party. Next day Nicolson saw an uncertain Mosley: 'If he strikes now he may be premature. If he delays he may be too late.' He said if he had '£250,000 [£8.5 m] and a press I should sweep the country'. Nicolson begged him to wait as he should not trust Beaverbrook.

The air was thick with talk of political realignment. On 19 November Morris's Council of industrialists called on politicians to discard party politics as it was 'long past when parties can or should be considered at all'. In a letter to *The Times*, Bill Allen said the conflict between the old men and the young was the 'only reality for each political party. We have no respect for grey hairs, grey theories, methods and conditions.' The *Observer* hinted at a Lloyd George–Mosley tie-up. Churchill was said to be working hand-in-glove with Lloyd George on a national coalition.

With Birkenhead's death in September, Churchill led diehard opposition to Indian reform. He opposed the Round Table Conference call for an all-India federation and a measure of self-government. He criticized Baldwin's failure to mount a sustained attack on the government's relaxation of British authority in Egypt and its recall of the imperialist-minded High Commissioner Lord Lloyd. Rothermere promised Churchill support for a crusade as India assumed 'cardinal importance in Conservative politics'. However, young Tories suspected Churchill of intrigue in his ambition to reach the top and considered his India diehardism wholly outdated.

The emphasis on a national solution above party was attacked in the Commons by Frank Owen, who accused Mosley of preaching the 'crudity of economic nationalism' and unleashing the 'jingo imperialism' of Joseph Chamberlain. Strachey and Bevan were prepared to swallow this 'as a business arrangement in a world that seemed to offer few immediate alternatives'. They did not criticize when, on 14 November, Mosley addressed a group of advertising men and hinted at parallels between his demand for action and the Continental movements, though he assured them that they would 'never see in England people walking about in black shirts'.

When, on 20 November, his group was criticized at a party meeting for failing to adhere to party discipline, Mosley retorted that 'if there is to be a scrap it shall be a scrap to the finish'. To jeers, he hastened to add, 'but it will not be fought out here but at the Labour Party conference'. There was ironic laughter, for the next conference was a year off. Attlee moaned to Dalton,

'Why does Mosley always speak to us as though he were a feudal landlord abusing tenants who are in arrears with their rent?' To the leadership's annoyance, he supported an ILPer standing at a by-election in opposition to the government's unemployment policy.

On 30 November Nicolson was at Cliveden with Lord Lothian, J. L. Garvin and the Young Tories discussing Parliament's future. They concluded the country was about to enter an economic crisis, which had to be dealt with 'on undemocratic lines'. Later he learnt that Mosley was going to launch his manifesto, thereby 'practically creating the National party'. Mosley hoped Morris would finance him and expected the Young Tories to join, with Beaverbrook's backing.

Baldwin was annoyed by the Young Tories' support for Mosley. Party Chairman J. C. C. Davidson was informed that Macmillan would probably join Mosley. However, as Boothby had predicted, their revolt was ineffective as they lacked coherence. They included the diehard Edward Marjoribanks; the maverick Macmillan; the moderate Victor Cazalet; and Churchill's supporter on India, Brendan Bracken. There were few common links except youth. Chances of forging an alliance were unrealistic. Bill Allen believed they were 'held back by a combination of personal mistrust of Mosley and pragmatic conformity to the established structure. Breaking away from the Conservative Party was not so attractive in reality as it had been to talk about.'

Mosley admitted his tendency was 'to drive things too hard'. When he tried to fix a date for action, the Young Tories' impotence was revealed. Elliott was lambasted by Baldwin, who condemned those who had strayed 'on strange trails', for supporting Mosley and made his peace. Pressure was put on the rest and the conspiring evaporated 'in the cold world of political realities'. The ideological differences between them and the Mosleyites turned out to be acute and could not be bridged. They could not contemplate the nationalization of the banks and a dominant role for the State.

By December 1930 there were 2,500,000 out of work. Mosley was convinced that 'in crisis Labour would always crack. I simply thought the leadership had built a party with a structure, character and psychology which was inadequate to great events.' The coming crisis would 'at last give the frustrated war-generation its chance to make its own independent impact on politics. The "modern mind" would take over.'

The first step was the 'Mosley Manifesto' – 'an immediate plan to meet an emergency situation'. The draft was purged of Mosley's rhetoric and the imperialist theme, and slanted leftwards by Strachey, Bevan and Brown. Their 'National Policy' began with a warning that the immediate question was 'not a question of the ownership but the survival of British industry'. Familiar proposals included high wages, targeted tariffs, planning, an emergency Cabinet, Import and Commodity Boards, imperial self-sufficiency and slum clearance. The State would constitute a public utility organization, turning out 'houses and building materials as we turned out munitions during the war'. Budget surpluses would subsidize prime necessities and the taxes of skilled, technical and managerial workers would be reduced. A Cabinet of five Ministers would legislate through orders in Council, with Parliament stripped of its privilege to block executive action. Parliament would become a business assembly to implement the 'national will'. It was a major assault on parliamentary democracy.

The signatories claimed they had lost none of their socialist faith, but action was needed: 'afterwards political debate on fundamental principle can be resumed'. Critics doubted whether spending £200 million over three years to employ 100,000 men annually could have had significant effect, but no one else 'was advancing plans to put 300,000 men to work'.

On 4 December draft copies were hawked around the Commons. Fenner Brockway was listed sixth in order of anticipated willingness to sign up (the first five – Cimmie, Strachey, Brown, Forgan and John McGovern – signed) but refused, as did Will Lawther and James Maxton, even though Brown had worked to modify the content to suit their concerns. The manifesto's denial of socialism's immediate relevance alienated ILPers, who thought it was 'orientated in such a way as to make it a buttress for the stabilisation of Capitalism'. Cole refused, as he viewed it as a 'conspiracy against the Government'.

Seventeen MPs signed; most were young and had entered Parliament in 1929, with half from the West Midlands. Mosley claimed others had offered to sign, but 'only wholehearted supporters were encouraged to do so'. The small number of signatories from Birmingham indicated Mosley's declining influence, though support came from mining constituencies in Wales, the North and Scotland, and the Miners' Federation's Arthur Cook did sign. Contemporaries believed his deteriorating physical state – he had had a leg amputated – contributed to a 'mental and moral collapse'.

The Mosley manifesto was printed in the *Observer* on 7 December, with edited versions ('A National Policy for National Emergency') in the *Telegraph* and *The Times*. Garvin saw merit in its 'unflinching recognition that without a national awakening to the necessity for "peace-energy on a war-scale" the Empire cannot be maintained and Britain's traditional greatness in the world cannot endure'. Mosley was the 'only leader of his generation who has the courage to strike out a new path, even though it may lead him temporarily into the wilderness'. There was no consensus among reviewers. The problem was its 'wonderful eclecticism' with something in it 'to attract every floating straw of current opinion'.

The manifesto was published on 12 December as a pamphlet to rally support, but it was not a success. Maxton condemned ILPers (Brown, Forgan, McGovern, Philips Price and Simmons) for supporting 'imperialist and autocratic' policies. In turn, Mosley accused Maxton of using the parrot cry of dictatorship as an excuse to prevent anything being achieved. 'If, in England, it is impossible to get things done, then England is done.' His argument was not helped by Harold Nicolson, who agreed in a BBC broadcast that in the coming crisis Parliament might have to be replaced by a junta of experts.

Cole distanced himself from Mosley and set up a New Fabian Group to rally the young with 'some decent Socialist literature instead of Mosley amateur clap-trap', though he believed the Mosleyites 'might be useful in a wider movement of a less melodramatic sort'. Herbert Morrison, who had not read the manifesto, described Mosley as having 'true-blue Tory blood in his veins'. He had been 'reared in upper class society and had become accustomed to giving orders purely because of their personal wealth or social position'. Dalton dismissed the manifesto with the quip that it would lead to 'Five Dictators and a Tariff', which was the view of the cartoonists, who compared Mosley with Mussolini. 'Would all the five chosen rulers be efficient and righteous men?' asked the *Spectator*. 'Would four be? Would there be three? Would two be? If not, there would only be one left?'

The only analysis came from Keynes, who liked its spirit. He said the central debate was between planning and laissez-faire. There were three views: firstly, Snowden's trust in natural forces; secondly, the hastening of natural forces and reducing wages; and thirdly, the manifesto's collective planning. Keynes was aware that the third option would shock those 'with laissez-faire in their craniums' but 'how anyone professing and calling themselves a socialist can keep away from the manifesto is a more obscure matter'. He said that in a previous generation, Lloyd George and MacDonald 'would be where Mosley is. Let them not, then, look too schoolmasterlike on his ebullience . . . We should be grateful to Sir Oswald Mosley for an effort to clear the air.'

The Young Tories fired off letters to *The Times*, praising the tariff and Empire policies. Macmillan assumed that those who did not support it, cared 'more about party machinery and the survival of the old party conflicts than about national unity and national effort'. They published their own manifesto on 17 December, acknowledging that 'representative government may be inconsistent with efficiency'. However, the tone was conservative with calls for spending cuts, reform of national insurance and reduced wages. Hopes of an alliance were dashed on the rocks of ideological divisions on planning. Whereas socialists viewed Mosley's national planning as an attempt to make capitalist society stable, sympathizers saw it as a 'dangerous challenge to that society'. The *Week-End Review* voiced Young Tory objections that his planned economy could only be enforced by 'something near dictatorship'.

It has been assumed that there was a consensus among planners – as pragmatic thinkers with a non-partisan technocratic faith in the application of the scientific method – which transcended party politics. Daniel Ritschell, however, rightly claims the variety of planning approaches has been glossed over. Planners who professed approaches rejected by Keynes have been converted into 'unsuspecting Keynesians'. Skidelsky attempted to rehabilitate Mosley's ideas by reinterpreting them in terms of their alleged Keynesian roots. He later stressed 'the distinction between the approaches of Keynesian demand management and physical planning' but the point is, Keynes was not a planner. There were distinct differences between his expansionism, Liberal mixed-economy, Labour gradualism, Tory industrial corporatism, State socialism and Mosley's proto-Fascist corporatism. Mosley placed planning on the national agenda and introduced it into the vocabulary of British politics in the 1930s, but he failed to make 'a deep impression on the general public or the Labour electorate'. This revealed 'the difficulties inherent in any attempt to secure a consensus around the idea of planning'.

The National Council of Industry and Commerce supported the manifesto and in a letter in *The Times*, Sir Felix Pole, Wyndham Portal and William Morris described it as 'a ray of hope'. It was the 'forceful gesture of a young and virile section of the Labour Party, providing concrete evidence of the possibility of the formation of a vigorous Industrial Party'. They visualized 'a homogeneous alloy of young men of clear vision and unclouded ideas, men of modern metal, who, rid of the baseness of old party policies and led by a mature brain, will combine to form a new element that will lead this country to security and then prosperity'.

Suspicions of Mosley were 'too long standing to be overcome by the secretive lobbying of known adherents'. He had set out his stall too early and, in December 1930, there were few takers. Repeatedly, his sense of timing was out: it had been over his resignation; it was over his manifesto. A shrewder politician, suggests W. F. Mandle, would have waited, 'for there were signs of change – to be followed, however, not anticipated'. The logic of his national planning did not yet coincide with contemporary politics and he found himself isolated. Fascism was to be his 'last Quixotic challenge to a political world that had rejected him and his ideas long before he came to reject this world himself'.

Boothby was horrified to learn Mosley was thinking of forming his own party. He sent an urgent letter warning it was not practical politics. The Young Tories 'won't play, and it's no use deluding yourself that they will. Even on the assumption that Macmillan decided to play, how many votes can he swing? Not two.' There was a possibility of Lloyd George but he was regarded as 'a shit'. Mosley could 'sway more votes than any other contemporary politician' but Boothby doubted he could recruit MPs: the mugwumps will be 'solidly arraigned against you . . . and the intelligentsia venomously hostile'.

There might be press support but Rothermere was 'beyond the pale. In any decently organised community his papers would be suppressed and he would be executed.' And Beaverbrook was 'in the impregnable position of being able to double-cross and let down the side at a moment's notice, without loss of power or even prestige'. How would people react to a 'Beaverbrook–Mosley–Rothermere–Lloyd–Macmillan–Stanley–Boothby combination'? They might say, 'By God now all the shits have climbed into the same basket.' Mosley had underestimated the power of the political machines. The 'shrewdest electioneer in the country', Dr Hunter, was convinced 'two only – right and left, will wield political power in this country in the years that lie ahead'. The only thing to do was to 'try and collar one or other of the machines, and not ruin yourself by beating against them with a tool which will almost certainly break in your hand'.

Perceptively, Boothby added that if there was an 'economic crisis this winter, there may be a widespread demand for a national Government, new men and new measures'. Then the situation would be 'fundamentally changed, and a game of a kind we cannot yet envisage may yet open out'. Mosley could 'do more for us than anyone else now alive. Only for God's sake remember that this country is old and tradition-ridden, and no one – not even you – can break all the rules at once. And do take care of the company you keep. Real shits are so apt to trip you up when you aren't looking.' Inevitably, it was prescient advice that Mosley chose to ignore.

Since Mosley's manifesto did not include food taxes, which were a non-negotiable part of his own policy, Beaverbrook would not, he told fund-raiser Philip Cunliffe-Owen on 6 January 1931, provide 'any cash contribution to Mosley's fund'. Mosley told the *Herald* that a 'Beaverbrook–Mosley Combination was all bunkum'. Soon support from the Young Tories drained away. The *Express* said the 'disquieting thing about the younger men' was that they had 'none of the boldness of youth'. When, on 27 January, Churchill resigned from the shadow cabinet over Baldwin's India policy, commentators thought there was an opportunity for Mosley. Churchill, however, had decided he had no intention of joining his 'Suicide Club'.

Mosley had not quite finished with Labour. Bevan and Brown asked MPs to convene a conference to debate unemployment. In committee room 14 Mosley delivered, according to MacDonald's biographer L. MacNeill Weir, 'one of the most effective and impressive speeches ever heard'. He appealed for action and the 'applause indicated to the leaders ranged along the platform that here was a man to be reckoned with'. MacDonald should have replied but, instead of 'facing up to Mosley as Greek would meet Greek', the PM – dismissed on the previous day by Churchill as the 'boneless wonder' – sheltered behind Henderson, who opposed the motion.

Henderson asked Mosley to withdraw his motion but he refused and, in doing so, again blundered. His oratorical triumph secured much sympathy; so much so that he appeared as a possible leader but, characteristically, he wanted an instant result. 'Like a revivalist, he was out for sudden conversions'

– but the vote, noted Weir, put members in a dilemma. 'As the Government was being indicted, every Member of the Government became an accused person, and to have supported Mosley's motion would have been self-condemnatory. Again, Members would naturally be reluctant to vote for this new-comer and against the well-tried leaders of the Party, especially when the said leaders were lined along the platform, keenly watching every hand that went up.'

Mosley was defeated by ninety-seven to thirteen. At dinner, Nicolson noted that democracy for Mosley was 'dead – and so it is for me. The people must be treated humanely but firmly.' The desire to enact his proposals obsessed Mosley and he now campaigned 'for a transformation of political life, this being the only way he could see his policies being carried out'. 'Action' dominated Mosley's article 'A New National Policy' for the *Week-End Review*. 'We create a new philosophy, the broad principles of which, like all dynamic forces, must be kept flexible and adaptable to the realities of whatever situation it confronts.' His National Economic Planning Organization, co-ordinating economic activities, implied a State-run economy and was far removed from any Keynesian notion of 'managed capitalism' and temporary State intervention.

Keynes was committed to finding a 'third way' alternative to Marxism and laissez-faire (and Fascism). He was a liberal, a believer in individual liberty, the rule of law and limited government. Mosley wanted sweeping regulation, with control over investment and production, prices and wages. In a crucial shift, he put 'national' in front of planning, and stressed his proposals' non-socialist nature. Talks continued with the Young Tories but their model of industrial self-government was designed to provide private enterprise with the 'chance of self-government, as an alternative to the dead hand of the Socialist or the Fascist State'.

H. Hamilton Fyfe in the *Queen's Quarterly* believed Mosley would 'play a prominent part in British politics, whether he becomes a Dictator (not on the Mussolini model) or gives back to the British people their faith in democracy as a working system. Now there is no more interesting figure in public life.' Bevan and Brown were alarmed when *Labour Monthly* labelled Mosley the 'advanced guard of fascism' with his call for a 'new psychology' and a 'renascent and resurgent Britain'. Boothby shared their feeling when he discovered Mosley was attempting through the NCIC's Colonel Portal to raise funds in the City to launch a party. He wrote to him on 30 January that this was madness. 'You have persistently disregarded every piece of advice or suggestion that I have ever ventured to offer. And so, my dear Tom, I cannot feel that you have greatly missed the benefit of a judgement which you obviously do not value highly!'

Mosley met with William Morris, a 'genuine and ardent patriot' but one 'less well versed in the technique of politics, a business genius who seemed rather lost outside his own sphere'. Mosley found the conversation tedious because he had come to talk money but 'that point never seemed to be reached'. However, at the end of lunch Morris handed him a cheque for £50,000 (£1.7 m). He had been 'studying me for some time – the object of the seemingly pointless conversations were now clear – and had developed full confidence in me and had decided to back me'. Morris liked risk takers and promised further support if Mosley looked like getting anywhere.

Speaking at Rochester on 2 February, Mosley confirmed he was 'in a hurry because we believe that if the present situation is allowed to drift on, a catastrophe will overwhelm the country'. He had concluded the national position was so grave that 'drastic and disagreeable measures will have to be taken'. Two days later Cimmie confirmed to Nicolson that her husband was about to launch a new party. He would do so in the midst of a world slump, which appeared to be opportune timing.

10

The New Party

The world slump at the beginning of the thirties was the most severe in history though Britain suffered less than some countries. There had been a world industrial boom during 1925–9 but not in Britain, which only managed moderate growth. After 1929 there was no financial collapse as suffered by Germany, but Britain still experienced a slump. Mosley was proved right in that the world depression ended hopes for an export-led recovery.

Against this background, Snowden rose in the Commons on 11 February 1931 to warn that 'some temporary sacrifice' was necessary 'in order to make future progress possible'. W. J. Brown said the speech represented the 'surrender of the whole philosophy of the Labour movement to the bidding of the financial interests of this country'. For his attack, he was expelled from the trade union group of MPs. 'The orthodox members of the Party were blind and deaf,' Jennie Lee recalled, 'but far from dumb in repeating the doctrines of the leaders. Their chief sport, then as always, was persecuting anyone who tried to tell them that the Emperor was stark naked.' Mosley enlivened the debate with his claim that putting 'the nation in bed on a starvation diet are the suggestions of an old woman in a fright'.

Brown half jokingly suggested to Mosley they set up a new party. On 13 February the pair lunched with Bruce Lockhart and talked about breaking across party lines, but admitted the 'young man's movement' could only come via Labour since the Conservatives were 'dead'.

On the following day Mosley suggested to H. G. Wells that 'the only chance of successful progress in this country is in co-operation with the more intelligent of the big business people'. Wells had recently published *The Autocracy of Mr Pelham*, which charted the rise of a Fascist leader of the 'Duty Paramount League'. He treated Mosley (Sir Osbert Moses) as a positive character, who pleads 'in vain with a sheepish crowd of government supporters for some collective act of protest' against the forced dissolution of Parliament. 'Moses' was half-Jewish and this was a common misconception even among those close to the Mosleys. Mosley noted that Wells detested 'anyone who physically was an entirely different type to himself'. The other literary figure admired by Mosley, George Bernard Shaw, urged him to break with Labour and start a new movement – 'The Activists'. Shaw, however, soon changed his mind and insisted he remain in the party, on the grounds that he was 'bound to succeed MacDonald'.

On the weekend of 15 February, at Savehay, the Mosleys were joined by Nicolson, Stanley, Macmillan and other MPs to create his New Party. The *Observer* reported Mosley would 'start a platform campaign, which will be opened in nearly all the big towns early in March'. Fifteen Labour MPs were expected to join. Cimmie found it difficult to follow her husband's 'repudiation of all the things he has taught her to say previously'. Nicolson said she was not made for politics but for 'society and the home'. Mosley wanted Nicolson to head the party's publicity committee, which was being advised by *Week-End Review* editor Gerald Barry. Cyril Joad attended the preparatory meetings where the atmosphere was an uneasy truce between 'a Socialism which is vestigial and a fascism which is incipient'. For the moment socialism had the upper hand.

It was rumoured that six Labour MPs were about to join Mosley, who hoped Aneurin Bevan would resign. Opponents thought Bevan suffered from a Mosley complex in that he only played the game on his own terms and, if thwarted, would break up things. Although he believed in the proposals, he told Jennie Lee 'it's the Labour Party or nothing. I know all its faults but it is the Party we have taught millions of working people to look to and regard as their own. We can't undo what we have done.' Allan Young said Bevan refused to join because he had an old mother and was 'dependent on his miners' trade union subsidy'. Bevan, however, wanted to know 'Where is the money coming from? Who is going to pay? Who is going to call the tune?' He warned it would 'end up as a Fascist party'.

Bevan tried to prevent Strachey's resignation, as did Amabel Williams-Ellis. She was fascinated by Mosley. He had the right views, was handsome but when he made sexual advances he 'had to be resisted'. She begged her brother not to resign because 'a cure should be attempted from within' but Strachey felt 'something very definite had to be done and quickly'. Amabel warned this meant Fascism. He 'swore that at the least sign of that, he would leave'. On 23 February Forgan and Strachey resigned, claiming there was 'a prospect of social breakdown and it had to be arrested'. Allan Young wrote to Cimmie that Mosley 'displayed all the qualities of intellectual courage and ability, combined with the caution great actions demand'. Caution was not usually considered a Mosley characteristic but at crucial moments he could hesitate.

Beatrice Webb regarded Mosley's defection an 'amazing act of arrogance . . . slamming the door with a bang to resound throughout the political world'. His one chance was to become 'the He-man of the newspaper lords' but his egotism would clash with Beaverbrook's and they would part company. He had already been nicknamed the 'English Hitler' but she believed the British would not elect a Hitler. He lacked fanaticism and deep down was a cynic who would be 'beaten and retire'.

Written by Strachey, Young, Brown and Bevan, the New Party's 'National Policy' was published on 24 February by Macmillan (run by Harold's elder brother). Planning, self-sufficiency, imperial preference and developing the home market were its main features. Protection was seen as the answer to the problems of newer industries such as electrical goods and aircraft. While 'every effort should be made to develop the Empire, there was no reason why trade should not be encouraged with other countries, for example, Russia'. Noticeably absent was Mosley, who was uninterested in the details since he would discard aspects with which he disagreed.

The NP programme had links to social imperialism, though Mosley went further in wanting a mass movement outside the party system and in advocating State direction of the economy. He explicitly identified the City as the chief obstacle to success, but shared the social imperialists' strategic and geopolitical views. Its economic nationalism was akin to Fascist notions of autarchy. Mosley wanted to put the solution of unemployment on 'an emergency war footing, abrogating normal, peace-time rights, riding roughshod over normal peace-time susceptibilities'. With its themes of nationalism, class harmony, leadership and anti-parliamentarianism, it was only a small step to Fascism. This new activist style of politics was recognized by the *Spectator* as a form of Fascism.

Beatrice Webb thought the 'National Policy' fell 'dead in the no-man's-land between those who wish to keep and those who wish to change the existing order'. The NP was just 'another bubble on the surface of political life'. The launch was eclipsed by the withdrawal of the official Conservative candidate, Ivan Moore-Brabazon, from the St George's Westminster by-election because he opposed Baldwin. The fielding of an Empire Crusade candidate, Sir Ernest Petter, in this safest Conservative seat in the country demoralized party leaders and Mosley hoped to take advantage, confident he would sweep the country. Things soon went wrong, however.

On 25 February Mosley went down with influenza. Three days later he staggered to his office, 'appealed for voluntary workers and funds, promised to run 400 candidates at the next election and then went to bed'. He told Nicolson this was 'the first serious collapse of my life, and what a moment!' In the end, only nine MPs defected to the New Party and, even then, most were temporary recruits. Mosley had expected more but they had 'melted like snow upon the desert's dusty face, for the good reason that the sun was still shining'.

Oliver Baldwin resigned on 26 February and styled himself as an Independent, but agreed to appear on NP platforms. Spoilt, unstable and homosexual, the son of the Conservative leader had not spoken to his father for nearly a decade. J. Lovat-Frazer and Frank Markham joined, but George Catlin distrusted the anti-American tone, though he helped Mosley's secretary, George Sutton, and Cecil Melville as 'fact-gatherers'. Bevan dissuaded some ILPers from joining, but many ILP branches tolerated dual membership. George Strauss erased his NP past and John McGovern fleetingly joined but was persuaded to withdraw by Brockway. Other ILP recruits included John Scanlon, Parliamentary Secretary to Sir Patrick Hastings, Leslie Cumings, a prominent London official, Bill Risdon, an organizer in the Midlands. Rebellious young left-wingers Iain Mikardo and Wogan Phillips, husband of novelist Rosamond Lehmann, also jumped. Mikardo soon detected an 'authoritarian attitude at odds with the mores of the Party' but it did not deflect him from supporting its 'socialist programme'.

In the *Observer* on 1 March, Mosley called for a 'mobilisation of energy, vitality and manhood to save and rebuild the nation'. Comparisons made between the NP and Hitler's movement alarmed Brown, who had second thoughts about joining a quasi-Fascist import given that the NP had been planned as a 'breakaway movement to the Left – not the Right'. He was leaned on by his union and, in order to stiffen his resolve, Mosley went by ambulance to see Brown. Carried into his living room on a stretcher, he told Brown he had obtained 'a guarantee from William Morris to cover his salary for several years'. Brown resigned on 4 March but still declined to join, fearing he would lose his union post. Mosley developed pleurisy and pneumonia, a serious matter before the discovery of antibiotics, and was laid up in bed. It was a stumbling start for a movement of energy and youth. Beaverbrook said Mosley had done 'a foolish thing' and should have stayed inside Labour and 'bombarded it from within'.

On 3 March Cimmie resigned, as did Sir Charles Trevelyan, but he emphasized he had 'not the slightest sympathy with the action of men like Mosley. Officers who command the battalions can retire, but they must not rebel.' His criticism of Baldwin was heard in silence and he received no cheers. The mood had changed. 'Like shipwrecked passengers in an open boat', David Marquand notes, Labour MPs 'assumed instinctively that their only hope of survival was to huddle together against the storm: when a few hardy souls jumped overboard, the rest clung to each other even more tightly than before'.

Although Young Tories and Liberals promised to work on the NP's behalf, only the Empire Crusader Bill Allen took the plunge. When Nicolson informed Beaverbrook he was joining Mosley, his boss expressed 'deep sympathy with me in my obstinacy and wrong-headedness'. A meeting was held on 5 March in Southampton Row; posters said the speakers would be Mosley, Cimmie, Allen, Strachey, Brown and Bevan. Mosley was ill and Bevan backed out after the Miners' Federation withdrew their sponsorship. Cimmie was 'undaunted by two ghastly hecklers, a communist and a drunken Labourite'. According to Irene, 'she dealt with them and the crowd finally got livid with them and wanted them evicted'. They were removed by stewards who were denounced as 'Fascist thugs'. Only the *Telegraph* reported the event. The press, wrote Nicolson, was 'determined to boycott anyone who tries to be independent of them'.

Strachey realized the enormity of what he had done, aware of the jibe it was a Fascist party. 'Maybe we have committed political suicide.' Young took charge of organization in its Great George Street headquarters, a Welsh Liberal and accountant, Sellick Davies, acted as treasurer and Robert Forgan was its whip.

On 10 March Mosley was officially expelled by Labour for 'gross disloyalty'. MacDonald wrote to him, mixing the regretful with the ironic: 'You remain true, while all the rest of us are false . . . We must tolerate your censure and even contempt; and, in the spare moments we have, cast occasional glances at you pursuing your heroic role with exemplary rectitude and stiff straightness to a disastrous futility and an empty sound.' An editorial in Birmingham's Labour paper expressed the general view that had Mosley 'devoted your ability and eloquence to the task of converting a majority of the people to the socialist policy of the Labour party, thus ensuring the return of a majority Labour Government at the next election, you would have been a great figure in our Movement – honoured for your service and well rewarded with office. But you could not wait.'

Michael Foot suggested that with his clumsy breach with the party, Mosley had 'tossed away the massive support he had been accumulating throughout the country'. By walking out of government in May 1930 and out of the party in March 1931, he had exposed his unsuitablity for leading the Labour Party. He had 'no love for it, no roots in it, no compunction at the breach with old comrades. He could leave as easily as he had joined, without a twinge of conscience or regret.' Mosley identified the party with himself, rather than the other way round, and did not appreciate that members' support was for parties not the politicians. A Birmingham colleague wrote that 'ambition is a good quality when it is directed to the service of one's fellows but it is a soul destroying tyrant when dedicated to self aggrandisement and the lust for power'.

A statement by the Birmingham Borough Labour president on 6 March reflected the determination to fight Mosley. Stories circulated that he was bribing candidates and agents to leave the party, in a wrecking move against the Labour movement. The sublimated suspicion about his motives 'manifested itself with venomous force'. Catlin recalled that Mosley's former associates 'took a speedy opportunity to clean themselves with scrubbing brushes'. Westminster rumour mongers had a field day with 'horrid tales of his bullying at Winchester', while plans were prepared to crush the NP at birth. *The Times* said a decision had been taken by Henderson, Dalton and Morrison to oppose the defectors as upper-class traitors.

Watching Cimmie being verbally assaulted at Stoke, Bill Allen said there was something 'supremely noble in her as she faced the angry audiences of disappointed Labour supporters'. On 15 March Oliver Baldwin's speech at Manchester's Free Trade Hall – 'Socialism is like a radish, red only on the outside, not like a tomato, red all the way through' – was disrupted. Organized disruption followed in Liverpool (29th) and, again, Manchester (30th), with meetings in Dundee and Hull closed down.

The St George's by-election on 18 March proved to be a turning point in the tussle between Beaverbrook and Baldwin, who had considered resigning but at the eleventh hour decided to fight back. He went to support the new candidate, Duff Cooper, and produced the famous line that Beaverbrook and Rothermere were pursuing 'power without responsibility, the prerogative of the harlot throughout the ages'. Cooper won decisively with the result that Empire Crusade was relegated to obscurity. The defeat indicated the difficulty Mosley faced in challenging the two major parties. On 20 March Margot Asquith warned Harold Macmillan about Mosley: 'Tom has played the fool to a degree I never thought possible as he is very clever – but not quite as remarkable as he thinks he is.' It was expected that Macmillan would defect, but his 'political antennae began to quiver' and he had second thoughts.

As commentators began to draw parallels between events in Britain and Germany, on 17 March 1931 the *Daily Worker* declared the NP to be Fascist. Nine days later Wyndham Lewis – the first writer definitely to link Hitler with Mosley – published *Hitler*, the first biography of the Nazi leader. Lady Rhondda, editor of *Time and Tide*, commissioned the biography from Lewis, who believed Nazism was responding to Communism. He found in Nazism his favourite themes – 'a hatred of parliamentary and bourgeois democracy, a horror of money and finance and a cult of youth'. He celebrated Hitler's young street fighters as pillars of the law who, in contrast to a culture eroded by feminine values, were 'morally pure, personally austere and enlightened'. Hitler was seen as a man of peace whose racialist ideology might unite Europeans against war. Frederick Voigt, the *Manchester Guardian* correspondent in Berlin, claimed Lewis had been taken in by Nazi propaganda and had been 'naive and gullible' in judging Hitler.

The press viewed *Mein Kampf* as the 'literary folly-of-youth of a failed putschist who had dispelled the boredom of prison by do-it-yourself philosophising'. Hitler was perceived as having the 'usual rag-bag of prejudices, resulting in the usual practices of social discrimination'. Lewis glossed over anti-Semitism as a 'curious Germanic idiosyncrasy'. When Hitler was compared with Mosley, he was seen as being no less respectable than Labour's *enfant terrible*. Lewis wrote of Mosley 'standing to attention as stiff as a puppet, clutching his cane, his heels together, with an enormous topper upon his moustachioed dandy's head'. He had 'wondered what a Credit-crank would be like in real life, and now I know!'.

In April Lewis was approached by the Nazi propagandist Dr Hans-Wilhelm Thost, correspondent of the *Völkischer Beobachter* and co-founder of the Anglo-German Club in Oxford of which Nicolson was a member. He said his biography was 'not at all bad for an Englishman' but criticized the assertion that the Jewish question was a 'racial red herring. If you do not understand the *Judenfrage* you have not understood Hitlerism. Without the Jewish question Hitlerism would not exist.' Thost had a social dilemma. His father had been a friend of Lord Curzon and he had a letter of introduction to Cimmie. He was, however, reluctant to present it because of her 'Jewish' ancestry. 'What a fearful obstacle-race life was', mused Lewis, 'for a member of the Nazi party, winding his way in and out of the family trees of his father's oldest friends.'

Beatrice Webb spent the first April weekend with Virginia and Leonard Woolf, and discovered that BBC director-general John Reith was a disciple of the NP. Mosley, she wrote, believed he will sweep the constituencies and become prime minister. She found it odd that he 'should be so completely ignorant of British political democracy, of its . . . slowness of apprehension of any new thought'. He was 'already choosing his Cabinet! Which argues megalomania.' NP policy was for an inner Cabinet of five. Wits said the five would be (1) Sir Oswald Mosley, (2) the late Chancellor for the Duchy of Lancaster, (3) Comrade Mosley, (4) Tom Mosley and (5) the member of Parliament for Smethwick.

Mosley, said Catlin, was 'a genuine experimentalist looking for a good plan – a Napoleon itching for any campaign'. He had returned from recuperating at Beaverbrook's villa in the South of France in an extremely enthusiastic mood. On 11 April an area office was opened in Birmingham, where Labour attacked local organizer Dan Davies, former Secretary of Aston Labour Party, and E. J. Bartlett, ex-Chairman of the Birmingham branch, for attempting 'to buy candidates, organisers and propagandists by offers of good jobs'. Labour Chairman J. Johnson warned the NP against putting up candidates because it would arouse 'more political bitterness than has been known for a generation'. Members were 'more united in their determination to fight the Mosleyites than they ever were to fight the Communists'.

Mosley decided to hit back 'in the place where it would hurt most'. A Lancashire cotton town with 46 per cent unemployment, Ashton-under-Lyme's Labour Member had died, leaving a majority of 3,407. The NP's by-election candidate on 30 April 1931 was Allan Young. At an NP propaganda committee meeting Mosley said he would ask Shaw, Wells and other intellectuals for their support. A committee member was former BBC Chief Engineer Peter Eckersley, who had been forced to resign over his affair with a married woman, Dorothy Clark. An RFC veteran, war had demoralized him and for a time he was attracted to the League of Nations. When that failed, he adopted pacificism.

Eckersley was a friend of Wyndham Lewis and his modernist flat in Swan Court became a centre of radical discussion. He knew Strachey as a BBC literary critic and was introduced through him to Mosley. Eckersley was driven to the right by his mistress who, like their artistic friends, was weary of democracy and became a 'passionate seeker after revolutionary causes'. He chaired the NP's London Committee and worked closely with Bill Allen, who donated his billboards to the campaign. Eckersley suggested hiring time on Radio Paris, an early indication of the interest in using radio for political broadcasts. Modernist in use of new media, they hoped to use cinema advertising and set up a newspaper.

Bill Risdon and Strachey's agent, Dan Davies, quickly created an organization of enthusiastic young officials. With Beaverbrook's agreement Bruce Lockhart attended NP planning meetings for the Strachey-directed campaign which, according to the *Herald*, cost £35,000 (£1.3 m). Labour made great play of the NP's 'hidden backers'. William Morris donated £50,000 and £5,000 each came from GWR magnate Wyndham Portal, who spoke at Ashton, and tobacco millionaire Hugo Cunliffe-Owen. Lord Inchcape was rumoured to be a backer but most finance came from Lancashire cotton interests. Mosley revealed that Labour had a secret fund solicited from rich men such as Bernhard Baron, another tobacco millionaire. Labour leaders were 'stricken with dismay at this subtle counter-thrust', which was represented as another piece of Mosley's treachery.

Red NP posters with the single word 'CRISIS' were plastered on giant billboards. The cotton town was suffering from an export slump and heavy unemployment. The NP's policy of a quota system for imports was designed to tackle precisely this situation. It was therefore surprising that the NP's campaign concentrated on parliamentary reform. *The Times* thought it 'fantastically remote from practical politics', though attempts were made to woo the 4,000 Catholic voters.

Parties employed professional speakers to put over the message in an era without microphones. Jack Jones was a working-class speaker for the Liberal and Communist Parties. At NP headquarters, he met the 'political flotsam and jetsam' of ex-candidates and ex-election agents, who were joining 'to do battle with "the old gang"'. He was taken on at £5 (£120) per week as a national propagandist. Also recruited was Herbert Hodge, cab driver and jobbing journalist. A socialist, he was 'antagonised by the Communist Party's rigid dogmatism and class-hatred', and thought Labour was 'staggering from one futility to another'. Here was a 'chance to build up something new and clean and vigorous, a party determined to break away from the old doctrines and prejudices'. He was enthused by the idea of 'men and women of goodwill in both classes working together for a class-less society'.

The free-flowing funds, Hodge found, attracted 'job-hunters, professional politicans, and smart-alecs of all sorts – like blue-bottles round a dropped cod's-head'. He considered Mosley 'an actor playing a part, perfectly rehearsed, but a part in which he had no personal belief'. His handshake was 'limp, his manner over-cordial'. His ability to switch on his artificial smile was 'uncanny. Like talking to a robot.' But at meetings in front of up to 7,000 people he was 'imbued with the sense of a great mission'. He was 'an impassioned revivalist speaker', Nicolson wrote, 'striding up and down the platform with great panther steps and gesticulating with a pointing index, with the result that there was real enthusiasm towards the end and one had the feeling that 90 per cent of the audience were certainly convinced at the moment'.

A street-corner speaker, Hodge was unsure of policy detail but was enthused by the 'beauty of the basic idea. Our slogan "Britain First" meant socialise Britain first . . . socialism behind the barriers of regulated imports and exports.' It also meant something different to every member. Jones made most of the second-string speeches as the 'X-Men of the first grade' were rarely available. Cimmie was a willing speaker and worked like a Trojan, addressing scores of street meetings for women, as did Strachey's wife, who 'could hold a crowd long enough to rest some of those whose throats were wearing'. A meeting on 23 April was disrupted, claimed the local paper, 'under the Communist banner'. Were these Communist actions or those of Labour supporters, as Henderson had promised?

On 27 April Mosley met with colleagues to discuss progress. Canvass returns indicated they might win but he had little confidence in their accuracy, though he believed they would beat Labour. At the by-election the Conservative vote was 12,420. Labour narrowly lost with 11,500 votes. For a third party, the NP achieved a respectable vote of 4,472. 'We just managed to save our deposit,' Jack Jones recalled, 'and in doing so made a present of what was a Labour seat to the Conservatives.' When the result was announced, the rowdy-ism intensified into violence. Labour supporters hurled shouts of 'traitor' and 'Judas' at Young and Mosley.

Mosley was advised by the police to make his getaway through the back of the town hall. He declined but agreed to his wife being smuggled out. The objective was the hotel on the far side of the square, which meant forcing a passage through the crowd. Dan Davies said he would be lynched if he did. Jones remembered Mosley, 'white with rage, not fear; he showed his teeth as he smiled contemptuously out on to the crowd'. He then remarked to Strachey, 'That is the crowd that has prevented anyone doing anything in England since the war.' Mosley later claimed the crowd had been manipulated by 'sophisticated communists'. With a police escort, he plunged ahead. 'Men cursed; women shrieked and spat at us,' recalled Jones. At the hotel, Mosley was almost cheerful.

Mosley claimed no harm was done by the violent scenes in Ashton, 'except to the psychology of Strachey'. His friend was, indeed, appalled and suspected they were on the wrong side. Labour blamed the NP for its defeat. 'Did not Brutus stick the knife into Caesar?' suggested Manny Shinwell. 'The stiletto in the back is as old as the hills.' The *Herald* cried 'WRECKERS'. Mosley 'poses as the champion of the unemployed. In fact, he is an ally of Mr Baldwin.' By-election swings throughout the country were running at 8.4 per cent against Labour and Ashton would have gone Tory anyway.

Neville Chamberlain told Beaverbrook that Mosley had 'no chance against the Labour machine'. Beaverbrook disagreed: he 'polled an immense vote. Remember, he had no newspapers backing him. I have always had the advantage of newspapers, as well as my own campaign. I do not write that fellow down. He may peter out, but if he does as well the next time, he will bring the pigs to market.' Tories now closed ranks around an anti-socialist agenda. Following by-election success on the back of a rise in unemployment to 22 per cent, Chamberlain believed they would make a clean sweep of the North with their message of economy and protection for the home market. The slump's impact forced a convergence between the Conservatives and the Liberal's right wing, headed by Sir John Simon, which signalled the eventual fall of the Labour government.

On 4 May Mosley recruited F. M. Box, the Tories' chief agent for Yorkshire. Box drew up plans for an electoral machine. A list of parliamentary candidates was compiled, including Nicolson. Beaverbrook said this was folly, since he 'cannot attract Socialist working-class votes'. Nicolson worried that NP policy was 'too intricate to be understood by the electorate' and urged on Mosley 'a new attitude of mind'. On 6 May they met Keynes, who said it was impossible 'to get across an economic programme when the only arguments the electorate can understand are the simple political slogans'. They were aware, however, that they were nearing a crisis. On 11 May the collapse of Austria's Kredit Anstalt bank brought German banks to the brink of disaster. The Bank of England was forced to step in to prevent complete chaos.

In the *Fortnightly Review*, Cecil Melville produced an overview of the NP, whose assumption was not that 'we have a class war so much as we have a class deadlock. We shall try to do something towards unlocking it.' This might be achieved by emulating the Nazi movement with which there were strong similarities. Both were National Socialist, had the support of industrialists and were 'protagonists of industry versus banking finance'. The NP proposed 'to help both industrial capital and the industrial worker to their mutual benefit'. It had a 'good chance of realising this hope, provided it can succeed in reconciling the many interests which it represents – to become the principal magnet for a new "Centrum" in British party politics'.

Melville shied away from Nazi methods but Cyril Joad suggested today's problems required a 'new political technique, making use of a new political machinery'. It would be carried through by a 'strong man with a strong policy'. He recognized that 'many of the tendencies have a markedly Fascist complexion' but when they ultimately take shape, 'it would be the nearest thing to Fascism which the British nation with its known peculiarities of political temperament, its centuries of political training, and its loyalty to Parliamentary institutions could manage'. Joad expected success among young men 'ready to dance in thousands to any tune Mosley may choose to pipe them'. But incipient Fascism may get 'the better of vestigial Socialism, and we shall have to deal with castor oil young men pure and simple'.

Believing the crisis had arrived, on 14 May Strachey, Young and Allen met secretly with Mosley, who claimed violence at meetings was organized by 'dedicated agents and warriors of communism', playing on 'the anarchy inherent in the Left of Labour to secure confusion, disillusion and ultimately the violence which is essential to their long-term plan'. After Joad suggested a Nazi-style defence force, it was announced that NP 'biff boys', led by Peter Howard, England rugby player and Oxford captain, would enforce order at meetings.

Evelyn Waugh had been at Lady Cunard's, where he noticed that Nicolson, attracted to 'virile and manly youths of the better classes', was inflamed with the 'forceful but terribly immature' Howard. Other Oxford graduates were introduced to the NP, including Christopher Hobhouse and Mosley's cousin, James Lees-Milne. Strachey wanted to recruit young workers to counteract the influence of the 'strapping Oxford hearties in their plus-fours and sports cars' but was repelled by the idea of a militarized defence force. Nicolson found the idea 'faintly erotic'. He was probably sexually attracted to Mosley. Lees-Milne noticed that he was 'fascinated, almost to a masochistic degree, by Mosley's compelling personality and autocratic manner'.

Mosley told the *Express* that the biff boys would use the 'good old English fist' but the *Evening Dispatch* warned that 'unless discreetly kept in the background, the brawny peace-preservers would probably have a provocative rather than tranquillising effect'. He was accused of 'cynically welcoming disorder at his meetings as a way of publicising his readiness to deal with "Red" disruption'. Mosley admitted the 'reserve function, its long-term purpose' was to 'take control in a revolutionary situation'. In a leaked memo, he claimed the Communist challenge 'will seriously alarm people here. You will in effect have the situation which arose in Italy . . . We have to build the skeleton of an organisation so as to meet it when the time comes. You have got to have an iron core in your organisation around which every element for the preservation of England will rally when a crisis of that kind comes.' He was restraining members who wanted to do 'something dramatic immediately if the movement is not to stagnate'.

Mosley tried to woo sympathetic Tories associated with Charles Portal (later Air Marshal) and Moore-Brabazon, who was considered a prize. There had been an encouraging response from those Young Tories 'distinctly fascist in character', and it was expected that if the NP won seats then they and the young Liberals and Labour MPs would join. There was, however, irritation at the lack of courage of Mosley's parliamentary supporters to declare themselves.

Labour Ministers delivered thunderous condemnations at meetings in renegades' constituencies. Dalton said the aim was to 'bomb the traitors out of their holes'. There was a press boycott. Strachey claimed 'explicit instructions have been issued that no mention must be made of the Mosley party. We're on the political correspondents' black list.' The NP failed to attract mass support; the *Herald* estimated that by June there were fewer than 1,000 members.

Mosley's inner circle upheld the Nazi movement as a model organization. In early June he sent two emissaries, Major Thompson and Leslie Cumings, to Germany – probably arranged through Dr Thost – to study Hitler's methods, though he said the trip was a 'holiday-cum-business affair'. Melville revealed that other NP members visited the 'Brown House', the Nazi headquarters in Munich. Strachey claimed a circular stated the NP 'will be the British equivalent of the Nazi movement'. The evolution to Fascism was dictated by Mosley, who controlled policy and funds. The NP's Fascist faction, however, was disappointed by the slow progress and the refusal to commit 'to a definite policy of dictatorship'.

Jack Jones travelled down to Denham with Strachey and Joad for an NP summer school. Strachey told him he was going 'to clear the air with a good-old fashioned Marxian speech'. At which, Joad 'sighed heavily'; he was already regretting joining the NP. When Hodge arrived at the old timbered Elizabethan farm he wondered, 'What did Mosley want with politics when he owned all this?' The weekend revealed the existence of a Fascist faction and a socialist one. Everyone disagreed about policy and discussion degenerated into oratorical wrangles. Activist Peter Winkworth spoke on the need for a revival of 'The Attic Spirit' enforced by 'absolute dictatorship'. Cimmie was troubled, as was Strachey's wife. Nicolson spoke like a diplomat and Forgan talked 'noncommitally – for they are all his friends'. Box stood in the background with 'a smile on his face' as Young 'squirmed impatiently' and Mosley talked 'soulfully of the Corporate State'. Denham, thought Jones, was 'a charming little place in which to agree to differ'.

Discussion took place on the proposed Morris-funded youth clubs. Joad argued the 'new Continental movements showed how the organisation of Youth supplied the impetus for change' and the necessity for 'Youth active-force propaganda'. Mr Papineau, Treasurer of Oxford University, wanted to appeal to reason not rowdiness and Young was 'uneasy lest the Party should be forced into Hitlerism'. The NP 'should not meet communist force with fascist force'. Nicolson wanted the 'cranky disaffection', which he dreaded, kept to a minority.

Few of Mosley's friends cared for his new associates. Georgia Sitwell lunched with him and his 'not very nice satellite' Bill Allen at the Carlton. The talk was all politics but she found 'Tom a little disappointing as a political figure'. He was 'too preoccupied with Freud. It may be a joke but it goes too far.' Mosley had joined the Birmingham Fencing Club. He viewed fencing as a 'natural extension of the sense of chivalry of the cavalry officer and airman'. It is, Richard Cohen notes, a 'dramatic, ritualistic and individualistic sport which obviously appealed to Mosley's sense of theatre'. It is also strongly embued with sexual imagery with obvious Freudian connotations. Strachey complained it was 'impossible to get him to transact important NP business because he was so busy fencing'. Despite his injured foot, he was an impressive fencer, being taller than his opponents. He belonged to Salle Bertrand and in 1931 was runner-up in the championship – proving himself to be 'one of the leading épéeists of the time' – and for two years a member of the national team.

Mosley joined the army and RFC officers of the London Fencing Club. He was, however, not popular with older members, mostly Tories, who felt he had been 'a traitor to their party'. He formed a close partnership with Charles de Beaumont, an upper-class antique dealer who embodied the sport. A boxer at university and founder of the Cambridge Scout Troop in the mid-twenties, he was in business in Italy, where he was introduced to Fascism. De Beaumont went out on a limb in supporting Mosley, partly as a means of promoting fencing.

The NP lacked publicity and the BBC refused it airtime. Beaverbrook said it required 'immense sums of money, and brilliant journalistic support, but of course there is a conspiracy of silence in the newspapers'. On 16 June Mosley invited Nicolson to edit an NP newspaper, Action, at £3,000 (£102,000) per year. Max Aitken thought he was 'a fool hitching his wagon to Mosley's star'. Mosley proposed setting up an evening paper and wanted Randolph Hearst, who was friendly with Mussolini, to invest £1,500,000 (£45 m) in the project. Nicolson disliked being 'financed by a foreign source'. A more modest idea of an 'Evening Wire' came from Robert Lynn, editor of the Northern Whig and Empire Crusader, whose Ulster seat had been taken over by Bill Allen. Lynn said he could gain a controlling interest in a wireless station on Sark; a scheme Mosley pursued four years later.

Morris agreed to back *Action* with £5,000 and guaranteed £15,000 per annum. Mosley admitted the car maker was his chief backer and that Portal's efforts at raising City funds were largely unsuccessful. Only Mosley had knowledge of the donors and kept his colleagues in the dark on finance. A reason for secrecy was that, he told Nicolson, the Prince of Wales was a supporter. He wanted to 'get a line on Lady Houston, who, being a snob, might be dazzled by the Prince's name, and might give us money'. To collect society donations, Sybil Colefax was employed under the 'vain glorious impression that "people of influence" would give the party substance'. Nicolson considered 'this cadging a most unpleasant necessity'.

With 25 per cent of the insured workforce on the unemployment register, the NP's inner circle debated its future direction. On 16 June Strachey wrote on the NP's progress for the *Week-End Review*. The NP was the 'only alterna-tive to waiting with MacDonald and Baldwin for immediate decline and ultimate catastrophe'. He repeated Melville's line that the NP was a 'Utopian attempt at social compromise', and wanted to fuse left-wing domestic aims and Commonwealth insulation in a form of National Socialism. Melville agreed the NP was a National Socialist movement, which sought to 'cut across existing conceptions of Right and Left' and 'combine the two in an advanced national form'. The central concept was National Planning, which Strachey supported as 'soundly socialist'. The class-conscious Young was not so sure.

When Mosley turned the temporary compromise of national planning into the permanent ideology of the Corporate State, Strachey and Young rowed with him over what this meant. The more he explained, 'the more it seemed to be remarkably like Capitalism: or rather it seemed to be Capitalism minus all the things which the workers had won during the last century of struggle'. They believed planning's reformist rhetoric was 'nothing but a reactionary trap for the unwary socialist' but were 'willing to carry self-deception very far in order to avoid a break which was extremely painful to both of us'. Aneurin Bevan told Strachey he had 'allowed himself to be subordinated to Mosley's superficially stronger personality'. At the time, his personal life was in turmoil. Celia Simpson, a strong character and committed socialist, encouraged him to break from Mosley.

At Birmingham's Cannon Street Hotel, on 30 June, Mosley spoke of a 'new political psychology, a conception of national renaissance, of new manhood and vigour'. Young was outraged and considered resigning. Three days later Strachey addressed the youth movement and repudiated the idea of disciplined violence to counteract disruption of meetings. Mosley angrily reprimanded him. He would 'allow no independence', Nicolson discovered, and 'claims an almost autocratic position'.

During the summer the youth movement – 'the iron core of the organisation' – became an autonomous section under the control of Peter Winkworth.

However, it proved to be 'an apple of discord'. The political section, under Cumings, Strachey and Young, was made up of ILPers deeply suspicious of these 'Fascists'. Mosley had boasted that if a revolutionary situation arose, these 'pioneers' would 'come down on the supine Government and the disorderly workers and knock their heads together'. Then they would impose the Corporate State. He declared there could be 'no corporate state without a private army' and referred to the NP as the 'British equivalent of the Nazi movement'.

While the NP was embroiled in factionalism, the government was in crisis over the rising cost of benefits. On 18 June the Anomalies Bill was introduced to increase the Unemployment Insurance Fund from £90 million to £115 million with variations in its availability. Mosley opposed the Bill and said the government by this measure had bought itself 'another short lease of your own miserable lives. You buy it at the expense of the poorest of your supporters who voted for you in more slavish days.' Ministers blamed their troubles on the City, but Mosley pointed out to Snowden that 'they did not walk out of the Bankers' palace until it fell about their ears'.

Strachey and Young assumed they 'would not dream of allowing to pass this opportunity of demonstrating that its whole policy was to oppose such "economy" efforts to solve the economic crisis by cutting down the workers' standard of life'. They were astonished, therefore, when Mosley wanted to vote against ILP amendments. They subsequently learnt that he had received an urgent telephone call from one of the NP's City supporters 'politely threatening us with the loss of financial support if we acted against the Bill'.

Strachey and Young threatened resignation unless Mosley opposed cuts to benefits. He reluctantly agreed, and Strachey and Cimmie worked with the ILP, and those Labour MPs who had signed the Mosley manifesto, in harrying the government. At an all-night session on 15 July Cimmie said, 'If I had shut my eyes in this debate I might well have believed that it was the Conservative Government bringing in a Conservative measure.' On 20 July Mosley sat with the opposition, displacing Brendan Bracken from his customary seat. The press said he had taken up 'the most reactionary attitude of supporting drastic economies at the expense of the unemployed'.

Kredit Anstalt's collapse led to a crisis which sent a shock wave through Germany, where unemployment rose to more than three million. By July, rumours circulated that MacDonald and Baldwin were planning a 'National government' to deal with the financial crisis. On 21 July Mosley and Nicolson met at Archie Sinclair's house with an assembly of political talent – Lloyd George, Churchill, Bracken, Garvin, Hore-Belisha, Henry Mond and Esmond Harmsworth – who had little confidence in the Labour government or the Tory leadership being able to cope with the crisis. Lloyd George dangled before them the prospect of a grand political alliance, under his leadership.

Mosley was tempted but Churchill refused to submit to another's leadership. Mosley concealed his presence from Strachey and Young, telling Nicolson there would be no split until the autumn. 'In other words he wishes to use them a little more before he flings them aside.' Mosley expected to be approached 'in the event of a National Government being formed to cope with the crisis' but worried that forming a 'National Opposition' might 'wreck the last hope of orderly solutions and play staight into the hands of the communists'.

The NP's own crisis arrived sooner than expected. On 20 July Strachey put forward a proposal for 'close economic relations with the Russian Government', which would require a break with the US. Mosley said only a Communist 'could possibly support such an extraordinary proposition'. The policy was rejected by Mosley, Cimmie, Forgan, Nicolson and Allen to Strachey's and Young's two votes. Two days later Strachey wrote to Mosley that the differences between them were 'really so wide as to make argument impossible'. Young said he had been 'aware of the dangers implicit in a movement such as ours', which 'could only have been avoided by a leadership above suspicion as far as working-class interests were concerned. You have not given us that leadership but rather have provided grounds for the suspicion that the party would become Hitlerist, Fascist, and ultimately anti-working class.'

On 24 July Strachey and Young, who was on the verge of a nervous breakdown, resigned. An emotional Strachey claimed Mosley's 'faith has left him. He is acquiring a Tory mind. It is a reversion to type.' Mosley said he was 'pathological'. Strachey's 'great hirsute hands twitched neurotically as he explained, with trembling voice, how unpathological he really was'. Mosley admitted his description was 'tactless' but he frequently teased Strachey with the suggestion that he was 'governed by Marx from the waist up and Freud from the waist down'. The observation, however, was accurate. Strachey left his wife for Celia, who joined the Communist Party, something he never did. After their marriage, Strachey and his new wife underwent a three-year course of analysis.

Having detected Fascism's 'cloven hoof', Joad feared the NP was 'subordinating intelligence to muscular bands of young men' and also resigned. Recent convert Osbert Sitwell told the *Week-End Review* he was aware Strachey's home was 'in Moscow rather than in London'. Hodge thought their resignations 'looked like desertion'. Mosley told *The Times* that Strachey and Young had tried 'to force on us the dogmas and doctrines they had promised to leave behind'. He purged the NP of 'all associations with Socialism'. Nicolson felt the party was 'heading straight for Tory Socialism', which, with its implied synthesis of Right and Left, meant Fascism.

Mosley appeared on 1 August at a rally at the Sitwell estate at Renishaw Park in Derbyshire. He told a crowd of 40,000 that 'for two years we have had a crisis in Britain, and what had British statesmanship done about it?

Nothing at all.' The Sitwells, wrote D. H. Lawrence, 'taught England how to be young'. Osbert, born in 1892, Edith and Sacheverell in 1897, grew up on the estate feeling 'very alien to its traditions'. The seventeenth-century laird George Sitwell had made a fortune from coal and iron. Until he met Mosley, Osbert said he had 'never encountered an English politician who was not living, in his own mind, before the year 1888'.

Osbert had been disillusioned by a war in which politicians 'indulged in all the treacherous democratic claptrap' and which was 'consummated by a million British deaths'. He was another writer, apprehensive about a second war, who put his feelings into print. Richard Aldington's bitter novel *Death of a Hero* appeared in 1928; a year later, R. C. Sherriff's *Journey's End*, a tragic portrayal of life in the trenches, was staged; hugely successful was Erich Maria Remarque's *All Quiet on the Western Front*. Henry Williamson, destined to become a devoted Mosleyite, revisited Ypres and in 1930 produced *The Patriot's Progress*, based on the experiences of a bank clerk invalided home and stripped of all illusions. The idea was created that the war had been 'a dirty trick played by the older generation on the young and that it was responsible for most, if not everything, that was wrong with England'.

The books were followed by popular films portraying the waste of war, including *Journey's End* and *Westfront 1918*, which introduced 'talkies' to audiences, including Mosley, who thought *Dawn Patrol* the 'best yet – overdrawn in personal things but wonderful flying pictures'. He was moved and depressed by it. It took a decade for the war to penetrate popular culture, principally, Robert Graves believed, because the war's danger had 'filled the blood with a kind of drug and it had taken that time before the blood was running fairly clear again'. Distance shaped personal experiences for the war's survivors among whom there had been confusion and aimlessness. By 1930 the cause for which they had fought was lost and youth had lost the peace. Believing the war had shown that 'the nation was a more binding ideal than class, that reason was weaker than instinct and feeling, that action was superior to and relatively independent of thought, that spirit was stronger than flesh', they were tempted by Fascism.

Osbert Sitwell admired Fascism's father figure, the poet d'Annunzio, who founded a state that attracted 'beautiful idealistic boys from all over Italy to fight in its army'. The Sitwells were among those dandified writers and intellectuals in rebellion against the old men, identified by Martin Green as the *Sonnenkinder*. They idolized the young as the Supermen, were preoccupied with style, were immature and selfish with a sexuality rooted in narcissism. These Children of the Sun associated with the cousins of the dandy – the naïf and the rogue. The naïf was the 'sun-bronzed young man with his shirt open, bringing the radiant candour of his gaze to bear on the mess the fathers have made of the world'. The rogue scorned the intellectual actions of both naïf

1. The Mosley family home, Rolleston Hall, was situated in the village of Rolleston-on-Dove, near Burton-on-Trent. Inherited in 1879 by Mosley's grandfather, it was described by Diana Mosley as 'ugly without and hideous within'

2., 3. Mosley's mother, Katherine Maud and his grandfather, Oswald (the model for 'John Bull')

4. The seventeen-year-old Mosley joined the 16th Lancers on 1 October 1914 and was soon transferred to France, where he served with the Royal Flying Corps as an observer

5. During the 2nd battle of Ypres in April 1915, Mosley witnessed the destruction of the town's celebrated Cathedral and medieval Cloth Hall. 'The work of centuries of genius took only hours to destroy,' he lamented

6. Suave, with a slight but suitably heroic limp from his 'aviator's ankle', Mosley already had the look, presence and manners in 1918 to succeed, and had a reputation as a seducer of women

(Left) 7. Mosley married Lord Curzon's daughter, Cynthia 'Cimmie' Curzon, on 11 May 1920 in the Chapel Royal, St James's Palace

(Above) 8. The Mosleys went to Portofino in Italy on honeymoon

9. Cimmie's younger sister, 'Baba' (Lady Alexandra Curzon) married 'Fruity' Metcalfe, equerry to Edward, Prince of Wales, in 1925. Baba had a crush on Mosley, which developed into a full-blown affair

10. Cimmie's other sister, Lady Irene Curzon (later Lady Ravensdale), was a popular member of the hunting set to which Mosley belonged

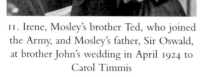

11. Irene, Mosley's brother Ted, who joined the Army, and Mosley's father, Sir Oswald, at brother John's wedding in April 1924 to Carol Timmis

12. Cimmie introduced her husband to Stewart Menzies (seen here on her left, in 1919 with his friend, Lionel Gable)

(Left) 13. Mosley got into trouble with his excessive attentions to Mrs Cole Porter

(Above) 14. Mosley, Cimmie and his brother John at Antibes, 1927

15. Bob Boothby at Isle de Marguerite, 1927

16. Mosley aquaplaning, 1927

17. Independent Labour Party school, 1926. Mosley with his important collaborator, John Strachey and Fenner Brockway (centre)

18. The Mosleys photographed at the Labour Party Conference at Blackpool, 1927

19. Savehay Farm in the village of Denham, Buckinghamshire was modernised for the Mosleys by the architect, Clough Williams-Ellis

20. Labour Party leader Ramsay MacDonald at the farm

21. Mosley canvassing for his wife in Stoke-on-Trent during the General Election. Irene gave her successful sister a bracelet with 'Stoke 1929' marked out in diamonds

22. The New Party was intended to break the log jam of British politics but the setting for its summer school at Denham in June 1931 was hardly new or modernising

23. New Party Chiefs, Denham, June 1931. *Left to right*, W.E.D. 'Bill' Allen, Robert Forgan, Cimmie, Mosley, John Strachey

24. Mosley showing off his body at the Lido, Venice

25. Conservative MP 'Bill' Allen in 1927

26. Bob Boothby advised his friend against starting up his own party. Here he is seen with Paula Casa Maury

27. The former diplomat, journalist and diarist Harold Nicolson with another member of the Mosley's social circle, Zita James

28. Photographed here by Cimmie in 1931, Georgia Sitwell also had an affair with Mosley

and dandy, being 'a Tory radical in politics, and yet their effective ally against the fathers'. Mosley was the brutal rogue, though a dandy in his 'conscious enjoyment of his own style and in his rebellion against responsible morality'. He was the narcissist, obsessed with his own sexual appetite.

'Byronic, Napoleonic, Nietzschean', Mosley was the nearest to a political leader the *Sonnenkinder* found. He briefly led a band of dandy-aesthetes – the Sitwells, Oliver Messel and Cecil Beaton – and political naïfs such as Oliver Baldwin, and the rogues such as the young Esmond Romilly. Among the NP circle were Empire Crusader Peter Rodd, model for 'Basil Seal' in Waugh's *Put Out More Flags*; frivolous dandy Hamish St Clair Erskine; naturalist and nude sunbather Cyril Joad; and Randolph Churchill, 'always in trouble and a trouble to his friends'. At its head was the Prince of Wales, the youthful, blond and pleasure-seeking royal with signs of a social conscience, who toyed with supporting the NP.

By the time the banking crisis spread to Britain, the government was in trouble as the Bank of England's reserves drained away 'in a golden haemorrhage'. At the begining of August 1931 bankers warned that Britain would go over the precipice unless foreign confidence was restored by a balanced budget. The May Committee recommended raising taxes, reducing wages and cutting the dole by 20 per cent. Keynes condemned the proposals as 'replete with folly and injustice'.

Despite the sense of crisis, the Mosleys set off in August to France. On the way, Mosley stopped at Oxford to talk to William Morris, who agreed to make more funds available. Mosley had been approached by Forgan for money. Having given up lucrative medical work, he suggested the NP could ill afford to lose another MP. Mosley gave him £500 (£17,000). Peter Howard was offered £650 a year to head the biff boys. He wrote to his fiancée, Doe Metaxa, daughter of a Greek family in exile, that Mosley was 'the most unpopular person in England today. But you have to be a rather big person to be as hated as that. He is rather Mussolini-like, you know, when you talk to him.' He agreed Mosley was the 'most vindictive hater of anyone I know' but he would 'never desert him while he still needed me in politics because he really does believe he can help the British working classes and no one else can'.

Nicolson hired for *Action* an 'intelligent Jew' named Hamlyn as general manager, and sub-editor Noel Josephs, 'an embittered ILPer with an inferiority-complex who should be able to give me the acid I require'. On 17 August he informed Mosley he had taken on as economic adviser a protégé of Keynes, Rupert Troughton, who had published *Unemployment: its Causes and Their Remedies*. He wrote that the 'criticism of "impractical" is the criticism which age levels against the ideas of youth, which conservatism levels against innovation'. Nicolson worked on an NP propaganda film with shots of the unemployed set to 'Land of Hope and Glory'. It 'cut to somnolent old gentlemen sitting on front benches in parliament filmed in slow motion'. A scene of Trafalgar Square had a jeering crowd shouting 'England wants Action'.

The Mosleys were joined for their holiday in Antibes by Cecil Beaton, Doris Castlerosse, Beatrice Guinness and daughters Baby and Zita Jungman, and Mosley's new girlfriend, the petite Lottsie, wife of the rich Alfred Fabre-Luce of Crédit Lyonnais. Mosley would whisk Lottsie off to Villefranche or to Monte Carlo. Cimmie, who was pregnant with a third child, did not know how to deal with the affair, which took place in full view of everyone. She was happy when her husband condescended to pay her attention but was usually in a blind rage.

With the financial crisis worsening, the government could either seek a loan to appease American investors or go off the gold standard and default on its obligations. The latter course was deemed unacceptable and so negotiations opened with New York bankers for a loan, conditional on a balanced budget and cuts in benefits. The Cabinet accepted the terms by eleven votes to nine but it was not enough to secure the loan. On 21 August more cuts were demanded, but the Cabinet refused. Nicolson wrote to Mosley that 'people may say that during the gravest crisis in present political history, you prefer to remain upon the Mediterranean. On the other hand, I do not see what you would do were you here at this moment, and I feel that it is more dignified to be absent and aloof, than to be present and not consulted.'

With the Cabinet split, on 24 August the Prime Minister resigned. To colleagues' astonishment, on his return from Buckingham Palace MacDonald announced he had accepted the King's invitation to form a 'National' government to implement emergency measures. Essentially a Conservative administration, there were four Tory Ministers (Stanley Baldwin was Lord President of the Council), two Liberals and three Labour Ministers, including Philip Snowden as Chancellor, who announced cuts of £70 million. However, Labour had already committed itself to £56 million, thus the National government 'came into existence for a task no more herculean than that of reducing Government expenditure by £14 million'. In view of this bitter betrayal for Labour, MacDonald was expelled from the party. G. B. Shaw wished Mosley had waited: 'If only he had known that MacDonald was contemplating political suicide!' He feared the new party was the National government, not Mosley's.

The joke around Westminster was that 'poor MacDonald has had to resign and Mosley has sent for the King'. The news only reached Mosley when he read the following day's papers. When H. G. Wells joined the Mosleys, 'they seemed not to think of anything except whether Mosley, who was going to England next day, ought to sit on the Opposition Bench and what should be the colours of the Mosley party'. Cimmie remained behind and Wells observed her drive over to the casino, where she 'danced deplorably in public, and then got drunk and smashed up her car driving it home'. To Irene's horror she 'fell asleep at the wheel and hit the rocks on the hairpin bend'. Wells saw it as an instance of their inability 'to exercise self-discipline even in a time of crisis'. Irene thought Cimmie had simply stopped caring what happened.

When he reached London on 26 August, Mosley told Nicolson 'we should build up rather than cut down'. It would be impossible, 'having been the first to preach crisis, to cease our lonely voice now that the crisis has come'. The NP had been derailed by the decision of the new Labour leader, Arthur Henderson, to go into opposition to its former leaders: 'In the end even the worm turned at the prospect of the final betrayal being demanded of it.' Mosley believed Labour supporters would 'no longer respond to our appeal since Henderson and the machine have transformed the crisis into a class conflict'. He would appeal to Fascism's traditional target: the 'little people, the shopkeepers, clerks who wore a white collar under their black coats' – the class 'most threatened by the economic crisis because they were not organised as were the blue-collar workers'. They might elect a few MPs if the election was delayed, or fail, in which case he would retire from public life for ten years. Even then, he would be 'no older than Bonar Law was when he first entered politics'.

Bruce Lockhart had been in Munich and was shown around the Brown House by Alfred Rosenberg, Hitler's adviser and editor of *Völkischer Beobachter*. On his return on 27 August he saw Mosley, who expected the National government would be compelled 'to remain longer than they intend, and without a constructive policy the revenue situation (which depends on industry) will get steadily worse. This is when the New Party will come in.' He admitted he had made a study of Hitlerism.

Mosley had been seeing Churchill and claimed the support of Lloyd George and Beaverbrook, who 'must join eventually'. On 31 August, through Randolph, Churchill approached Mosley to join him and the 'Tory toughs' in opposition. Randolph spoke at the NP Club where, to loud applause, he said 'castration was a modern remedy for ineffectives in the hygienic world of thought. It ought to be applied to political ineffectives. It would, however, be unnecessary in the case of Baldwin and MacDonald as they were old women already.'

On 8 September, following Parliament's reinstalment, Mosley gave one of his last Commons speeches. He attacked those who believed a 'bankers' ramp' had subverted the government. 'If the Labour Party had said that it was the banking policy of the last ten years, a policy they supported, that was responsible for this situation – a policy which their Chancellor of the Exchequer supported and which they supported him in supporting, then they would be getting at the root facts of the present situation.' He agreed with Douglas Cole's article 'Was it a bankers' conspiracy?' that the crisis was a direct result of defects in Labour thinking. He urged MPs to adopt a constructive policy and added, in a line taken from Keynes, that he did 'not care who does it. I do not care so much what the policy is.' The way out was 'not the way of the monk, but the way of the athlete. It is only by exertion, by a great attempt to reorganize our industries, that this country can win through, and I venture to suggest that the simple question before the House is whether Great Britain is to meet its crisis lying down or standing up.' The diehard Leo Amery observed that Mosley had been 'free to make the speech I should have liked to make'.

At a Trafalgar Square rally on 14 September Mosley claimed there was 'an element of farce in the tragedy' for Labour in that it had 'every resource of the State at its command. What happened? The great day dawned, and Labour resigned; cleared out just when they had the realisation of their greatest wish. What must we think of a Salvation Army which takes to its heels on the Day of Judgment?'

By mid September a Mosley luncheon group in the Commons comprised Amery, Jowitt, Bracken, Boothby, Hore-Belisha, Randolph Churchill and Terence O'Connor. On 16 September he attended a meeting at which Keynes said current policy was 'perfectly mad. We have been making in the last few weeks as dreadful errors of policy as deluded statesmen have ever been guilty of.' In order to reduce unemployment he wanted more spent on 'education, public health and public works and as little as possible on the dole'.

Throughout September the rift widened between the NP's political and youth sections. Nicolson was alarmed that Glyn Williams, with his 'extraordinary flair for working-class movement and organisation', wanted uniforms for the youth section since they had 'a thirst for colour and for drama'. The 'active force' of stewards was built up by Edward 'Kid' Lewis, a former England welterweight boxing champion and Whitechapel Jew. Incongruously, he was accompanied on his tours by the effete Sachie Sitwell.

Cecil Melville published *The Truth About the New Party* and suggested the modern movements had been 'born of a state of crisis, and depended on the acuteness of that crisis for their success'. It was happening with Hitlerism and Mosley believed 'it will happen with Mosleyism'. Accused of 'political Douglas Fairbanksism' and sneered at for being 'un-English', Mosley was determined to create a movement that would 'justify as qualities those very things which his opponents stigmatised as defects'. He believed that when the country faced a crisis as catastrophic as was the crisis of war, the English 'will then again be flamboyant and he is getting ready to give them a flamboyant leadership'. However, 'suppose this calculation on the crisis should misfire? Suppose the calculation should be avoided, got round, got over, in some ordinary, hum-drum sort of way? In that case the political evocation of Romanticism would fail. That would be the end of Mosleyism.'

On 20 September Mosley addressed 20,000 people on the Green at Glasgow. He warned that 'before the crisis is ended the nation will welcome more drastic measures'. To counter the disruptive hecklers, the biff boys advanced on a group of 'Communists'. At which point a stone was thrown and hit Mosley on the head. His personal bodyguard fought off the attackers but not before three were slashed by razors. Eventually, he 'drove away, waving his hat to the crowd, and still smiling'. On the following day he told colleagues that 'this forces us to be fascist and that we no longer need hesitate to create our trained and disciplined force'.

The National government imposed deflationary measures in order to restore confidence in sterling but to little effect. On 21 September Snowden had to suspend the gold standard. Hearing the news, former Labour Minister Tom Johnston commented that 'no one ever told us we could do that'. For Montagu Norman, Governor of the Bank of England, it was a blow to the Bank's prestige and 'the shattering of his plans for world capitalism'. He then suffered a breakdown. There was, however, a sense of renewal as the 'cross of iron' was lifted, thus ending a decade of deflationary finance. Abandoning the gold standard led to a more accommodating monetary policy and when the bank rate fell it provided the stimulus for recovery.

On 22 September Mosley learnt that the Young Tories were 'forcing an Election for October'. There had been a meeting between Empire Industries Association members – Henry Page Croft, Lord Lloyd, Sir Patrick Hannon and Leo Amery – and Baldwin, which agreed to Tories going to the country under MacDonald. During a discussion on *fascismo*, Mosley forecast a rapid increase in Communism. Nicolson feared the 'black-coats' would vote National, the workers Labour, and the Communists would 'collar our imaginative appeal to youth', leaving the NP without a constituency. He wanted Mosley to join with the National Party but predicted the Communists 'would win with a revolution'. The NP needed a theory and a vigorous youth movement but he shied away from Fascism, which 'unless based on class hatred, would not make a significant enough appeal'. He supported a National Socialism of social reform, the organic state and disciplined planning. He described the NP platform as 'State capitalism' which caught well the 'peculiar character' of Mosley's national planning.

Mosley was not ready for an election. Nicolson told his wife, Vita Sackville-West, he was 'not optimistic about any single one of us being returned to parliament except perhaps Cimmie'. They expected to be annihilated. They would concentrate upon becoming a movement rather than a parliamentary party.

Hodge recalled that Mosley seemed happiest on the platform. On 25 September at Birmingham's Rag Market, he was protected from hooligans by 'half-baked college-boys out for a lark'. Mosley 'hoped they'd have some "fun"' and was like a 'big sixth-form boy, the captain of his side, telling them to go and win'. When the heckling began, Mosley jumped into the crowd with his bodyguard, but was forced back under a barrage of chairs and bottles. Hodge noticed a 'flash of a smiling Mosley surveying the scene of desolation', before he 'escaped through a side exit on police advice'. He blamed the chaos on Mosley: 'To go to speak at a meeting accompanied by a strong-arm squad was asking for trouble.'

On 30 September Peter Howard was asked to set up provincial 'Pioneer Clubs'. The man behind this initiative was detective novelist Peter Cheyney, an impulsive physical type who had been severely wounded in the war. A journalist, he published a pro-Fascist journal for Ukrainian émigrés. During the twenties he ran a private detective agency with retired Special Branch Detective-Inspector Harold Brust. In the General Strike he worked with Colonel Ralph Bingham, a British Fascisti member and co-founder of the extreme National Fascisti, known for its provocative violence, running a depot of the Organization for the Maintenance of Supplies. It was in this atmosphere of authoritarian discipline that Cheyney developed his love of policing and Fascism. When Bingham was appointed Secretary of the Order of the Hospital of St John of Jerusalem, Cheyney renounced his faith and became editor of its journal, *Chivalry*. He was almost certainly associated with the British Fascisti. He was a special constable but kept this 'very secret', perhaps because he was an informer.

On joining the NP, Cheyney took up fencing and was tutored by Charles de Beaumont, soon winning the Salle Paul Club épée championship. He carried his patriotism to such extremes that he challenged to a duel 'anyone who sneered at Britain'. Nicolson took a violent dislike to this 'unpleasant Jew fascist' who thought like 'a gangster and talks in terms of a soap-box politician'. Despite his protests, Mosley supported Cheyney. When asked about him he was evasive and dismissed his politics as 'immature and unimportant'. However, Nicolson, who did his best to persuade Mosley 'to get rid of the thugs', believed Cheyney 'sinisterly wielded power' over policy and his 'malign influence and thick-eared philosophy' influenced Mosley into seeking mastery of the streets.

On 1 October Mosley secretly met Neville Chamberlain. The Tories were 'anxious to get some of us in and are prepared to do a secret deal'. Election organizer Box was invited to meet their Chief Agent to see if a bargain could be struck. Five days later it was announced a general election would be held on 27 October. Forgan saw John Reith about political broadcasts and it was agreed that 'if they were putting fifty candidates in the fold . . . they would have a claim'. The NP manifesto, 'A National Plan for a National Crisis', was issued on 7 October, omitting any reference to corporatism. The party was unclear whether or not to oppose the National government and chose to reiterate calls to put the 'interests of the National above those of the Party'. In his last parliamentary speech, Mosley appealed for a planned industrial policy. Buttressed by a meeting with Keynes, he criticized the obsession with budget balancing – 'deficits are the fashion nowadays. All the best countries have deficits.'

On 8 October appeared the first of the thirteen issues of the Nicolson-edited *Action*, costing 2d. The ideological content was developed through Mosley's front-page leader and Nicolson's '*Action* Looks at Life' column, which stated man's intelligence is 'capable of creating a Modern State as organic as the human body. A State in which all will possess their function, and in which there will be no division and no conflict of interest.' The means to accomplishing this was the Corporate State – co-ordinated, co-operative and controlled. He drew attention to the Continent and said the same phenomenon was certain to occur in England but 'framed to accord with the character and high experience of this race'. Mosley wanted a movement which 'grips and transforms every phase and aspect of national life'. It would be one of 'iron resolution and reality', cutting 'like a sword through the knot of the past to the winning of the modern State'.

Nicolson knew he was not suited to run a journal. *Action* was intellectually subtle but journalistically amateurish. Iain Mikardo was surprised by its mixed bag of contributors and contents: politics and economics, including a sympathetic account of the Soviet system; the arts and sciences; the environment; the generation gap. Among its contributors were Christopher Isherwood, Peter Quennell, Vita Sackville-West, Raymond Mortimer, the Sitwells and Alan Pryce-Jones.

Pryce-Jones was assistant to J. C. Squire, editor of the *London Mercury*. His pacifist views found a platform in the journal of the Promethean Society, whose members included W. H. Auden and Wyndham Lewis. The *Twentieth Century*'s first editorial in 1931 proclaimed a scientific attitude – 'the only method of approach for anyone who cares more for intellectual honesty than for party, creed, or shibboleth'. They believed a state of crisis was natural since they had 'never known any other'. For a brief period these poets and writers flirted with the NP. In reviewing Auden's *The Orators*, John Heyward noted the striking images of a 'sick England with a sick people, its industries closed and its workers idle; its middle classes fearful and defensive, afraid of change, afraid of life; and the young, feeling the need for action, but uncertain and afraid, and wanting a leader'.

Looking back at this period, Auden admitted he was someone 'near the border of sanity, who might well, in a year or two, become a Nazi'. Peter

Quennell said it was impossible to tell if the thirties poet was 'a Communist or a young Hitlerite' since the 'prodigious melodrama of modern Europe cast its shadow in some form on to his mind'. Mosley offered a radical solution but within a year Auden and the Prometheans turned to the left as Mosley proved to be too impatient to be the leader they sought. Politics was not the area – 'too heavily patrolled by father-figures' – to win success.

The NP rejected Chamberlain's offer and would accept 'no coupons from the National Coalition' in the election. Nicolson warned his readers to expect no dramatic NP successes: 'Our day will come in 1933 . . . within a measurable time this country will be exposed to the dangers of proletarian revolution and massacre, starvation and collapse.' Mosley saw the election as an opportunity for propaganda. On 16 October Reith met with Box and agreed to a political broadcast 'if they had forty candidates but they only have twenty-three so they are out'. Peter Howard agreed to stand at Merthyr – one of Labour's safest seats. He had not seen before the poverty of the Welsh valleys. Watching at play children who were suffering from malnutrition, 'in a moment, anger, pity, humiliation, a compound of every deep feeling of the human heart rose within me. For I saw that almost every one of these children had mis-shapen legs or ankles.' The indifference he experienced back in London infuriated Howard. Nicolson admitted he was the 'best of a fantastically bad bunch'.

London organizer Albie Smith told Hodge the other parties had 'scooped all the competent election agents in the country and we were left with duds'. To his surprise, Hodge was asked to stand at Limehouse; and in Whitechapel stood Kid Lewis, an East End legend for fighting his way up from the gutter to fame as a boxer. 'Yet here he was,' recalled Joe Jacobs, 'back in the gutter, so far as we Communists were concerned.' He had heard people pay tribute to Mosley's political ability but wondered how this could be explained, 'other than that he was out for cheap publicity'.

In presenting the NP as a centre party, Mosley played down corporatism and informed *The Times* (18 October) he had 'no use for Fascism or anything else that comes from abroad'. He tried, unsuccessfully, to buy time on commercial radio. The NP film, *Crisis*, was banned by the censor on the grounds that shots of snoring MPs were calculated to bring Parliament into disrepute. People were 'urged from walls and hoardings to "Take Action"'. The election was roughly fought but it was NP meetings which were subjected to the worst disruption. On 18 October at Birmingham, Mosley was mauled by the crowd despite his bodyguard. Violence had been expected and the local branch had been issued with small clubs, the size of a policeman's baton, with instructions only to use them if attacked.

The 15,000 crowd became restive when Mosley's microphone went off. When he strode into the crowd and appealed for silence, scuffles broke out (he was accused of assaulting two men but was later acquitted). Howard claimed the 'Communists tried to kill us with chains and bottles and I got cut on the head just before the real fighting began. I and Mosley had just been fighting with batons and clearing the space around the platform.' A section then 'charged the platform, brandishing chairs and chair-legs, hurling bottles, and swept all before them'. A hundred police restored order. London organizer C. F. Kendrick was carried 'unconscious from under the feet of the mob, where he had fallen after being struck with a bottle'. Dozens of people received minor injuries and Mosley emerged with lacerations. Hurrying away through the Bull Ring, Lewis 'pulled his hat down over his eyes and turned his coat-collar up. Opponents, seeing Lewis's smallness, chose to attack the boxing champion – with the result that Cheyney and de Beaumont stood by watching until they shook with laughter.'

On 19 October, 10,000 people turned out in Glasgow, where the crowd ended up stoning Mosley. Jack Jones had warned that to bring bodyguards would invite trouble. After the meeting Mosley refused to be hurried away by car and walked back to his hotel under police guard. He 'smiled all the way at those who from both sides shouted "traitor" at him'.

Five days later the *Manchester Guardian* reported that at the Free Trade Hall there was a microphone, but Mosley had it disconnected. 'I hate these machines,' he explained. The audience was 'stirred and finally swept off its feet by a tornado of peroration yelled at the defiant high pitch of a tremendous voice'. Mosley was 'already thickly encrusted with legend. His disposition and his face are those of a raider, a corsair; and his place in the history of these times will be won, if at all, with the sword.' Campaigning for the NP, James Lees-Milne thought him a hypnotic monster. 'He brooked no argument, would accept no advice. He had in him the stuff of which zealots are made. The posturing, the grimacing, the switching on and off of those gleaming teeth, and the overall swashbuckling ... were more likely to appeal to Mayfair flappers than to sway indigent workers. I did not think the art of coquetry ought to be introduced into politics.' Beatrice Webb predicted voters would reject the political showman and the excitement at meetings did evaporate.

A wave of patriotic fervour swept the National government into office on 27 October 1931. The Conservatives won 473 seats and the Liberal vote virtually disappeared. It was calamitous for Labour. Four-fifths of its seats were lost because of anti-Labour pacts which gave National parties a free run against socialists. Labour was represented by only forty-six MPs and five ILPers; also elected were thirteen National Labour MPs supporting Ramsay MacDonald. The notion that the election was a form of 'Fascist *coup d'état*' was both 'a characteristic response by Labour people to the enormity of their defeat, and a legend that would endure for over a generation'.

The election was a disaster for the NP. Mosley obtained 10,500 votes at Stoke but was bottom of the poll. Sellick Davies in Wales achieved 30 per cent of the vote in a straight fight with Labour, but Kid Lewis attracted a derisory 154 votes and, like all but two of twenty-four NP candidates, lost his deposit. The total votes cast for it were 36,377, compared with 74,824 for twenty-six Communist candidates. With a reduction in the number of three-cornered contests, a third party was destined to do poorly. The NP's election organization was ramshackle and a tactical error – based on Mosley's delusion that 'working-class areas would catch fire by his daring policies' – was the targeting of safe Labour seats. Mosley told Nicolson that 'we have been swept away in a hurricane of sentiment' and that 'our time is yet to come'.

The election re-established the two-party system, though it was disguised by the existence of a 'National' coalition in which the Tories formed the dominant element. Churchill suggested to Mosley that he stand in a by-election, with promises to come out in his support. He decided he would wait until the 'reaction against the National Government assumes a more definite shape'. In fact, he found himself 'marooned in the loneliness of political independence'.

NP members argued that from such defeats their Continental counterparts had 'returned with fresh strength to triumph over their opponents'. The identification with Hitlerism coincided with sweeping internal changes. The headquarters was closed, regional groups were disbanded and officials were sacked. *Action*'s employees left or were sacked. Sellick Davies was discovered taking £270 (£9,000) from the till and a candidate was found to have several aliases. Only Box, Forgan and Howard were retained. Hodge thought there had been one benefit from the election failure – 'it shook off some of the blue-bottles. The cod's head was now a bony skull.'

The NP had been infiltrated by adventurers and crooks, and their dismissal for incompetence and corruption heralded the destruction of its orthodox side. The youth movement's triumph over the political faction was symbolic of Mosley's rejection of electoral politics as he readopted Corporatism as the main policy plank. The new movement 'must differ fundamentally from the old political parties in both ideology and organisation. It must be a movement of youth which willingly accepts the discipline, effort and sacrifice by which alone great executive purposes can be achieved, and by which alone the modern state can be built.'

11

The New Movement

Mosley abandoned conventional politics. An unintended result of the massive vote for the National government was to push fringe parties to extra-parliamentarianism and a more physical response. Harold Nicolson, who hated the violence associated with Fascism, was fearful of the change of the direction Mosley was taking. 'He believes in fascism. I don't. I loathe it,' he wrote on 2 November 1931.

Mosley said increased violence made it impossible to hold meetings – 'just as it had driven many Conservatives away from towns where the hooligan element was particularly strong'. An ILP recruit to the NP, John Beckett, had been convinced by his trips to Italy that 'here was a great new conception of civilisation'. If Fascists were 'brutal reactionary thugs, then also they were the finest and best informed actors I have ever met'. Following Communist disruption of his meetings in Peckham, Beckett set up his own defence force led by a local boxer, anticipating, his son Francis notes, 'one of Mosley's least respectable initiatives'. Mosley cited the disruption at Birmingham as a key reason why he organized Blackshirts to prevent 'red' violence curtailing free speech. He would 'not tamely submit to intimidation and ruffianism'.

'New men came to us,' said Mosley, 'who were ready to fight for their beliefs, in type the dedicated blackshirt.' The youth movement recruited 'splendid young Britons who shared a vision of national rebirth'. Herbert Hodge heard of mysterious goings-on at King's Road, Chelsea, where, Albie Smith told him, graduates were 'drilling and doing all sorts of military dags under the orders of ex-officers'. He noted Mosley's friendship with a 'distinguished general of known political and intellectual proclivities', and another high-ranking officer, known as 'the British von Seeckt'. The Fascist-style youth clubs in Greenwich and Birmingham alarmed Nicolson, who feared Mosley shared the fantasies of Peter Cheyney and Ralph Bingham. 'They really are the devil.' The clubs were designed to produce Spartans skilled in fencing, boxing and public speaking. Needless to say they attracted a number of thugs who, Mosley admitted to *The Times*, carried truncheons.

The young toughs were initiated into the NUPA (New Party) elite corps of 'shock troops'. Cheyney said they would 'learn realism as opposed to bunk, vibrant nationalism as opposed to sloppy internationalism, discipline as opposed to the post-war ideal of sloth, and a comradeship unknown to the Red "comrades" of the sickly sickle'. The aim was to establish national 'NUPA-Shock-Propaganda Controls' by 1933 and a 'Political-Shock-Youth Movement' by 1935. Newspapers were alarmed: HITLERIAN STORM TROOPS and MOSLEY'S THUGS ran the headlines. Before long, the Communists and NUPA were inter-reliant and constituted the main audience at the other's meetings, with the result that a tradition was born.

Mosley intended to 'concentrate on clubs and cells within clubs: a new movement cannot be made within the frame of a parliamentary party'. Italy was the primary source of the new faith, but he also turned to Germany for inspiration. On 3 December Bruce Lockhart met with Nazi ideologue Alfred Rosenberg, who was in London, and then discussed the situation in Germany with Mosley, who 'talked a great deal about the necessity for militant organisation against Communism', since 'the man who could control the streets would win'. On 10 December an *Action* editorial praised Hitler's achievement. The new direction was evident from talks to NUPA recruits – 'Hitler's nephew on Hitler'.

Addressing socialists on 13 December, Keynes said Labour had been 'out of sympathy with those who have had new notions of what is economically sound . . . such as Lloyd George or Oswald Mosley or myself'. Because of his association with Mosley, Keynes was viewed with suspicion by Labour, which had set its face against his strategy of demand management through active monetary policy and public investment to achieve full employment. It was a 'dangerous illusion' as only socialist planning could end the 'anarchy of unregulated private enterprise'. Keynes sympathized with the National government and told Mosley there could be prosperity in ten years, though the 'transition between a battered capitalism and the organised State would be slow and bitter'. However, he 'portends no disasters': Mosley disagreed.

The only protection against Communism was the Corporate State, which was the 'conception of a society working with the precision and the harmony of a human body. Every interest and every individual is subordinate to the overriding purpose of the nation.' This was National Socialism – 'the subordination of the individual to the State'. In the Corporate State, *Action* said, 'if something is not in harmony with this then it must be a microbe, a virus harmful to the body'. It was not clear what would happen in the event that 'something' was not in harmony but reducing enemies to the level of a virus was common among anti-Semites. NP philosophy contained elements of eugenics with the desire to protect the British race through contraception, abortion and sterilization. Nicolson wondered why the 'most civilised race on earth was retrograde in matters which vitally affect the future of the race' and wanted a Royal Commission of Eugenics appointed to 'gaze with virile eyes upon the implications of such a decision'.

Action was losing £340 (£11,000) per week and its thirteenth issue on 31 December was its last before it was amalgamated with the *Saturday Review*, which published Mosley's articles. Mosley admitted they had failed 'both as a party and as a paper to arouse the people to any sense of their necessities'. If normality returned, Britain would be subject to a 'slow and almost imperceptible decline', but he had no intention of allowing that to happen. 'Better the great adventure, better the great attempt for England's sake, better defeat, disaster, better far the end of that trivial thing called a political career than strutting and posturing on the stage of Little England, amid the scenery of decadence, until history writes of us the contemptuous postscript: "These were the men to whom was entrusted the Empire of Great Britain, and whose idleness, ignorance, and cowardice left it a Spain." We shall win; or at least we shall return upon our shields.'

Mosley's funding of the NP and Cimmie's legal costs involving the Leiter estate left them with large overdrafts and forced them to let out Savehay Farm and Smith Square. Cimmie and the children moved into a flat in Ebury Street. He was desperate for allies but industrialists were appeased by the National government's ditching of the gold standard and the introduction of protectionism, and united behind its promise of attacking socialism. On 8 December NUPA's Christopher Hobhouse learnt that Mosley wanted money from the Fascists and Nazis. Three days later Mosley revealed that Rothermere wished 'to place the whole of the Harmsworth Press at his disposal'; however, he wanted to 'lie low for a bit but would be grateful for it later'. Cimmie detested Rothermere, who accelerated Mosley's drift towards Fascism, arranging an introduction to Mussolini. She disassociated herself from Fascist tendencies and contemplated putting a notice to that effect in *The Times*.

Rothermere followed closely the career of Mussolini, whose significance had been grasped by the *Mail*'s correspondent in Rome, Sir Percival Phillips, who honoured him in his 1923 book, *The Red Dragon and the Black Shirts: How Fascist Italy found her Soul*. The paper portrayed him as 'the Napoleon of modern times, a leader who worked hard, had given up alcohol and smoking, and sacrificed his social life'.

On 30 December Bruce Lockhart heard that an NP delegation was off to Rome. 'Tom is taking his épées with him and hopes to fence his way into Mussolini's presence.' Bill Allen went, as did Esmond Harmsworth, who later joined Mosley in Berlin. Esmond was witty and attractive but not a commanding figure such as Rothermere. A former Tory MP, he had not sought re-election in 1929, in order to chair the *Mail* group. Obsessed with his wealth, Rothermere had stepped down as he did not want to lose his dividends in the face of new cut-throat competition.

The group studied the 'new political forces born of crisis, conducted by youth and inspired by completely new ideas of economic and political organisation'.

They wanted to be prepared for 'when this country comes to pass through great events'. In fact, Nicolson hoped Mosley would be discouraged by witnessing Fascism at first hand. They arrived in Rome on 2 January 1932 and were joined by Christopher Hobhouse, who arrived from Munich, 'full of Hitler'. Aged twenty-one, Hobhouse was the son of a mentally unstable Canon of Winchester and a mother who had died young. A reckless character, he was another Oxford graduate seduced by Nicolson. Hobhouse said the Nazis believed they had 'tried to do things too much on the grand. We should have begun in the alleys.' The following day a worried Nicolson wrote to his wife that 'the Führer contends that we British hitlerites are trying to do things like gentlemen. We must be harsh, violent and provocative.' Mosley gave Vita 'the creeps'.

The Italians treated Mosley with the utmost deference – regarding him as a '*duce in erba*'. *Lavoro Fascisto*'s editor told them about the Fascist electoral system, which impressed them as 'not electoral at all'. On 5 January Mosley said the future lay with NUPA, which would correspond to the Nazis' SS or Schutzstaffel organization. Hobhouse argued it should be working-class, while Nicolson insisted it be constitutional. Mosley thought they might succeed with the backing of Rothermere. Nicolson handed him a copy of a State-controlled newspaper devoted to Mussolini. Mosley 'grinned with delight, slapped his leg and joked: "I'd like to make Max [Beaverbrook] produce a paper like that."'

The British ambassador, Sir Ronald Graham, arranged an interview with Mussolini. While they waited, they met Princess Jane di San Faustino, who addressed a delighted Mosley as the 'beautiful boy'. He was amused when a guest 'asked if I was still a Bolshevik!' He talked to Prince Philip of Hesse, nephew of Kaiser Wilhelm II, married to Mafalda of Savoy, daughter of Italy's King. Hesse enthusiastically supported Hitler's hopes for a German–Italian alliance and became a key intermediary between the Führer and Mussolini. On 6 January the group spoke with Mussolini's Party Secretary Achille Starace, known for his vanity and mindless loyalty, and toured the Pontine marshes and land-reclamation schemes. When queried about opposition, Starace shrugged: 'We do not understand! We believe in *solidarietà*.' Mosley informed Cimmie that the State's powers were enormous and that Corporatism 'interferes immediately with inefficient ownership and management'. She wanted to know about the condition of the workers.

State intervention through public works – housing, reclamation and roads – was impressive but assistance to industry was unsuccessful and the Corporate State achieved little. The economy was depressed, industry was in recession and growth was lower than in all other European countries. The million unemployed were controlled by 'brutal repression just as those in work were disciplined by fierce paternalism'. Mussolini's policies were a mixture of self-advertisement and opportunism, and failed to make Italy self-sufficient. Nicolson was shocked that Mosley was impressed by Fascism. He cannot 'keep his mind off shock troops, the arrest of MacDonald and Thomas, their internment on the Isle of Wight, and the roll of drums around Westminster. He is a romantic. That is a great failing.' Certainly, Mosley had an image of himself as the self-created hero. In *The Holy Terror*, H. G. Wells described him as a 'Byron without the limp'.

On 7 January Mosley met Mussolini at the Palazzo Venezia. He was received in the fifteenth-century Hall of the Mappamondo, with its first globe of the world. They talked in French until the dictator insisted on speaking in poor English. 'No one who knew him could deny his charm or sense of humour,' Mosley recalled. 'He had the quickest and clearest mind of any statesman I have met except, possibly, Lloyd George.' He was an 'Elizabethan swashbuckler', who liked Wagner, read Byron and Nietzsche, and shared with Mosley an interest in Caesar.

Mussolini was, his biographer R. J. B. Bosworth concluded, 'no more than an ambitious pseudo-intellectual from the provinces who convinced others, including many foreign observers, that he was a supreme leader who could lead Italy through a forced process of modernisation into top nation status'. Mosley reinforced Mussolini's inflated view of his standing in the world and the belief that the measures taken in Italy could be turned into 'a coherent political doctrine of universal validity'. He had previously pleased British Conservatives by stating that 'fascism is not an article for export' but now wanted to develop it as part of Europe's rejuvenation.

Mussolini invited Mosley to stand with him during a Fascist parade. In public, he looked like a silent screen villain but he governed by terror, suppressing civil liberties, banning trade unions and imprisoning people without trial. Nicolson was appalled and refused to appear in public with the murderer of Matteotti. He quarrelled with Mosley, packed his bags and left Rome. Mosley travelled on to Munich to study Nazism. He was advised by Boothby, who lectured in Germany on the economic crisis. Boothby's friend was 'Putzi' Hanfstaengl, Hitler's personal private secretary and court jester, who introduced him to the Nazi leader, who read his speeches with interest. Nothing is known about Mosley's visit.

On 13 January, in London, Nicolson was visited by Cimmie, who was pregnant and in poor health. Her relationship with her husband was 'wretched' and had rendered her 'miserable, angry and confused'. She said she loathed Fascism. Five days later Mosley returned, buoyed by Mussolini's advice to call himself a Fascist. He hoped in the autumn to rope in Rothermere but feared he could not be kept 'on ice for so long, and that we may be forced to do something violent in the spring'.

Hitler announced he was a candidate for the presidency on 22 January

1932. In the *Evening Standard* Boothby said Hitler had 'youth, abundant vitality, and passion', and that 'deeply felt passion retains the power to move men to heroic action and painful sacrifice'. On the same day Nicolson and Hobhouse arrived in Berlin on a fact-finding mission, even though the former felt the Nazis had been 'a catastrophe'. He wrote to Vita that he had learnt that if Hitler came to power 'he will get rid of all the Jews'. Nicolson was an upper-class anti-Semite with attitudes rooted in his reaction against Bolshevism and was pro-Zionist because it removed Jews from the country. He was appalled by Nazi methods but admitted he 'disliked Jews'. Nicolson spent time in a debauched tour of Berlin nightclubs after meeting Peter Rodd and the bisexual Tom Mitford. 'Everyone looked hungry, with eyes like wolves, and Hitler was the sole topic of conversation.'

The NP had East End Jewish ex-servicemen members, who met in a Jewish-owned property in Bow. They marched with the NP because they were afraid of being portrayed as unpatriotic. Philip Sylvester, father of the art critic David, was a member. A Russian émigré with an antique shop in Chancery Lane, Philip was a prominent Zionist, who preferred gentiles as friends and invited leading speakers to his synagogue for debate. He did express disquiet over NP policy and sought from Mosley 'reassurances that the movement was not anti-Semitic'.

At the beginning of 1932 Kid Lewis – born Solomon Mendeloff – visited Mosley with his son, Morton, with a similar request. Mosley sat at his desk flanked by brown-shirted bodyguards who gave the Fascist salute. When Lewis demanded to know if he was anti-Semitic, Mosley smiled at his naivety and replied, 'Yes.' At which point Lewis allegedly 'struck an open hand across Mosley's face, sending him and his chair crashing against the wall'. Nicolson told Mosley an openly anti-Semitic movement would be counter-productive, in terms of converting public opinion, because of Britain's underlying liberal culture.

Rothermere gave Mosley space in the *Mail* on 1 February to outline the 'new psychology'. With Mussolini, 'Every moment possible is wrung from time; the mind is hard, concentrated, direct – in a word, "Modern".' The secretive King's Road club became the core of the new movement. Hodge thought it 'girl-guidish on the surface' but there was the 'urge of elderly leaders to achieve power at any price'. He disliked what he saw and left the NP. Fired up by the trip to Italy, Mosley set about turning NUPA into a 'Union of Fascists' and searched for allies in the obscure world of Fascist groups. Robert Forgan approached the Imperial Fascist League (IFL) and the British Fascists (BF) with a proposal that they accept Mosley as leader and merge with the NP.

These Fascist parties recruited from the ranks of the British Fascisti, which had recalled the jingoism of Chamberlain's social imperialist campaign and adopted similar nationalist beliefs and use of anti-Semitism. Before the First World War, politicians had faced militant action by suffragettes, trade union-ists and Ulster Unionists, while diehards bent on national regeneration revolted against the liberal State. They praised men of action and supported a militancy which 'shaded off imperceptibly into a cult of violence'. A leading figure was Henry Page Croft, whose National Party, created in 1917, campaigned for the organic State, in which citizens would work to end unemployment and poverty. In his call for a joint council of employers and employees, and policies of a minimum wage, profit-sharing and Imperial Preference, one glimpses a 'body of opinion which foreshadowed 1930s fascism'.

Croft countered the idea of workers' revolution with 'national socialism'. His Nietzschean socialism of the Right idealized a nation threatened by 'alien' influences. His backing of anti-alien laws owed much to wartime anti-German and anti-Jewish riots instigated by the thugs of the Anti-German Union whose founder, Sir George Makgill, alleged that a 'hidden hand' of German Jews controlled events. His network of spies investigated disloyal elements, reports of which went to MI5 Director-General Sir Vernon Kell. At the war's end the AGU was transformed into the British Empire Union, with funds from William Morris – Mosley's principal backer. Makgill's son, Sir Donald, became a BUF member and his wife headed its women's unit. Croft's sister also became a Blackshirt.

Croft lacked magnetism and his National Party was wiped out at the 1918 general election. Industrial unrest resumed post-war as workers tried to pre-serve wartime gains. The Labour Party's growth and the emergence of the Communist Party unnerved employers, who turned to Makgill, who set up the Industrial Intelligence Board (IIB) to keep them abreast of unrest. It supplied intelligence to Lieutenant-Colonel John Carter, a former senior MI5 officer responsible for the Special Branch. Makgill recruited ex-officers to launch assaults on strikers. These 'gentleman soldiers', defending 'Old England' from Jews and Bolsheviks, figured prominently in post-war fiction.

Sapper's Bulldog Drummond (1920) battled 'Bolsheviks, Anarchists, members of the Do-no-work-and-have-all-the-money Brigade', who organized industrial unrest by 'using the tub-thumping Bolshies as tools', so that Jewish financiers could make fortunes. Mosley conformed to the stereotypical Sapper hero who had been in France where 'the salt of the earth went to Play the Great Game'. Captain Drummond was the decent Englishman who believed the working classes needed gentleman sportsmen to lead them against the Communists. In The Black Gang (1922) Drummond's vigilante squad give the Bolshevik Jews 'a taste of their own medicine – a taste of the whip'.

Virginia Woolf observed that strikes 'broke in to our life more than the war did'. Fear of revolution hung over society and thrust 'itself into consciousness whenever the people came out on to the streets en masse'. The threat of general strikes in 1920–21 was crucial in the development of Fascist groups. Croft used paramilitaries to disrupt strikes and promoted the Corporate State as a way of eliminating class and industrial confrontation. His ideas were disseminated by currency crank Arthur Kitson in the *Age of Plenty* (later the pro-Mosley *New Political Economics* journal). The National Party had the elements of a Fascist movement and Croft compared his failed effort with Mosley's: both were 'tilting at windmills'.

The National Party was absorbed in 1922 into a wider movement headed by the Duke of Northumberland, an influential diehard figure with MI5 connections. He established the *Patriot*, which detailed the conspiracy against the Empire. Anti-Communism transformed his racialism into anti-Semitism, largely by way of Nesta Webster, wife of a police official from an Anglo-Indian family. As the daughter of a bank director, it was ironic that she dedicated her life to exposing the conspiracy of international finance. Her writings influenced Churchill, Lord Sydenham, Henry Hamilton Beamish, founder of the Britons Publishing Society, A. K. Chesterton, senior BUF propagandist, and Arnold Leese, leader of the Imperial Fascist League.

The sense of impending crisis and the example of Mussolini were the motivating factors in Northumberland's creation of the British Fascisti (BF). 'All those brutal attacks on Christianity, individual liberty, patriotism and loyalty to the throne,' he warned, 'under which – but for the coming of Fascism – Italian civilization had perished, are to be reproduced here in Britain in 1923.' In May, twenty-six-year-old Miss Rotha Lintorn-Orman asked for recruits in the *Patriot*, whose offices housed the BF headquarters. She had served in a volunteer ambulance corps founded by her mother, who provided funds of £50,000 (£1.25 m). Lintorn-Orman shared premises in Great Russell Street with the Partito Nazionale Fascista Italiano who marched alongside their BF counterparts. The BF, however, was not truly Fascist. Members, who wore black handkerchiefs in their top pockets, were card-carrying Conservatives, with a 'Thatcherite' agenda of secret ballots in trade unions, abolition of picketing, consumption of Empire goods, State economy, promoting agriculture, suppression of Communist Sunday schools and anti-alienism.

According to its President, Brigadier-General R. B. D. Blakeney, the BF would, in 'the spirit of intelligent patriotism', prevent the 'swarms from the slums' being used by Bolsheviks through its paramilitary force maintaining vital public services in the event of a general strike. Military and upper-middle-class members joined from the Anti-Socialist Union with which it co-operated in anti-Communist activities. Propaganda written by Nestor Webster pushed Empire co-operation and social reform in a manner similar to Mosley. *Express* editor Ralph Blumenfeld was one ASU supporter who flirted with Fascism, as did Sir George Makgill, whose contact with the BF was future Tory MP John Baker White.

White sat on the BF's Fascisti Grand Council as its first Intelligence Chief. Running Section D of Makgill's IIB, he investigated 'subversion, communism, and the international traffic in drugs and women'. He was in regular contact with MI5's Brigadier Jasper Harker – an example of the alignment between Fascism's anti-Communism and MI5's counter-subversion work. A branch of the War Office staffed by army officers, MI5 duties included detecting espionage and seditious movements directed against the armed forces. Its funding was drawn from the Secret Service fund administered by the Foreign Office's Permanent Under-Secretary of State. Because MI5's work was confined to British territory, enquiries against 'suspicious individuals and subversive political movements' abroad were carried out by MI6, using agents run by Carter's SB unit.

Makgill's leading operative in Liverpool was the BEU's James McGuirk Hughes, who had a gift for intelligence work against left-wing groups. Under the pseudonym 'P. G. Taylor', he later ran the BUF's Department Z. Born to Katherine McGuirk and tram owner Arthur Hughes, he was granted a commission in the RFC. In 1920, working as a political organizer, he married Valerie Taylor Tahan, whose father was connected to shipping. BUF member Alex Miles said Hughes boasted he had been 'expelled from Soviet Russia for espionage and from his membership of the CPGB for the same purpose'. His 'Special Propaganda Section' was financed by Cunard, to whom he provided a blacklisting service. His infiltration agents obtained plans on strikes and undertook agent provocateur activities on behalf of the BF. During 1924, in a 'severe blow to the Reds', he burgled the headquarters of the International of Labour Unions and the Minority Movement. Hughes claimed the help of Scotland Yard and received funds from SB liaison officer John Carter.

One of White's agents was Maxwell Knight, later responsible for MI5's infiltration of Mosley's BUF. That he served as BF Director of Intelligence (1924–7) was later confirmed by BF member and BUF Director-General Neil Francis Hawkins. Knight was responsible for the paramilitary units, counter-espionage and intelligence gathering, and establishing Fascist cells in trade unions. A colleague was William Joyce, with whom he shared a girlfriend, Hazel Barr, a member of the BEU.

Born in New York, Joyce was a naturalized American citizen. In 1909 his family returned to Ireland, where they rented land from Lord Clanmorris (his son John Bingham became an MI5 officer in Knight's section). Brought up as an 'extreme Conservative of strong Imperialistic ideals' with an inflated sense of patriotism, he grew up in a world of feud and betrayal. He elevated his work as a fifteen-year-old informer for the Black and Tans to 'service with the regular forces of the Crown in an intelligence capacity against the Irish guerrillas'. Chillingly, a teacher predicted he would 'either do something very great in the world or he will finish on the end of a rope'. In 1922 the family moved to

England and he enrolled in the University of London's Officer Training Corps. A year later he started an English Language course at Birkbeck College and became president of its Conservative society, working as a volunteer for Lord Howe, Lord Curzon's son.

In January 1924 the seventeen-year-old Joyce joined the 'K' society, a shadowy group of BF working-class thugs who battled with Communists. They eventually gained the upper hand and, White claimed, 'forced the Communist Party to abandon much of its militant activity, such as breaking up constitutional meetings by force, denying its opponents free speech'. This is what Mosley hoped to achieve. While protecting Jewish Tory candidate Jack Lazarus during the 1924 general election, Joyce was razored by a 'Jewish Communist'. The *Mail* featured his photograph after the attack, with the caption 'Victim of Hooliganism'. With a scar running from his right ear to his mouth, Joyce became a youthful hero of British Fascism.

In 1924 the BF was renamed the British Fascists to avoid the charge that it owed loyalty to Italy. Membership was estimated at 100,000, with the Women's Units accounting for a sixth of the total. This included ex-suffragette Mary Allen, who created the Women's Police Auxiliary and went on to become a Mosleyite. She was part of an upper-class lesbian subculture among militant women's groups on the extreme right.

Knight's section became notorious as a result of its operations, which prompted newspapers to suggest the BF was a more serious menace than the Communists. The kidnapping in March 1925 of Harry Pollitt, Secretary of the National Minority Movement, caused outrage. Despite this, Knight was invited to an Intelligence Persons' Club dinner hosted by Vernon Kell at the Hyde Park Hotel and was asked to join a reserve of intelligence officers in case of a national emergency. When the BF began recruiting in military circles, the Army Council prohibited serving personnel from joining any Fascist body to prevent it from exploiting its military associations. Similar fears were expressed when Mosley and 'P. G. Taylor' planned to set up Fascist 'cells' in the armed forces.

With its army-style units designed to organize transport and communications in an emergency, the BF provided a model for the semi-official Organization for the Maintenance of Supplies (OMS) but the government was hostile to BF offers to provide volunteers for the strike-breaking OMS. Having previously turned a blind eye to BF activities, Home Secretary Joynson-Hicks threatened to withdraw support for the OMS if the BF request was accepted. The Home Office portrayed the BF as an eccentric movement surviving on the resources of Lintorn-Orman, who was dependent on alcohol and drugs. 'Jix' objected to the BF's vague commitment to corporatism and Fascism, and requested it dismantle its paramilitary units, which was accepted by most members when the General Strike erupted.

A rival National Fascisti was formed by disaffected members. One defector was Colonel Bingham, an important influence on Mosley's thinking on Fascism, and Arnold Leese, who reacted against BF policy of allowing Jewish members. The NF was a small, highly visible group of militant blackshirts, inspired by Mussolini and advocates of the Corporate State. The NF ran a boxing and fencing club to train members for direct action. However, it quickly dissolved following public ridicule of its militarism, which included parading with drawn swords. NF members later formed an East End BUF branch in Bow.

The failure of the General Strike dissipated the threat of revolution and, with the Communist Party in decline, the BF was left without a cause. Diehards such as Croft subsequently used the BF's 'Q' divisions of 'able bodied men of pure British race' to steward meetings. They were led by an officer bearing a Union Jack, who took the platform salute as the speaker passed through. In a manner copied by Mosley, hecklers were removed by BF stewards placed throughout the halls.

In the 1929 General Election the BF proclaimed the solution to national bankruptcy was a 'man of great patriotism', who would impose tariffs, cut expenditure and institute a State lottery. The BF, however, was soon splitting into factions. One centred on the North Riding's Lady Downe and the director of the Children's Clubs, Lady Sydenham. A second sought a Fascist ideology and was tied to the British Institute in Florence and its director, Captain Harold Goad, who had been on the first Fascist march in London, and James Strachey Barnes of the Royal Institute of International Affairs. In spring 1923 the Institute moved into the Palazzo Antinori and Goad worked hand-in-glove with the Fascists. Like Mosley, he believed the guilds contained elements of Fascism and his books, *What is Fascism?* and *The Making of the Corporate State*, transposed Italian principles into the British experience.

A relation of John Strachey, Barnes was brought up in Italy and converted to Catholicism. An RFC pilot, post-war he served under Harold Nicolson as an expert on Albania and became a friend of Mussolini. Barnes said Fascism would 'create harmony in the universe by transcending the decadence of western society'. In 1927 he became Secretary of the Lausanne-based Centre International d'Etudes sur le Fascisme (CINEF). A year later he published *The Universal Aspects of Fascism*, with a foreword by Mussolini, and agitated for a Fascist international to promote corporatism and European union. On 27 October 1930 Mussolini acclaimed Fascism as a 'universal phenomenon'. From this moment, wrote Dino Grandi, later ambassador in London, Mussolini 'tried to help the "grotesque" imitation of fascism abroad', including the 'ambitious Mosley'.

Barnes eulogized Fascism in a volume for the 1931 Everyman Home Library and criticized the BF for its lack of ideology. It did subsequently call for corporations and attempted – possibly at Mosley's instigation – to co-ordinate activists into a single body. In May the BF, Unity Band, Legion of Loyalists, Kensington Fascists and Imperial Fascists called for the abolition of the 'system of parliamentary party government'. The BF co-operated with the National Citizens' Union (NCU), whose Vice-President, Esmond Harmsworth, employed the 'Q' divisions to steward its 'Hands Off Our Empire' crusade. The BF colour guard at the Croft-organized Albert Hall rally was led by Francis Hawkins, formerly of the OMS. At the same time, Rothermere's United Empire Party affiliated with the Unity Band, a group of anti-Semitic Christians. BF members were anti-Semitic – of the 'mild, doctrinaire type which excludes Jews from golf clubs' – but it was only sanctioned as official policy after Mosley's approach.

Maxwell Knight resigned from the BF in 1931 to join MI5, where he recruited agents to penetrate the Communist Party. Hawkins went to a meeting at the War Office where Knight revealed he was assisting the BF's anti-Communist work. At the same time Knight sounded out Joyce 'on whether he would go to Germany as a British agent, become naturalised and join the Nazi Party'. That he ran Joyce was confirmed by the latter's brother, Quentin, who was separated from fellow internees in 1940 because he knew of his interrogator's Fascist past.

Graduating with a first-class honours degree from London University, Joyce married Hazel Barr. He joined the Junior Imperial League as a speaker in Chelsea. He avoided expressing his anti-Semitic feelings among the upper classes, who were 'so intermarried with Jewish grandees that half of them were half-Jewish themselves'. He befriended solicitor Captain Charles Lewis (later editor of the BUF's *Blackshirt* newspaper) and hoped to become an MP. He was not, however, liked and when it was discovered he had seduced one of his pupils and wanted a divorce to marry her, moral pressure was brought to bear and he left the 'Imps' just before the National government was formed. Rebuffing MI5's approach, Joyce took up psychology at King's College. Knight noted the emergence of 'a natural aptitude for intrigue and an abhorrence of compromise'.

Knight later used his BF connections in operations against Mosley. Hawkins's ex-Communist father-in-law, Arnold Bristol, was recruited and his brother-in-law also spied on the BUF. While Knight was sympathetic to an anti-Communist version of Fascism, he was antagonistic to German Nazism; it was a common prejudice on the extreme right. However, it raises the issue of Joyce's role within the BUF. Was his extremism explained by his action as an agent provocateur?

Mosley met with Hawkins of the BF's Grand Council. A short, tubby salesman of surgical instruments and lineal descendant of the Elizabethan sailor, he attended several NP meetings. His political imagination was limited to the idea that 'the country needed tidy, orderly administration to replace the confusions of democracy' but he had been impressed by Mosley's intention to achieve power speedily and introduce a Corporate State, and recommended acceptance of Mosley's terms.

Mosley's personal life was at the time undergoing a major upheaval. On 28 February, at the twenty-first birthday party of Barbara St John Hutchinson – soon to marry Victor Rothschild – he sat next to Diana Guinness. Tall, slim and blue-eyed, the beautiful twenty-one-year-old knew of his reputation as a lady killer. The two discussed politics all through dinner but she had decided she had met her fate. They began an affair, which neither bothered to keep secret. From that first encounter she followed him 'absolutely blindly'; fell wildly in love and 'knew it would never end, except with death'.

The Hon. Diana Freeman-Mitford was born on 10 June 1910, the fourth child of seven born to Sydney and David Mitford, Lord and Lady Redesdale. The 'unconventional personality of their father and the toughness needed to survive the bullying of the eldest sister, Nancy, had honed a personality with a core of steel'. Already a star, at eighteen she married the Hon. Bryan Guinness, the rich poet-heir to Lord Moyne. His father was Colonel Walter Guinness, Minister of Agriculture and brother of the chairman of the Guinness brewery. James Lees-Milne said Diana was 'a goddess, more perfect, more celestial than Botticelli's sea-borne Venus'. An infatuated Evelyn Waugh, who dedicated his 1929 novel, *Vile Bodies*, to her, thought her beauty 'ran through the room like a peal of bells'.

The couple had two children, Jonathan and Desmond. In summer 1930, when boredom 'left her longing for the metropolitan pleasures', Diana returned to London, determined to be 'unlike anybody else'. She was intelligent and witty, and quickly made an impact on the small, close-knit London society. Her house in Buckingham Street, wrote James Knox, became a 'haven for her husband's most amusing friends', notably Waugh, who was in love with her, the homosexual writer Robert Byron, the poet John Betjeman, the Anglo-American Brian Howard and Harold Acton. Through such friends she enjoyed the intellectual company she craved. Diana was designated to take over the leadership of London society from Lady Cunard, who called her 'Golden Corn' and treated her as a surrogate daughter.

Vaguely pro-Liberal, Diana admired Lloyd George. She was anti-Tory and would not vote for her father-in-law. Mosley was not her 'genre. None of my other friends was the least bit like him.' But she did have a tendency to hero-worship and welcomed 'a single, strong leader who would accomplish wonderful things'. Mosley was sure of himself: 'He knew what to do to solve the economic disaster we were living through; he was certain he could cure employment. Lucid, logical, forceful and persuasive, he soon convinced me.'

Her son Jonathan suggested, 'It was the passion of Juliet and the conversion of St Paul; emotion and conviction were inseparable.'

Cimmie had been unwell for months, suffering from fainting spells. On 8 March Nicolson learnt she had 'kidney trouble' and there was concern she might lose the baby. Throughout the spring, Georgia Sitwell clung to her position as Mosley's chief mistress as his relationship with Diana blossomed.

The Guinnesses moved to Cheyne Walk, to a house which had belonged to the American artist James Whistler. Diana's social life was taken up with endless parties and new social friends were added, including eccentric composer Lord Berners, surrealist Edward James and dancer Tilly Losch, with whom Diana's brother, Tom Mitford, was in love. However, this was not enough for Diana. When Mosley said she could help him achieve his dreams, she felt she had been enlisted in a crusade. In Mosley, Lees-Milne observed, Diana 'found her hero, the man of her dreams. His cause became her cause and she subordinated everything to his dynamic interests.' Randolph Churchill remarked that she had 'no fundamental moral sense'. She rarely did anything wrong, but 'did not actually see anything wrong in sin'. Diana became a political animal with a potential for extremism.

In March 1932 Mosley wrote in the *Political Quarterly* that the crisis would produce 'new parties, new types and new forces'. He intended to meet the crisis with a movement for those who 'turned their backs on the old world and on the old political system'. Communism would supersede the 'woolly-headed Social Democrats and flabby conservatism' but the old parties whose organization 'rests on women's buns and tea fights will not put up five minutes resistance against the new and modern reality'. Only the Corporate State could defeat Communism. The new movement 'must be indigenous and peculiar to the British mind and nature', since its supporters would be dismissed as 'fanatics and romantics'. At a meeting with Forgan and Howard, it was suggested NUPA 'keep fascismo alive in this country and that the NP can now acknowledge its own death'. On 5 April the New Party was dissolved. Five days later Hitler came second to Hindenburg in the German presidential election.

Howard greeted the end with relief, since Mosley's thoughts were with Fascism, which he detested. Mosley's 'shirt darkened as day followed day'. He decided to adopt as the movement's symbol the fasces, the bundle of sticks symbolizing unity, and the axe, as carried by the lictors of ancient Rome, signifying the power of the State. Soon afterwards, Nicolson 'picked his hat off the peg', while Howard was handed his, and they both walked out of the NP together. Howard joined Beaverbrook's Empire Crusade Club and became a ruthless political journalist of 'unbespoken hatred for the men in power' and a prominent figure in Moral Rearmament. Peter Eckersley, who left to take up consultancy work, said he was 'only a Mosleyite when it seemed to me that he was leading a movement to bring about the true reforming spirit of the Labour Party. I cannot feel that Mosley's present methods are bringing that about.'

Nicolson hoped Mosley would retire into a 'studious life for a bit', and then emerge fortified to become Prime Minister. If he became entangled with the 'boys' brigade', he would become 'a revolutionary – and to that waste land I cannot follow him'. Nicolson joined National Labour; Colin Coote thought this 'another lost cause which consisted of himself, MacDonald's father and son – and the unfortunate J. H. Thomas'. Cyril Connolly regarded him as 'too upper-class and international to fit into the Labour Party, too patrician to accept the Tories' appeasing worldliness, too infected with the New Party's pristine desire for change and action to vote Liberal'. Soon afterwards, Nicolson published a novel, *Public Faces*, which envisaged a Churchill–Mosley government by the mid thirties.

Establishment friends had not abandoned Mosley. On 15 March he was approached by Tory whip David Margesson to stand as a National Independent, and J. M. Kenworthy MP, who suggested he lead the Labour Party. He said it 'would be impossible for him to re-enter the "machine" of one of the older parties' and 'place himself in a strait-waistcoat'. The country was entering a new phase and he felt he could accomplish more as a Fascist. Nicolson argued people would not stand for violence and if he resorted to it, he would be 'detested by a few and ridiculed by many'. He was prepared, however, to run the risk of 'further failure, ridicule and assault, rather than allow the active forces in this country to fall into other hands'. When Georgia Sitwell lunched with him, she found him 'a trifle absurd as usual about Superman, Nietzsche, Schiller and Napoleon'.

On 27 April Mosley chaired a NUPA meeting at which Henry Hamilton Beamish of the Britons Society and Arnold Leese of the Imperial Fascist League spoke on 'The Blindness of British Politics under the Jewish Money-Power'. Son of an admiral, brother of a Tory MP, underpinning Beamish's anti-Semitism was the disillusionment of the post-war years, which he channelled into resentment and prejudice. A retired veterinary surgeon and authority on camel diseases, Leese had been a member of the BF and the National Fascists. The IFL was very much his private affair. With only 500 members, it would have been without importance if the Nazis had not chosen to promote it. The ILF's magazine, *The Fascist*, received a donation from a 'National Socialist' – Dr Thost of the *Völkischer Beobachter*, who wrote in the journal that Hitlerism was peacefully working for the unity of the Nordic race. MI5 reported that the IFL, whose flag featured a swastika superimposed on the Union Jack, 'sought to maintain the closest relationship with Germany'.

On 8 May NUPA held a rally in Trafalgar Square attended by 1,500 people, who heard its new Fascist anthem. 'Communists' heckled speeches by Robert O'Hagen, Patrick Moir and Vincent Collier, but were held in check by grey-shirt stewards. Ten days later they spoke on 'The New Party's Approach to Fascism' to sympathetic IFL members who insisted on the primacy of the Jewish question. Leese's comment, that he accepted corporatism but anti-Semitism would obscure it, led to an intense debate within NUPA. Moir was 'anxious to conduct an entirely anti-Jewish campaign at the expense of all other interests'. NUPA said that if Jews 'impede our movement's constructive policy, they will be dealt with as occasion demands'.

Leese disliked Mosley's 'muscling in to the fascist field' and was unwilling to sacrifice his leadership to an opportunist who rejected racial nationalism. 'Hitlerism at its base is the true Fascism of the Northern European, and true guide to our own politics in the years ahead,' he declared. The psychologically impaired Leese said Mosley was a 'kosher fascist' run by Jews to discredit Fascism. Mosley regarded the IFL as a crank society, which existed purely for 'the purpose of Jew-baiting'. He considered the Protocols of the Elders of Zion, which it and the Britons promoted, a silly forgery, and the existence of a world-wide secret conspiracy a ludicrous fantasy. He had, however, no qualms about their members joining NUPA.

The crisis of Cimmie's health passed and on 25 April she gave birth to a third child, Michael, who was christened at Morden Church with Nicolson, Forgan and Zita James as godparents. In pain with the kidney infection, Cimmie had 'the exuberance that could light people up when she came into a room', but she was no longer elegant. In order to regain her health, she left for the Villa d'Este. She wrote to her husband on the occasion of their twelfth wedding anniversary, hoping the year would be 'better than beastly 1931' and that 'loveliness and understanding and sympathy be with us and between us'.

Mosley was in discussion with Hawkins, whose aide was E. G. Mandeville-Roe, a schoolmaster and the editor of British Fascist. He argued that the BF must adapt its ideas 'to suit the truth of the moment' which required the Corporate State and an anti-Semitic policy barring Jews from public posts. The adoption of Fascist ideology was less the result of the economic crisis than of the state of the BF, which was reduced to a small hard core. The Communist Party was not a serious threat and the General Strike's end proved the threat of revolution had passed.

A memorandum setting out a basis for fusion with NUPA ran into opposition from an angry Ms Lintorn-Orman, who considered Mosley a near-Communist. The three BF Grand Council women's units representatives rejected the merger, whereupon Hawkins and Mandeville-Roe resigned to join Mosley. With them went the BF's most effective official, Lieutenant Colonel

H. W. Johnstone, chief of the men's units and, importantly, the membership lists.

There was little radicalism in the BF's authoritarian reaction but it did link itself to Italian Fascism, even if in a diluted form. Mandeville-Roe wrote a book on the Corporate State which, together with the work of Alexander Raven Thomson, was the source of such ideas in the BUF. The BF also provided a model for organization and a recruitment pool for his administrative clique. However, its paramilitarism and foreign style offended public opinion. Ultimately, it failed because anti-Communism and nationalism had more respectable outlets.

A worried Nicolson told Mosley it would prove impossible to disassociate NUPA from 'young Bermondsey boys with *Gummiknüppel*'. It was the 'more active element which colours the whole. If we ever have fascism in this country, it will creep in disguised in the red, white, and blue of patriotism and the young conservatives.' The NP's transition to Fascism was marked by the integration of 'nationalist, socialist, imperialist and racist attitudes into a coherent theory of National Socialism'. This version of social reform, disciplined planning and the organic State partly originated with Nicolson's friends in Vienna, some of whom joined the SS.

Support for National Socialism came from A. R. Orage, who on his return to England joined the Economic Freedom League, and Maurice Rickett's Chandos group, formed by social creditors and distributivists attracted to the new age philosophy of Dmitri Mitrinovic, an émigré Serbian sage. The group was effectively the editorial board of Orage's fresh venture, the *New English Weekly* (*NEW*). Edited by Philip Mairet, contributors included T. S. Eliot, A. J. Penty, Hilaire Belloc and Italian apologists Ezra Pound and Odon Por. The *NEW* praised Mosley for being the political champion who gave expression to the revolt of youth. It disliked the violence associated with Fascism but pleaded that its excesses were 'as peculiar to Italy as are particular manifestations of communism to Russia'.

On 25 May Lord Tavistock addressed NUPA on the 'Douglas System of Social Credit'. A vegetarian pacifist, writer on the care of parrots and heir to the Duke of Bedford, his National Credit Association wanted a 'just and equitable system of finance, scientifically adjusted to the needs of the nation'. Tavistock, MI5 reported, had flirted with Communism and 'fell into the hands of every kind of crank and eccentric'. Despite promoting autarchy and repudiating the liberal-socialist past, he was dismissed by ex-ILPers Marshall Diston and Leslie Cumings on the basis that Britain's dependency on foreign food supplies was a more important issue than 'this dubious system'.

ILP input is a striking feature of the NUPA debates. The Communist Party's Rajani Palme Dutt argued the Blackshirts emerged from 'the heart of the Labour Party and the ILP'. So did BF members who dismissed Mosley's

ILP-style propaganda as 'merely a Socialistic attack on capitalism under the name of Fascism'. Certainly a NUPA faction believed Mosley's objectives were 'frankly socialistic'. Fascism, claimed Bill Risdon, was 'custodian of the ideals of the early Socialist pioneers' and Mosley was the twentieth-century equivalent of Robert Owen.

John Strachey thought Bill Allen was surprisingly left-wing and accepted that Mosley had developed a *fascisme du gauche*. It was an economic revolt against obsolete capitalism and a spiritual reaction against materialist Marxism. Labour Party critics noted the similarity with the authoritarian socialism of Hendrik de Man of the Belgian Workers Party and the French neo-socialists around Marcel Déat. These Front Generation socialists, notes Philip Rees, were 'equally disillusioned with the dogmatic sterility of socialism, concerned with the gap between radical rhetoric and conservative practice, disturbed by the bureaucratisation and embourgeoisment of the official labour movement'. In trying to broaden socialism's appeal to the middle classes and youth, the neo-socialists accepted the need for authority and order, and above all nationalism.

NUPA policy, said Risdon, rested on nationalism, preservation of private property and the notion that 'the interests of the State as a whole comprised the interests of every section within the State'. ILP deserter John Scanlon believed that if technicians, managers and workers 'could combine to produce for use, they could end the fear of poverty and the fear of war tomorrow'. Ideas came from left sources but the emphasis was not on class conflict, but on a productivist alliance of all classes within the nation to produce national unity. This black socialism, wrote Oswald Spengler, was about dominating life: 'We need a class of socialist mastermen. Once again: socialism means power, power and yet again power.' Leadership and discipline were the keys to integrating the working class into the community and the basis for national regeneration. Thurlow notes that Mosley's aristocratic image of society, the technocratic belief in progress and vision of men as machines, enabled him to slip easily from socialism to Fascism.

On 28 May Randolph Churchill celebrated his twenty-first birthday at Claridge's. Rude, spoiled and unstable, he was related to the Mitfords through his maternal grandmother, Lady Hozier, sister of their maternal grandmother, Lady Clementine Mitford. His best friend at Eton had been Tom Mitford and, at sixteen, he fell in love with Diana. He dropped out of Oxford, took to drinking and gambling, and became notorious as a boorish party guest. Mosley attended his party with Rothermere and Esmond Harmsworth, Beaverbrook and Max Aitken, Viscount Hailsham and Quintin Hogg, Lord Hugh Cecil, Austen Chamberlain and General Sir Ian Hamilton. Mosley was still a respected figure.

Although contemptuous of MacDonald's leadership, Liberal free trader

Robert Bernays feared Mosley's extra-parliamentarianism and Churchill's agitation over India might become inter-twined and undermine the National government. Churchill's ally was Rothermere, who wanted to involve Lord Lloyd in the India Defence Committee, whose Secretary was ex-British Fascist Patrick Donner. After a visit to Rome, Churchill, who believed Fascism had saved Italy from the Bolsheviks, was greeted in the Commons with ironic cries of 'Mussolini' by MPs who suspected his dictatorial ambitions. A vague kind of corporatism was accepted by the Milnerites Lord Lloyd and Henry Page Croft, who were favourably disposed to Fascism. However, Austen Chamberlain, whose wife wore a Fascist pin, said that Mussolini's methods, though admirable in Italy, would not work in Britain.

Mosley had not abandoned ideas of an anti-Semitic campaign. He obliquely outlined the policy in 'The New Movement Fights for the Corporate State': 'International financiers who to-day control our financial system in the interests of foreigners, and the alien agitators whose propaganda seeks to destroy the greatness of Britain in the interest of foreign powers, will be sent where they belong. Britain First will be the motto of the Corporate State.' This was code for Jews and Communists, who, in the conspiracy theory, were one and the same.

Mosley was writing *The Greater Britain*, an outline of Fascist policy. His reference to a conspiracy of 'international Jewish bankers' was dropped when Nicolson complained it displayed a 'destructive platform manner'. Jewish banks are the 'villains of the piece' but there is a 'Nazi note in these denunciations which will cause many people to question your seriousness'. Readers were 'impressed by propagandists who take off their boots before they start kicking below the belt'. Mosley thought Nicolson 'unsuited to the rough and tumble of a new movement advancing novel ideas'. The idea attracted him 'but he was repelled by the process; he loved the end, but could not bear the means'. Nicolson told Cimmie the passage had been cut but Mosley merely deleted the overt Jewish references. 'We have within the nation a power largely controlled by alien elements, which arrogates to itself a power above the State, and has used that influence to drive flaccid governments of all political parties along the high road to national disaster . . . No State can tolerate within its body the irresponsible superiority of such a power.'

Such representations saturated British society long before they were institutionalized by Mosley. The image of the Jew which, Bryan Cheyette argues, was central to modern literature, was ambivalent, in that the Jew was constructed as spectacularly civilized but also as an unchanging Semitic other. It followed there were 'good' Jews (Mosley's friends) who adapted to patriotic and cultural norms, and 'bad' Jews, who conspired to undermine the national interest. It was in this latter tradition that Mosley's anti-Semitism was grounded. Unlike the Nazis and the IFL, he rejected the idea that biology prevented Jews from changing their behaviour, allowing him to make a distinction between different forms of Jewish conduct.

Before the First World War, national anxieties were projected on to Jews. J. A. Hobson labelled them international financiers par excellence, with a mixture of radical and reactionary politics; Catholic authors Hilaire Belloc and G. K. Chesterton highlighted 'Jewish' finance scandals, such as the Marconi affair, and depicted Jewish financiers as an alien force destroying Britain. Post-war socialist suspicion of capitalist power was transferred into fear of the 'golden international', while nationalists, wary of any propensity to form a nation within a nation, attacked Jewish influence.

The chief interest that Mosley challenged was not capitalism but finance, a power within the State. He argued the system of international finance was kept going 'for the sole reason that the process is a means of collecting the usury of the City'. Finance allowed 'quick jumping financiers' to gamble with the prosperity of industries and nations. It broke governments 'by cracking the whip of a financial logic to which all parties in the state subscribed'. People must organize against the 'giant rogues' of international finance 'their own police force to deal with the enemy and the exploiter'.

In attacking the City, Mosley would be targeting his own class. Given that abolition of class conflict was central to Fascism, the solution was to have the Jews represent all that was bad about finance. 'You can hardly exhort your storm-troopers to street fighting', Cecil Melville wrote, 'with an involved analysis of the difference between productive capital and loan capital.' So, 'instead of just downing the Banker for being a Banker, let's down the Banker as being a Jew!' This removed the 'anti-capitalist sting' and united both right and left by enabling them to 'project their own foreignness vis-à-vis the English political culture on to the Jew'.

A Liberal MP, Belloc tested 'the limits of liberalism from the left – by maintaining a rabid anti-capitalism – and from the right – by positioning at the heart of his politics an exclusivist vocabulary around "race" and nation'. He supported Action Française, whose leader Charles Maurras provided the model for Mosley's anti-Semitism. Belloc presented a vision of an all-powerful 'Anglo-Judaic plutocracy' dominating the country but claimed 'no-one can say with truth that I have ever objected to the practice of Judaism'. However, 'I do object most strongly to Jewish cosmopolitan financial influence.' Mosley, too, reacted to 'facts' about Jewish power in a 'rational' non-fanatical way. He had believed anti-Semitism was for 'halfwits' but began to think about Jews as 'unpleasant foreigners, with no right to interfere in "British" business'.

Melville recognized that anti-Semitism was 'integral to fascism and essential for the purpose of mob politics'. Maurras thought it a 'methodical necessity, a real historical requirement'. It all seemed 'terribly difficult without the providential appearance of anti-semitism'. Things were 'smoothed over, and simplified. If one were not an anti-semite through patriotism, one would become one through a simple sense of opportunity.' Melville agreed there was in Mosley a 'good deal of the dross of political opportunism'. He became an anti-Semite because he had to. 'The masses could not be taught to hate capitalism, since he only wanted to control it, and he hoped for business donations.' He needed anti-Semitism as an ideology of radical nationalism to retain the devotional core and realized the propaganda gain of 'concentrating all his fire on a single opponent'. During the summer Mosley sanctioned a debate within NUPA on Fascist ideology.

The debates were partially recorded in the three issues of the internal newsletter, the *New Times*, edited by John Proctor. Mosley said it would express 'the vigour and virility of the Movement. Without fear or favour, it will cut through the cant and humbug of current thought and politics to the building of the constructive conception of the Corporate State.' Patrick Moir's survey of policy stated strikes would be ended and financiers prevented from acting against the interests of the State. They would 'clear away the slums, and promote imperial and economic unity, with a firm hand in India'. What needed to be resolved was which variety of Fascism to emulate.

L. G. Waterman worried members placed 'too much emphasis on learning the lessons of the exceptional conditions under which Mussolini came to power'. The use of force was 'only one aspect of the Italian fascists, whereas its underlying aspect was the ideal of a moral revolution'. Sympathy for Leese blinded them to the 'most important object of our movement – the establishment of the Corporate State'. He identified a schism between supporters of Nazism and backers of Italian Fascism. He bemoaned the obsession with Hitler: 'We have more photos of Hitler in the Club than Il Duce.' Waterman argued Mussolini and the Corporate State were superior and regretted the adulation of the 'provocative and disorderly violence of the Nazis'.

Mosley continued to fence all over England and was elected to the committee of the Amateur Fencing Association. Observers noted that, as a symbol of 'Savile Row Fascism', he dressed like a 'fencing instructor with a waist fondly exaggerated by a cummerbund and chest and buttocks thrust out'. Runner-up in the British Épée Championship was a formidable achievement for a man with a gammy leg. On 15 June Mosley and Charles de Beaumont, founder of the All England Club, put on a fencing display for NUPA women. It was unpopular with the head of the Defence Squad, who believed 'a Youth Movement such as ours will lose its manhood the day the first woman enters as a member'. Women 'should never have anything to do with the running of the country. Let's confine women to a monthly Ladies night.'

Cimmie returned from the Villa d'Este in pain but was able to attend, on 19 June, a dinner to which Georgia and Sachie Sitwell were invited. Irene was

shocked by the loucheness of the Mosley set with its 'gossip and "muck"'.
On 7 July the Mosleys went to a party in honour of Diana's sister, Unity, who
arrived with her pet snake, Enid. The 300 guests did not fail to notice that
Diana, in a 'pale grey dress of chiffon and tulle and all the diamonds I could lay
my hands on', spent the evening dancing with Mosley. Next day, she told Cela
Keppel she was in love and wanted to leave Bryan. Soon after, Mosley left for
Paris on the way to his family's holiday in Venice. Diana, too, made her way
through France, where he planned to run into her as if by chance. When they
met at Arles, they went sightseeing and borrowed Bob Boothby's room for
their liaison. Cimmie was aware of the threat posed by the dazzling Diana,
twelve years her junior, and was in pain both physically and emotionally.

Before he left, Mosley told colleagues he was keen to launch an anti-Semitic
campaign against the bankers and appointed a gung-ho Moir to head research
and Cumings to lead the propaganda. Newspapers reported that speakers in
Westminster were attacking Jews. On 7 August a NUPA loudspeaker van in
Croydon broadcast anti-Semitic slogans. When Jewish passers-by objected,
two greyshirts were arrested for shouting 'Down with the Jews'. Members
took exception because 'they think this should be corrected to "Down with
the Bloody Jews"'. Three weeks later, nineteen-year-old J. Maddocks was
convicted of posting anti-Jewish stickers, bearing the words 'Nationalise the
wealth of the Jew Banks' and 'Expel all Jews from the Country'. A NUPA
statement said 'anti-Jewish propaganda is neither authorised nor approved by
Sir Oswald'. The *Jewish Chronicle* on 26 August said these assurances meant
nothing unless Mosley rid his movement of anti-Semites, but this he refused
to do.

With Mosley back in London, bickering continued within NUPA over
anti-Semitism and the means of seeking power. Cumings told the *Herald* the
'young men of our clubs will undoubtedly form the nucleus of Storm Troops'.
In August, *Chatham News* carried a letter from Patrick Woodroffe, dissociat-
ing himself from NUPA because of its Italo-German Fascism, its Corporate
State policy and Nazi salute. Rumours of an imminent change of name to
Fascist were confirmed by a letter from Mosley sent to those on the membership lists provided by Hawkins.

The adoption of Fascism was boosted by the appointment as Italian
ambassador of Dino Grandi, who had 'won his spurs as a brutal squad leader
during the fascist conquest of power'. In July, Mussolini took over the reins
at the foreign ministry with an aggressive Fascist policy and demanded the
Anglophile darling of the Cliveden Set take the post. Tall, good-looking, with
a pointed beard, Grandi attracted women and he took it for granted that he
could play away from home. His first conquest was Mosley's sister-in-law,
Baba Metcalfe.

Grandi informed Rome that every day he explained to admiring audiences Fascism's merits. On 13 August he cabled that H. G. Wells was proposing '*un nuovo "fascismo"*'. Mosley wrote to Wells, who had considered joining the NP, to congratulate him on a speech supporting 'Liberal Fascism'. He included a copy of *The Greater Britain*. 'I am afraid the word "Liberal" has not much relation to my book, but it certainly is an attempt to create a scientific Fascism which is free from the excesses and repressions of the Continent.' Mosley added that 'like most prophets, you will probably have the unpleasant experience of recognising many of your own teachings of the past reproduced and reshaped by less capable hands'. Wells, however, objected to the 'displacement of the power of reason with the charisma of "leaders"', and disliked Mosley. Grandi believed British Fascism had a formidable future and told Mussolini he had advised Mosley to take 'revolution into the streets'.

Instead, Mosley sought out business support. Irene was asked to arrange a meeting with Israel Sieff, Chairman of Marks and Spencer and the man behind the think tank Political Economic Planning. Launched in June 1932 to produce a programme of national reconstruction by way of capitalist planning, the PEP grew out of Max Nicolson's 'National Plan', published in the *Week-End Review*. Mosley hoped there would be a meeting of minds between PEP and his anti-socialist version of planning. PEP was committed to political activism along the lines advocated by its 'young Prometheans', led by Nicolson, head of the Technique of Planning (Tec Plan) study group, which promoted Wellsian technocratic policies of 'scientific' modernization.

Mosley was 'a remarkable talker, with an acute and well-stocked mind', Sieff discovered. He wanted PEP to be the 'brainbox' of his movement. When Sieff declined because of its non-political nature, Mosley said he was 'making a mistake'. Perhaps Sieff thought he had because he invited Mosley to address a group of businessmen looking for a leader. Mosley impressed him as a 'dynamic figure, of that rare charismatic type which when suitably motivated can work wonders in the service of their fellow men'. A highly controversial meeting took place at Sieff's home in Regent's Park in early September.

The businessmen belonged to the Industrial Group, an elite from which the TEC planners hoped to enlist support. They had the backing of PEP Chairman and Bank of England Director Sir Basil Blackett, who was convinced of the need for closer economic ties with the Empire. Although their planned economy would be 'made to conform with British ideals of freedom', the idea so disturbed members that Blackett had to resign. The TEC Plan was subsequently scuppered as Sieff turned against planning and promoted industrial self-government. The ideological differences with Mosley grew rather than diminished.

Industrialists, according to Irene, admired Mosley's energy and would have financed him, but for his 'high-handedness and tactlessness'. According to

Sieff, Mosley said 'a political party must ultimately be based on emotion. Only feeling could win power and carry plans into effect. A new movement must find somebody or something to hate. In this case it should be the Jews.' Sieff's nineteen-year-old son Marcus confirmed his father's description of the meeting. Mosley 'did not seem to think that he had said something particularly unacceptable, but the effect on the company was instant'. Mosley added, 'Of course, it doesn't apply to Jews like you, Israel,' but the insult had been made and Sieff asked him to leave. Mosley denied the story but why would both Sieffs lie? He had repeated to Irene that 'a dynamic creed such as fascism cannot flourish unless it has a scapegoat to hit out at, such as Jewry'.

A former Communist and Oxford graduate, E. D. Randall, wrote in the *New Times*'s September issue that 'yelling anti-Jewish slogans from vans, shrieking death and murder to the Jews' was not the way 'to convert people to the ideals of the NP'. However, he did not dismiss anti-Semitism. Jews 'being largely responsible for the present political, economic and social chaos, ought to be publicly denounced and deserve to be howled down'. He did not advocate 'the elimination of the anti-semitic element from our propaganda. No member of this club has greater cause to hate the Jew than I, nor carries in his heart more bitter hatred.' However, he recognized the Jews'

power and cunning to smash any organisation directed against his race. A tiny movement such as ours simply cannot afford, in its early stages, openly to make anti-Semitism its main plank . . . Let us wait until we have become a power in Britain: then we can translate our hatred of the despicable parasites – who seek to profit in our downfall – from futile words to deeds! The public have long succumbed to the incessant hidden prompting and whispering of our Jew-ridden press, and are quite unprepared for a sudden, bitter anti-Jew movement. We have got to clear away all the old rubbish from their minds – Jew-manufactured lies, distorted facts, twisted opinions, international-mindedness.

This was official NUPA policy and that of the shortly to be launched BUF. Anti-Semitism was central but could not be advocated openly until the movement was strong enough to confront the inevitable backlash. There was an ironic conundrum here: Mosley could not openly attack the Jews because they were too powerful; the precise reason he gave as the basis of his own 'rational' anti-Semitism. The campaign was pre-planned and worked to a timetable. For the moment, however, Mosley manoeuvred to keep the policy secret, while at the same time attempting to keep on board the pro-Nazi faction.

Beaverbrook advised Mosley to 'tour the Empire and return as its expert to rally the forces of an imperial conservatism'. He would dedicate himself to 'a national renaissance' and replied on 9 September that he believed 'in the constructive conception of Fascism which I am preaching, and am indifferent to the fact that this course probably means "political suicide". If by any chance the normal political system does not endure, it is perhaps better from the nation's point of view that Fascism be built by me than by some worse kind of lunatic.'

Mosley tested the waters by turning the Newcastle branch into a prototype Fascist one. Manufacturer's agent Michael Jordan, Bill Risdon, parliamentary agent for Gateshead, and Bill Leaper, another ILPer and journalist on the *Newcastle Evening Chronicle* and Mosley's northern organizer (who turned out to have Jewish ancestry) floated the new movement on a self-financing basis. With instructions from Forgan, Jordan launched branches across the north-east; resembling the Salvation Army in structure, they became the model for Fascist organizations. Jordan was rewarded with the post of Area Administrative Officer for Northumberland, Durham and Tees.

Cimmie had fallen from a loft and suffered a back injury, which induced a bacillus coli infection of the urinary tract. Since childhood she had suffered with a spinal curvature and lumbago attacks. To regain her health, she went to Contrexeville in France. She wrote home that she was looking forward to 'you building up your organisation, coping with sales of your book, having a happy time with your family – and some stolen moments with lovely sillies but not too many'. All she wanted was a 'little public demonstration, want to show off a bit, and it is that part that gets hurt and upset'. Mosley said he was 'back at the grindstone – far, far away from Venice pleasure and temptations'. She was distressed by his affair with Diana and wanted him to be frank with her, but felt he was 'only sweet to me when you want to get away with something. I would understand if you give me a chance, but I am so kept in the dark.'

On Cimmie's return, the Mosleys attended a fancy dress ball at Biddesden. Writer Rosamond Lehmann, there with her husband and NP member Wogan Phillips, recalled that a beautiful Diana, wearing a white Grecian dress, danced with Mosley, who was suitably dressed in black, the pair looking 'as though they were magnetised together'. Lady Pansy Lamb said Diana told everyone 'how thrilling she found him, like having a crush on a film star'. However, it was 'the most awful evening, Tom in triumph with this dazzling beauty, and Bryan, the host, looking like a shattered white rabbit'.

Cimmie's misery was compounded by her husband's confession of all the women he had slept with: 'But they are all my best friends!'

Mosley told Boothby what he had done.

'All?' asked his incredulous friend.

'Yes, all. Except, of course, for her sister and stepmother.' Mosley apologized to Cimmie for being 'such a Porker', but his life was 'so strenuous and hectic'. Leaving behind his distressed wife, he departed on a secret visit to Rome in pursuit of funding from Mussolini. He wrote home that he had received a tremendous reception.

On 29 September, dressed in a grey shirt with a gold Fascist badge, Mosley met with Bruce Lockhart. 'His British Fascism is Mussolini in policy: corporate state, Parliament to be elected on occupational franchise . . . House of Lords to be replaced by a National Corporation which will act as Parliament of Industry. Organisation on Hitler group system . . . members to wear grey shirts and flannel trousers. Storm troops: black shirts and grey bags.' There was no mention of anti-Semitism but *Herald* journalist Hannen Swaffer knew about the debates. He wrote on 1 October that it had been decided not to attack the Jews as such. They would, however, be criticized if they were either Communists or international financiers acting against British interests. The forecast proved to be right.

A. J. P. Taylor, often sympathetic towards Mosley, described the New Party as the 'greatest personal miscalculation since the fall of Lord Randolph Churchill'. Colin Coote considered it a 'catastrophic blunder' since it had been founded upon 'an abysmally wrong political judgement – that there would be a Communist revolution'. Mosley 'wasn't really a very sound man in many ways. I always felt that the outward bonhomie that he engendered was a bit phoney. Indeed the man started with a great sense of logic but he never had really much sense of either strategy or tactics.'

Had Mosley waited, Harold Macmillan said, he 'might have been supreme. He struck too soon, and fell for ever. In politics the essence of the game is "timing".' Bill Allen admitted he was 'constantly questing and uncertain – the New Party had failed before it had been launched'. Perhaps Mosley struck too late. It might have worked had he been Fascist from the start but now the Tories pulled the strings in an authoritarian and patriotic National government which pre-empted his appeal by adopting economic ideas that brought about a recovery of technology-based industries, though the 'drastic overhaul of the state machine which he wanted, and the ambitious programme of state intervention which he proposed, were resisted'. Labour had been routed and the Liberals split. There was 'little for Mosley to bite on beyond the controversy over India'.

The NP was another 'third force' which unsuccessfully tried to break the mould of British politics. Mosley spent large sums of money and had used modern campaign techniques, but to little avail. The two-party system was impervious to new ideas and new parties. Whatever the nature, popularity and strength of the third force – Communist, extreme right, Liberal, social democrat – the political system's regressive structure ensured that only immense organization and vast resources for a media and electoral campaign could sustain a breakthrough.

Mosley decided he had lost a battle rather than a war. What was required was the 'grip of an organised and disciplined movement, grasping and permeating every aspect of national life'. He now stepped outside the party racket and turned to pure Fascism. He jettisoned much of the theoretical baggage and search for economic ideas. He had 'finished with people who think, henceforth I shall go to the people who feel'.

Macmillan said Mosley was doomed when he 'tried to bring Fascism into England'. When he said 'he was thinking of putting his supporters into black shirts', Macmillan replied, 'You must be mad. Whenever the British feel strongly about anything, they wear grey flannel trousers and tweed jackets.' Walter Elliott thought it 'courting failure to tell people that they have first to dress themselves in black shirts and throw their opponents downstairs in order to get the corporative state'. The growing acceptance of new economic ideas alleviated the need to travel the low road of street corner politics.

For the social imperialists – opposed to Germany and Fascism – Mosley was a great talent gone 'badly and perversely wrong'. Whereas he preached revolution, Carlyon Bellairs (MP 1915–31), who joined the NP, merely wanted reform to strengthen the status quo. 'It was a tragedy', wrote Leo Amery, 'that such real gifts, instead of being constitutionally employed within the Socialist Party, should, through lack of balance and patience, have been subsequently frittered away, not only in aping the theatrical posturings of continental dictatorships, but also in adopting their more odious features.'

John Strachey wrote to Boothby that the saddest thing about Mosley was that, 'contrary to general opinion, he had a heart'. Genuinely concerned about social problems, 'he can't break his heart, it was broken very early . . . There was some left when we first knew him – but now, I fancy, none.' He was seen as suspect, putting principle before party and engaging in a personal political odyssey across the spectrum of high politics. Macmillan regarded Mosley as the most able man he had met. Boothby said he was the 'only man that I have ever known who could if he played his cards rightly have been the leader of the Conservative or Labour Party', but had destroyed 'a great parliamentary career, because of his own idiosyncrasies, because of his character. He smashed it for no good reason.' It was his 'arrogance, his insolence, his persecution complex', which was responsible. Colin Coote agreed it was hubris.

In summarizing his career thus far, the *Evening Standard* said Mosley was an 'astonishing man' but also an 'astonishing failure'. He had thrown away a succession of opportunities and was destined for an 'ultimate and tragic retirement into obscurity'. He sarcastically replied that he was

clearly a great gambler, who prefers backing a horse at 5 to 1 with a prospect of winning great stakes, to backing an even-money favourite with the prospect of winning stakes too small to attract him. To his peculiar mind, the blue and gold prizes of democratic statesmanship – the pomp and decoration without power of achievement – are not worth the having or the buying. He prefers a great gamble on abnormal events, on the winning of a position which might enable him to re-write the pages of history in terms of achievement for the British Race.

12

The British Union of Fascists

Approaching his thirty-sixth birthday, Mosley launched the British Union of Fascists at 12 Great George Street on 1 October 1932 with thirty-two founder members. He asked them 'to march with us in a great and hazardous adventure. We ask them to be prepared to sacrifice all . . . to dedicate their lives to building in this country a movement of the modern age.' They will 'face abuse, bitter animosity and possibly the ferocity of struggle and danger. In return we can only offer them the deep belief that they are fighting so that a great land may live.' Rothermere telegrammed support from Monte Carlo and welcomed the BUF as the only alternative to socialism.

The BUF's black shirt was modelled on Mosley's fencing tunic, with button fastening over the shoulder; his own was tailor-made in black silk. Recruits received a badge representing the fasces and were required to recognize the necessity for 'discipline and loyalty to its leadership'. On the back of the membership card was the official creed: 'To win power for Fascism and thereby establish in Great Britain the Corporate State.' Mosley's Fascism was largely based on his reading of Shaw's interpretation of Nietzsche, with fantasies of cleansing the world of decadence, and owed a great deal to Orage and the *New Age*. However, he misread Nietzsche, whose superman hopes 'by seeing people's struggles for power and their capacities to delude themselves about these, to have some power over himself'. He was never intended to have power over others.

Mosley wrote in the Italian review *Ottobre* that modern forms of dictatorship were an 'eternally recurrent phenomenon of British history, which invariably coincide with our great periods of dynamic achievement'. The virility of the Tudor dictatorship re-emerged in the 'so un-English personality of the yet so English Chatham, who founded the British Empire by overawing a corrupt Parliament with the power of his popular support'. His Fascism derived from Sorel and Nietzsche, but he had been influenced by English men of action such as Hobbes, Bolingbroke and Carlyle. His 40,000-word synthesis of these inputs was published as *The Greater Britain*, with a cover designed by one of the foremost graphic artists of the day, Ted McKnight Kauffer. Salesmen from Mosley's publishing company sold the book, at 2s. 6d., all over the country. It received wide publicity and 10,000 copies were quickly bought.

The *Manchester Guardian* said it was

an extravagant eulogy of the Fascist State (according to Mussolini and Hitler), a denunciation in familiar vein of the 'old gang' of politicians and parties, and an exposition of a domestic policy for Britain which contains – with Fascist flavouring – most of the mixed Socialist and Protectionist ideas with which Sir Oswald endowed his ill-fated New Party. The Corporate State is to be created, but instead of a dictatorship there is to be a Government with 'absolute power to act'. The Crown is to be maintained but the House of Lords is to go, and Parliament must look out for itself. Violence is not ruled out. If the situation degenerates rapidly, 'something like collapse may come before any new movement has captured Parliamentary power'. In this case, 'other and sterner measures must be adopted for the saving of the State in a situation approaching anarchy'. But, Mosley says, 'in no case shall we resort to violence against the forces of the Crown; but only against the forces of anarchy if and when the machinery of the State has been allowed to drift into powerlessness'.

Mosley said the parties could not halt the 'spineless drift to disaster'. They 'squat impotent in front of the problems of the day like a hypnotised rabbit in front of a snake'. Those fed up with the Baldwin–MacDonald old gang would turn to the BUF. The Corporate State would deal with mass unemployment. Producers' interests had been sacrificed to the interests of cosmopolitan finance. 'In every struggle between producer and financial interest in recent years, the latter power has been triumphant to the detriment of the national interest.' State intervention would ensure finance served the national interest. 'The Gordian knot must be cut.'

By permanently correlating wages, prices and rising output at the maximum level of production, the Corporate State would 'submerge social conflict in an equitable distribution and make possible the material utopia of socialism without any of the economic anarchy associated with this creed'. In drawing together ideas of planning and technocracy, Mosley rejected the anti-scientific thinking associated with Fascism. His rhetoric was Wellsian: 'Science shall rule Great Britain.' It provided the means by which to conquer the material environment and 'the means of controlling the physical rhythm of civilisations'. Many Fascists feared 'Brave New World machine-fantasies' but Mosley hoped to master the machine 'to meet modern fact'.

The Corporate State seemed to be revolutionary but it was merely superimposed upon capitalism, rather than substituted for it. 'Just as the centralised authority of the Tudor kings protected the citizens from the depredations of the robber barons, so', Mosley wrote, 'the corporate system will protect and promote a genuine private enterprise in face of the large industrial combines and concentrations of financial power.' Worker participation would be within limits imposed by the 'over-riding authority of the organised State'.

'He who talks of planning within the limits of the present parliamentary and political system', Mosley went on, 'either deludes himself, or physically shrinks from the effort and the danger of real and fundamental reorganisation.' Planning could not succeed without strong executive government. Fascism would 'not hesitate to act when the State interests are threatened and the action of such a power will be decisive'. In a Mosley regime, economic power would rest with an authoritarian State 'ultimately controlled by no one but himself'. He annunciated its totalitarianism: 'There will be no room in Britain for those who do not accept the principle "all for the State and the State for all".' When anyone rejected this principle, 'so that his activity becomes sectional and anti-social, the mechanism of the Corporate system descends upon him'.

The Corporate State would handle security, defence, foreign affairs and national propaganda. Mosley envisioned a self-contained Empire with a 'permanently functioning machinery of economic consultation and planning in place of haphazard conferences'. He assumed 'white commonwealth' countries – South Africa, Canada and Australia – would join the project, while those that refused would be forced to co-operate. A 'Britain First' policy ensured 'we shall never pursue the folly of an aggressive Imperialism'. In a reorganized League of Nations, he would 'call a halt to the flabby surrender of every British interest which has characterised the past decade, and has reduced this nation to the position of a meddlesome old lady holding the baby for the world'. He would work for universal disarmament but, recognizing that the Air factor had 'altered the position of these Islands', he would raise Britain's Air Force 'to the level of the strongest power in Europe'.

Fascism, said Mosley, was a revolt against the materialism of the modern world, 'where there are no spiritual landmarks' and in which the young were reared 'to venerate metallic fetishes, factories and machines'. The hope was 'youth dedicated to the resurrection of the nation's greatness and shrinking from no effort and from no sacrifice to secure that mighty end'. Their ideal was a 'morality of the Spartan pattern tempered with the Elizabethan atmosphere of Merrie England'. He appealed to his countrymen 'to take action while there is still time' but if 'the Empire is allowed to drift until collapse and anarchy intervene, we shall not shrink from that final conclusion, and will organise to stand between the State and ruin'.

In the *Fortnightly Review* Cecil Melville said *The Greater Britain* was 'an exposition of the English variant of National Socialism' and noted its closeness to the 'philosophic violence of Georges Sorel'. It had the brilliant qualities of many of Mosley's ideas but 'the unfortunate thing about it all is that probably the majority of average Englishmen will be put off, by a not unnatural distaste for fascist theatricality'.

His deputy, Dr Robert Forgan, followed Mosley into the BUF from personal loyalty but also for the salary of £700 (£23,000). These were exciting days for Forgan; his office was his home and the movement his life. He organized the first rally on 15 October in Trafalgar Square. Following riots at Stoke, Mosley declared, 'We do not want to fight but if violence is organised against us, then we shall organise for violence in reply.' He told the *Morning Post*'s W. F. Deedes that Mussolini had said 'the road to power lay in creating fierce opposition. Against every ten adversaries, you recruited one staunch ally.'

According to Britain's ambassador in Paris, William Tyrrell, Mosley had been given a 'terrific dressing down' by Mussolini. On 14 October he told Mosley's former mentor, Lord Cecil, that he had said Fascism was 'quite unsuitable for England'. Colin Coote, whose visit to Rome had given him 'a horror of the police state', said Italians had a proverb: 'An italianised Englishman is a devil incarnate.' That is what 'the public came to think a British adaption of Mussolini to be'.

Forgan went to Rome to solicit funds but Mussolini did not think it a wise investment. Lord Sydenham was there with former ambassador Rennell Rodd when Mosley's name was mentioned. 'Ah,' said Mussolini, 'he has been spending most of this summer on the French Riviera. I spent quite a lot of time on the Riviera myself, but I was in exile struggling to make a living with my hands. It's not a place for serious reformers to linger in private villas for more than a few days. He wants too much the best of both worlds.' A. J. P. Taylor thought Mosley was 'not a sticker. Often at a moment of crisis the self-appointed saviour of his country was not to be found: he was at a fencing match.' True dictators 'thought of politics and nothing else. Mosley gave the impression that politics were for him an exciting hobby. Though he spoke repeatedly of action, this worked out in putting on a performance rather than of practical work.'

Diana countered that Mosley worked incredibly hard. The fencing was used as cover for his political activities. Taking part in championships in Paris, Rome and Milan enabled him to meet European Fascists, safe from the prying eyes of the security services. Diana accompanied him and recalled that he fenced with skill and an immense will to win. His 'whole character was in evidence when he was fencing: the "happy warrior"'.

On 24 October Mosley said at the Memorial Hall, Farringdon Street, that hostility would be directed only at those Jews who were anti-British or financed Communism. At the heated meeting he abused hecklers, who were violently removed by his Fascist Defence Force, as 'three warriors of the class war – all from Jerusalem'. Blackshirts later marched to the Cenotaph where police ordered them to disband following shouts of 'to hell with the Jews'.

Irene was at the meeting with Baba and wondered why Mosley descended to 'the Jerusalem inanity', since the 'little man in the balcony was quite inoffensive'. He was a 'silly schoolboy only proud of some silly scuffles and glorying over his menials throwing two lads down the stairs . . . all this vanity to [Diana] – much muck muck'. When Israel Sieff saw her on 31 October, he was so bitter at Mosley's 'inane jibe to the heckler' that he decided 'not to give him money for his industrial investigations. Oh! how tactless Tom is. It makes me sick.' Mosley subsequently issued an order barring Jew-baiting – indicating it was a problem that had to be curbed.

There was speculation that Wells and Shaw would throw in their lot with Mosley. Kingsley Martin noted a resemblance between Wells and Mosley with their planning and contempt for old party games. 'Both describe themselves as revolutionaries: both aim at the formation of a corps of young people pledged to the fulfilment of a single social ideal.' Wells saw his supporters as 'Liberal Fascists or Communist Revisionists or enlightened Nazis' and preached an 'Open Conspiracy' of a directorate of managers, scientists and engineers. However, Wells's society did not acknowledge allegiance to 'any unit smaller than the world', whereas Mosley was a pure nationalist.

Shaw told a Fabian meeting on Bonfire Night that Mosley was 'one of the few people who is thinking about real things and not about figments and phrases'. People disliked him because he is 'going to do something and that is a terrible thing. You instinctively hate him, because you do not know where he will land you; and he evidently means to uproot some of you.' He recognizes Fascism is the only 'practical alternative to Communism'. Shaw reminded the audience that Mussolini began with twenty-five votes but it did not take him long 'to become the Dictator of Italy. I do not say that Mosley is going to become Dictator of this country,' but 'you will hear something more of Mosley before you are through with him'.

The BUF considered Shaw a Fascist. In *On the Rocks*, Prime Minister 'Chavender' nationalizes everything, forbids strikes and institutes compulsory public service. The working classes were 'ready to go mad with enthusiasm for any man strong enough to make them do anything, even if it's only Jew baiting'. Shaw celebrated progressive Jews, but also believed Jews 'did not encompass a "biologically" ordered future' and supported eugenic means of dealing with racial difference: 'extermination must be put on a scientific basis if it is ever to be carried out humanely and apolitically as well as thoroughly'. When Nazis shouted 'Down with the Jew Shaw', in an attempt to clear himself of suspicion of pro-Jewish bias he claimed 'a pro-Fascist bias', to give weight to his protest.

To Mosley it seemed the ingredients which were to bring Hitler to power existed in Britain. He expected the system to collapse into chaos, thus provid- ing Communism with its historic opportunity. Mass unemployment, a failing social democratic party and middle-class insecurity indicated an opening for the Communists to exploit. With the political vacuum and a middle class searching for a saviour, new ideas, argued Mosley, 'will come violently, as they have come elsewhere'. In the crisis, 'reason, persuasion vanish and organised force alone prevails. Either Fascism or Communism emerges victorious.'

Mosley claimed his meetings were threatened with disruption by 'hundreds of men, accompanied by violence often prepared in semi-military fashion'. At Battersea, 'Communists' armed with broken bottles attacked BUF stewards, who countered with rubber truncheons. The stewards included ILP militants who brought to the BUF 'both a hatred of communism and considerable experience of street fighting'. Alexander Miles said the violence had the effect of 'fanning to a white hot flame the faith of these young men in Mosley'. They recalled a 'spirit of brotherhood, equal to the early days of the Socialist Crusades'.

Fascism grew 'out of chaos, with bloodshed, rioting and revolutionary conditions', thought Irene, but she could not see it spreading to Britain without the 'cataclysmic whip of national bankruptcy'. Mosley insisted Fascism would succeed by constitutional methods and only when confronted by 'red terror' would he meet force by force to save the country. When the crash came, the 'man who could control the streets would win'. It became clear, however, that Fascist aggression was used to provoke Communist retaliation in the hope that it would precipitate the crisis which would thrust him into power. He had 'a curious ability to transmute thuggery into a kind of idealism'. Public order was threatened by political extremism and it seemed something like a revolutionary situation had developed. At his party's conference, Labour's Stafford Cripps declared that 'the one thing that is not inevitable now is gradualness'.

A challenge came from the hunger marches of the Communist-dominated National Unemployed Workers' Movement (NUWM). With 40,000 members, mostly in South Wales, Lancashire and Scotland, Harry Pollitt admitted it had 'a greater degree of support than either the Communist Party or the BUF could command'. In the autumn, there were disturbances in Glasgow and Belfast, where two demonstrators were killed and fifty injured, and several days of rioting on Merseyside. Demonstrations were forcibly put down in North Shields and London by mounted police. The treatment meted out to marchers was more severe than anything experienced by the BUF. The trail of violence throughout the country aroused disquiet but the government insisted a firm line was necessary because there was 'the very material connection between those in Moscow' and the NUWM.

Attempts were made in late 1932 to bring in an Act with sweeping powers to prohibit marches, which alienated moderate opinion. The violence, however, was not on a revolutionary scale and the NUWM was more often the loser than the beneficiary of the 'politics of violence'. It acted within traditional British restraint and was more constitutionally minded than Mosley's Black-shirts. The working class, Ross McKibben argues, 'was never a revolutionary one; more than that, its political culture was undoubtedly defensive'.

Communism rarely emerged from the political fringe and Mosley later recognized he had overrated its threat. Communist Party membership was only 6,000, with half concentrated in the mining areas. The unemployed who joined – 3,000 during the thirties – soon left. When industry revived, support collapsed beyond the hard-core activists. At the same time Labour's vote rose and the 'chance of a vacuum for extremist parties to exploit had gone'. Even with the slump at its worst, unemployment produced apathy and a 'remarkably quiescent' political scene.

It was an open secret among Diana's friends that she was planning to leave her husband. Mosley encouraged her in her decision 'to devote the rest of my life to him'. She confided in Cela Keppel how 'marvellous was his lovemaking compared with her husband's inexperienced advances'. She knew he had not given up his other affairs, including that with Baba. He had no ethical boundaries, though he never considered women of the middle or working classes worthy of his attention, only making advances to women 'he thought were equal to him'. Caesar was a favourite character because he could 'dally with Cleopatra, but as soon as the call came from politics or battle he could drop it and stay away'. He did, however, Nicholas noted, 'risk a lot of his politics by his overt relationship with Diana while still married to my mother'.

Diana was only twenty-two but was 'convinced of the permanency of what I had decided to do; other people gave it a year at most'. She was never unfaithful and was uninterested in sex: 'beauty and art are what matter'. With her goddess-like quality, she was almost sexless. The exquisite manners and disdain for the opinion of others disguised a vulnerability as she hid her jealousy. There was a coldness about her affair. Everyone knew Mosley had had many affairs – so she did not think Cimmie would mind: 'What difference would it make?' The Mitfords were horrified. Nancy wrote on 27 November that her social position 'will be nil if you do this. You are so young to begin getting wrong with the world.' On Christmas Eve Diana's father-in-law, Lord Moyne, and her father, called on Mosley – 'dead white and armed with knuckle duster' – to see if he would give her up. Rebuffed, they decided to put detectives on him. Bryan did not want a divorce and left for Switzerland having forbidden Mosley to enter their house.

At a Christmas party given by the Maughams, an excited eighteen-year-old Unity Mitford met the 'absolutely charming' Leader, who was not the wicked monster described by her family. He did his eye trick of raising his eyebrow which, one mistress noted, 'he obviously thinks is very fascinating and which indeed has a great effect on some people'. The Mosleys held their celebrations at a house at Yarlington, in Somerset, where they were joined by Baba and Fruity Metcalfe, who played Santa Claus, and by Diana, which made for an interesting time.

Diana left her husband and moved with the children to Eaton Square, close to Mosley's bachelor flat. She subordinated her movements to his furtive visits; he announced his arrival with a tap of his cane on the window. Only friends 'so intimate that they would understand her cancelling at the last minute in the event of Mosley turning up' were invited. Lady Cunard remained close and Diana continued to see Nigel Birch and a director of London Films, John Sutro, who had been asked to stand as a New Party candidate. John Betjeman was a non-political friend, as was the wealthy collector of surrealist paintings Edward James. The affair caused complications. A New Year's Eve party at Baba's was a trying event as Diana turned up without her husband. Everybody knew she was 'Tom's new girl', though most were unaware she had left Bryan. The pair revealed all to Georgia Sitwell but were 'very irritating'.

In the *Observer* on 8 January Lloyd George lamented that the world was like 'a lunatic asylum run by lunatics' as no leader commanded confidence. MacDonald was senile, Baldwin was disparaged, Churchill was unreliable and even Lloyd George was discredited. There was a possibility of economic chaos and the National government might fall. If it did, *The Times* believed Mosley would appear a credible figure who was prepared 'to save Britain in a struggle of violence with the Communist Party'. The *Manchester Guardian* warned he was 'deliberately inciting physical opposition and public disorder', like Hitler in Germany.

On 30 January 1933 Hitler was sworn in as Chancellor. The *Mail* said it was 'one of the most historic days in the latter day history of Europe'. There was a reluctance to criticize Hitler. On 10 February the *Jewish Chronicle*'s Berlin correspondent claimed his programme was 'not the Nazi programme at all'. The paper was alarmed by BUF anti-Jewish innuendoes but when Mosley said 'we do not attack Jews because they are Jews, we only attack them if we find them pursuing an anti-British policy: any Jew who is not anti-British will always get a square deal with us', it asserted he had 'arrived at the safe haven of tolerance and common sense'. Anti-Semitic feelings, however, ran high in BUF branches in Hull and Leeds, where walls were plastered with posters. In Manchester, Jews were threatened with violence, shops were painted with the slogan 'Perish the Jews' and a synagogue had swastikas chalked on its walls.

In the *Blackshirt*'s first issue in February, Mosley declared: 'Fascism alone today can hold open meetings in "Red" strongholds without police protection.' It was important to demonstrate the BUF's ability to stand up to 'Communist' disorder. On 24 February Mosley spoke against his old ILP colleague Jimmy Maxton in a debate, later the subject of a libel suit against the *Star*. Maxton challenged him as to what his Defence Force would do if faced with a left-wing takeover. Mosley – 'dressed for the slaughter in his black shirt' – replied that behind the Labour Party 'will emerge the organised communist, the man who knows what he wants; and if and when he ever comes out we will be there in the streets with Fascist machine guns to meet him'. The *Star* said Mosley was ready to take over the government with machine-guns. A jury disagreed and awarded him £5,000 damages. In his summing up, Lord Chief Justice Hewart asked the jury whether Mosley 'did not appear to you to be a public man of no little courage, no little candour and no little ability?'

A week later the clash between Fascism and Communism was the subject of Mosley's table talk at Lord Dufferin's. Conservatives thought they could control the situation but even Rothermere 'did not realise what is coming'. Mosley admitted he needed 'disaster here to give him a chance' but maintained 'England is the country best adapted to Fascism'. A few years ago, 'six men started the Nazi movement. After a year's struggle they numbered only 63 men in the whole country – what slow progress compared to the great strides of our British Union of Fascists in these first five months of its existence!'

On 5 March the Mosleys listened to a wireless address by President Roosevelt at Lloyd George's house. Cimmie wrote to Roosevelt that they had been 'terrifically excited' by his speech. He wrote back that he admired Lloyd George and hoped he had started 'a liberal trend of affairs in this country'. Mosley criticized Roosevelt's policies. Exports, agricultural incomes and industrial production fell by a half, and during 1933 unemployment in the US rose to fifteen million. He said the failure was due to 'the absence of a coherent national plan to check forces inimical to the stability of the State'. America had 'made a god of unregulated anarchy in private enterprise'. The 'very energy of American libertarianism' was the best argument for Fascism but only corporatism could set the temporary boom on a permanent footing.

Mosley admitted in Italy's *Gerarchia* that the BUF had had a difficult start with the 'weapons of ridicule and defamation used against us' but was now progressing. He said the BUF was 'not imitating Italian fascism. Fascism is a national creed and the English are a very insular people.' However, he announced his support of the 'iron realism of universal fascism' and played host to foreign Fascist leaders and admirers.

In March Eric Campbell, leader of the Australian New Guard, contacted Mosley, following a suggestion from Rear-Admiral Gerald Dickens, the Chief of Naval Intelligence. The New Guard had a following of 100,000 ex-servicemen, with a hard core of 20,000 'Ironsides'. In London, Campbell found Fascism was not frowned upon and, in the circles around Lady Dalton, heard 'high praise for Mussolini's objective approach to problems that beset his country'. He found Cimmie 'elegant and charming', and Mosley a 'fine cut of a man with more than an ordinary share of personal magnetism, if perhaps a trifle dramatic'. He attended a BUF meeting chaired by Cimmie but thought the Blackshirts 'unpleasant and unconvincing types'. Mosley provided him with letters of introduction to Italy and Germany.

Fascism was considered more curious than disreputable and Mosley was welcome at Establishment functions. He debated Fascism at a Foyle's Literary Luncheon with Megan Lloyd George and was involved in a verbal contest at the Cambridge Union with Clement Attlee, who thought he talked 'pretty fair rot. It is really Mosley and nothing more.' Mosley explained Fascism to the English-Speaking Union, though it had 'only been in existence little more than ten years' which was too soon for it to 'have assumed a crystallised form'. It was a practical creed of action based on a Spenglerian approach and Caesarism. Only Fascism could secure 'order out of the economic chaos which exists today'. Blackshirts believed they were living through a crisis and that selfless efforts were needed to save the country. Britain was in 'acute danger' and they were determined, in a crusading spirit, 'to act as a modern St George'. Most believed the BUF was there to solve the 'devil's decade's' social and economic crisis – namely unemployment.

Mass unemployment was the popular image of the thirties, but it was also true, noted A. J. P. Taylor, that 'people were enjoying a richer life than any previously known in the history of the world: longer holidays, shorter hours, higher wages. They had motor cars, cinemas, radios, electrical appliances.' The two sides of life, however, did not join up. Higher consumption helped fuel industrial growth and by the summer of 1933 unemployment began to decline as the revival gained pace. New industries forged ahead, but exports from staple industries declined. The result was that unemployment reached one and a half million, mostly concentrated in the deprived areas of south Wales, Scotland and the north of England.

In these areas, many people felt degraded by their experience of the dole with its invasive Means Test and loss of self-respect, which revealed the 'utter sham of party politics'. Mosley was the only leader, said Blackshirts, who was proposing a cure for the evils of the thirties. However, George Cole wrote in the *New Statesman* that 'conditions do not exist in Britain for the growth of fascism. We have no ruined middle classes . . . we have no economic suffering extreme enough to drive men to desperate ventures and . . . we are not suffering under the psychology of defeat.' The crisis never had, Ross McKibben notes, the 'same socially disintegrating effects that it had elsewhere. It was contained within the existing state structure and within traditional party allegiances.'

In an attempt to break these allegiances, J. Paton, a Covent Garden porter and ex-leader of the National Unemployed Workers Movement in Battersea, formed a Fascist Union of British Workers (FUBW) as the 'forerunner of the one big administrative union which will represent the workers' interests under fascism'. The FUBW aimed to 'protect the interests of workers, whether in employment or unemployed. To fight against wage cuts and all reductions in the standard of life, to fight the Means Test and all means to bully the unemployed.' It encouraged the unemployed to join Fascist clubs.

In April Charles Bradford, an ex-Communist steel erector, took charge of the FUBW, which enjoyed some success in representing workers at public assistance committees, and gained a foothold among non-unionized workers in the Midlands and the North. It attempted to infiltrate selected union branches by organizing Fascist cells. Special Branch reported in May that a Brown Shirt Section was recruiting 'unemployed manual workers of the navvy type as distinct from the younger and rather better educated men who make up the Black Shirts'.

A BUF Women's Section was established in March, under Lady Mosley, with premises at 233 Regent Street, which had been donated by a Fascist sympathizer. Female Blackshirts, who made up 20 per cent of the membership, held the St John Ambulance certificate and were trained in ju-jitsu – 'a precaution made necessary by the behaviour of Communist women at some of our rougher meetings'. The BUF attracted former suffragettes, though Mosley's advocacy of women's rights was superficial: 'The part of women in our future organization will be important, but different from that of the men; we want men who are men and women who are women.' The men still dictated policy on birth control, sterilization and abortion.

Essential to Fascism, notes Julie Gottlieb, was a stress on the masculine. Macho Fascism was personified by the Duce himself; an example which Mosley emulated. He was a man who 'thinks and feels for Britain as a man, and all true men, all true women, recognise his lead and follow him unfalteringly through ordeals which only they can face and they can survive'. With 'his tall athletic frame, with its dynamic force and immense reserve of strength; his unconquerable spirit, with its grandeur of courage and resolve', he was a model of virility. There was an element of homoeroticism in the BUF, paralleled by homophobia, which created rifts in a movement with homosexuals in key positions. Blackshirt propaganda 'symbolically castrated opponents' by ascribing to them feminine characteristics, which were associated with softness and weakness. Fascist sexuality was measured against the effetism and decadence of intellectuals, and the old women who ruled Britain.

Against the old who ran Britain, there was 'a curious cult of hatred', George Orwell noted. Their dominance was 'held to be responsible for every evil known to humanity . . . throughout almost the whole nation there was a revolt of youth versus age'. Alex Miles acknowledged being 'swept up in this hot flood of feeling that here was a Leader who typified Youth'. Silke Hesse made the point that the model Fascist society is of a gang of adolescent youths.

There was heated discussion on whether clubs should be mixed or exclusively male. The latter conception won the day, despite warnings that to confine them to young men would be emulating Nazi organization.

Mosley's revolutionary patriotism attempted to supersede Conservative love of King and Country with 'a determination to build a country free from unemployment, poverty and despair'. However, he knew Fascism would not pose an attraction for an increasingly prosperous middle class insulated from economic insecurity, so hoped the loss of Empire would put patriotism to the fore. The spectacle of Britain 'increasingly belittled and bewildered, her former glory and power diminishing', angered diehards and he dropped economic policies in favour of an Empire-orientated, self-sufficient unit. Indian constitutional reform was the National government's crisis and one Churchill's supporters exploited. Robert Bernays discovered Rothermere had hosted a dinner party of 'all the crooks in politics' – Beaverbrook, Lloyd George, Bracken, Boothby and Mosley.

In choosing India as the issue 'best calculated to dissociate the Conservative Party from Mr Baldwin and break up the National Government', the *Economist* judged Churchill chose well. On 6 April Samuel Hoare observed that Churchill was convinced 'he will smash the government . . . and thinks England is going Fascist and that he will eventually be able to rule India as Mussolini governs north Africa'. With Mosley waiting in the wings, the scenario of a Churchill-led proto-Fascist diehard ramp was not implausible. Fascism was in the air. Hitler had forced through the Reichstag the enabling law, the prelude to the establishment of dictatorship.

In response to events in Germany, Mosley was determined Fascism would come to Britain but wanted 'to avert the collapse which has led to bloodshed and violence on the Continent'. However, he anticipated a positive role for his paramilitary force if he was 'called upon to save the nation in a condition of anarchy'. Skidelsky believed the violence was 'at least as much the result of anti-fascist demonstrators interrupting meetings or attacking fascists'. Stephen Cullen argued Fascists were 'far more the victim than the perpetrator' of violence and that it occurred almost exclusively in connection with the defence of their meetings. Although he did not look for fights, avoiding them was not Mosley's priority and he admitted that at times the fighter took over and the soldier came to the fore. He denied his Defence Force carried weapons, but it soon became apparent that the I Squad used weapons to impose its will. In Manchester, Fascists set the pattern of violence.

On 12 March, at the Free Trade Hall, Mosley said his stewards did not want violence but would insist on the right to free speech. He began, reported the *Manchester Guardian*, 'smilingly with some references to his legend, but he has not got very far before the smile disappears and the face says clearly "into battle". It is an earnest, gripping mood. First that apathetic audience is arrested, then stirred, and finally swept off its feet by a tornado of a peroration yelled at the defiant high pitch of a tremendous voice.' Hecklers were harshly dealt with. When one was felled by a blow from a steward, the audience's mood became hostile and fights broke out. To quell the disruption, the I Squad used lengths of hosepipe supplied by Defence Force leader Eric Hamilton Piercy, a former salesman and special constabulary inspector often seen at Mosley's side. The police eventually closed the event by ushering the stewards into the lobbies. Manchester foreshadowed future disturbances.

Mosley went out of his way to parade the uniformed Defence Force, whose jackbooted I Squad inner core regarded itself as an elite within an elite. Even within the BUF its members had a reputation for brutality. Mosley stated the use of weapons was forbidden but, two days after Manchester, Fascists used rubber hoses – loaded with lead shot – and others knuckledusters, to attack a jeering crowd on Rochdale's town hall square. Arthur Fawcett recalled a coachload of members travelling to the north-east with the sole intention of 'doing over the Reds'. The BUF strategy was to carry out campaigns in working-class districts where the Defence Force actively sought a fight.

The violence originated with I Squad members imported from London to bolster local 'pansy gangs'. According to north-east organizer Michael Jordan there was little violence until the I Squad intervened and unleashed a campaign of provocation. They hurled insults at crowds, or launched unprovoked assaults, to goad the crowd to react. The violence then developed a momentum of its own and proved to be infectious. Within a few months local members were involved and adopted the new tactics as their own. Jordan was convinced the violence had been deliberately orchestrated by the leadership.

Edward Bailey organized Reading's Defence Force, which worked to the strategy of Piercy and regional organizer Captain Keenes. In secret, Mosley had said 'there must be a fight in Reading to secure the mastery of the Blackshirts over all others'. Bailey attended training sessions for plain-clothes members to practise disruptive heckling for the pre-arranged violence. For the Belle Vue rally, after which Italian Fascist Party Secretary General Achille Starace congratulated Mosley on his 'gallant performance', two weeks' training and rehearsal took place. Bailey claimed the tactics were 'usually successful' and enabled blame to be attached to the Communists.

Piercy had allegedly said that, although the BUF claimed to be seeking power by the ballot box, it was in fact preparing to seize power by force. It was not organized for elections and Blackshirt Arthur Beavan admitted that with 'most of us being ex-Servicemen', it seemed 'perfectly natural' that it was organized as an army. Mosley drew a parallel with the New Model Army. With 20,000 disciplined members, the BUF represented 'a force equal to Cromwell's and more experienced in war'.

It has been argued that 'the glorification of war and violence was not to be found amongst the ideas of the BUF'. It was true its propaganda said war was 'an evil to be avoided', which suggested it was pacifist, but that was not the case. Spengler had written that 'armies will in the future take the place of parties', and Mosley turned explicitly to an army-like model for the BUF structure, which was based on a number of headquarters in the main urban areas, organized as military barracks, in which squads of uniformed Black-shirts would live and train for crisis day. The *New Statesman* believed the BUF's militarism was an 'incitement to violent resistance', designed to help bring about the very situation Fascism was intended to meet.

Piercy boasted to Bailey that in the event of a crisis – which could be engineered – Mosley would, under the guise of 'saving England from Mob law', take power by force. Fascists enlisted in the army would 'bring companies of soldiers and arms and ammunition', allowing the BUF to have a 'machine gun in every street'. No doubt this was bravado but others reported that the BUF 'would step in following the crisis of a resurgent Labour Party'. Experienced politicians such as Forgan argued that to gain power, 'we had 10 years of hard, slogging, painful endeavour, slow organisational activity to face'. Mosley was not prepared to wait. 'He wanted power almost at once,' Alex Miles realized, 'and thought he knew how to get it.'

On 9 March 1933 the Nazis won 43.9 per cent of the vote in the Reichstag election, whereupon Hitler created the Gestapo, which persecuted Jews. The *Jewish Chronicle* now took Nazism seriously and published smuggled-out photographs of Jew baiting. With 60,000 Jews fleeing Germany, the paper supported a boycott of German goods to 'extinguish the fire of persecution at its source'. Organized Jewry feared intervention would unleash an anti-Semitic backlash from Tory MPs, such as J. J. Stourton and Peter Agnew (later members of the anti-Semitic Right Club), who were in touch with the BUF. In Parliament, Edward Doran asked the Home Secretary on 9 March to 'take steps to prevent any alien Jews entering this country from Germany', while Stourton revealed the Jewish identities of the refugees. Two days later Doran referred to the resentment caused by the 'invasion of undesirable aliens' and asked that the Home Secretary 'give them notice to quit before serious trouble develops'. Mistrust of refugees led inexorably to the rejection of 'refu-Jews', in a campaign in which the BUF played a leading role.

The government did little to help Jewish victims of the Nazis because it was convinced that allowing their entry would fuel anti-Semitism. A number gained entry to fulfil employment needs as maids and nannies to wealthy families. Ironically, a private organization serving this need, the Anglo-German Servants Agency, was run by the German wife of Alexander Raven Thomson, who was about to join the BUF. The general ill feeling towards the refugees reminded Aldous Huxley of Wordsworth: 'The land all swarmed with passion, like a plain devoured by locusts.' That was Europe in 1933 – 'the awful sense of invisible vermin of hate, envy, anger crawling about . . . Let us hope we shall not have to scuttle when Tom Mosley gets into power.'

Communism's official position on Fascism was determined by a Comintern resolution on 1 April 1933, which set the tone for the decade not only by condemning social democracy for leading to Fascism but also by confronting Fascism via the United Front. There was little guidance on how to apply the principle to Britain. Communist Party policy was to work with the ILP and Labour against Fascism, but it was the rank and file, not the leadership, which campaigned. The *Daily Worker* recorded many local initiatives but turned a blind eye to CP involvement in anti-Mosley activities which were deliberately played down by the Central Committee. There was opposition to the BUF in the North but the CP leadership felt Fascism's threat came from the National government. Reporting in the summer to the Central Committee on the European Anti-Fascist Congress in Paris, Ted Bramley dismissed the fight against the BUF as irrelevant to the main anti-Fascist struggle and said CP leaders had 'waged a fight against the line of breaking up fascist meetings'.

Despite Communist and Labour Party reservations, cross-party activists fought BUF efforts to establish a bridgehead in Manchester. R. H. S. Phillpott reported to the TUC that local Blackshirts were 'undoubtedly anti-Jew'. BUF membership legitimized for some youth gangs already present feelings of anti-Semitism and violence towards other gangs. Blackshirts were engaged in frequent street fights with anti-Fascists from the Jewish Young Communist League, who responded to 'a violent situation which was not of their making'.

Mosley disclaimed any interest in the 'Jewish Question', as did the *Blackshirt*, which was edited by Cecil Lewis, a solicitor who had served in the Indian Army and as a political officer in Iraq. He spent time in Italy where he acquired his Fascist convictions and was employed by Mosley as a legal adviser. Lewis pioneered a Fascist literary style of violent invective with opponents described either as 'scum' or 'sub-human'.

On 1 April 1933 the *Blackshirt* stated that the idea that the BUF was anti-Semitic was old gang press propaganda. Jew baiting in every shape and form was forbidden. 'The early propaganda of the Nazis against the Jews has considerably complicated their accession to power and their ability to deal with Socialist, Communist and financial enemies of the State.' It was lying propaganda that the Nazis were persecuting the Jews: 'Dr Goebbels, Minister of Propaganda, has offered a challenge to anyone who can name one single Jew who has met his death in the course of the national revolution.' It all seemed to indicate that, because of an internal policy debate, anti-Semitism was being curbed. A few speakers were removed from their posts but the statement was entirely to do with Mosley's visit to Rome.

*

The Mosleys attended the International Fascist Exhibition, celebrating Fascism's founding. According to Irene, Cimmie was going through hell over Diana, who was recklessly ruining her life because of 'her crush on that vain insensate ass'. She was happy to be away from London, whose gossip columns were trying to dig out details of the affair. With the banner headline 'FASCISM AND PEACE', the *Blackshirt* announced on 17 April that the 'firm friendship of fascist nations will build the new Europe'. In Rome were representatives of other movements, including Hermann Goering. The Exhibition, Mussolini said, 'was a thing of today, therefore very modern and daring, with no melancholy memories and decorative styles of the past'. It emphasized the regime's desire to live in the age of machines, in which technology's dehumanizing effects would be subdued through the Corporate State returning machines to their role of 'serving man and the community as instruments of liberation, not as a means of increasing misery'.

Mosley was received by Arturo Morpicati, Vice-Secretary of the Fascist Party, and Achille Starace, who presented a banner to the BUF delegation. Mosley appeared with Mussolini on the balcony of the Palazzo Venezia and handed him a parchment BUF membership card in a leather case. Mosley was advised not to copy Nazi aberrations: 'anti-Semitism is a symptom, not of Fascism but of Germany'. Holding up Fascism for emulation, Mussolini criticized deviations from its ideals by the German imitator. He branded the Nazis heretics for their pagan racism. Mussolini was intrigued by Hitler, perhaps even jealous. Thus his anti-Nazism became more pronounced as his standing on the European scene was weakened by Hitler's success. Throughout the spring of 1933 he warned Hitler that his anti-Jewish measures were causing outrage throughout Europe.

On 20 April the *Manchester Guardian* reported that the terror in Germany 'has become a war of extermination waged by Brownshirts against the entire left'. In Rome, Mosley said the BUF was not anti-Jewish and that Hitler 'had made his greatest mistake in his attitude towards the Jews'. The *Blackshirt* quoted Goering: 'The German Government will not tolerate persecution of a person merely because he is a Jew' and thought it 'unfortunate that this policy was not maintained in the Nazi Movement from their early days'. There had been anti-Semitic outrages in Germany and the 'disciplined movement of world Fascism looks to the Government to suppress them'. It praised the single-mindedness of Mussolini, who 'avoided conflict with Jews, with Church, with sectional interests of any kind'.

It is argued that anti-Semitism was unknown to Fascism outside the Teutonic races, but though Italy was considerably less racist than Germany, it was racist nonetheless. Of a Jewish population of 45,000 in 1938, 10,000 ended up in concentration camps. Racism was endemic in Fascism, as was borne out by the regime's harsh treatment of the Libyans and Ethiopians.

Mussolini harboured anti-Semitic prejudices and saw Zionism as a threat to Italian nationalism. He exploded that 'the Jews are my worst enemies' when his daughter Edda told him she was going to marry a Jew. Radicals wanted to go down the anti-Semitic route but were prevented from doing so by institutional limitations which blocked racial versions of Fascism. Even so, Jews were excluded from public positions. Head of the Science Academy and father of radio Guglielmo Marconi was a Fascist hatchetman and systematically blocked Jewish candidates at the behest of the dictator. Anti-Semitism was less virulent than in other European countries (for social and historical reasons) but there existed 'an anti-semitic ferment, a subterranean movement that became open only with the racial laws'.

The Mosleys were honoured by sharing Mussolini's platform at a march past of Fascist contingents. However, he failed to appear and they, *Blackshirt* editor Captain Lewis and John Celli, BUF organizer in Italy, had to stand in the pouring rain for two hours, as 35,000 Blackshirts marched past. The *Telegraph* reported that Cimmie wore a 'light mackintosh, brown felt hat and – for the occasion – black gloves, which are the correct wear when giving the Fascist salute. This she did repeatedly as unit after unit obeyed the order "Eyes left!".'

The Mosleys returned to London praising Fascism. The Pontine Marshes had been drained and villages built. They had seen evidence of Communist crimes, such as 'holding the heads of living men in steel furnaces until they were burnt off'. Cimmie had been impressed but Nicholas disputed Diana's claim that his mother was a Fascist convert. She made an extra effort to be loyal. Irene 'expressed the hope that the man she worshipped and adored had finally pegged his creed to a pattern that he could serve without any more deflections'. An early infiltrator into the BUF had 'reason to believe that she is not in full accord with his activities'. Cimmie devoted many hours in her failing health to working out a card-index system for the BUF. Spotted at a meeting, a reporter asked her about her politics. She replied, 'I am a member of my husband's Party.'

Mosley sent his aide-de-camp, twenty-four-year-old Ian Hope Dundas, to Italy to study Fascism. The son of Admiral Sir Charles Dundas, ADC to King George V, he was educated at the Royal Naval College, Dartmouth. Well-dressed, handsome and arrogant, he resigned his commission in 1929 to become private secretary to Brendan Bracken, who recommended him to Mosley, for whom he performed special duties. A daughter from his second marriage, Lynette, believed he was 'probably into Mosley for money and not for ideological reasons'. He was introduced to Mussolini by Harold Goad, an important contact for the BUF. Goad lectured at the University of London and was a member of a pro-Fascist Corporate State study group within the Royal Institute of International Affairs, which included Sir Charles Petrie,

Muriel Currey and Major Strachey Barnes, who never joined the BUF, believing anti-Semitism was for idiots. The group was too political for the RIIA and its meetings were moved to Miss Curry's flat where Ambassador Grandi was a frequent guest.

Fascism, Beverley Nichols observed, was 'mercifully confined to Italy. The youth of England had not yet begun to prance about the street in black shirts, like perverted Morris dancers, pushing the palms of their hands in the faces of the startled bourgeoisie.' Faith was put in Mussolini's remark that Fascism was not for export but his Grand Council announced the 'expansion of fascism in the world' as official policy and, after Dundas's visit, there developed close relations between Italy and the BUF. Dundas was regarded as a friend by *Italia Nostra* in whose columns he frequently appeared. Italian papers reported at length on Mosley and, in particular, his references to a pan-European policy and his willingness to join others in developing universal Fascism.

Prompted by restlessness among Fascists who looked to Galeazzo Ciano for fresh energy, Mussolini subsidized foreign groups as part of a widespread propaganda campaign. A decisive factor was Hitler's emergence. If Italy failed to institutionalize these contacts, a Fascist International might be co-opted by the Nazis, which was intolerable to Mussolini. In London, Grandi told friends Mussolini was 'becoming unbalanced and thinking of himself as the Pope of Fascism, infallible, above criticism and surrounded only by satellites, toadies and flatterers'.

'Our deep and abiding friendship with the fascist movement in Italy', Mosley stated in May, 'is based on the solid rock of our friendship between men who hold in common a vast conception and a greal ideal. Such friendship raises no question of subordination, it raises only a question of common service to a common cause.' A delegation of Italian Fascists were welcomed at a reception at Denham. The interpreter was the Italian-born BUF district officer for Liverpool. 'It was a shock', Alex Miles wrote, 'to discover that the "British" Union of Fascists required the service of an Italian and a further shock was provided by the extremely close relations I found to exist between the staff of the Italian Consulate in that city and local Fascist headquarters.' The BUF constitution forbade enrolment of foreigners but Italians were made honorary members. A consequence of Mosley's Rome visit was that Italian intelligence was allowed to insert agents into the BUF.

Mosley was influenced by the 'adventurous, irresponsible and intelligent' Bill Allen who, John Strachey said, would provide 'a useful façade of theory'. He argued emphasis 'on the conception of the nation does not preclude that Universalism which is the antithesis of Internationalism. A revolutionary movement, developing in different countries as the expression of the will-to-power of a generation already decimated by war, would hardly seem likely to envisage the initiation of new wars as the over-riding objective of its inspiration.' An integral universalism built around European racial culture would 'assure to Europe, peace – and to the world, order'.

To bring the pro-Italian groups under his control, in June Mussolini created the Comitati d'azione per l'Universalità di Roma (Action Committees for Roma Universality, CAUR). Under Eugenio Coselschi, CAUR developed secret links and distributed funds to the burgeoning Fascist groups, including the BUF. Asvero Gravelli, the militant editor of *Ottobre* and a leading propagandist, used CAUR to promote Fascism as the 'solution to the crises besetting the West'. He wanted to 'group together the best elements in Europe, to instil the experiences of fascism, to nourish the revolutionary spirit and to establish devotion to the cause of European dictatorship'. CAUR, however, attacked the Nazis because of their racial theory.

In *Ottobre*'s survey of British Fascism, Gravelli praised Mosley for rejecting Nazi racial doctrine, for acknowledging Fascism's Italian origin and adopting corporatism. He accepted newspaper reports of 17,000 members were 'a gross underestimation' and claimed there were 370 branches and from 'a calculation of the income of the BUF, one can infer that there are about 700,000 members'. The figures were created by the BUF, which made every effort to give the impression that it was 'larger and more powerful that it actually is'. Gravelli said the emphasis had been 'on those aspects of fascism which are particularly British but the international alliance of fascism is the superior form of organisation for the young fascist forces. Fascist youth must be able to build up a new European and world entity. British fascism will get strength from this.'

Mosley denied the BUF was subordinate to Italian Fascism but 'the truth is', Johannes Steel wrote in *The Nation*, 'that the actions of political parties are determined less by the terms of their formal programmes than by the sources from which their funds are drawn'. Mosley did not slavishly copy Mussolini but policy was shaped by his opinion. He temporarily buried anti-Semitism in order to secure funding and for this reason attacked Nazi racial policies. He followed up with a public hymn of praise to Mussolini 'as the chief architect of European peace and thanked the Duce's genius'. The dictator was now satisfied that the BUF was worth long-term investment.

BUF finances fluctuated wildly. Some weeks there was no money to pay officials' salaries. At other times the movement was flush with funds, financing propaganda on a scale as large as Conservative Central Office. TUC infiltrator H. R. S. Phillpott reported that 'a couple of months ago the BUF was ... doing a relatively small amount of propaganda work and not very much money was being spent. Since then, however, there has been a considerable speeding up both in activity and in expenditure. Whether the extra money is "new" in the sense that it is not Mosley money it is, of course, impossible to say.' He was unaware of the Italian subsidies which had come on stream.

Mosley made clandestine arrangements for banking of the money. When, after the war, Home Secretary Chuter Ede raised the issue of Italian funds, Mosley claimed all BUF activities were 'paid for direct from its own bank account. The wage bill and all the considerable expenditure or propaganda and organisation were met by cheques drawn on that account. This account . . . was in the hands of the Government of the day. If Italian money was paid into this account how and when was it paid and through what accounts did it pass?' Journalists tried to question Count Grandi, who had taken refuge in Portugal, but he refused to respond. The *Spectator* (14 June 1946) noted that 'no one could seriously suppose that traces of a transaction of this kind would be allowed to appear in any accounts'.

Bill Allen's secretary, Major G. J. H. Tabor, later told Special Branch that his boss had opened a confidential account at the Westminister Bank Charing Cross branch in March 1933. Tabor said he had been given 'large payments of foreign notes by Allen to pay into the account, but he never had any idea where the money came from'. MI5 believed Tabor, who with Allen and Dundas controlled the account, lied. It has been suggested that Allen was an MI5 agent, but though he was very briefly interned and questioned by Francis Aiken-Sneath, the files show he was hostile to MI5, which regarded him as 'completely amoral and politically unstable'. Allen contacted MI5 in 1941 and only told the truth about the account after being shown evidence from telephone taps. When asked about Allen being an agent, author Dorothy Carrington said 'one would absolutely hesitate to think that he was reliable. Perhaps he was a dark horse; he may have been more intelligent than he looked.'

From spring 1933 the BUF received suitcases of large parcels of mixed European currencies, worth around £5,000 (£170,000). According to Grandi, the first 'present' was handed to Mosley. Forgan, who paid in cheques into the Charing Cross account – the first on 6 June – claimed he had no knowledge of the source of the parcels but assumed they came from the Italian embassy. During 1933 a total of £9,500 (£313,000) was banked, though most Italian cash was never deposited. Mussolini supported the BUF to the tune of £60,000 (£2 m) a year.

In contrast, the Germans were cautious in dealings with Mosley. Alfred Rosenberg, Hitler's chief Jew baiter and head of the NSDAP's Foreign Policy Office (APA), was interested in an association of kindred movements but attacked their racial confusion. Through its director for Britain, Otto Bene, the Overseas Organization (AO) was regularly informed about the BUF's attitude to the Jewish threat, which the Nazis feared would drive Britain into the service of Jewish interests. The Jewish question dominated policy, which favoured 'anti-semitic-national protagonists', such as the IFL's Arnold Leese and the Britons' H. H. Beamish over Mosley, who had 'Jewish blood'. He was treated coolly by Nazi journalists, who recognized that, given the 'health of imperialist Englishness', what was required was not so much a movement such as the BUF but a 'rejuvenation of the political leadership'.

Rosenberg visited London on 5 May, as guest of Sir Adrian Baillie, a Unionist MP who later joined Mosley's pro-Fascist January Club. The fact-finding mission was a diplomatic disaster, best remembered for the placing on the Cenotaph of a wreath bedecked with a large swastika. An annoyed Hitler thereafter gave the key role on foreign affairs to former champagne salesman Joachim von Ribbentrop, who was independent of the Foreign Office. The APA retained contacts with the BUF but these were short-term. The *Blackshirt* asserted that once Hitler had remodelled Germany, the 'so-called atrocities and harshness would end. Three-quarters of the reports were not true . . . for the Reds had begun the violence.'

There were Jewish protests against Rosenberg's visit and assaults on BUF news vendors in Piccadilly and the Strand. Inspector Wells believed 'Jews visiting the area will not tolerate the arrogance of the fascists' and recommended Mosley 'be told that in view of the breach of the peace his proposed action is likely to cause, it cannot be allowed'. Special Branch subsequently began monitoring the BUF, particularly in the East End following reports of Jew baiting.

The BUF was identified by the public with Hitler and, influenced by events in Germany, Jewish activists organized an anti-Nazi lobby to oppose it on the streets. Skidelsky argued this was 'an advanced point in an interactive chain of provocation and counter-provocation'. According to the BUF, a British Union of Democrats 'sent van-loads of Jews all over the country to break up Blackshirt meetings' – the 'organised bands of Communists' about which Mosley complained. Skidelsky claimed violence occurred because of 'the attitude of Jews themselves, and they must take a large share of the blame for what subsequently happened'. Following criticism, he changed 'a large share' to 'some' in the paperback edition of his Mosley biography.

Although the police reports Skidelsky cited were inconsistent, he claimed 'some local Jewish communists were more violent than anything produced by East London or any other branch of British fascism . . . Whether they deliberately used Jews as front-line troops in order to expose fascism's anti-semitic potential, or whether Jewish communists showed particular relish for this work, is difficult to say: probably a mixture of both.' The original conclusion read: 'A Jewish malaise of this time was to be obsessed by fascism. If some Jews found it intolerably provoking they certainly went out of their way to be provoked. Fascist meetings drew them as a magnet. The very sight of a blackshirt in uniform was enough to make their blood boil.' Skidelsky deleted this passage for a less provocative one.

Mosley found it difficult to hold back the activists. William Joyce, who was studying for a postgraduate course in Philology at King's College, joined the

BUF and, as Area Administrative Officer for West London and then Director of Propaganda, used his influence 'to give the party a strongly anti-semitic direction – and I may say that I succeeded in that direction. These were marvellous times.' Joyce cloaked an inferiority complex behind an arrogant manner, but was a brilliant public speaker with a passionate but cold, clinical voice. 'Thin, pale, intense, he had not been speaking for many minutes before we were electrified by this man,' a Fascist observed. 'Never had I met a personality so terrifying in its dynamic force, so vituperative, so vitriolic. The words poured from him in a corrosive state.' Joyce was lost in a 'colourful dream-world where he was the universal teacher, the model patriot and the scourge of the Jews'. MI5 files made note of his mental instability and his romantic streak, which made him 'doubly effective and doubly dangerous'.

For months Cimmie had been unwell with severe abdomen pains and unhappy with her marriage. In early May the Mosleys spent the weekend at Savehay Farm but after a row over Diana, Mosley stormed out. On 8 May, after a wretched night, Cimmie wrote her last letter to him. 'I do love and adore you so as much as 13 years ago and in a way more frightenedly as then I had confidence and was happy and now I cannot figure anything quite out any more . . . I am feeling too done in to cope much more.' That evening she was rushed to a London hospital with appendicitis. The operation appeared to go well. Next day Mosley went to Diana's for lunch with Unity, who recorded that 'the Leader was feeling happier'. Cimmie, however, developed peritonitis. Diana worried that if she died 'people would say that she had lost the will to live' and she, Diana, would be seen as being responsible. For several days she did not see 'a very busy, very miserable and tired' Mosley. Cimmie continued to go downhill and died on 15 May.

Dr Kirkwood told Irene that Cimmie had 'never fought from the start. Both mentally and physically she had never lifted a finger to live.' He informed the *Telegraph* that 'she must have meant far more to her husband than the world knows . . . they had a very beautiful time together during their last few days'. As Cimmie lay dying, 'poor Tom was trying to get through to her how magnificent her life had been . . . Tom murmuring to her his last words of love.' When he went for a walk in the garden, Irene asked her fiancé, Miles Graham, to hide Mosley's revolver, in case he did 'something dreadful'. When Cimmie was laid out, he sat for hours gazing at her coffin.

Cecil Beaton was in Rome when he heard of Cimmie's death. He responded on 16 May: 'I am so upset I could cry. I owe much of my happiness and success to her appreciation and friendliness.' Her body was taken to Smith Square, where lilies surrounded the coffin, with a garland of roses plaited by Lady Diana Cooper trailing from it. On 19 May a memorial service was held at St Margaret's, Westminster, presided over by the Archbishop of Canterbury.

It was 'unbearably sad', wrote Georgia Sitwell. The King and Queen and the Prince of Wales sent their condolences; among the mourners were Lloyd George, Ramsay MacDonald and a tearful Churchill, who appealed for a memorial fund which resulted in the building of a Day Nursery in Kensington.

A gushing obituary in the *Observer* marks her out as the Princess Diana of her day. Her death 'removes from politics an extraordinary gracious and charming personality. She had been given the balanced sanity of many gifts – patience, the unrelenting strength of life, the divine relationship of life's continuity. Cynthia Mosley's death is a tragedy, her life a service, possibly a sacrifice. Thus she leaves a man of destiny – to fate, and this is the greatest tragedy of all.' She had 'stepped from grandeur at its blazing ephemeral uncertainty to the gutter to help the humble and the meek, the poor and the desolate, the mother-woman who understood the Nazerene's injunction "to suffer little children" '. *Reynolds News* reported that 'the whole nation wept at her death'.

Opinion was divided on whether Cimmie's health had been undermined by Mosley's 'romping from bed to bed as from party to party'. Nancy Astor considered his grief theatrical and that it would 'pass like a mirage'. Harold Nicolson believed her death really did fill him 'with grief and remorse'. Her death, however, only added to the hatred MPs felt towards him. Mary Hamilton, a Labour MP in the 1929 government, said Cimmie had been 'sacrificed to the hurried ambitions of her husband. Everyone liked her, and not only her lovely face: everyone felt her sincerity, we should have written off Tom much sooner but for her.' Irene thought 'it was best she had gone to suffer no more at Tom's hands'. Devoted Fascists idealized Cimmie for her womanly virtues and, above all, her loyalty.

For a year, Cimmie's body lay in a chapel at Cliveden. An elaborate tomb was designed by Sir Edwin Lutyens and his son, Robert, on the banks of the River Colne, at Savehay Farm. It consisted of a terraced sunken garden, with a tomb of pink marble and a sarcophagus in gold travertine stone, engraved with the inscription 'Cynthia Mosley, my beloved'. Mosley, the bearers and two workmen were the only people there when the coffin was finally interred.

Cimmie's estate was valued at £20,951 (£712,300), with income from her Leiter Trust (£8,000 a year) divided between her three children. Mosley's own fortune was around £300,000 (£10.2 m). His stocks and shares were looked after by his brother John, who worked for City brokers Spurling, Skinner and Tudor. Edward looked after the trust of Lord Anslow, who had been made a peer by Lloyd George and was a next-door neighbour to Rolleston. His medieval doll's house near Horsham had been left to John, who was six foot three inches tall. John lost money in the Crash but by the end of the thirties retained control of his stockbroking firm. John's son, Simon, did not consider the Mosleys a close-knit family as the brothers rarely met. John was 'very laid back' about Mosley's activities. 'He disapproved a bit but not a great deal. He was philosophical.'

Irene, Baroness Ravensdale became guardian to the Mosley children and dedicated herself to the role of surrogate mother, especially to Michael. Nicholas and his sister Vivien found Aunt Baba (Lady Alexandra Metcalfe) a more distant figure, but they were impressed with her air of glamour. Nicholas recalled that his father 'saw his role with children as making jokes'. He wormed it out of his nanny that his aunts were hostile to Diana because they felt she was responsible for his mother's death. 'Peritonitis is what killed her,' Vivien acknowledged, 'but with Diana there, she didn't want to live.' After Cimmie's death, Baba embarked on an affair with her bereaved brother-in-law, much to the anger of her adoring husband. Mosley later told Nicholas that 'it was taboo for a young man to go to bed with an unmarried girl; this would spoil her for the marriage market. Married women, however, after they had had a legitimate child or two, were free to play the game.' Irene did not object, even though the two sisters were great rivals. They united, however, in discouraging Mosley from seeing Diana.

Diana said Mosley found Cimmie's death shattering. He 'blamed himself for having allowed her to work too hard – he thought her physical resistance had been undermined by her political exertions'. In consequence, he became overprotective towards Diana. 'If I was ill he thought I was going to die; he imagined it might be a result of the tension caused by his own life of struggle and strife.' Diana could now nail her colours to his mast, 'colours which to most of her friends were of a most disturbing hue'. High society was shocked to learn that she had asked Bryan for a divorce, to which he agreed. After attending the Women's League of Health and Beauty, Diana and Unity would dine at the Eatonry with Mosley, occasions which laid the groundwork for their obsession with Fascism.

Mosley said he would devote himself to Fascism as a 'fitting memorial' to Cimmie. His public and private life were put in separate compartments and no BUF officials were invited to Denham. He gave up his social pleasures in London, as well as Mediterranean holidays, and occupied himself with speaking tours and administration. His mother took over Cimmie's public role. 'There must be someone to help him in his work and I am going to do my best to fill the gap.' Diana was content to be a mistress to Mosley and dedicated herself unswervingly to his cause, which led to 'a certain blindness to flaws in either the man or in his ideals'. On 6 June she informed Unity about Mosley's love affairs. Years later she was 'quite meticulous' in doing the same to Nicholas. 'She gave me the instances and the dates of all the women he'd flirted with.'

Around this time Mosley asked Baba, whose intense sexual and emotional attraction to him was mirrored by her loathing and jealousy of Diana, to join him on a trip through Bavaria. He persuaded Diana that, until her divorce became final, seeing Baba would be useful cover for him. There was a row, though Diana claimed she did not mind the affair. 'I might be jealous of a deep friendship but not sexually jealous.' Mosley and Baba 'had this thing for each other, and it's life. And with sex, opportunity is so important.' She said he would always come back to her, though Irene hoped his obsession with Baba would oust Diana. The permutations of deception and self-deception seemed endless, as he juggled people and passions. On 16 June the dissolution of Diana's marriage was announced.

At a house party given by Mrs Richard Guinness, Diana and Unity were introduced to Dr Ernst Hanfstaengl, an official of the Nazi Party's foreign press department, who was attending a World Economic Conference to assess reactions to Hitler. 'He is David to Hitler's Saul,' the hostess told Diana, who had 'often met drawing-room communists who breathed fire and slaughter' but he was her 'first drawing-room Nazi'. The eccentric son of a Munich fine-arts publisher and an American mother, at six feet four inches tall, he was awkward-looking with his huge frame. 'Putzi' – Bavarian dialect for 'little fellow' – was among the first of the middle class to join the Nazis and the 'Chauffeureska', Hitler's inner circle. Irene referred to him as the jester lover 'bugger' Hanfstaengl – 'a magnificent type of man who plays the piano beautifully, is anxious and oily and utterly evasive on any real question'. The British embassy in Berlin cabled London that anything he might say should be taken with a large pinch of salt, as his ideas were 'fantastic'.

Putzi recalled meeting Unity – 'she was very much second string to her sister, tagging along'. Diana asked him about the Jews. He replied that 'people here have no idea of what the Jewish problem has been in Germany since the war. Why not think for once of the 99 per cent of the population, of the six million unemployed. Hitler will build a great and prosperous Germany for the Germans. If the Jews don't like it they can get out. Let them leave Germany to us Germans.' Putzi invited them to visit Munich. Otto von Bismarck, Counsellor at the German embassy, contacted him with a request to introduce them to Hitler. 'After that I had Unity on my hands.'

Unity was born at the outbreak of the First World War. The choice of her middle name, Swastika (the Canadian town where she was conceived), was prescient. Almost six feet tall, with big hands and feet, she could look beautiful and was sometimes mistaken for Diana. Romantic by nature, rather dreamy and somewhat unruly, she secretly joined the BUF behind the backs of her parents, to whom any mention of 'that man' Mosley was taboo. His mother viewed her with suspicion: 'This wretch is wanting to sell black shirts and walk in parades and attend all meetings – for what reason?' Claud Phillimore observed that she was 'determined to do something against convention. She had a strong masculine streak in her. She was immensely influenced by Diana, and I suppose not well balanced. She wore the fascist emblem to flaunt her outrages, to bait her parents.'

On 1 July the BUF marched in London with Mosley amassing his Fascists in Eaton Square, near his mother's house. The march of 1,000 young Black-shirts and 100 girls in black shirts and skirts was 'a splendid show', reported Irene. Among those watching from Colin Davidson's window in Grosvenor Place were Zita James, Beatrice Guinness and Hanfstaengl. Mosley had a knack of attracting disreputable figures and on the balcony were new members, Joseph Hepburn-Ruston and his wife, Baroness Ella van Heemstra, parents of Audrey Hepburn. The Baroness was a Christian Scientist of mixed Dutch–French–Hungarian origin and Jewish ancestry. The family's Castle Doorn, near Utrecht, had given sanctuary to the Kaiser following his abdication. Her husband, variously described as an adventurer or financial adviser, had been born in Bohemia of Scottish (he wrote a book on Fascism's Celtic roots) and Austrian parents. During 1923–4, he met his future wife while serving as British consul in Sumarang, Java, then part of the Dutch East Indies, where he may have been acting for British Intelligence. The couple returned to Europe and settled in Brussels where he supposedly managed a branch of the Bank of England. It has been suggested Hepburn-Ruston was employed on undercover work of a 'delicate' nature by the Bank's Governor, Sir Montagu Norman. More likely, he dabbled in investments as an independent broker.

Mosley was proselytizing among the titled. A meeting of upper-class ladies was held on 6 July in his house, where Anthony Rumbold, whose father was ambassador in Berlin, heard Mosley speak 'much more of Italy than of his own movement'. The BUF, suggests Julie Gottlieb, was a cult in veneration of one man. His matinée idol persona helped pack meetings with ladies in evening dress, who 'come to watch fascist brutality in order to pander to appetites which everything else decadent in the world can no longer satisfy'. The middle-aged Lady Pearson was one titled woman, with a crush on Mosley, who flirted with Fascism. His dandified appearance, however, also facilitated the derision of his many detractors and his 'political Douglas Fairbanksism' was a ready target.

Aristocrats joined the BUF, but most despised Mosley as a traitor because he attacked inherited wealth. 'No longer will the country house of the decadent plutocracy stand empty for three-quarters of the year while their owners disport themselves in the night clubs of Europe, while the peasants, because they have no land, are relegated to the care of the "local authorities".' He excused himself of the charge of hypocrisy. Some felt the patrician in the faultlessly tailored black shirt was unpopular with his own class but 'too scornfully aristocratic to be beloved by the masses'.

Mosley was buoyed by articles in the *New Statesman* in July by Keynes on national self-sufficiency. He believed Keynes had validated his own thinking but when he wrote to congratulate him, the economist said their purpose 'was to save the country from me, not to embrace me!' The rise of Fascism alarmed him and he wanted to ensure it would not be imposed on the country. Diana admitted Mosley met Keynes 'a few times but they were not close'; he admired him but 'his influence was overrated'. Mosley was finding it difficult to attract allies.

13

Universal Fascism

Following negotiations with Nazi representative Dr Thost during July 1933, *The Times* published 'purified' extracts from Hitler's *Mein Kampf*. Despite hundreds of articles on Germany, editors disconnected Nazi ideology from practice. Its essence – race theory – was 'so remote from the liberal *Weltanschauung* that few were willing to come to grips with it'.

On 10 July the *Daily Mail* announced 'YOUTH TRIUMPHANT'. George Ward Price urged 'all British young men and women to study closely the progress of this Nazi regime'. Any acts of violence were 'exaggerated to give the impression that Nazi rule is a bloodthirsty tyranny'. Germany was 'falling under the control of its alien elements. In the last days of the pre-Hitler regime there were twenty times as many Jewish government officials in Germany as had existed before the war. Israelites of international attachments were insinuating themselves into key positions in the German administrative machine . . . It is from such abuses that Hitler has freed Germany.' Rothermere believed Jews were playing a malevolent role and complained they were 'everywhere'. Goebbels thought the article 'wonderful' and had it reprinted throughout Germany.

Three days later Ward Price met with the Prince of Wales who, in conversation with Prince Louis Ferdinand, his cousin and the Kaiser's grandson, was 'quite pro-Hitler'. He said it was 'no business of ours to interfere in Germany's internal affairs re Jews, and added that dictators were very popular these days and that we might want one in England before long'.

In an effort to retain Mussolini's favour, Mosley clamped down on anti-Semitism. Interviewed by the *Jewish Chronicle* on 28 July, he said attacks on Jews were 'strictly forbidden'. Anti-Semitism was not known in Italy. 'The attacks on the Jews in Germany do not rest on any Fascist principle but are manifestations of an inherent quality in the German character. For many centuries religious and racial tolerance has been part of the British character, and I give my assurance that under Fascism that great tradition will be preserved.' He attempted to close down other Fascist groups. BUF members resented that they 'might be blamed for the display of hostility towards the Jews' because of the actions of others. When British Fascist members counter-demonstrated in Hyde Park against an anti-Hitler protest and began shouting anti-Semitic slogans, they followed it up with an attack on the BUF. Later, Blackshirts raided the BF headquarters and caused considerable damage.

At the end of July, Grandi met with Mosley, who expressed his 'profound gratitude for the precious assistance'. Grandi assured him Mussolini followed his progress 'with particular interest' and that arrangements had been made for the 'delicate operation of the consignment to be carried out in the most secret way' via the diplomatic bag for delivery by 'Dottore Enderle'. A courier, Enderle's nephew Arturo Resio, was 'told to carry out the assignment with the maximum caution', because his uncle 'could be easily singled out, since he has carried out similar tasks in the past'. Resio left Rome on 26 August and was responsible for 'slipping unobtrusively' the instalment of £5,000 in packages of used notes to Mosley.

Former Labour Home Secretary J. R. Clynes observed that Mosley was becoming 'the Greta Garbo of British politics'. He was 'surrounding himself with a fog of mystery so dense that even his own followers must be finding it difficult to penetrate it'. During his wartime interrogation Francis Hawkins, who controlled the fund collectors but not foreign donations, said money had been sent abroad to hide the identity of British donors and that Mosley put money into his solicitor's account to conceal his own contribution. He was aware money came from France but never knew its source. Cheques from Ireland (Bill Allen's) and Switzerland (allegedly Nazi funds) were also deposited. The Italian funds were laundered via Minculprop, the Ministry of Culture and Propaganda headed by Count Ciano, Mussolini's son-in-law. Only Mosley was privy to the details and relied on his collector for France, Ian Dundas, to visit the Italian embassy in Paris once a month to receive money through the Italian Press Attaché Amadeo Landini.

Grandi informed Mussolini that the

underground movement in English political life has given rise to manifestations not without significance ... these Chinese of the Western world prepare, slowly but surely, their Revolution. They may come last but they will find out that the Revolution has taken place anyway ... Even here there is the noise of a pick-axe. Mosley picks up fights in the streets, the mass of young Tories is in open rebellion and the theme of every group, tendency, party, is the following: one must concentrate the power of the State in a few people.

Rothermere was pushing 'an openly fascist campaign', which was considered 'good business in selling more copies of a major newspaper. In my view this is an interesting indication, don't you think?' The important point was Grandi's acknowledgement that, on Mussolini's behalf, he had studied the 'Summer Autumn programme of action Mosley plans to undertake. Upon my suggestions and advice he has prepared the programme enclosed *for your approval*.'

Flush with Mussolini's subsidies, in August the BUF moved into headquarters next to the Duke of Wellington's Barracks in Chelsea. Previously the Whitelands Teacher Training College, the grey pseudo-Gothic pile at 232 Battersea Park Road, was renamed the 'Black House' – by its opponents the 'Fascist Fort'. A Union Jack floated over the entrance and the walls were plastered with posters: 'Shall Jews Drag Britain Into War?' An inmate said 'it was filled with students eager to learn everything about this new, exciting crusade; its club rooms rang with the laughter and song of men who felt that the advent of Fascism had made life worth living again'. With its ex-serviceman, ex-officer complexion, the Black House operated in a paramilitary fashion. Army terms and methods were used; 'discipline, fitness and obedience were proclaimed as virtues; the need for leadership emphasised'. Mosley said he had 'reverted to type and lived in the spirit of the professional army where I began; I was half soldier, half politician.'

Within the Black House existed a Ruritanian atmosphere. Day-to-day activities of the Defence Force, who slept, ate and trained there in readiness for meetings, were 'regulated army fashion by the sound of the bugle summoning them for parades, mealtimes and lights out'. Reveille at 7 a.m. heralded a programme of drill and administrative work. Enhancing the martial image was the military band. Mosley wanted Sousa's 'Stars and Stripes' as a Fascist anthem, with words by Osbert Sitwell.

The Black House was expensive to run and attracted an oddball collection of recruits. There were fights, disobedience and petty thefts. Special Branch reported an incident in which a man was badly wounded by a knife during horseplay between inmates. It was rumoured the cellars were used for punishment purposes. Headquarters was run by an administrative clique recruited from the BF, led by the trusted Francis Hawkins, who was always at his desk. Officials who did not commit their lives to the task were labelled clock-watchers by 'FH', who denounced them as unworthy of the cause they served. Colleagues found Hawkins always accessible but difficult to get close to. A homosexual, he surrounded himself with unmarried men but was disliked for the favouritism he granted to his 'Mafia'.

The best leaders employ constructive dissenters 'prepared to tell them, when the time comes, that they are crazy', but Mosley surrounded himself with uncritical loyalists who, Diana said, were 'faithful and had integrity'. Captain Brian Donovan was Assistant Director-General. He had been wounded in the war in France and received the Military Cross. He was said to have served in the Middle East with Lawrence of Arabia. He was posted to Turkey and fought with the Indian Cavalry on the North-West Frontier. Donovan had been a school headmaster and had recently interviewed George Orwell for a teaching post. A devout Catholic, he had a religious conception of the State. Blackshirts regarded him as 'inflexible, exacting and an incompetent martinet'.

Next in importance came Mosley's long-time secretary George Sutton. Wounded in the war, Sutton had chaired the North St Pancras Labour Party. As the 'only man alive who can make head or tail of what Mosley writes', there was always a queue of people, Diana recalled, 'waiting for Sutton to decipher notes they had received from OM'.

Within the BUF elite there was a preponderance of highly educated youth. Another characteristic was the number of middle-class business-professional-farming-independent types and lower-middle-class journalists and travellers. They displayed a high degree of restlessness, with changes in jobs and locations. Senior officials were often ex-officers with varied travel experiences around the world. A typical official was Northern Organizer Richard Bellamy, who had been a Black and Tan, later a jackaroo in the Australian outback and then a coffee grower in New Caledonia. Experiences such as his were not untypical of the feelings of rootlessness engendered by war. Bellamy said of his Blackshirt comrades that often their 'minds lay rooted in the halcyon past which had ended abruptly in 1914'.

Bill Allen said Fascism appealed to those 'younger-minded middle class who are conservative by temperament and strongly nationalist in spirit, and to those rarer and more dynamic individuals who, naturally revolutionary in their outlook, have been disappointed and exasperated by the failure of all leadership from the left to approach any fulfilment of their aspirations'. Many of the best recruits came from the ILP, including Bill Risdon, who 'gave a cool, logical exposition of economic policy' and became Director of Propaganda.

The BUF's left wing achieved some success with the Fascist Union of British Workers, which criticized the TUC, Labour and the Communists for putting the welfare of foreigners before British workers' interests. The Communist International found the FUBW was achieving results with its propaganda against the means test and demands for work with decent wages for the unemployed, and was concerned about this 'deceptiveness, because in the ears of so many workers it rings true'. Alex Miles expected FUBW activities would be expanded but he ran up against Mosley's 'distrust of a working class wing of organised character'. In the end, its appeal did not prosper since working-class occupational groups were unwilling to disown the trade unions. Efforts to win support in non-industrialized sectors with weak unionization attracted groups outside traditional labour-capital confrontations.

A Home Office report said BUF membership comprised marginal members of all social and economic classes and occupational groups – working-class domestic servants, lower-middle-class shopkeepers and middle-class cinema owners in competition with large chains. They were unpoliticized and had not voted for the major parties but supported 'a "hero" in an "heroic" age'.

*

In August Mosley travelled with Baba through France, where they began an affair. When Nicholas asked his aunt about it, she 'drew herself up in the best Lady Bracknell manner and said, "I'd never have gone to bed with your father while your mother was alive!"' Irene noticed the kindness Mosley showed Baba, which he had never displayed to Cimmie. He told Diana that sexual flings were to be treated almost as a joke.

Diana and Unity were on a sightseeing trip to Bavaria. Their interest in Germany had been fired by their brother Tom, a strong advocate of German culture, who read Schopenhauer and Kant, and in common with friends believed Germany had been unjustly penalized by the victors at Versailles. They were accompanied by Mosley's friends Lord Hinchingbrooke and Nigel Birch, and had an invitation from Otto von Bismarck for the first big Nuremberg rally. The Nazis were now controlling propaganda abroad. In a report on British–German relations on 16 August, Ambassador Leopold von Hoesch counselled against any 'vehement and blatant' propaganda campaign and suggested sponsoring prominent Britons for trips to Germany as the best way to strengthen support for National Socialism. A BUF contingent had visited Osthofen and toured a 'concentration Camp for political prisoners, communists and other Reds'.

Arriving in Munich, the Mitfords realized Hanfstaengl was not as well accepted in official circles as they expected. Putzi 'fished haphazardly in the social currents that flowed his way and, as often as not, when his temper flared, rejected prize catches'. He said the sisters were pretty but had 'no chance of meeting Hitler if you don't wipe that stuff from your faces' – it conflicted with the Nazi ideal of womanhood. They did so but were dismissed by Rudolf Hess – 'too much make-up'.

On 21 August the pair attended the Day of Victory, celebrating the Nazis' seizure of power. It was a huge political circus with nearly a million performers. Part of a BUF delegation, Unity wore a black shirt. Also present was William Joyce who, in applying the previous month for a passport for 'business travel and holiday purposes', had falsely claimed to be a British subject by birth. Like many BUF officials, he preferred the Nazis to Italian Fascists because of their racial policies. Diana described witnessing a 'demonstration of hope in a nation that had known collective despair'. British newspapers barely mentioned the Parteitag and, when they did, it was to describe it as militaristic, though Diana thought it 'not even as militaristic as a torch-light tattoo in England'.

'A feeling of excited triumph was in the air,' Diana wrote home. When Hitler appeared, she felt 'an almost electric shock pass through the multitude'. Unity 'underwent nothing less than a religious conversion'. Nazism appealed to her on a very simple level. She told the *Evening Standard* that on seeing Hitler, 'there was no one I would rather meet'.

Diana's parents were horrified that she accepted hospitality 'from people we regard as a murderous gang of pests'. Friends wondered how a 'passionate subscriber to all that was most civilised in their world, should be in thrall to such a dark and ugly creed'. Diana was aware of where it might lead and wrote to Roy Harrod asking if it was 'not preferable that in a movement such as this one, that might so easily become barbaric, there should be some civilised persons throwing in their weight with the inevitable boxers, old soldiers, suffragettes and oddments'? Mosley was 'so clever and in his way so civilised and English' that the BUF 'could not be comparable to the German movement. But if everyone of sensibility, charm and intelligence shuns him, there is definitely a danger that he will come to regard these virtues as vicious and the possessors of them as enemies.'

Diana's activities were now directed towards one aim, 'that of her Führer at home'. She intended to forge close links with officials who could be of use to him. She went to stay in Rome with Lord Berners, an ageing homosexual, who was almost a P. G. Wodehouse creation. However, he had been an assistant to Sir Rennell Rodd at the embassy in Rome, where he encountered the Futurists. Novelist, composer and dilettante, he had the instincts of the diehard right. Many of his friends were less naïve but held extreme views, including fellow diplomats Harold Nicolson and Gerald Wellesley, future Duke of Wellington, and his one-time fiancée Violet Trefusis.

At the end of August Claud Cockburn wrote in *The Week* that Mosley and Lady Houston, owner of the *Saturday Review*, had joined forces to publish a new weekly. When, two months later, the *Fascist Week* appeared, Lady Houston denied involvement. She had been left £6 million (£120 m) on the death of her third husband and donated large sums to patriotic causes. When in 1931 the government refused to pay for the RAF entry to the Schneider trophy, she provided £100,000 to commission a plane, which spawned the Spitfire. Lady Houston contemplated writing out a cheque for £100,000 (£3.4 m) for the BUF because she admired their 'revival of English manhood'. Unfortunately for Mosley, she changed her mind and tore it up.

Mosley hoped to prosper in rural areas, where campaigns were waged under the patronage of wealthy agriculturalists such as Lady Pearson, who said the BUF would 'restore the Land to the service of the People'. The American wife of the tenth Viscount and lady-in-waiting to Queen Mary, and former leading British Fascisti, managed her Hillingdon estate in Norfolk. The BUF received numerous £100 (£3,000) subscriptions from such supporters. Ralph Bellamy saw Mosley speak in an East Anglian market town. 'A light would flash in his eyes [which] seemed to indicate some inner flame or fire. He showed extensive knowledge and a deep understanding of the many aspects of his subject, memory for facts and figures, and above all there remained with me the recollection of his strong magnetism in that strong voice as he spoke on and on, without strain and affectation in political but unaffected prose.'

Mosley wanted to exploit the 'Tithe Wars'. Tithes had been paid to the Church based on the value of the corn crop, but with the restoration of free trade prices fell. However, farmers were still required to pay the same tithe. If it was unpaid, Church Commissioners could seize property. BUF member and East Anglian farmer Ronald Creasey recalled many poverty-stricken farmers being pushed 'to the utmost despair and many suicides'. They 'shot themselves with their own guns, because of the mercilessness of the Church and the tithes'.

On three occasions from the summer of 1933, Blackshirts appointed themselves defenders of downtrodden farmers with instructions to obstruct bailiffs collecting the tithe. Despite police warnings, they took over a farm near Wortham, Suffolk, run by an East Anglian novelist, Doreen Wallace, who refused to pay the tithe. When the Church sent in bailiffs, Creasey persuaded Mosley that it was an opportunity to ally the Fascists with a popular cause. National Political Officer Dick Plathen was sent to mount an operation. Blackshirts set up camp at the farm, fortified the entrance with trenches and prepared for pitched battle with the Church's agents. The BUF remained for sixteen days, until a busload of fifty London policemen arrested nineteen Blackshirts who pleaded guilty to unlawful conspiracy to effect a public mischief. National Farmers Union branches rejected militant action but direct action did have an effect. In 1936 a law was passed which provided for the tithe's phased abolition, though farmers paid the anachronistic tax into the mid seventies, and it was only in 1996 that it finally passed into history.

Despite widespread depression in agricultural areas, the modernized character of British agriculture – highly mechanized and cushioned by generous government subsidies through Walter Elliott's 'socialist' Agriculture Act – ensured that wealthy landowners were largely impervious to BUF propaganda and did not desert the National government.

Mosley's romantic nostalgia for a rural past found favour with Nietzschean Tories of the organic movement, who feared modernity and cosmopolitanism, and dreamed of a pure and spiritual national renewal. They favoured the English Mistery, led by US-born Lord Lymington, educated at Winchester and a Conservative MP. Besides a return to the soil, they advocated selective breeding for the development of racial traits and the elimination of alien control of finance. 'We felt that outside influences were corrupting our standards and national purpose,' Lymington wrote. 'We believed in ritual as man is a ritualistic species.' Royalism was at the core of their belief along with an admiration for Mussolini.

Influential in the movement for an organic socialism was A. J. Penty. A member of the Rural Reconstruction Association, Penty praised Mussolini for creating a Corporate State – in essence the 'Regulative Guild State'. He supported Belloc's and Chesterton's Distributist League, which wanted property vested in the many, mirroring the Middle Ages, when peasant property was the distinctive form of landholding. Belloc had met Il Duce, who shared his belief that the 'International Financiers govern us'. One commentator noted that the League, 'once a Jacobin Radical organization which owed pretty well everything to Mr Chesterton, is now partly Tory and partly Fascist'. Corporatism disposed distributists, such as Douglas Jerrold, to accept Fascism. Mosley recognized allies among them, such as Penty, who said Fascism was the best defence against Communism even if he recoiled from its totalitarianism. His son Michael wrote articles for the BUF. Mosley made an unsuccessful attempt to subsume the League within the BUF.

The link between English Mistery, the distributists, social credit and BUF thinking was elucidated by John Strachey's former friend H. F. Ludlam, who edited a financial paper, the *Age of Plenty*, and acted as a BUF expert on corporatism. There were similarities between the Fascist and the social credit analyses. Raven Thompson said, 'the class war becomes a sheer absurdity in an age of plenty, for what object can there be in struggle between the classes when there is plenty for all?' Pro-Fascists such as aviator A. V. Roe, military writer J. F. C. Fuller and Catholic convert Christopher Hollis, brother of the future head of MI5, all adopted social credit. The Green Shirt Movement for Social Credit felt so threatened by the BUF's apparent appropriation of its ideas that its leader, John Hargreave, publicly dissociated himself from Mosley.

Artist and social creditor Wyndham Lewis met Mosley for the first time in 1933 – Mrs Naomi Mitchison having arranged an appointment. Lewis thought him 'a good fellow'. The meetings were an excuse for cloak-and-dagger theatricals. 'Lewis used to come to see me in most conspiratorial fashion at dead of night with his coat collar turned up,' Mosley recalled. He feared assassination, 'but the unkind said he was avoiding his creditors'. Despite the promptings of Lewis and Ezra Pound, social credit never took centre stage in BUF thinking. Mosley disliked its anti-puritanical attitude to work and the social equality implied by the idea of a national dividend. Ludlam was considered an unpleasant 'little man who wanted to be a god' and there were rivalries between the BUF and the Green Shirts, whose Liverpool headquarters was broken up by Blackshirts.

In autumn 1933 a cousin to G. K. and Cecil Chesterton threw in his lot with Mosley. A Fleet Street sub-editor, A. K. Chesterton's wife Doris was a Fabian socialist who belonged to Wells's Federation of Progressive Societies and Individuals. She said her husband had called himself a socialist but was really a prophet in search of a creed, who fell for Mosley. Chesterton believed in Carlyle's suggestion that you should 'find in any country the ablest man that exists there; raise him up to the supreme place and loyally reverence him;

you have the perfect government for that country; no ballot box, parliamentary eloquence, voting, constitution building, or other machinery whatever can improve a whit'.

Chesterton was a volcano about to erupt. He believed Fascists were the 'soldiers of Britain's civil life'. Mosley said that 'more than any writer of this time, he expresses in dynamic and passionate prose the resurgent soul of the war generation . . . he could find no home but Fascism'. For Chesterton, the personal was political. When life is 'depraved and insupportable, as when it is called a decadent age', the Fascist 'is able to come to grips with his personal problems by dealing with the problems of society in which his own, either directly or symbolically, are exteriorized'.

During September on a visit to Rome, John Beckett decided the Italians were 'achieving all those things – national unity and abolition of class privilege – for which I had hoped from the Labour Party'. Approached by Dr Forgan, he was reluctant to commit to the BUF since he 'never had any faith in Mosley's character'. He was 'completely insincere and his judgement seemed erratic'. Forgan said he now took his mission 'extremely seriously' and arranged several meetings with Mosley. According to a report to the British Foreign Secretary, Beckett's conversion was given large headlines by many papers in Italy, which represented it as an important political event.

Beckett put aside his reservations partly for financial reasons – Mosley offered a stable income. Beckett and his wife Kyrle Bellew, a Labour councillor in Peckham, managed the Strand Theatre, which during 1933 made substantial losses, which bankrupted him. Their relationship then disintegrated, each blaming the other for the financial disaster. Beckett went to Forgan's tailor, bought a black shirt and quickly became one of the best-known Fascists in Britain.

Beckett claimed his BUF speeches were 'practically the same as those I had made in the ILP because my change of organisation had no effect upon my socialist convictions'. One difference was the anti-Semitism, which surfaced after his mother's death in 1932. Dorothy Solomon was Jewish; a secret he guarded so well that his son only discovered it years after his father's death. There were those in the BUF, however, who knew he had a Jewish background. A rabid anti-Semite, initially influenced by Joyce, he was convinced he 'just opposed international money power which happened to be controlled by Jews'.

Another important recruit was thirty-four-year-old Alexander Raven Thomson, the BUF's leading intellectual and chief propagandist. He had been in Germany, where he read economics at university and married the daughter of the German inventor of X-rays. Thomson had learnt the process for silver paper and on his return to England set up a factory to manufacture it. He had a private income and devoted several years to studying politics. For a brief period he was a member of the Communist Party in Battersea. In 1931 his wife formed the Anglo-German Agency for Domestic Servants, which accepted Jewish refugees from Germany as well as 'Aryan' servants.

In 1932 Thomson published his reply to Spengler's *Decline of the West, Civilisation as Divine Superman*, which Mosley thought exceptional. 'His approach differed from mine because his conclusion was as pessimistic as Spengler's, and his concept of the future seemed to me an almost ant-heap collectivism.' Thomson argued civilization could avoid decay if it adopted a communal spirit of the type found in insect communities. Civilization was the master, not the servant, of man, granting him 'the immense advantages of co-operation and specialism only as a reward for surrendering his freedom to the higher aims of the communal spirit'. Bill Allen wrote that Thomson 'professes to see in this superorganism the true superman. Civilization is not a biological process in the upward progress of mankind; it is a "super-biological" force governed by "super-biological" laws, directing the actions of mere men to the realization of its higher aims, the very realization of the "superman".'

Thomson had discovered a 'hidden key' which 'seemed to shed a flood of illumination over so much that was obscure and inexplicable'. With his belief in religion restored, he believed Fascism provided a Utopia closest to his ideal. A romantic reactionary, he dreamed of a cleansed and united nation but also shared the radical ethos of the BUF's left wing which attacked laissez-faire. He claimed Fascism came from the left, emerging not from Marxism but syndicalism. Building on his ideas, Mosley developed a complex system of industrial self-government, based on delegates from corporations being elected to a national chamber to decide industrial policy. In a rare confession of an error, he later admitted his Utopian structure was too bureaucratic. He had falsely assumed mere national will could reconcile sectional conflicts.

Raven Thomson was known as a fighter-intellectual, who 'breathed political and philosophical truth'. He created a 'feeling of something approaching euphoria among his audience, disarming his opponents before they were able to utter anything in opposition'. He was Mosley's personal representative in discussions with the Nazi Party and on visits to Germany, but many regarded him simply as a 'yes man'. When Blackshirts supported strikers at the Firestone factory in Brentford, TUC General Secretary Walter Citrine warned they were 'using the methods of the Communists. They were using every strike, every grievance, as a means of agitation.' Supporting the strike was divisive and, on the advice of Captain Lewis, the BUF legal adviser, Mosley sent Thomson to ask Nazi representatives in London 'whether the Nazi Party had ever supported strikes'. He reported that they did not support strikes.

The Foreign Office's Permanent Under-Secretary of State, Sir Robert Vansittart, learnt in September that 'a close watch is being kept on Nazi activities in this country'. Of particular interest was Otto Bene, a salesman for a German company, but in reality a Nazi official reporting to Rudolf Hess. Attitudes towards the BUF were confused by the anatagonism between the NSDAP, which preferred contact with individual Fascists, and the German Foreign Office, which had yet to be nazified.

Initially slanted towards Mussolini, BUF publications now paid homage to National Socialism, reflecting the divisions within the movement. During September the *Blackshirt* portrayed Hitler as a messenger of peace. Nazi official Gunther Schmidt-Lorenzen visited England to study at first hand British Fascism. A guest of Viscount Downe and Lady Downe at their 42,000-acre farm at Wykham Abbey, Yorkshire, he found among their circle of military and aristocratic figures a friendly view of Germany. They told him of a 'rising wave of rejection of international Jewish capitalism' and introduced him to British Fascist leaders, who exaggerated the BF's membership at 400,000, attacked Mosley for 'accepting money from Jews' and being friendly with 'men such as Baron Rothschild and Sassoon'.

Lady Downe introduced the German to the 'un-English' Mosley. 'His dark hair, his very expressive features, perhaps playing for effect, show this. He knows how to put himself and his political views over through his style and is without doubt a skilled and man-of-the-world fighter for his cause.' The British might not accept Fascism, but Mosley claimed the 'bad world-wide situation and the resulting distress in agriculture and industry and the desire and hope for improvement were pushing astonishing numbers of supporters to him'. He had 'great sympathy with the great Hitler movement and wished for nothing more than to be able to remain in close contact with events in Germany'. He was sending 'capable men' to Germany to make direct reports, since there had been 'no contact with the representatives of our embassy for a long time'. When the German expressed concern regarding his leniency towards Jews, Mosley insisted 'it wasn't correct that he was paid by the Jews; his attitude and tactics with regard to the Jewish question was one more suited to the English character and which appealed more to the English sense of fair play. It is better to say "Here is a man who brings in international finance and is flooding us with interest – here is another who is in touch with international communists and who are damaging English industry – both are Jews". Judge for yourself what happens to them.' Mosley admitted it was a 'machiavellian policy'.

Mosley bent policy to attract potential suitors. At the end of September, the BUF attacked the 'international finance of the City of London, which is of course largely Jewish' and the 'low type of foreign Jew . . . who are to the fore in every crooked financial deal'. In Manchester, Mosley claimed Jews were dominating British life, although he carefully distinguished between 'good' and 'bad' Jews. For the first time the BUF revealed how it would deal with the alien financier: 'They will go out of the country . . . for these are the elements which the Fascist state cannot and will not absorb. They are a cancer in the body politic which requires a surgical operation.'

Schmidt-Lorenzen's report was studied in Berlin with key passages outlining BUF policy on the Jews underlined. Hans Thomsen, responsible for the foreign press in the Reich office, thought the comments on the rival British Fascist movements 'unusually to the point and fascinating'. Schmidt-Lorenzen recommended 'it should be our first task to support the growing fascism in England'. A copy was passed on to Hitler. To deal with any misunderstandings, BUF Chief of Staff Ian Dundas sent Mandeville-Roe to Germany to meet Hitler in order to bring about 'the mutual harmonisation of press reports'.

Mosley remained close to the Italians and on 30 September wrote for *Antieuropa* on 'Dictatorship'. He praised Cromwell's Ironsides as a 'determined minority, who carried through one of the most efficient and ruthless revolutions in the history of the world, and in the space of a few years completely transformed the character and psychology of the nation'. Modern dictatorship came from 'an organised and disciplined movement hammered into shape, coherence and corporate sense in the struggle in the streets – possessed by a religious sense of national renaissance, and therefore set apart almost as a priesthood, dedicated to the service of its country'.

Mosley was back in favour with Irene who supported his political efforts. He told her dramatically that his 'life was over, he wanted to put fascism on the map and he did not mind if a bullet met him'. Cimmie talked to him and was 'always by his side'. On 11 October Harold Nicolson visited him at Ebury Street, where he was recovering from a bad back and still grieving for Cimmie. Mosley told him he was making 'great progress in town and country alike. He gets very little money from the capitalists but relies on subscriptions. His aim is to build up from below gradually.' During the autumn a recruitment drive in Scotland created twenty branches. This picture was repeated in Yorkshire, with twelve branches, Manchester boasted eight and a further ten were active in Lancashire towns.

The *Blackshirt* referred to 'the emotion surrounding the dipping of the Union Jack and BUF flags at the Cenotaph' during a march in Manchester. Northerners had 'looked with respect on these sturdy silent men marching with a precision brought about by organised control'. However, the Metropolitan Police Commissioner attributed the rise in disturbances to the wearing of military style uniforms. Special Branch began compiling reports on the BUF, based on an agent in its headquarters.

The expansion was funded by Mussolini's subventions. In late October his Foreign Ministry asked Grandi to 'get the above sums into Mosley's hands in whatever form your Excellency considers best'. The courier Resio was 'doing all in his power to ensure that the sum arrives in Mosley's hands in the easiest way for him to withdraw it secretly'. Grandi confirmed a package had been delivered to Mosley, who signed the 'usual letter of thanks'. On 21 October £1,900 in notes, $7,150 and 25,000 Swiss francs were dispatched. Twelve days later Swiss francs worth £1,533 (£52,000) were deposited in the Westminster account. An infiltrator, W. H. Stevenson, was able to inform his TUC contact, Mr Dunbar, on 24 October of rumours that Mosley 'received from Italian sources a subsidy of £5,000 a month. This is to continue until the aggregate sum is £200,000 [£6.8 m], and then the position will be reviewed.'

Stevenson's information was better than that of MI5. He said a 'good deal of bickering appears to be going on in the ranks'. There was discontent because Mosley's programme 'lacks novelty and virility; for example, Walter Elliott has put through his plans for agriculture, and Cripps has stolen his thunder about dictatorship'. Irene went to a dinner at the Italian embassy and sat next to Elliott. Grandi was 'thrilling on Tom'. He watched his every move and, 'as the press gives no fair verdict of his speeches, writes home himself the truth'. He predicted the spread of Fascism after a Labour government.

In late 1933 writers and politicians associated with *Everyman* and the *English Review* expressed sympathy with Mosley as part of a campaign which looked as though it might create a genuine Fascist threat. This paralleled Mosley's attempt to 'permeate' the Establishment, a task given to his deputy Dr Forgan.

The *English Review* Circle included its Catholic editor Douglas Jerrold, and foreign editor Sir Charles Petrie; *London Mercury* editor Sir John Squire; brewing magnate, intelligence officer and co-editor of *Air* Norman Thwaites; Muriel Curry, co-author with Harold Goad of *The Working of a Corporate State* (1933); Arnold Lunn, Lord Lymington, Sir Arnold Wilson and, indirectly, Leo Amery and Sir Edward Carson. They admired Mussolini's revitalization of Italy as a great European power and his accommodation with the Vatican. They were less impressed by Germany because 'corporative ideals have made no appeal'.

Led by Jerrold, the Circle wanted the Conservatives to take on corporatism. The campaign was co-ordinated with diehard leader Lord Lloyd, with the aim of ousting Baldwin. Grandson of a director of Lloyds Bank, Conservative MP until 1925 and High Commissioner for Egypt (1925–9), Lloyd chaired the Empire Economic Union and attracted the interest of fifty MPs. It was rumoured Lady Houston was funding him to found a new party. Tory parliamentary candidate Sir Henry Fairfax-Lucy argued in the *Saturday Review* for a 'fascist or corporative' government. Jerrold wanted a 'strong central government to speak for the nation, and not merely for a class, on national issues'.

Prominent in the campaign was Indian Cavalry officer Francis Yeats-Brown, author of *The Lives of a Bengal Lancer* and from September editor of *Everyman*. He shared the Fascist outlook with his restlessness and mysticism.

He resembled the 'best type of his fellow-countrymen in the Elizabethan age, who combined the spirit and courage of the warrior with the gentler qualities of the scholar'. Born in Italy, Yeats-Brown had met Mussolini many times. Visitors to his house at Portofino included Harold Goad, of whom he wrote he had 'never met a man who is nearer a saint'. He had spent time among Germans 'living on the brink of ruin' and, though worried by the anti-Semitism, believed Hitler – his favourite book was *The Bengal Lancer* – 'promises them a way out'. Yeats-Brown outlined his intentions in *Everyman*: 'We must be governed by a small group of men or one man with dictatorial power.' England needed a 'systematic cleansing' and a Corporate State.

The National government was racked with internal dissension, particularly over India. Mosley waited in the wings for the political rupture he hoped would provide an opening. Another chancer was Churchill. That summer, the India Defence League (IDL) was launched with the support of peers, MPs and military figures, and funding from the Duke of Westminster, Lady Houston and Rothermere. Its autumn campaign, led by Lloyd and Churchill, fuelled not implausible Conservative fears that a 'Churchill-led destructive proto-Fascist diehard ramp' might emerge. At the end of October a by-election in East Fulham produced a swing of 29 per cent to Labour. It raised the possibility, said Churchill, of 'socialists' sweeping the election. Sir Stafford Cripps would be in power and 'Fascism would follow'.

Everyman's directors withdrew their support from Yeats-Brown and on 10 November sacked him after only seven issues. MI5 had expressed concern about his editorship, his advocacy of 'alien' ideas, his links to Lloyd and position on the fringes of the royal circle. MI5 learnt that his activities had been funded by a foreign source – almost certainly Mussolini. The diehard campaign reached its climax on 21 November at the Savoy. Jerrold wrote there was 'enough anti-political dynamite in that room to have unseated half a dozen leaders'. Intended as the launch pad for a campaign against the government's neglect of distressed areas where the Tories were losing votes, the dinner was a disaster after Lloyd failed openly to challenge Baldwin. Afterwards, Jerrold spoke to three friends. 'Two had decided to become Fascists; the third was by ten o'clock a convinced Communist.' Mosley hoped to pick up the diehard remnants.

Forgan was tasked with building links with those whose support was 'crucial if the BUF was to gain respectability within the political and social establishments'. He operated from the BUF's Central London branch, which had expensive offices in Curzon Street, Mayfair. Its members were titled people and high-ranking military officers, who helped publicize plans for a forum for discussing Fascism and corporatism. Those invited included Yeats-Brown, Squire, Petrie and, key behind-the-scenes, Thwaites and Captain H. W. Luttman-Johnson.

Wounded during the war, Thwaites was posted on special duties to the United States, after which he retained close ties to the intelligence community. Attached to the Prince of Wales's staff, in 1924 he stood as a Conservative candidate. A Bengal Lancer and like Yeats-Brown a Cavalry Club member, Luttman-Johnson left India and moved to Scotland, where he enjoyed shooting on his Perth estate. Following the death of his wife in 1930 'Uncle Bill', according to his nephew, sold Railton cars and for financial reasons had 'fallen in with Mosley, who employed him in some capacity'. He hated Communism, extolled Mussolini and, somewhat less so, Hitler. In December he helped create a club to 'inquire upon modern methods of Government'. Its remit was vague so that those 'who did not wish to openly embrace membership of the BUF could nonetheless support it'. Mosley saw it as an opportunity to build a wider Fascist movement.

Forgan's debating club was established in the new year as the January Club. MI5 identified Forgan, Sir Donald Makgill, Yeats-Brown and Luttman-Johnson as co-founders. Sir John Squire and Luttman-Johnson became Chairman and Secretary respectively of a front organization controlled by Forgan, who nominated its officials. Squire said he was happy to be one of Mosley's lieutenants: 'I have been one in spirit ever since he resigned his Cabinet job over unemployment.' Luttman-Johnson admitted the Club had been founded as a platform for Mosley. Lord Midleton, former Secretary of State for War, put his Mayfair flat at the Club's disposal. It was run by George Makgill's son Donald, whose wife, Esther, ran the BUF's Ladies' Section – an example of continuity with twenties proto-Fascism.

MI5 viewed the Club as a powerhouse for the development of Fascist culture. It 'brought fascism to the notice of large numbers of people who would have considered it much less favourably otherwise'. Patrons included the *English Review* Circle and a network of aristocrats, diplomats and military men from Mosley's social circle. It attracted 200 influential figures who dined at the Savoy or the Hotel Splendide, with reports featured in the *Tatler*. Members included Rothermere, Lloyd, Basil Liddell Hart, Sir Henry Fairfax-Lucy, General Sir Hubert Gough, Sachie Sitwell, Sir Philip Magnus-Allcroft MP and Ralph Blumenfeld. Those in regular attendance were Wing-Commander Sir Louis Greig, Gentleman Usher to the King, Lord Erskine, eldest son of the Earl of Mar and an assistant government Whip, and Lord William Scott, brother of the Duke of Buccleuch. Guests included ex-BF member the Earl of Glasgow and Lady Russell of Liverpool, and directors of Siemens, London Assurance, Vickers, Handley Page and Morgan Grenfell. Speakers included Forgan and Raven Thomson, and BUF sympathizers such as Miss Muriel Currey, Commandant Mary Allen and Air Commodore J. A. Chamier.

Jullio Sanducetti of the 'Friends of Italy', Giovanni Telesio, a journalist on *Lavoro Fascista*, and Italian propagandist Luigi Villari were Club regulars.

MI5 monitored the leading lights of Fascio di Londra, in particular Mussolini's agent Camillo Pellizzi and Villari, who kept in touch with Mosley's circle. Attached to the University of London, Pelizzi told Rome he was inundated with requests for information on Fascism. He gave funds to journalists to present a positive image of Italy.

Diehards joined the Club in opposition to Baldwin, which resulted in 'a remarkable, if temporary, upsurging of Fascism'. Edward Grigg hoped Mosley 'would not exploit a huge crisis for the next election, thereby antagonising men in the Conservative ranks who might join him if not intimidated by extreme methods'. Petrie said they were not Fascists as such, but were 'so weary of the drabness of the Baldwin regime that they were prepared to embrace almost any alternative. Whether, had Mosley succeeded, they would have liked what they would then have got is another matter.' Fascism was seen as foreign and his interpretation of corporatism was different from theirs. Many agreed it had 'nothing necessarily to do with fascism, or the colour of men's shirts'. However, admitted Petrie, 'this cannot blind us to the fact that at one moment it was a very considerable force indeed'.

From November the BUF slid into anti-Semitism, attacking alien financiers and highlighting alleged Jewish rackets. On 4 November Jews were blamed for the mounting criticism against Germany. The *Blackshirt* editorial 'Shall Jews Drag Britain to War?' said a campaign existed to force Britons to intervene in German affairs. Jewish power was widespread: Conservatism was subservient to Jewish international finance and socialism was dominated by Jewish intellectuals. It has been argued this outburst was initiated by an 'anti-Semitic vanguard' but this was untrue, as evidenced by Mosley's speech six days later, at Ealing town hall, where he opposed 'Jewish interests fostering a spirit of war' and accused the Jews of 'organising a minority race within the nation'. He objected to German Jews finding refuge in Britain and 'taking jobs from Englishmen'. He stated that 'whatever happened in Germany is Germany's affair, and we are not going to lose British lives in a Jewish quarrel'.

Mosley later said that 'violent things were said and written on both sides when tempers were up in a bitter controversy', but denied culpability since 'party journals were in other hands, because I was often absent from London'. Chesterton chided him for forgetting the 'meetings of the policy directorate over which he presided every week to read page proofs' of the paper. Another official confirmed Mosley 'vetted every issue before it was put to bed, if he was out of London he checked it over the phone'. Mosley regularly tested reaction to anti-Semitism in order to assess opposition strength. When the *Jewish Chronicle* responded strongly to these 'stale and trashy oddments, taken from the rag-bag of the pedlars of Continental anti-semitism', he retreated to a more reasoned position.

*

On 6 November Nancy Mitford wrote to Diana after attending a BUF meeting at Oxford full of Tories 'who sat in hostile and phlegmatic silence'. Mosley was wonderful but there were 'several fascinating fights, as he brought a few Neanderthal men along with him and they fell tooth and nail on anyone who shifted his chair or coughed. One man complained that the fascists' nails had pierced his head to the skull.'

Nancy had been in love with the Earl of Rosslyn's homosexual son, Hamish St Clair Erskine, with whom her brother Tom had had an affair at Eton. While Nancy was naive, Hamish – a socialite member of the New Party – was self-centred and wanted to escape from her overbearing expectations. Hamish's sister, Lady Mary, intimate of Bruce Lockhart and friend of Unity, married Philip Dunn, son of the steel magnate and Beaverbrook partner Sir James Dunn. She announced her engagement on the same day Hamish announced his to Philip's sister Kit. It exemplified the incestuous nature of the circle around Mosley. Lady Dunn's obituary described her as a passionate anti-appeaser, even though she attended Mosley's secret pro-peace meetings.

At the end of 1933 Nancy married Peter Rodd, son of Lord Rennell, former ambassador to Italy, where he had spent much of his childhood. A correspondent for *The Times* in Germany and now working for an American bank in London, Peter was enthused by Beaverbrook's Empire Free Trade campaign. Politically erratic, he had been a Communist at Oxford but was fascinated by Mosley and joined the January Club. Both he and Nancy wore black shirts, but she finally ended in the socialist camp. Nancy was 'politically immature, her opinions too frivolous to be taken seriously' but that did not restrain her from airing her opinions. Diana thought Rodd an 'excruciating bore' and a 'very superior con man'.

After Nancy's and Peter's wedding, Mosley fell ill with phlebitis and was ordered to rest. For most of the summer and the autumn, Diana had deliberately not seen Mosley, who was courting Baba, or 'Ba-ba Blackshirt', as she was dubbed by Chips Channon. As a counter to Diana, Irene encouraged the affair and told Fruity he 'must learn to put up with this sort of thing'.

Mosley's womanizing was the subject of intrigue within the Black House as officials manoeuvred to gain his ear. 'Baroness Marovna' – film actress Mary Tavener – had met Mosley a month after Cimmie's death, when he visited a studio with a view to making a film on Fascism. According to Tavener, Mosley begged her to come to him, otherwise he might have to marry Diana. 'A deep mutual love of Spirit and mind as well as body', Mosley wrote, 'can help to set the final seal of greatness on destiny.' In a bizarre reply, Tavener claimed royal descent – according to Diana, she said she was the reincarnation of Mary Queen of Scots – and urged him to stay away from 'that blonde lady of easy virtue who you mentioned was pursuing you' and who had tried to break up his happy marriage with Cimmie. 'This type of woman will stop at nothing to satisfy their urge to possess.' Marrying Diana would 'bring endless scandal to your name by confirming the hysterical and fantastic stories that this pitiful creature has caused to be circulated about your alleged love for her prior to Cynthia's death'.

Unfortunately for Mosley, the letter fell into the hands of Joyce, who was emerging as a rival to the Leader. Tavener said she had been spurned by Mosley, who ordered his secretary not to return her calls and had barred her from the Black House. Mosley's response to any hint of blackmail was a categorical denial. He had countered a threat from a maid with a demand that she produce cast-iron evidence. According to Diana, he confronted Tavener, who claimed 'she had sexual relations with OM at Smith Square in 1933. She hadn't.' Shortly after, Tavener received a series of threatening anonymous notes. Four years later she launched a lawsuit for slander against Mosley, on the grounds of breach of promise and for displaying a photograph of her, which his associates dubbed the mermaid portrait.

By the time of the lawsuit, Joyce had left the BUF, at which point he wrote to Tavener detailing the peculiar goings-on in the Black House. The interception of mail, including Mosley's, was one of the 'sordid trifles' which were an everyday event. A gold love token had been taken from her letter which itself had been copied and distributed among the 'Kamaraden'. It had also been translated into French and Italian, so useful was it as 'a poisoned dagger for Tom's back', and a copy had been given to the 'huntress' (Diana). 'Did you never anticipate that said Nymph's possession fixation, as you so aptly described it, might include espionage of the movements to her unsuspecting "target" and that she would yet again inevitably pay handsomely for "aid" in the removal of any possible rival.'

Diana dismissed enquiries about Tavener with a wave of her hand, but she was more jealous than she admitted. Her all too noticeable charm was used to protect herself from personal questioning and she was practised at feigning indifference. Tavener was being followed – those doing it sent her details of her movements – but whether Diana paid is unknown. Joyce's ranting letter displayed his mad side but it did reveal the intrigue that swirled around Mosley. The deceivers – 'Tom's Judas Chorus' – included one who had a grudge against him because he had been a victim of the Leader's practical joke: a castor-oil cocktail.

In order to establish links with the Nazis, on 5 November, Mosley sent Raven Thomson to the Reichspartei at Nuremberg. Saxony's Minister of Justice, Thierack, reported to Dr Lammers at the chancellery that Thomson, who was staying at a Brownshirt camp, was 'so enthusiastic about his experience that he told me quite openly that Germany's rise was now unstoppable and that it was high time that people in England sought an alliance with this re-awakened nation'. BUF branches were opened in Cologne and Berlin, which the British consul reported were run with Nazi approval. The BUF had arranged 'to supply through the Gauleiter a monthly list of the members of the Branch and their addresses for the information of Premier Goering'.

The Nazis were happy to liaise with the BUF but were unsure about adopting formal relations. Thomson sent a signed Mosley photograph to Thierack, who requested one of Hitler to send in return. The request was considered but, after receiving another report from Schmidt-Lorenzen, Thomsen said that because the British Fascist movements were 'in conflict with one another', he did not 'consider it proper to enter the conflict'. He added that Mosley's 'personal relationships with influential Jewish circles in England do not seem prudent'. Dr Lammers agreed 'it would be more expedient to allow the matter to rest'.

This decision was noted by Special Branch whose note takers had been at a London NSDAP meeting, where Otto Bene told members it was 'strictly forbidden for any Nazi to discuss or participate in English politics and particularly they were not to fraternise with members of fascist organisations here'. Frustrated by the ruling, Mosley instructed the I Squad to end the festering row between the groups. A Blackshirt attack on an IFL meeting in Great Portland Street resulted in Arnold Leese being thrown to the ground, 'half-stripped of my clothes, struck on the face with a leaden "kosh" and much bruised by kicks'.

BUF official photographer Kay Fredericks was among the fifty Blackshirts involved in the attack. Each was given a Communist badge to wear. Thomson was in charge and at a signal from him 'we were to break up the meeting and if possible beat up Leese'. The IFL leader had 'no sooner opened his mouth when Thomson gave the pre-arranged signal. The hall burst into uproar' as the Blackshirts attacked Leese. Newspapers described it as the 'biggest fight that had ever been seen at a London meeting; our enemies deliberately smashed as many chairs as they could, knowing that we, who had no large fund behind us, would have to pay the owners of the hall for them'. Leese realized the idea was to 'finish and silence the IFL'.

The attack and the use of false badges had been co-ordinated by P. G. Taylor, whose responsibilities included investigating rival organizations. 'Taylor' (aka James McGuirk Hughes) had recently left his employment in the offices of *The Aeroplane* and joined the BUF, having disclosed his security service work to Mosley. He said he knew about his secret role in paying off the Austrian woman blackmailing Ramsay MacDonald because her rooms had been 'bugged' by MI5. Mosley accepted Taylor because his closeness to Special Branch 'need not have clashed. He was "on our side", which seemed good enough.' He told him 'we will observe your methods with interest. Carry on.' Taylor served as the BUF's Chief of Intelligence in 'Department Z' (the letter on the door of his office), which operated as a secret service from a room on the second floor of the Black House. Inside was a piece of theatrical showman-ship with black-painted walls and no furniture except for a small table in the centre, over which was suspended an electric lamp. Taylor had 'three separate telephone lines each under a different name'.

BUF officials were suspicious of the 'Chief Snoop'. 'Why does he avoid even our own cameras?' Until 2005, no photographs of him had been found. Taylor sported a small moustache, every inch a cultured Englishman – a typical ex-army major. When headquarters worker 'Mrs B' saw him leave a local Catholic church with a woman and a teenage girl, he cut her dead. 'It was as though he didn't want to mix family with business.' Fredericks recalled Taylor hinting that he had once been a highly placed agent in the Communist Party, extracting as he did so 'the last drop of drama from the word'. He was 'fond of telling in breathless whispers of his escape from Russia "with a price upon his head" and of his connections with high police circles in Britain'. A BUF member who had served with the British Military Mission in Russia was later surprised to see Taylor speaking on the BUF's behalf as he knew him to be an agent. Mrs B said his Home Office affiliation was general knowledge. He grinned whenever asked 'if he had caught anyone today'.

Charles Dolan, formerly an ILPer and Communist, employed in the Propa-ganda Department, said Taylor had 'contact with all political units. Trades Unions and workers' organisations, the Labour and Communist parties especi-ally being among their happiest hunting grounds.' Fearful of the menace of Moscow in our midst, he organized the 'shadowing of the mildest of Labour MPs'. Taylor ran a nationwide network of agents, according to a leaked paper. In Edinburgh, 'only the District Branch Officer knows anything about them. They are members of some parties and may even be respectable members of a committee. They are men of the night who will probably never be known.'

There was support for 'our German cousins' at the highest level of British society. Grandi told Mussolini, 'the only person who told me that the British are stupid to be upset at Hitler has been the Prince of Wales one evening after dinner.' On Armistice Day, Edward confided in Count Albert Mensdorff, former Austrian ambassador, of his fondness for Nazism. 'Of course it is the only thing to do, we will have to come to it, as we are in great danger from the Communists here, too.'

As if in response to the German rebuff, Mosley expanded BUF activities. 'The leader was going to have a big push around England,' Unity learnt on 13 November, but Diana 'couldn't go as a result of the divorce which had been made absolute'. Five days later the *Blackshirt* came out against the 'oily, material, swaggering Jew' and the 'pot-bellied, sneering money-mad Jew'. The TUC's spy reported that the BUF had 'taken on a definite anti-Jew com-plexion'. There had been disciplinary trouble at the Southampton branch when 'some Jews were asked to leave and others left of their own accord'.

Subsequently, 400 Jews left the BUF and their recruitment was discouraged.

At the end of 1933 Mosley claimed it was 'quite untrue that we organised provocative marches and meetings in Jewish areas'. The authorities viewed the BUF as a threat to public order, particularly in the East End where incidents arose from selling the *Blackshirt* in Jewish districts. The newspaper vendors acted within the letter of the law but their behaviour was considered 'deliberately provocative'. Mosley complained of Jewish attacks on his sellers and assured the police he would 'do everything in my power to prevent any breach of the peace and to carry out any regulations laid down by the police'. He affirmed, however, the 'right of Englishmen to pursue any legal and peaceful activity in this country without molestation and assault'.

Mosley addressed hundreds of meetings, the vast majority of which were peaceful. However, the BUF set out 'to goad, incite and provoke a violent response from their adversaries. The purpose was to establish a pattern of confrontation and escalating cycle of violence from which it was hoped the movement would derive benefit.' Reports document incidents in which Blackshirts engaged in provocation and unprovoked assaults, and that the tactic of organized anti-Fascists was generally disruption and not violence. By December Northern Organizer Michael Jordan had been dismissed. Men of violence arrived, at which point, 'all hell was let loose'.

Employed as a paid speaker, Charles Dolan alleged his speeches were designed to incite the audience to react, thereby engineering the intervention of the National Defence Force. A document sent by Defence Force Control on 22 December in respect of a meeting at Finsbury Park revealed that '50 plain clothes (The Knuckle Duster Boys) and 12 Defence Force will be on duty. The boys want trouble, so let it rip.'

Dolan linked the violence to Mosley's strategy for acquiring power by way of political disorder. He publicly professed to wanting to win electors' support, but knew he could not win a majority and 'intended to use eventually the Defence Force when the time comes to seize power'. Dolan claimed Mosley knew such a strategy required military support, so the BUF sought army, navy and air force recruits, who were to be appointed to lead Defence Force units and help establish contact with serving army officers. This was conducted covertly and such members were 'known only to and controlled by headquarters'.

Mosley tasked P. G. Taylor with an ambitious scheme to establish fascist cells in the armed forces, Civil Service and trade unions. This was considered vital if the BUF was to combat the Communist Party on its own ground. Mosley admitted the Blackshirts were designed as a counter-revolutionary force. Dolan believed this was why he 'organised contacts within left wing organisations, such as the Trade Unions, the Communist Party, and wherever discontent appears capable of stampeding into some sort of action that fits in his secret plan'. The contacts were to act as agents provocateurs, 'advocating violent action or spreading criticism of existing leadership in order to foster the time for a strike or riot'. Mosley would then step in to 'save the Nation from The Red Terror'. Dolan heard Mosley say: 'Rats will always take my cheese.'

Mosley maintained there was nothing illegal in his activities, and the fact that he recruited Taylor, who was deeply involved in his more secret activities, suggests he 'played a complex intelligence game with the authorities'. He wished to acquire early intelligence of what measures were planned against him but was also aware that the views of MI5 officers with regard to Communism were similar to his own. He recognized that 'some security service personnel were far less anti-fascist than anti-communist'. Mosleyite John Warburton speculated that Special Branch inserted Taylor into the BUF so as to be 'in a position which they thought might be useful in the organisation of BUF's well known fighting qualities should a "Red Revolution" erupt and threaten a take-over of the State'.

MI5 was undergoing a major reorganization. Institutional rivalry, factional hostility and ambition delayed the emergence of a co-ordinated security service until 1 October 1931 when the Secret Service Committee transferred Scotland Yard's intelligence staff, including its leading subversion expert Guy Liddell, to MI5 to create a new security service to centralize information on subversion. Designed to save money, operations against the Communist Party were transferred to MI5 from the Special Branch. Security work was underfunded and B Branch under Jaspar Harker had a staff of only six officers for counter-espionage work against German and Italian intelligence agencies, which MI5 feared were in contact with the BUF.

The agency employed by the Secret Intelligence Service to supply it with information on Communist activities was transferred to the control of MI5's 'M Section'. Maxwell Knight, British Fascist's intelligence chief and Section D member, officially became an MI5 officer and M Section's head. In 1943 Knight stated he had been involved in investigating Fascism for sixteen years, and an MI5 officer for twelve. His tasks included penetrating agents into the CP, known enemy secret service agencies and the BUF. Fascist membership did not cause Knight any difficulty with MI5, whose former army personnel were strongly anti-Communist. Continuing to report to his SB handler, Taylor's BUF duties were identical to those which Knight carried out for the British Fascists: compiling intelligence dossiers on rivals and enemies, supervising counter-espionage and sabotage operations.

Taylor, who lived at 144 Sloane Street, close to Knight's flat at number 38, was immortalized in Knight's anti-Semitic novel *Crime Cargo* (1934). It was memorable only because of teasing references to Taylor, who appears as the villain and 'pig-eyed Irishman' 'Baldy McGurk'. Intriguingly, the dashing hero is 'Dennis Joycey' (Joyce). That all three were connected by the British Fascists and intelligence activities confirms the impression of collusion between the secret state and Fascism in the area of anti-Communism. The fact that in the fifties Knight visited Mosley in Paris only adds to the view that MI5 surveillance of the BUF was not a straightforward affair.

Fredericks said Mosley paraded the 'mythical bogey of Communism in the hope that it will scare into his ranks the middle classes, who are even more worried than the aristocrats by the thought of a proletarian rising in our land'. He knew Fascism's progress was hindered by the weakness of the Communists but Sorel suggested 'the middle classes allow themselves to be plundered quite easily, provided a little pressure is brought to bear, and that they are intimidated by the fear of revolution: that party will possess the future which can most skilfully manipulate the spectre of revolution'. The *Blackshirt* bragged 'the organised and disciplined masses of fascists today will have little difficulty in repelling Red terror'.

The Communist Party was too small to pose a real threat. The figure who did frighten the middle classes was Stafford Cripps, MP for Bristol East since 1931. A successful barrister, his father (Lord Parmoor) and an uncle (Sidney Webb) served in the first Labour government, but his political background was, if anything, Tory paternalist. Cripps became a socialist, 'not as the result of a Damascene conversion, but because Labour needed a solicitor-general and offered him the job'. His move to the left was a shock. Hugh Dalton dismissed him as a 'dangerous political lunatic'. During 1932 he became leader of the Socialist League and argued Labour should develop a full socialist programme and implement it by assuming emergency powers and ruling by decree. There was widespread hostility from both wings of the party to this strategy, which smacked of dictatorship, and his argument that it was designed to forestall Fascism failed to convince trade union leaders. Although there was little chance of his ideas coming to fruition, Cripps did instil fear on the right, in particular with Rothermere.

At a conference on 23 November, Home Office officials, Police Commissioner Lord Trenchard, MI5 officers and Special Branch Head Superintendent Canning decided the BUF needed monitoring and tasked the SB with collecting intelligence on Fascist and anti-Fascist activities, and MI5 with collating this material. MI5 feared the BUF had a secret organization for action in an emergency and wanted to influence the armed services. It believed it received funds from Mussolini but lacked evidence and wanted warrants for mail openings and telephone tappings, but faced resistance within the Home Office.

Mosley knew he would attract MI5's attention and made arrangements to conceal his secretive activities. In addition, he compiled a list of members whose identity was to be kept secret. This included women's policing proponent Mary Allen, one of a number of suffragettes who became Fascists. Its militants, Cecily Hamilton noted, were the first to use the word 'Leader' as a reverential title. On a smaller scale, Emmeline Pankhurst was the 'forerunner of Lenin, Hitler, Mussolini – the Leader who could do no wrong!'

Mosley hoped Allen would provide him with advance warning of moves against him by the authorities. In 1932 Allen set up the paramilitary Women's Reserve (WR) to deal with strikes. Police observed Allen visiting the British Fascist's headquarters in search of 'particulars of the people in key positions in the electrical and gas undertakings in London', but with the BUF's formation there was a realignment towards Mosley. Conforming to a Fascist tradition, Allen and other officers placed their aircraft at the disposal of the WR, which organized pilot training at private aerodromes. Allen made overtures to the authorities, seeking official recognition of the WR's usefulness. It is possible she aimed to place her cadets in positions where they might obtain useful information.

In the following spring Allen was present at a BUF-held air rally in Gloucestershire, attended by 250 Fascists. Commander Godman said the aim was to give members a chance to acquaint themselves with aeroplanes. Mosley's interest in aviation led to the formation of a Fascist flying club with plans to train forty pilots. The prospect of a BUF Air Defence Force led to questions in the Commons. Mosley sympathizer Michael Beaumont defended the move, saying it was 'no more than a flying club, on all fours with other flying clubs in this country'.

On 19 December Mosley was best man at Ian Dundas's wedding to debutante Pamela, daughter of Geoffrey Dorman and niece of Ernest Shackleton. The ceremony was rich in symbolism. The bride's gown was trimmed with golden fasces and the cake, in the form of fasces, was placed on a table draped with the Union Jack. Dorman had been with Mosley in the RFC and wrote for the pro-Fascist *Aeroplane* until 1930, when he began writing adventure books. BUF organizer for South London, Dorman wrote on aviation and motoring in *Blackshirt* under the pseudonyms 'Blackbird' and 'Bluebird'. The BUF attracted aviators such as Sir Alliot Verdon Roe, the first Englishman to fly in 1908 and designer of Avro aircraft; Air Commodore Sir J. A. Chamier of the Air League, a generous funder to the BUF; and Norman Thwaites, the League's Secretary. The airmen, thundered Bill Allen, were 'Caesar-men' – modern warriors of the Faustian world who stalked with 'cynical laughter over the ruins of the Reichstag. These men are the expression of some new potent consciousness – the Fascist revolution.'

H. G. Wells wanted an elite of airmen to rule 'without scruples about using violence'. His Modern State Movement of disciplined air force shock troops was portrayed in *The Shape of Things to Come*, released in 1933. In a war's aftermath, black-costumed airmen of the Air Dictatorship create a technocractic world State. Wells believed socialism was about the scientific replacement of disorder by order, which required dealing with the alien nationalism of the Jews, whose behaviour was irrational. Mosley still hoped to gain his support but there was always a fundamental divide between his own ultra-nationalism and Wells's belief in world government.

In December the head of Berlin's Economic Policy Association, Dr Margarete Gartner, arrived to monitor Fascist progress. In the twenties she had welded propaganda agencies into a network of contacts for the foreign policy-making elite. Funded by Krupps and with the support of Goering, as air representative, she promoted commercial intelligence. The German ambassador made her aware of the delicacy of her mission.

Gartner first talked to BF member Madame Arnaud, who bad-mouthed the BUF for its 'Jewish capital and Jewish members'. On 15 December Forgan dismissed the slur and said they attacked Jewish propaganda against Germany. Mosley said 'England will be fascist in four to six years', but Gartner reported to Berlin that the press did not support that impression. They dismissed Mosley with 'a scornful hand gesture'. The BUF was financially 'badly off', membership was 'not growing too well' and there was 'no mood of idealism in England as in Germany and Italy'. However, 'intelligent and discerning acquaintances' considered the prospects for BUF MPs were 'not so bad'. On her return to Berlin, officials admonished her for telling Mosley that, contrary to the Führer's position, the colonial question was not urgent in Germany. Shortly afterwards Gartner, who was not a Nazi, became aware she was under Gestapo surveillance.

In the *Blackshirt* at the end of 1933 Mosley wrote that he expected great progress in the new year. 'The light spreads over England at Christmas and the marching legions in their ordered strength move forward to a new and Greater Day.'

14

Mosley approached newspaper barons for support. The BUF's women's organizer, Lady Makgill, was Beaverbrook's former secretary and it was arranged for him to meet the Leader. Nothing came of the meeting, but two weeks later Blackshirts became aware discussions were proceeding with Rothermere. A *Mail* executive, Collin Brooks, said Rothermere's prevailing mood was 'politically one of the deepest pessimism. He was convinced Britain had entered a phase of decline, had lost her old militant virtues, and, in her softness, was lusting after strange idols of pacifism, nationalisation, and everything which would continue to sap self-reliance.' His pessimism partly related to his financial woes. He wanted to be the richest man in Britain and, though he had not lost in the Crash, his fortune had declined.

Rothermere's emissary, George Ward Price, who wore a monocle, hob-nobbed at the dictators' courts and authored Nazi eulogies, which appeared under his boss's name in the *Mail*, the only popular newspaper to condone the Nazis. In interviews, Nazis were provided with a platform to soft-sell their policies. Hitler, readers were assured, was 'obviously sincere. There is no man living whose promise given in regard to something of real moment I would sooner take.' He would save mankind from Communism but Rothermere also recognized 'Hitlerism means war' and advocated air rearmament to meet the threat.

Mosley, who was about to visit Rome, received a telegram from Rothermere affirming his support. Although the Italian Foreign Ministry thought it an 'inopportune moment', since the British Foreign Secretary was due to arrive, they would 'see to it that all goes smoothly, without indiscretions'. The previous autumn, senior BUF officials noted 'funds were not coming in as expected' and recognized the urgency of Mosley's visit.

On 8 January Grandi sent to Rome a Mosley letter relating to the instructions concerning the receipt of payments. Mosley was 'persuaded it is better to leave out his lieutenants from the thing and receive personally the money'. He asked Grandi 'to convey his gratitude' to Mussolini when Rome sent a fourth instalment of £5,000 (£170,000). MI5 discovered later that during

1933 the BUF received a total of £20,000, of which only £9,500 was deposited; the remainder was used to cover existing debts.

Mosley travelled on 9 January from France to see Mussolini, one of half a dozen meetings over a period of three years. On this occasion he had the 'most violent arguments with Mussolini on the subject of anti-semitism'. Mosley made his allegiance to universal Fascism by enrolling in his Fascist CAUR international, though his support was ambivalent, as he feared domestic reaction. With Diana's divorce finalized on 15 January, Mosley asked her to accompany him to Grasse, where they rented a house from Sir Louis Mallet.

On his return, Mosley met with Grandi who told Mussolini he had 'never seen him so sure of himself and so confident. He told me that the talk with you had enriched and illuminated him and he left the Palazzo Venezia more determined than ever to do battle.' Payments arrived in larger denominations. BUF officials recalled seeing bundles of foreign notes. Mosley told those eager for their salaries: 'We'll put you right up now.' Baba had been encouraged to develop her relationship with Grandi. She suspected the origin of the funds but never discussed it with her lover. On 24 January a courier left Rome carrying £20,000 in seven packages of foreign currency. Six days later they were given to Mosley, who verified the contents. The BUF received monthly payments of £5,000, which during 1934 totalled £77,800 (£2.66 m), representing almost all the BUF's annual expenditure, which Hawkins later confirmed averaged £70,000 during 1934–6. Grandi reported to Mussolini that Mosley expressed his gratitude for the money and had told him 'how, with generous spontaneity, you had accepted his requests for future material assistance'.

MI5 did not learn details of the Charing Cross branch account until July 1940 when Dundas was briefly detained. It suggested the Italian subvention 'puts the Fascist Movement in this country in an entirely new light'. Where once 'it seemed to have roots in this country, these roots now appear to be very much frailer and to have been kept alive only by artificial means'. The BUF was dependent on foreign funds without which it 'would probably cease to exist'. Mosley admitted to Grandi that he owed the definitive conversion of Rothermere and his newspapers entirely to the Italian dictator.

For months, Mosley had worried about associating the BUF with the 'too-much-discussed' Rothermere. Grandi, however, had managed before Christmas to overcome his doubts 'by pointing out the immediate and practical advantage that would accrue to his movement by suddenly gaining, without effort or expense, the group of newspapers which, because of its circulation and influence on the masses in Great Britain (above all in the provinces), is by far the strongest of them all'. Rothermere was second-rate but that was 'another reason for not taking too seriously any harm that may later come out of the fact of being associated with him'. He convinced Mosley but Rothermere only made up his mind after Ward Price went to Rome. 'If Mussolini believes in Mosley, then let's get strongly behind him, with the whole newspaper group.' Then the headlines, recalled Mosley, 'came pelting like a thunder-storm'. There was no consultation, just 'Hurrah for the Blackshirts!'.

Rothermere, who with Harmsworth and Ward Price joined the January Club, feared a Communist insurrection, against which event he set about preparing estates in Hungary. He worried militants were rallying to Stafford Cripps's Socialist League, and he and Mosley were rival candidates for an inevitable dictatorship. Both were Wykehamists and outsiders, driven by an inner, unshakeable conviction of their own righteousness. They were fine orators who adopted theatrical methods for their rallies. The *Mail* said the BUF offered 'an alternative at the next general election to rule by Cripps'.

The prospect of a Fascist takeover following a Labour election victory was not only entertained by maverick press barons. Like other MPs, Bob Boothby believed the National government was moving towards 'a very considerable electoral debacle'. He thought the Conservative Party was rotten to the core and 'so terrified of Communism that it would welcome a Fascist counter-revolution'. Rothermere said 'no strong anti-socialist policy can be expected from a Conservative party whose leaders are themselves tainted with semi-socialist doctrines'. Socialist activists saw Britain as a battleground over which Fascist forces were advancing with the only effective resistance being a Labour government armed with emergency powers. The National government was 'quasi-Fascist', though, in fact, it was 'Labour's electoral advance that was responsible for making the threat of Mosley credible'.

Rothermere regarded the Blackshirts as an adjunct to the Tory Party in the same way as the Socialist League operated as a Labour ginger group. Their function was to provide a defence against Communist-led insurrection. Their example would embolden Tories to rediscover their traditions and end the National government. His aim – shared by January Club members – was to use the BUF as partner in a diehard triumph over Baldwin. Although he had not read *The Greater Britain*, he supported its anti-socialism, its stance on India and call for a stronger air force. On 15 January the *Mail* announced the Great Switch-Over. 'Hurrah for the Blackshirts!' claimed the 'spirit of the age is one of national discipline and organisation' and that Britain's survival depended on 'the existence of a Great Party of the Right with the same directness of purpose and energy of method as Hitler and Mussolini have displayed'. The danger of Cripps necessitated a Fascist movement. Rothermere added, 'The socialists who jeer at the principles and uniform of the Blackshirt being of foreign origin forget that the founder and High Priest of their own creed was the German Jew Karl Marx.'

Mosley was portrayed as a protectionist in the tradition of Joseph Chamberlain. Unsullied by contact with the National government, he represented for the middle classes sound Conservatism. His Blackshirts were 'ready to take control and prevent national bankruptcy and disaster'. Prominence was given to developing the Empire and expanding air defences (the *Mail* advocated 'a programme of building at least 5,000 first-line machines without delay'). The Corporate State was ignored by Rothermere who promised to preserve Parliament after implementing a few wise reforms. The tag Fascists was dropped in favour of Blackshirts, who were praised for their authoritarian style, not their revolutionary nationalism.

The *Observer* on 21 January suggested Mosley had 'stolen the thunder both of the Left and the Right'. As with the Nazis, there was a BUF 'reactionary wing composed of violent anti-Socialists, and a revolutionary wing, recruited from the ILP and the Communists', which was 'considerably stronger than the Right'. Headway had been made with the unemployed in the 'big industrial centres of the North. This success in the areas that have remained unshakeably loyal to Labour for so many years is the most impressive fact about the Fascist movement.' The paper was impressed by its presence in Manchester and the fact that Mosley had addressed 100,000 people in Birmingham's Bingley Hall, in his biggest ever rally.

Grandi reported that Rothermere's 'sudden conversion to fascism was, in political circles in London, for several days the object of angry comments on many sides, but its effects were immediately seen. The fact that the most widespread group of newspapers in England gave a whole page to the Birmingham meeting "forced" *all* the English papers, from the conservative *Times* to the anti-fascist *Daily Herald*, to give a full and faithful account of it.' What should have been a triumph was, however, undermined when Mosley's phlebitis flared up again and confined him to bed.

On 22 January in the *Mirror* Rothermere attacked the alarmists who whimpered that Blackshirts are 'preparing the way for a system of rulership by means of steel whips and concentration camps'. George Catlin said that behind Mosley's 'eloquent appeals Englishmen visualise the concentration camp'. However, few panic mongers, the *Mirror* countered, had 'any personal knowledge of the countries that are already under Blackshirt government. The notion that a permanent reign of terror exists there has been evolved entirely from their own morbid imaginations, fed by sensational propaganda.' Blackshirts 'were disciplined to defend free speech' but were prepared to 'meet like with like'.

Blackshirts, Rothermere said, had 'no prejudice either of class or race'. They would stop war as the 'only safeguard against crafty and ruthless men', operating 'secretly with the aid of foreign money to promote the class war'. An upcoming hunger march by the unemployed was 'evidence of the hidden hand of Bolshevism in our midst' and showed the need for a 'steel framework of patriotism and discipline'. A trade union infiltrator into the BUF reported that it intended to run an agent provocateur-style operation against the march. 'Their plan is to ferment disorder through a few individuals apparently unconnected with the BUF, and then to come on the scene as a body of Blackshirts to restore order.' On 29 January the *Mail* claimed Cripps had changed his tune as the result of the BUF.

The *Jewish Chronicle* feared the BUF had adopted anti-Semitism. Although such propaganda was downplayed, in an interview on 2 February, Dundas said Jews were excluded from membership because of the 'physical opposition on the part of a certain section of Jews towards their movement', and Mosley called for a ban on Jews as officials and MPs. In reply to a question on the class war during a Chiswick meeting, Joyce said Jews were not a class: 'I regard them as a privileged misfortune. The flower or weed of Israel shall never grow in ground fertilised by British blood!' When Jewish groups called on Mosley to repudiate the speech, under pressure from his new partner he was forced to smother the incipient anti-Semitism in BUF propaganda – a telling commentary on Mosley's claim that he was unable to control what went into his papers.

Grandi acknowledged collaboration with Rothermere would not be easy. 'The first differences have already begun to show,' he told Mussolini. Mosley was asked to put up 'candidates (among whom Rothermere naturally wants to infiltrate his old friends from the failed Empire Party) for the municipal elections'. Grandi said it would be a mistake and told Mosley it was 'in the provinces that we must begin and from there that we must move on to the besieging of the city'. He added that 'what happened in our own Revolution will happen with Rothermere: the reactionaries believed they could use us to defeat socialism and democracy and then be in charge themselves; when they realised that the threat of socialism was a joke compared with the Revolution which you were preparing, they were alarmed and tried to withdraw, but it was too late'.

As a newcomer on the political scene, Fascism made compromises in the quest for power and chose to ally itself with conservative forces. Their elites' willingness to work with the Fascists, 'along with a reciprocal flexibility on the part of the fascist leaders', were, therefore, important factors.

Grandi characterized Britain as a hippopotamus 'slow, fat, heavy, sleepy and weak-nerved'. He felt sympathy for Mosley as the 'expression of something absolutely new and unexpected in England . . . He wants to bring back Tudor England, the England of Elizabeth, an England that wasn't "natural" but sectarian, that ate oxen roasted on the spit, chopped off people's heads, tilled the soil and committed piracy on the high seas.' If Mosley 'knows how to play his cards, this is the moment because the Labour Party was divided'. Labour's only leader of value was Cripps but he was 'no more than an aristocratic intellectual, ready to put out brave ideas, but not equally ready to risk his own skin to defend them. Mosley is considered an unscrupulous adventurer, but he has guts and a personal scorn for danger, exactly the qualities which the masses like to see in their leaders.' Grandi said 'England must get ready to choose between fascism and labour'.

Rothermere kept on friendly terms with Germany and hoped to curtail its military threat by offering concessions on its ex-colonies and by giving Hitler a 'free hand' in the East. But in case of failure, he also campaigned for rearmament. 'There is nothing in modern politics', the *News Chronicle* reported, 'to match the crude confusion of the Rothermere mentality. It blesses and encourages every swashbuckler who threatens the peace of Europe – not to mention direct British interests – and then clamours for more and more armaments with which to defend Britain, presumably against his lordship's pet foreign bully.' Mosley sought closer links to the Nazis. At the end of January the British ambassador in Berlin reported the BUF had opened a branch in the capital.

Mosley's problem was that diehards believed in the superiority of British ways and were hostile to foreign concepts. He was like a Continental politician and 'not quite respectable'. The *Everyman* said he did not have 'the instinctive understanding of the English character that would enable him to transform an intellectual concept from Italy into a typical English political movement'. Catlin said he had 'yet to discover a characteristically English formula such as that which enabled Cromwell to combine individualistic liberty of the Puritan with the authoritarianism of the Protectorate'.

In February police charged three Blackshirts with inflicting grievous bodily harm on George Richardson, an infiltrator for the Labour movement, who sold information to the *News Chronicle*. He told his handler Mosley was 'quite apart from the members generally. He used to go into the headquarters, and go straight to his room, and the rest of them never saw any more of him.' Dundas was described as a 'poor type', Forgan was 'not important' but Joyce was 'very able and idealistic'. The general run of officers were 'of the hooligan type who think nothing of "beating up" people they dislike'. Richardson's role was soon uncovered by Taylor's Department Z and he was denounced as 'a crawling rat'.

Alex Miles claimed 'no member could afford to laugh at "Z" because it spied on every officer', and at the first sign of disaffection 'that man became suspect'. Taylor conducted the courts of inquiry which punished recalcitrant members involved in squabbles and feuds. Opponents claimed the cellars were used for punishment purposes and Special Branch alleged a man had been seriously wounded during horseplay between Fascists. Richardson said he had been struck and pinned to the floor by Blackshirts before castor oil was forced down his throat. At a subsequent trial the Blackshirts denied the incident, though Richardson's stomach when pumped did contain castor oil. One defendant admitted striking Richardson but was acquitted because the evidence was not strong enough to convict.

MI5 had an 'unimpeachable' source on contacts made by January Club members with army officers. Major-General J. F. C. Fuller was a prominent guest, as were Conservative MP Brigadier-General E. L. Spears and General Sir Hubert Gough, a leader of the 1914 Curragh Mutiny. These contacts led MI5 to believe the Club was forging dangerous ties to the army. The Service was obsessed with the belief that such links were the beginnings of a potential 'fifth column', though the evidence was thin.

Aneurin Bevan and Jennie Lee were alarmed at the prospect of a Fascist revolution and made arrangements to go into hiding. Such views were not uncommon. Virginia Woolf listened to the 'nearly mad' outpourings of the German conductor Bruno Walter, who had recently fled Germany. His talk on the poison of the Nazis made a violent impression on her. 'These brutal bullies go about in hoods and masks, like little boys dressed up, acting this idiotic, meaningless, brutal, bloody pandemonium.' She feared the Blackshirts and on 15 February told Quentin Bell, 'We are to have Mosley within five years. I suppose you and Julian [his brother] will be for it.'

Friends of Lord Marley, opposition Chief Whip in the Lords and previously Under-Secretary for War (1930–31), feared Mosley's progress and founded an anti-Fascist society, which had been promised funds. He told the editor of the *Manchester Guardian*, W. P. Crozier, they would keep track of BUF activities and organize counter rallies. Marley had an overheated view of the dangerous Mosley, who had plans for a march on London and had organized a private aeroplane squadron. Mosley was 'so hot-headed that he was capable, if his march on London were interfered with, of ordering the squadron to drop bombs on the city. Conditions were conceivable under which certain Tory politicians and Generals would connive at Mosley's coup and abstain from putting it down.' He told Crozier that if Mosley was rebuffed, 'he might then lose his head completely and order his various sections to take any violent measures that were within his power'. This was not based on reality but Marley, who acted as the innocent cover for Communist-inspired bodies, expressed the fears of many authoritative figures.

Mosley's Fascism was a crisis-dependent phenomenon with hopes of power being contingent on Labour's electoral challenge being interpreted as a real threat. Convinced Fascism would displace 'flabby conservatism', he angled his appeal at those dissatisfied with the National government. He argued, like Rothermere, that the threat came from Cripps's Socialist League, which was in a 'unity front' with the Communists. He played on the fear of a socialist takeover, believing Cripps's emergency powers rhetoric was his greatest propaganda asset. He hoped such fears would take root among the middle classes and 'events would transform this apprehension into crisis proportions, which would be his route to power'.

Events moved Mosley's way when, in a trio of by-elections in February, Labour achieved large swings against the National government. The upsurge in its fortunes conferred on the BUF a fashionable popularity, even though Herbert Morrison claimed Cripps's 'socialism in our time brigade' had been killed off. Tories considered aligning themselves with a 'suitably house-trained' Mosley. Backbencher Cuthbert Headlam believed colleagues 'might well fall in with a Fascist *coup d'état*, preferring a bourgeois revolution to a proletarian one'.

There was deep unease within government circles about Mosley's success. On 16 February Foreign Secretary Sir John Simon warned Home Secretary Sir John Gilmour of the 'danger of letting this silly business of playing at Mussolini go on in this country' with the 'folly of coloured shirts and tin trumpets'. However, 'as long as people imitate Germans or Italians without breaking the law, one can only deplore their want of national spirit'. Gilmour and Metropolitan Police Commissioner Lord Trenchard wanted the black shirt uniform banned. Trenchard claimed the BUF was in contravention of the 1819 Act which proscribed 'unauthorised exercises, movements or evolutions' and that it was 'to all intents and purposes an unauthorised military formation'. His reactionary style and apparent friendship with Mosley, who championed the RAF which Trenchard had founded, led Lord Marley to claim he protected BUF demonstrations. In fact, by February he wanted an end to uniformed stewarding of meetings and a stop put on 'movements of this kind while they are still comparatively small and easy to deal with'.

Trenchard complained to the Home Secretary that the BUF had passed false information (presumably from Taylor) about a Communist plot to attack its Holloway branch and an alleged IFL plan to attack its headquarters, and suggested that this 'mischievous nonsense' would best be dealt with by outlawing the Fascists. Discussion culminated in the drafting of a 'Bill to Prohibit the Wearing of Uniform'. Three attempts to bring forward a Public Order Act were dropped as it became clear that Labour and Liberal MPs were lukewarm to the idea.

Rothermere's deployment of an 'arsenal of gutter press' techniques had an immediate impact on Blackshirt recruitment. There was 'terrific enthusiasm and it seemed there was no limit to what we might achieve'. The Home Office reported that the BUF was attracting 'a better class of recruits and its membership is increasing'. There was a surge of 17,700 paying members, including an influx of 'Generals, Admirals, big business men, and the Debs of the period with Union Jacks around their lily-white shoulders, who probably saw just the one side of it; the patriotic side'. It helped boost the reactionary wing of former British Fascists.

The BUF's growth led the government to query its funding. In the Lords, on 28 February, Lord Feversham admitted the 'exact source is unknown, but it is obvious that substantial financial backing is forthcoming from various sources other than that of the private wealth of the leader and the dues or subscriptions of members'. John Strachey wrote that the BUF was 'an extremely expensive undertaking' but Mosley's 'private fortune is not unlimited'. He remained sphinx-like on the funding and, officially, was removed from direct contact with the BUF's financial side, in order to confuse MI5, for whom it had 'not been possible to obtain reliable information on this matter since the facts are known only to Mosley and his most trusted assistants'. A side effect was that he never exercised effective financial control. The 1940 Advisory Committee inquiry into the BUF Trust found there was a deficit for 1933 and surpluses for 1935 and 1936 but there was no way of verifying the subscriptions and donations.

The *Mail* claimed the BUF's annual income was £70,000 (£2.38 m). The 30,000 to 40,000 members at the height of its success paid a shilling a month if employed and fourpence if unemployed, which brought in £12,000 (£408,000) a year. Expenses largely consisted of salaries totalling £20,000. Dr Forgan was paid £750 as Deputy Leader, John Beckett received £700 as editor of *Action*, while the total salaries of the twenty officers in the lower rank were in the neighbourhood of £500 (£17,000).

With the injection of Italian funds, BUF activity increased dramatically. It cost nearly £2,000 to transport five hundred Fascists from London to Manchester and a similar number to Birmingham for meetings. Propaganda was produced on a lavish scale, at around £3,000 a week. The *Blackshirt* and the more highbrow *Fascist Week* (which cost a penny and tuppence respectively, with circulations of 25,000 to 30,000) paid their own way. They were run by companies in Lady Mosley's name as a means of protecting them from libel suits.

In seeking funding Mosley had been influenced by the Italians who said 'they had got the money from capitalists and had double-crossed the capitalists and gone over to the working-class which they intended to serve'. This money did not go through the books. 'It was a joke among our people the lengths these people would go to conceal their connection.' Rothermere insisted on personally handing to Mosley a gift of money.

In 1940, in front of the Advisory Committee, Mosley admitted that Morris (Lord Nuffield) had given 'large sums of money but he went as far as to publish in the *Jewish Chronicle* that he was not supporting us because his cars would have been subject to a boycott'. In his July letter to the *Chronicle*, Nuffield denied he was anti-Semitic – which was untrue. He enclosed a cheque for £250 (£8,500) for the fund for German Jewry which, his biographer notes, 'was very small by his standards'. There was no record of financial support in his cash books but there were larger than normal payments to the National Council of Industry and Commerce, which 'may have been a way of channelling the money to Mosley'.

A Labour research document claimed Mosley received money from Lord Inchcape, Lord Lloyd, Baron Tollemache, Air Commodore Chaumier, Vincent Vickers, the Earl of Glasgow and Sir Charles Petrie. Rumoured contributors included Sir Henry Deterding of the Royal Dutch Petroleum Company, whose name was linked with Mosley by both anti-Fascists and ex-Fascists. A BUF official, G. P. Sutherst, said Lancashire cotton mill owners donated. 'Very rarely we would approach a person who Mosley had reason to believe might put his hand in his pockets,' recalled a fund-raiser, but 'it was sizeable small fry stuff'. The income from small funders was £12,500. Richardson claimed 'there were no wealthy persons giving secret contributions'.

In fact, Mosley hid significant contributions from prying eyes. A millionaire, later peer and Conservative Minister, bitten by enthusiasm for Fascism, contributed £40,000 (£1.36 m) and collected £50,000 from friends. The *New Statesman* later identified him as Wyndham Portal, a New Party fund-raiser. He became Chairman of the Commission on Unemployment and 'expressed regret for being misled' but his pro-Fascism remained a secret and, as Viscount Portal, he went on to serve as wartime Minister of Works. Portal was close to the Prince of Wales who, it was rumoured, contributed anonymously. Donors included the stockbroker and contributor to the Empire Industries Association Alex Scrimgeour, and the Tory MP Henry Drummond Wolff (£1,000). Scrimgeour was a friend of Joyce, through whom he channelled £11,000 to the BUF as a bulwark against Communism.

Branches such as Hull were funded by local businessmen who formed clubs to collate support. Contributors ranged from directors of regional companies to small firms and were the saviours of Headquarters, which had 'a perpetual struggle to find money'. Fund-raising luncheons presented by Mosley were organized at the Criterion and January Club gatherings were lucrative. Wealthy landowners such as Viscountess Downe in Norfolk and Lady Pearson, who ran the Canterbury branch and was the sister of Henry Page Croft, and Jorian Jenks, a farmer and activist in Surrey, put on garden parties. Regular subventions came from rich members such as Bill Allen and Sir Alliot Verdon Roe, who served on the BUF finance committee. On temporary loan as its financial secretary, Allen's accountant, Major Tabor, said the BUF 'must do what Allen wants because it is his money which keeps them going'.

In February 1934, under the pseudonym 'James Drennan', Allen published his Spengler-derived *BUF: Oswald Mosley and British Fascism*. He had married Mosley's former companion, Paula Casa Maury, and spent much of his time in Ireland writing his *History of the Georgian People* and helping Oliver Wardrop, former British Commissioner of Transcaucasia, create an exile

Georgia Committee. Allen celebrated Fascism as 'an insurrection of feeling –
a mutiny of men against the conditions of the modern world'. He presented
Mosley's career in heroic terms and argued for a collectivist 'Elizabethan'
model of society, instead of a failed liberal bourgeois system. It was British
Fascism's most systematic defence.

Allen leaned heavily on Stirling Taylor's *Modern History of England* (1932),
which posited an Elizabethan golden age. 'In the great days of the Tudors . . .
were laid the foundations of a national state of a seriously planned economy.
Had the Elizabethan system been maintained the coming of the Industrial
Revolution and of the Age of Mechanics might have been a slower process,
but it must undoubtedly have been steadier and more ordered.' Blackshirts
linked 'feudalism, the guild system, Tudor centralised authority and the spirit
behind the achievement of Empire to their own conception of the corporate
state'. Fascist synthesis would combine the 'virility of the Elizabethan with the
intellect and method of the modern technician'. The ideal was Mosley who
represented 'the spirit of the Tudor aristocracy'.

Mosley said Fascism was a movement 'to secure national renaissance by
people who felt themselves threatened with decline into decadence'. He prom-
ulgated the image of a national community, purged and rejuvenated, rising
phoenix-like from the ashes of a morally bankrupt system and its soft culture.
The revolution consisted of 'hardening the character and purifying and energis-
ing the community rather than making the social structure or the economic
system more just or free'. It provided a means for checking social change
rather than advancing it. Fascists used nineteenth-century degeneration theories
of national decline and decay of empire, and demonized those who were
perceived as different.

For Allen, Fascism was a 'counter-revolution against an industrial revolution
which had uprooted man from the open country and cooped him up in the
city'. He viewed with horror and fascination Spengler's megalopolis, which
sucked 'into its iron belly the insignificant units who swarm in from all the
outlying lands of the old "culture"'. The city, progress and modernity were
'paradoxically, the very agents of decline'. The contradictions were evident in
the hopes of BUF Utopians such as Birmingham schoolteacher Louise Irvine.
Fascism was 'hostile not only to dark satanic mills and soulless factories but
to the very cities which contained them'. After the slums had been destroyed,
people would be rehoused in small and self-sufficient communities, in rural
environments.

Mosley discussed the ideas of German philosopher Oswald Spengler with
Allen, Mandeville-Roe, who wrote a book on the Corporate State, and
Alexander Raven Thomson, the BUF's principal philosopher. Mosley said
Thomson, who during 1932 published his Spengler-derived *Civilisation or
Divine Superman*, 'intellectually, towered above the men I had known in the

Labour Cabinet'. It was Spengler who provided the broad background of Fascist thought and Mosley's reading of his ponderous *Decline of the West* confirmed his analysis of Britain in decay and helped inject an apocalyptic edge.

World history, Spengler claimed, exhibited a cyclical pattern based on the growth and decay of cultures, which could be understood by an 'intuitive spiritual organic logic of existence' which he termed destiny. As each culture neared the end of its cycle the creative stage closed and a stagnating stage began, whose collapse into barbarism could only be delayed by heroic Caesar-type figures.

The new Caesars relied on blood, instinct and *realpolitik* to control the masses and govern nations. Representing the ultimate in the will to power, the natural aristocratic leader had returned 'in the grim serenity of Mussolini, in the harsh force of Hitler'. Mosley was the dramatic figure who dominated his audience; under physical attack, 'men shrank back from his giant frame and giant spirit'. The *Blackshirt* said 'a stone that struck his head flew apart at the impact'. He cast himself as a fact-man who would lead his people to a higher destiny. The 'original will of devoted masses, subject to revolutionary discipline and inspired by the passionate ideal of national survival' would replace 'the will to power of a higher order of the individual superman'. Every Blackshirt was to be 'an individual cell of a collective Caesarism'.

Mosley claimed the Fascist fact-man would rescue Europe from the external threat of Bolshevism and internally from the Jews. He rationalized his anti-Semitism in terms of Spengler, who distinguished between 'good' Jews, who assimilated to the national culture, and 'bad' Jews, who did not. The inner spiritual difference between Jews and Faustian Europeans was responsible for the inevitable hatred between the two groups, which could not be overcome. Spengler's cultural anti-Semitism was derived from an apartheid perspective and a belief that mixing cultures led to stagnation. Mosley envisaged a policy of separation for Jews (and later for blacks in Africa).

In contrast to Spengler's pessimistic conservatism, Mosley believed Fascism could renew European culture in 'a mutiny against destiny'. Caesarism and science would evolve Faustian man and a civilization which renewed its youth in a persisting dynamism. It would produce a 'final union of will with thought to a limitless achievement'. Fascism would create a society in which man 'could become like a God and control like a magician the forces of the universe'. In a mystical note, he told Peter Liddle that after the Caesarist stage there would be 'eternal light'. Thomson saw Fascism as the twentieth-century expression of 'the will to infinitude' and Mosley as the leader who would transform the world.

For Mosley, Fascism would 'respiritualise the thought of the people until the principles of religion return to their hearts – the militant service and mystical love'. Blackshirt Olive Hawks recalled the 'desire to merge into the greater unit of nation or faith', which derived from Fascism's spiritual instinct of self-sacrifice, which set them apart from 'people who drifted along'. Fascism, Mosley preached, comes 'with the force of a new religion'. It was infused with ritual as an alternative to Marxist faith. Its core was the idea of national rebirth in which the individual would be fused with the mass to overcome oppositions between private and public, individual and collective. It had the totalizing aim of a millenarian cult led by a charismatic leader, whose 'dynamism was recharged in the liturgies of mass meetings where irrational forces of the chosen and the symbolic took over from individualism and rationality'. Freud believed surrendering to the mass generated a feeling of safety so that 'all individual inhibitions fall away and all the destructive instincts . . . are awakened'.

Fascism contained a passion for destruction and could not fail to end in ruin. BUF songs drew on the image of the revolutionary spirit arising over the martyred bodies of the dead. The 'Marching Song' (sung to the tune of the 'Horst Wessel') called up 'the voices of the dead battalions', who 'still march in spirit with us'. A verse of 'Onward Blackshirts' (sung to the Italian anthem 'Giovinezza') reads, 'Heroes: your death was not in vain! . . . For a free and greater Britain, Stand we fast to fight or die!' E. D. Randall wrote, 'Mosley: Leader of thousands! Lead us! We fearlessly follow to conquest and freedom – or else to death!'

The forbidden became legitimate when Fascists put on the black shirt. 'Our Blackshirt Sons', wrote Anne Preston, 'get into black shirts and at once they are in a fine new world. The transformation of a bored and aimless youth into an active Fascist is nothing short of a miracle. From a slouching and selfish young cynic he is changed as if by magic into a keen confident lad . . . His eyes grow steely and his flabby muscles seem to harden overnight.' Anti-Fascist journalist Winifred Holtby was outside the Black House when she saw a woman with 'close-cropped black hair, black beret, black blouse and party badge'. Her uniform was

business-like, her walk determined, her air pleasantly self-confident. Perhaps she saw the Blackshirts as crusaders, marching to sweep away from their beloved country decadence, lethargy and confusion. They would smash the foul slums and build a new Jerusalem; they would take the unemployed youths, rotting their lives away in squalid by-streets and give them a part in the corporate state, a faith, a hope, something to live for.

She suspected, however, 'the civilisation of the concentration camp' and 'did not relish a country in which men are afraid to speak their mind'.

There existed within the BUF a strand of 'Fascist feminism', which attracted former suffragettes to the possibility of a carefully controlled revolution, opening new fields of activity to women but avoiding social and class dislocation. In April Women's Section Head Lady Makgill was forced to resign for embezzling funds. She was replaced by Mary Richardson, one of the first suffragettes to be forcibly fed and threatened with confinement in a mental home. After working in London's East End, she stood for the ILP and then joined the New Party. She saw in the Blackshirts the 'courage, action, loyalty, gift of service, and ability to serve which I had known in the suffrage movement'. A colleague, Norah Elam, argued that Fascism 'is the logical, if much grander, conception of the momentous issues raised by the militant women of a generation ago.'

In April Commandant Allen, who met Mosley through Elam, spoke at the January Club, dressed in a 'dark blue tight-fitting tunic, dark blue breeches, black top-boots and a peaked cap'. She had visited Germany 'to learn the truth of the position of German womanhood', and talked about her audience with Hitler and Goering. Her zest for National Socialism was reflected in the pages of the *Policewoman's Review*, which carried Nazi and anti-Semitic propaganda. At a BUF meeting at Oxford University she endorsed Mosley as head of a movement which sought 'to put country first, and not to interfere with other nations'. Allen maintained she was 'not herself a Blackshirt', but officials assumed she was a secret member.

Baba Metcalfe strengthened her intimacy with Mosley by donning the black shirt and regularly attending his meetings, which Irene thought 'unnecessarily provocative'. Peter Rodd had recently joined the BUF and bought black shirts for himself and his wife Nancy. She had just begun work on a book, *Wigs on the Green*, with a heroine modelled on her sister Unity. It contained a comic sketch of the leader of the 'Union Jackshirts', 'Captain Jack' (Mosley). Neither Unity nor Diana was amused.

Rothermere backing of the BUF had always been intended as a short-term measure to put pressure on the National government. The ruse worked and he received undertakings from the Prime Minister for radical changes with more spending on aircraft and the creation of a ministry of propaganda. The promises, in fact, came to nought, which left him feeling cheated. Esmond Harmsworth told Leslie Hore-Belisha that espousal of Mosley's cause intensified after this setback. At the same time Mosley's diehard friend, Ivan Moore-Brabazon MP, discussed with him 'the future policy of the BUF'.

Rothermere published Mosley's articles, advertised BUF demos and printed accounts of his meetings. Randolph Churchill said Mosley's speech at Leeds was 'one of the most magnificent feats of oratory I have ever heard. The audience . . . were swept away in spontaneous reiterated bursts of applause.' His 'eloquence has often been compared to that of the leaders of Fascism in other countries. He does not thunder like Mussolini. He has most in common with Dr Goebbels. Both possess a voice with a real ring of conviction which carries a thrill to the audience.' When there was a disturbance at Manchester's Free Trade Hall, blame was heaped on the Communists.

In Germany, Mosley drew praise from the shaven-headed and sadistic whip-wielding Julius Streicher, whose Jew-hating newspaper, *Der Stürmer*, had previously abused the BUF as 'a Jewish "catch-up" movement' and Mosley as having 'Jewish blood in his veins'. With its disgusting articles, obscene cartoons and slogans advocating terror against Jews, *Der Stürmer* had one of the highest circulations of all German periodicals, with a claimed readership of 500,000. Its spring issue, available through *Blackshirt* sellers, was devoted to 'ritual murder' and openly incited Germans to physically exterminate the Jews.

Der Stürmer had said 'the Party which in England strives in this anti-Semitic spirit is led by a certain Mosley. This man acknowledges nothing of a Jewish or a race problem. He is therefore not opposed by the Jews, on the contrary they praise and support him.' In March, editor Karl Holz admitted a mistake had been made. An agent sent by Streicher convinced them of the genuineness of the BUF's anti-Semitism. 'We are now glad to be able to state that this movement is furiously combated by Jewry and thereby proves that it is anti-Semitic.'

During March Mussolini ordered an attack on Jews. Leftists arrested in Turin were referred to as 'Jewish anti-Fascists in the pay of expatriates'. The Germans realized this was 'the first time a distinction had been made between Jews and non-Jews in Italy'. With competition between Rome and Berlin for the allegiance of foreign Fascists, Mussolini gave his blessing to anti-Jewish currents and urged the Austrian Chancellor to add a 'dash of anti-Semitism' to his programme in order to take the wind out of the sails of Nazi-backed Fascists.

Hitler responded by allowing a pro-Nazi German lawyer based in Zurich, Dr Hans Keller, to found the 'International Union of Nationalists', whose expensive-looking pamphlets extolling a 'nationalism of Race' were subsidized by Goebbels. Keller promoted a German Europe opposed to ideas of collective security as a 'limitation of power'. Eventually run out of the embassy in London, the IUN was anti-Semitic, anti-Italian and referred to CAUR as the 'Vatican-Fascist International'.

The existence of two internationals posed a dilemma for Mosley. Was he to support CAUR, given that he relied on Mussolini for funding, or the IUN, since many Blackshirts admired the Nazis? But too close a relationship would be counter-productive if his diehard supporters perceived the BUF as a foreign movement. 'We were sometimes suspected of being organised in a fascist International,' Mosley wrote. 'On the contrary, we were too much national. There were sporadic meetings between leaders but no form of systematic organisation.' That is not quite true. He built up branches overseas and created covert links, which avoided MI5 surveillance, with similar movements abroad.

The fostering of ties with Fascist movements was left to the secretive Foreign Relations Department run by Dr Georg Pfister and his mysterious 'German' second in command. A Swiss subject born in Naples, Pfister's family left in 1906 for Australia, where he was naturalized four years later and served with the Australian Army during the war. He was connected to the German Auslands Organisation and moved to England in the 1920s. His department made arrangements for BUF deputations to Germany and Italy, and senior officials who were 'continuously disappearing on mysterious visits abroad'. On 18 March the British consul in Genoa reported a visit by forty BUF members.

Interviewed by H. P. Knickerbocker, Pfister told the American journalist of Fascism's worldwide expansion. The BUF had branches in Berlin, Cologne, Milan, Rome and Paris. There were ties with the Ulster Fascists, the Australian New Guard, and the Canadian Union of Fascists boasted of its receipt of 'fighting support funds' from Mosley. His representative in Winnipeg, Hubert Cox, reiterated that anti-Semitism formed no part of CUF policy, emphasizing that Mosley had condemned it. During the summer BUF representative Edward York travelled via New York to the West Indies to set up branches. In New York he called on the German consul and said he 'hoped to do justice to the German viewpoint'. On the Riviera Branch Secretary Captain R. Coates lectured to expats on Mosley's success.

Mosley's adherence to universal Fascism was kept secret from members. They were predominantly from urban areas, with the main area of strength in London and the South-East. There was support in Liverpool, Leeds and Manchester, which had premises in the heart of the Jewish area, but apart from outposts in south Wales and Scotland, the BUF could not be classed a British union. It made efforts in Ulster but, except for Joyce and Allen, was largely indifferent to Ireland. The North was a different matter and Blackshirts made their presence felt under the title 'Ulster Fascists', with a badge of the Red Hand of Ulster imposed on the Fascist axe and bundle of rods. They were autonomous but closely associated with the parent BUF and sharing a common corporatist policy. The attempt to transcend divisions between nationalists and unionists within a framework of imperial unity was short-lived, as Mosley called for the imposition of economic sanctions 'until Southern Ireland behaves herself as a loyal member of the Empire'.

A committed supporter of Unionism, Rothermere claimed in April that he and Mosley were 'entirely at one . . . in thinking that Ulster must have from now on unyielding support'. All the momentum came from Rothermere, whose mother was from County Down. During a visit to Belfast on 6 April, Northern Ireland Prime Minister Lord Craigavon urged him to use his influence with Mosley to stop BUF criticism of his government. Rothermere told Mosley he was disappointed that the *Blackshirt* had attacked Stormont: 'This is a very grave mistake.' The province was the 'most valuable recruiting ground of anywhere in the United Kingdom and did not want my enthusiasm for your cause to be diminished by such an unnecessary and unfair attack'. Mosley was conciliatory but the most Rothermere achieved was a suspension of *Blackshirt* criticism and Mosley's agreement not to visit Belfast to support the Ulster Fascists.

During April MI5 began investigating Mosley's links with Italy and Germany. Kell enquired of the Home Office Permanent Under-Secretary, Sir Russell Scott, whether he expected him 'to take any special steps about Nazis in this country'. Scott said that unless MI5 'discovered in the ordinary course of its work any case of subversive propaganda or other inimical steps against the interests of this country' it was 'to leave them alone'. MI5's remit had been expanded to cover Fascist movements with international ramifications, whose significance as instruments of foreign powers were as the 'potential nuclei of a "Fifth Column"'. It was unclear whether this covered the BUF.

Jack Curry, formerly of India's Intelligence Bureau, was first to grasp the nature of the Nazi threat, though there was no knowledge of direct contacts with the BUF for subversive purposes. Fascist growth, however, worried the Home Secretary, Sir John Gilmour, who, on 9 April, blamed disorders on the BUF's semi-military and provocative behaviour. When MI5 discovered Mosley's visits to Rome involved making arrangements for funding, a decision was made to investigate the BUF.

MI5's B Branch was responsible for the investigation and Maxwell Knight's M Section was assigned the task of penetrating the BUF. Enquiries indicated contacts between the Auslands Organisation and senior BUF officials centred on a pro-Nazi faction led by Allen, Joyce, Thomson and Pfister. MI5 noted, however, that 'when these contacts showed signs of getting out of control Mosley issued orders forbidding any contact with foreign organizations except under the control of his own headquarters'. Mosley was conscious of MI5 operations, in fact, so security conscious, suggests Thurlow, 'that he appeared to be more concerned with limiting and controlling the information the authorities received about his activities than with running an efficient organisation'.

In the *Nation*, Johannes Steel warned in 'Is Britain Going Fascist?' that the BUF was run with 'fascist efficiency and employs the same methods of organisation and propaganda that the Hitlerites use'. The Black House was staffed with Nazis 'who have been sent by Hitler to instruct Mosley's stalwarts in political terrorism'. Rumours that the Nazis had contributed £50,000 (£1.7 m) to the BUF led MI5 to investigate German propaganda agencies which aimed to influence public opinion 'in Hitler's forward policy in Europe'.

Grandi informed Mussolini on 15 April that he told Mosley 'to disregard the popular districts of London and to speak in the open air in the small backstreets and at street corners. Revolutions are made in the streets.' After recovering from another bout of illness, Mosley put his energy into a meeting at the Albert Hall on 22 April, organized by Bill Risdon.

When Mosley entered the Hall, the 10,000-strong audience raised their right arm in the Roman salute. He 'limped across the length of the hall to the rostrum; his chin was high and his face, deathly pale, wore a relaxed, confident expression'. Robert Bernays MP found the meeting 'horribly impressive'. His 'description of Baldwin as the perfect representative of Britain asleep, with the Blackshirts as the incarnation of Britain awake, was perfectly done'. The audience was riveted. Ward Price said he had 'heard Mussolini, Hitler, and Goebbels, the three great Fascist orators of the Continent, address vast meetings. None of them, to my mind, equalled Mosley, who, in his eloquence, thrilled his huge audience in a way that men are rarely moved in their whole lives by public speech.'

L. MacNeill Weir could not 'believe that the soft-spoken, courteous, seemingly shy young man, without a hint of hauteur' he had known in the Commons 'had metamorphosed into the haughty attitudinarian who, the cynosure of a thousand eyes, stands a majestic figure, in the blazing spotlight of the Albert Hall, to receive the clamant homage of a multitude of worshippers'. Mosley resembled in the veneration of his supporters German Socialist Lassalle, founder of the Social Democratic Party. 'Hot-blooded Rhinelanders received Lassalle like a god. Nothing was lacking – garlands hung across the streets, maids of honour showered flowers upon him, interminable lines of carriages followed the chariot of the "Leader".' Both were young, wealthy, clever and ambitious. The resemblance of their careers was 'too close to be casual'.

The audience, observed Bernays, were 'exiles from Empire outposts, disgruntled Conservative women, hard-faced beribboned ex-servicemen and young toughs from the shops and the banks. It was the lower middle classes. It was the people of England who, as in Chesterton's poem, have not yet spoken. God help England if they ever do for they are a mass of prejudice, ignorance, intolerance and cruelty.' At the end, they rose to their feet as Blackshirts chanted: 'MOSLEY – Mosley! We want Mosley!'

Mosley was the last of the great platform speakers. He made 200 speeches a year and spoke without notes. He recorded a draft and learnt it off by heart. Bernays said the content was 'nothing more than extreme Toryism . . . the so-called reform of parliament, the strong hand in India, parity in the air, extreme economic nationalism . . . But it was expressed in superb language.' He exerted every resource of his will-power to persuade his audience, who demanded the same surrender of the will as other demagogues. 'Admit all this,' Weir added, 'and the preposterous pageantry and cheap demagogism falls into place as the merest stage properties of the "act".'

Mosley hoped to attract intellectuals but Wells, who was at the Albert Hall meeting, now mocked Mosley. The 'little snob-cad has found his advantage in over-expressing the secret desires of the upper classes, and the political adventurer has found an abundant following at this social level, needy, yet passionately eager to feel a "bit superior"'. Anyone who saw Blackshirts 'running like the wind down Regent Street from the Jewish prize-fighters, who broke up their demonstrations, knows the real quality of this weedy reactionary riff-raff'. Their model was the Empire ideology of Kipling's *Stalky and Co.* 'in which the idea of nasty little quasi-upper-class boys taking the law into their own hands was glorified'.

T. S. Eliot's wife, Vivienne Haigh-Wood, did join the BUF. An emotional wreck with her marriage disintegrating, she found the idea of a Jewish conspiracy appealing. Although he believed 'reasons of race and religion combine to make any large number of free-thinking Jews undesirable', Eliot distanced himself from the 'infection' which emanated from Ezra Pound. In the *Church Times* on 2 February 1934, he invited Catholics who sympathized with Fascism to question its orthodoxy that absolute monarchy 'can never return' and that the State was an absolute. On 12 March Eliot warned Pound against Mosley. Not long after, he drafted *The Rock*, satirizing totalitarianism with a scene of Blackshirts chanting anti-Semitic abuse. Mosley was unable to turn intellectual flirtation with Fascism into allegiance to the BUF. Few remained members for long and those who did were 'not particularly bright'.

The Albert Hall meeting produced the German embassy's first report on the BUF. Its author, Prince Otto von Bismarck, grandson of the Iron Chancellor, and his wife Princess Ann-Mari were popular in social circles. He disclaimed interest in the anti-Semitism which characterized Nazi accounts of the movement. On 25 April he said the BUF had 'grown stronger in industrial areas'. He was impressed that Mosley, an 'effective but moderate orator', attracted 10,000 people to a 'totally undisrupted meeting'. Berlin noted with interest Mosley's comment that no one should be persecuted because of his race and that 'in fascist England, the Jews would be ruled and not vice versa'. Bismarck concluded that Mosley's 'fight to seize power seems difficult since the economic improvement in England and the reduction in unemployment has reduced the number of disenchanted people'.

Hitler viewed British domestic politics as a conflict between 'Jewish-Bolshevist' and national political groups. The German Foreign Office cautioned against official contact with the BUF and within the Nazi Party there were 'considerable misgivings about an opening of official relations with the BUF' because of Hitler's desire not to endanger chances of an agreement with the British. Even more so, Mosley's official rejection of anti-Semitism and his alignment with Mussolini were significant hurdles to an alliance.

According to Special Branch, Mosley had designated Dr Pfister as his sole channel of communication with Germany. Faced with Hitler's reluctance to embrace Mosley, Pfister set up a back channel via Berlin publisher and former owner of the *Bergisch-Märkische Zeitung* Walter Bacmeister. Contact had been made at the end of 1933 when Pfister sent him a copy of *The Greater Britain* with the aim of securing a German publishing deal. He was asked for a revised edition with a 'more comprehensive appreciation of German National Socialism'. It was translated by Emil Chalet, who was made a honorary BUF member.

During April 1934 Pfister told Chalet he was looking forward to 'significantly closer co-operation and a better understanding between our two movements', particularly on the Jewish question since Mosley now took a 'completely unambiguous stance'. The Jewish question 'can be finally settled only when it is resolved here. The centre of Jewish power is here in London. To hope that the present government would get rid of this Jewish bondage, would be self-deception. That we will take over at the helm everyone knows who has his hand on the pulse of the nation. Draw your own conclusions.' Pfister added that the BUF was the 'most effective means in England so far for Nazi propaganda' and quoted Mosley's recent speech: 'We stand by our friends and against our enemies.' He wanted a German 'well-disposed towards us' to visit, in order 'to pave the way for a private meeting in Germany between Hitler and Mosley'.

The *Mail* said Mosley was the 'paramount political personality in Britain' and claimed the BUF was 'caught up on such a wave of deep-seated popular enthusiasm as must sweep it to victory'. Membership had doubled to 34,000 and Blackshirts believed that their time had finally arrived. In some towns the BUF 'had taken hold like wildfire' with forty-two London branches and 112 in the provinces. During recruitment drives, speakers arrived with a coachload of Blackshirts who would march with a band through the streets to meetings, with new recruits encouraged to fall in behind. Support was concentrated in a chain of branches along the south coast from Margate to Plymouth, with a few branches in non-industrial towns such as Blackpool and Harrogate. In the industrial Midlands and the North, branches were flourishing with support from small traders, shopkeepers and the middle classes.

Mosley claimed to have twenty branches in Scotland. After a speech suggesting 'Scottish people should be allowed to manage their own affairs', MI5 spotted him talking to Sir Compton Mackenzie, Scottish nationalist and later author of *Whisky Galore*, who had been hounded for breaching the Official Secrets Act by publishing in 1932 *Greek Memories*, about his time as an intelligence officer. The Communist Party's Harry Pollitt claimed Mosley offered Mackenzie 'Wales and Scotland and I will have England only'. The BUF was itself a victim of Scottish sectarianism. Its association with Catholics 'created a great hostility between them and Protestant extremists who were bitterly opposed to all things Catholic'.

With high unemployment, Lancashire was thought to have the 'best potential for revolutionary action'. The BUF found favour with cotton workers wanting to protect their jobs from foreign competition. Mosley claimed it was possible to recover the markets for British cotton in India and restore no fewer than 65,000 jobs in the process. Nearly 5,000 members were recruited among the middle class and businessmen, who were discreet in their support. Mosley appealed to both working-class Tories and Labour voters with his patriotic and anti-capitalist rhetoric, and posed an electoral threat to local Conservative MPs.

According to the Home Office, the increasing number of middle-class *Mail* recruits Mosley was attracting were derisively called 'Albert Hall Fascists' by Blackshirts. In fact, all kinds of people joined for a variety of reasons. Stuart Rawnsley's study of the North uncovered cotton workers, self-employed, small businessmen, shopkeepers and Catholics, but also those from across the social classes. In rural areas farmers became members; in Manchester the majority were non-unionized or unemployed working-class recruits. New adherents came from the Left and the Right, and those with no experience of conventional politics. There is no one theory which explains this spread but Communists were probably right in suggesting that Fascism appealed to different classes at different times.

MI5 noted that Mosley drew the support of sympathetic Tory MPs such as Moore-Brabazon, Drummond Wolff, and Colonel (later Sir) Thomas Moore wrote in the *Mail* on 25 April that there were no 'fundamental differences of outlook between Blackshirts and their parents, the Conservatives'. All were 'filled with the same emotions, pride of race, love of country, loyalty, hope'. The *Mail* said Mosley expressed views 'identical with those of the robuster minds in the Conservative Party. Like them, he stands for law, order, free speech and English methods.'

Blackshirts were weary of the 'uncanny conspiracy among our friends and our enemies to regard us as the future propaganda machine for the Tory Party'. Fascism was being watered down. Fredericks said the BUF 'rapidly lost all semblance to the true ideas of Fascism'. Pioneers were overshadowed by newcomers: 'We did not want to become the shock troops of the Tories – taking all the kicks and getting nothing.' The Left faction wanted the new recruits to be the basis of a mass movement, which would be 'obtainable only if we outrivalled the Labour machine'. Miles said Mosley wanted 'a quicker method' – a *coup d'état*, albeit a law-abiding one, in which Tories, forced to make a choice between Mosley or Moscow, would invite him to take over.

When H. R. Knickerbocker asked Mosley about the preconditions for Fascist rule, he admitted middle-class despair was 'not as severe or sudden in

Britain but there is a mass of white collar people who will become unsupported unemployed in desperate straits in a probable depression'. He did not yet see a danger of Communist revolution but 'if Labour win the next election and then acts simply to retain power the radicals will feel deceived and will revolt. The moderate socialist government will either be dissolved or will go the way of the extreme left. Either way will lead to upsurge of fascism.' He was wary of Tories 'wanting fascism without fascists. Impossible.'

Herbert Morrison told Knickerbocker Fascism succeeded where the economy and the government were in a state of collapse. But 'this was not going to happen. If fascists think we will allow power to slip away without a fight, as happened in Germany, they can think again.' Knickerbocker concluded Mosley would not succeed because he 'came on the scene when economic recovery had already started' and 'government institutions still have public support'. His appeal to the middle classes was only temporary. Fredericks thought they were 'horrified when they found its socialist side'. Many potential supporters refrained from enrolling or, having joined, soon faded away.

In the spring MI5 prepared its first report on 'The Fascist Movement in the United Kingdom'. Kell asked chief constables for information and 'their opinion as to the importance to be attached to this movement in their areas'. He discovered the BUF was 'more active and successful in the industrial areas and that their achievements in the majority of the Counties may be regarded as negligible'. However, monitoring was deficient and he did not know whether it had a 'secret organisation in being, or under preparation, which would enable them to take effective action in an emergency', or if it intended 'to influence the Armed Forces by direct propaganda or otherwise'. Nor did he have evidence of funding from Italian or German sources.

MI5 knew little of Mosley's attempt to build links with the Nazis. In May he wrote a foreword for a German edition of Bill Allen's book, which Bacmeister passed to Thomsen at the Reich Chancellery. The BUF, 'like the movement which today rules Germany, springs from the very soul of the mass of the people. It rises from the inner spiritual urge of the new generation to find new and higher forms of European civilisation.' Hitler has said a European war

can only result in the triumph of our common enemy, the international Marxist movement, which lies ready to destroy forever European culture. He is right. Such strife between fascist nations would be a crime against fascism and against European civilisation ... Individually we will each fight to save our great nations from the dark forces that menace them with destruction. Together we will strive to save Europe from the dangers that encompass the highest of all civilisations and to build in the future a Europe which is worthy of the modern mind and spirit.

On 4 May, Bacmeister informed Secretary of State Lammers that his agent, Chalet, was exchanging letters with Pfister. He said the BUF inner circle believe 'the takeover of power by Mosley in England is only a question of time'. If this was true, then 'a strong German interest could be supported in the near future for the presence of unofficial relations between the BUF and German authorities'. It was underlined by Lammers who passed it upwards and noted that Pfister had talked of 'British efforts to arrange a meeting of the German Führer and the British leader'. Bacmeister believed it was his national duty to continue the contacts and wanted to meet with a chancellery official 'who has a broad view of the political significance of the matter', so that he could 'judge the delicacy with which this matter must be handled'. He met with Lammers who referred the matter to the party's Foreign Affairs Office and the Minister of State for Foreign Affairs. Thomsen 'now officially made Mr Chalet your middle man' with the BUF but said it would be necessary 'to guard against undesirable errors'. During May, Unity Mitford returned to the Munich home of Baroness Laroche to learn German but also to contact Nazi officials.

The Germans were in receipt of reports on the BUF from a secret informant. On 2 May he told them questions were being asked about 'whether the link with the big business press lords will bring about the long-term survival of the movement or whether inner tensions could destroy it'. The Jewish question created problems since 75–80 per cent joined on the basis that policy 'would follow the German example'. Mosley had to tread carefully because he had been married to a 'half-Jewess' and had 'accepted financial support from Jewish Circles'.

Mosley's attitude to Jews was outlined in Allen's book in which he said, 'national pride has no need of the delirium of race. The English and the Italians are strong enough to ignore – and to absorb – the Jews, but in Germany they remain a constant intellectual provocation to a people sensitive to the newness of their nationhood.' Mosley's paymaster, Mussolini, attacked Nazi racialism, 'drunk with a stubborn bellicosity'. On 6 May, at Liverpool, Mosley's claim that 'there will be no racial persecution, no man will be persecuted because he is a Jew', was noted by German observers.

Mosley, however, concluded with a warning that Jews 'will have to put the interests of Britain first', instead of putting 'their own race before the interests of the country in which they reside'. They could not join the BUF because they showed 'bitter hostility to Fascism, victimised our people and bitterly attacked us in the press. It would be folly to admit declared enemies to our ranks.' To counter accusations that Fascism was a foreign creed, Grandi suggested Mosley mention that 'the founder of the Conservatives, Disraeli, and that of socialism were Jews'. On 12 May he attacked Tories for worshipping 'at the shrine of an Italian Jew'. A worried Rothermere wrote to a Jewish friend, Eric Wollheim, authorizing him to reveal his 'true feelings in regard to the anti-Semitic question'.

The Nazi informant reported that young Tories wanted to use the BUF to give their party 'fresh blood and frontline troops'. Walter Elliott 'is close to fascist thinking even though he does not approve of the model chosen by Mosley' but the Tories and aristocratic classes 'are preparing themselves to seize upon the new fascist trends'. They are 'preparing for the widely expected day of violent conflict with Marxism. A battle with the Communist Party is hardly expected but rather with the Socialists [led by Cripps] who are currently gaining supporters in massive numbers.' He noted that Mosley had 'more points of contact with Italian fascism than National Socialism'.

Mosley benefited from internal Tory disputes over India. John Strachey noted that when diehards demanded Empire Free Trade, he called for protectionism and fortification of 'islands on the Cape route to India'. Lord Lloyd, who spoke to the January Club, warned in the *Morning Post* that 'you cannot be surprised if the Conservative Party will not look after the interests of this country as well as of India, that more and more people in this country will prefer a black shirt to a White Paper'.

Lloyd George told Lord Bledisloe of the widespread unease in Tory ranks, 'not only in regard to Baldwin's India policy', but 'in regard to the general Socialist and Liberal principles with which he seems to seek to infest all Conservative thought and actions'. The right wing might 'break away from Conservatism to Fascism'. The only obstacle was Mosley's personality but the *Manchester Guardian* warned he was 'making headway, as Rothermere wants him to do, by attracting Tory die-hards and creating a new Tory party of intolerance and reaction'. Assistant editor Arthur Cranfield admitted Rothermere, with his 'whims and telephone calls', set the paper's policies. He specified 'to the inch the space to be given to Mosley and his absurd blackshirts'.

Beaverbrook was too wedded to the parliamentary system to be seduced by Mosley and his papers ignored the BUF. He thought it 'strange indeed' to see *Express* Chairman R. D. Blumenfeld, 'a Jew, even one so comfortably assimilated', a member of the January Club. Beaverbrook liked Mosley and even when attacked by him told Rothermere on 7 May that he did not 'mind how much or how often Mosley dresses me down. You and I have sent too many arrows forth, to complain of the self same shafts.' Rothermere offered that 'if he attacks you I shall drop his Blackshirts', but Beaverbrook did not want Mosley 'to feel restrained in this respect . . . politics thrive on personalities'.

'If people of this country in great numbers were to become adherents of either Communism or Fascism,' Baldwin warned, 'there could only be one end to it. And that one end would be civil war.' MI5 reported that 'it is impossible to resist the impression that taken as a whole', civil servants 'tend to underestimate the importance of Mosley's movement'.

The BUF's high profile led to hostile popular opposition. When John Beckett returned to the North, he had to run the gauntlet of 3,000 anti-Fascists at Gateshead and 5,000 at Newcastle. At Leicester, Chesterton was prevented from speaking. 'Physical assaults', recalled Richard Bellamy, 'became frequent and dangerous. Open air meetings often ended in trouble, affrays and minor riots.' Anti-Fascist disruption and the ruthlessness of the BUF Defence Force attracted publicity. One Blackshirt thought the tactics unnecessarily provocative and complained that people were 'apt to feel they were at the mercy of any "whipper-snapper" in big boots'. Julius Streicher said the baptism which the BUF has 'already received in bloody battles in public halls and streets assures it a happy future, provided it continues in its way without compromise'.

Leaked Fascist orders for meetings at Edinburgh's Mound, the equivalent of Speaker's Corner in Hyde Park, London, described tactics adopted by the Defence Force. Once the speaker arrived, 'the Plain clothes section drifts along in ones or twos and take up any position they think fit. They never communicate with each other and always take the side of the people around them.' They can 'yell Communist slogans. If any trouble breaks out they do not take any part in it. Their orders are to let the uniformed men look after it. When the uniformed men are being overwhelmed the speaker gives a signal to the leader of the section. He gives the order for the Plain clothes men to enter the skirmish. It is their duty to get the uniformed men out of the crowd.' On 28 May the Home Office came round to Trenchard's view that it was 'becoming difficult to distinguish these Fascist performances' from the 'military exercises, movements or evolutions' prohibited by the 1819 Act.

Rumours circulated in the Black House that thirty MPs were secretly sympathetic to Mosley and 'wait only for the day when open advocacy of Fascism may become a politically profitable manoeuvre'. The only converts who broke ranks were Carlyon Bellairs, former social imperialist and author of *The Ghost of Parliament*, and H. M. Upton, son of Viscount Templeton. Miles claimed pledges of support were reinforced by the presence in the Lords of 'some twenty-two peers of the realm. The Earl of Erroll is not the only belted bulwark of the aristocracy who has accepted membership of the BUF.'

A week before his thirty-third birthday, Scotland's Lord High Constable Joss Erroll visited the Black House and was spotted at Quaglino's at a table with Otto von Bismarck. A founder member of the British Fascists, he joined the January Club and discussed with Mosley plans to launch Fascism in the colonies, as a solution to Africa's agricultural depression. He added his voice to Mosley's rallying cry to develop Empire trade 'in a long-term plan to make the Empire a great self-contained economic unit' with 'the highest standard of civilisation in the world'. Erroll attracted publicity and when *The Times* announced his appointment as BUF representative in Kenya, Mosley's every move was covered by the press. It helped that he was friends with figures such as Ribbentrop.

At the end of May the Savoy hosted a Blackshirt Dinner, publicized by the *Tatler*. Attending were close friends of the Prince of Wales, Fruity Metcalfe and Count and Countess Munster. On 31 May the Home Secretary button-holed the Prince and told him of his anxiety over the growth of the Blackshirts. John Aird, an equerry of the Prince, talked to Edward on the way back. 'We agreed that, without knowing much about them, we both thought it quite a good movement except for Mosley.'

Pfister sought increased exchange of information with the Nazis and hoped for more reporting on the BUF in the German press. As the most effective channel for NSDAP propaganda in England, he told Bacmeister he was 'personally ensuring that all readers of the *Blackshirt* have the material to place the new Germany in the most favourable light'. There followed a visit to the Black House by Nazi agent Dr Thost, who was introduced to P. G. Taylor, who showed him a purloined 'plan which was currently being prepared on the Jewish side for a general attack – Press, finance, trade boycott etc. – against Germany'. Thost was impressed and his report to Berlin opened the way to a change in relations with Mosley. On 2 June the Nazi Party's Foreign Office assured Bacmeister that 'considering the significance of the questions raised, some decisions have not been made', but the German press would report extensively on the forthcoming BUF rally at Olympia – against which anti-Fascists had agreed to organize a counter-demonstration – and that the close ties between themselves and Mosley would be emphasized.

15

Olympia

The BUF's rally at Olympia received wide advance publicity from Rothermere's papers, which offered free tickets to readers who sent letters under the heading 'Why I like the Blackshirts'. Anti-fascists responded looking for the opportunity to disrupt the meeting. 'It soon appeared', L. W. Bailey recalled, 'that nothing, however ludicrous, could fail: "I like the Blackshirts because I want to die for my country and they seem to offer the best opportunity." Fired by curiosity rather than commitment, I sent my letter.'

Special Branch knew of anti-Fascist preparations for action and a plan to carry out 'something spectacular'. A report on 7 June said Communists were 'active among the Jewish elements in the East End, from whom they hope to obtain a large number of demonstrators'. This report probably came from P. G. Taylor, who was in receipt of information from an agent inside the Communist Party. Claims of collaboration between the police and the BUF were fuelled by rumours that Mosley lunched with Trenchard on the eve of the rally.

No information on BUF preparations appeared in the SB reports, which suggested to Skidelsky that the BUF 'took no special precautions'. In fact, Alex Miles recalled, 'The hall had been surveyed in order to discover how many men were required to control each exit and entrance.' Men were shipped in from around the country to swell the ranks of the Defence Force, whose section commanders received sealed orders. On the day, alcohol was on sale and money flowed freely, 'almost as freely as blood flowed during the course of the meeting'. Officials said the idea was to 'teach the bloody Reds a lesson'.

Former *Herald* editor Hamilton Fyfe saw in Oxford Street 'bands of young men, mostly Jews, on their way to the meeting . . . in a fighting mood'. Over 1,000 anti-Fascists were involved in a counter-demonstration against a similar number of Fascists who marched from the Black House to Olympia; another 900 Blackshirts, mostly stewards, made their way separately.

The *Daily Worker* forecast readers would see 'hundreds of Rolls-Royces and fine cars – showing the class who want more fascist action against the workers – to maintain their dividends'. Lord Erroll, Sir John Rhodes and Sir George Duckworth-King wore black shirts. Diana's friend Lord Berners composed a 'dreary little tune' for the event. He told Mosley, 'You'll never win because you've taken on both the Jews and the buggers.' Diana did not attend because she was running a temperature. Peter Rodd's father sounded a warning note to Nancy Mitford: 'Can you not persuade him to stick to the business at hand and not to advertise himself in these Fascist demonstrations? If he becomes identified with an anti-semitic campaign you must see yourself what that would lead to.' He admired the BUF spirit, 'but things are manifestly taking a wrong direction'.

Collin Brooks, Rothermere's fixer and author of 'shock' thrillers, was a guest. BUF members who read his column in the *Sunday Dispatch* considered him a Fascist fellow-traveller. Anti-Semitic, he belonged to the English Mistery and the Grosvenor Kin, which aimed 'to recover the lost values of older England, and to nurture men of all classes who might be worthy of leadership'. Brooks was accompanied by journalist John Bingham (shortly to join Maxwell Knight in MI5).

At 8.45 p.m. searchlights scanned the end of the hall. Along the centre, Blackshirts waited as 'trumpets brayed as a mass of Union Jacks passed towards the platform'. 'Hail Mosley!' swept the hall. Irene felt that Cimmie 'must be there and seeing all that she would be glad'. Unfortunately, Mosley's entrance failed to coincide with the fanfare. Eventually, he mounted the platform and gave the salute – 'so high and so remote in that huge place that he looked like a doll from Marks and Spencer's penny bazaar'. His speech was largely inaudible as the loudspeakers were not tuned in.

'From time to time in the history of great nations comes the moment of decision, the moment of destiny,' he began. 'This nation again and again in the great hours of its fate has swept aside the little men of convention and delay and decided to follow men and movements who dared go forward to action.' It was all, George Catlin noted, 'familiar to anyone who knew Mosley in his Socialist days'. 'The old gang of politicians do not confront unpleasant facts . . . What is required is to confront with courage the situation; to maintain and raise the standard of living by developing the home market; to turn out the old politicians.'

Opponents had been silent but 'then began the Roman circus', Brooks recalled. Orchestrated heckling could be heard: 'Hitler and Mosley mean hunger and war.' The interruptions were answered by chants of 'MOSLEY!'. He then launched into virulent anti-Semitism, talking of European ghettos pouring their dregs into the country. There was pandemonium as stewards hurled themselves at a heckler. Brooks saw him being 'battered and bashed and dragged out – while the tentative sympathisers all about him, many of whom were rolled down and trodden on, grew sick and began to think of escape'. It was brutal. 'There is no pause to hear what the interrupter is saying: there is no request to leave quietly: there is only the mass assault.'

Special Branch's Sergeant Thompson reported that 'removals and interruptions from all parts of the arena' lasted for an hour. As hecklers were removed, others took their place. The fact that many were Jewish was used by the BUF as fuel for its anti-Semitism. Brooks found it interesting that Mosley was 'cock-a-hoop when an interrupter was battered out and growing apologetic as the psychological tone of the audience changed into disgust and personal fear'.

The breaking of glass 'added to the trepidation of the old ladies in the audience who had come to support the patriots'. *The Times* noted the many

people of middle age who wore neither blackshirt nor badge: people with a tired expression and wrinkled brows: some of the people who bore the strain of the war . . . they seemed to be looking for the reason beneath this resurgence of youthful enthusiasm and militant spirit, lest they should have missed a chance of deliverance which those in their inexperience had miraculously found. The impression gained was that the inquirers had neither found the secret nor caught the enthusiasm.

Many disliked the theatricality. Yeats-Brown's biographer John Wrench 'could not envisage anyone as devoid of humour as Mosley becoming a great national leader, able though he was'.

Brooks's party left at 10.30 with 'the loud speakers still preventing our hearing a word Mosley said'. The hall was half empty. Georgia Sitwell found it 'very unpleasant. Terrifying crowds of roughs, dozens of fights, casualties, broken heads and glass.' She left feeling ill. One of Brooks's party, previously sympathetic to the Fascists, decided that 'if it's a choice between the Reds and these toughs, I'm all for the Reds'. Fredericks claimed that ejections were 'accomplished by the simple method of throwing him or her down the iron staircases leading to the corridors and outer hall. If the unfortunate still retained consciousness after this unpleasant experience, he probably thought he had been thrown out and that was that.' It was, Wrench said, a 'disgusting exhibition of force'. When stewards claimed a female comrade had been slashed with a razor, violence escalated.

In the corridors 200 Blackshirts, aptly called 'the wolves', were already drunk. Their role was to beat up those ejected from the hall. 'The fact that so many received quite serious injuries', Fredericks claimed, 'originated in this double beating-up process. It was not a matter of six to one this time, but about twenty or thirty.' *News Chronicle* editor Gerald Barry 'saw a man lying on the floor, obviously powerless and done for, being mercilessly kicked and horribly handled by a group of Blackshirts'. They were 'kicking a miscreant in the stomach and all over the body more brutally than anything I have ever seen in my life short of the war. It made me feel physically sick.' At one entrance 'policemen were so disgusted that they drew their truncheons, driving the blackshirts back into the main hall and calling them "bloody bastards"'.

A BUF official complained that the police had no right to be in the hall and they were forced to leave.

The log entry at Hammersmith police station stated the meeting passed off without serious violence. The report to the Home Office said thirty people had been ejected 'with a certain amount of violence'. Fredericks thought it a miracle that no one died: he had not seen 'so much blood in all my life'. Five people were detained in hospital and fifty needed treatment. A doctor said it was obvious weapons had been used.

Baldwin's Parliamentary Private Secretary, Geoffrey Lloyd, told the *Yorkshire Post* he was 'appalled by the brutal conduct of the Fascists. There seems little doubt that some of the later victims of the Blackshirt stewards were Conservatives endeavouring to make a protest at the unnecessary violence.' He said Mosley's 'tactics were calculated to exaggerate the effect of the most trivial interruptions and to provide an apparent excuse for the violence'. Mosley was a 'political maniac and all decent people must combine to kill his movement'.

When Bob Boothby and Archie Sinclair met Harold Nicolson on 12 June, they said the Commons was 'up in arms against the Fascists and that something will be done about them'. Isaac Foot argued violence was Mosley's policy and that he had adopted the Italian method of using agents provocateurs to incite disorder. He wanted an inquiry into the wearing of uniforms and their 'setting up a kind of glamour of civil war to attract youth'. Mosley said those MPs who claimed to witness Blackshirt violence at Olympia were 'liars and jackals'.

Brendan Bracken told Baba that the Tories were 'so frightened of the BUF that they might rush a bill through forbidding the wearing of black shirts'. Unity wrote to Diana commiserating with her for missing the rally: 'Too awful for you. It does sound such heaven.' Was it a success, she wondered. 'Does the Leader think so? All these absurd attacks in the papers are bound to do the Party a certain amount of harm.'

Mosley refused to apologize. Appearing on BBC radio with Gerald Barry, he claimed it was all the fault of organized 'Red violence'. 'We knew all about it, and so did the authorities. For weeks before the meeting, incitements to attack it were published, and maps were printed to show how to get to the meeting.' Blackshirts never attacked their opponents, but when the victim of violence, they hit back hard and 'so would any Briton worthy of the name'. Ex-suffragette Mary Richardson wrote that she admired Blackshirts 'the more when they hit back, and hit hard'.

Mosley published a pamphlet, 'Red Terror and Blue Lies', with a photograph of him examining weapons taken from the Reds. According to Fredericks, who took the photograph on instructions from a Defence Force officer, the weapons had not been taken at the rally. He had previously been asked by Mosley 'to fake some pictures . . . to give the impression that it was the blackshirts who had been attacked'. He swathed the head of a Blackshirt in bandages and dabbed it with red ink. It was 'published as representing an atrocity of the red front'.

Mosley's refusal to condemn the brutality suggested to many that the BUF was composed of sadistic thugs. The *Telegraph*, hostile to the idea of a Defence Force, said on 11 June there was 'no room here for private armies'. Former Blackshirts acknowledged the violence was overdone. Mosley, however, continued to believe Blackshirt spirit had 'smashed the biggest organised attempt ever made in this country to wreck a meeting by Red violence'.

Olympia is often portrayed as a turning point in Mosley's fortunes: from then on his respectable support fell away. Even if it had been a memorable experience, Brooks thought the 'whole thing was a fiasco and . . . the personal appeal of Fascism has been drowned by such a display of un-English methods'. Jon Lawrence argues Mosley had been exposed harnessing the rowdy techniques of Edwardian politics to an avowedly anti-democratic purpose. 'It did not help that Mosley underlined the organised character of his "force of arms" by swapping a conventional steward's arm-band for a blackshirt uniform.' In fact, support did not evaporate. Many admired his defence of free speech. Letters in the *Morning Post* were pro-BUF, which was seen as the victim of the violence.

Opinion in the Carlton Club was divided: anti-Baldwin rebels voiced support for Mosley. In a Commons debate on 14 June pro-Mosley MPs, including Sir Patrick Hannon, Moore-Brabazon, Drummond Wolff, Thomas Moore and Vice-Admiral E. A. Taylor, one of Rothermere's Empire crusaders, kept silent. T. F. Howard and Earl Winterton said reports of Blackshirt violence were exaggerated and asserted the disruption had been organized by Communists. Patrick Donner said, 'Communists were armed with razors, stockings filled with broken glass, knuckledusters and iron bars . . . Can it in equity be argued that the stewards used their fists, when provoked in this manner, with more vigour than perhaps the situation required?' MPs cheered Mosley's readiness to suppress Communism. T. P. O'Connor said the BUF 'thrives on the feeling that is prevalent in the Conservative Party, that it is utterly fed up with interruption of meetings – organised interruption and hooliganism'.

Dubbed the first parliamentary Fascist convert by the *Chronicle*, Michael Beaumont claimed 'respectable, reasonable and intelligent people' were joining the BUF. MPs elected in the 1931 National landslide feared it might split the anti-Labour vote by running its own candidates. F. A. Macquisten said Mosley is 'going to do all the things they said they would do but have not done yet. That is very awkward for the Conservative Party but this is a matter on which Hon. Members had better talk to the Conservative leaders.'

The view among Ministers, noted Deputy Cabinet Secretary Thomas Jones, was that 'organised Communists had got not only what they asked for, but a great deal more with excessive brutality'. Mosley 'cut a poor figure the moment things went astray' and had 'not got the personality which would carry his movement to victory'. Although Blackshirts had physically won the battle of Olympia and the Communists the propaganda war, the fallout proved to be complex.

Rumours circulated that Rothermere's papers would no longer promote the BUF. In fact, the *Dispatch* justified Fascist behaviour and continued to endorse Mosley. This was a cause of concern to MI5, which placed Rothermere high on its list of 'important personages' backing Mosley. 'Support lent to a fascist or extreme nationalist movement by a powerful section of the English press might prove very convenient to the Weltpolitik of the Third Reich at this juncture.' Ward Price enthusiastically reported that 'Red hooligans savagely and systematically tried to wreck Mosley's magnificently successful meeting. They got what they deserved.' When the 'necessity is forced on them, the Blackshirts are able and willing to meet violence with violence'. This reaction explains why Mosley was delighted with Olympia.

George Catlin observed that 'only one thing can make Mosley – and that one thing is the Communists'. Blackshirt violence at Olympia had a tactical purpose: it produced a visible spectacle of public disorder. 'This was', Nick Smart suggests, 'necessary so as to make the sense of crisis immediate. People might read newspaper reports of socialist uprising in Vienna with more than usual attention if they considered the same would soon be on their doorstep.' On 10 June Rudoph Gessner, an adviser to 'socialist' Vienna, told an East End audience at Limehouse not to think 'British people are different from the Germans or Italians and that you will have an easy going Fascism. After Olympia from now on all the brutally inclined Britishers will join the Fascists because then they can be as brutal as they want with impunity. Very soon it will be capable of committing the brutalities and atrocities which happened in other countries. The Mosley meeting proved that.'

Many people found the fighting exciting rather than offensive, and Cuthbert Headlam feared that all the attention was 'doing a good deal to advertise the Fascists'. Olympia, noted the Home Office, 'provided an unprecedented fillip to recruitment. For the next two days people of different classes queued up from morning until night at the National Headquarters.'

Olympia changed the Nazi viewpoint. Unity told Diana that German press accounts of Olympia were marvellous. On 11 June, *Völkischer Beobachter* acclaimed the 'energetic defence of the Blackshirts in a bloody battle' and attributed the violence to Communists. Previous embassy reports on the BUF were 'not calculated to arouse the interest of the leading Nazis' but Berlin was now informed that Mosley had a great success. Foreign Ministry Director Dickoff underlined Bismarck's conclusion that Olympia was 'symptomatic of events which are occurring throughout England: growth of support for British fascism, lively activity in meetings and recruitment together with the growth of an aggressive and defensive rejection of fascism by its opponents'.

Dickoff circulated a memo suggesting Mosley was welcome to visit Germany but 'the time should be carefully chosen'. The Nazis worried the British government might move against Mosley even though Bismarck said no action would be taken because of the law of free speech. Dickoff said Mosley could meet Hitler at the Nuremberg party rally 'without too much clamour'. A few days later he wrote to Bacmeister and it was decided correspondence between the two representatives would refer to individuals in code – Pfister (Georg), Oswald (Oskar), Hitler (Arnold), Charlet (Emil) and Bacmeister (Wilhelm).

On 11 June Mosley talked with Pfister about Germany and a verbatim report was sent to Charlet. 'It is beyond question that the present and future outlook brings my operation ever closer to Arnold's so that close co-operation is absolutely necessary. *We both have the same aims.*' To emphasize the point Mosley declared, 'we are in excellent agreement with our business friends in the south [Italy] but Arnold's business is of greater importance.' He also made clear his commitment to anti-Semitism: 'As far as our opponents of non-Aryan race are concerned, we will have to take the most drastic measures as soon as we are in power, or we will have no rest.' Pfister said they could pass on the statements to the right quarters.

On 14 June Cimmie's will was published, leaving property valued at £20,951 (£710,000) with the residuary estate held in trust for her children. Mosley was left Savehay Farm and appointed executor with the Public Trustee. Leiter Trust money could be used for the family but not to support his Fascist activities. Despite Mussolini's funds, expenditure outstripped income and Mosley was forced to make economies. Taylor was told to offload all his salaried agents, except one in the Communist Party (still useful to MI5). He was given new responsibilities as the FUBW was merged into the Industrial Section of the Propaganda Department. Resigning in protest at Mosley's action its head, Andy Barney, warned Miles that 'we are distrusted by those who control the Movement. Time will prove whether we of the working-class are wanted.'

The Home Office built up a profile of Mosley drawn from the 'observations relayed by some of his associates'. He was a poor administrator and, while he had contributed considerably to the ideological content, the true thinker was Bill Allen. MI5's first report, released on 18 June 1934, devoted considerable attention to Allen, intrigued by his relationship with Mosley, his financial dealings on behalf of the BUF and Establishment links, through membership of White's and people such as Lord Glenconner, a director of his poster firm. MI5 was interested in Forgan's propaganda, which 'turns a smiling face to every section which might feel that its interests would be endangered by the introduction of a fascist regime. While it attacks the financiers of the City of

London, it promises investors that their interests will be safeguarded. While it is more active and successful in the industrial areas, it makes special efforts to attract farmers and rural communities.'

Fascist theory, MI5 noted, 'contemplates the use of force to defeat insurgent anarchy in an emergency.' A Fascist coup was far away but it was concerned that 'since the Armed Forces of the Crown would be a factor in such an emergency, the Fascists ... must adopt a definite attitude towards them, directed to securing their sympathy, more or less active – or even the power to control them, if and when the ultimate issue arises'. MI5, however, did not yet know Mosley's intentions.

The *Mail* rejected the 'utterly baseless fiction that the Blackshirt movement is anti-Jewish', but in an interview with Reuters in early June, Julius Streicher said he had information from an envoy that the BUF 'has positively defined its attitude towards the Jewish problem'. Mosley 'realised that the tactical reserve hitherto observed by him in this question is no longer expedient'. Pfister wrote to Bacmeister, an old pan-German, who regarded the BUF's 'attitude towards Germany as crucial – but not its attitude to Judaism'. It is clear from his letters that his friends were wary of his involvement with the 'Jewish-dependent BUF'. To counter such views, on 29 June Pfister forwarded material to be used for a book Bacmeister was planning on Mosley's attitude towards the Jews.

In July Pfister visited the Nazi Party to negotiate a meeting between Mosley and Hitler, but Otto Bene refused to pursue the matter and, moreover, informed Dr Bohle, head of the Foreign Department, that Mosley was of 'little importance'. Pfister arranged a secret meeting to resolve the matter. Mosley told Bene, 'We have never received a penny from Jews. I give you my word of honour.' Pfister noted it was 'an expression which I have never heard him use before. For him it is the highest compliment.' Mosley outlined the BUF's covert strategy. It was made explicit it was an anti-Semitic movement and had intended to be so from its inception. 'During the first months I intentionally said not even one word against the Jews. If I had done so we would never have been able to withstand the power of the Jews. We would have been simply crushed. We were not strong enough then. Today we are so strong that we are feared.'

Mosley said his plan had succeeded. 'The Jews have attacked us, at first sporadically, then more and more. From "underground" methods they have moved to open attack in the press. Now we must defend ourselves against these attacks and have been forced into counter measures.' He was 'adamant that we should attack no Jew on the grounds of his religion or race. We attack them because of their damaging influence on the people, because of their internationalism, because of their many activities of all kinds against the good of the people. The outcome is the same.' He told Bene the 'anti-German world boycott by the Jews is led from London. And I imagine that you are well aware in Germany what it will mean if we break Jewish power here . . . Open war – raising hell – will probably come in two or three months . . . I will contribute my part in order to hasten this explosion and I have so organised my plan of campaign that they will find us ready, whatever they do.' Bene made a report of the meeting which for the moment would be kept secret. 'We don't want to disclose any of our intentions to the children of Israel,' wrote Pfister. 'When the critical moment comes we will let the actions speak for themselves.'

On 30 June 1934 Hitler liquidated internal rivals, including Ernst Röhm and other Brownshirt leaders in the 'Night of the Long Knives'. Hitler told the Reichstag he had given 'the order to burn down to the raw flesh the ulcers of this poisoning of the wells in our domestic life'. Deputies greeted this with wild acclaim. Many people had believed the Nazis were like other parties, but now, even the *Express* was shocked. 'There has never been anything quite like it in the history of the world. Jews are still murdered in the concentration camps; they are still beaten in the streets. But from this week-end the screw tightens. There is nothing they can do except run round helplessly in circles until they die.'

Not everyone was squeamish. On 1 July Unity wrote to Diana that when she heard about the purge, she felt 'so terribly sorry for the Führer. It must have been so dreadful for Hitler when he arrested Röhm himself and tore off his decorations. Then he went to arrest Heines and found him in bed with a boy. Did that get into the English papers? Poor Hitler.'

MI5 observed that Rothermere and Mosley were alone in adopting a friendly attitude to Hitler. On 2 July the *Mail* said Hitler had saved Germany by making a clean sweep of his enemies. On the same day Pfister sent congratulations to the German Foreign Ministry for the 'brisk way in which A. H. cleaned out the stables. Such matters are just unavoidable.' Mosley had said it would 'be a mistake if a party such as ours, when it comes to power, carries on with any minister of the old regime. Mussolini had regretted it' and, Mosley said, 'I will be on my guard against that. Even today, from my well tested officers who have the right spirit, I could put together a better ministry than England has had for many, many years.'

Pfister revealed that Rothermere's wings had been clipped by Jewish threats to withdraw advertising from his papers. BUF speakers were working 'to expose Jewish lies' and requested material on emigrants to England so that they could 'expose these filthy Jews. If we can prove that even just a half dozen "undesirables" have gained good posts, then that will make a big impression on the public.' It would be used in questions on Jewish refugees by anti-Semitic allies in the Commons.

Pfister said the Jewish question had been 'brought to the fore in our policies'.

Mosley knew at the beginning, when the party was weak, that the Jews could have rendered us harmless. So he waited until the rulers suddenly became aware that our policies were diametrically opposed to theirs and that we were to be taken seriously. Then they attacked us. Mosley wanted that. Then at the Albert Hall Mosley explained that he was obliged to defend himself and took up the gauntlet. The battle is now not quite open but it will soon be.

Pfister's committee was dealing with the matter. It included Joyce – 'too impulsive and would best like to get stuck in straight away'.

Mosley argued 'there was no shadow of suspicion that we were an anti-semitic movement when Jews attacked our Olympia meeting'. Because he did not attack Jews on account of race or religion he was not, therefore, anti-Semitic, even though he admitted to Bene the outcome was the same to racial versions. He claimed the 'quarrel arose . . . for clearly discernible reasons. There is not the slightest doubt that some Jews began it in Britain.' They were 'in a state of considerable alarm and liable to jump to unjustified conclusions'. During his wartime interrogation he gave a slightly different version. Jews had seen how their co-religionists were being treated in Germany and they no doubt said, suggested Lord Birkett, 'this Fascist Movement in Britain is the same type of movement existing in National Socialist Germany?' to which, Mosley replied, 'Yes.'

Mosley's claim that the Jewish question was 'a topic which had no place whatever in party policy' was simply untrue; it had merely been suppressed during the Rothermere period, which indicated the degree to which it was under his strict control. Birkett asked him whether his attitude 'to the Jewish problems arose because they had attacked your meetings, so you thereupon gave the problem some consideration?' 'Mosley agreed. He had thought it 'the work of cranks. But then I wondered "why are they so opposed to us?" We want to stop certain things. We want to stop international usury, we want to stop the whole money-lending racket. We do not like price-cutting. We do not like the sweating of labour. Gradually it dawned on me that certain people were very much engaged in these things.' This was, of course, a smokescreen. Mosley chose for the task of researching the matter A. K. Chesterton, who was hopelessly anti-Semitic with a conspiratorial view of Jewish activities.

Chesterton claimed 'Jewish money was being poured into anti-Fascist activities; the Jews were forming organisations which carted toughs around in vans to create uproar at Fascist meetings; the influence of Jewry was making itself felt through all the media of "national" propaganda; and that no less than 50 per cent of persons convicted of assaults on Fascists bore Jewish names'. He confirmed Mosley's view that Jews were 'prominent in the attack on us at Olympia', even though Harold Laski had been troubled by 'the refusal of the Jews here to adopt a fighting attitude'. He warned that 'Jews could not save themselves by pretending to be more English than the English'. Initially, the Board of Deputies of British Jews viewed the BUF as a minor threat. Laski attributed this to fear of being seen as collaborating with Communists.

Chesterton wrote in 'The Tragedy of Antisemitism' that his report left Mosley 'genuinely puzzled' about why Jews attacked the BUF. Then, Mosley recalled, Chesterton found the reason in the close ties between anti-Fascism and Jewish interests. There was 'no great financial, industrial, or commercial trust or combine which was not dominated by the Jew, whether acting in person or by proxy. The whole capitalist racket, the whole of the national Press, the whole of the "British" cinema, and the whole bunch of purely parasitical occupations were found to be Jew-ridden. Every vitiating and demoralising factor in our national life was Jew-influenced where it was not Jew-controlled.' His report was not published but Chesterton produced a summary claiming Jewish donations influenced political parties and that they ran the Communist Party.

In 'Jews and Fascists' Mosley claimed the report revealed the 'victimisation of our people by Jewish employers and the pressure of Jewish interests on our supporters'. He told Birkett of the example of a female Blackshirt who was dismissed. 'This occurrence forced the Jewish question on the attention of many who had paid no more attention to Jews or their particular problem and character than any other section of the community.' Blackshirts complained 'our girls were dismissed from shops owned by Jews. Our people were persecuted. Our supporters were blackmailed by Jewish interests.'

Mosley imagined he had stumbled on some great secret. The BUF was not anti-Semitic but was countering financial and political interests which happened to be run by Jews. So was not the BUF justified in openly retaliating? Chesterton declared that Jewish domination of national life 'precludes the possibility of an economic square deal for the British people . . . until that power has been politically crushed'. In the knowledge that a transcript was unlikely to be made public, Mosley admitted to Birkett that 'having looked at the Jewish problem, I developed what is called anti-semitism'.

The traditional account of Mosley's anti-Semitism argues the BUF's violent tactics at Olympia eroded its support and created the desperate need for a new dynamic to revitalize an ailing movement. The Jews were thus 'the helpless victims of a cynical and politically-motivated campaign'. Others suggest the anti-Semitism is best understood 'as a result of the interaction of bitterly opposed fascist and anti-fascist elements'. The interactionist model places a share of the blame for the anti-Semitic campaign squarely upon the shoulders of the Jewish community itself, because of its attacks on Fascism, though the proportion of blame attributed varies. Skidelsky's analysis – in many ways identical to Mosley's exercise in retrospective self-justification – went as far as to suggest that Jews should take 'a large share of the blame' for what followed. A more sophisticated interactionist account suggests the progression towards anti-Semitism was not cynical political opportunism but a genuine, integral part of the movement.

A Special Branch report on anti-Semitism identified the inner leadership of former BF members, such as Joyce and Hawkins, as primarily responsible for pushing Mosley in that direction. It was true that they wanted it immediately implemented, but anti-Semitism had been accepted as a core policy prior to the BF's absorption into the movement. Nor can it be concluded, as did Skidelsky, that from 1932 to 1934 Mosley 'regarded the Jewish issue as more of a liability than an asset, a diversion from his main task'. Nor did he decide to go ahead only after long deliberation. The theory of the reluctant Mosley is an attempt to absolve him from his responsibility for reintroducing into politics an abhorrent policy which, as communications between Pfister and Germany reveal, he fully endorsed.

Mosley said he rejected the Jewish conspiracy theory and biological racism. There was, he insisted, 'no evidence of occult Jewish power, simply the determination to fight by men who in this case had the means to do it, which I had not'. He accepted anti-Semitism's ability to smooth over contradictions in Fascist ideology but was 'genuinely puzzled' on how to present it in 'rational' terms; the Chesterton report solved the problem. Its pseudo-research and its conclusions, which presented anti-Semitism in terms of a 'well-earned reputation' argument, were exactly what he had been seeking in order retrospectively to justify a campaign which he had decided would be launched in the autumn.

Mosley needed to assure the Nazis that he was worth supporting. The Pfister communications reveal the extent to which he attempted to appease them in expectation of a meeting with Hitler and the possibility of funding. Dietrich Aigner believes Mosley's 'turn to anti-semitism without a racial stamp, happened more under the influence of the German example than under German propaganda'. He cemented relations with Germany in terms of the Jewish question. The Jews were provoking conflict between the two countries and their goal was to instigate war. This became the leitmotif of BUF foreign policy. At one with Hitler's policy, Germans should have one greater Reich with their former colonies returned. That autumn, 'amid scenes of tumultuous enthusiasm', Blackshirt reported, Mosley 'took up the challenge flung at his movement by Jewry'.

The almost simultaneous occurrence of the Night of the Long Knives and Olympia drew MI5's attention to the BUF's close affinities with the Nazis. It had no hard information about funding, though there were rumours of a £50,000 (£1.7 m) gift from Germany – via Rosenberg's friend, Deterding. MI5, however, found it difficult to obtain permission to investigate the BUF's Continental links. During June Guy Liddell asked to intercept correspondence between the Nazi Party in London and Berlin, on the grounds that it was 'acting as an agency of the German Secret Police', but the Home Office refused and only allowed interception of a few minor BUF figures. Permission to monitor Mosley's correspondence was denied because he had been an MP and was known to be litigious. MI5 relied on agents who were unaware of Pfister's back channel to the Nazis.

During the summer MI5 promoted the line that 'red violence' was responsible for Fascism's growth and accused Communists of promoting violence by publicizing such activities against the BUF. The Fascists were 'aware of plans to break up their meetings and regarded it as an incitement to violence, justifying direct action'. Labour and trade union circles were criticized for accusing the authorities of pro-Fascist bias; an accusation which MI5 deemed unjust, since Fascists 'had never made organised attempts to break up opponents' meetings'.

There was a degree of discrimination among police, who had a greater suspicion of Communists than of the BUF. They were more scrupulous about the law when dealing with Fascists as opposed to anti-Fascists. They did not baton-charge Fascists, though there were numerous occasions when police acted violently against anti-Fascists. Locally, pro-Fascist prejudices – such as in York where the Chief Constable and other policemen were BUF supporters – did exist, though impartiality was maintained at senior levels of the Metropolitan Police.

Indoor meetings passed off peacefully as Mosley, wary of the Home Secretary introducing new police powers, modified his tactics. MI5 argued parliamentary and press hostility had persuaded him to abandon the policy of using Blackshirts to overwhelm hecklers. The ban on police at indoor meetings was rescinded and stewards were instructed to threaten disrupters with prosecution under the Public Meetings Act. Branches were 'discouraged from distributing free tickets to all-comers, and reminded that they could ask the police to eject persistent interrupters'. When Mosley asked police to steward a proposed rally at White City, officers said he was trying to engineer a situation whereby they would be blamed for any disturbances. In the end, he had to abandon the rally. Fearing another Olympia, Trenchard persuaded the owner that he 'might consider the size of the bond to be deposited by Mosley to be sufficiently large to make it impossible for him to agree'.

During the summer the *Blackshirt* attacked the 'tottering Tories'. In an interview on 4 July with Signor Franzero of *Il Giornale d'Italia*, Mosley announced the BUF 'would present itself to the voters as soon as its electoral machine was ready, mainly in working class towns'. Rothermere, however, was concerned Fascist candidates might put the National government in jeopardy by splitting its vote. Ironically, it was his parliamentary strategy, rather than the violence, which undermined Mosley's position with Rothermere. In

July the National government appeared to acquiesce to his demands when it announced an increase in RAF squadrons. This was the news he had been waiting for as it satisfied his ego that 'he had the insider influence he felt was his by right'. Believing the government 'would not collapse from within and that diehard resistance to the India White Paper policy would be contained', Rothermere decided he no longer needed Mosley.

'Then came a sudden message,' Mosley recalled. Rothermere decided not to fund a manufacturing project, costing £70,000 (£2.38 m), in which the BUF would be an outlet for Blackshirt cigarettes. Learning of the scheme in which members would be instructed to smoke, an official chortled: 'Truly the way of Fascists will be hard if their taste in cigarettes is to be made to conform with their political convictions.' Mosley had established New Epoch Products and registered a factory for production. Rothermere saw it as an opportunity to use spare capacity in his Canadian paper mills. On the Board of Directors sat his associates, Sir Max Pemberton and Ward Price, as well as Mosley and Dundas. Mosley envisaged the project as the basis of an industrial empire to include banking and retailing. However, he learnt that Rothermere was 'in trouble with certain advertisers, who had not liked his support of the blackshirts and in company with many other people had now heard of the tobacco business and liked it still less'.

Two days before the split, Mosley spoke at Portsmouth on the theme of 'No Compromise' with the message that Fascists would never tarnish their creed by working with Conservatives. There followed a contrived exchange of letters heralding Rothermere's withdrawal. In a letter to Mosley on 14 July he confirmed he was not interested in Fascist ideology, but also pointed to a possible resumption of co-operation: 'You have a unique gift of personal appeal, and the assistance which I have rendered you was given in the hope that you would be prepared to ally yourself with the Conservative forces to defeat Socialism at the next and succeeding elections . . . I do not see why we should not come together on the foregoing lines.' Mosley responded that 'you are in accord with many aspects of our policy, such as the strong maintenance of the British Empire, notably in India, and the creation of a British air force second to none in the world'. But 'you are a Conservative, we are fascists'. The break with Mosley, however, was not final. That weekend Rothermere filled the *Dispatch* with pro-Fascist articles, which Collin Brooks thought missed the point, namely 'that to answer Communist brutality by Fascist brutality in the middle of an orderly audience of peaceful citizens is to undermine the whole theory of the modern State'.

The German Press Attaché FitzRandolph forwarded to Berlin copies of the Rothermere/Mosley exchange. The uncertainty surrounding his position and the 'relatively insignificant power that Mosley could bring to the political scene make it necessary to maintain our principle of indifference towards the

BUF. This position could well be advisable in view of the sneering critical attitude of the press at the present; the same view would have to consider a "private" approach towards the Fascists (Reichspartei Day – Nuremberg) as not appropiate with regard to timing.' Bismarck said Rothermere was 'trying to show a rapprochement with the Mosley policy; the subsequent exchange of correspondence was to demonstrate to the English readers the relationship of R. to M. and M. to R. since this relationship seems not always to be properly appreciated'. The Nazis were informed by 'reliable sources' that 'the Jews threatened to remove their advertisements' and Rothermere had 'quickly to decide between the future of his newspaper and expressing his political opinions. He decided for the continuation of his newspaper.' Protests had come from the Jewish firms, Lyons and the Carrera Tobacco Company.

Mosley claimed Jewish advertisers had exerted pressure 'at the point of an economic gun'. Hugh Cudlipp agreed they had become uneasy and 'the Jews provided a large slice of his income'. Esmond Harmsworth had warned the economics were unsustainable and that readers were affronted by the Mosley campaign. He was alarmed by the circulation decline but 'had given up trying to understand his father's motives'. MI5 referred to Rothermere's decision as 'a matter of business, no doubt'.

Mosley believed the dispute could have been settled if Rothermere had stood firm. He had asked him what his brother, Northcliffe, would have done. He would have said, Mosley claimed, 'One more word from you and the *Daily Mail* placards tomorrow will carry the words "Jews threaten British Press". You will have no further trouble.' Rothermere felt he was 'asking too much, not for himself but for others who depended on him'. In the *World's Press News* he was asked whether his support of the BUF had been a crusade or an incident like the *Mail*'s standard bread campaign involving Mosley's grandfather. He replied, 'Definitely an incident.'

In his letter to Mosley Rothermere said he had 'made it quite clear in my conversations with you that I never could support any movement with an anti-semitic bias'. Mosley said he was 'not prepared to relax our attitude towards Jews' because – using the Chesterton research – '80 per cent of the convictions for physical attacks on Fascists were pronounced on Jews, while the Jewish community represents only 0.6 per cent of the population'. Chesterton recalled there was 'a sigh of relief when his Lordship repented in haste and celebrated his dropping of the Blackshirts with two leading articles full of ridiculous praise for the Jews'. As soon as the break was made, Mosley mounted a campaign of anti-Semitism. On 20 July the *Blackshirt* linked socialism with Jewish finance and 'the unsavoury Oriental'. Bismarck reported that within the BUF anti-Semitism was 'unquestionably developing apace'.

Robert Forgan opposed anti-Semitism as tactically unwise. He cultivated through the January Club prominent Jews, including Gladstone's biographer

Sir Philip Magnus-Allcroft, who was 'not quite the only one of my faith to have embraced the Club', though H. L. Nathan, a Jewish Liberal MP for Bethnal Green, did speak out against Mosley. During the summer Forgan had talks with BoD Deputy Dr J. Blonstein, and Chairman of the BoD's Parliamentary Committee Sir Lionel Cohen (later Lord Justice of Appeal), to thrash out a Jewish–Fascist agreement. Joyce claimed the BUF was offered £100,000 (£3.4m) by Edward Barron, son of the proprietor of Carreras, to end its anti-Semitism, but without consulting Mosley he rejected it with 'an impolite message'. Given Carreras's role in the *Mail* boycott, this is not implausible. When James Lees-Milne attended Mosley's funeral, Magnus-Allcroft told him Mosley had approached his cousin, Lionel Cohen, with an offer to call off the persecution of the Jews for a suitable payment.

On 28 July Forgan met BoD President Harold Laski, who thought him a 'pathetic figure'. Convinced the anti-Semitic infection of the BUF was irreversible, he said he could no longer work with Mosley as he visualized a Fascist state assuming 'a different form to that adumbrated by Mosley in his speeches'. He admitted the BUF was collapsing but refused to provide details. MI5 claimed a rapid decline and high turnover in membership from a peak of 50,000 in July. However, Olympia had increased numbers because 'people thought the reports of the meeting were exaggerated' and after Rothermere's desertion people realized Mosley was not going over to Conservatism, though events in Germany harmed the movement and Olympia eventually proved to be a decisive setback.

In Olympia's aftermath and only six months after retiring from the army, the acclaimed military theorist Major-General J. F. C. Fuller wrote to Mosley, 'This is the worst day of your life; you should always join a man in his worst moment.' He was 'glad the position between you and Rothermere has been cleared up. The press is valuable, but its danger is that it always aims at mastership, and that its principles are regulated by dividends. As it can only create great emotions and not great movements it cannot destroy a great movement. Every great movement starts off in a minority of one. The strength of a new movement is in indirect proportion to the resistance offered to it.'

Fuller – the BUF's most important recruit – had been placed on the retired list following differences with the War Office over the future of mechanized operations. He ridiculed the army's amateurishness. It was widely held that Fuller and his mentor, Lord Ironside, were the two 'most conceited men in the Army'. Ironside, who had supported Mosley when he stood for Parliament in 1918, considered him 'straight and fearless' but military strategist Basil Liddell Hart held that his inability to tolerate criticism was the reason for his attraction to Fascism, which brought out 'all that was unsavoury and unappealing in both his character and his thought'.

A misplaced intellectual, who admired Carlyle and Cromwell, and wrote poetry in the style of Swinburne, Fuller's main friends were Douglas Jerrold of Eyre and Spottiswoode (publisher of his books) and Francis Yeats-Brown. He was intrigued by Aleister Crowley and disillusioned with democracy. His attraction to Gurdjieff's Law of Three was reflected in his belief in the threefold order. He shared Mosley's interest in Spengler, social imperialism, Mackinder's geopolitics and a vision of a technocratic elite. He had, Mosley noted, an 'exaggerated intolerance of bureaucracy of any kind' and believed in the 'fallacy spread by social imperialism that if the administrators were changed, then a more efficient policy could be introduced'. Fuller's prime concern was liberating man's mind from the 'mechanical monster it has created ... to intellectual and spiritual ends'.

Fuller lectured to the New Britain group, political dissenters who held Communist, Fascist and pacifist attitudes, who were pro-European. Dissatisfied by its vagaries, he concluded Fascism had come to stay and was admitted to Mosley's inner circle as his adviser on military matters; he would have been Minister of War had Mosley come to power. Fuller persuaded Liddell Hart, who joined the January Club, to visit the Black House to dine with Mosley. Liddell Hart eventually became repelled by the enthusiasm for violent action and, after the shock of the Night of the Long Knives, considered the BUF absolutely Nazi and would have nothing to do with it.

Rothermere's support had brought in public schoolboys, ex-officers and Tories, but unifying them into the movement proved too big a task for Mosley. They wore 'boss-class' black shirts and privileged members such as Lord Erroll had their BUF badge copied in silver and ate in a separate canteen. Special Branch reported unrest among the rank and file who grumbled about 'class-conscious officers'. When Mosley threw a ball, it was at venues where they felt out of place. On 27 June a Blackshirt Cabaret Ball was held at the Prince's Galleries in Piccadilly, hosted by Lady Mosley. The Blackshirts' Dance Band provided the entertainment for the lords and ladies.

The Policy and Propaganda section, controlled by socialists under Risdon, aimed to put 'reality into the Socialist phrases in the Party's programmes' but clashed with the organizational wing, which was supported by the influx of ex-officers. This conservative side eventually stripped Risdon of authority and proceeded 'to weed out any and every speaker who showed even the faintest tinge of "Red"'. Frequent purges took place, with propaganda officers carpeted by Box for indiscipline.

On 15 July, at a rally in Newcastle, John Marchbanks, General Secretary of the National Union of Railwaymen, accused the BUF of being active in the armed forces, compiling blacklists on its rivals and foes, and for 'assembling in the guise of a military machine with the object of overthrowing by force the constitutional government of the country'. He based his claims on the testimony of Charles Dolan, who had approached him in April, disillusioned with the BUF's paramilitarism. With his loss of faith, Dolan transferred his loyalty to Methodism, eventually becoming a pastor. After his defection he was approached by Alex Miles, a former ILP colleague, who offered him £100 (£3,400) to emigrate to Canada; an offer authorized by higher officials. Predictably, Mosley sued Marchbanks for slander. The case was not heard until February 1936. Mosley won but the jury only awarded him a farthing in damages and recommended he pay legal costs. The judge stressed the technical nature of the decision, adding that Marchbanks's remarks were so close to the truth as to be fair comment.

The movement, wrote Richard Bellamy, had drawn to itself 'almost every unstable person and adventurer'. G. S. Gerault admitted some 'hoped to cash in in a big way eventually out of victory, but meanwhile were content with chicken-feed from petty theft and mean little rackets'. Others exploited the lax security and opportunities for criminal activity. Brixton's branch was organized as a brothel and Newcastle's secretary was convicted of burglary. People, Bellamy recalled, 'felt that they could not afford to be associated with the types congregated at the local headquarters. In these spots nothing remained but a bad odour, still lingering three or four years later.'

Gerault sent Mosley a negative report. Although his policy on the Jewish question had been 'very sound and appealed much to the public mind', he was now 'going definitely in for the persecution of Jews on German lines, and that has produced very grave repercussions'. There was a 'feeling that the leader is being jockeyed either knowingly or unknowingly into an impossible position by Joyce; and there are those who say that he is now, to all intents and purposes, the Movement'. Mosley wrote in the margin, 'Joyce!!!' MI5, aware Joyce was trying to supplant the BUF's Chief of Staff, relied on an optimistic appreciation of him by Maxwell Knight, who said that although he was a fanatical anti-Semite with a 'mental balance not equal to his intellectual capacity', it was unlikely anything could 'shake his basic patriotism'.

It was becoming clear, Kell reported, that with Olympia Mosley 'suffered a check which is likely to prove decisive'. He was 'not making progress anywhere' and BUF membership was 'nearer 5,000 than 10,000' (later confirmed by Forgan). January Club members resented Mosley's efforts to dominate the Club and, according to MI5, those 'erstwhile members who had been pleased to be identified with Mosley when the climate had been mild' now scrambled to safety. In rural areas enthusiasm for the BUF faded among farmers once the tithe war ceased to be an issue and it lost support in the middle-class areas of the South and the East. In addition, it lacked funds.

With Rothermere back on side, Chancellor Austen Chamberlain's key supporter, Joseph Ball, approached editors requesting they deprive Mosley of publicity. He had been attached during the war to MI5 and, as a full-time officer, handled subversion and espionage against the armed services. He played a significant role in the Zinoviev story and in 1924 – still an MI5 officer – joined Tory Central Office to look after propaganda and intelligence. He subsequently directed the Conservative Research Department and from 1934 ran the National Publicity Bureau, a Tory front which campaigned for the National government. The Bureau's pro-appeasement policy was run through the anti-Semitic *Truth* magazine, which Ball used to attack Chamberlain's critics. Although staff supported Mosley, *Truth* 'feared and distrusted Hitler and loathed Nazism', which accounted for its ambivalent attitude to the BUF.

Inspired by an article in Lord Lothian's *The Round Table* and another in *Harper's* magazine, which suggested Mosley's prominence was due to the 'unmistakable alliance between would-be-dictators and desperate industrial-patriots' and to Conservative fear of socialism, MI5 speculated on whether the economic situation suited Fascist growth or, reflecting a view held in industrial circles, that economic failure could lead to socialism. It stressed conditions were very different from those on the Continent but if economic recovery collapsed, 'apprehension in regard to socialist progress' might 'induce a number of leading industrialists to contribute large sums, in order to keep the movement in being'. With this in mind, Ball met with the heads of ICI, Morris Cars, Courtaulds and the League of Industry, which had once courted Mosley.

Ball helped provide a conduit for funds from executives 'precluded from subscribing to any party organisation'. The aim was to accommodate industrialists tempted to back Mosley with promises of sympathetic concern for their interests, including increased rearmament spending. Morris transferred his support away from Mosley and his biggest donation of the period – £75,000 (£2.5m) – went to the Bureau. Ball received a KBE for his propaganda work in Tory constituencies.

Those disillusioned Tories who had supported Mosley returned to the fold. They liked the excitement of the Blackshirts but were frightened by the violence. Britain, notes Martin Blinkhorn, generally lacked an authoritarian tradition and its 'social order was considerably less convulsed' than on the Continent. Industrialists also returned to a Tory Party they saw as the best defence against a unionized and politicized working class with whom they were perpetually in conflict. Despite corporatism's promise of breaking the violence of faction, they refused to put their faith in the 'superior wisdom of an authoritarian leader', whose prediction of an apocalyptic economic collapse failed to materialize.

Mosley recognized conditions were more favourable in Italy and Germany, where the severe depression led to mass unemployment. The British economy performed much better than he envisioned and unemployment never reached Continental levels. He blamed the lack of progress on this factor. National and personal income increased by 20 per cent and industrial production by 46 per cent in the period 1932–7. The reason for recovery was partly due to an upturn in the economic cycle and the surge in house building, fuelled by a 'cheap money' policy. 'The whole thing is economic,' Mosley later wrote, 'and if the war hadn't come the economic situation would have returned and in my view today quite calmly and in retrospect we should undoubtedly have won.'

Unemployment was a regional problem with higher rates north and west of the Humber–Severn line. Except for some success with its cotton campaigns, Fascism's main centres were south and east of this line. Mosley launched another cotton campaign at the Floral Hall in Southport, where he repeated his plans for Lancashire. A letter to the *Cotton Factory Times* said he 'has promised to put you on the same footing as your Italian and German counterparts. What more can you ask him for? Hail Mosley – the man with a mission.' Apart from Lancashire, he made little impact in areas of high unemployment such as central Scotland or north-east England. Cumings was sent to organize in south Wales, but soon left the BUF.

The unemployed voted for Labour's reformism rather than radical solutions. The depression 'blunted rather than sharpened the edge of social discontent', which was also a problem for the Right's *bête noire* and alleged 'Communist' sympathizer Sir Stafford Cripps. In the autumn Wyndham Lewis did a drawing of Cripps, wearing 'steel-rimmed spectacles and a frosty curl to the lip', which appeared in the *London Mercury* next to a portrait of Mosley in Blackshirt uniform, with projecting jaw, under the ironic byline 'Two Dictators'. 'The Governess and the Gorilla', Mosley commented when he saw them. He found Lewis 'agreeable but touchy'. He recalled they had 'considerable mental sympathy but I would certainly not claim he agreed with me in all things'. Lewis considered men were essentially weak and craved authority, not freedom. 'We should naturally seek the most powerful and stable authority that can be devised.' Lewis's disdain for ordinary humanity led him to advocate Fascism until 1938, but though he contributed to the journals he was too individualistic to join the BUF.

Ball closely liaised with newsreel companies and persuaded them not to film BUF demonstrations; the unofficial ban remained in place for the rest of the decade. Mosley had written to BBC Director-General Sir John Reith asking 'to be allowed to participate with other political movements in all future series of wireless talks', but the BBC imposed an unofficial ban on extremist views, and denied both Fascists and Communists, as well as independent mavericks such as Churchill, wireless time. Neither Mosley nor the Communists were allowed to broadcast for another thirty years.

Despite setbacks, Blackshirts 'worthy of the cause stuck it out', Mosley recalled, 'and found that the almost universal hostility put more iron into their souls'. There was a new emphasis on struggle. During July Nancy Mitford wrote that Mosley had 'the character, the brains, the courage, and the determination to lift this country from the slough of despond in which it has for too long sheltered, to a utopia. Soon the streets will echo beneath the feet of the black battalions, soon we will show the world that the spirit of our forefathers is yet alive within us, soon we shall be united by the sacred creed striving as one man for the Greater Britain.' *Blackshirt* editor Bill Leaper observed that the movement's spirit was 'more powerful, the character is more steel-like, the determination to keep itself unsullied is stronger than ever'.

16

The Nazis

During the summer of 1934 MI5 reported that Mosley had been making 'crude attempts' to establish relations with other Continental Fascist movements. These were largely secret as he was concerned how such contacts might be viewed by those who were hostile to foreign ideas and, in particular, the radicalism and racism of the Nazis.

An early visitor to London was José Antonio Primo de Rivera, son of the late Spanish dictator. An Andalusian playboy with a social conscience, José founded Falange Española, basing it on Italian Fascism rather than his father's authoritarian model. It appealed to students with its call for national violence but was largely insignificant and survived on Italian funds. Léon Degrelle's Belgian Rexists were also student-based but developed a broad base through yellow press exposure of scandals. A friend of Bill Allen, Degrelle met Mosley at the Allen family home. He was, Martin Conway notes, 'a man of great charm whose personal magnetism disarmed even the most suspicious of opponents'. At different times the Rexists – in receipt of Italian subsidies – were Catholic authoritarians, Poujadist populists and National Socialists.

Another recipient of Mussolini's funds and Mosley visitor was a former Norwegian General Staff officer who had resided at the British legation in Moscow and was regarded as a British Secret Service agent. Minister of Defence Vidkun Quisling was an anti-Bolshevist, who during 1931 underwent a political transition from liberalism to National Socialism and founded the National Union. He promoted a racist interpretation of the Nordic race as part of a grand coalition beginning with Great Britain and Scandinavia. He was 'neither particularly German nor Italian in sympathy. Culturally he was above all pro-British.' Norwegian Greyshirt Terje Ballsrud had talks in London with Mosley and in Dublin with Eoin O'Duffy. With a flair for publicity, former police commissioner O'Duffy set up the Blueshirts as a section within the Fine Gael Party to promote the reunion of Ireland, oppose Communism and alien influence in national affairs, and support corporatism.

An acquaintance of Commandant Allen, O'Duffy admired Mosley and there were rumours that the two were in league to organize Blueshirt units in Northern Ireland. The initiative, however, was disastrous, especially since

Stormont wanted to ban BUF literature. It contributed to O'Duffy's political demise and the collapse of the weakened Ulster Fascists. In the autumn, a faction under Captain Armstrong regrouped as a regional branch of the BUF. With the termination of Rothermere's support, Mosley found little reason to concern himself with either part of Ireland, though he remained hostile to Stormont.

Mosley's most intriguing visitor was Armand Grégoire of the French Françiste. Founded in 1933 by Marcel Bucard, formerly of Action Française, it adopted the trappings of Italian Fascism but was violent and anti-Semitic. They only had 1,500 members and the funding from François Coty – perfume millionaire and publisher – and Mussolini was relatively small. It was too pro-Nazi to win popular support.

Grégoire was described in a French Sûreté report as 'one of the most danger-ous of Nazi spies'. Swarthy, with a duelling scar, he had been born in Metz and was awarded the German Iron Cross during the war. He practised law and was attorney for the German embassy. He wrote in Le Françiste that 'naturally, we hope with all our heart for an alliance with Nazi Germany. We fully realize that this alliance constitutes the only possible means of avoiding the universal corruption of the world.' He represented Ribbentrop, Hess, Goering and later German ambassador Otto Abetz, and acted for Wallis Simpson and dealt with Mosley's affairs in Paris. He had contacts with the BUF and, as a prominent Nazi collaborator, was possibly a conduit for Nazi funds to Mosley.

MI5 kept tabs on Raven Thomson, Mosley's representative to Germany, though they differed on relations with the Nazis over the question of anti-Semitism. Around Mosley there was serious rivalry, which was exacerbated by Nazi meddling. MI5 considered Mosley 'a puffed-up mediocrity, finding difficulty in holding his position in the eyes of colleagues and foreign associ-ates'. He had to balance support for Italian Fascism and Nazism – 'a strategy which accounts in part for his failure to insist on uniform commitment to a central policy'.

According to Eric Drummond, British ambassador in Rome, the Italian press promoted Mosley, whose objective now was to secure a meeting with Hitler. Dr Pfister was a personal friend of Julius Streicher, whose son, Lothar, came to London during August under government restrictions. He told Pfister he would be 'happy to arrange a meeting with Hitler'.

In its second report on 1 August MI5 had no information on Nazi funding though it believed that any such link was likely to derive from the 'close connection between the BUF and Austrian Nazis'. During 1934 Italo-German differences over Austria increased and the failure of Mussolini's meeting with Hitler, and the murder on 25 July of Austrian Chancellor Dollfuss, in which Austrian Nazis attempted a coup in Vienna, created tensions. When Mosley arrived in Rome, he found Mussolini 'in such a rage that none of his associates dared approach him on the subject'. If 'this country of murderers and paederasts were to overrun Europe', it would be the end of civilization. Hitler was a 'sexual degenerate, a dangerous fool' and National Socialism was 'savage barbarism'.

In response to the threat on Italy's border, Mussolini rushed troops to the Brenner Pass. Mosley believed he was even contemplating war. The problem for Mosley was that he was playing both sides. Pfister was intriguing with the Austrian Nazis and his officials had met Otto Skorzeny, later notorious for his special forces exploits.

Pfister was one of the few BUF figures trusted by the leading Nazi in London, Otto Bene, who regarded Mosley as a 'political adventurer of no serious consideration'. Visiting Nuremberg on 4 September, he told Hitler the BUF was a 'powerful movement' but Dundas, Pfister and Thomson were 'more worthy than Mosley of recognition and co-operation'. MI5 considered Joyce a man of 'great energy but not of the calibre to take Sir Oswald's place as leader'. Much of the disruptive factionalism was a result of the rivalry between Joyce and Pfister. An informant to Maxwell Knight, Joyce briefed against Mosley to the Nazis. He was partly responsible for the eclipse of Pfister and suspension for intrigue with Austrian Nazis.

Mosley planned a big rally in Hyde Park against which, for the first time, the Communist Party decided to support a mass anti-Fascist demonstration. Its leaders' main concern, however, remained the 'encroaching Fascism' of the National government. Palme Dutt told Harry Pollitt he was 'right about the danger of seeing only Mosley and not NG. But in fact the danger is a double one. The other danger is to see NG as a whole issue and Mosley as a minor detail . . . What is essential is for our people to see and explain all the time the twofold character of the fascist offensive, both NG and Mosley, and the effective division of labour and INTERPLAY of both.' Though Joe Jacobs was right to maintain that the CP was reluctant to take part in anti-BUF campaigns, this time preparations were undertaken by a Co-ordinating Committee for Anti-Fascist Activities, under the guidance of John Strachey. Such campaigns led to bigger recruitment for the CP and increasing militancy. Mosley's response was to order all BUF branches to attend.

On 9 September in Hyde Park, up to 100,000 people were ranged against the 2,500 Fascists protected by 7,000 police. Mosley let fly at his tormentors: 'Behind the Communist-Socialist mob were Jewish financiers who supply the palm-oil to make them yell.' The police kept the Fascist and anti-Fascist meetings apart and only eighteen people were arrested. Special Branch suggested the crowd came for the political theatre, with the Fascists generally seen as objects of derision. Fascist gatherings were being outnumbered by anti-Fascist crowds which, in London, helped to check the momentum of the BUF.

The *Morning Post* said public interest demanded the government ban such rallies outright. It also suggested, to Mosley's annoyance, that both Communists and Fascists had been intent on turning the rally into a pitched battle, and that only good policing had preserved order. The *Telegraph* declared 'public opinion has sensibly hardened against Mosley during the past three months'. Fascism was seen as a threat both to free speech and public order. Pleased with its success, the CP announced it intended to fight Fascism on a broad United Front. However, Labour Party leaders were unwilling to support it, in the belief that Mosley was overrated and that passive measures denying him publicity were the correct response.

Bismarck reported to Berlin that Hyde Park was 'an absolute fiasco and will not be likely to lend new drive to Mosley's movement which at the moment is losing ground'. Apparently, Mosley was so depressed that Forgan doubted his leader's sanity. However, Bismarck also reported that BUF growth had led to a 'much more serious judgement of the "Fascist danger"'. The Cabinet 'considered it necessary to wage a campaign against fascism. According to certain information available to the embassy, the press lords . . . jointly agreed to throw down the gauntlet to fascism . . . the press attacks on Germany in the last few months, stems from this moment.'

That autumn Baba planned to go to the Nazi Congress at Nuremberg, and sent Mosley a picture postcard of Hitler's house with the query, 'Is Mrs G still at Denham?' In fact, on 11 September Diana, Unity and Tom Mitford attended the Congress, where they made friends with Streicher's youngest son, Elmar. Wearing a black shirt, leather gauntlets and a BUF badge, Unity said she believed in uniting the Nordic races: 'Sooner or later we'll all be fascists.' Back in London, Diana and Mosley formulated a plan to promote his cause.

Around this time MI5 became suspicious of Diana and placed her under surveillance whenever she travelled abroad. It knew she had visited Rome, to 'study fencing', but her studies had 'thrust her into the society of fascists'. She went back to Munich, rented an apartment and enrolled on a German language course. Diana claimed her activities were 'entirely connected with business and not at all with propaganda', but they were inextricably intertwined.

The next stage in the launching of an anti-Semitic campaign were Mosley's speeches in Manchester and at the Albert Hall. On 29 September 3,000 protesters, including Young Communist League militants, opposed 1,500 Fascists. Mosley was protected by the lake at Belle Vue, with his Blackshirts assembled on the dance floor in front of it. Searchlights picked out anti-Fascists and fire engines with water cannon were on standby. When Mosley tried to speak, he was greeted by shouts of 'Down with Fascists'. Despite powerful amplifiers, a *Manchester Guardian* journalist, 'sitting in the midst of Sir

Oswald's personal bodyguard within three yards of where he was speaking', was barely able to hear a word.

Mosley made a venomous attack on 'these Jewish rascals'. They were the 'sweepings of the continental ghettos, hired by Jewish financiers'. Drawing on the Chesterton report, he attacked 'the organised corruption of Press, Cinema and Parliament which is called democracy but which is ruled by alien Jewish finance'. He referred to the 'yelpings of a Yiddish mob' and 'foreign Yiddish faces'. Mosley used all his theatrical tricks to make an impression but, according to an observer, 'without any effective sound he appeared like a demented marionette. Defeat stared him in the face and he knew it, as did his audience which slunk away as soon as the police bodyguard was removed. The humiliation of the fascists was complete.' The only sound was the singing of 'bye bye Blackshirt' to the tune of 'bye bye blackbird'.

Manchester passed off with little disturbance, Bismarck reported. Berlin underlined his comment that 'the anti-Jewish attitude of the English fascists is expressed in ever stronger terms'. He did not know if Mosley's utterances 'come from his own convictions or whether he is pushed this way by the rank and file of his comrades', but the new stance 'brought about a more unfriendly attitude in the whole of the press', which barely mentioned the meeting. In October MI5 decided the BUF no longer constituted a serious political threat.

Grandi's influence over Mosley concerned officials. Box was credited by Special Branch with confirming Mussolini's funding when he commented it was 'a pity that Rome was now deciding Mosley's policy' and that 'the man who pays the piper calls the tune'. Grandi wrote to Irene hoping to deepen his relationship with Baba. She was aware of her sister's 'dominating ways and influence' over Mosley, whose adoration of Baba was 'tempered with tenderness and the yearning to control this love and not to mar it all'.

On 12 October, Baba attended a Blackshirt Ball at the Gargoyle Club, whose owner, the Hon. David Tennant, wanted to promote the club. Mosley lent his support to a programme of épée fencing with Scottish champion Charles de Beaumont, which attracted 'Britain's loveliest women', including Miss Diana Churchill, Ladies Mary Lygon, Mary St Clair Erskine and Sylvia Ashley who, the *Express* reported, 'applauded the English Hitler as he cut and thrust, parried and returned with immense fire and exquisite precision'. The Jackson twins, Derek, who married Pamela Mitford, and Vivian had a ringside table.

The Jacksons were rich and intelligent. Their parents died when they were young and newspaper magnate Lord Ridell became their guardian. Derek was recruited by Professor Lindemann for the Clarendon Laboratory at Oxford, specializing in spectroscopy, and Vivian was an astrophysicist. Impulsive, during the fencing the twins heckled, egging each other on. Mosley told them

to keep quiet but the heckling turned into a political argument and they invited
him to 'come outside'. At five foot eight, they were no match for Mosley's
six-foot-two frame. The situation was defused by Tennant with champagne:
'If not oil, then let wine be poured.' They all shook hands and became friends.
Derek often expressed support for Mosley, though his reactionary politics had
strict limits.

During the autumn Forgan was sent to inspect Scottish branches as a way of
getting him away from headquarters. His wife had recently attempted suicide.
He was out of his depth in the BUF with its discipline and his administrative
methods were 'more akin to those of an army orderly room than to a political
office'. Officials disliked him for failing to take them into his confidence and
his choice of subordinates. He was a 'kind man, who lacked judgement of
character'.

On 8 October Fuller delivered his 'Report on the organisation of the BUF',
which was described as chaotic. They 'cannot fail to succeed if certain radical
changes are made in organisation and discipline' but if they were not carried
out, 'either the movement will decline or it will break up into hostile factions'.
'Blackshirtism' was developing into a 'Frankenstein monster'. It appealed 'to
the young and inexperienced, but if it is unchecked, it will lose more votes in
the next elections than anything else'. Britain was an 'old country, very solid,
stable and . . . their instincts are against violent change. Most of the Blackshirts
are too young to realise this. In a revolutionary country they would be right,
but in a conservative country they are wrong.' Fuller wanted their enthusiasm
channelled into winning seats but doubted 'whether a single seat will be won
in 1935 or 1936'.

BUF propaganda – Forgan's responsibility – lacked both 'art and common-
sense'. John Strachey wrote that Forgan 'will never be able to organise the
propaganda of the British fascists with the reckless brilliance that Goebbels
achieved in Germany'. Fuller wanted 'to concentrate propaganda on potential
districts which show a marked Fascist inclination'. Fascism should be presented in a British guise, with foreign influences 'rigorously exorcised and
every endeavour made to register it acceptable to British traditions'.

The movement had been pushed into a militarism with the result that its
political organization had been superimposed upon its defence organization.
Fuller wanted this reversed with the Defence Force 'to automatically slide
from a semi-military to a fully political footing'. Mosley agreed to it being
kept as an elite propaganda instrument but Fuller warned the existence of the
BUF was precarious as it was 'a one-man show'. Without Mosley it would lose
its finance and disintegrate. They were 'sadly lacking in able men'. Fredericks
observed that Mosley was 'surrounded so thickly by professional political
racketeers that he only knows what they want him to know. Of latter days he

has become almost as inaccessible as the Great Mogul. It is quite impossible for an ordinary member to get anywhere near him.' Even his mother found it difficult because of the intrigue: 'Insubordination from people whose word you preferred to take to mine and who would disappear from the movement by your instructions.' Fuller wanted a triumvirate to discuss important issues: headquarters should be 'a Corporate State in embryo. It is the acorn of the eventual oak.'

It was difficult for Mosley to implement Fuller's report, as he was overwhelmed by internal problems. It was one reason why, on 12 October, Forgan resigned, ostensibly on the grounds of ill health. Differences in philosophy, coupled with his organizational and financial failings, were noted by the Home Office as reasons for his resignation. Internal rivalries dated back to the spring when Box, Beckett and Risdon attempted to reshape the BUF along party lines. However, Hawkins's military faction resisted the restructuring and during the summer a military-style Court of Inquiry, comprising Captain Reavely, Major Lucas and P. G. Taylor, was established to stamp out factionalism.

The resignation of Forgan, who was popular with the left wing, caused a revolt that nearly split the movement. It was led by Charles Bradford of the Industrial Propaganda Department, who 'plotted to take over the movement by force and oust those officers who had crawled in during the boosting period of the *Mail*'. Mosley 'flew into a tearing rage and threatened to shoot them in the guts'. At the October court martial – presided over by Piercy, Hawkins and Taylor – Bradford and Frederick Knowles were accused of threatening deputy Chief of Staff Archibald Findlay and conspiring to 'seize the building and make demands to Mosley that certain officers be dismissed'. Risdon was said to be one of the disenchanted Blackshirts involved in the 'subversive plot'. He was nursing a grievance because people who had joined the movement after he did had been given prominent positions.

Mosley summoned staff to the club room, where the I Squad was armed with lead tubing. Two hundred Blackshirts stood by, while Mosley and 'his satellites considered how to deal with the mutineers'. News of the upheaval reached provincial branches, which voted in favour of the rebels. When Mosley entered the room, the atmosphere was 'sullen and brooding. A spark would have set light to the tinder of discontent already smouldering.' Members were aware of rumours about Forgan's resignation but Mosley convinced them he 'had not left the ranks for ever and would return when health permitted'. Being financially dependent on Mosley, the mutineers realized 'if they went too far there was considerable danger of them being without jobs'. He assured them that 'those who march with me to Fascist victory shall have their reward'. The revolt was crushed and the ringleaders were later expelled.

Special Branch reported that Mosley had decided 'to purge the movement of undesirable elements', including 'ex-members of the Communist Party and

National Unemployed Workers Movement' whose presence hindered 'the recruiting of the better class of citizen'. The movement was beset by scandal. Piercy was engaged in an affair with Joyce's wife, who was pregnant. While women were expelled for sexual misconduct, Piercy was reappointed Chief Inspector of Branches, away from London, to avoid any scandal. Six months later he left the BUF

One result was P. G. Taylor's promotion. He assumed the title 'Industrial Adviser' with responsibilities for the disbanded FUBW. Miles commented that if this 'means that one controls a number of people who burrow into organisations such as Trade Unions . . . so that the controller of these ferrets may "advise" his employers of their intentions and actions, then, of course Mr Taylor was rightly described'. Taylor oversaw the shift in BUF policy to 'permeation' of the unions. The burrowers included agents provocateurs.

Such events highlighted the contradictions between Mosley's ideas on leadership and his delegation of administrative functions. He had previously said Fascism's leadership 'may be individual or preferably in the case of the British character, a team with clearly allocated functions and responsibility', but in the 1934 edition of the *Greater Britain* now wrote that 'undoubtedly single leadership in practice proves the more effective instrument'. His intellectual stature and the lack of any credible alternative figure ensured he had little coherent opposition but only retained consistent support from inexperienced political mavericks.

MacNeill Weir knew Mosley to be an extremist but thought 'his vaulting ambition accompanied by a lofty pride, seems to have completely changed his character. He would have been saved from this by a wise restraint.' He was unable to accept criticism and operated in 'an autocratic fashion where he brought the tablets down from the mountain to his adoring supporters'. His disciples' adulation, however, fed his arrogance and 'led him to excesses of pompous ostentation'. Blackshirt hero-worship was religious in its intensity. John Charnley recalled meeting Mosley: 'I saluted him in the customary fashion and stood to attention. Even to write of this episode after fifty years still fills me with emotion. Then he stood up, looked at me with those penetrating eyes, which seemed to be alive with electrifying sparks, shook me vigorously by the hand and said, "Charnley, I need men like you." From that moment I have been his man.'

The devotion was reciprocated by Mosley, who never believed a Blackshirt was ever at fault. At the end of a rally he would gather them together and ask for further sacrifices. He would stretch out his arms and cry, 'You are blood of my blood, spirit of my spirit!'

'Crikey, has the old man gone off his head?' whispered E. D. Randall, author of the BUF marching song. Randall represented a cultish faction, who saw themselves as engaged in a spiritual revolution.

Mosley argued that the Fascist 'transformed his own life into the new man ... free from the trammels of the past'. To become a Fascist was to be stripped of ego boundaries and thus become absorbed into a regenerated national community. The 'post-Fascist utopians, such as Randall and Thomson, despised modern values and sought a total spiritual revolution', though their criticism of bourgeois decadence 'paled before their hatred of Marxist decadence'. They demanded the liberation of the race from 'materialism and from the repression of natural tendencies'. Randall called for 'youth to leave the unreality of cities for the reality of cosmic harmony ... for the truths of Blood and Spirit; to return to the life of the soil and sun'. This implied ridding England of the Jews.

On 28 October the BUF held a rally at the Albert Hall. Rumour spread that Mosley was 'going to attack the "Yids"'. There had been some discussion beforehand about the speech's content, which revealed the influence of Chesterton and Fuller.

Fuller wrote to Mosley that 'the Jews cannot destroy Fascism unless Fascists create a fulcrum from which the Jews can operate their final lever. This fulcrum is anti-semitism in such force as will lead to a popular outing in their favour.' These sentences were underlined by Mosley with the admission that he was 'in favour of putting the onus of aggression on to the Jews' since it 'can be shown ... that the Jew is the aggressor'. Mosley highlighted the statement that 'what the big Jew yearns for, that Fascists will knock little Jews on the head, so that non-Jewish opinion will be shocked. They will spend millions to exploit this situation.'

Inside the Albert Hall there was an electric atmosphere when Mosley took to the rostrum. He said he had 'encountered things in this country which, quite frankly, I did not believe existed. And one of these is the power of organised Jewry, which is today mobilised against Fascism.' He opposed Jews because they attacked Fascists. Jewish employers victimized Fascist employees and 'big Jews' in advertising frightened off potential Fascist support. In referring to Rothermere he claimed, 'big business men have come to me and said: "I dare not come out for Fascism, or dare not remain with you, because if I did the Jews would ruin me and my business."' These 'big Jews' were more of a menace than the 'sweepings of foreign ghettos' allowed to enter Britain. He said 'a new phase had entered the history of Fascism'. The BUF would fight organized Jewry as 'an unclean, alien influence in our national and imperial life'. It marked 'the end of the sparring with the issue, and the beginning of the real fighting'.

He whipped the audience into a frenzy: 'They have declared in their great folly to challenge the conquering force of the modern age. Tonight we take up that challenge: they will it: let them have it!' The applause lasted fifteen minutes. It was a classic performance in describing a conspiracy 'as far-ranging as ever Rosenberg conceived' and a commitment to anti-Semitism 'as firm as Hitler's'. The BUF was presented with 'the glittering example of the Nazis who had come to power as an avowedly anti-Semitic party'.

Irene had gone out of loyalty to her dead sister, 'in case some awful accident should happen to this new dictator'. She found his anti-Semitism 'terrifying'. Nonetheless, it 'excited terrific applause from packed audiences, whom he could get fighting mad with enthusiasm with the Mosley rhetoric'. Hearing the 'ranting attack on the Jews', Francis Yeats-Brown felt sick but his female companion was thrilled. Prompted by revulsion at the anti-Semitism, he wrote to Wrench on 1 November forecasting the collapse of the January Club. Its social functions had been successful but MI5 wrote off the Club, now chaired by Norman Thwaites, secretary of the Air League. A recent dinner had 'very few persons of note and no young officers'. Thwaites soon afterwards dissolved the Club, which Yeats-Brown welcomed, as it became evident that Mosley saw in the Club a 'ready-made opening for propaganda'.

On 2 November 1934 the *Blackshirt* heralded 'The Leader's Great Clarion Call' and the coming battle between the 'cleansing spirit of Fascism' and organized Jewry. It no longer differentiated between 'good' and 'bad' Jews. They were the 'symbol and source of all evil' and 'organized as a racial minority within the State to conduct a furious agitation with all the force of their great money power, which can have no effect except to drag this country towards war with Germany'.

Reaction in Germany was positive. *Der Stürmer* said Mosley was 'an intrepid fighter' and featured a photograph of a BUF meeting with the comment that he 'has long angered and provoked the Jews'. His Defence Force 'gave the Jews and the Reds a good hiding whenever an opportunity arose'. Bismarck reported to Berlin that Mosley, 'with a frankness not previously heard', had 'turned against the jews'. But the *Mail*, 'mouthpiece of English fascists did not mention the meeting with a single word'. MI5 was not entirely convinced Rothermere had dropped the BUF and believed he still had 'a more than sneaking regard for Mosley' and that the BUF was still a viable political force. On 6 November Robert Bernays mused that even without Rothermere, Mosley had been able to fill the Albert Hall: 'No other politician could come within measure of that . . . It seems to indicate that Hitlerism is not nearly as unpopular as we would like to imagine.'

Mosley and Diana visited Paris, where he bought her a Voisin car, which she drove to Germany to join Unity as press representatives at the Nuremberg Rally. An acquaintance, Rosemary Macindoe, recalled that when Unity saw Jews being beaten up she used to say, 'Jolly good, serves them right, we should go and cheer.' There were jokes about the concentration camps. 'If somebody does anything bad, they said, "We'll send them to Dachau."' The young Macindoe was swept off her feet by Diana's admiration of the Leader, which was shared by Unity, who 'may have been in love with Mosley too'. Diana's flat was visited by SS men from the Brown House with access to its senior officials arranged through Putzi Hanfstaengl.

The BUF's new stance was criticized by Roberto Farinacci, a rabble-rousing journalist on the Fascist Grand Council, for copying Nazi aberrations. He added that the 'trouble with British Fascists was that, though they adopted the black shirt and the Roma salute, they were British patriots first; they opposed Italian claims on Malta [where Italian secret service funds were used to influence the island's elections]'.

Taking Fuller's advice, Mosley concentrated on targeting propaganda on particular groups and regions. Ex-miner and boxer 'Tommy' Moran was sent to south Wales; Beckett concentrated on Tyneside; and rural areas were assiduously wooed. There was an anti-Catholic campaign in Edinburgh and an anti-Protestant one in East Anglia. Late 1934 saw efforts in East London to champion grievances against Jewish immigrants. The manipulation of ethnic hostility and hatred, notes John Brewer, was 'reserved for those areas where it was assumed to have the greatest effect on the host communities'. It was 'cynical opportunism of the worst kind'.

Lancashire was again the centre of attempts to revitalize the movement. In Manchester on 25 November Mosley attacked the government's recent report on India for its toleration of Indian nationalism, its failure to tackle sweated labour and for allowing Japan to swamp Indian markets with cheap cotton goods, the cause of unemployment in Lancashire. Japan was attacked as the 'almost almond-eyed cuckoo'. He wanted trading arrangements with the white dominions to lead, in the long term, to a planned imperial economy. Fuller advocated an Imperial Council to co-ordinate imperial defence.

MI5 recognized that Mosley wanted to turn Lancashire into a Fascist stronghold but dismissed his ideas as weak, though his speeches were 'punctuated with prolonged cheers' when he blamed 'international Jewish finance' for destroying jobs. Bill Risdon had expected support among former ILP colleagues but hostile memories of Mosley ensured he made little progress. The working class remained wedded to the Labour movement and the BUF's main appeal was directed towards the petty bourgeoisie, unorganized sections of the working class and the small independent businessmen. These groups were deemed likely to succumb to the anti-Semitic appeal.

Mosley's emphasis on India impressed the diehards, including Leopold Amery, Sir Edward Grigg and Churchill, and rumours spread that Lord Lloyd was contemplating financing the BUF. In a repeat of the British Fascists' relationship with the Conservatives, Sir Arthur Steel-Maitland MP used Blackshirts to steward a meeting in Brighton, organized by peace lobbyists who were considered by local anti-Fascists as BUF fellow-travellers. Mosley hoped to gain a foothold in ruling circles but they rejected British Fascism 'while continuing to indulge in fantasies regarding the comfortably distant continental variety'. Sir Charles Petrie believed Mosley's 'flirtation with Hitler and Mussolini caused his movement to be regarded as something not far removed from a foreign conspiracy: had he put his followers into blue pullovers instead of black shirts much would have been forgiven him. Then, again, there was grave distrust among the more sober-minded of the implications of his anti-Semitic policy.'

In Kenya the *East African Standard* reported that Joss Erroll had returned 'with a constructive and energetic plan to convert the Colony to the Blackshirt policy'. Elspeth Huxley's mother, Nellie Grant, was at the first meeting in December when he addressed settlers in the Rift Valley. 'Everyone cheered to the echo' what he said. 'British Fascism simply means super-loyalty to the Crown, no dictatorship, complete religious and social freedom, an "insulated Empire" to trade with the dirty foreigner, higher wages, lower costs of living.' When he said Fascism stood for complete freedom, 'you could hear Mary Countess at the other end of the room saying that within five years, Joss will be dictator of Kenya'.

In Zurich on 5 December the neo-Nazi International Union of Nationalisms held a conference, followed by a congress in Berlin. Keller regarded the delegates, who had been invited by Goebbels, as representatives of their peoples rather than their governments. With a slogan, 'Nationalists of all centres, unite!' Keller wanted 'to unite the peoples against the Communist International, which is their mortal enemy'. Mosley avoided the congress, whose British delegates centred on English Mistery and included Michael Beaumont MP, T. P. Cornwallis-Evans, Viscount Lymington and the Marquess of Graham. The IUN lacked a coherent ideology and all that united the disparate groups was anti-Semitism.

Under CAUR's auspices, the Italians held a meeting of their own international at Montreux in Switzerland. Mosley, in the city for a fencing competition, attended in a private capacity. Irish Blueshirt General O'Duffy was elected to its co-ordinating committee, which included Mosley's acquaintances Coselochi (Italy), Clausen (Denmark), Bucard (France) and Quisling (Norway), with the task of establishing an 'Entente de Fascisme Universel' around Mussolini's conception of corporatism. The Congress agreed to Mussolini's moderate policy of 'defensive' anti-Semitism against 'certain Jewish groups in certain places which have installed themselves as in a conquered country, openly or secretly exercising an injurious influence on the material and moral interests in the homeland'. The conflict, however, between Rome and Berlin on the question of anti-Semitism 'exposed the impossibility of a coherent Fascist International'.

On 20 December the German Consul General in Danzig reported that he had met George Pitt-Rivers of the Wessex Agricultural Defence Association and self-confessed Mosleyite. He believed that while Fascism and National Socialism were 'embraced because of the necessity through the lack of any other way out of a confused situation, Britain will have fascism not because it must embrace it but because it wants to'. Pitt-Rivers was 'worried by the increased Jewish population and the control exercised over the press, cinema and the economy, especially banking'. The BUF had grown dramatically in just two years – he claimed 'two million members!' – and he believed Mosley 'will be playing a significant role in the near future', which will 'benefit England's relationship' with Germany.

The Prince of Wales admired the Nazis and established a study group to analyse events in Germany. He was introduced to Mosley in January 1935 by society hostess Lady Cunard, whose drawing room was 'alive, night after night, with excited conversation about the merits and demerits of Mussolini and the Führer'. He questioned him on 'the strength and policy of the BUF. These were explained at length by Mosley.' He later claimed 'Tom would have made a first-rate Prime Minister'.

Emerald Cunard embroiled Edward's lover, the married American socialite Wallis Simpson, in the Nazi connections that dogged her for many years. A favourite courtier was an opera set designer, Gabriel Wolkoff, brother of the late Tsar Nicholas II's naval attaché in London. Admiral Wolkoff had been awarded the Order of the Bath in 1915, in recognition of his services to Britain. The Wolkoffs settled in London, running in South Kensington the Russian Tea Rooms, a centre of anti-Bolshevik intrigue. The Admiral headed a group of anti-Semitic, pro-Nazi White Russian exiles determined to crush the Soviet Union. His daughter Anna, who was naturalized in 1935, was a dressmaker for Princess Marina, who introduced her to Wallis and Pamela Jackson (formerly Mitford). Anna allegedly became a Nazi agent and was of interest to Special Branch.

Treasury stinginess and the Air Ministry's technological conservatism ensured that Britain was 'peculiarly weak in the air'. Fuller's argument that offensive power would increase in the air with a parallel decline of ground forces was adopted by Mosley, who wanted to 'immediately raise the air strength of Britain to the level of the strongest power in Europe'. He was influenced by Fuller's belief that only Fascism could tame the 'mechanical monster' and wrote in mystical terms about air power: 'Not until man has mastered the machine and the machine has mastered material limitations will the soul of man be free to soar beyond the fetters of materialism.'

Enthusiasm for the aeroplane was a right-wing phenomenon. Airmen included wealthy aristocrats associated with aircraft companies such as Geoffrey de Havilland and the Duke of Buccleuch. The Prince of Wales bought a De Havilland Gypsy Moth, which he flew from his private aerodrome in Windsor Great Park. The Air Ministry was overseen by Lord Londonderry, a man known to be sympathetic towards Nazi Germany. *The Aeroplane* was pro-Fascist and anti-Semitic, and deputy editor Geoffrey Dorman took pleasure from young people's interest in aeroplanes, which made them 'good Fascists'. He reported on 'a youth's joy at the sight of a Nazi sign on an aeroplane'.

That Rothermere had not cut his links to Mosley was confirmed when in 1935 he created a National League of Airmen (NLA). He feared that in the coming war, 50,000 enemy aeroplanes, 'laden with bombs and gas, will rise into the air and set off at more than 200 miles an hour to rain destruction on this country'. He spent £50,000 (£1.7 m) on a campaign to 'awaken the country to its dangers and the need for rearmament in the air'. The NLA was headed by Norman Macmillan, former RFC flyer and the *Mail*'s air correspondent, and supported by Fuller, Freddy Guest, the Duke of Westminster and Admirals Sir Murray Sueter and Mark Kerr. Sueter, a wartime naval aviator, belonged to a number of pro-German organizations.

On 23 January Rothermere arranged a meeting with Mosley, along with his newspaper executives, including Brooks, Brittain, McWhirter and Sir George Sutton. Brooks found Mosley was 'less aggressive than one imagined – much more stalwart in build. He dominates a table, but not unpleasantly.' At this meeting, with Mosley centre stage, the 'League was practically formed'. That Rothermere was interested in a wider political agenda was evident from a letter he sent to Lloyd George two days later. 'I am quite sure that right-wing politics are going to rule this country very soon. The right-wing movement has captured Italy and Germany and is capturing France. Come out very strongly on India and air armaments and I believe at the end of a couple of years you will be the leader of the Conservative Party and once more Prime Minister.'

The NLA was supported by *The Aeroplane*'s editor C. G. Grey: 'Thanks largely to Adolf Hitler and Signor Mussolini, we are now well on the way towards building up an Air Force which in due course will enable us to help them and the United States to meet the real enemies of civilisation, the Russians and the Japanese. Perhaps I should say enemies of the White race, or human sub-species as Prof. Huxley would have us say.' Such views, and Mosley's attack on Japan during the Lancashire cotton campaign, led Japanese Foreign Minister Hirota to instruct the ambassador in London, Matsudaira Tsuneyoshi, to monitor the BUF. He wired Tokyo that it was 'quite newly established so political influences in and out of the country is esteemed not large at this stage. Ideology: 1) Absolute loyalism to Nation, King. 2) England as No. 1.'

MI5 told the Home Secretary, Sir Russell Scott, that the BUF 'has failed almost everywhere'. Where it 'seemed to have roots in this country, these roots now appear very much frailer and to have been kept alive only by artificial means'. It was 'for all practical purposes dependent on foreign funds'. In

February 1935 the PM was told BUF weekly expenditure was £8,225 (£300,000). The Home Office estimated the true figure for total annual expenditure at between £40,000 (£1.36m) and £80,000 (the latter was close to the truth). MI5 believed that without such funds, British Fascism would have ceased to exist. Mosley 'is, in fact, reported to have sent a message to Mussolini to that effect'.

The BUF was not in receipt of Nazi funds but Mosley was in regular contact with Joachim 'von' Ribbentrop, who 'had been in London and in touch with us even before he came to power'. Having spurned Foreign Office channels, Hitler improvised. Ribbentrop set up the Dienststelle Ribbentrop or 'Buro' under Rudolf Hess's secretariat to prove that Nazi methods were superior to those of traditional diplomacy. Special Branch reported that Otto Karlowa had 'completed' the Nazification of German organizations in Britain.

A former wine merchant who impressed Hitler with claims to contacts in London's politicial and social circles, Ribbentrop was a self-styled 'England expert'. He regularly sent Hitler a précis of the British press, which on 14 January included a *Mail* article – 'possibly the best to appear in the British press' – on the Saar plebiscite, which returned the region to Germany. Two days later a wireless broadcast from the Saar sounded to Yeats-Brown 'like the paean of triumph of the new world – keen and clear and purposeful – nationalistic, patriotic, romantic, over the turgid hypocrisies of the old order. But God save us from Mosley in this country! He is no good.' Ribbentrop included Mosley's *Despatch* article, 'Why I want friendship with Germany'.

Hitler forebade spying in Britain because, if discovered, 'it would endanger his grand policy. The tidbits of information that espionage might bring in were not worth this risk.' Ribbentrop created Information Post III, using unconventional diplomats, but it did not engage in espionage. He gained access to Mosley through the geopolitical thinker Albrecht Haushofer. At the behest of Goebbels, his son Karl visited London 'to test the feelings of leading politicians and their reactions as well as to put the German viewpoint'.

With the BUF drawing closer to the Nazis, Mussolini sent his own emissary to assess whether his annual subsidy of £86,000 (£2.9 m) was a worthwhile investment, with membership dropping to 5,000 and no sign of the 'strict disciplinarian, authoritarian, centralised character of mass movements'. Policy was made by the Policy Directorate, whose membership was fluid, depending on the management of internal power.

BUF leadership was divided into mutually hostile cliques. The two most influential factions favoured an electoral strategy with a view to contesting parliamentary seats at a general election. However, they remained divided and a perpetual battle raged in the Directorate between the 'politicals' and the 'bureaucrats'. The central issue was whether resources should go to building up the organization or to mounting propaganda. The dispute was between

those such as Hawkins, Box and Dundas, who supported a military organization with an emphasis on disciplined marches, and those who wanted to
convert the masses to Fascist ideology. The second faction of Joyce, Beckett,
Thomson and Chesterton hoped a socialist government would come to power
and provide them with 'an opportunity to lead a reaction'. They were a distinct
elite and, as 'intellectuals', were in conflict with the autocratic Hawkins, who
put a higher value on reliability.

The doctrinal Fascists considered Mosley too cautious and advocated
uncompromising anti-Semitism. The black shirt would be retained as a symbol
of virile, heroic struggle. They wanted to build a popular movement in the
factories, with the goal of electoral success. Under Box, Beckett and Risdon
plans were drawn up for election agents and propaganda officers. Like Fuller,
Box favoured the development of conventional party campaigning and
opposed Blackshirt 'physical force' methods and Joyce's Jew baiting. MI5's
Maxwell Knight said Joyce was 'a born leader of men, and a rare combination
of a dreamer and a man of action'. Fuller, however, had a poor opinion of
him and friction was present from the start. Mosley liked Box and tended to
side with Fuller's assessment.

Box was appointed as Forgan's successor with a brief to reduce expenditure.
The Box/Fuller axe fell heavily on the movement's radical wing. The paramilitary complexion was de-emphasized with the abolition of the national and
local defence forces. The network of Fascist social clubs was eliminated and
the I Squad was allowed to dwindle to fifteen 'storm troopers'. Centralization
was extended with the liquidation of area headquarters, with branches supervised by a system of national inspectors. Box's 'victory', however, proved to
be pyrrhic. Indeed, MI5 considered him to be 'defeatist' in his confrontation
with the paramilitary Hawkins and Dundas.

Beckett thought headquarters a 'mess' with 'a huge staff of badly paid and
useless people'. The 200 speakers 'made trouble wherever they went, and their
only qualification seemed to be their cheapness and extreme servility'. Senior
officers were 'quite happy if they could sit at their ease while a few underpaid
hacks clicked their heels and saluted'. Box 'did succeed in averting the administrative chaos which threatened almost daily with the inflow of hundreds of
new members and the outflow of a number almost as great'. The Vauxhall
branch had 160 members but only forty paid the subscription. Most were
'young men and women of an average age (19–20)' and 'of the illiterate type'.
The pattern was repeated at other branches with no more than a quarter
classed as 'active'. Internal discord eroded membership while the reorganization and purge of criminal elements had 'inadvertently, motivated the resignation of those unable to concede to the absence of democracy within
the BUF'.

Mosley accepted Fuller's recommendations and plans for an electoral machine were institutionalized on 21 January 1935. A Political Section embraced a new category of non-uniformed members, with executive powers to develop local constituency organizations to cover electoral wards. Although 'Blackshirt Command' held joint executive powers with the Political Section, the thrust of the reforms, as Box and Fuller intended, was in the direction of conventional party politics. The radical Blackshirt units were expected to inject the 'vital spirit of endeavour' with regard to doorstep canvassing and street propaganda, but they were subordinate to the Political Section on political administration matters. However, the BUF structure was ill equipped to cope with Britain's political system and the Box/Fuller initiative proved to be a failure. Appeals to struggle might be ennobling, Thomas Linehan notes, but they were 'qualities too vague and eclectic to cope with the technical and quantitative machinations of electoral politics'. Paramilitarism attracted volatile recruits, who 'alienated potential support from more conventional constituencies'. The conservative ex-military elements proved as bad for the BUF's image as the radicals.

Special Branch said Beckett was 'spreading stories to the effect that the Blackshirts are finished and that all their past efforts have been in vain'. He blamed Box and demanded his removal. Innumerable internal disputes revolved around the personality and leadership clash between Joyce and Mosley, which was chronicled in detail by MI5. Such disputes were settled by Mosley who, in accordance with advice from Blackshirt Command head Francis Hawkins, mostly sided with the administrators.

Dissension extended to relations between Box and the Women's Section, which was characterized by 'personal antipathies, professional incompatibility and conflicts of interests'. On 12 February Lady Mosley wrote to her son, upset that he had 'succeeded in making me look a complete fool'. She said she was being squeezed out, unable to travel around districts and left without a desk from which to work. Little more was expected of her than 'looking pleasant on all occasions'. She did not think the Leader had 'any idea of the difficulties I had to face . . . when we moved to N. HQ. Intrigue the whole time. Insubordination from people whose word you preferred to take to mine and who have since disappeared from the movement by your instructions . . .'

The situation deteriorated when Mosley appointed Mary Richardson to organize the Lancashire area. Box opposed this executive decision and threatened resignation over her 'dishonest inefficiency'. Lady Mosley said she 'would like to resign, and would do so if it were not that such an action might cause damage to the movement and harm the prestige of her son'. Shortly afterwards Richardson was expelled from the BUF for organizing a meeting protesting at the unequal pay for women employed by the movement. Because the Women's Section contributed to the increasing conflicts, its independence was eroded and its profile was downgraded.

*

During 1935 Mussolini appointed Ciano as Under-Secretary for Propaganda to extend the message of universal Fascism. Mosley was a member of the British épée team, which came fifth at the European Championships at Lausanne and he was invited to a CAUR conference at nearby Montreux. Ciano regarded some of the delegates as an embarrassment. Dr Clausen was a 'notorious' Hitler supporter 'absolutely financed by him', while Bucard was 'a noted pederast' only 'interested in Italian lire'. The Jewish question split the meeting which, Ciano acknowledged, 'showed that the issue of racism went very deeply indeed into the structure of European fascism'. A meeting in Paris on 30 January proved to be 'the next-to-last gasp' of Mussolini's Fascist International. Shortly afterwards he decided to withdraw the BUF subsidy, with a final payment in February.

On 9 February, having tried for months to catch his eye, Unity Mitford was introduced to Hitler at the Osteria restaurant in Munich. Most days, Hitler would lunch until 3 p.m. with a relaxed but influential group of companions, including Martin Bormann, architect Albert Speer, photographer Heinrich Hoffman, Munich's Gauleiter Adolf Wagner, Hitler's Adjutant Julius Schaub, Dr Theodor Morell and Press Chief Otto Dietrich. Talk for Hitler, Dietrich said, 'was the very element of his existence'. According to Schaub, Hitler knew nothing of Unity's background. She wrote to Diana that Hitler 'felt he knew London well from his architectural studies'. He talked about war and said 'international Jews must never again be allowed to make two Nordic races fight against one another. I said no, next time we must fight together.' After 'the greatest man of all time' had left, she wrote to her father that she was 'so happy I wouldn't mind dying'. Unity wrote at once to Diana, with the idea of her too meeting Hitler.

Unity, Speer recalled, was 'in love with Hitler . . . her face brightened up, her eyes gleaming, staring at Hitler. Hero-worship. Absolutely phenomenal.' Dietrich said she was an 'enthusiastic follower' of Mosley and had 'many private conversations about Anglo-German relations with Hitler, whose secret itineraries she accurately guessed. Hitler frequently included her among the guests who accompanied him on his travels.' She introduced Hitler to her father and her brother, when they passed through Munich. Farve, wrote Diana, 'has been completely won over to him and admits himself to have been in the wrong until now'. Mosley urged Diana to return to Germany, where she was in turn introduced to Hitler and quickly established a friendship with the Nazi leader. Irene was 'saddened deeply' by tales from Baba of Mrs Guinness, who was 'wriggling her way into Tom' and 'goes everywhere with him in a black shirt', and was acting as his 'entrée to Hitler and Goebbels'.

The Prince of Wales, who admired Hitler, was admonished by the King for expressing views contrary to official Foreign Office policy. He continued, however, to develop indiscreet relations with the German ambassador, Leopold von Hoesch, and criticized the Foreign Office for being 'too one-sided' in its approach to negotiations with Germany over the naval agreement in March 1935. He made clear 'his complete understanding of Germany's position and aspirations'.

MI5 was worried by the 'revolutionary nature' of Mosley's 'bitter attacks' on existing institutions'. An SB agent purloined minutes of the Research Directory, which revealed plans to infiltrate trade unions, including 'the permeation of the Miners' Federation'. In early spring MI5 claimed the BUF was trying to form 'cells' in Civil Service branches and feared a 'highly placed' source was leaking information. When William Rogers in the Treasury Solicitor's Department was identified as organizer of the BUF's Queen's Gate branch, it created even more concern. MI5, however, later admitted that attempts to establish cells had met with little success. It also reported that the BUF had an ambitious scheme to investigate 'all Jewish firms throughout the world' prior to 'detailed attacks on Jewish financial houses and the whole system of international finance'.

When the National government failed to deliver promised policy changes, Rothermere again applied pressure on the Tories. He backed an unofficial Conservative candidate on a diehard ticket at the Liverpool Wavertree by-election, during which twenty-three-year-old Randolph Churchill was attacked as a Mosleyite. Rothermere's newspapers fully supported the *Sunday Dispatch* journalist who was paid an annual subvention of £2,500 (£85,000). Donations were made by the Duke of Westminster, his father and Lady Houston. In the event, Randolph split the Tory vote and handed a safe seat to Labour.

Rothermere expected support from the India Defence League (IDL), which had widened its scope to 'all Imperial questions including Defence and the general maintenance of Conservative Principles'. On 12 February Randolph told Collin Brooks that 'his father and Lord Lloyd had both wanted the seat to be fought' but the League 'turned down the project'. He decided, therefore, to build an organization, using remnants of the IDL and the support of the National League of Airmen, which Brooks wanted to fight a by-election at Norwood. Rothermere, however, said 'the pilots might think we had merely organised them for a political ramp'. Instead, Randolph plunged into the contest with a candidate of his own, Richard Findlay, an RFC flyer who 'resigned' from the BUF on 22 February. Two days later Rothermere told Brooks 'he'll get the women's vote. They like 'em over thirty. With hair on their chests.'

The backdrop to the by-election was the Committee stage of the India Bill. Mosley took up the issue 'in hope of attracting the well known Conservative leaders opposed to the Bill to join the BUF'. He moved staff to Manchester for a new cotton campaign in order to 'take advantage of developments'. According to Special Branch, Lord Lloyd had approached Mosley through Rothermere with an offer to join the party 'in any capacity'. In this context, Findlay's decision was in line with BUF policy but, as a candidate seeking a wide support, he had to distance himself from Mosley.

There was manoeuvring going on between Randolph and Mosley. Churchill said his son had 'got a considerable fund through Lady Houston and appears disposed to form an organisation to run candidates not only at by-elections, but against Government supporters at the general election. His programme seems to be to put Socialists in everywhere he can in order to smash up MacDonald and Baldwin.' Houston also signed a cheque for the BUF for £100,000 (3.4m). However, 'she changed her mind and tore it up'. Commandant Allen reported in the *Saturday Review* that Houston was still angry with Mosley for an attack on her in the *Blackshirt*.

Churchill tried to induce his son 'to withdraw his candidate who is an ex-Fascist airman (not much good)'. Rothermere withdrew his backing after consulting the City – he was obsessed with his wealth. He feared their candidate might split the vote and allow in a socialist, which would 'precipitate a crisis'. In the March by-election, Findlay polled 2,698 votes and lost his deposit. The official Conservative, Duncan Sandys, won the seat against a Labour opponent. Mosley remained in contact with Findlay but, knowing MI5 would monitor their correspondence, played down the connection by claiming he had merely received many 'long and tedious letters' to which he politely replied.

The failure of the by-election was a blow to Mosley's attempts to build an alliance with Conservative forces and create a political space in which the BUF could operate.

In March Diana drove her new Voisin car through the Black Forest snow to Munich. On the 11th Unity introduced her to Hitler. Diana later told Nicholas Mosley she believed this meeting had ruined her life, and 'your father's'. However, in letters to Unity, she referred to Hitler as 'beloved' and admitted 'we were very great friends', though 'I didn't love Hitler any more than I did Winston'. She was 'very, very fond of him'. Diana Tennant, a friend of Unity staying at a German finishing school, admitted they were 'Nazis to a T, the whole lot of us, and I'm not ashamed of it'. Mosley encouraged Diana to stay on in Munich 'as I was naturally interested to hear more of developments in that country and of these personalities. They were introduced to his whole circle.'

Diana found Hitler 'incredibly frank and wonderful, charming'. He was 'neat and clean looking, so much so that beside him almost everyone looked coarse. His teeth had been mended with gold.' He did 'imitations of marvellous drollery which showed how acutely observant he was. I never heard him rant. He was extremely polite to women. He bowed and kissed hands . . .' Hitler described the two Mitford sisters as 'angels'. They were the type of beauty he admired, 'so much so that both sisters got away with wearing the make-up of which he so disapproved'. Hitler was both fascinated by and afraid of women, but they were entranced by him. The truth was, Diana wrote, that in private, 'Sweet Uncle Wolf' 'inspired affection'. She claimed that she never heard him mention the Jews: 'I know that he didn't like them, that he hated them, that he murdered them . . .'

Diana made a telling point to Nicholas about the difference between Hitler and Mosley. When people met his father they thought: 'Here is this wonderful man who has an answer to everything himself so what is there for us to do? When people met Hitler they thought: here is this wonderful but unfortunate man who seems to have all the cares of the world on his shoulders, so we must do all we can to help him.' This was not an isolated view. In a review of *Mein Kampf*, George Orwell said he had 'never been able to dislike Hitler'. He had 'the face of a man suffering under intolerable wrongs. In a rather more manly way it reproduces the expression of innumerable pictures of Christ crucified, and there is little doubt that that is how Hitler sees himself. He is the martyr, the victim. One feels . . . that he is fighting against destiny, that he can't win, and yet that he somehow deserves to.'

'Masterful' was the wrong word to use about Mosley, Diana thought. His followers 'adored him and looked up to him and thought him perfection and thought that he could lead them into a promised land'. With Hitler it was different: 'He had a very soft side to his nature, so that people terribly felt they would like to help him; and that tremendously applied to women. There was something almost vulnerable . . . about him which made men want to help him and made women want to cherish him.' She admitted Mosley 'had not got that at all'.

At the beginning of March it had been expected the BUF would announce it would put up candidates at the general election, but MI5 reported on the 11th that it did not do so because Mosley could not reveal, even to senior officials, the real state of the movement's finances. Reports from chief constables indicated that, except in Manchester, BUF 'membership had declined, branches had closed, sales of the *Blackshirt* had dropped, and enthusiasm had cooled'.

Mosley was forced to impose swingeing cuts, including closing the expensive Black House. In the *Blackshirt*, in 'The Next Stage in Fascism', he said discipline was to be tightened in a movement organized on army lines with every Blackshirt attached to a small unit as part of a Section, which, in turn, would belong to a Company. At the top of the hierarchy would be the Leader. Only those committed to door-to-door canvassing would be entitled to wear a black shirt. The aim was to establish a BUF branch in every constituency.

The changes entrenched the position of the paramilitary faction and provoked outbreaks of unrest among members, with serious dissatisfaction in London, Liverpool, Manchester and Leeds. When Scottish branches threatened secession, Mosley sacked administrative staff and replaced them with those of proven loyalty. As Director of Organization, Hawkins was responsible for the entire movement and restricted the Political Section to providing technical instruction for Blackshirt officers.

The Italians had grown weary of Mosley's excuses for the lack of progress. Sceptical about the merits of universal Fascism, Grandi told Mussolini he was 'flushing money down the sewer. At the moment you are spending a great deal of money in England. Until a few days ago, you were giving Mosley about 3,500,000 [£60,000] in monthly instalments of about 300,000 lire. All this money, believe me Duce, even on the best supposition simply goes down the drain. At the present time we should concentrate our efforts in a different direction. With a tenth of what you give Mosley, I feel I could produce a result ten times better.' Mussolini agreed and the funding was reduced. Even so, during 1935, £86,000 (£2.94m) was deposited in the BUF's secret account.

Baba saw Grandi constantly and he confided both his personal and political worries to her, including the worsening situation in Africa, where Mussolini wanted to build an empire. When she was later asked about the funding of the BUF she replied, 'Of course, I thought I knew what was going on. But if you ask me "Had I got evidence?" the answer is "No".' Dundas was sent to Rome to plead with Mussolini to reconsider his decision.

The wartime Advisory Committee studied the audited account of BUF Trust Ltd for the year ending February 1935. That the total deposited in the Charing Cross account was close to the published income of the movement during 1934 (£36,812) and 1935 (£75,606) gave credence to MI5's claim that the BUF was only kept going by Italian money. According to MI6 sources, during 1935 Mosley received a one-off payment of £35,000 (£1.5m) from oil magnate and Nazi associate Henry Deterding.

Despite Mosley's meeting with Bene, London Nazis continued to shun the BUF. They reported that the movement was collapsing and that without Italian subsidies it would 'run into the sands very quickly'. In mid-March Fuller and Allen returned from a trip to Germany, where they had met Finance Minister Hjalmar Schacht. They had been hindered by Bene's reports. Fuller had been received by Hitler 'not as a member of the BUF but as a British officer visiting Germany'. He 'could not understand why senior high officials were so ignorant of the activities of the BUF and of the Political situation in

Great Britain generally'. Pfister, in regular contact with Schacht, who had a high regard for Mosley, discovered from German friends that a memorandum sent to senior officials, though not to Schacht, indicated the BUF delegation was not '*persona grata*' and was to be offered 'as little assistance as possible'.

Pfister learnt that the snub had arisen because 'a certain high Nazi official who visited this country had not been favourably impressed by a meeting he had with the Leader'. On a visit to Berlin, Archibald Findlay 'had not created a favourable impression' and on a second visit 'a still less favourable impression' with his demands to see Hitler. A third reason was Lady Mosley's interview with a French journalist in which she said 'Hitler was the greatest enemy of the BUF since people in this country would not join on account of the brutal methods in Germany'. When Berlin expressed 'disappointment that the Leader had shown so little appreciation of their victory in the Saar', Pfister knew something was wrong since Mosley had personally delivered a special message to the Nazi press representative in London. He discovered the message had been suppressed.

Despite doing what Pfister thought was in the best interests of the movement by contacting Austrian Nazis, it had been against Mosley's express orders. Mosley later said he 'wanted to combat the growing up of any international idea. I forbade any of our leading people to visit Italy or Germany without express permission.' The real reason was that he feared surveillance by the intelligence services. Pfister, who was briefed against by Joyce, was suspended from his post for six weeks and ordered to break off correspondence with Germany. This caused Pfister problems with his rent and he was forced to go cap in hand to the Leader. Mosley kept properties in London which were rented out to officials, including Findlay, who was responsible for the movement's financial affairs, including secret funding. Pfister was considered by MI5 to be an 'agent of the Nazi party in the headquarters of the BUF' and was sacrificed by Mosley, who took care to avoid known Nazi agents. Pfister later moved to Germany and became a member of the Nazi Party.

Italian attempts at a Fascist international collapsed in the spring with the last CAUR meeting in Amsterdam on 1 April 1935. CAUR and the Nazis' own Fascist international faded into the background as a clear detente developed between Rome and Berlin. Mussolini helped consolidate the secret alliance with Germany by sharing confidential British Cabinet documents, which had been supplied by a 'pro-Fascist' MP.

Foreign contacts were developed in an even more secretive manner by Captain Robert Gordon-Canning, a Research Directory member and Chairman of Action Press. The forty-seven-year-old Etonian was Mosley's foreign policy adviser. Like Mosley, his niece, Mary Redvers, recalled that he came from a hunting and shooting background, whose family estates in Hartbury,

Gloucestershire, had been sold after the First World War. Diana said he was 'a typical English gentleman who thought the country was going downhill quickly'. He was a descendant of the nineteenth-century Prime Minister and Foreign Secretary George Canning. He had a distinguished war record (10th Hussars, MC), had travelled in Palestine and India, and had a special interest in the Arab world, having served on the staff of the Rif leader, Abd-el-Krim.

According to his daughter Louise, 'Bobby' was 'very highly regarded by the Arabs and had a large number of contacts with them'. He thought the Rifs had been unjustly treated, which brought him into conflict with the Foreign Office. He was a romantic in inclination, modelling himself on Lawrence of Arabia, and published several plays. Because of his interest in Morocco, Louise said, 'the French were very anti him'. He was employed by MI6 and was presented with a cigarette case inscribed with 'for services to the Secret Service' for help in France during 1926–7. His daughter recognized that he had been involved in 'a lot of undercover activities'.

Gordon-Canning's reasons for joining the BUF were, according to his daughter, tied to his experience of the war: 'He was there on Christmas Day when both sides stopped fighting.' He had been at the Somme, wrote poetry about the war and became pro-German. Although 'a cold, emotionally frigid man', he was also 'very active, very charismatic, very kind, though extremely innocent'. Strongly anti-Bolshevist, in Fascism he discovered a 'certain barbaric splendour' and a 'warrior spirit opposed to that of the nightclub'. He also found an outlet for his anti-Semitism. He disagreed with Mosley over the use of uniforms. He told his daughter that 'Britain had never had a standing army and the British people would not stand for it'.

Gordon-Canning had married well and 'threw money at the BUF', acting as Mosley's banker and contact man with Hitler. In 1935 he made a special trip to Berlin and, fearful for his life, took out an expensive insurance policy. In March he created the January Club's successor, the Windsor Club. Its confidential membership was by invitation of its front man, Luttman-Johnson, who attracted to the Club well-connected right-wingers such as Sir Henry Fairfax-Lucy and Douglas Jerrold.

Despite setbacks, Mosley packed out meetings and on 24 March addressed 8,000 people at the Albert Hall. He attacked 'international Jewish finance', which was 'sweating the East and ruining the West, destroying the Indian masses and filling the unemployment queues of Lancashire'. The enemy was 'that nameless, homeless and all powerful force which stretches its greedy fingers from the shelter of England to throttle trade and menace the peace of the world. This is the force which . . . challenges Germany with chatter and menaces of war, using the power of the Press to insult and to provoke the new world force of Fascism.' He warned that 'Jews must either put the interest of Britain before the interests of Jewry, or be deported from Great Britain'. He brought the crowd to its feet with a rousing finale. 'This shall be the epic generation which scales again the heights of time and history to see once more the immortal lights – the lights of sacrifice and high endeavour summoning through ordeal the soul of humanity to the sublime and the eternal. The alternatives of our age are heroism or oblivion. There are no lesser paths in the history of great nations. Can we, therefore, doubt which path to choose?'

That night there was an attempt to contact Cimmie through a medium. Lady Mosley claimed she had sent a psychic message saying she did not want the children to be with Mrs Guinness. Mosley was an absentee father who took little interest in his children's lives. His youngest son was almost a stranger. Irene worried about Michael, whom she had come to regard as the son she had never had, and Vivien, who was subjected to her father's 'unpredictable moods and sudden ferocious teasing'. His overriding interest was politics and the Curzon family solicitor was convinced he would sell Savehay Farm to fund his ambitions. Mosley had thoughts of asking his children to refund him any money he spent on Denham when they came of age.

On 4 April Ian Hope Dundas returned from Rome, where he had presented radio broadcasts supporting Italian Fascism, with the news that 'although he had been successful in interviewing highly-placed officials, Mussolini refused to see him'. Shortly afterwards Mosley made an unscheduled trip to Italy but he, too, was unsuccessful in restoring funding to previous levels and was forced to make further cuts.

The National League of Airmen had some success. People, Collin Brooks wrote on 27 March, 'are very much alive to the German menace and very angry at the lack of an adequate air force'. Care was taken 'not to attack Germany, though when any incautious speaker does so it is only a few Fascists who object'. Churchill was incensed by Rothermere's appeasement. He told his wife on 13 April, 'he thinks the Germans are all powerful and that the British are hopeless and doomed. He proposes to meet this situation by grovelling to Germany.'

The Mail urged building 10,000 planes and pleaded for 'a British Goering' to cut through interdepartmental wrangling. 'Blackbird' (i.e. Dorman) wanted the aviation industry run 'under a modern fascist system of government with an Air minister who knew his job'. Mosley supported the 'thoroughly fascist sentiments' of the rearmament campaign. Britain had a thriving aviation industry and was the world's largest exporter of aeroplanes. It was achieved by the sort of planning and co-ordination between ministries of which Mosley approved. With help from Lady Houston, Rothermere paid Bristol Aeroplane to build a prototype aircraft, dubbed 'Britain First' – the slogan of the BUF. The Blenheim light bomber flew for the first time on 12 April 1935 and was presented as a 'peace gift' to the Air Ministry. Ordered by the RAF, it played a significant role in the Second World War.

On 14 April in Leicester Mosley opened a new crusade against organized Jewry 'so that relations with leading representatives of National Socialist Germany could be intensified'. Mosley learnt 'there was a body of opinion' among Nazis in Munich that was 'not nearly so keen to avoid offending Great Britain' and wanted to establish relations with the BUF.

Alfred Rosenberg was responsible for 'arranging a possible visit to Germany by Mosley'. He had spoken 'to the Führer about it numerous times' but 'a secret meeting was not expedient, since such a meeting would probably become public. Rather, the Führer informed me that he would not stand in the way of a possible visit since he wanted to grant a hearing to every British politician (regardless of party-political affiliation) who is endeavouring to do justice to Germany.' Rosenberg then discovered that a meeting with Hitler was being arranged in 'great secrecy' by Ribbentrop, who scored a diplomatic triumph by negotiating the Anglo-German Naval Treaty. By agreeing to limit the German fleet, he eased British fears of a German sea threat and a naval arms race. Hitler believed the treaty freed him from British interference in his own plans.

Mosley travelled to Munich on 25 April and was received at the Führer's flat in Prinzregentenplatz. Hitler 'slipped shyly into a room', Mosley recalled. 'His bombast was reserved for the platform. Unlike Musso, who was all bombast and impossible to talk to. Not so Hitler.' His 'hypnotic manner was entirely absent; perhaps I was an unsuitable subject; in any case, he made no attempt whatever to produce any effect of that kind. He was simple, and treated me throughout the occasion with a gentle, almost feminine charm.'

The conversation was translated by Paul Schmidt but no record survives. According to Mosley, Hitler 'talked in a very cool fashion', clarifying the relationship between the Nazis and the BUF, which had to be subordinated 'to his foreign policy goal of coming to an agreement with Great Britain'. Hitler was a 'completely inert, white, exhausted creature', until they discussed the possibility of war between Britain and Germany, which Mosley said would be like 'two splendid young men fighting each other until they both fall exhausted and bleeding to the ground, when the jackals of the world would mount triumphant on their bodies'. Hitler spoke 'passionately against fighting the English. He had developed a complex that he must avoid fighting us if he could.' Mosley said, 'if you get into a war with the English they will never stray, they're like that, you understand that, don't you? They will go on fighting till the bitter end.' Hitler replied, 'Yes, I do.'

Herbert Dohring, a member of the Führer's bodyguard, recalled that Hitler's favourite film was the 1935 production of Yeats-Brown's *Lives of a Bengal Lancer*. It influenced his thinking and he 'would always praise how a small country like England could run and manage this huge Empire. Hitler always wanted to have a friendly relationship with England.' Mosley later told James Lees-Milne that, had he spoken German, he believed he could have influenced Hitler. He 'wanted unity with us in the fight against Bolshevism'. But, Lees-Milne replied, 'he wanted war with other, smaller countries which he could overwhelm'. Mosley tacitly agreed.

Hitler and Mosley talked for an hour but 'the word Jew was never mentioned'. They moved to the drawing room for lunch with the Duchess of Brunswick, only daughter of the Kaiser and a great-granddaughter of Queen Victoria; Winifred Wagner, English-born daughter-in-law of Richard Wagner, who ran the Bayreuth Festival, and was connected to the Mitfords via the grandfather Redesdale, a great friend of her husband's; and Unity Mitford. Hitler hoped Unity would be surprised at meeting Mosley but was unaware they already knew each other. Mosley remembered her 'stage-struck by the glamour and panoply of the national socialist movement and the mass admiration of Hitler'. She asked Hitler what he thought of Mosley. He replied, '*Ein ganzer Kerl*! [Quite a man]'

Also present were Hitler's Minister of Propaganda, Joseph Goebbels, and his wife Magda, Ribbentrop and Werlin, a director of Daimler-Benz. Mosley had a discussion with Hermann Goering and his wife, actress Emmy Sonnemann, known for her vulgarity and Wagnerian appearance. The 'small, dark and (ironically) Jewish-looking' Goebbels was the only one of the Nazi hierarchy with whom foreigners found conversation amusing. Diana thought him 'intelligent, witty and sarcastic'.

Goebbels hero-worshipped the Führer as the 'natural creative instrument of divine destiny. I stand by him profoundly moved. What a fellow, what a man.' The little Doctor with the club-foot claimed his limp was the result of a war wound but it was probably due to infantile paralysis. According to Staff Officer Wilfred von Oven, it was partly bitterness about his deformity – psychologically crippling in the context of National Socialist eugenics – that made Goebbels a malevolent monster. He had hatreds he never lost. A virulent anti-Semite, Goebbels was absolutely loyal and Hitler appointed him national director of the Ministry for Propaganda (ProMi). Goebbels thought Mosley made 'a good impression. A bit brash, which he tries to conceal behind a forced pushiness. Otherwise acceptable however. Of course, he's on his best behaviour. The Führer has set to work on him. Wonder if he'll ever come to power?'

17

1935

Mosley boasted Hitler liked him, admired Diana and had been entranced by Unity, who was influential with Hitler as part of his Osteria group, though he learnt 'only afterwards that she was a follower of Mosley'. Unity's diary records every meeting with the Führer in red ink. The red-letter days number 140 – about two or three times a month. She wrote to Diana that Hitler said Mosley was unwise to import Fascism and adopt the black shirt – both were foreign to British traditions. He said he should have referred to the revolution of Oliver Cromwell – and called his men 'Ironsides'.

Hitler, Albert Speer recalled, said 'it was a mistake to export ideas such as National Socialism. To do so would only lead to a strengthening of nationalism in other countries and thus a weakening of his own position.' Other movements had produced 'no leader of his own calibre'. Mosley was one of the 'copyists who had no original ideas. They imitated us and our methods slavishly and would never amount to anything.' He believed that 'in every country you had to start from different premises and change your methods accordingly'. Speer's claim that Hitler 'thought nothing of Mosley' changed as the Führer learnt more about the British Fascist.

Speer believed Hitler used Unity for unofficial leaks. She was not a spy but 'it was amazing that someone not German was around Hitler and could listen to details of party politics and far-reaching policy. Hitler made no secret of his thoughts [but] his outspokenness was calculated, talking secrets knowing that rumours would be spread.' Unity was tight-lipped with journalists as to the details of her conversations; to private individuals she argued his case, often to shock. She talked freely with Hitler and pressed him on his relations with Britain. He said he wished to cement an alliance with a fellow Nordic nation. Unity fed his admiration of 'the English cousins', amid 'profound and widespread German ignorance of British politics, national life and wider history'.

The BUF praised Hitler's pledge of friendship to Britain in his May 1935 Reichstag speech as 'the most important European event for a decade'. It welcomed the 'rough, gauntleted handshake of the New Germany, glad to feel again the iron grip of a worthy foe now comrade in the struggle against

... the perfidious advance of Communist World Revolution which would assuredly otherwise overrun Europe'. Mosley conceded the right to aggressive expansionism, based upon the desire to unite the Germanic people. Hitler's desire to achieve 'racial union' was considered legitimate and he argued that even if Britain and Germany pursued different political aims, they could still complement each other in striving for peace.

On 7 May Diana and Unity lunched at the Osteria with Hitler. Also present were BUF members Baroness Ella van Heemstra and Joseph Hepburn-Ruston, who attended Nazi rallies, and she contributed articles to the *Blackshirt*. 'The Call of Fascism' (26 April) was dedicated to 'King and Empire, the Corporate State, and the revolt against alien domination of banking'. Hepburn-Ruston's role as a covert propagandist for Mosley included frequent visits to the Brown House and led the Dutch government to question Nazi influence among its citizens. Queen Wilhelmina asked the Baroness's father, a court official, to speak to his daughter on the subject. Hepburn-Ruston took umbrage at the interference and supposedly walked out of the marriage. In fact, the Baroness found her husband – a lookalike for Hollywood idol Ronald Colman – in bed with the governess. He was next heard of in Berlin working for German Intelligence and then running several 'businesses' in London with fellow Mosleyite Dr Arthur Albert Tester.

Tall, well-dressed, monocled, Tester described himself as a financier, though the Foreign Office considered him a 'first class crook, who lives by swindling the public through the formation of bogus companies'. Born in Stuttgart, the son of a British consul and a German mother, he was imprisoned during the First World War. At the war's end, developing a reputation as a racketeer, he was connected to naval security and may have undertaken 'intelligence work for the occupying forces'. In 1927 Tester was expelled from France, suspected of spying for German Military Intelligence. Three years later he was imprisoned for fraud and, on release, moved to England where he bought Naldera, on the Kent coast near Broadstairs, for his German wife and six children. The house had been built for Lord Curzon as a seaside retreat; Cimmie spent her summer holidays there. Tester bought the *Lucinda*, a luxury steam-yacht on which he held lavish parties, and ran an expensive office in St James's Place with Hepburn-Ruston. Most of Tester's time was spent in Europe where he set up bogus companies and absconded with investors' funds.

In 1932 Tester joined the BUF. He admitted – when a personal letter from Mosley was found on him in a security check – that he was a great admirer of the Leader. A German Foreign Office report revealed that Tester's brother-in-law, Arthur Uckert, had been 'active with the Secret State Police since 1933'. He had moved with Tester from Berlin to England and stayed until August 1934, when he returned to Germany and joined the State Security Head Office. The files reveal Tester's links to 'the inner circle of Reichsführer Himmler'.

He was 'leader' of the Broadstairs BUF and told the *Express* he was Mosley's personal aide-de-camp and wished 'they were not called Fascists in England. National Socialists would describe us better.'

Tester predicted to the *Herald* that Mosley would attain power. When Mosley was later interned, Tester wrote that 'the highest principle which determined my life and directed its course' was 'to achieve his freedom so that he, whose calling is to lead England out of chaos, remains alive and can fulfil his objective. I accept him alone as my judge; he will one day judge whether I have the right to be called one of his shield bearers.' Despite the negative press Tester received, Mosley never denied his role.

German documents acknowledge Tester as a 'representative of the Mosley Party to Germany' and the man 'who got Mosley, who was previously turned towards Italy, interested in National Socialism'. British Foreign Office files refer to allegations that Tester 'finances Mosley's movement'. He claimed he 'did not receive either directly or indirectly any financial benefit for my political and propaganda activity. From the German Government or from private German organisations or people.' A number of authorities disputed this. According to captured US Counter-Intelligence Corps (CIC) files, Tester was the one genuine Nazi agent in the BUF. The CIC regarded Tester as 'an official of the BUF' and an 'S. D. official'.

MI5 surveillance of Naldera confirmed Tester 'entertained many visitors from abroad and many Englishmen, some avowedly connected with the Fascist movement', including Joyce and Mosley. During 1935 he was granted an interview by Belgian Premier Graf de Broqueville, which was published in *Action*. In the same year he arranged for a Hamburg-based barrister assisting the German Foreign Office, Dr Behn, to interview Mosley. When a second interview was arranged, Behn was banned from entry to Britain. Joyce later told the Germans he had known Tester 'personally' but warned them of his activities. He was known to Fritz Hesse in the German embassy in London, who wrote that 'he smells of a smart businessman with whom it is best doing no business'.

On 9 May Unity and Diana had lunch at Hitler's flat, where they were joined by Gordon-Canning. Mosley's representative later met with Rosenberg and officials of the Nazi Party Foreign Department to 'deliver a request' which he felt 'unable to set down in writing'. Rosenberg subsequently had an audience with Hitler to put to him the request for funds.

Manchester Guardian journalist Paul Willart found Unity 'a good contact' but also 'a stupid girl, illiterate. She had mopped up everything in the *Stürmer*.' She told Lady Phipps, wife of the British ambassador, that Streicher was 'her favourite among the Nazis'. She said 'Jews were traitors' and wanted 'everyone to know she was a Jew-hater'. During a home visit with Diana, Unity produced an autographed photograph of Streicher, which proved too much for their sister, Decca, who remembered Diana drawling: ' "But, darling," opening her enormous blue eyes, "Streicher is a kitten." '

German diplomats in London realized anti-Semitic propaganda should not be given too much prominence and, since they received no guidance from Berlin, used their own discretion. Streicher, however, displayed little restraint as he now praised Mosley for his anti-Semitism. On 9 May at Nuremberg he congratulated Mosley for a speech at Leicester which drew attention to the Jewish Question. Mosley replied and on the following day, Streicher's *Fränkische Tageszeitung* published the telegram (reprinted in the *Herald*) under the headline THE AWAKENING OF THE PEOPLES. 'I value this message of yours, in the midst of our hard fight, greatly. The might of J e w i s h c o r r u p t i o n [as reprinted] must be overcome in all great countries before the future of Europe can be assured in justice and peace. Our fight is a difficult one. Our victory certain.' Skidelsky chose not to publish this telegram and, David Pryce-Jones noted, did not even hint at 'the relation of Mosley and his movement to Streicher'.

MI5 saw Mosley as vain and unrealistic but possessed with sufficient machi-avellian cunning to keep his activities within the law. He was perceived as 'a renegade aristocratic dilettante and traitor to the labour movement, a figure of ridicule rather than a threat to the ability to protest'. From the summer of 1935 the BUF was viewed as having only minor political significance but there was concern about the growing links with Continental counterparts. Maxwell Knight's Fascist sympathies waned when he learnt of Mosley's contacts with Germany. Margaret Leighton makes the point that he 'could have been por-trayed as the reliable tool of fascist Italy and Nazi Germany in the same way that communist leaders were said to be pawns of Moscow'. In fact, most official pronouncements on Mosley 'bore an air of bemused tolerance'.

At the end of May Mosley flew to Rome, accompanied by Dundas and Peter Symes, National Inspecting Officer in Birmingham, to revive the subsidies. Funding was resumed but Mussolini extracted a high price, insisting he support his Abyssinian campaign. MI5 learnt that he also insisted the BUF demonstrate its potential for achieving power. Once in power, it was agreed a Mosley government would recognize Italy's legitimate interests in the Mediterranean, which included Malta.

On 5 June Diana learnt that a flat had been found for her on the orders of Hitler. 'It belongs', Unity wrote, 'to a young Jewish couple who are going abroad.' Their brother was introduced to Hitler. Tom 'adored the Führer – he almost got into a frenzy like us sometimes, though I expect he will have cooled down by the time he gets home'. On 18 June Unity wrote to *Der Stürmer* bemoaning the fact that

the English have no notion of the Jewish danger. Our struggle is extremely hard. Our worst Jews work only behind the scenes. They never come into the open, and therefore we cannot show them to the British public in their true dreadfulness. We hope, however, that you will see that we will soon win against the world enemy, in spite of all his cunning. We think with joy of the day when we shall be able to say with might and authority: 'England for the English! Out with the Jews!'

Streicher invited Unity to Hesselberg for the midsummer 'blood-and-soil' festival on 22 June. A crowd of 20,000 heard her brief speech praising Streicher. On the same day the *Münchener Zeitung* published 'Confessions of an English fascist girl'. She said Mosley was 'a man imbued with his sense of mission and an unshakeable belief in the victory of his cause . . . we English fascists are behind him with the same enthusiasm as today the whole German people are behind their wonderful Führer.' She added that 'the moment our Jewish enemies are ready to attack us – the time for this, we know, is likely to be soon – then our struggle at last will reach its final decisive stage'. A copy was forwarded by the British embassy with a note that 'Miss Mitford, although only 20 years of age, appears to represent Sir Oswald Mosley at Munich'. The Foreign Office added that 'the Embassy do not seem to know about Miss Mitford's acquaintance with the Chancellor which is very curious indeed'. It was 'true that her family are friends of Mosley' but the official could not believe she 'represents' him, even though 'she sees Herr Hitler very often'.

When, on 24 June, the *Fränkische Tageszeitung* asked Unity about the low profile of the Mosley movement, she said it was 'ignored in the main papers, as once happened in Germany to the National Socialists'. She acknowledged Mosley had not originally been anti-Semitic, but he 'very soon recognized that the Jewish danger . . . fundamentally poses a danger to all the peoples of the world'. She said the BUF would 'put up some candidates in the certain hopes of winning seats . . . But that will be only one more springboard and there can be no looking back until we have swept the whole nation with us.'

Mosley was aware of Unity's activities in Germany and, if they annoyed him, on no occasion did he admonish her for her statements. He was happy for her to develop contacts within Nazi circles at the very highest level. Nancy Mitford mocked her: 'We were asked to stay with somebody called Himmler or something, tickets and everything paid for . . . Actually he wanted to show us over a concentration camp, now why? So that I could write a funny book about them.'

Nancy sent an advance copy of *Wigs on the Green* to Diana. The book is a mild satire but Diana removed passages she thought damaging to Mosley. Nancy recognized their point of view, 'that Fascism is something too serious to be dealt with in a funny book at all. Surely that is a little unreasonable? Fascism is now such a notable feature of modern life all over the world that it must be possible to consider it in any context.' She believed the book 'far more in favour of Fascism than otherwise'. The heroine, Eugenia Malmains, is a fair-haired eighteen-year-old who spouts Fascist ideology. Eugenia, re-cognizable within the family circle as Unity, is not wholly a figure of fun. She says things Nancy believed: 'The rich have betrayed their trust, preferring the fetid atmosphere of cocktail-bars and night-clubs to the sanity of a useful country life.' One of the young men (based on Peter Rodd) is the voice of Nancy: 'Western civilisation is old and tired, the dark ages are practically upon us anyhow, and I should prefer that they march in with trumpet and flag than that they should creep upon us to the tap of a typewriter.'

Diana was angry and 'felt that when Mosley and his supporters were being attacked in real street fights she could not have much to do with a sister who was publicly laughing at them'. Nancy told Unity she wished she 'had never been born into such a family of fanatics. Please don't read the book if it's going to stone you up against me.' The book attracted little attention but Mosley banned Nancy from visiting Diana.

After her disparaging remarks about Hitler, Mosley avoided his mother. On 26 June she wrote that she had been 'troubled for a long time because it is obvious to me that I was not really wanted by you in the BUF any longer. If my position is going to be made difficult by your showing me, as you have so often done, that *you* do not want me, then the best thing is for me to go.' He let her down in front of all her subordinates, despite 'the time and money I have spent . . . I do not suppose you will ever realise what it has cost me to write this letter.' The breach was healed but she no longer played a part in the BUF.

BUF opposition to the India Bill was organized by Joyce, who described its backers as 'one loathsome, fetid, purulent, tumid mass of hypocrisy' hiding behind 'Jewish dictators'. By forcing through the India Act in July, the govern-ment took a step towards Indian self-government. The India Defence League had support in the country but 'the bitter battle fought within the Tory ranks over the issue was never to be repeated'. Nor again did Mosley have an opportunity to exploit the issue.

Mosley did, however, take the opportunity to exploit anti-Semitism, particu-larly in London's East End. The Bethnal Green and Bow branches had been formed in the previous autumn and, during the winter, a Shoreditch branch whose organizer was J. F. 'Duke' Sutherland, a Catholic law clerk and racing driver who was an important contact with Germany and conduit for Nazi funds. In the summer of 1935 Richard 'Jock' Houston in Shoreditch and Edward 'Mick' Clarke at Victoria Park Square, Bethnal Green began to gain receptive audiences. Within six months eighty meetings were held in Bethnal Green alone and within the year nearly half of the BUF membership was to be found in Bethnal Green, Stepney, Shoreditch and Hackney.

The East End remained rooted in traditional industries – the docks, clothing, shoe and furniture manufacturing – which were severely hit by an economic downturn. It was not a 'Depressed Area', as it suffered lower unemployment (15 per cent) than the worst-hit regions, but many families were crowded into run-down, insanitary Victorian slums. Blackshirt Fred Bailey recalled that conditions were appalling: 'My father was out of work for ten years. He laboured to keep our heads above water. He would earn a shilling as a bookie's runner or a look-out for a game of dice. We were means tested. My family was brought to the means test because of that and they had to go before the Board. You had to sell everything before there was any money.'

Bailey was typical of East Enders featured in the novel *What hope for Green Street* (1945) by another Blackshirt, Olive Hawks. It is a highly partisan account 'of why so many working class families in East London supported "Imperial Socialism" and the social factors that prevented the wishes of ordinary people from materialising'. According to Mosleyite John Warburton, 'There was no hope. The one thing they had was patriotism and to them Mosley brought that hope.' But instead of turning their anger against the powerful, Mosley's working-class recruits sought a scapegoat for their situation. Bailey 'resented the way the East End was being used as a sweatshop'. Warburton admitted, 'they didn't like the people who a generation earlier had come from Russia and Poland and who now lived in Aldgate and Whitechapel.'

Britain's Jewish poplulation in 1935 was around 330,000 (0.8 per cent of the population). During the late nineteenth century there had been an influx of 100,000 Ashkenazi Jews from Russia who mostly settled in Leeds, Manchester and the East End, which by 1935 contained about 150,000 Jews. The Jewish community was easily identifiable with its 'East European culture, Yiddish language, respect for Jewish law and deeply held traditionalist religious practices'. This was, notes Robert Wistrich, 'the single most potent factor in the new anti-semitism which attained a new virulence in Britain'. It combined 'negative stereotypes of poor immigrant Jews with a whole range of "rich Jew" anti-semitism, intellectual racism, Social Darwinism and class snobbery, with vulgar conspiracy theories about Jewish plans for world domination. The newcomers were closely identified with the practice of sweated labour, disease-ridden, clannish, materialistic, criminal and unpatriotic.'

A key BUF figure was ex-Liberal Mayor Charles Bennett, whose chemist shop in Green Street was 'a centre of vigorous resistance to the menace of the price-cutter and chain store'. A former Vice-President of the Bethnal Green Chamber of Commerce, Bennett organized shopkeepers on behalf of a BUF front, the British Traders' Bureau. The Nazis had a high regard for Bennett, who had married a German and whose children were educated in Germany. Ribbentrop identified him as 'one of the most active comrades of Mosley' and his trips to Berlin were sponsored by Goebbels, who noted that he 'made use of every opportunity to learn about German rebuilding and to carry our philosophy back to the Mosleyites'. Bennett was invited to Hitler's last birth-day celebration before the war.

There was long-standing anti-Jewish feeling in the area and BUF speakers made a direct link to the British Brothers' League, which had earlier gained support for anti-alien legislation to control immigration. Among those who listened to BUF speakers were parents and grandparents of Blackshirts who had supported the League. Founded in 1901 by Captain Shaw, it attracted local Conservative and Liberal MPs. Its tactics of mass meetings, inflammatory oratory and popular mobilization were highly successful but also led to anti-Jewish violence. Speakers referred to 'savages' and 'scum of humanity' but made few direct references to Jews because the leadership believed overt anti-Semitism would harm the League's progress. The legislation was tame but the League lived on until 1923, providing an outlet for G. K. Chesterton's Distributists in their veiled attacks on Jewish influence. 'A generation of East Enders', noted Colin Holmes, 'were familiarised with a populist movement, basing its tactics on the mass meeting, that allied jingoistic nationalism with anti-alien feeling.'

Both in the local furniture trade, Owen Burke and Mick Clarke – the only important grass-roots leader thrown up by British Fascism – spearheaded the Blackshirt assault in Bethnal Green. The pair spoke at street corners to jeering audiences. 'Night after night,' recalled John Beckett, 'squads of their comrades used to receive the riot-call, and from Chelsea the old vans would rush to extricate the venturesome speaker from a hostile crowd.' Gradually they developed receptive audiences, particularly among the Stepney Irish – tra-ditionally anti the Jewish community – who came to dominate the local BUF. Speakers played on local resentment against Jews who were accused of taking over the furniture, tailoring and hairdressing trades, and of being engaged in local government corruption.

Fred Bailey claimed the campaign 'was verbal more than anything else'. That is certainly not how those subjected to it viewed it. William J. Fishman, a sixteen-year-old Stepney Labour League of Youth activist, said the BUF 'deliberately played on the irrational fears and hatreds of the slum dwellers. Fascist incursions were mounted against the Jews. Attacks . . . were stepped up as blackshirt gangs made daily, more often, nocturnal, forays into the ghetto . . . East End Jews, in the front line of attack, had no alternative but to resist.'

The Jewish establishment response aimed to deny Mosley publicity. They advised, recalled Joe Jacobs, that Jews 'should not draw attention to them-selves by taking part in anti-Fascist action on the streets. They seemed to think that it would only play into Mosley's hands if he could point to more and more Jews as Communists.' They pleaded for 'trust in the authorities' but events in Germany 'didn't seem to show that this attitude was right'. As the

BUF campaign intensified, East End Jews joined the Communist Party in increasing numbers.

The Popular Front idea was formalized at the Seventh World Congress of the Comintern in July and adopted by the British Communist Party at its National Congress in the autumn. It was, however, opposed by the Labour movement and CP leaders remained wedded to the idea that the National government posed the real threat. Mosley represented a 'lightning conductor' for the government whose 'reformist leaders point to Mosley as representing the sole menace of fascism'. This allowed them to promote the National government's repressive measures of preparation towards Fascism as a lesser evil compared with Mosley, while the masses' attention was fixed on him.

Individual Communists, however, were preoccupied with the BUF. When Mosley's 'travelling circus' tried to penetrate south Wales and Lancashire, it encountered fierce resistance. 'We would physically throw them out as well as politically throw them out,' a Manchester Communist recalled. Joe Jacobs's account of Communist–Fascist rivalry in the East End illustrates the divide within the CP over strategy. Philip Piratin favoured a more sophisticated approach but Jacobs advocated 'the maximum force available'. A Special Branch report details how Communists 'succeeded in driving the fascists from the streets of Camden Town and forced them to vacate their branch there'. The same tactic was attempted in the East End, but 'did not meet with the same success'.

In the summer, links were established between BUF officials and Otto Bene, now leader of the NSDAP's foreign division, though they were not without stress, since 'Bene's entourage regard both Mussolini and Mosley with some contempt as being financed from Jewish sources'. Nevertheless, Joyce sent the Germans a report, in which the BUF's anti-Semitic agitation was stressed. Mosley made his first East End appearance at Stratford Town Hall, West Ham, on 17 July 1935. He told the crowd he was 'going to tell you who your masters are ... Who backs the Conservative Party? who but international Jewish financiers? They are the people who put razor gangs on the streets. Who finances the Labour Party? The Little Jews in Whitechapel who sweat you in your sweatshops.' Two days later he turned on the 'decadence of our legislators' who were 'hysterically seeking to protect the negroid savage of Abyssinia'.

Italy announced it wanted to run a railway through Abyssinia to link Eritrea with Somaliland. Addis Ababa refused permission and Mussolini called up his troops. When Emperor Ras Tafari made a 'stirring appeal' to his people, Mosley denounced them as a 'black and barbarous conglomeration of tribes imbued with not one single Christian principle'. How was it possible 'to envisage the "equality" of one of the Four Great Powers of Europe with a barbarous Negro state existing in the conditions of the Dark Ages?'.

Alongside Garvin in the *Observer* and Lady Houston's *Saturday Review*,

Rothermere led opposition to sanctions against Italy. He claimed 'an Abyssinian victory over a white race would raise in the Dark Continent and other
continents far worse and more far reaching problems than any it could solve'.
In an article on 24 July he said, 'all sound-thinking Britons will wish Italy well
in the great enterprise to which she has set her hand.' The *Mail* suggested 'the
British public take no interest whatever in the slave-owning Abyssinian
Empire. And in this war which now seems inevitable their sympathy is wholly
with the cause of the white races which Italy is so firmly upholding.'

Once a supporter of the League of Nations and its right to act against illegal
interventions, Mosley was now in Mussolini's pocket and claimed a change
of heart 'due to the League's transformation into an instrument for maintaining the status quo and the personal weaknesses of League delegates'. In
The First of the League Wars (1936) Fuller claimed that 'what the League
definitely wanted was a war to smash Fascism, for that was the object of
the occult power that was controlling its destiny ... socialists, communists,
half-sane and deluded people shouted for military sanctions and the closing
of the Suez Canal. These meant world war, the destruction of Europe and the
expansion of atheistic Bolshevism – here the occult powers revealed themselves.' Behind it all was the Jewish conspiracy, whose only opposition was
Fascism – 'a powerful religious conception – divinely manifested in
nationalism'.

Mosley's problem was in getting his message across to the public. On 26 July
he was informed by the BBC that a broadcast of a talk by him might be
possible in the autumn and rumours spread through BUF headquarters that a
talk was planned. The BBC's Gladstone Murray reported to his controller
that 'this communication has given Sir Oswald great satisfaction and should
keep him quiet over the summer and autumn. I do hope, however, that the
plan succeeds this time.'

Two days later Mosley set off with his two elder children and Baba, who
somehow believed his relationship with Diana was platonic, for a holiday in
a villa owned by her friend Lady Rennell at Posillipo on the Italian Riviera.
As they left England, Diana was involved in a car crash. Her face was cut so
badly that her looks were only saved by a leading plastic surgeon, Sir Harold
Gillies (later a national figure for his work restoring the burnt faces of Battle
of Britain fighter pilots), whose skill left her without a scar.

Diana eventually made it to the villa, arriving during a dinner at which
Mosley and Baba were entertaining Italy's Crown Princess, a childhood friend
of the Curzon sisters. Vivien remembered hearing a row between the grown-
ups that night with doors being banged. Next day Mosley took Baba and his
children for a three-day trip on his yacht (named after Vivien) to Amalfi,
during which he managed to convince Baba of his devotion. As Anne de
Courcy notes, 'the status quo that so suited Mosley both temperamentally and

physically had been satisfactorily restored.' Diana tended to treat Mosley's philandering as he had once advised Cimmie to do, as a tiresome 'silliness' that he could not help. She admitted she suffered 'agonies of jealousy', but was confident 'he'd always come back to me'. Diana, too, attracted admirers, and Mosley was apt to be jealous when he was apart from her. She became pregnant during the stay and later had an abortion.

Franco Zeffirelli's film *Tea with Mussolini* was factually based on the strong British community in pre-war Tuscany. Most were civil servants and army officers retired from far-flung posts of the British Empire; a number were wealthy and lived in grand villas. Most were sympathetic to Italian Fascism and the 'head of the English Fascists' in Italy, John Celli, recruited them to the BUF. The irony was that they were often not only regarded as potential spies by their hosts but were later vilified as traitors in their homeland. Military records list 114 ex-pats, including Celli, classed during the Second World War as 'renegade British subjects' and liable for arrest. Unfortunately, Foreign Office records on those facing arrest have not survived.

'English women adored Mussolini because he was macho and well mannered,' recalled Zeffirelli. 'Only in the end did they realise what a bastard he was.' One was Diana's friend, Violet Trefusis, whose mother, Alice Keppel, had been Edward VII's lover. Violet was a lesbian; one of her lovers was Harold Nicolson's wife, Vita Sackville-West. Her parents had bought a 'super-luxurious villa full of treasures' in Florence. Her friend Vitetti had moved from the London embassy to the Foreign Office in Rome and arranged for her to see Mussolini. Trefusis recalled skidding on the marble floor as they were introduced, 'scattering the contents of my bag, lipstick, cigarettes, bills, compact, love letters. What could Mussolini, who prided himself on his way with women, do but help me pick them up?' She wondered why 'Oh God, why had we interfered in Abyssinia, interfered without interfering, brandishing threats, recoiling before acts?'

At the end of August Mosley tried to enlist Rothermere in his anti-sanctions campaign. Gordon-Canning approached his personal assistant, Harry Morrison, and invited Collin Brooks to Ebury Street for lunch which, Brooks recalled, 'was set on a balcony entered by stairs that might have been designed for *Macbeth*'. Mosley was joined by the 'rather silent' Gordon-Canning and they talked freely for an hour, mostly about the National League of Airmen, which Brooks said had 'inevitably attracted crooks'. Mosley recounted 'the trouble he had had in purging the Fascist movement of such fellows'. Mussolini told him 'discipline must be a light rein at first and only gradually tightened'. He instanced Hitler as 'one suffering from clever scoundrels, which made the night of the knife inevitable'.

Brooks thought that 'on the mastery of the streets', Mosley was convincing. When he asked whether he contemplated a *coup d'état*, Mosley said, 'Look at Hitler, he was legal to the point of ridicule – "Legality Hitler".' Only 'in strange unforeseen circumstances' would there be a coup. When Brooks suggested his moment would come in 1938, he expected 'another economic crisis then. What has amazed me has been our progress despite trade recovery.' Brooks thought he had misjudged the situation: 'Discontent is not evident in bad times, but always in improving times, when the share-out is in question.' Mosley was 'rather wrathy with Rothermere not for withdrawing support but for starting the supporting campaign too violently'.

It was from this time of Mosley's open support of Mussolini that MI5 began to regard the BUF with 'very grave suspicion'. It feared Mosley might have a secret organization ready for action in an 'emergency'. In response, the Committee of Imperial Defence set up a subcommittee chaired by Sir Claud Schuster, Permanent Secretary to the Lord Chancellor, to devise emergency legislation in the event of war. It was concerned what role the BUF might play in aiding a potential enemy. To counter the threat, MI5 used penetration agents, 'most but not all of whom were controlled by Knight's M Section and the shadowing staff'. Knight's agents revealed that Italian Military Intelligence was recruiting within the BUF and that some of Mosley's close aides and friends were assisting Nazi propaganda agencies.

According to German files, Fuller wrote intelligence reports on British organizations and individuals for Goebbels and Himmler, chief of the SS. In September he attended the German Army's manoeuvres at Lüneburg and reported in the *Mail* on 9 September on 'a great national demonstration'. Hitler had been present, 'moving from point to point and taking the keenest interest in what he saw'. He met Hitler's senior staff, some of whom were suspicious that he might be a spy. In fact, he did report on such visits to the War Office. Hitler told Diana that Fuller was 'a difficult man to work with', though Mosley found him, 'absolutely logical'. Hitler admired Fuller but was acutely embarrassed, Mosley discovered, whenever the subject of his association with Aleister Crowley was broached.

Mosley was in Italy when Mussolini invaded Abyssinia. Beckett took control of propaganda, launching a campaign against sanctions under the slogan 'Mind Britain's Business'. BUF income 'swelled mysteriously until it was able to spend over £3,000 [£102,000] per month'. With Fuller's 'organisational experience, a great deal of useful spade work was done'. Mosley had set the tone with meetings on 1 and 2 September in Manchester and at London's Adelphi Theatre. When an Englishman secured an oil concession for an American oil company from Abyssinia, Mosley saw it as evidence of the role of international financiers. 'Over the whole dispute rises the stink of oil. And stronger even than the stink of oil rises the stink of the Jew.' The Free Trade

29. Boxing champion Ted 'Kid' Lewis joined Mosley's New Party and trained its defence force, the 'Biff Boys', originally made up of Oxford rugby players and undergraduates but eventually a group of East End toughs

30. The violence associated with Mosley's NP meetings, particularly the wreckage caused at Birmingham's Rag Market in September 1931, led to Mosley embracing a more militant movement

31. With the break-up of the New Party, Mosley took time away from politics. Mosley with daughter Vivien and son Nicholas at Morden Park, 1932

32. Diana and first husband Bryan Guinness photographed by Cimmie at the Lido, Venice, 1932

33. This framed photograph of Mosley, taken by Cimmie, was by her bed when she died in May 1933

34. Mosley sought the backing of
Mussolini, seen here addressing the people
from the balcony of the Palazzo Venezia,
Rome in 1935

35. Destiny. Mosley in the black shirt
modelled on his fencing tunic

36. Mosley enlisted his aristocratic friends
into the BUF. At the Blackshirt Ball in
October 1934, Mosley gave a fencing display
with fencing champion Charles de
Beaumont

37. Lord Rothermere's *Daily Mail*
enthusiastically endorsed the Blackshirts.
Although fearful of another European war,
he praised Hitler and the Nazis

38. Mosley was best man at the fascist wedding of his Chief of Staff, Ian Hope Dundas, and Pamela Dorman in 1933. Dundas was the channel for funds from Mussolini to Mosley

39. Geoffrey Dorman had been an airman in the First World War and became editor of the BUF newspaper, *Action*

40. Director of Research, George Sutton was Mosley's long serving secretary

41. Director of Publicity, A.G. Findlay was one of the very few within the BUF to know about the secret funding from Mussolini

42. Mosley hoped for success in agricultural areas. He is seen here addressing farmers at Aylesbury, Buckinghamshire, in September 1933

43. Neil Francis Hawkins was the BUF's director general and surrounded himself with heel-clicking young Blackshirts

44. Hawkins's deputy in Administration was a Catholic former schoolmaster, Brian Donovan. He was intensely loyal to The Leader

45. During 1934 the Blackshirt Defence Corps, seen here with its specially adapted vans, was largely responsible, with its heavy-handed stewarding, for the violence that came to be associated with BUF meetings

46. Mosley attracted huge counter-demonstrations by anti-fascists. Hyde Park, 1934

47. Director of Propaganda Bill Risdon represented the left wing of the BUF, which included a number of former Communists and members of the Independent Labour Party

48. A cousin of G.K. Chesterton, A.K. Chesterton was responsible with William Joyce for the movement's extreme anti-Semitic propaganda

49. A BUF delegation to the 1933 Nuremberg Party Rally included Unity Mitford, William Joyce (flanked by French fascists in the front row), Alexander Raven Thomson (with moustache) and Captain Vincent (adorned with medals)

50. Diana Mosley with Putzi Hanfstaengl, responsible for foreign press relations at the 1934 Party Rally

51. Unity opened many channels for Mosley to leading Nazi officials. Unity speaking at Hesselberg in 1935 with the regime's leading anti-Semite, the notorious Julius Streicher

52. From 1935, Captain Robert Gordon-Canning, MC, an Arabist and financial backer of the BUF, was Mosley's personal foreign affairs adviser with responsibility for relations with Nazi Germany

53. During 1936 the BUF supported Italy's invasion of Abyssinia with its 'Mind Britain's Business' campaign which was heavily subsidised by Mussolini

54. Blackshirts flooded London streets during the Abdication Crisis, December 1936, in support of the young king, who was regarded as a Fascist monarch

55. With his new Nazi-style uniforms, Mosley inspects his storm troopers before the Battle of Cable Street, October 1936

56. An anti-fascist demonstrator is arrested by police in the East End of London, October 1936

Hall audience responded with several minutes of applause. He insisted the BUF was willing to take up arms in times of war, 'but we shall not fight in foreign quarrels for foreign ideals, or for foreign finance'. No Briton ought to die for Abyssinia: 'Britain is against all war and ... not one drop of British blood shall ever be spent except in defence of Britain and our Empire.' The main burden of his speech was that collective security was 'collective madness': 'keep out and stay out' was his policy.

Daniel Waley, in his study *British Public Opinion and the Abyssinian War*, claims the BUF campaign against British government policy in the Italian–Abyssinian dispute was 'isolationist and anti-League rather than pro-Italian'. In fact, Mosley opposed the League because his sympathies lay with the aggressor. Grandi told Irene that Mosley was 'the only man talking sense in England'. Michael Pugh notes that BUF support for the Italians was predictable but 'the militancy of its campaign could not have been foreseen' and does not 'explain why the BUF took so determined a stand against the trend of British foreign policy' given that a Peace Ballot survey showed that over eleven million people favoured League sanctions against the Italians. The explanation is that Mosley had to prove to Mussolini he was receiving value for his money.

Mosley unleashed his costly campaign with dozens of Blackshirts appearing in the streets carrying placards with the slogan 'Mind Britain's Business'. The BUF organized a 1,000 pro-peace meeting during September and chalked 'Mind Britain's Business' in 175,000 places and 'Mosley Says Peace' in 100,000 others.

The BUF's extremist version of the conventional right-wing mixture of imperialism and isolationism was championed in the House of Lords by Lord Mottistone, Churchill's Under-Secretary for Air (1919), and the pacifist Labour peer Lord Ponsonby. The former portrayed the Italians as underdogs – 'You have 200,000 young fellows – we all know what a charming people the Italians are – up against 600,000' – and accused Abyssinia of committing 'the most frightful atrocities'. The theme was echoed by Italian propaganda in the *Blackshirt*, which on 13 September published photographs purporting to show victims of Abyssinian torture. To counter such savagery, the BUF said a lesson in white civilization from Italy was long overdue.

The Foreign Office estimated that during the first nine months of its peace campaign the BUF received monthly payments of £5,000 (£170,000) from Italy. It was, however, not enough to change British public opinion. Grandi recognized it would require considerable time to convince the British that Italy needed to protect its interests in Africa. BUF door-to-door canvassers collected signatures for a petition but the results were never revealed. On 18 September Grandi requested and received extra funds from the Ministry of Popular Culture.

*

Mosley had reason to celebrate when on 3 September 1935 Sir Malcolm Campbell, in a Rolls-Royce-engined *Bluebird* adorned with the pennant of the BUF Volunteer Transport Service, broke the land speed record at the Bonneville Salt Flats. He achieved 301.1292 mph. A romantic adventurer, educated in Germany, he had served with the RFC and had been a pilot to the Prince of Wales. He made his money selling cars, dealing in diamonds and formulating libel insurance for newspapers. The *Mail*'s motoring correspondent and one of Rothermere's diehard friends, he unsuccessfully stood for the Conservatives in Deptford in 1935. Campbell was a 'convinced fascist and the nominal head of the propagandist British Movietone News, which displayed thinly disguised attacks on Trade Unionism and Parliamentarianism'. He frequently visited the Black House and was part of a racing-car network which embraced the BUF's Automobile Club.

Automobile Club regulars included former RFC observer Captain D. M. K. Marendez, seen frequently in his Alvis at Brooklands, and Miss Fay Taylour, Britain's leading female racing driver. In partnership with Marendez, Campbell bought two airfields and, at government request, set up a flying school at Barton to train airmen for war. Marendez not only knew Mosley but also Reichmarshall Goering. He was once caught photographing RAF installations and was threatened with imprisonment. Marendez worked with Thomas Godman, son of the Mayor of Gloucester and Receiver of the Hampton car company. Nicknamed 'Goering of the West', Godman often visited the Black House and was remembered as an important member of the BUF's Gloucester branch and its Blackshirt Flying Club, which was viewed as a dangerous development by MI5 when members began flying to Germany.

After the Second World War the US Counter-Intelligence Corps interrogated a Nazi official, Lothar Eisentraeger, about pre-war ties to the BUF. He said 'his only contact with Mosley was through a Commander Godman who also contacted the former Finance Minister Dr Hjalmar Schacht'. Schacht claimed 'he never met or heard of a Commander Godman'. However, it is clear from the transcript that the CIC was intrigued by the story. In particular, Eisentraeger's reference to 'an affair involving Admiral Canaris [chief of *Abwehr* intelligence] and Mosley', the nature of which remains unknown.

After the holiday at Posillipo, Diana joined Unity for a visit to Nuremberg. Before festivities began, they were guests of honour at the Congress of Nazi Groups Abroad held at Erlangen, Bavaria. The sisters, reported the British United Press, 'were given seats at the speaker's table, where Julius Streicher, Germany's Jew-baiter Number One, was addressing the congress'. It was a characteristic mixture of folk dancing and racial hatred. According to the *Fränkische Tageszeitung* (10 September), he interrupted one of the speeches to introduce the ladies at the top table: film-maker Leni Riefenstahl, Frau

Troost, the wife of Hitler's architect, and the Mitfords, who were treated as official BUF representatives and had 'the Nazi message in their blood'. Mosley was a 'courageous man' who had 'set himself the task of solving the Jewish problem'.

The next day Unity and Diana attended the Nuremberg Congress, sitting behind Hitler, with Tom Mitford and journalist Michael Burns. They were accompanied by Putzi Hanfstaengl, Riefenstahl and Sigismund FitzRandolph of the London embassy. Attending as the BUF representative was Gordon-Canning, along with a number of sympathizers. Funded by the Ministry of Propaganda and guests of the Führer were Henry Williamson, the Mosleyite novelist, and his friend the journalist John Heygate, who had married Evelyn Waugh's first wife. Heygate worked at UFA Films in Berlin as a propagandist for Goebbels and supervisor of English versions of German films. He was impressed by Hitler's movement of 'blood-brotherhood' with its 'pride of race' and wrote that 'there are innumerable young men like me who are waiting for a great leader'. He later disowned his National Socialist past in his 1940 book *These Germans*.

The Mitfords heard Hitler read out the Nuremberg Laws, which deprived Jews of their citizenship. Williamson was overcome by 'the romantic mixture of military parade, rousing speeches, together with elements akin to Wagnerian opera and religious ceremony'. Struck by the way people 'gave up all for an idea and bound themselves together for their beliefs, and fought the forces of gold and disintegration and rival ideas', he was moved to exclaim 'Heil Hitler!'. He was convinced Germany 'would create her own destiny, no more crowd hysteria or mass panic, no more political parties fighting for power'.

Williamson returned home a convert 'to a dreamy, idealised Hitlerism (rather than Nazism)'. Heygate recognized that his friend 'lived on fantasy'. He needed hero figures to venerate and he turned Mosley into an heroic idol. Following the death of T. E. Lawrence (who had considered joining the January Club) in a motorcycle accident on 19 May 1935, Williamson created the myth that he had been going to see his hero on a matter connected with a peace mission to Hitler. With Lawrence of Arabia's name to attract them, ex-servicemen would gather in the Albert Hall and begin 'a whirlwind campaign which would end the old fearful thought of Europe (usury-based) for ever. So would the sun shine on free men!' Williamson's blood-and-soil Fascism was romantic with its 'quest for perfection and idealism' but he had a 'distinctly unChristian attitude toward Jews'.

Hitler deeply impressed Gordon-Canning: 'As an Englishman proud of the heritage and tradition of my country, I can say without hesitation as he passed by us from the depth of my heart "Heil Hitler".' He gave an account to Mosley, who also received reports from BUF personnel in the Reich. Phillip Spranklin worked in the Munich Foreign Press Office run by Henrich Hoffman under the aegis of Goebbels's Ministry. Beckett's wife remembered him as one of 'the wilder young men on the publicity side, still in his late teens'. Clever but mischievous, he was a friend of leading Mosleyite journalist Bill Leaper and E. D. Randall, now teaching in Germany. Spranklin identified with Nazism to the point of losing his British nationality.

There was an increasing exchange of visitors between London and Berlin. In September Herr Hildebrand of the Hitlerjugend organization visited Mosley and presented lectures to the BUF, which were published in the *Blackshirt*. Two months later the British authorities ordered his deportation. The Communist Party observed these events and sent a file on Hildebrand to Moscow. Dr Karl-Hans Galinsky, a Manchester University lecturer who had spoken at the January Club on Hitler, wrote a laudatory account of the BUF for the Germans. After describing Mosley's speech at the Albert Hall – 'We fought Germany once in our British quarrel. We shall not fight Germany again in a Jewish quarrel' – he observed that there was 'something of the Elizabethan in his gallant, rather arrogant air. He is the Englishman of the Carolean tennis-court; of the duelling-ground rather than of the Pall Mall Club. He is a big man of blood and bone, of strong tones, no feeble creature of grey shadings. He is a personality with all his individual qualities and faults, no self-complacent bladder of conventions.'

During the autumn the BBC decided to produce a series of educational talks on 'The Citizen and His Government'. It gave Mosley reason to hope an agreement had been reached with regard to him being allowed to broadcast. The last talk was to feature lectures on Fascism and Communism by Mosley and Harry Pollitt. On 13 September the Foreign Office's Rex Leeper contacted the Controller of Programmes, Alan Dawnay, urging the BBC to drop the Pollitt talk. The Foreign Office's Permanent Head, Sir Robert Vansittart, then expressed concern to Sir John Reith that Mosley was being allowed to broadcast. Prompted by Italy's recent attack on Abyssinia, he worried as to the use Mosley might make of the opportunity. These points were considered by the Board of Governors but were rejected after assurances that Mosley would not be allowed to refer to Abyssinia. Vansittart remarked at a meeting on 27 September that he saw little possibility of the international situation developing in such a way that a talk by Mosley would be innocuous. Mosley was 'an agent of Italian fascism taking his orders from Italy'.

The Foreign Office threatened to bring the BBC to heel. The Minister for League of Nations Affairs, Anthony Eden, outlined the government's objections in a memorandum to Cabinet. It would be unfortunate if publicity were given to 'a man who was known to be in close touch and sympathy with Mussolini'. He suggested the BBC class the talks as 'not in the national interest'. Vansittart said that 'should it be decided that Mosley should not speak then there would be no need to inform the public that it was because of

Mosley, but merely to say that, owing to the present situation, it was not considered desirable to go forward with this particular series of talks; it should be left to listeners to form their own conclusion as to why the series had been dropped, but probably 90 per cent would assume it was the Mosley issue'. In the event, an imminent general election solved the problem and provided a pretext for postponing the talks. The BBC Board agreed 'not to say anything about the private discussions that had been taking place between the Foreign Office and ourselves'.

Mussolini viewed foreign policy as a means of invigorating 'moribund fascism' by channelling internal frustration into external violence. At 5 a.m. on 3 October 1935 his legions began a mission, Grandi declared, 'to civilise the black continent'. The British Minister in Addis Ababa reported that the first bomb from the opening air raid on Adowa fell on a hospital building marked with a red cross. General Rudolfo Graziani's Expeditionary Force killed thousands of civilians and starved infants in concentration camps; his men posed for photographs holding severed heads. General Pietro Badoglio's planes sprayed mustard gas over villages. Acting as an agent for the War Office, Fuller said in the *Mail* that 'it proved a decisive tactical factor in the war'. The head of a Red Cross hospital commented, 'This isn't war – it isn't even slaughter. It's the torture of tens of thousands of defenceless men, women and children with bombs and poison gas.'

The BUF defended the tactics. On 7 October Fuller visited Mussolini with a letter of introduction from Mosley. He introduced himself as 'a full-blooded Fascist' and said press hostility to the invasion was the result of Jewish influence. He offered his services as Rothermere's special envoy on Abyssinia 'attached to BUF HQ', who could 'get away from the other correspondents. As a soldier I shall know how much not to report.' Passage was arranged for Fuller on a troopship to Abyssinia, where he spent three months observing the war. The *Mail* and the *Morning Post* were the only papers to support Mussolini, though a number of Fascist-inclined writers and academics reported sympathetically on the Italian action.

Fuller was joined by Reuter's correspondent James Strachey Barnes and Muriel Curry, former branch secretary of the League of Nations Union and BUF member, who became a war correspondent after travelling to the area on a permit from the Italian government. She was adopted as a mascot by General Villa Santa's Gavinana Division, broadcast from Rome and received the Croce di Guerra. Evelyn Waugh believed Italian control of Abyssinia 'would be for the benefit of the Ethiopian Empire and the rest of Africa'. Such writers were helped by Grandi's secret funds of around £2,000 (£68,000). He reported to Rome on 25 October that 'much has already been done'.

Beckett organized BUF propaganda but direction came from Grandi who sent Rome 'samples of the leaflets distributed in Grosvenor Square during the attempt to demonstrate against the Italian embassy'. At his request, British Fascists 'marched carrying placards with the words "Why should Britain assist Abyssinia?"'. Members filled out audiences at newsreel shows – 'so that they can clap and counteract any criticism'. Grandi told Mussolini he sent his request to Mosley, who 'tells me that it will be done'.

BUF propaganda suggested Afro-Asians had similarities with Jews. Haile Selassi – 'Jewry's new idol' – was portrayed in cartoons with exaggerated Jewish features. The *Blackshirt* said 'the powers of Jewish international finance and Jewish-controlled Bolshevism' were ranged against 'the regenerated Fascist nations of Europe, prepared to fight to the last ditch for the principles of white civilisations'. Radicals wanting an overt anti-Semitic campaign were let off the leash to exploit the issue in the East End. On 5 October Joyce told a Bethnal Green crowd, 'If war comes and you have to leave your land for a foreign battlefield, the Jew will not march with you; but he will stay here and advance unchecked, into possession of your opportunities, your homes, and all that you dare call your own.'

Mosley portrayed himself as a restraining influence on his lieutenants' extreme anti-Semitism, but this runs counter to the evidence of his own speeches. When he spoke to branches in the West Midlands, members heard speeches dominated by abusive anti-Semitism. He refused to veto the vehement anti-Semitism of the BUF press and in the East End walls were daubed with the slogan 'Perish Juda'. Complaints about BUF behaviour multiplied with stories of Fascists terrorizing Jews. The Communists reacted after Italy invaded Abyssinia but, again, the upsurge in anti-Fascist activity came from the rank and file. This was the case even when the emergence of the BUF in the East End proved to be 'a great boost to morale, strength and membership'. In some areas anti-Fascism proved to be the CP's only successful platform.

Mosley warned in *Giornale d'Italia* that the anti-Italian drive was directed by Jews who wanted to plunge the Western world into a fratricidal war. 'While this propaganda had little effect on opinion in the Western democracies', Mosley claimed it had 'a profound impression on Mussolini and many members of his entourage'. Meir Michaelis suggests the idea of a 'Jewish' sanctionism was 'encouraged not by Hitler (who adopted a policy of neutrality between Italy and the League), but by Western anti-semites, especially in England, who supported the fascist aggression'. There followed anti-Jewish polemics in the Italian press attacking 'world Jewry' and its responsibility for Anglo-French hostility to Italy. Secret police reports to Mussolini claimed Foreign Office Minister Anthony Eden, who was denounced as a 'special enemy of Italy', was 'of Jewish extraction, the bastard son of King George V' and a 'most beautiful Jewess'. Mosley's role illustrated the degree to which he was willing to submerge the movement's nationalist ideology in his desire to court Mussolini's support.

Grandi flooded Britain with propaganda through BUF contacts, Carlo Camagna, secretary of the London Fascio, Camillo Pellizzi of University College, Cesare Foloigno at Oxford, and Luigi Villari, a member of Mosley's Windsor Club. The *British-Italian Bulletin* produced a supplement edited by Camagna, which included articles by Ian Hope Dundas, Ezra Pound and Harold Goad, who defended Italy's imperialist role because of Abyssinia's 'scandalous and barbaric' conditions. Out of Muriel Curry's flat propaganda efforts were run involving Barnes, Yeats-Brown and Sir Osbert Sitwell. Curry was the BUF's chief enthusiast for the organization of womanhood in Italy and an intelligence asset of Grandi. Sitwell wanted a 'respectable fascism' with government 'allowed to get on with its business, to be given a good bus service and punctual trains'.

Liberal opinion was thrilled when the British government on 11 October condemned Italy's aggression. However, the desire to preserve Italian participation in the Stresa front against Germany meant that military intervention was unlikely. A week later Mosley ended the Peace Campaign and, announcing that since military sanctions had been abandoned, released members from special duties. It was, however, 'a hollow triumph'. He miscalculated the public mood and 'popular indignation with Italy outdid the BUF's own brand of patriotism and threatened to smother the movement'. On 18 November the League passed a blockade resolution and Britain took the lead in imposing economic sanctions. In fact, it was privately preparing to back down but it was a blow to Italy and the Fascist movements that had tied themselves to Mussolini.

With the perceived 'success' of the campaign, Mosley persuaded Mussolini to reinstate funding to previous levels. According to the Secret Service in a report of 22 October, Mussolini resumed monthly payments of £3,000 (£102,000). Italian agents forwarded to Rome highly favourable assessments to justify their salaries and exaggerated their accounts. They claimed there were 500,000 pro-Mussolini, pro-BUF Fascists. 'Most Englishmen, and most true English intellectuals', announced Villari, 'supported the war.'

Mosley made 'any investigation into the finances of the BUF impossible' and MI5 investigators 'had to content themselves with the observation that the funds were derived for the greater part from "unknown sources"'. Jack Curry believed the details were known only to Mosley's inner circle, 'one of whom went regularly either to France or Switzerland to collect the money in pound notes'. In sharp contrast, the Service knew from intelligence intercepts, deciphered by the Government Code and Cipher School under the codename

MASK, that the CPGB was receiving £3,000 (£112,000) per month from Moscow.

MI5 had no evidence of 'serious Italian espionage in this country' since it had no 'reliable information which would enable us to see the purely espionage aspects in clear perspective'. It conducted an inquiry into the Nazis' worldwide Auslands Organisation (AO), which had been created as the Party's foreign division by a Hess protégé, Bradford-born Ernst-Wilhelm Bohle. Members were organized into 'cells' and collected political information in their host countries and occasionally military affairs. Its chief contribution 'was in providing the names of potential spies'. MI5's B Branch warned that 'we should not lose sight of the fact that ... the whole energy of the machine could be utilised in the reverse direction'. It was 'a ready-made instrument for intelligence, espionage and ultimately for sabotage purposes'.

Also of concern to MI5 was the Ribbentrop Büro, whose staff tried to establish contacts in the upper echelons of British society sympathetic to the idea of an Anglo-German alliance. Home Office files on the BUF make a reference to Margarete Gartner, 'well known as a Nazi propagandist', who developed the contacts she had made in the previous year. She had been responsible for creating the Anglo-German Association which had been dissolved in April over allowing Jews to join. Richard Meinertzhagen, a former AGA member and wartime British Intelligence officer, had been in touch with the German embassy and 'an influential body of businessmen' with a view to creating a new organization more assertive in its support of Germany.

Backed by Ribbentrop, who had been introduced to prominent figures by merchant banker Ernest Tennant, the Anglo-German Fellowship (A-GF) was created in October. Its German twin, the 'Deutsch-Englische Gesellschaft', was active in the 'para-diplomatic sphere'. Fellowship members took part in the celebrations to mark the opening of the D-EG in Berlin in January 1936. Under its Chairman Lord Mount Temple, the A-GF – its secretary was outspoken anti-Semite Elwin Wright – drew its support from Tory backbenchers, peers, retired officers, industrialists and financiers, who wanted 'to promote good understanding between Britain and Germany' without necessarily implying approval of National Socialism. Walter Hewel was an A-GF member and Ribbentrop's personal liaison to Hitler, enjoying immediate access to the Führer.

Goebbels later told Wilfred von Oven that 'there were quite a number of influential Tories who entirely agreed with the Führer's championing of a policy of Anglo-German conciliation'. Goebbels who, Diana admitted, never liked Mosley and resented Hitler's interest in him, added

In saying this, I don't even take any account of Mosley. He was an outsider of small political significance. Fascism is a plant that does not grow in the soil of Britain. It does not seem to go down well with the English. And what Mosley was doing over there with his Blackshirts, harmed rather than benefited our cause. Far more important were a number of Conservatives who pleaded for a close association with Hitler although, from the ideological point of view, they had nothing in common with him.

To the Nazis, the Anglo-German societies were ideal propaganda platforms from which prominent Germans could lecture foreign audiences. They were also part of the Büro's intelligence network, whose 'permanent escorts' questioned guests about the state of British public opinion. Although the A-GF could be seen as a pro-Nazi bridgehead – its members 'an anti-communist conspiracy in business, high finance and high nobility of the island kingdom who did important work for Hitler, including trying to strengthen the anti-Soviet and "pro-German" alignment of the British government' – its influence on British foreign policy decision making was 'insignificantly small'.

During October MI5 noted that BUF officials had 'distinctly pro-Nazi tendencies and social relations between the two have been fairly close'. They 'attended gatherings of Nazis in London and the effect of such intercourse on both sides must be considerable'. Mosley was finding a sympathetic audience in Germany as Unity's efforts bore fruit. On 24 October she was invited to tea with Goebbels and Hitler, who talked about the German–English relationship. Goebbels believed the Führer's 'thoughts are gaining a foothold in England'. It looked that way to Special Branch, which reported that Dr Thost, who had 'a reputation for political intrigue', was under some sort of cloud with Otto Bene for an indiscretion. His 'association with certain British politicians, and with members of the BUF has caused the trouble'. Spreading the Nazi gospel was legitimate but spying would cause a problem for Hitler's efforts to court the British government. In November, Thost's residency permit was withdrawn and he was asked to leave Britain because 'his stay would not be in the public interest'.

On Diana's return to London, she broke her rule of not involving herself in politics by attending her first and only demonstration. On 27 October in Hyde Park she came across a large demonstration organized by the Non-Sectarian Anti-Nazi Council, among whose speakers was Labour leader Clement Attlee. When a boycott of German goods was proposed, a sea of hands went up in support, then a single hand to vote against it. The *News Chronicle* reported that Diana 'stood in the crowd on her own and recorded a lone vote . . . During the singing of "God Save the King", while the crowd stood bare-headed, Mrs Guinness raised her hand in the fascist salute.' The crowd jeered and turned nasty. John Warburton and a fellow Blackshirt were close by and escorted her to safety. Unity recorded that Hitler was pleased with what 'Diana had been doing at Hyde Park', rallying support for the Nazis. Diana did not 'regret getting involved. National Socialism was a great fact. You couldn't just evade it at that time.'

At the end of October, Prime Minister Stanley Baldwin, who six months earlier had taken over from MacDonald, called a general election. Mosley had said the BUF would win a majority of seats in two successive general elections before implementing the full programme of the 'Fascist Revolution'. He had considered standing in Evesham or Ormskirk but the BUF was not in a state to launch an election campaign. On 28 October Mosley announced he was not fielding candidates and would campaign for voter abstention with the slogan 'Fascism Next Time'. Supporters were 'not to waste a vote for a farce. Wait for the real battle. This election is a sham battle, which at the next election will be followed by the real battle: not until Fascist candidates enter the field as challengers for power will any reality be introduced into British politics.'

The Windsor Club did support candidates against the 'old Gang'. Sir Henry Fairfax-Lucy did 'what I could' to help a Committee member and Tory MP, Colonel Alfred Todd, at Berwick-on-Tweed. A friend of Lord Erroll, Fairfax-Lucy, who had land in Kenya, wanted a 'drastic reform of parliamentary government' and would support Fascism if that was what was required. There was help through U. C. S. Hayter of the Indian Empire Society for those opposing the government's India policy. The pro-Nazi MP for Basingstoke, Henry Drummond Wolff, had resigned, ostensibly for health reasons. However, he and the previous constituency MP, Lord Lymington, shoehorned into the seat Patrick Donner, British Fascist and Secretary of the India Defence League. Before Donner's adoption the local agent wrote to Wolff that he understood Donner 'had a successful interview' with Mosley, suggesting he was 'adopted with Mosley's approval or co-operation'. Protest letters in *The Times* attacking sanctions against Italy were organized by Club Chairman Luttman-Johnson. Round robin names included Douglas Jerrold, who advised on whom to approach, Lord Salisbury's nephew Algernon Cecil, Arnold Wilson, Ronald Graham and Lord Phillimore.

The 1935 general election was a comfortable victory for Baldwin's National government. A loss of ninety seats still left a parliamentary majority of 255 for the Conservatives. The return of 154 Labour MPs increased the party's strength but was considered a poor showing that did not materially alter the situation, since the Liberals dropped from thirty-three to twenty seats. The National government's comprehensive victory showed what little impact Fascism had made on the public.

According to Ambassador Grandi, on the day after the election he was called by Sir Robert Vansittart 'and we started to work on what became known as the proposal Hoare–Laval which should in fact be called Vansittart–

Grandi'. Having assured voters he was not trying to 'do a disreputable deal' behind the League's back, Foreign Secretary Samuel Hoare agreed on a peace plan with French Minister Pierre Laval, which rewarded Italy by giving it Abyssinia's fertile plains and more territory than it had captured. In return, Abyssinia would gain an outlet to the sea. The pact undermined the policy of collective security and legitimized Fascist aggression by seeking to reward it.

There was an outcry that Baldwin had won the election on a League pro-gramme, which he immediately jettisoned. 'Never', reported French ambassa-dor Charles Pineton, 'has Italian support for Mussolini been more complete.' The Duce turned a squalid colonial adventure into a patriotic crusade and sent a more vigorous commander to Abyssinia. The *Express* published a picture of Grandi and captioned it 'The Winner'. In fact, with a narrow circle of friends in London, Grandi had sent Mussolini misleading information about the government's willingness to stand up to Italy. Even so, the championing of Grandi bruised Mussolini's ego and and he was recalled back to Rome. A war against Britain was now spoken of with confidence by Mussolini and Britain's weakness gradually consolidated Hitler's enthusiasm for a 'combi-nation of the Fascist powers' that might be 'transformed into a world-wide anti-British alliance'.

Contact between the BUF and Italy was strengthened after Mosley agreed in December that Dundas become the permanent liaison with the Italian Fascist Party (PNF). Dundas and his wife had cruised around the Mediterranean with Mosley and Diana, and had spent a few months in Italy. In Rome, they were housed in the Villa Albani with a butler and servants. Ciano sent roses and the couple regularly met Mussolini. Dundas's daughter, Lynette, recalled that they had a good life and 'always had lots of money'. All they had to do was 'reach under the bed into a trunk of cash'. Dundas ran English broadcasting from Italy. His broadcasts were numerous but no recordings appear to have survived. There was comment in the British press and he can be seen as the first of the radio 'traitors'. His daughter admitted he was 'a kind of Lord Haw Haw'.

Box criticized Mosley's obligations to Rome. MI5 sources and the peace campaign now left no doubt as to the source of the funds. There was, recalled Guy Liddell, an air of triumph in MI5 at the discovery of the Italian subsidies. When Mosley told Box 'We will be ready for the next election', he replied, 'You won't be ready in ten years' time.' Disillusioned with Mosley, Box decided to resign; a decision kept secret for fear of the disastrous effect on the movement's morale.

When Chesterton went on a fact-finding tour of the Midlands, he reported that in one district the offices were 'part thieves kitchen and part bawdy house'. Many branches were moribund. The lack of a close relationship between centre and periphery was partly blamed on Mosley, whose 'political background and experience lay in the British party system not in organising extra parliamentary movements'. He was forced to sell the lease of the Black House for a rumoured £50,000 (£1.7m). New offices purchased in Sanctuary Buildings, Westminster, bizarrely also housed the Home Office. The landlord was approached by Special Branch but could not prevent Mosley taking the lease.

After Box's departure, Hawkins's ex-officer class dominated the BUF. Beckett had no time for his 'heel-clicking and petty militarism' but, notes his son, 'does not seem to have realised that all this was an intrinsic part of the creed'. Hawkins was promoted to Director-General, ranking second to Mosley, who reserved for himself absolute control of policy and propaganda. The secret of Hawkins's influence was his unquestioning loyalty, a quality to which Mosley attached high value when so many were deserting him. Mosley received adulation and expected it. Blackshirts, Colin Cross noted, 'even saluted him when he went into the sea to bathe at the Movement's summer camps at Selsey'. They 'whispered his name in religious awe and every Fascist speech had its quota of praise for the Leader, who was presented to the public as a superman. Criticism was totally taboo and humour nearly so.' A minority complained of his megalomania. Beckett referred to him as 'The Bleeder'.

The political leaders – Beckett, Chesterton and Joyce – quarrelled with Hawkins's choice of men for posts. Brian Donovan, Assistant Director-General (Administration), was one of his martinets and was considered 'too taut, inflexible, exacting'. The new system, which was intended to provide an unbroken chain of command from the Leader to the active member, was in practice riddled with personal jealousies. Beckett later blamed the 'malicious intrigue rampant in the BUF' for which he was partly responsible. Factional civil war broke out with rumours of favouritism and of promotions based on homosexual friendships. In the long term, Mosley kept the allegiance of the bureaucrats far better than that of the political idealists 'for whom the BUF in the end proved an inadequate vehicle for their ideas and ambitions'. In the short term, however, the BUF's anti-Semitic campaign remained in full swing.

The BUF was among the weakest manifestations of Fascism in Europe. It was unable to make inroads into the Conservative and Labour vote, and failed to elect a single MP or local councillor. It had been 'squeezed out' as a major force in both conventional and extra-parliamentary politics. John Stevenson argues that failure stemmed from developments outside of Mosley's control; British Fascism had to operate in an unpromising climate, both politically and economically. There was no economic collapse, national humiliation through defeat, street violence, or polarization into two armed camps.

George Orwell wrote that a foreign observer in England 'sees only the huge inequality of wealth, the unfair electoral system, the governing-class control of the press, the radio and education. But this ignores the considerable agreement that does unfortunately exist between the leaders and the led.' There was little reason to throw off their electoral allegiance to the Conservatives or to dismiss Baldwin's leadership.

The middle class did well economically. Those living in the South experienced the 'most sustained period of growth in the whole inter-war period'. Mosley noted that exports to imperial markets rose from a third to two-fifths of her total exports, while the proportion of imperial imports into Britain rose dramatically. He could argue it was the result of mild protectionism, which eased pressure on the balance of payments and the pound, and allowed cheap money, with bank rate at 2 per cent. The housing boom brought home-ownership to the lower middle classes for the first time; exactly the group that turned to Fascism abroad. Mosley's case for public works schemes was weakened since 'such a project's main beneficiary – the construction industry – was already flourishing'. Instead of 'the outsize concrete monuments of a British Mussolini', three million homes were built and jobs increased by a third during the 1930s. The long-term consequence was a distortion of the British economy and the weakening of manufacturing.

Unemployment remained high at 2.4 million and was seen as 'the greatest threat to the stability of the state as well as to the welfare of families and communities'. At the end of November the Prince of Wales was reported in the *Illustrated London News* as saying of unemployment that 'something should be done'. It was, however, largely confined to specific areas, of which the middle class remained ignorant. The BUF opened propaganda centres in Lancashire and enrolled hundreds of members, which worried the Labour Party. 'If any totalitarian creed stood a chance of adoption by the Lancashire workers,' commented H. Pelling, 'it is likely to be fascism.' Risdon, however, could not deliver the expected breakthrough. When propaganda eased off through lack of funds, Fascist support melted away.

Rearmament helped drive down unemployment to below two million. The Treasury, however, regarded public works as futile and snubbed Germany's 'debatable doctrines' despite the fact that they had an almost immediate effect. The Nazi cure was much discussed within BUF circles. When Lady Downe spoke to the King's Lynn branch after returning from Germany, 'she explained how unemployment had been reduced from five to two million since the Nazis came to power'. With exports still only 75 per cent of their 1929 level, it was hard, as Mosley had predicted, to claim that increased industrial efficiency was 'a sufficient cure for unemployment'. However, his natural backers were out of recession, doing well and had no need of his shock troops.

Mosley hoped the crisis of the loss of Empire would attract support because 'fascism not the Conservative Party' was 'the true mantle of patriotism'. However, contrary to Lloyd George's fear that Baldwin's moderation would drive diehards into Mosley's arms they joined, instead, with Churchill.

The organizers of disorder 'were content to stop short of generating the kind of violence seen on the Continent'. The Fascists acceded to police instructions, which fitted in with Baldwin's view of the English and their antipathy to Continental methods. Having adopted a position which necessitated waiting for history to take a particular turn, Mosley was left marooned when history did not turn in the required direction. So long as the Communists were kept in check, there was no reason for the middle class to feel threatened. Ultimately, Smart suggests, 'it was the Labour party that let Mosley down. Its failure to fulfil that change-agent purpose Mosley had mapped out for it was the killer blow.' The Socialist League had presented a challenge, but 'at the moment when it frightened its opponents most, the party reverted to type: becoming as before the epitome of loyal oppositional respectability, imbued with parliamentary values. The non-materialization of the socialist threat was what rendered the Fascist challenge stillborn.'

The BUF degenerated into an organization increasingly dependent on a localized campaign playing on populist anti-Semitism. Paying membership had fallen but it recovered at the end of the year, tripling to around 15,000, at which level it remained for the next fifteen months. The surge in recruitment was partly a result of the Abyssinian peace campaign, which 'tapped into an authentic anti-war feeling amongst many East End workers'. When Gordon-Canning dined with Bruce Lockhart on 15 November, he was 'full of optimism for the future of Fascism'. He took 'comfort from the large percentage of non-voters in the election (30 per cent) and thinks Fascism will recruit most of this'.

Mosley was just as optimistic when in early January 1936 he addressed staff, and affirmed his admiration for Nazism and a desire to emulate its methods. According to an SB informant, Mosley dreamed of a 'disciplined troop of BUF MPs marching into Parliament and giving it "the shock of its life"'. Favourable 'as the police frequently were, they were often obliged to protect Red hooligans', nevertheless, the BUF would triumph over the 'droning dirge of the "Red Flag"' and replace it with 'discipline, confidence and challenge – and nothing can stop them'. The Home Office warned that Mosley's rhetoric 'must be taken seriously for what it was, a genuine statement of intent to undermine the political stability of Britain'.

18

The East End

With the country swept by a harsh winter, George V developed bronchitis. On 19 January 1936 the King died and was succeeded by the Prince of Wales. The Duke of Saxe-Coburg Gotha, a Nazi Party member and President of the Anglo-German Fellowship, attended the funeral as Hitler's emissary. He told Edward the Führer wanted friendly relations with Britain and asked him if it would be 'useful' for Hitler and the PM to meet. 'Who is King here?' came the reply. 'Baldwin or I? I myself wish to talk to Hitler.' Minutes of the meeting were sent direct to Hitler. The BUF lauded the 'steel-true' King as an 'airman hero', who was destined 'to throw the whole influence of his brave spirit into Britain's resurgence'.

Major-General Fuller returned from Abyssinia and reported on the Italian Army's 'staggering inefficiency' to Rothermere, who was 'mentally staggered' by the news. Fuller wrote to Mosley on 8 February warning that Continental Fascism 'will not fit the English. Both Hitler and Mussolini are riding for a fall. They may get up, but we do not want to fall with them; because we may never be able to get up again.' He realized his ideas 'would not be popular with many of your staff' but 'we are not Italians, we are not Germans, we are British – this is the fundamental fact to guide us'. Mosley ignored the advice and, with an eye to new funding, switched his allegiance from Italy to Germany. The anti-Semitism campaign and the dropping of the label 'Fascism' and its replacement by 'National Socialism' marked the shift in thinking.

A favourite slogan was 'If you love your country you are National, if you love her people you are Socialist – Be a National Socialist'. The *Blackshirt* praised Hitler, while Blackshirts emulated the Nazis with their uniforms, songs and salute. Under the BUF's first Constitution, they were organized according to the German model of black guards and storm troopers. Mosley enhanced the standing of the elite corps by issuing a special uniform. He referred to the Germans as 'Our Blood Brothers' and could 'say without any hesitation . . . from the bottom of my heart, "Heil Hitler"'.

In late January, when Ian Hope Dundas and Mosley visited Rome, Mussolini decided to reduce the subsidy by £43,300 (£1.47m) per annum. Because of the funding crisis, Bill Allen sent Mosley a letter on 11 February guaranteeing to back any loan to the BUF of up to £10,000 (£340,000). On the following day Allen sent him a proposal to develop a commercial radio station on Sark. The Italian leader was not convinced the BUF was making progress and sent his agent to make enquiries. In response, Mosley made 'extravagant claims' about the East End campaign and decided to concentrate resources in the area.

Anti-Semitism united all sections of the BUF in their hatred of Jews. Half of the national membership was concentrated in the East End boroughs. In Shoreditch, a working-class subculture within the rank and file approved of provocative physical force Jew baiting. The volatile mix of populist anti-Semitism and Fascist violence threatened to get out of control. The Bethnal Green campaign was led by mob orator Mick Clarke, who had the ability, according to John Charnley, 'to take hold of an audience and ring it until their very withers withered away'. A genuine Cockney, Clarke was labelled the 'Julius Streicher of the BU', due to his parading about in a full-length black leather coat and to his rabid anti-Semitism. Those skilled in populist street-corner agitation, such as Bill Bailey and Jock Huston, who had a lengthy criminal record, brought much adverse publicity to the movement.

Mosley still believed he might be allowed to take part in a BBC discussion, *The Citizen and His Government*, but Anthony Eden's memorandum for a Cabinet meeting on 12 February suggested the BBC 'withdraw the objectionable items of their programmes' as not being in the national interest. The BBC felt 'there could hardly be a period in the history of Fascism when Fascist arguments would be less likely to commend themselves to the British public'. However, the PM was able to report a week later to relieved Ministers that the BBC had agreed to withdraw the Mosley talk and had agreed to make 'no public reference to government intervention'. The Controller of Programmes wrote to Mosley on 17 March that the BBC had taken 'no decision to exclude Fascism in Britain from the microphone'. His 'invidious treatment' was raised in the Commons by Sir Reginald Blair, who had known Mosley in the War Office at the end of the war, but to no avail.

The Foreign Office had reason to worry about the deteriorating situation in Europe. German troops marched into the Rhineland on 7 March 1936 but Hitler hoped this breach of the Locarno Treaty would not provoke military countermeasures from the Allies. Mosley welcomed the reoccupation as helpful to peace by removing one of Germany's main grievances. When the troops entered, Diana and Unity were in Cologne to greet Hitler.

On 10 March the German ambassador, Leopold von Hoesch, persuaded Edward VIII to threaten abdication if Baldwin wanted war over the Rhineland crisis. After seeing the PM, the King telephoned von Hoesch to report success. Listening in was Press Attaché Fritz Hesse. Edward had seen 'that bastard' Baldwin and given him a dressing down. 'I told him I'd resign in the event of war. There will be no war. Don't worry.' Hearing the news, Hitler said, 'At last. The King of England will not intervene. He is keeping his promise.'

As a result of a 70 per cent cut in Italian funding, on 11 March Mosley announced a reduction in Headquarters personnel. With active membership estimated at 4,000, he began a new recruitment drive. The *Blackshirt* adopted 'The Patriotic Workers Paper' as its sub-heading and devoted itself to 'matters appealing to workers'. George Orwell saw evidence of the new direction at a meeting on 16 March in London of around 700 mainly working-class people and 100 Blackshirts. He was dismayed by their reaction to Mosley: 'He was booed at the start but loudly clapped at the end.' They were 'bamboozled' by Mosley, who spoke from 'a Socialist angle, condemning the treachery of successive governments towards the workers. The blame for everything was put upon mysterious international gangs of Jews who are said to be financing ... the British Labour Party.' Mosley extolled Germany but dismissed a question about concentration camps. 'We have no foreign models; what happens in Germany need not happen here.'

For a rally at the Albert Hall on 22 March, the *Daily Worker* organized a counter-demonstration. Around 8,000 anti-Fascists demonstrated against Mosley's last meeting at the Hall, where he said 'it was the intention of British Fascism to challenge and break for ever the power of the Jews in Britain'. Those Jews who did not 'put Britain first' would be deported.

The Beckett-edited *Blackshirt* and *Action* launched an attack on Jewish influence. On 2 April *Action* implied that Lord Camrose, owner of the *Telegraph*, was of Jewish extraction and his paper was subservient to international finance. In the subsequent libel case the jury agreed the article was defamatory and awarded damages of £12,500 (£425,000) to Camrose and £7,500 to the *Telegraph*. This had little effect, since the company publishing *Action* 'folded up' following the award. It had been set up in such a way as to avoid libel damages.

In April Mosley changed the movement's name to the British Union of Fascists and National Socialists – 'British Union' for short. The fasces symbol was superseded by a circle of unity enclosing a flash of lightning – dubbed by opponents the 'flash in the pan'. The changes coincided with a new peace campaign. Blackshirts wrote 'Mosley Says Peace' in whitewash on walls across Britain and on the doorstep of 10 Downing Street. He envisioned a United Fascist Europe, with the Empire a key factor, to replace the League of Nations as the body to maintain peace. He claimed there was no conflict between Britain, whose 'world mission' was Empire-centred, and Germany's quest for a union of German people. The BU tried to reassure the public that the Germans did not want a worldwide Empire, for that could lead to 'racial deterioration'.

At the end of April Diana was dispatched to Berlin with a wild money-making scheme. Goebbels was told the idea was 'to make available £50–100 million [£1.7–3.4 billion] through loan bank Morgan. That would be wonderful. And Mosley would be saved by it. Führer will pursue the matter. Baron v. Schroeder is to test the ground in London.' An excited Goebbels brought the Führer to Schwanenwerder for a discussion with Diana, who repeated the offer from Mosley. 'Sounds very positive. A representative of Morgan's Bank must come to Germany and negotiate with v. Schroeder. We'll see what comes of it.'

Kurt von Schroeder managed the Cologne bank J. H. Stein and belonged to the 'Keppler Circle' who donated large sums to Hitler. Stein owned a share of the Schroeder banking houses and Kurt was a frequent traveller to its London branch, J. Henry Schroeder. Chaired by Baron Bruno von Schroeder, the bank was a large underwriter of German debt. It supported the Anglo-German Fellowship and was banker to the Allens. Bruno's son, Helmut, a partner in the bank, had married Margaret Darell, whose grandfather, Justinian Heathcote, was Mosley's maternal grandfather. In the summer Bruno rented Rutland Gate from the Redesdales and stayed with Nancy Mitford.

According to Diana it was all Bill Allen's idea. 'I remember thinking, "Why should Morgan bring Allen into it?" They could have gone straight to the German government. Allen dealt in fantasies.' Mosley said he was 'a Walter Mitty character' but, Diana noted, 'it was he who suggested the radio advertising, about which he knew a great deal as advertising was his family business' and which Mosley fully supported. The proposal was that they would receive a commission for their efforts.

J. P. Morgan was not a name plucked out of the air; Mosley knew Thomas Lamont, the bank's Chairman, having met him at Lady Colefax's. It had floated the loan for the Dawes Plan to resolve the reparation dispute that burdened the German economy and the Young Plan, which established the Bank of International Settlement. It had been involved with the Du Pont family – controllers of General Motors and financiers of Fascist and anti-Semitic groups – in the 1934 attempted *coup d'état* launched against the 'Jewish-controlled' President Roosevelt. According to Charles Higham they received the support of Baron von Schroeder. The bank's London branch was Morgan Grenfell, among whose officials was Francis Rodd, brother of Diana's brother-in-law Peter Rodd. Francis was regarded as 'suspicious' and Kingsley Martin classed him as a Nazi 'fellow-traveller'. Quite what happened to the loan idea is not known; presumably it collapsed, but three years later Francis was in discussions about a half-billion-dollar gold loan to Germany through the Bank of International Settlement, which proposed the restoration of its colonies, a removal of the embargo on its goods and a non-aggression pact.

When shown details of the Allen scheme Diana added, 'George Drummond was involved.' Disfigured in the second Battle of Ypres, he chaired

Drummond's Bank, the London Branch of the Royal Bank of Scotland, in which Diana held an account. High Sheriff for Northamptonshire, he gave money to the BU and knew Mosley through their mutual love of hunting. A friend of Montagu Norman, Governor of the Bank of England, Drummond was regarded by MI5 as a 'Nazi sympathizer'. He was like a life model for Kazuo Ishiguro's 1989 novel *The Remains of the Day*.

Captain Drummond entertained royalty at Pitsford Hall, where the Prince of Wales had been a regular participant at the Pytchley hunt. It appears Edward was the father of Drummond's daughter Edwina. It was known within the family that he was in love with Drummond's wife. In 1937 Edwina greeted the King when he visited Munich, where she was at finishing school. King George VI was a godfather to his first-born son George. Drummond was a prominent member of the British Union for the Abolition of Vivisection. He thought Britain was 'spineless', its 'spirit had gone'. Everyone was aware of his German connections through membership of Anglo-German friendship societies and visits to Germany. His chauffeur, Jack Brooks, recalled him meeting Hitler and Heydrich. Ribbentrop visited Pitsford, where guests allegedly changed into Nazi uniforms.

Alf Goldberg worked at Moon's garage, near Victoria Station, in which Mosley stabled his cars. 'I would see Mosley or other members of the BU hierarchy arrive, change to a suitable limousine and depart for Croydon Airport, which was then the main London aerodrome for the Continent.' They returned with German officers and 'would then transfer to smaller cars and proceed to destinations best known to themselves'. Goldberg believed this included Brocket Hall in Hertfordshire, home of Lord Brocket, an industrial magnate and a Hitler admirer. Brocket cultivated relations with Germany and entertained Ribbentrop and Mosley lavishly at Inverie House on his Knoydart estate in Scotland. Because he was closely connected with leading Nazis, Halifax 'used him as a channel through which to communicate to Hitler and Ribbentrop the views of the Government'.

On 29 April Grandi talked with Edward VIII on restoring friendly relations between Britain and Italy. When Grandi said people were suggesting the Suez Canal be closed, the King asked, 'Why? To stop the victorious Italian troops from returning home?' Diana's friend Gerald Berners came back from Rome talking of Italian fury at the Secretary of State for Foreign Affairs, Anthony Eden, and his pro-sanctions policy. The Duchess of Sermoneta had told him she wished she could open a vein and let out every drop of her English blood.

The Italians occupied the Abyssinian capital and on 9 May King Victor Emmanuel was proclaimed Emperor. Grandi reported to Rome that everyone in England was hanging on Mussolini's every word. He was 'glad to find himself in a world where even respectable journalists, while not obvious Fascists, could be persuaded to write favourable articles on Italy in return for a small monthly payment'. There was marginal influence from 'a number of street rallies' organized by the Anti-Sanctionist League and the BU. Mosley mounted protest meetings in Hyde Park on 6 June and in the East End against the presence in London of the exiled Emperor Haile Selassie.

Luigi Villari, employed by the Ministry of Foreign Affairs, wrote in *Nuova Antologia* that he was grateful to Mosley for support over Abyssinia and his proposal that while Malta should remain part of the Empire, Italian should be taught in schools. In an otherwise balanced picture of the BU, he wildly overestimated membership at 800,000.

Sanctions against Italy failed to achieve their objective and were quietly withdrawn, confirming Mosley's contention that they would lead either to war or to a humiliating retreat. James Strachey Barnes said Italy 'won the contest of 1935–36 hands down by dint of the daring spirit and vitality of youth, reminiscent of England's Elizabethan age, when, as a little country, she successfully challenged the might of Spain'. Mosley claimed his campaign had played a part and he attracted large audiences but Italian aggression was so naked that the BU emerged 'not as a party of peace concerned with British interest, but as an unofficial ambassador of Mussolini, and an apologist for fascist violence'.

Nazi philosopher Alfred Rosenberg believed the BU was damaged by its campaign. The British government's anti-Italian stance had majority support, yet the BU, though it stood for 'British interests exclusively', by supporting the Italian cause could not help but be suspected of being in league with Mussolini. Rosenberg pointed out the error of duality of loyalties in BU policy. It was a psychological mistake for Mosley to call his movement 'Fascist'. 'Using a label of foreign origin conflicted with the pride England possessed for her own traditions.' His view, however, was not believed by all leading Nazis.

Mosley's officials returned from Germany with messages of support and 'glowing reports of national efficiency, aesthetic grandeur and happy women'. As chief Women's Propaganda Officer, Anne Brock-Griggs attended the May Day celebrations when 80,000 German youths gathered to praise Hitler in 'a feast of colour and an example of orderly discipline'. The *Völkischer Beobachter* welcomed 'the open words of the Leader of the British Union which reach the core of the British question. Every national patriotic movement – even if it is not anti-Semitic in its beginnings – must some day come up against the Jewish question and seek a solution for it.' On 16 May the *Blackshirt* alleged that 'no leading paper in this country dare publish anything which is at all contrary to Jewish interests for fear of losing its advertisements'.

On Empire Day, 24 May, Mosley used a march in Watney Street to unveil the BU's new uniform – a military-style outfit with coat, peaked cap, belt and buckle, and jackboots. It reminded observers of Hitler's SS. The resemblance was confirmed by the adoption of an armlet bearing the lightning-flash emblem in red, white and black. The uniform was restricted to Headquarters officers and stewards, which reinforced the idea of a sinister Nazi elite. Mosley later admitted that its introduction had been a mistake.

On the following day Mosley spoke at a meeting at the Carfax Assembly rooms, Oxford, whose disruption, Skidelsky suggested, resulted from an organized Communist conspiracy. An observer, Arthur Exell, claimed the local anti-Fascists' intervention was aimed 'not to smash up the meeting' but to 'prevent the Fascists from adopting their customary brutal methods with interrupters and to secure a fair hearing for all genuine questions put to the platform'. Future Labour MP Christopher Mayhew, who was fiercely anti-Communist, also claimed workers were there 'to stand by our comrades if rudely treated'.

Skidelsky maintained that Communists were encouraged to disrupt the meeting and named Basil Murray as a culprit. In fact, Murray shared the Liberal politics of his father Gilbert Murray. Mosley was looking for a confrontation. Future Labour MP Patrick Gordon Walker said he 'provoked the audience beyond endurance'. Protected by 'a squad of twenty tough-looking Blackshirts', he described Labour as 'pink rabbits in the pay of the Jews'. It looked as though the meeting would end peacefully but Mosley's decision to eject a heckler marked the point at which the 'audience's sense of decency had been outraged' and the meeting descended into chaos. The hall became 'a struggling mass of people'. Frank Pakenham claimed he was punched and four Blackshirts ended up in hospital.

The first East End BU rally took place on 7 June in Bethnal Green. It was left to Joe Jacobs, secretary of the CP's Stepney branch, to mount a counter-demonstration. CP leaders 'did not see the anti-Mosley/BU movement as particularly important when ranged against the need to ... mount a mass movement against the "pro-fascist" National Government'. The 5,000 crowd grew so hostile that it was dispersed by the 600-strong police. The pro-Mosley Collin Brooks attended for the *Mail*. 'It was the anti-Jewish references that drew the cheers. These references the *Mail* took out because they thought Jewish advertisers would be offended. This is the power of the Jew. Here is the justification of Fascism.'

Two weeks later, in Finsbury Park, 20,000 anti-Fascists shouted Mosley down. Stepney CP branch remained divided over tactics. Jacobs wanted to 'drive Mosley out of East London', using 'maximum force'. Phil Piratin wanted more than 'Fascist baiting' since Mosley had attracted many ordinary working-class people: 'Do you bash ordinary people?' Jacobs wrote an open letter to Stepney's three Labour MPs – Clement Attlee, Dan Frankel and J. H. Hall – asking them to join a united front 'to smash the Fascist menace now, when it is beginning to show itself'. After a bitter debate, Piratin's view prevailed.

Mosley said, 'the great and powerful were afraid when our Fascist movement opened its crusade against Jewry . . . Up to three years ago anti-semitism was unknown as a strong force in Britain. Today, in any audience, the strongest passion that can be aroused is the passion against the corruption of Jewish power.' With meetings every night, rallies every weekend and violence against Jews from Fascist thugs, the BU created 'in miniature the mass psychology of fascism', even if by German standards the violence was comparatively modest.

Mosley advocated withdrawing citizenship from all Jews. 'All nations have a right to say that foreigners who have abused their hospitality shall leave the country.' He admitted before the Advisory Committee in 1940 that 'in the fascist state, Special Commissions were to be set up to decide whether individual Jews were more Jewish or British in their attitude, and those who failed to pass the test would be expelled'. His 'final solution' was to resettle Jews in one of the 'many waste places of the world possessing great potential fertility (excluding Palestine)'; Madagascar was mentioned. When Diana was asked for her own solution, she suggested they could have gone 'somewhere like Uganda: very empty and a lovely climate'.

At the end of June, after Mosley left a meeting at Hulme Town Hall, Manchester, he was confronted by a 3,000-strong crowd. The police had to escort his car to the local BU headquarters. However, a hostile crowd gathered outside, and windows were broken and the Fascist flag was torn down. Nellie Driver, a BU Nelson member inside the headquarters, believed it was the action of drunken 'Reds' which had inflamed them, after it was rumoured Blackshirts had trampled to death a three-year-old boy. After a night of violence, order returned. The *Manchester Guardian* concluded, 'the crowd had been so numerous that, had it wanted, it could have caused far greater damage.'

The violence led Beaverbrook to remark that Mosley had embarked on a 'path that can never lead him anywhere'. MI5 reported that his only success was in the East End but even there it was limited and generally discredited because of the violence. Mosley, however, believed the BU would make a breakthrough and told officials it would contest the 1937 London County Council elections and prove it had the East End's overwhelming support. He planned to stage a big BU rally through Jewish areas to demonstrate that the movement was a significant force and merited Mussolini's aid.

Mosley was desperate for money and Diana tried to persuade the Germans to fund the BU. She admitted 'Mussolini sent money for a while' and said she 'begged the Germans – not Hitler himself – for money, but they never gave any'. This was untrue. On 19 June Goebbels recorded that she had been successful. Funding the BU was highly significant. Hitler's support of foreign movements was rare, and occurred only if they advocated pan-Germanism and therefore fitted into his expansionist foreign policy. 'Mosley needs money,'

Goebbels wrote. 'Wants it from us. Has already had £2,000 [£78,000] ... £100,000 necessary. £60,000 [£2,040,00] promised. Must submit to Führer.' On the following day he 'got hold of £10,000 for Mosley'. This was a substantial sum, given Germany's foreign currency shortages. Arrangements were made by Franz Wrede, head of the press office, for it to be secretly smuggled to Mosley. Described by Otto Dietrich as 'an arrogant, stupid, fanatic Nazi', Wrede was posted as correspondent of the *Berlin Lokal-Anzeiger* to London where, according to German documents, he was 'in close association' with Dr Tester, Mosley's aide-de-camp.

In June 1936 the Joint Intelligence Committee recommended directing attention 'to the potential danger of Nazi and Fascist Party Organisations in this country'. However, no more staff were made available for an already over-stretched Security Service. It was easy for Mosley to organize a courier service for the Nazi funds, evidence of which was never uncovered by MI5. Only after the war did it discover the extent of Italian operations among BU personnel.

On 8 July 'Mr Bianchi', who had enrolled him 'in the Fascist Intelligence Service', asked Theodore Schurch 'to join the Royal Army Service Corps as a driver'. The eighteen-year-old lived with his British mother and Swiss father in Stoke Newington. He joined the BU because 'he was persecuted at school' and 'rapidly assimilated its doctrines' – including anti-Semitism – noting that 'many more illustrious people than himself held these views'. From 1936 he supplied Italian intelligence with information. The BU had been in touch with him 'through Edward King and according to his instructions I volunteered for overseas service in the Middle East'. He eventually embarked on 11 November 1937 for Palestine, where he was put in touch with a friend of Bianchi. Schurch claimed 'he only gave the Italians information which he knew they already had. He never gave accurate information to the enemy but false information.' His defence later alleged Schurch had been 'caught young when he knew no better and jockeyed into a position from which he could not recover'.

Diana returned to London, staying with Gerald Berners at Halkin Street or with the Dunns near Regent's Park. Mosley had left Ebury Street for a flat at 129 Grosvenor Road, a former nightclub on the Chelsea river front, decorated by Diana in a Greek style. She managed to keep her friends, including Jewish ones, though some thought her mad for her views. 'What a bully you are,' she wrote to Roy Harrod. 'I thought we had a divine day and not a hint of dread politics. As you know, I feel very strongly about these things so very likely it shines out of me willy nilly.' Her son Jonathan pointed out that 'in polite society anyone attacking another on politics puts oneself in the wrong', and guests who disliked Diana's views would normally have kept their feelings to themselves.

Diana lunched with her cousin, Winston Churchill, who wanted to hear her opinion of Hitler. The others present – Lord Ivor Churchill and Sarah Churchill – were 'simply fascinated' when she said the Führer had asked her about him. She was the only person who knew them both well on a personal level and suggested the two should meet. 'Oh, no. No!' Churchill replied. He had recently helped found Focus, a loosely organized group intended to convince the public and government of Hitler's aggressive intentions. He helped Harold Laski produce *The Yellow Spot*, documenting anti-Jewish measures in Germany, including the murder of thirty-four Jews in Dachau concentration camp. Mosley was still welcome at Churchill's influential Other Club and was never expelled.

Mosley was in trouble with the Courts about the provision of the children's money for Savehay Farm: a judge reduced the payments on the grounds that they enabled their father to spend more of his own money on Fascism. Shortly afterwards Diana went to live in Staffordshire, at Wootton Lodge, a beautiful Elizabethan house but icy cold and completely unmodernized, owned by Captain Unwin VC. Mosley agreed to rent it for £400 (£12,800) a year with an option to buy. Diana installed the central heating out of her yearly allowance from Bryan Guinness of £2,500. Wootton was ideal for Mosley, as it was close to Manchester, where there was strong BU support, and for meetings in the Midlands and the North.

The couple spent much time together at Wootton with its wild and beautiful countryside. They no longer holidayed on the Mediterranean and the children stayed during the summers of 1936–7. Nicholas, who was at Eton where 'the whole business of my father fell away', was as unlike his father 'as it is possible for father and son to be'. In his detached way his father 'was fond of him and was anxious for him to enjoy his holidays'. Mosley loved fishing for trout in the pools or stalking rabbits with a .22 rifle. 'We lay on the grass in the sun in summer,' Diana recalled, 'and trudged through snow in winter. We were alone as a rule living in the moment.'

During July Mussolini's agent, journalist C. M. Franzero, sent Rome a negative report on the BU. Monthly contributions were subsequently reduced from £3,000 to £1,000. On 10 July MI5 had information from 'an absolutely reliable source' that the funding had stopped altogether. Mosley had made 'some advances' with the Nazis but it had no evidence that financial help was actually forthcoming. Its source had little evidence of significant outside funding. However, the secret BU bank account uncovered by Special Branch during the war showed that during 1936, £43,300 had passed through it and an astonishing £224,000 (£7.6m) had been laundered into BU funds between 1933 and 1937 by way of foreign currency transactions.

Mosley's foreign affairs adviser, Robert Gordon-Canning, was involved with leading Catholic Mosleyites, MI6 friends and Spanish Fascists in the clandestine transfer of Generalissimo Francisco Franco to Morocco at the outbreak of the Civil War. Gordon-Canning had served as a cavalry officer in Palestine and with the Rif leader, Abd-el-Krim, and envisaged himself as a latter-day Lawrence of Arabia, siding with the Arabs against the Jews. Spain's over-officered army had sought to preserve some imperial prestige in campaigns of pacification against the tribes in Morocco and Franco had commanded the Spanish Foreign Legion in 1923–7 during one such campaign.

By 9 July 1936 Franco agreed to assume command of the African army and fly from his hideout to Tétouan. The operation was organized in London by Spanish monarchists with ties to British politicians and businessmen. Junta Nacional included the Duke of Alba, *English Review* editor Douglas Jerrold and aviators. Jerrold thought Mosley an important man, who was 'telling the truth as he sees it, and he is one of the few people in England who are even trying to do so. He has sacrificed the certainty of office for the certainty of a life in the political wilderness.' The BU did not campaign on the Spanish Civil War but it had the backing of a large number of Catholic members; 12 per cent of its leading officials were Catholics. The *Catholic Herald* and the *Tablet* were among the few journals which sympathetically reported on Mosley and the BU.

The company carrying out the clandestine flight was chosen by aeronautical inventor Juan de la Cierva, whose Autogiro was built by A. V. Roe (Avro), a generous funder of Mosley. ABC's London correspondent, Luis Bolin, made the arrangements with Olley Air Services, whose chief pilot was Mosley's friend Lord (Jeffrey) Amherst, later a founder of British European Airways. Mosley knew Amherst at Sandhurst. Wounded in the battle of Loos and winning a Military Cross, he subsequently joined the RFC. They were both acquaintances of Roger Senhouse, a guiding light behind publishers Secker and Warburg. The Bloomsbury-linked Senhouse was a friend of the Mitfords and a cousin of Cimmie's father. His suitcase of letters, many from Mosley, whose 'discretion was much the lesser part of their content', later disappeared. Employed at Heston Aerodrome, headquarters of the British Intelligence-linked Airwork Services, Amherst was a frequent visitor to Berlin and met Hitler. He subsequently joined Olley Air Services – 'Fly Anywhere: Anytime' – which was backed by Sir Hugo Cunliffe-Owen, Chairman of BAT and one-time backer of Mosley, and like so many of Mosley's friends (and senior MI6 officers), a member of White's.

The £2,000 (£64,000) for chartering Olley and a de Havilland Dragon Rapide came from Spanish millionaire Juna March, who channelled the funds through Kleinwort Benson, a bank with strong ties to MI6. Amherst was told the London insurance market footed the bill. On 11 July the Dragon Rapide – flown by ex-RAF pilot Captain Cecil Bebb – helped by Major Hugh Pollard, a retired British Intelligence officer – took off from Croydon en route to Las

Palmas to collect Franco. Told that his mission was 'to get a Rif leader from the Canary Islands to start an insurrection in Spanish Morocco', Bebb thought it 'a lovely challenge'. The plane landed in Lisbon on 12 July. Two days later the Spanish Civil War began and five days after that the exfiltration operation was carried out. Bebb returned to Croydon, promising to keep quiet about his mission.

On 16 July Mosley announced the BU would fight seats in the municipal elections in the following March: 'East London will be asked to choose between us and the parties of Jewry.' This broke with the BU's claim that 'it was a waste of energy to fight local elections, Fascism being capable of implementation only at national level'. It was a risky move as the municipal register was unfavourable but with Mussolini threatening to end the subsidy, Mosley had little alternative but to demonstrate that his movement was making progress.

MI5 acknowledged that his attacks on the Jews struck a chord in the East End but there was 'a good deal of anti-semitic feeling there and anti-semitic speeches are therefore welcome. There does not seem to be any reason for believing that public opinion in the East End is becoming seriously pro-Fascist.' However, in a Commons debate on 10 July MPs viewed the BU's campaign as a 'threat to traditional political values that could not be tolerated'. Home Secretary Sir John Simon subsequently insisted the police enforce the law, with shorthand writers taking notes of what was said at meetings and inspectors charging speakers contravening the law.

The police not only permitted anti-Semitic abuse to go unchallenged but also engaged in unnecessary violence against anti-Fascists. Reports describe them using batons and fists with little discrimination, causing injury to bystanders. But it was not only East End meetings that attracted violence. On 17 July BU hard man Tommy Moran was at 'the roughest and toughest meeting that I ever attended'. At the Corporation Field, Hull, 'the reds did everything that was filthy'. After the meeting police collected 'bicycle chains, brush staves with 6-inch nails in the end, chair legs wrapped with barbed wire and thick woollen stockings containing broken glass in the heels'. Twenty-seven BU supporters and over a hundred Communists were injured. A bullet pierced a window of Mosley's car. The incident attracted little publicity, which suggests it was not a 'genuine attempt' to assassinate him, and the BU did not exploit its propaganda value. However, Mosley's behaviour under attack added to his mythical status among Blackshirts. Moran said, 'The Leader was superb, if we loved him in the past his courage last Sunday made us his for life.'

On 19 July the Board of Deputies of British Jews set up a Co-ordinating Committee 'to unify and direct activities in defence of the Jewish communities'. Its President, Harold Laski, organized a number of agents to report on BU activities and provide advance notice of meetings. The key mole was Captain Vincent Collier ('Captain X'), an Irish ex-officer, former New Party and Sinn Fein member who admired Mosley's support for Irish independence. Laski submitted regular reports to the BoD on the progress of the campaign.

On 3 August Metropolitan Police Commissioner Sir Philip Game issued a memorandum on 'Anti-Jewish Activities', which ordered the police to carry out the policy as outlined by the Home Secretary. Formerly Governor of New South Wales, Game's actions during the constitutional crisis of 1932, when he dismissed the Prime Minister, provide an insight into his behaviour towards the BU. From an English liberal background, he genuinely believed, notes Australian academic Andrew Moore, 'in the superiority of "constitutional methods" and objected when it seemed that these may have been subverted'. His 'adherence to democratic processes was sincere', and his opposition to the Fascist New Guard, when it adopted a paramilitary complexion, 'would prove to be enduring'.

In response to the new instructions Mosley ordered speakers to obey the law. During August the SB reported that he had 'given a definite warning to its speakers to refrain from attacking the Jews at public meetings, it being emphasised that arrests of its members for Jew baiting is likely to do the fascist movement more harm than good'. The order was opposed by Joyce and Beckett, who urged a policy of courting arrests and imprisonment to 'intensify antagonism towards Jews'.

After settling into Wootton, Diana left for Berlin where she joined Unity for Hitler's invitation to the Olympic Games. On 23 July they were at the Goebbelses' villa at Schwanenwerder with Hitler. Diana conveyed a plea from Mosley. 'He boldly asks for an infusion of £100,000 [£3.4m],' recorded Goebbels. On the following day Hitler talked with them about 'Richard Strauss . . . the Jews and Bolshevist danger. He will keep that danger down in Germany. The rest of the world can do what it wants.' Diana always insisted Hitler never raised the subject of the Jews. She was too clever to admit to the use of anti-Semitic language, but letters to Unity show that there was such talk. At a dinner with Hitler she referred to brother Tom's Jewish sympathies. 'I said, "The lackey of the Jews has almost become a National Socialist" and he roared with laughter and said, "Your brother is a splendid young man."'

In August Goebbels received 'Wrede's reports of his English visit and the delivery of money. Very informative. Mosley must work harder and be less mercenary.' Diana, however, 'wants money again for Mosley', he wearily recorded on 6 August. 'She was fed with hopes. Should help themselves sometimes.' Goebbels checked with Hitler: 'The Führer has turned down giving money to Mosley for the moment.' Goebbels recalled his own penniless start and expected the BU to begin the same way.

There had been rumours that Mosley might be picked for the British Olympic fencing team. He was not, on this occasion, but was for the national team the following year, after which he retired from the sport. In any case, he believed attendance was not politically expedient and there had been opposition to English athletes going to the Games.

While in Munich, Diana asked the advice of the British consul about arrangements for getting married in Germany. 'He told me British subjects were married by the ordinary registrar in Germany, and vice versa.' Hitler agreed to 'ask the Berlin registrar to keep the marriage quiet'. Diana later explained that they knew the press would soon be on to it 'if they married in a registry office in England'. Mosley said Cimmie had been subjected 'to the most blackguardly abuse from some sections of the press and it was my desire that no woman should again be subject to such treatment merely because she happened to be married to me'. Diana was fond of Magda Goebbels, who helped with the wedding, which was arranged for October.

An intelligent middle-class woman, Magda's background was high society. She was brought up by her Jewish stepfather, Max Friedlander, whose name she took for her own. Married to a Russian Zionist activist, Victor Arlosoroff, who became foreign minister of the Jewish Agency and was murdered in 1933, she was converted to Nazism by a speech by Goebbels. She divorced and became his secretary. The attraction was not physical; she felt the need to attach herself to charismatic, rich and powerful men. A 'noted philanderer, sometimes carrying on liaisons in the bedroom next to hers', Goebbels's affair with Czech film star Lida Baarova was blatant. Magda, as 'first lady' of the Nazi regime, appealed to Hitler for a divorce but he insisted they remain married and that Goebbels give up his lover. Their Berlin home was a magnet for Hitler and top Nazi officials.

The Mitford sisters were driven to the Games each day and travelled with Hitler to the Wagner Festival at Bayreuth, where they met Winifred Wagner. Diana found the festival 'an experience as heavenly as the Olympic Games were boring. For the first time I heard *Parsifal*.' Mosley told the Birkett committee that, with Frau Goebbels and Frau Wagner, Diana was one of the three women for whom Hitler had the highest regard in the whole world. They returned to Munich in his private train. 'Thousands of people were shouting "Heil! Heil!" along the track and we didn't sleep a wink in the excitement.'

One of few women whom Hitler considered as a near equal, Winifred was English by birth. Adopted by the German anti-Semitic Klindworths, friends of the Wagners, she married Siegfried, the composer's son, and ran the Bayreuth Festival to 'present the pure art of Richard Wagner' after her husband's death in 1930. After the attempted putsch in Munich 1923 she had declared her alliance to Hitler. Winifred immersed herself in anti-Semitic Nazi ideology and visited him in prison, providing the notepaper on which *Mein Kampf* was written. He once asked her to become his wife. Hitler regularly went to Bayreuth where Wagner's music reduced him to tears.

Hitler praised the anti-Semitism at the core of the music of Wagner, who had been influenced by Schopenhauer and the idea that Christianity was polluted by its Jewish origins and required purification, and the pioneer of 'racial science' Joseph Gobineau. Wagner conflated the two in *Parsifal*, whose hero is an Aryanized, racially pure Christ figure who seeks mankind's redemption. 'It is so poisonous', suggests David Cesarani, 'because it forms a compendium of German nationalism, racism, and anti-semitism.'

That the Mitfords were descended from Bertie Redesdale, backer of racial ideologist Houston Stewart Chamberlain, was of huge importance to Hitler. An Englishman by birth and a German by choice, after marrying Wagner's daughter Eva and settling in Bayreuth, Chamberlain became the chief link between Wagnerism and the extreme Right, meeting Hitler in 1923. When the first international writer to align himself with the Nazis died in 1927, Rosenberg praised him as 'the founder of a German future'. Hitler mentioned the Redesdale–Chamberlain relationship constantly, regarding his meeting the Mitford sisters as no mere chance. They were the living embodiment of his racial theories. Bertie believed racial origins determined almost everything. Through Chamberlain, he became a friend of Siegfried Wagner and Winifred told Diana her grandfather's photograph always stood on Siegfried's writing table.

The BU opened its election campaign at the end of July with a Raven Thomson speaking tour of the East End. The crowds were bored by his restrained utterances but applauded when he moved on to violent invective. He warned 'the gloves had been taken off. The fight is on. It is Gentiles against Jews, white men against black men.' Blackshirts chalked details of meetings on the pavements – 'All Out Aug 16th for Pogrom' – and posters – 'Kill the Jews'. Over the following two years the BU held over 2,000 meetings in East London. BU speakers placed an emphasis on the notions of 'blood and soil' and the *Blackshirt* said National Socialism was necessary for Britain's salvation.

Hitler's expert on the United States, Colin Ross, and colleague Albrecht Haushofer, asked Mosley to write an article on BU foreign policy. It was for publication in Rosenberg's *Zeitschrift für Geopolitik* (*Journal of Geopolitics*), edited by Karl Haushofer, who with his concept of '*Lebensraum*' for the German people helped legitimize the border expansion of the Third Reich. One of Haushofer's pupils was Dr Fritz Hesse, a propagandist attached to the German embassy who cultivated British Establishment members. A member of the Dienststelle Ribbentrop, Hesse was its foremost 'England expert' and went on to edit the Haushofer journal. A version of Mosley's article was published in the July issue of the *Fascist Quarterly* as 'The World

Alternative: European Synthesis within the Universalism of Fascism and National Socialism'.

Based on the Italo-Abyssinian crisis, Mosley said the balance of power idea had put world peace in jeopardy. Failure had been due to attempts 'to restrain particular nations within circumstances which denied them not only the national honour of great nations but also the means of free and prosperous existence'. He wanted a return 'to the fundamental conception of European union which animated the war generation in 1918 and has been frustrated by the perversion of the League of Nations to exactly the opposite purpose that it was intended to serve'. He warned of 'the jackal of oriental Communism summoning the Western peoples not only to the suicide of Europe but to an oriental Armageddon which will finally make the world safe for anarchy and Jewry'. Using Haushofer's concept of geopolitics, he advocated 'a Union of European people of German race in a closed economic system' against Soviet Russia. An alliance of Fascist governments would form the basis for world peace, from which both Communism and capitalism would be banished.

Although Italy's friendship was necessary to safeguard Empire trade routes, Mosley's article was a paean of praise for Nazi Germany. 'In proceeding to build first a system of European union we shall naturally begin with Germany', whose objective was 'the wealth and happiness of its people'. To secure this she would require 'an adequate supply of raw materials and full outlet for expanding population. But less than any other great nation of today her philosophy leads her to think of limitless colonial Empire – which to the Nazi mind suggests loss of vital energy, dissipation of wealth and the fear of detrimental admixture of races.' Her objective lay 'in the union of the German peoples of Europe in a consolidated rather than a diffused economic system which permits her with security to pursue her racial ideals'. On this 'profound difference of national objective between the British Empire and the new Germany' rested 'the main hope of peace between them'.

Haushofer promoted the idea of 'leader' nations and Mosley agreed 'nations must be either hammer or anvil'. They had the 'duty to lead the more backward countries in their sphere of influence and thereby enrich not only themselves but the world by the production of fresh resources for civilisation'. Mosley envisaged a carve-up of the world's resources by the Fascist powers, who were 'enthusiastic imperialists'. Seditious Indian nationalism would be rooted out and its advocates would answer 'with their lives and their property'. On the basis of 'British power throughout the world and German power in Europe' the two could become 'the main pillars of world order and civilisation'. However, there was a need to 'remove all cause of friction between Britain and Germany'.

In a speech at Hastings, Mosley warned that 'Britain, holding in very feeble hands the vast Empire won by the heroism of our forefathers, is denying the right of the great and virile populations of Germany, Italy and Japan to advance into territories where British interests are nowhere affected . . . Sooner or later these virile nations expand or explode. Which do you want? Do you want colonial development or a world war?' In return for excluding from India its goods which competed with Empire produce, Mosley would support Japan's exploitation of northern China. If its colonies were returned, it would eliminate the possibility of German explosion in Europe 'by the provision of means of her peaceful expansion'. This chimed with Hitler's view of Britain as an ally to control the world's trade routes while he marched east to gain access to raw materials and 'living-space' for Germans.

Mosley's 'rationalisations for trying to keep peace in Europe, to avoid a "brothers' war" between the two representatives of the Faustian culture, Britain and Germany', owed, notes Thurlow, 'much to Spengler as well as his desire not to repeat the political and human disasters of the First World War'. With Britain free to pursue an imperial policy, he was prepared to sacrifice its influence in Europe. The half-Asiatic Russians of Spengler's nightmares would be told 'Hands off Europe and back to the East where you belong!' while Germany would be allowed to carve up Eastern Europe and Ukraine. Mosley intended that such a policy would be negotiated from a position of sufficient defensive strength to render Britain invulnerable to attack if Hitler turned on the West. Taking up the ideas of Fuller, rearmament in the air and the mechanization of the army became central planks of his defence policy.

Karl Haushofer praised as 'important' Mosley's article. In Ribbentrop's office Rudolf Karlowa thought that 'as the independent view of an Englishman [it] needs no criticism by us and fits our standpoint well'. 'Das grosse Entweder Oder' appeared in September and attracted considerable attention among Nazi officials. Diana was in Berlin when it was published and was invited to luncheon at the Reichskanzlerei. Hitler was holding it in his hand: 'You know they say I never read anything.' He said he greatly admired it.

During August, Mosley was recuperating following an operation for appendicitis. Baba, who had been at the Olympic Games, had been due to go to the French Riviera with him but refused to go when she heard he had also invited Diana. Temporarily, their relationship was off. Mosley and Diana stayed in Sorrento and he was out of the fray for two months' convalescing. In his absence the East End campaign appeared to be in decline, which MI5 put down to his lack of staying power. Officials bemoaned his 'unwillingness' to keep up the momentum and 'fear' of police pressure. Joyce was seen as a more potent figure among those who had contempt for Mosley's opportunism. This reflected a body of opinion among the London-based Nazi elite.

On 14 August Magda Goebbels wrote to Diana with a date of 17 October for the wedding. 'You are taking on difficult tasks, and just as in the past, so even more in the future you will need your strength and health. Give my best wishes to the Leader. A thousand kisses to you too. I am so fond of you.' On 11 September Ribbentrop told Hitler he had heard from Gordon-Canning that Mosley had recovered and was in Rome where he had 'several conversations with Mussolini. I have informed Mosley that the Führer has agreed to receive him.' Ribbentrop's envoy, Stammer, organized details in London. When Diana went to the registrar's office, an official queried her father's Christian name – 'David?' In Germany it was regarded as a Jewish name and the official thought the marriage might contravene the Nuremberg race laws. The adjutant accompanying Diana assured him that in England a David could be perfectly Aryan.

On 17 September Hitler asked Magda if their house could be used for the wedding. Goebbels was 'not too keen. But the Führer wants it. Magda is too closely involved. Greater reserve would be appropriate.' He was not pleased with the arrangement, since he discovered that one of the witnesses was to be Bill Allen, whom he did not trust. But he did not like Mosley either and quarrelled with Magda about the wedding.

Mosley later explained to the Birkett Committee that around this time he discovered the BU was nearly bankrupt. 'I was advised by those responsible for our funds that substantial contributions to HQ had practically ceased.' He blamed

the growing hostility of the capitalist, which had begun with my public refusal of Rothermere's suggestion to adopt a more conservative policy and to abandon anti-Semitism, appeared to have resulted in the entire hostility of the money world and a practically complete boycott of our funds. Capitalism had discovered that we were a genuine revolution and were not to be bought off or used for their own purposes.

In fact, they ended their funding in 1934 and he was dependent on foreign subsidies, and it was this aspect which Mosley wished to hide.

'I was therefore', Mosley wrote, 'confronted with the classic problem of the revolutionary – lack of money. So far the problem had been solved in one of two ways. (1) The Socialist way: to take money from capitalism and stay bought. (2) The Fascist way: to take money from capitalism and to double cross the capitalists in the interests of the workers.' The pompous language obscured the reality that Mosley was desperate and was willing to pursue any means of raising funds. The means was chosen 'partly by design and partly by accident'.

In February 1936, during the accession of King Edward VIII, the government became interested in the propaganda potential of Radio Luxembourg. Thought had been given to transmitting the King's speech through Luxembourg, as it would give a much wider circulation in Europe than the BBC could provide. The BU had been frustrated at its inability to secure airtime either on the BBC or even Luxembourg. Since the days of the New Party, Allen and Mosley had sought a radio outlet but Luxembourg raised the possibility of exploiting radio advertising.

As director of David Allen & Sons, which was diversifying into the new medium, Allen was in a position to steer Mosley into profitable commercial radio ventures. The development of sponsored radio had impressed Bill's brothers, Geoffrey and Sam, during visits to America. The success of programmes from Luxembourg and Radio Normandy demonstrated that Britain offered an expanding market for radio and confirmed the practicability of broadcasting sponsored programmes in English from Continental stations. Mosley's friend, Robert Boothby, was a representative of the Jack Buchanan Radio and on the Allen board, and had invested money in an Allen company, Mills and Allen.

The Allens' rival was wealthy Conservative MP Captain Leonard Plugge, a cross between 'a playboy-sportsman-buccaneer and a dilettante electrical experimenter'. He owned Luxembourg, which broadcast popular dance music interspersed with talk in English and advertisements by British firms. He had extended his operations from Radio Normandy to stations at Toulouse, Lyon and Paris, running the network through the International Broadcasting Company. Limited in power and confined to the late hours, these were minor operations compared with Luxembourg, which had one of the most powerful transmitters in Europe and reached peak audience figures of four million in Britain.

Hiring a former Plugge employee, the Allens sought concessions to set up commercial radio stations in Continental countries. The project appealed to the Allens' flair for action and they set up a company to deal with radio advertising, though there was opposition from the BBC (supported by the Foreign Office) to advertisers using Continental wavelengths. Mosley was enthusiastic: as 'an added incentive to the great fortune this would have meant for my cause was the good crack it would give my old enemy the Press. For they have ever been terrified of the development of radio advertising as a great threat to their advertising income.' He hoped radio advertising 'would crack up much of the National Press' and planned to use profits to purchase local newspapers.

The project began in September 1936 following the return of Frances Eckersley from a holiday in Germany. She was a member of the literary Stephen family and married to Peter Eckersley, former BBC engineer and New Party member. Dorothy, whose son James Clark was tutored by William Joyce, joined the Anglo-German Fellowship and became a fanatical admirer of Hitler. A former ILPer, Dorothy and her husband visited Germany, noting the progress in combating unemployment. Peter was a delegate at the Union Internationale de Radiophonie and had pioneered pan-European ideas for a United Europe. He also chaired the League of Nations Union and wrote for the pacifist magazine of Lord Allen, who was notorious for meeting Hitler. Peter feared another war and believed Hitler was a man of peace. He also went through a period of anti-Semitism.

On his return from holiday Peter, who was involved in private ventures in broadcasting technology, fell in with the Allens, who unfolded their plans for commercial broadcasting in English to a British audience, offering advertising airtime to British businesses. It was to be a great money spinner. He accepted their generous offer of the use of their aeroplane and a salary of £1,000 (£34,000) per year (Mosley paid him an additional £2,500) to be their technical adviser. The Allens retained a 'controlling interest' in patents of Eckersley's Wired Wireless System, for which they found backers, including the brother of Foreign Secretary Samuel Hoare, Oliver, who worked with the Allens and had the ear of Lord Perth, Secretary General of the League of Nations, and was an amateur radio enthusiast; Stanley Baldwin's former Private Secretary and a friend of both Diana and Mosley, Lord Hinchingbrooke (who relinquished his title to revert to his name of Victor Montague); and Simon Harcourt Smith, attached to the British embassy in Brussels where commercial radio was flourishing.

The whole venture was shrouded in secrecy and the Allens explained that Mosley was the silent partner in the project. The syndicate would present itself as a British commercial venture. In their six-passenger plane, the Allens scoured Europe from Finland and Latvia to Greece and Portugal looking for suitable opportunities. The authorities in Ireland and Iceland were canvassed, and visits were paid to Sark and Lundy. Germany also became a target.

On 15 September the Allens stayed at the Hotel Adlon in Berlin, a place frequented by the Nazi hierarchy, and approached the German Post Office about setting up a commercial station. The Allens knew Germany was short of foreign currency and emphasized the rewards which would flow from the influx of foreign currency. A senior member of Hitler's staff, however, informed them Germany had no need of a foreign-owned radio station and turned the scheme down. They then moved to Italy where Eckersley interviewed Senatore Marconi. On 8 October he was in France to see if Andorra could offer a site but the situation was compromised by the closeness of the Spanish Civil War. Negotiations were started with Radio Toulouse for transmissions of English programmes.

Invited as a guest to the Nazi Parteitag, Irene found it 'breathtaking in its splendour' and felt the 'aloneness' of Hitler 'in his colossal undertaking'. Vera Brittain watched Goering followed in by a 'procession of Fascist flags – the most highly organised pageantry in the world, to which Mosley's Wagnerian displays are childish toy demonstrations'. A BU delegation headed by A. K. Chesterton fulsomely praised the Nazi regime. His wife recalled that he found it 'difficult to sleep because of recurring nightmares of the horrors of the First World War. This, combined with his selfless work for Mosley, proved to be too much even for his iron constitution.' Beckett remembered 'finding him, drunk and filthy in some dive, and returning him to his wife to be cleaned up'. Mosley paid for him to attend a German clinic and he spent the winter of 1936–7 mixing convalescence with observation of the Nazi regime, through the efforts of a senior Nazi official who was 'able to command the opening of all gates'.

The German Foreign Office avoided contact with BU personnel while Lloyd George was on a private visit to Germany. Accompanying Lloyd George, Thomas Jones wrote that 'Hitler was forty-six, Ll G was seventy-three, alike only in their perfect grooming and the brilliance of their blue eyes, these two actors exchanged courtesies'. Hitler gave a signed photograph to his guest, who replied 'how honoured he was to receive the gift from the greatest living German'. In England, he confided to friends that Hitler was 'a mixture of mystic and visionary. He likes to withdraw from the world for spiritual refreshment; that he has no vices, or indulgences or ambition.' Despite evidence of Nazi terror, such views were not uncommon. Ward Price thought Hitler 'the saviour of western civilization'.

After the Parteitag, Diana wrote to Unity that Hitler was 'so wonderful and really seemed pleased we had gone'. On 20 September she had a late-night meeting with Hitler and Goebbels, who watched films about Mosley's BU. 'Perhaps it will work,' wrote Goebbels. 'We began in the same way.'

Commandant Mary Allen secretly visited Germany at the invitation of SS Chief Heinrich Himmler; a trip she later denied making. She returned wanting a British 'Hitler of the spirit'. She secured an interview with Sir Thomas Inskip, Minister for Co-ordination of Defence, and offered the assistance of her Women's Reserve to counter the conspiracy to 'inflict a Communist dictatorship on England'. The matter was referred to Sir Hastings Ismay who turned down her request since he was in receipt of an SB report that she was 'a secret adherent of Mosley's BU' and was 'in a position to obtain useful information for the Union through her contacts'.

The Home Secretary had no doubt that the BU campaign was 'stimulating the Communist movement so that the danger of a serious clash is growing'. Joyce refused to stifle the anti-Semitism in the face of pressure from the authorities. In fact, he wanted to intensify the campaign in the belief that any arrests would increase anti-Semitic feelings in the country. There were clashes in Manchester, Hull and Bristol with anti-Fascists – 'or more often between anti-fascists demonstrators and the police'. These climaxed on 27 September with violent rioting on Holbeck Moor, Leeds. Forty Fascists were injured in an ambush mounted by anti-Fascists, who rained down rocks on Fascists. The event was 'one of the things which inspired a dread of what was going to happen in Cable Street'.

The BU announced it would celebrate its fourth anniversary by marching through East London on Sunday 4 October 1936. The Communist Party, facing a grass-roots rebellion if it did not respond, called on workers to oppose Mosley. A Popular Front organization, the Jewish People's Council against Fascism and Anti-Semitism, gathered 77,000 signatures for a petition to stop the march. Slogans such as 'Bar the road to fascism' and 'They shall not pass' – echoing the stance of the Spanish Republican government against Franco – were chalked on walls. The BU was infiltrated by Communist agents – a medical student provided much of the information about BU plans – who enabled the CP to organize the counter-demonstration.

On the eve of the march, Mosley's front-page article for the *Blackshirt* said the BU fought 'the great Jewish interest which controls much of our national life', and that the fight had begun when Jews had forced the issue: 'We did not begin the struggle until we had overwhelming evidence of its necessity. We did not begin – the Jews began.' With business pressure, victimization and physical attacks, Jews had provoked the BU. Mosley forbade unchecked racial anti-Semitism which, he argued, made the Jews appear 'as a wronged and persecuted people'. It was 'bad propaganda and alienates public sympathy'.

Metropolitan Police Commissioner Sir Philip Game wrote to a journalist friend in Melbourne that Mosley was 'making a blatherskite in East London. The antis have sworn not to let him pass and have collected to the tune of 10–12 thousand in the route and are causing a bit of trouble and danger. I expect there will be some fun and a few broken heads before the day is out. I shall be glad if it brings things to a head as I hope it may lead to banning processions all over London.'

At 2.30 p.m. 3,000 (including 400 female) Blackshirts assembled at Royal Mint Street, Stepney. Three-quarters were said to be under eighteen, some wearing the BU Cadets grey uniform. London's full complement of mounted police were present with 6,000 foot police. At 3.25 p.m. Mosley arrived in a bullet-proof car with motorcycle escort. He wore the new SS-style uniform of black military jacket, grey jodhpurs, Sam Browne belt, jackboots and a peaked cap; round the left arm was a red-and-white armband. He inspected his 'storm troopers' prior to a march east for a meeting in Summer Lane, Limehouse, and then on to Victoria Park in Bethnal Green for a final rally.

The Fascists were surrounded by 1,000 police who isolated them from the 100,000 counter-demonstrators – the largest anti-Fascist demonstration yet seen in London. An observer noted 'their grim determination, Mosley was that day to be denied the streets of Stepney'. Before the march could start, police led baton charges to clear Mint Street of demonstrators, who let off fireworks that sounded like gunshots. Scuffles broke out and three Fascists were injured – almost the only BU casualties on the day. Newsreel showed Tommy Moran picking off his attackers one by one. He was finally felled by a blow to the head from a chair wrapped in barbed wire.

Commercial Road, a continuation of Summer Lane, thronged with a hyped-up crowd. An eyewitness recalled three bus loads of police arriving, some giving 'Hitler salutes' and shouting 'Jew bastards'. Anti-Fascists had information from a police inspector that Mosley's route would take him through Cable Street. Jack Spot claimed to have lain in wait with his gang: 'Some had knuckledusters; many had coshes. Others were armed with old-fashioned cut-throat razors with a hollow-ground blade that sliced through flesh like butter.' It was the police, Phil Piratin recalled, who 'then attempted, not the fascists, to come into Cable Street . . . and it was the police who were beaten up. It was the police whose batons we took away.' Anti-Fascists had broken into a builder's yard and a lorry loaded with bricks was overturned and used as a barricade. Police were met by a shower of concrete and glass. Gladys Walsh claimed she saw 'Communists with their clenched fists rolling marbles under the police horses' hooves and stuffing broken glass up their noses to bring the mounted police down'. She made up her 'mind from then on to be an active BU member'.

Seeing the police struggle to clear a way for Mosley to proceed with his march, Fenner Brockway telephoned the Home Office demanding the march be called off. After an hour Game decided it would be impossible to get the crowd to make way for the Fascist march and telephoned the Home Secretary, Sir John Simon, for permission to give orders for the march to be called off. Simon agreed but officials said he had no powers to ban a legal march and that it was inadvisable to make a martyr of Mosley, who was litigious and had never lost a case in court. They were therefore loath to overreach police powers in dealings with him. Game therefore used the only legal power at his disposal and re-routed the march to the West End.

'As you can see for yourself,' Game told Mosley, 'if you fellows go ahead there will be a shambles.' Journalist Bill Deedes was standing next to them. 'Mosley declared he must have direct orders to cancel the march, and retired to consult his officers.' At this point rioting was reaching its height in Cable Street. On Mosley's return 'Game repeated his order. Mosley consented and the march was turned west' – down Great Tower Street and Queen Victoria Street towards the Embankment. Among the Blackshirts were 'cries of disappointment'. The BU said 'the decision was immediately obeyed because the British Union obeys the law and does not fight the police'.

Blackshirts set out through empty streets to the Embankment at the Temple, where they dispersed. Some made efforts to hold meetings in the Strand and

Trafalgar Square, where minor fights broke out. Back in Aldgate, the crowds and the barricades disappeared from the glass-and debris-strewn streets after assurances were given that Mosley's march had been cancelled. In Cable Street the police scaled the obstructions without injury and, according to a policeman, 'the few defenders gave up and ran into their houses. We cleared the obstructions and stood by to prevent any further trouble. The whole episode was over in roughly an hour and when we were recalled to our contingent all was quiet, with not a soul in sight.' Between 100 and 200 anti-Fascists were hurt. Anti-Fascists gained a victory without ever sighting the opposition. Jack Spot was arrested and was sent down for six months.

At 5.30 p.m. in Aske Street, Blackshirts were told that 'owing to the influence of the forces of the left and of the Jews the leader will be unable to speak. He was persuaded not to come on here only because his life would have been in serious danger.' Many made their way to the Great Smith Street headquarters to hear Mosley speak from an upstairs window. 'We never surrender. We shall triumph over the parties of corruption because our faith is greater than their faith, our will is stronger than their will, and within us the flame that shall light this country and shall later light the world.' Irene and Baba agreed 'the Jews and communists created the disorder'.

The day ended with an outbreak of violence against Jewish businesses in Roman Road with shop windows smashed. Many of the local Jewish community had arrived from Eastern Europe and the Fascists 'seemed to them to be analogous to the East European perpetrators of pogroms. To them, Mosley loomed as an even greater threat than his actual activities may have warranted.' The violence had been, compared with events on the Continent, relatively minor. Of the eighty-eight arrests, eighty-three were anti-Fascists. Anti-Fascists had defended vulnerable Jewish communities and Mosley's image was dented and the disturbances eventually led to the Public Order Act, which impacted on BU activities.

Cable Street suggested that Mosley was not a serious revolutionary. A Shoreditch member blamed the humiliation on his legal policy: Blackshirts 'were disappointed 'cause a lot of them thought, we should have gone forward. There would have been bloodshed . . . It would have either finished the party completely or you would have made the breakthrough. You would have hit the Reds! But Mosley was very law abiding. He was too law abiding!' He was, Nicholas suggests, 'someone who gambled for power on his own terms, but was not prepared to put everything into the gamble; which is why, although he lost, he survived'.

The fact was that Mosley was due in Germany for his wedding and had he been arrested would not have been able to get to Berlin the next day. On 5 October the Ribbentrop Büro confidentially told the *Frankfurter Zeitung* that Mosley 'is coming to Berlin for a few days. Nothing concerning his visit must appear in the German press. This ban extends to the controlled foreign reports.' According to Diana, Ribbentrop, now ambassador in London, 'invited the couple to dinner in the hope that they would confide in him, which they did not. Ribbentrop was visibly annoyed, and the Mosleys extremely embarrassed.'

Diana and Unity stayed at the Goebbels' Berlin house, where the wedding was to take place, and Mosley at the Kaiserhof. Diana was dressed in a pale gold tunic. Standing at the window of an upstairs room, she saw Hitler walking through the garden that separated the house and the Reichskanzlei: 'the leaves were turning yellow and there was bright sunshine. Behind him came an adjutant carrying a box and some flowers.' Unity and Magda Goebbels were Diana's witnesses, Bill Allen and Gordon-Canning were Mosley's; the only other people present were Hitler and Goebbels. After the short ceremony Hitler said, 'This is an occasion which we must not speak about, it is a secret and we must ensure the news does not get out.' He ordered the registrar to put the marriage certificate in a drawer.

The Goebbels gave Diana a leather-bound twenty-two-volume edition of Goethe's works inscribed to 'Liebe Diana'. Hitler gave her a photograph of himself in an eagle-topped silver frame which had pride of place in their bedroom at Wootton. Magda invited the guests to lunch at Schwanenwerder. Diana said their contacts that day were purely social but Unity recorded that 'a Dolmetscher [interpreter] arrives and the Führer and the Leader go and talk alone'. Hitler was careful in his relations with Mosley. At the lunch was Henriette Hoffman, daughter of Hoffman the photographer. She already knew the Führer kept his distance from the BU and had asked him why. He said that 'if he joined forces openly with Mosley he would lose his prospects of manoeuvring with other politicians, like Lloyd George'.

The rest of the day was spent at the Sportpalast where Hitler, Sefton Delmer reported in the Express, attacked European democracy and Bolshevism. Mosley understood no German, but was interested in observing his theatrical performance. Behind him sat Unity and Diana, who distinguished themselves by giving the Nazi salute on every possible occasion. Mosley gave an interview to the Lokal-Anzeiger and urged as 'a contribution to peace' the return to Germany of former colonies now held as British mandates. Nothing would then stand in the way of a close alliance between England and Germany.

The party went back to the Reichskanzlei for a dinner hosted by Hitler. During the meal the new Lady Mosley gave Goebbels the inside story of the affair between Edward VIII and Mrs Simpson. The King wanted to marry an American woman, already divorced from one husband but still married to another. Goebbels was dismayed at the depths to which 'a proud Empire could sink'. This was 'the King who had openly praised Hitler's social programme'.

Goebbels and Hitler were shocked and agreed to forbid newspapers to print news of the scandal. This was the last time Mosley saw Hitler. The newly-weds stayed the night at the Kaiserhof but had a quarrel and 'went to bed in dudgeon. Next day we flew home to England.'

Although it was supposed to be a secret, the wedding was known to the Foreign Office. St Clair Gainer, the British consul in Munich, had been asked to be a witness. 'He had been dreading it, prevaricating as best he could,' recalled his wife, 'and he was very pleased when they switched to Berlin. Why keep the wedding secret? I asked Unity, and she said she could not imagine why it was all so secret.' Mosley said he was protecting Diana from attack by his political opponents but there were other reasons. Baba came to believe he insisted on keeping the marriage secret so that he could continue his affair with her – a liaison she would have ended if she had known of his marriage. There was also the radio project and its confidential negotiations to consider. He had kept his own involvement a secret and did not want to risk exposing his ties to the project by way of Diana.

Mosley denied to his children that the wedding had taken place and did not tell his mother, despite the fact that she idolized him and, with her religious convictions, was troubled by his living in sin. Diana did, however, tell her parents and her brother Tom. In the *Express* on 11 October Delmer wrote that 'Mosley arrived unannounced on Monday and slipped away quietly on Thursday. His stay in Germany was devoted to studying the organization of the Nazi party.'

By autumn 1936 there was a rising tide of anti-Fascist activity, as the events of Cable Street moved into the realm of myth. Anti-Fascists portrayed it as a 'great rising of East London workers against Mosley'. Mosley condemned it as 'the first occasion on which the British Government has openly succumbed to Red Terror'. The police rejected the idea that the entire population of the East End had risen against Mosley and claimed the main activists had been Communists. *Blackshirt* editor John Beckett suggested the anti-Fascist mobilization was 'a revolutionary dress rehearsal' and Joyce claimed it had all been orchestrated by 'the combined resources of Jewish Finance and Muscovite subversion'. Ten days after Cable Street, at Salmon Lane, Limehouse, Mosley insisted a 'Red army mobilised from all over Britain' had been at the forefront of it.

Part of the Cable Street mythology was that it 'effectively checked Mosley's campaign in east London'. The police, in fact, argued it threw 'out of perspective the events of the month as a whole'. The BU was 'steadily gaining ground' in Stepney, Bow, Shoreditch, Bethnal Green and Hackney. 'A definite pro-fascist feeling has manifested itself throughout the districts mentioned, and the alleged Fascist defeat is in reality a Fascist advance.' In the following week, Mosley addressed a series of successful meetings in Stepney, Shoreditch, Bethnal Green and Stoke Newington, without any interference, in front of 'manifestly pro-fascist' working-class audiences. Police said the BU's London membership had 'increased by 2,000'.

Cable Street, however, proved to Mussolini that opposition to the BU was greater than Mosley had indicated. In Rome for his customary meeting with Mussolini he was interviewed instead by Foreign Minister Ciano, who asked him whether it was true that he had just been in Berlin. Mosley replied 'without further explanation, "Yes"'. He 'did not entirely trust' Ciano's discretion and did not give him the reason for the visit, which he admitted, 'ruptured my relations with Mussolini'. Mosley was told that Cable Street was viewed as a defeat and they were considering ending the subsidy. Mosley's excuse was that the 'real' East End had been 'overwhelmed' by 'Alien Jews', and boasted that the depth of Fascist support would be expressed at the LCC elections in March 1937. His Blackshirts would sweep the polls, demonstrating the BU's inevitable advance to power. A message arrived saying Mussolini was ill and could not see him. He had, however, relented on the subsidy and would postpone a final decision until after the elections.

The BU's East End campaign saw an increase in attacks on Jews by young Fascist hooligans. The breaking of shop windows, the desecration of Jewish cemeteries and synagogues, and the spread of anti-Semitic graffiti led to a highly charged atmosphere. Increased street corner meetings at which BU speakers made anti-Semitic remarks inflamed passions still more. BU speakers played a game with the police to see how far they could go in abuse without breaking the law. At a meeting in Bethnal Green, Mick Clarke said it was 'time the British people knew that East London's big pogrom is not very far away now. The people who have caused the pogrom to come near in East London are the Yids . . . Mosley is coming every night of the week in future to East London and by God there is going to be a pogrom.'

BU speakers felt they had little to fear from the police, who were regarded as their natural allies since many were ex-army men who were 'extremely patriotic' and, therefore, agreed with their views. Jeffrey Hamm recalled police laughing at points made by speakers and enjoying the meetings. One eyewitness claimed the police were 'very anti-semitic' and 'corrupt in the way they obtained convictions against Jews'.

Policemen were disciplined for not arresting blatantly abusive anti-Semitic speakers, but Sir Philip Game admitted speakers' tactics kept mostly within the law, which was vague and difficult to enforce. Attempts to prosecute them foundered on the belief of the Director of Public Prosecutions that proceedings would probably fail, because Fascists criticized the Jewish people as a whole rather than those present at meetings. The BU claimed it was defending the right to free speech, even though it was responsible for the bulk of the violence, particularly against the opposition who were usually attacked after meetings. MI5 claimed Fascists never attempted to break up opponents' meetings but this was challenged by a Home Office official who marked the report with the comment: 'This is not true.' It indicated that 'not all officials automatically branded the communists as chief culprits'. However, they all agreed that the two extremes fed off each other. In a memorandum on 9 October Game, who wanted a ban on all political marches, suggested 'the real clash may come eventually not with Fascism but with Communism. If that does come would it not strengthen the hands of whatever Government was in power, if the nettle of Fascism had been grasped, and received drastic treatment today.'

A week after Cable Street, Mosley did march through the East End. On 11 October he spoke to an enthusiastic 12,000-strong crowd at Victoria Park Square. At the end, John Warburton recalled, Mosley announced he was going to speak in Limehouse. 'He was told he couldn't march there. "Very well," he said, "I'll walk." The crowds followed and as he walked, they started to shout "Good old Mosley". People were leaning out of their downstairs windows to try to shake his hand.' There was also a victory parade by 10,000 anti-Fascists, which was charged by Fascists, resulting in scuffles and arrests. While 2,000 special constables were occupied with the affray, in the Mile End Road a group of 200 Fascist youths set fire to cars, smashed windows and looted Jewish shops, attacking anyone who looked Jewish. There was a razor-slashing and one Jew, a hairdresser, was picked up and hurled through a plate-glass window; after him the Fascists threw in a four-year-old girl. The 'Mile End Road Pogrom' was the most violent anti-Semitic outbreak the East End had seen.

For Bill Deedes, who lived in Bethnal Green, that Sunday 'offered a disturbing glimpse of the bitterness and hatred which six months of active political and race strife have generated in the East End . . . Political passions have reached a pitch when ordinary, apparently decent citizens are ready to vilify, spit upon and injure their neighbours.' Deedes believed he was 'witnessing a mild version of what was happening in Spain between the extremes of right and left'. The police drew truncheons and mounted police were used against anti-Fascists. Of the eighty-five arrests, seventy-nine were anti-Fascists, while seventy-three police and forty-three demonstrators required medical attention.

On 13 October the President of the Board of Deputies of British Jews, Neville Laski, met Labour's Herbert Morrison to urge him to keep his people away from Fascist demonstrations, since Mosley thrived on the publicity the confrontations produced. Laski arranged an unattributable meeting with Harry Pollitt, CP General Secretary. The three agreed that Jews themselves helped stimulate anti-Semitism through poor housing conditions, low wages and bad workshops. Jewish employers could help solve the problem if they ceased using sweated labour and if landlords looked after their houses. 'Jews ought to be super-correct in their economic conduct,' Morrison said. In local politics 'Jews play too prominent a part. They should keep in the background . . . and leave it to the Gentiles to fight for them.' His attitude was no better than Mosley's who wrote in *Action* that 'the Jew himself created anti-Semitism. Created it as he has always done by letting people see him and his methods. Even Hitler was not an anti-Semite before he saw a Jew.'

Also present was Felix Frankfurter. 'It is heart-breaking', he wrote, 'that the three spokesmen could not agree on a public campaign of meetings jointly sponsored by their organisations to counteract the well-organised gangsterism' and the 'beatings-up of Jews', which 'will one day mean minor pogroms'. Morrison was afraid of joint action with Pollitt, and Laski was 'afraid of an appeal to the CP and its effect on the rich Jews'. Laski's final comment was that 'even rich Jews will risk fascism in the hope of buying themselves off rather than strengthen the working-class cause'.

That night Mosley addressed a crowd of 12,000 at Bethnal Green and then marched to Limehouse. Mosley told the crowd, 'I challenge and expose tonight the corrupt power in England of international Jewish finance.' Collin Brooks was in touch with BU officials. He thought 'anti-semitism is a rising force, as everywhere'. The Nazi hierarchy, too, believed anti-Semitism was beginning in England. The National Socialist press created the impression that in London 'Jews and Communists walk arm in arm'. The exultation which greeted Mosley, the ominous 'Perish Judah' on walls of houses and the rioting in the East End, notes Dietrich Aigner, 'left no doubt that anti-semitism was in the air. England was becoming "Jew Conscious".'

Mosley insisted the BU had few links with the Nazis and stated that Diana represented him alone, not the BU; though he and the movement were, in effect, one and the same. Diana would make at least fifteen trips to see Hitler; all of which were monitored by the Secret Intelligence Service (MI6). On one occasion her luggage was searched by Special Branch, which found the autographed photograph of Hitler that he had given her as a wedding present. Mosley's standing within the Nazi movement changed from month to month and depended on who was making the assessment. On 20 October 1936 Goebbels, who disliked him, recorded that 'the Führer issued a damning judgement about Mosley. Exactly my opinion. He is not a great man.'

Ribbentrop was more sympathetic and on the same day told the British ambassador, Sir Eric Phipps, that he had recently had a good talk with Mosley about the 'terrible danger' of Communism. Phipps, who regarded the German as 'ignorant and boundlessly conceited', concluded that the Nazis were waiting to see if he could woo Britain. 'If he fails the "party" will give up playing *la carte anglaise* and will strain every nerve to isolate us, and then *Gott strafe England* will be their motto.'

Mosley considered the idea that Unity, 'immature for her age, who amused Hitler, had any influence at all' ridiculous. Military Adjutant Gerd Engel, however, recalled how her light-hearted talk was 'taken seriously by Hitler, because he had fixed ideas about things, and once he got an idea into his mind it was very difficult for him to get it out'. He depended on personal impressions and Unity, described in an MI6 report as 'more Nazi than the Nazis', helped shape his perceptions of Britain. Speer said she was the sole exception to an agreement among Hitler's personal entourage that politics should not be mentioned. Reinhardt Spitzy recalled her making 'withering jokes about its ruling class, thus encouraging him to believe that the British people would soon grow weary of this privileged clique. Here was another fatal misunderstanding.'

Magda Goebbels described a lunch at Schwanenwerder at which the Mitford sisters attacked Hitler for Ribbentrop's appointment. Unity predicted he would become a joke in London but, despite her dislike of him, she strengthened his admiration for 'the used-to-ruling Tories'. Ribbentrop courted 'eccentric' aristocrats on the fringe of decision making. 'Each of them', recalled Spitzy, 'specifically cultivated to make cheap propaganda and generously supplied with foreign exchange.'

In London, Mosley was trying to recruit intellectuals to his new *British Union Quarterly*. Ezra Pound was a 'bustling and practical person, making the shrewd observation that Englishmen of my class never grew up until they were forty'. There was a lunch with Wyndham Lewis and the former editor of the *Review of Reviews*, Lovat Dickson, at the Leader's flat in Ebury Street. Attended by Joyce, the meal was served by 'heel-clicking blackshirts who raised their arms in 45-degree salute on entering or leaving the room'. Lewis agreed to write 'Left wings and the C3 mind', which was unequivocal in its loathing of Marxism as 'an enormous evil'.

Lewis intended to visit Germany and Joyce told him 'it had been arranged that I should see the Führer'. In his 1937 essay, 'Insel und Weltreich', Lewis praised Mosley's 'great political insight and qualities as a leader', and portrayed Hitler as 'the most unassuming and simple of men'. His anti-Semitism was a 'mere bagatelle' and understandable, given the character of German Jews. Jewish immigration to England would mean that men 'of the same blood as Chaucer and Shakespeare', who had not had the 'low cunning' to accumulate money, would be forced to abase themselves before 'some off-spring of an Asiatic bazaar tout'. He sketched Mosley and portrayed him as dramatically handsome and 'poised on the brink of some gesture or action'.

Lewis wanted Roy Campbell to meet Mosley, in the belief that 'these two men would be on the same wavelength'. The South African-born poet had been brought up like Mosley in 'a wholly pastoral, pre-industrial world, became proficient in every form of outdoor activity and had a belief in the excellence of physical action'. The reactionary nostalgia of *Broken Record* (1934) rejected the values of urban, democratic society and the 'herd-like masses'. A militant Catholic, he admired Fascism for being 'religious, not fanatical; human and not mechanical'. He failed 'to see how a man like Hitler makes any "mistake" in expelling a race that is intellectually subversive'.

The crucial event in Campbell's life was the Spanish Civil War, in which he was badly wounded and decorated 'for saving life under fire'. He saw the Civil War as 'the ultimate encounter between light and darkness, tradition and chaos, Christianity and atheism, Europe and Asia'. According to Tom Buchanan, he was 'an isolated (and even hated) figure in literary circles' for his support of Franco. Campbell insisted he was simply 'pro-European, anti-Soviet'. He was far from alone among Catholic intellectuals in his attitude to Spain, which 'reinforced the distance between Catholics and mainstream intellectual life'. Campbell recalled that the BU was 'at its zenith and I was regarded as a hero of the Right'.

In the new year Mosley proclaimed his support for Franco, who was 'performing a good work for the whole of civilisation', but said 'the whole of Spain is not worth one drop of British blood, and if we were in power we would not interfere in the quarrel in any shape or form'. It was denied there were Italian and German troops fighting for the Nationalists despite overwhelming evidence that Italy had supplied planes and German pilots were practising dive-bombing techniques. The BU press denied reports of Nationalist atrocities even to the extent of claiming Guernica had been destroyed not by German bombers but by the Republican government. From spring 1937 Major-General Fuller made frequent visits to Spain and insisted stories of killing prisoners were 'pure invention'. He sent his observations to an interested War Office. He recognized the war had 'ushered in the new era of the airmen'.

BU secret member Mary Allen also visited Spain, establishing links to the Falange. Guy Hamilton, journalist, sometime admirer of Mosley and a contact agent for MI5, provided the authorities with evidence that Allen was 'Franco's most dangerous agent in Britain'. A dossier on her visit to the Nationalists was kept by Republican Foreign Minister Julio Alvarez del Vayo, who showed it to Hamilton. She was highly regarded by Falangists and was the guest of Franco, who was told that Mosley planned to launch protests in the event of the British government siding with the Republicans. By championing Franco the BU increased its prestige among Catholics.

Mosley's meeting with Campbell was unsuccessful. While he found Lewis 'touchy but agreeable', Campbell, who was offered the post of Fascism's official poet, was a 'more robust character'. Campbell's wife recalled that he said, 'It's no good, kid. He's as bad as the others.' Lawrence Durrell wrote that if he loved Campbell, 'it was precisely because he turned down Joyce's overtures'. He decided he was 'going back into the ranks to fight Red Fascism, the worst and most virulent variety, and that when the time came I was ready to fight black fascism and that I could (although badly disabled) knock out both their brains with my crutches there and then!' Campbell did, however, contribute to the *BU Quarterly*'s first issue.

Despite points of convergence, modernist intellectuals of the authoritarian persuasion did not join Mosley. Lewis could not stomach the 'repression, violence and concentration camps'. Campbell was horrified when Mosley 'calmly discussed . . . using mortars in local conflicts'. Douglas Jerrold put it directly to Mosley: 'Fascism had the crudity to destroy; it lacked the subtlety to create.' As Leslie Susser argues, modernists 'might invoke discipline as a cure-all for the spiritual malaise of the modern age, but in Britain they would never surrender their ingrained notion of politics that respected individual needs. They could sympathise with a fascist analysis of the modern predicament, but not go the whole way with its cure.'

Strangely, it was Joyce who courted the artists of modernism, which the BU identified 'with the decadence of the dying culture, the fascist phoenix was supposedly rising to replace'. He wrote that 'intellectuals – who form the nuclei of decadence in the capital of the great industrial societies – please their own morbid mentalities (and incidentally fill their pockets) by a propaganda of filth which engulfs an increasing proportion of the youth of each generation'. He wanted Fascism to apply 'the stomach-pump of common sense to the unclean system of English intellectualism. If our intellectuals are still seeking new sensations we have something original for them.'

Through his propaganda efforts Joyce was recognized as the BU's most skilful officer and the immediate post-Cable Street period entered Fascist folklore as 'a golden age, when the BU appeared an unstoppable force'. In the East End, the feverish rate of recruitment continued and support more than tripled by November to around 20,000. 'Respectable' middle-class Fascism was undergoing a revival, particularly in southern England where it was intended to contest seats in a general election. Collin Brooks learnt from Mosley's circle that, as part of their appeal, they 'wish to reduce gradually the usage of the title from "British Union of Fascists" to "British Union" and to eliminate foreign savour. If the Government forbids uniforms, this transition will be the simpler.' Spurred on by the likelihood of legislation, councils allowed them halls on condition uniforms were not worn. George Orwell wrote that 'if, some day, an authentic fascism were to succeed in England, it would be more soberly clad than in Germany'.

MI5 reported the BU was 'being captured by the personality of Joyce', who was tipped as 'a possible successor to Mosley and a future Viceroy of India in a BU-headed government'. If Fascism was to be taken seriously, 'it seems likely that Joyce will continue to play a prominent part'. His leadership qualities were 'much more potent than Mosley's'. For radical Blackshirts, Joyce represented the expression of revolutionary 'rank-and-file' National Socialism, through his 'unwavering adherence to fascist ideology and principles'. Maxwell Knight repeated his assessment that it was unlikely that anything 'could occur to shake his basic patriotism'. This was so even though MI5 intercepted a wildly optimistic intelligence report Joyce sent to Berlin about the BU.

The ambitious Joyce was opposed by Francis Hawkins who, on 19 October, as Director-General of Organization assumed control of the headquarters, internal affairs and political machinery. Promoting his henchmen, such as Brian Donovan as his assistant, into key personnel positions enabled him to outflank Joyce and win the war for Mosley's ear. Joyce argued Hawkins's takeover of the training of the party speakers left him as a glorified office boy. He was convinced Mosley was a figurehead controlled by Hawkins, who was named by a Special Branch report as 'the most powerful figure in Mosley's Council'. By early November Joyce was gradually marginalized.

At a luncheon for wealthy sympathizers at the Criterion, Mosley presented his anti-Semitic policy which, he confirmed, had been planned from the beginning. An infiltrator for the Jewish Board of Deputies reported that Mosley said, 'since the international financier and speculator in our midst is our real enemy it became clear why we did not raise the Jewish question during the first two years of our party's existence ... we were told when we first raised this question of vital interest that we would be crushed in six months. Every attempt was made, but, like Englishmen, we have fought back.' The government was under criticism for its failure to deal with the violence associated with the East End campaign. The PM believed the banning of uniforms would eliminate a major source of provocation and clear the government of the charge of inactivity. On 9 November 1936 the Home Secretary, Sir John Simon, introduced the Public Order Bill with tough powers to control both political disruption and public protest in general. Tory MP Oswald Lewis acknowledged the government had taken advantage of the consensus against the Fascists in order to introduce wider measures.

The official Italian periodical *Nuovo Antologia* played down the role of anti-Semitism within the BU, which had 'no racial policy against the Jews, but encourages them to be British before being Jewish'. It admitted, however, that Mosley was 'not much liked by the public, partly because of the numerous changes during his political career'. The word 'Fascism' was also 'not much liked by the general public, it sounds very foreign, and therefore suspicious'. BU similarities with foreign movements were all too obvious. 'Few facts of Nazi anti-semitism were left unstated by the Press,' notes Andrew Sharf. 'And the Press, with the few exceptions ... was uniformly disgusted by these attitudes.' What made matters worse was that Mosley was at no stage critical of the dictators' actions. Laudatory articles on Mosley and his movement appeared in glossy Nazi propaganda magazines such as *Europea will leben*. On 12 November the Home Secretary confirmed rumours that the BU received foreign funds, without going into detail.

There was good reason to be concerned about Mosley identifying with the Fascists and Nazis. Mussolini declared an 'Axis' had been formed between Rome and Berlin. Robert Mallett found in Italian archives 'abundant evidence that Mussolini actively pursued an alliance with Hitler's Germany, and prepared Italy for a "parallel" war of expansion alongside the Third Reich against Britain'. On 15 November Goebbels admitted they had turned 'anti-English'. They were 'pouring unbelievable amounts of money' into armaments. 'We'll be prepared. Domination in Europe is as good as ours.' That day he saw Diana. 'Mosley wants money again. Not at the moment.' Mosley's reaction was almost instant. MI5 noted his 'closer approach to the German spirit in his more pronounced attacks on the Jews'.

In mid-November Mosley asked Baba to undertake 'some important secret service work' for him in Italy. Infatuated with the Leader, she asked Irene to go with her, to act as a smokescreen for her undercover task. MI5 believed details of Mussolini's subsidies were known only to a few people around Mosley. One courier was Dundas and another may have been 'Michael F.', a solicitor in the City, prominently connected with the BU and a 'responsible person for receiving funds for the Fascist Party from abroad'. Small amounts had already come from Hitler and 'a rather larger sum from sources in Switzerland'.

One differentiation from its Continental counterparts was the BU's absolute identification with and sycophantic reverence with which it beheld the young King. He was portrayed against a Union Jack with the title 'England's Sore Need – A Benevolent Dictator'. After Edward VIII visited distressed areas in Wales, Collin Brooks noted on 18 November that 'the suggestion has been made in many quarters that he could, if he wished, make himself the Dictator of the Empire. Some minds see in the South Wales activity and brusqueness a sign that he may yet dominate the politicians.' Chips Channon said the King was 'pro-German' and Ribbentrop described him as 'a kind of English national socialist'. Blackshirts regarded him as a 'member of the war generation, a kindred spirit'. Edward, wrote Raven Thomson, was 'the stuff of which Fascists are made'.

'He who insults the British Crown thus insults the history and achievement of the British race,' the BU stated. But there was the problem of the King's relationship with American divorcee Mrs Simpson. 'The King', Mosley declared, 'has been loyal and true to us. My simple demand is that we should be loyal and true to him ... The recompense of his country for twenty-five years' faithful service is the denial of every man's right to live in private happiness with the woman he loves. Let the man or woman who has never loved be the first to cast the stone ...' The *Blackshirt* headline – not long after Mosley's secret marriage – was LET KING MARRY WOMAN OF HIS CHOICE.

Prime Minister Stanley Baldwin warned the King he would resign if he married Mrs Simpson. His opposition was founded not on morality but on the quality of Edward's friends (Churchill, Lloyd George, Rothermere and Beaverbrook) and the undermining of the monarchy. Secretary of State for India Lord Zetland wrote privately on 27 November that Edward 'had been encouraged to believe Winston Churchill would be prepared to form an alternative government'. This would raise 'a problem compared with which even the international issues, grave as they are, pale into comparative insignificance'. Brooks thought the King 'may do anything – he may even dismiss Baldwin and send for Mosley, and attempt a fascist *coup d'état*'. Ministers feared this was 'not impossible'. Churchill might form a government and call an election, which might lead to a Fascist government. Mosley was organizing for this very possibility.

The BU's 'Save the King' campaign was directed by Beckett and attracted the support of ex-servicemen. He attempted to rally public opinion with leaflets, chalking the walls and a special newspaper, *Crisis*, which sold 37,000 copies. *Action* published a photograph of the King getting out of an aeroplane with the byline 'A Symbol of the Modern Age which the old men hate'. The campaign, however, was spectacular for its lack of impact. BU organizers soon realized they had misjudged the country's mood. Richard Bellamy found 'reports were extraordinarily unanimous'. The middle classes, particularly the lower middle class, regarded the proposed morganatic marriage (by which Mrs Simpson would be Edward's wife but not Queen) as 'an affront to petit bourgeois respectability and considered that Edward should abdicate, some said the sooner the better'. The working classes 'were solidly for the King. They knew he sympathised with their plight.' Even this was wishful thinking. Observers noted most people were 'resolutely hostile'.

With the crisis front-page news, Mosley was in Liverpool, where he was joined at the Adelphi Hotel by Joyce and Beckett, who found him 'in a state of great excitement'. He claimed 'to be in direct communication with the Court. The King was strengthened by the knowledge of the support of his movement, and for this reason would accept Baldwin's resignation and call upon Mosley to form a government.' Mosley later admitted he had been in secret correspondence with Edward. He denied seeing Edward but he had a number of close contacts with the King, such as Fruity Metcalfe. There was a feeling within the BU that 'something was going on and that they were going to achieve power'.

Mosley detailed plans to Joyce and Beckett 'for governing without parliament'. He 'strode about the room in excitement as he explained that millions of pounds would be available to fight an election in such a cause, and that as Prime Minister he could broadcast as often as he wished. This, he was certain, could not fail to turn the electorate in his favour.' There was then a telephone call and Beckett recalled that when Mosley replaced the receiver 'he turned to us and explained that he had received most important news from Court. He apologised for speaking in cipher, but said he always used it because his calls were intercepted by the CID.' Beckett thought Mosley's secretiveness schoolboyish but was sure he 'really believed he was on the threshold of great power'. He was certainly under surveillance. MI5 was worried by his attempt to organize support for a 'King's Party'. 'Certain delicate enquiries' were also made under Baldwin's direction involving 'matters touching on the Constitution and ultimate issues of sovereignty', which MI5 recognized were 'far removed from any question of guarding the King's Realm from penetration by external enemies or of rebellion by a section of the King's subjects. They involved its innermost integrity . . .'

On 4 December Beaverbrook and Rothermere picked up Mosley and Lady

Houston as recruits to their own campaign, but Lloyd George was in the West Indies convalescing. The Chairman of Associated Press, Esmond Harmsworth, promoted the idea of a morganatic marriage. The King had been seen by Churchill, who told him he 'must allow time for the battalions to march'. Harmsworth said Churchill would 'take office if only to be Prime Minister for a day'. Edward's defeat 'would be fatal – tantamount to silent civil war. In any issue between the King and a democratic Premier, the monarchy would go, even if – as is possible – the King's party won an election.'

On the following day Tory Chief Whip Margesson told the PM that forty Tory MPs supported the King. Lacking a majority, Churchill would be compelled to seek a dissolution. 'And therein,' Zetland concluded in a second letter, 'lies the supreme danger, for the country would be divided into opposing camps on the question of whether the King should be permitted to marry . . .' General Sir Ian Hamilton, former Commander-in-Chief at Gallipoli, who had seen Hitler secretly under cover of British Legion trips to Europe, told Baldwin 'there would be an ex-servicemen's revolution if the King abdicated'. Detective author Anthony Cox ('Francis Iles') heard from military friends of 'a conspiracy by certain young hotheads, junior captains in the Household Brigade, to take up arms against the Government and for the King and putting the Prime Minister under arrest'. Ceremonial guards outside Buckingham Palace were said to have been issued with live ammunition. In Berlin, Diana talked to Hitler and Goebbels about the King's plight. The latter was disgusted by the news: 'That an empire can sink so low.' He recorded that Hitler 'approves money for Mrs Guinness' and had released the money as arranged. 'As a result there will be peace. But they need so much.' Mosley was back in favour.

The Director-General of the BBC, Sir John Reith, feared 'we might have the King as a sort of dictator, or with Churchill as PM, which is presumably what that worthy is working for'. Sir Mark Pepys, Earl of Cottenham, had already chosen Churchill's government: 'Duff Cooper and Sassoon were to take the Exchequer and the Air Ministry, and Hoare and W. S. Morrison could be counted on.' A descendant of the diarist, Cottenham was a racing driver and air ace for Vickers. A Fascist sympathizer, he told Brooks that 'some change of leadership must come' but Mosley's record was 'too bad', as demagogy was 'less essential here than it was in Germany or Italy'. At the beginning of the war, Cottenham was recruited into MI5's Transport Section, but soon resigned to live in the United States because he 'could not reconcile himself to a war against Germany'.

The King had 'a night of soul-searching' about supporting a King's Party. 'In the end, I put out of my mind the thought of challenging the Prime Minister. By making a stand I should have left the scars of civil war.' The idea had been doomed to failure. The Imperial Policy Group, founded around the India issue, sought to convince governments that Britain's secret foreign policy was to keep out of European conflicts in order to give Hitler a free hand against the Soviet Union. Its secretary, Kenneth de Courcy, hoped to persuade Edward there was support for a King's Party but Thomas Dugdale MP told him MI6 had a case against Mrs Simpson; a stain of scandal which doomed the idea. The King decided to abdicate and summoned Baldwin, who called a Cabinet meeting for 6 December. The King sent messages to Mosley of 'polite thanks for his offers of support', of which he had 'felt unable to take advantage'.

On 8 December Goebbels talked with Wrede who had returned from London. 'Our attitude regarding the Royal crisis is much praised over there. The question of money for Mosley has been settled. Wrede wants to go to London to contact Mosley. I welcome that.' Hitler said, 'the King is to be pitied. The men in England have no guts.' It was not until the Abdication Bill was laid before Parliament on 10 December that German people learnt the truth. Ribbentrop lunched with J. C. C. Davidson, a confidant of Baldwin, and warned 'there would be shooting in the streets' when the King's Party restored Edward to the throne. Davidson reported that Ribbentrop talked 'more nonsense than I have ever heard from anyone in a responsible position'. It was 'quite obvious he had been stuffing Hitler with the idea that the Government would be defeated'.

Senior Lords civil servant Colin Davidson congratulated Edward on his 'determination not to encourage a "King's Party". It was within your power to create civil war and chaos. You had only to lift a finger or even come to London to show yourself, to arouse millions of your subjects to your support.' On the night of 10 December Scotland Yard flooded central London with policemen hours before Edward's abdication. Special Branch feared a 'public uprising' spearheaded by Blackshirts. Part of a crowd of 5,000, 500 Fascists were outside Buckingham Palace chanting, 'One two three four five, we want Baldwin, dead or alive!' Fascist youths led 800 demonstrators to 10 Downing Street and others picketed Parliament with placards reading 'Sack Baldwin. Stand by the King!' In the end, only five arrests were made. That night Jim Lees-Milne was with Diana at Wootton. They listened in tears to the King's abdication broadcast: 'I remember it well, and Diana speaking in [baby talk] to Mosley over the telephone.'

Ribbentrop told Hitler the abdication was 'the result of the machinations of dark Bolshevist powers against the Führer-will of the young King'. The Führer said the reason was because the King wanted Anglo-German rapprochement. There was now 'no other person in England who is ready to play with us'. A depressed Hitler said that with Edward on the throne 'there would have been no differences – and no war – between England and Germany'. Diana claimed, 'if the King and my husband had been in power, there would have been no war with Hitler.'

'We would have stopped it dead in its tracks,' claimed Mosley. 'I know this to be true. Although [Edward] and I considered it unwise for us to meet, we maintained a correspondence before and after the abdication crisis. The King already had a strong aversion to war with Germany. We would have told Hitler that he could do what he liked in the East. If he wanted Ukraine, he could have it as far as we were concerned, but we would have told him not to touch the west.' Edward admitted as much in a 1960s interview: 'I thought the rest of us would be fence-sitters while the Nazis and the Reds slogged it out.'

Mosley still entertained illusions of grandeur. He was thought by MI5 to be working for the ex-King's return. On 11 December 3,000 people attended a meeting in Stepney where he demanded the abdication issue be put to the people. Windows were smashed and there was a street battle with anti-Fascists.

The telephone call between Mosley and his royal contact proved to Beckett that the Leader was 'dangerously near the borderline between genius and insanity'. He knew the man as 'a dilettante society friend of Mosley's, who lived in as fictitious a world of grandeur as Mosley himself'. Beckett had left Mosley 'convinced that he already believed himself in charge of the nation's affairs'. His 'powers of self-delusion had finally conquered his sanity. He could not realise that nobody except himself and the comical little group of ex-peddlers and humourless ex-officers with whom he was surrounded took him at all seriously.' Critics who complained about his concentration on the East End whispered that Mosley 'liked the East End for reasons of vanity; that in the East End he could pretend that he was already the idolised Leader of the people'.

MI5 had been surprised by the display of pro-Fascist sentiments in the East End but 'instead of keeping the situation at boiling point' the BU 'allowed it to subside'. By December the enthusiasm of the 'Cable Street Fascists' waned, with many drifting away, never to return. Given the huge propaganda effort, the number of recruits who stayed was modest. Mosley decided ideological Fascism made few converts and, for reasons of conviction and economy, supported Hawkins, who argued populist campaigns based on activism and discipline attracted recruits, who could then be converted to Fascism.

As a result of an increase in violence the government rushed through the Public Order Act, which became law on 1 January 1937. Home Office officials were cautious about restricting civil liberties but police chiefs wanted the banning of uniforms – the definition of which was left to the courts, with prosecutions the responsibility of the Attorney-General – as well as controversial marches and public meetings. Insistence that uniforms led to trouble stemmed in part from an aversion towards a 'rival organization'. The attitude was not pro-Fascist but pro-police. Section 2 of the POA made it an offence to organize meetings 'for the purpose of enabling them to be employed for the use or display of physical force in promoting any political object'. A 'reasonable number' of stewards were permitted for private premises but forbidden at open-air meetings. Police were given the power to ban for a period of three months marches if thought likely to cause a breach of the peace. The Cabinet opposed the extension of the ban outside East London, where it was used to ban both Fascist and anti-Fascist processions, and trade union marches.

According to Sir John Simon, the Act worked like a 'charm'. Herbert Morrison claimed 'it smashed the private army and I believe commenced the undermining of Fascism in this country'. It deprived the BU of the propaganda value of its paramilitary displays. Mosley addressed a meeting at Hornsey wearing a black shirt and tie under his suit, and set the fashion for speakers. Members took to wearing high-necked black sweaters. Fascists continued to wear the uniform at private gatherings but did not challenge the new Act, though the author John Mortimer recalled walking with his father on the Embankment and seeing Fascists carrying their uniforms on coat-hangers. In many ways it was a relief to Mosley, who realized the Nazi-style uniform had been a mistake as it 'made us much too military in appearance ... The old soldier in me got the better of the politician.'

'One thing is clear,' wrote Kingsley Martin, 'Sir Oswald's form of Fascism is making less than no progress in England at the moment.' In fact, the number of meetings rose and during 1937 the Metropolitan Police supervised over 7,000 Fascist or anti-Fascist marches and meetings. The POA halted BU recovery but only temporarily. It forced Mosley to become more 'respectable' to attract the middle classes and in the long run the BU increased its support so that by the beginning of the war it was higher than at any time since the peak in 1934.

To gain respectability, lunches were arranged at the Criterion and attempts were made to 'popularise books calculated to awaken sympathy for fascism'. The Right Book Club (RBC) was created in 1937 to counter the success of Victor Gollancz's Left Book Club. Its moving spirit was the anarcho right-winger Christina Foyle, who received the support of Conservative Central Office and former January Club members Francis Yeats-Brown, Charles Petrie and Douglas Jerrold. It was responsible for publishing Ward Price's *I Know These Dictators* and Sir Arnold Wilson's *Thoughts and Talks Abroad*, which expressed admiration for Nazi Germany. Chairman of the book committee was Norman G. Thwaites, who also chaired the BU's Windsor Club. A rival National Book Association (NBA) was organized by the historian Arthur Bryant and published Hitler's *Mein Kampf*. The NBA's pro-German tenor overlapped with the RBC's pro-appeasement stance, but in Bryant's view true Fascism had 'no resemblance whatever to the foolish, provocative and completely unnecessary play-acting under the name of Fascism which we know in England'. He did not consider Mosley to be a bona fide Fascist leader.

The combined middle-class membership reached 15,000, but their influence was limited.

A BU official mentioned Italian funding in letters from Rome intercepted by MI5, where there was an air of triumph at the discovery. When it became known that Mosley had been subsidized to the extent of 'about £100,000 [£3.4m] and when it was probable but not established that he was being subsidised by the Nazi Party', Sir Robert Vansittart interceded on MI5's behalf with Sir Russell Scott, Permanent Under-Secretary of State at the Home Office, with the new information in an attempt to secure a warrant for 'a carefully restricted examination' of Mosley's correspondence. However, Scott refused because of his status as a former Minister.

The BU was, in fact, nearly bankrupt. Mosley had to mortgage his estate for £80,000 (£2,720,000) and put £100,000 into BU funds. He could no longer afford his share of the unkeep of Savehay Farm and decided to let it and allow the children to stay at Wootton. The Curzon sisters were horrified by the thought of Cimmie's children being in the same house as the woman they held responsible for her death. Mosley suggested Irene pay for the upkeep and make arrangements for the children to repay her when they came of age. The blackmail worked. To the outrage of her solicitor, Irene agreed to pay her brother-in-law's share out of her own pocket.

Miss Black of the BU Accounts Department told a Special Branch informant that no proper balance sheets were kept, the subsidiary companies were in a state of chaos and accountants simply arrived at some figures to satisfy Mosley. If 'we don't make drastic improvements the whole movement in the North will blow up'. On 13 January 1937 Goebbels gave Wrede 'the job of finding out what state the Mosley Movement is in. I'll get a report in three months.' Wrede's role in channelling funds to Mosley was revealed in secret documents of the Luxembourg Nazi Party, later obtained by Frederick (later Lord) Elwyn Jones. A socialist barrister involved in fighting cases arising out of the BU marches in the East End, Elwyn Jones supported the anti-Nazi underground, particularly in Germany and Austria. According to the documents, on 22 January, francs worth £4,000 (£128,000) were dispatched to the BU through 'Agent 18'.

Joyce wanted to intensify the East End campaign but Mosley was unwilling to challenge the law. Special Branch reported that Joyce's 'manner had steadily been becoming more parade ground like and his head was cropped closer than ever before'. Maxwell Knight observed that he 'knows what he wants in life, and is out to get it. I feel somehow, despite the fact I dislike the man intensely, that in him there is someone who might one day make history. With all his faults he remains in my mind one of the most compelling personalities of the whole movement.' He was, however, 'an expert at intrigue' and Knight was 'acutely conscious that he is irritated sometimes to the point of insanity by the men above him, especially the old men'. Joyce was in correspondence with Christian Bauer, a German journalist in London believed by MI5 to be engaged in espionage. He was deported in November.

Putzi Hanfstaengl did not like Unity. He had confided in her his 'criticisms of the influence of Goebbels and Rosenberg on Hitler', but his fatal error was to comment on the Nazis' war culture. She passed this on to Hitler. On 6 February 1937 he proposed a practical joke: Putzi would be told to report to a military airport for a secret mission. A pilot would take him up and would hand him orders that he was to be dropped behind the Republican lines in Spain. After circling a few times, Putzi would be dropped off at Munich, none the worse. Diana and Unity laughed at the plan, not supposing it would be carried out, but it was – exactly as planned. Putzi was shaken to the core and left Germany for Switzerland, and travelled on to London, terrified the Gestapo was after him.

Following government pressure on prominent BU backers to stop donations, Mosley was forced to hand over regular sums to keep the BU afloat. He took out a loan from Lord Amherst of £12,000 (£408,000) in February, followed by another £5,000 in June. Mosley's own income was £17,000, made up of dividends worth £10,000, Lady Mosley's £3,500 and a grandmother's legacy of £2,300. The day after the Putzi incident Diana saw Goebbels, who had decided Mosley was 'spending a fortune and not accomplishing anything. Now I'm not doing any more regarding this business. I'm referring them to Wiedemann.'

Mosley decided to gamble and devote his limited resources to putting up six candidates for the East London council. MI5 discovered that a decision had been made to put 'the Jewish question' at the heart of the campaign. Mosley wanted the enemy attacked where his corrupt power was strongest. They were going to fight the 'parties of Jewry' and speakers were instructed to show 'that all the present democratic parties are completely Jew-ridden' and were 'the flunkeys of finance and the jackals of Judah'. Raven Thomson explained that every vote cast would be a vote on the 'Jewish question'.

Mosley sought to attract the votes of Irish Catholics, who 'run like a bright thread through Mosley's chequered career' and in the East End supported the BU as a vehicle for their local grievances. The campaign was run by two local Irishmen, Owen Burke and Mick Clarke, along ethnic lines by playing the Irish off against the Jews. Clarke said 'the best thing to do when you meet a good Jew is to shoot him'. Catholic anti-Semitism was a source of anxiety to Anglo-Jewry in the inter-war years and Mosley found an ally in the popular *Catholic Herald*, which was 'an irritant in the life of the Jewish community'.

The election addresses were written by Mosley, accounting for their virul-ently anti-Labour tone. The *Pioneer* said voters 'tried to secure revolutionary changes through the Labour Party and you have failed because that Party and their Communist allies are also controlled by the Jews'. Jewish landlords, shopkeepers, employers and councillors were all strongly criticized. On the hustings in Bethnal Green Mosley said electors 'must choose between us and Jewry', and appealed to them to 'give the Jews notice to quit'.

On 8 February Special Branch passed a report to MI5 on the growing differences within the BU. Joyce was at the heart of the in-fighting. His 'irritability of manner' was a sign that he felt his talents had not been properly recognized. He was going through major personal changes. His marriage to Hazel, who had been subjected to regular physical abuse by him and had had to put up with his numerous affairs, had ended in divorce. Hazel's second husband was Eric Piercy, former head of the I Squad. Joyce married fellow BU activist Margaret White on 13 February at Kensington Register Office.

Mosley's campaign in the East End was a massive affair and by February police were required to attend up to 1,400 meetings, which was equalled by anti-Fascist demonstrations. The POA did not stop the street-corner meetings which heightened tension in the area and Police Commissioner Game acknowledged it did little to protect the Jewish community. Since 'most assaults occurred at night and the victims could rarely identify their fascist assailants, the police were hardly ever successful in tracing the offenders'. Jewish groups felt police deliberately minimized the extent of the anti-Semitism in reports to the Home Office. The Commissioner argued that routine reports of Jew baiting could now be discontinued since 'criticism and heckling' was being 'kept within the bounds usually considered permissible at election times'.

Colin Cross noted 'a widening divergence in policy and methods between the powerful East End movement and the isolated, idealistic provincial Fascist branches', where 'patriotism was the mainspring and anti-Semitism an embarrassment'. Mosley addressed large audiences but Beckett knew it was 'a stage army which attends him everywhere. In the north the same 100 or so have been his "brothers in arms" in every place at which he speaks.' They were bussed in and 'given reserved seats in the front rows, and they behave as hysterically as film star fans'. Mosley drove through streets 'alive with opponents shouting his name, to a hall where admirers greet him with enthusiasm all the more boisterous because of the "dangers" which their hero has just escaped'. Only in Bethnal Green and Shoreditch did the Fascists represent growing strength.

Right up to the count, Mosley was certain of victory and predicted they would win four seats. He said canvass returns proved it but Beckett knew they showed they could not win. Mosley was furious he had seen them and reprimanded the man responsible. Beckett said Mosley was 'capable of inspiring great love and great enmity', but 'not one person of integrity has remained his associate, although his brilliance and magnetism have drawn to him the best of his generation. This is the fault of his enormous ego, combined with a peculiar shallowness of judgement and ability to deceive himself. The man who brings him good news is his friend, the carrier of unwelcome tidings slowly becomes his enemy.'

In the election on 6 March 1937 not one BU candidate was elected. The highest vote was 23 per cent in Bethnal Green where the BU came second. In Limehouse 16 per cent was achieved and 14 per cent in Shoreditch. Labour's vote held up and denied Mosley the benefit of any anti-Labour sentiment. Its proportion of the vote fell only in Shoreditch; elsewhere it was the Liberals and anti-socialists who lost out. Mosley made little headway among the 'ordinary' working class, and his failure to win over the Irish constituted a decisive check to attempts to establish a secure power base and was a telling blow to the Fascists. The BU lost, and lost heavily.

On hearing the results Mosley smashed his fist into his palm and exclaimed, 'Better than Hitler!' He explained that in 1928 Hitler had polled only 2.7 per cent, but had returned twelve members to the Reichstag and five years later was in power. He told a German newspaper, 'Our position is now nearly equal to that which was formerly in existence with you in Germany. In the east end of London we have now gained the absolute majority . . . Our struggle against the Jews has helped us to win.' It was true that young supporters were ineligible to vote, but he never captured the East End, where 'the forces of anti-fascism always remained stronger than those of fascism'. The reality was that Hitler had won a national vote whereas Mosley fought a small number of constituencies that offered the best prospects of success. Goebbels was un-impressed. 'The red majority has only been strengthened. Mosley didn't win any seats. He came away empty-handed.' At the rate of progress shown in the LCC election it would have taken half a century for the BU to come within reach of power.

Mosley had not fulfilled the promise made to Mussolini and the BU experi-enced its most serious crisis to date when, on 10 March, the Italian leader told him he was ending his subsidy. The decision was final. Two days later Special Branch reported the 'foreign money has to a considerable extent ceased'. Dundas was ordered back to London from Rome. His family were temporarily homeless and stayed in one of Mosley's London properties. Shortly afterwards Dundas and his wife separated. Not only Mussolini but also domestic backers withdrew support, discouraged by the lack of success.

The Charing Cross Westminster bank account was closed in May 1937. The total Italian subsidy, which includes money not banked in the Charing Cross account, was £234,730, worth around £8 million in today's money. A. G. Findlay handled the final cash subsidy for 1937 of £7,630; not greatly different from the previous year for the same period. BU expenditure for the year dropped to about £20,000 (£680,000), less than half the usual amount. Special Branch reported that Mosley was shocked by Mussolini's decision, which plunged the movement into a series of internal crises from which it never really recovered. Mosley announced he would give his whole income to the movement, but this was not enough to maintain all of the BU's salaried posts.

The cuts in every sector were set against factional infighting between the 'politicals' such as Beckett and administrators like Hawkins. Beckett heard from Joyce an authoritative rumour that Mosley wanted rid of both of them. Beckett was bitter about the conduct of the campaign and considered Hawkins and Donovan to be 'utter fools and that if Mosley was not as great a fool as they are, he is certainly far too complacent'. The officials sent to the East End had been 'worse than useless'. Raven Thomson was 'a dangerous idiot who frothed about the Jews and boasted that he would soon be elected and giving orders'. Exasperated by the lack of realism on the night of the election, Beckett had 'very nearly resigned'.

On 11 March Mosley handed many officials envelopes containing money and a letter giving them a week's notice. Headquarters was cut from 143 to a skeleton staff of thirty and expenditure, hitherto running at £2,000 per week, was cut to £500. Many paid speakers of the Propaganda Department were dismissed in acrimonious circumstances. The cull included the legal officer Captain Lewis, Joyce and Beckett, and, according to the latter, 'every other man or woman on his staff who had ever reasoned with or contradicted Mosley or his henchmen'. Joyce had a face-to-face confrontation with the Leader but it did him no good and he was expelled for 'financial irregularities'.

A week after the dismissals John McNab, an official in the Jewish sub-department of the Propaganda Department and editor of the *Fascist Quarterly*, complained about the treatment of Joyce. 'Mosley went livid and thumped the desk and shouted that Joyce was nothing but a traitor; that he would never rest until he had broken him; that he would roll him in blood and smash him.' When McNab returned to his office, a uniformed guard gave him ten minutes to leave the building. In a private document Mosley wrote that 'those no longer on the salaried staff have offered voluntary service in their spare time, which is gladly accepted, and will consequently be available to the Movement as speakers, writers or voluntary organizers. The exceptions are Messrs Beckett and Joyce who have not emerged in the same manner from this stern test of character.' He thought Joyce 'intensely vain, a quite common foible in very small men'. He 'did his best to create a revolt in the party, which I overcame without difficulty. He failed to shake our members, whose morale was much too strong for him.'

Joyce claimed the charges against him were based on a forgery that black-ened his name. He sued for wrongful dismissal and won an out-of-court settlement. He formed, with Beckett, the National Socialist League, along with McNab and Vincent Collier, a propaganda officer and agent of the Board of

Deputies of British Jews. Financed by stockbroker Alex Scrimgeour, who had given £10,000 (£340,000) to the BU, the violently anti-Semitic NSL was committed to a pro-Nazi racial nationalist ideology. It was never a serious political force but attracted enough support to give Joyce a living.

It is a matter for conjecture, noted Robert Benewick, 'whether the Blackshirts who succeeded in stirring up some racial hatred in East London made real converts or only prodded a latent anti-semitism into action'. BU candidate Charles Wegg-Prosser, whose writings betrayed 'a faint "Communism is Jewish" trend', resigned when he saw anti-Semitism in action. He issued an open letter through the BoD to Mosley, denouncing anti-Semitism as 'a smokescreen to cloud thought and divert action with regard to our real problems . . . You sidetrack the demand for social justice by attacking the Jew, you give the people a false answer and unloose lowest mob passion . . . I tried to interest these people in real problems, unemployment, wages, housing, and so on. I watched with dismay the mentality which said "Get rid of the Jews, and you will automatically get rid of unemployment, slums, sweating".'

The criticism did strike home. *Action* issued a reminder that 'this task of repelling Jewry is a small and incidental feature of the British Union Campaign. Our task is to build a prosperous Greater Britain. From that task we shall neither deviate nor allow ourselves to be driven; and the Jews are only important in so far as they stand between us and our objective and will not be allowed to distract us from the great ends to which Mosley has called us.' On 14 March Collin Brooks met with Yeats-Brown and Fuller who were leaving for Spain to see Franco. 'Fuller says that Mosley is now intent upon dropping the label of Fascism' and 'still thinks his day will come when the next economic stress affects people'.

The reduction in personnel was followed by a restructuring of the organizational machinery, which included closing northern regional offices in Manchester and combining administrative and political functions in the London headquarters. MI5 reported that 'the significant feature of this upheaval is the complete victory of the Hawkins "blackshirt" clique, which has practically eliminated those who were opposed to its conception of the BU as a semimilitary organisation rather than an orthodox political machine'. A former propaganda officer complained the BU was 'bureaucracy run mad'.

The propagandists believed 'National Socialists had been driven out' and 'were being victimized because they tried to enlighten the Leader as to the true state of affairs in the organization'. As Hawkins took control, it seemed the movement had succumbed to 'heel-clicking and petty militarism'. His role, however, was overstated. It was to P. J. Taylor that Mosley turned to salvage the disaster, rather than Hawkins, who waited outside Mosley's office while the Leader consulted with Taylor – a fact officials noted with surprise.

Luckily for Mosley, on 17 March he received 22,700 francs (£91,000) from

'Agent 18'. In total, he had delivered nearly £220,000 in today's money – a not inconsiderable sum. MI5 believed the Nazis subsidized the BU 'for purposes of propaganda likely to be favourable to German policy'.

Unity wrote to Diana on 26 March that she had stayed in Nuremberg 'with the lovely Gauleiter'. The only irritation was the presence of Streicher's son, Elmar, who made 'the most amazing statements about England [he had been there the previous year to survey the BU] and he is always believed in preference to me'. On 9 April Diana reported that Goebbels admitted 'Mosley is slowly winning through'. He was still plagued by financial problems. The Public Order Act frightened away contributors, since it empowered the authorities to audit the finances of any organization deemed to be violating the law and required it to reveal the sources of its funds. The statute created difficulties with regard to the secret subsidies to which Mosley had become accustomed. It therefore became essential that he find other sources.

Geoffrey Allen had secured a concession to operate a station in Andorra but its construction was stopped by the civil war in Spain. An agreement had been made with Kieztoushi and Tremoulet of Paris and Toulouse to run two 'English hours' per day on Radio Toulouse. A programming company was set up in London and the English programme was opened in grand style by a speech on Anglo-French friendship by Winston Churchill and a talk from Peter Eckersley. The station intended to provide people 'with an entertaining alternative to the dreary schoolmasters at the BBC'. Mosley hoped to compete directly with Luxembourg by serving the British market from west, south and east Europe. Ireland was to be the western supply; Sark or Belgium the southern; Denmark or Germany the eastern. The Allens visited Dublin, where Radio Athlone had commercial channels and could offer studio time. After Bill Allen told Mosley about it, thought was given to a station on Sark in the Channel Islands, where the BU had a supporter.

Exploiting commercial radio had been suggested by Captain Dudley M. Evans, invalided home from the war in 1917. An Anglo-German Fellowship member, he was impressed by Nazi achievements. He was classed on MI5's Suspect List as 'a fanatical BU member'. Evans introduced Mosley to Colin Beaumont, a BU member with family connections to the Mosleys, who knew about commercial radio through contact with Captain Plugge. His mother, the Dame of Sark, the island's quasi-feudal ruler, admired Mosley, as did her friend Lady Dunn. During the war Sibyl worked in the War Office's Postal Censorship Department and in the Foreign Office. In 1932 the first flight was made to the island by Fascist sympathizer Lord Sempill. That Christmas she became the first woman to land on the island by aeroplane. The Home Office noted she was not wealthy but was 'anxious to do all she can for the island within her means'.

The current Seigneurie de Sark, J. M. Beaumont, remembers his father 'talking of this idea of a radio station to be based loosely on Radio Luxembourg. My father was always full of money making schemes!' Sark was outside the BBC's jurisdiction and Evans hoped to persuade his friend to allow a station to be built there. Beaumont 'got on very well' with Mosley and agreed a thirty-year contract whereby Mosley would create a holding company to finance the construction costs and Beaumont would receive 25 per cent of the profits. The Allens would share the profits and advanced money to the BUF Trust and New Era Securities, obligations later cancelled.

Mosley set up holding companies to obscure his partnership with the Allens, including to negotiate contracts, Air Time, whose principal directors were Bill Allen and Peter Eckersley, and the New Museum Investment Trust to conclude agreements. Mosley's investment of £10,000 was obscured by accountancy smokescreens created by James Herd. The system of loans and guarantees between the directors and Mosley was set out in a secrecy document which obliged signatories not to divulge his role. Diana stuck to the pact and even Unity was unaware of the real reasons for her trips to Germany. Mosley later asked Skidelsky to delete names connected with the project from his biography. He did not want the business 'to be traced to various well-known men who were engaged in it . . . It would not embarrass me, but it might embarrass them.'

In March, Allen completed the agreement with Sark to host a station, even though Eckersley advised the Post Office would never allow it and the BBC would seek an injunction to block transmission. Mosley was optimistic the courts could be convinced Sark was not bound by British law because of the legal autonomy granted it by Elizabeth I. The matter would need to be settled by the Privy Council.

Mosley employed Frederick Lawton, a colleague of Tom Mitford in the chambers of C. T. Le Quesne KC, a silk with roots in the Channel Islands. A future Lord Justice of Appeal, Lawton was the son of Wandsworth Prison's sadistic governor. He flirted with Communism, converted to Roman Catholicism and founded Cambridge University's Fascist Association. Called to the Bar in 1935, he helped Mosley in a libel suit and in 1936 almost stood as a Mosleyite candidate in Hammersmith and defended Blackshirts accused of offences under the POA. After visiting Sark and researching medieval land law, Lawton advised legal prospects were fair. Mosley recognized government opposition was 'likely to be much more intense if they discovered by any means fair or foul that I should benefit, and consequently it was of immense importance to cover my connections with the island and the business'.

Mosley claimed he 'attempted to get the German concession some time after getting the Sark concession. It was an entirely new idea to them, and it took over a year of very hard work through intermediaries to get them to entertain the project.' By March, Eckersley was presenting 'practical ideas'. He wrote to his wife from Berlin that Diana Guinness was 'the only one in the [Allen] team who is neither hysterical nor fantastical. It is a relief to get a little honest pessimism, coupled with determination.' Diana was never referred to as 'Lady Mosley', as everyone was anxious not to alert the press as to what she was doing. Eckersley insisted he was not engaged in 'some political racket' but he did see an Anglo-German station as a means of fostering co-operation between the two countries as part of his passion for peaceful coexistence in a 'United States of Europe'. Eckersley travelled on to Vienna, where the Allens failed to find studios, then to Copenhagen, again with no success, then back again to Berlin to meet 'DG'.

Returning from Germany in April, Chesterton was promoted by Mosley to Director of Propaganda. He became editor of the *Blackshirt* and published a series of articles, 'Aspects of the German Revolution', full of sycophantic praise for 'the splendid Nazi manhood and womanhood of Germany, old strugglers and young enthusiasts alike. "Comrades! The Blackshirts of Britain salute you! Heil Hitler."'

Nazi thinking was evident in the 'blood and soil' philosophy. Novelist Henry Williamson recognized that the BU had the most supportive agricultural policy, with increasing stress placed upon the 'moral' advantages of rural life. In a speech on 24 April Mosley warned 'the roots of Britain are being dragged from the soil'. The 'drift of population from country to town' was a symptom of decadence. 'Any civilisation that is to endure requires constant replenishment from the steady, virile stock which is bred in the health, sanity, and natural but arduous labour of the countryside.'

Chesterton wrote that 'unless they know, mystically, that beneath the concrete lies the earth which has nourished their race for a thousand years and . . . that it is their own earth from which their blood is shed and renewed, then they are a lost people and easy prey for those who have lacked roots for many centuries'. BU agricultural expert and Sussex farmer Jorian Jenks had been educated at Harper Adams Agricultural College and Balliol, and held agricultural appointments in England before becoming a victim of the slump and emigrating to New Zealand. Returning to England, Jenks was a leading light in the Rural Reconstruction Association and wrote studies of the organic movement. The combination of blood and soil mysticism and modernism, however, resulted in an unstable pledge to 'repeople the land' and encourage the 'small working farmer', while making 'every method of modern science available to British agriculture'.

On 12 April Goebbels celebrated Baldwin's retirement and hoped his successor, Neville Chamberlain, would be better for 'Europe's deliverance. In

Anglo-German unity lies the key to the new times.' He praised Rothermere for 'speaking out very warmly for the return of our colonies and for an Anglo-German bloc'. There was little difference between the Conservatives' policy of appeasement and Mosley's foreign policies.

Frustrated in domestic politics and subject to important defections, the adoption of a peace campaign provided Mosley with an issue around which to capture popular support. The ex-serviceman of the last war, he asserted, would rally to the BU because 'we have fought Germany once in a British quarrel and we shall not fight her again either in a Socialist or a Jewish quarrel'. Mosley 'grasped at what straws of hope still blew in the increasingly turbulent international atmosphere.'

Mosley's appeasement of Nazi Germany was denounced by Basil Liddell Hart, who regarded 'as double-dyed traitors those who wish to import methods of government that are contrary to the English traditions of justice and freedom, and uphold the aggressive policies of Great Powers which can be a danger to us – thereby playing into the hands of the enemies of England'. He could not forgive Fuller, who had aligned himself with Mosley and Hitler, and ceased communication with him.

Domestically, the BU remained a threat to public order, occupying police time and manpower. Prosecutions following the Public Order Act were almost entirely confined to the BU, which gave rise to Fascist complaints of discrimination. The impact of the POA, however, was limited and at the end of April BU anti-Jewish activities resumed.

Mosley maintained he had expelled the hardcore of the anti-Semites but had no problem with BU's publications claiming that 'to go to a swimming pool anywhere near London or the large cities is as efficacious as baptism in the Jordan; one becomes positively anointed with Semitic grease'. Jews were referred to as 'an obscene sub-human mass . . . these ape-like creatures'. With declining access to the press, Blackshirts resorted to outbreaks of slogan and emblem painting and chalking. The provincial press reported many cases of young members caught scrawling the anti-Semitic 'Perish Judah'.

Banned from marching through the East End, the BU used other London routes, such as through Bermondsey where serious disturbances took place. The police reported that marchers were 'often carried away by their anti-Jewish feeling, and acts of damage occur. The unfortunate inhabitants are deprived of sleep, and some of them are more or less terror-striken, for to the Jewish resident of the East End, the Fascist is a source of grave apprehension.' In the first year of the POA there were 3,904 Fascist meetings and 4,364 anti-Fascist demonstrations. The difference was that the latter did not set out to terrorize a section of the populace.

On 28 May Diana saw Goering, who asked her to see Putzi 'and persuade him to go back'. She did so but informed Unity on 8 June that he was 'quite mad'. He said, 'The truth is they wanted to [kill me] and they didn't manage it, so now they pretend it was a joke.' MI5 raised the subject of the BU's links to Germany with the Home Office on 9 June. It wanted to open Mosley's correspondence and that of Gordon-Canning, Dundas and Findlay – who were 'connected with the negotiations for, or payments of, German and Italian subsidies and were suspected of being intermediaries for the communication of secret information'. MI5's concerns arose from 'a source which had been tested over and over again and always found to be extremely reliable'. A week later Special Branch reported that Mosley wanted 'to keep the BU patriotic and respectable, at the same time fomenting industrial trouble in order to get the support of the workers when a slump comes'.

By 1937 unemployment had fallen to one and a half million but exports declined and imports rose sharply. With signs of a depression, defence spending came into its own as an anti-slump instrument. Germany's share of military spending rose in 1937 to 28.2 per cent and by the next year to 42.7. Within the BU there was anxiety that war would be used to avert a slump: 'Although there can be no question that war on a big scale would end depression overnight, we appeal to the sanity of the British people to choose the lesser of two evils. Surely a slump, however bad, is better than another war.'

On 4 June an agreement between New Museum Investment and Sark was signed. Mosley would finance construction of the station, with Beaumont receiving 25 per cent of the advertising profits and a £1,000 fee. Four days later, in Liechtenstein, agreement was reached for a radio concession with Roditi International, run by the Jewish Roditi brothers. Eckersley had undertaken the negotiations in Paris with his Roditi contact ('Kenmare'). He did not reveal his backers' identity when he approached the International Broadcasting Union to attend meetings on the strength of the Liechtenstein licence.

On the back of these two agreements Mosley launched 'Gemona' to involve the Germans in a similar project. Throughout the summer Diana acted as a negotiator on Mosley's behalf and timed her visits to Berlin to match periods when Hitler was present. Occasionally 'we dined and watched a film or talked by the fire'. She told Nicholas they spoke of events in England and Germany, of Mosley and the BU, and the state of the world. Mosley admitted 'it was a habit of Hitler to convey to me his view of events through Diana'. She broached the idea with Hitler of establishing an English-speaking radio transmitter on German soil to broadcast to England. He was non-committal as 'it was the sort of thing that bored him and was left to his ministers'. Hitler handed the project over to Wiedemann, whom Diana 'ceaselessly badgered in letters'.

Goebbels, through Radio Zeesen, and Mussolini, through Radio Bari, broadcast continuous anti-British propaganda. Mosley claimed that all propaganda would be specifically forbidden in the new stations for fear of scaring away advertisers. The aim was to make money, with light music, sport and beauty hints to advertise domestic products to housewives. Mosley and Diana planned a range of 'own brand' cosmetics and other domestic items to be sold over the airwaves. The opportunity, however, for propaganda, even of the mildest kind, to the mainly young audience that such a station would attract was incalculable, though Diana refuted that this was ever on the agenda. Bill Allen, however, later revealed the real purpose of the enterprise. The broadcasting company would be used as a safe channel for funds from the Nazis.

On 11 June Irene was shocked to receive a call from *Mail* journalist Ward Price, informing her of a report that Mosley had married Diana in Berlin and that the Führer and Goebbels had been witnesses. 'My heart stood still,' Irene recorded, 'though he denied it to all of us and his children.'

Fuller complained that Mosley 'will not see sense' over the BU's future. 'He goes rampaging on talking of fighting 400 seats. This is all absurd.' Fuller wanted to concentrate on 'gutter electorates' in the East End before branching out. In fact, gutter anti-Semitism was becoming more virulent, which pleased *Der Stürmer*. 'Exactly as the human blood stream, infected by a poisonous bacillus, responds by mustering germ devourers to attack and eliminate the invader,' Chesterton wrote on 26 June, 'so does a race conscious community at once mobilize its forces to fight the alien influences which instinct teaches would imperil its very existence.' He said of Jewish culture that 'when parasites crawl in and out of art like wood-lice, then culture is decadent and the people are brought face to face with doom'.

BU delegations visited Germany as enthusiastic admirers of Hitler's regime. Correspondence between an SA Division officer and BU members led to a twenty-strong group visiting in July for a study trip. Approved by the Ribbentrop Bureau, the group visited SA facilities on the 'guarantee no report of this visit will appear in the British or German press. The trip must be seen as that of private people and in no way as that of representatives of Mosley.' Streicher told his guests that he considered them 'brothers and comrades in the fight' against the 'one common enemy, and that is the Jew'. The BU spokesman replied, 'We rejoice that we have seen the world leader in the fight against Semitism.'

Goebbels still had reservations about Mosley and on 1 July stated, 'the Führer is only supporting Mosley because he does not believe in his victory. But he is a nuisance to the government.' Unity often saw the Führer alone, which his aides regarded as potentially dangerous. They were concerned about the role she had established for herself in his life.

Hitler rescinded the prohibition on spying and gave the green light to the *Abwehr* to resume operations. MI5 lacked resources to deal with German espionage but monitored Nazi journalists who were seen as agitators and spies. On 7 August the Home Office refused to renew the permits of Werner Crome, chief correspondent of *Lokal-Anzeiger*, his assistant Herr Wrede and Herr von Langen of the Graf Reischach Agency. Through them Goebbels had contact to Mosley, though MI5 was unaware that Wrede was the conduit for Nazi funding. 'Mosley was spending a fortune and getting nowhere. I think his cause is hopeless,' wrote Goebbels after a request by Diana for funds. Mosley managed to repay £17,000 of the loan he had taken out by obtaining a mortgage from Car and General Insurance of £60,000. He was investing his own money in his movement at an ever increasing rate. The total would reach £100,000 (£3,400,000).

Diana saw Hitler on 14 August when she watched films of 'the revolution here, the coming of the Führer, 1923 Parteitag, meetings, Schlageter being shot, Jews, Nazis . . . It was pure heaven.' Both Mitford sisters referred to Hitler as 'Wolf' – the name he went by to his intimates. Unity saw him lose his temper and regarded the incident with awe. She wrote to Diana that 'at last he thundered . . . It was wonderful.'

Despite MI5 fears of German intelligence penetration of the BU, the Service still made use of the organization. On 18 August four BU members – Ford, Dawson, Mann and J. C. Preen – burgled the home of Major Wilfred Vernon, a technical officer at the Royal Aircraft Establishment, Farnborough, where innovations in fighter and bomber equipment were designed. Vernon belonged to the Labour Party and Socialist League, and had set up a Self-Help Club for the unemployed. He was regarded as a Communist for meeting hunger marchers and MI5 intercepted his mail. During his absence Vernon's home was ransacked by burglars, who were caught by police making their getaway in a car sporting a BU flag. In the boot were an imitation revolver, a hammer, chisel and aluminium knuckleduster. Defended by BU barrister Frederick Lawton, the four were found guilty of larceny and bound over for twelve months.

'Nobody has ever explained', asked *The Aeroplane*, 'why four amiable-looking young men led by a self-confessed ex-Irish gunman should have been moved to extract these documents . . . We should so much like to know what is behind it, and who instigated these young men.'

During the trial the men stated that they wanted to expose the 'Communist' Vernon and not to rob him. A defendant was asked if he 'had been reading Bulldog Drummond'? He replied, 'No, I happen to be a patriotic citizen.' Preen said they had carried out the burglary on the orders of 'a senior intelligence officer' – later identified as P. J. Taylor, who hoped to secure evidence for MI5 that Vernon was spreading Communist propaganda among troops. However, at his hearing before the Advisory Committee, Preen explained that Taylor, having disclosed his MI5 credentials, said Vernon had stolen secret plans to pass on to the Soviet Union. He wanted Preen to raid Vernon's home and to bring whatever documents were found to the Intelligence Department at Scotland Yard. Among the papers stolen were 'sensitive' blueprints of the Avro Anson and Blenheim aircraft engines, which Vernon had taken to work on at home. Vernon was charged under the Official Secrets Act and fined £50 for failing to take proper care of secret documents, and dismissed from his job.

In 1940 MI5 sent a note to the Advisory Committee stating that the interned Preen should be released – a payoff for services rendered. The Committee was intrigued by the ambiguity of his action; he was working both for and against the Fascists. It illustrated the strange relationship between the BU and MI5, which regarded some officials as patriotic and used its personnel to carry out its freelance operations.

Hitler felt at home at the Osteria Bavaria where Unity was a regular guest. Privy to these occasions was Phillip Spranklin, BU correspondent in Munich, whose SS badge denoted his high status. American journalist Ernest Pope used him 'to lift the veil off Unity's love life with Hitler, or other goings-on within the walls of inaccessible Nazidom ... Phillip enjoyed proving how close he stood to the Nazi leaders.' Diplomatic columnist Bella Fromm wrote on 16 September that Unity was unpopular with Ribbentrop, having 'quarrelled about the methods of advancing the Fascist movement in England'. His mission in London had been unsuccessful and he blamed the British for his failure. Much to his chagrin, there were still 'saboteurs' in the Führer's entourage who hankered after a settlement with Britain. This included Unity and Wiedemann, Hitler's adjutant and wartime commanding officer.

Hess was suspicious of Unity, Fromm discovered. He repeated, 'where it will do the most good, Röhm's remark about her: "She pinches her lips so tightly because she has crooked teeth."' Hitler used her for political ends. He 'questioned her in a conversational way about England, English politics and Anglo-German relations'. Mary Ormsby-Gore recalled that Unity and Hitler 'used to comb through the Tatler every week to mark the names of those who might come over to them when he occupied England. They had great lists.' She observed that Mosley 'was treated seriously but not intimately'.

Hitler, his adjutant Nicholaus von Bülow noted, 'expected that his thoughts would be passed on in England' by Unity. On 25 September she 'complained freely about Mussolini'. Goebbels could not 'understand why the Führer lets it happen'. The British ambassador forwarded a report of a conversation with Unity who had learnt the Duke of Windsor was due in Berlin. Hitler had told her, 'If Mr Baldwin had not turned out King Edward VIII I might have been receiving him today instead of Mussolini,' though the visit 'was useful in demonstrating to other countries the strength of the Berlin–Rome Axis'.

Unity was 'as open in telling' the ambassador 'what Hitler had said to her as she undoubtedly was in telling Hitler what [he] thought'. The Foreign Office minuted that if Unity's account 'is true, Hitler will not have committed himself to Mussolini in Berlin'. It was initialled by the Foreign Secretary, Anthony Eden, who shortly after was seen by Ribbentrop, who talked about Communist activities, which seemed to 'obsess him to the exclusion of all other considerations'. He asked Eden 'what was the state of affairs in England. I replied that we had virtually no communists in this country, except those whom Sir Oswald Mosley was creating.' This puzzled Ribbentrop, who asked Eden 'to explain how it was conceivable that fascism could create communism'. Three months later Eden resigned, 'pincered by the Berlin–Rome axis, to the considerable pleasure of both Hitler and Mussolini'.

The Fascists and the Communists needed each other, 'for their mutual vilification gave them a significance which they otherwise lacked'. The CP benefited from opposition to Fascism at home and abroad. Rallies opposing the BU provided a major part of its activities. The CP achieved its peak, 'not when unemployment was at its worst, but on the eve of the Second World War', when membership rose to over 50,000.

Police Commissioner Game reported that the Public Order Act 'seems to have killed the wearing of political uniforms without any need for prosecution'. The BU had 'dwindled steadily into insignificance'. The autumn, however, saw serious disturbances. A march through Bermondsey celebrating the movement's fifth anniversary on 5 October culminated in a street battle on the scale of Cable Street. In Liverpool Mosley was hit on the head and was taken half conscious to hospital to treat a 'punctured wound of the skull'. On 12 October Goebbels noted that Mosley 'was going through the same thing we did'. The Home Secretary was bothered by the marches but, according to the Cabinet's deputy secretary, did 'not want to squash them in a hurry because the Civil Liberties group in the House is numerous and vocal'.

The disruptions led to increased support from Der Stürmer: 'Mosley's fight is truly courageous, truly honest, and truly chivalrous . . . We stretch out our hand to this man and tell him: "Adolf Hitler said in 1925, when the Jewish doctrine is opposed by a non-Jewish doctrine which fights with the same brutality but with greater truthfulness, then the non-Jewish doctrine will be victorious, if only after a very heavy fight." The day of Mosley's victory will come if he persists in his fight against Judah.' The BU now discussed the 'means of eradicating this pest from England once and for all'.

20

The Radio Project

Coverage of BU activities dwindled in the press, as that received by Anglo-German peace movements and Nazi apologists grew. Mosley, however, was careful not to associate himself directly with groups other than his own as he knew such ties might be used against him by the authorities. Instead, key BU members were used to maintain contact. Mary Allen's growing prominence among 'fellow-travellers of the Right' led to an invitation to join the Council of the National Citizens' Union, whose leadership was dominated by Conservative diehards and aristocratic closet Fascists. Anti-Semitism and pro-Nazism were increasingly characteristic elements of such groups.

The Link was founded in 1937 by C. E. Carroll, a badly wounded RFC pilot who edited the British Legion paper and became editor of the *Anglo-German Review*. Around 4,000 people joined the Link, which was more populist and active than the Anglo-German Fellowship. Its Council included pro-Nazis such as Professor A. P. Laurie and Sir Raymond Beazley, and had the support of Major-General Fuller, the Duke of Westminster and Lord Tavistock. Under the leadership of Admiral Sir Barry Domvile, Director of Naval Intelligence (1927–30) and member of the A-GF's Council, the Link strove for a German–British alignment.

Domvile's operation evolved through consultation with Dr Gottfried Roesel, the Anglo-German Information Service Head who was his next-door neighbour. A journalist on Goering's *National Zeitung* and party leader for Central London, Roesel had considerable sums of money at his disposal and worked closely with the BU. He cultivated 'white lists' of potential collaborators with a director of the *Anglo-German Review*, Dr Erich Hetzler, who allegedly sent to Berlin a list of 4,000 Nazi sympathizers. The Link was aptly named. Not only did it provide a channel for Ribbentrop and Goebbels to try to influence British public opinion, but Domvile saw his role as the key link man between pro-Fascist and anti-Semitic groups. He wrote for the BU newspaper under the pseudonym 'Canute' and was one of its secret members.

During the First World War, Domvile had concluded that 'behind the scenes controlling the actions of the figures visibly taking part in the government of the country' was 'the Judaeo-Masonic combination, which has wielded such a baneful influence in world history'. He blamed his early retirement in 1936 on falling out with MI5's Vernon Kell over criticisms of British Intelligence. During the previous year Domvile had visited Nuremberg and been fêted; he liked Himmler and his book, *By and Large* (1936), was a paean of praise for Nazi Germany.

Domvile belonged to an anti-Semitic 'subversive group' set up in co-operation with Nazi journalist Thost by Philip Farrer, a wartime intelligence officer related to the Mitfords and a friend of Mosley. Members included Fuller, who sent reports on the A-GF to Ribbentrop; Richard Findlay, Vice-Chairman of the Link's Central London branch, who had stood at the Norwood by-election in 1935; 'Billy' Luttman-Johnson, leading light in the Windsor Club, who offered German propagandist H. R. Hoffman help in the event of a Communist revolution. Luttman-Johnson's wife said he regarded Communism 'as a cancer which, if it took root here, would have to be cut out, if necessary, with foreign aid'. Other members such as George Drummond, President of the Northampton section of the Link, were recorded by MI5 as potential subversives and were put on the 'Suspect List'.

Der Stürmer talked of a secret organization in Britain whose object was 'to spread national and racial consciousness'. The Nordic League had been created in 1935 by Nazi agents sent to London to establish a branch of the Nordische Gesellschaft, run by Alfred Rosenberg, and used by the *Abwehr* and SS as a rival organization to Ribbentrop's A-GF. The Germans regarded the NL as the British branch of international Nazism.

A clandestine body with upper-middle-class support, the Nordic League had its origins in a racist and occultist order, the White Knights, Britain's nearest equivalent to the Ku Klux Klan. The White Knights and the NL shared a headquarters in Lamb's Conduit Street, and both aimed to 'rid the world of the merciless Jewish reign of terror'. In a room festooned with swastikas, master of ceremonies T. Victor Rowe heard members swear a blood-curdling oath to King Edward I, responsible for expelling the Jews from England, for the initiation ritual. A BU member, Rowe was described by Mandeville-Roe as a 'German agent'. An importer of kitchen equipment from Germany, he was alleged to have a 'close association with prominent persons in the Nazi regime'. The League's 'chancellor' was Commander E. H. Cole, a retired naval officer and member of the IFL, whose extreme anti-Semitism derived from his exposure to the Protocols of the Elders of Zion when he 'had been involved with allied help to the White Russians in the Civil War'.

The NL's extremism was the reason Mosley refused to get involved, but his lieutenants, Fuller, Gordon-Canning and Oliver C. Gilbert, had been founding members. Gilbert's contacts with German and Japanese agents were viewed with suspicion by MI5. NL membership was a who's who of the Fascist political fringe, with Maule Ramsay MP, Brigadier-General R. B. D. Blakeney

(BF), William Joyce (NSL), H. H. Beamish (Britons), Arnold Leese and P. J. Ridout (IFL), and 'Professor' Serrocold Skeels (United Empire Fascist Party and known Nazi agent). Meetings were often held under the auspices of the BU and Nazi propaganda was distributed. Through these ties, members of Lieutenant-Colonel Seton-Hutchison's pro-Nazi National Socialist Workers Party were integrated into the BU. The faithful exchanged views on the evil of Jews and watched films of the ritual slaughter of animals. Commander Cole said Parliament was full of 'dirty corrupt swine' and declared that 'extermination is the only solution to the Jew problem'. Audiences responded with shouts of 'Kill the Jews' and 'Heil Hitler'.

The League was aided by 'fronts', the Militant Christian Patriots and the Liberty Restoration League. Between them they encompassed MPs, aristocrats, industrialists and financiers – the Duke of Wellington, Lord Brocket, Lady Dunn, Lady Douglas-Hamilton, Lady Alexandra Hardinge, Sir Abe Bailey's son, Lord Carnock, Sir Michael O'Dwyer, Sir Louis Stuart and Commander Bowles MP. They were, however, relatively minor figures and the NL provided the Nazis with a distorted 'insider's' view of the British ruling class. One trusted Nazi agent in the League, Anna Wolkoff, had been associated with the inner circles of the BU since the time when Joyce had been an up-and-coming BU figure. Officials visited the Russian Tea Rooms owned by her White Russian parents, where Wolkoff held court. Special Branch noted her presence at BU London Administration luncheons held at the Criterion where Mosley addressed titled ladies.

Although Hitler forbade the *Abwehr* to create an intelligence network inside Britain, the *Abwehr* and the SD engaged in the 'development' of secret agents on a long-term basis. *Förscher* (scouts) searched among the BU and the mushrooming anti-Semitic clubs for people who could be enticed into espionage.

MI5 had penetrated the German embassy and recruited the Press Attaché 'Klop', father of Peter Ustinov, Counsellor Theodor Kordt and junior secretary Wolfgang zu Putlitz, who told them of 'improper contact with underground activities' by German officials. A report sent to the Home Office on 27 January 1937 emphasized that BU members 'would support Italy or Germany against their own Government in the event of war'. Mosley was surrounded by a group of 'reckless individuals with a revolutionary outlook. Ultimately, they hope to see a Socialist government in power when they would be able to "go into the streets" and imitate the tactics which brought the Fascists and Nazis to power in Italy and Germany.' MI5 backed Schuster's proposed Emergency Powers (Defence) Bill. He warned that 'in a future war ... there is a serious danger that attempts to impede the war effort might be made by persons actuated not by sympathy with the enemy, but by "internationalist" affiliations or by disinterested opposition to the war'. He wanted the government to have powers to intern anyone 'whose detention appears to the Secretary of State to be expedient in the interests of the public safety or the Defence of the Realm'. It was approved by the Committee on Imperial Defence but was deemed so controversial that the Cabinet was not told.

By late 1937 the Nazis had little use for Anglo-German rapprochement, preferring the Berlin–Rome axis. Hitler realized the pronouncements of visitors such as the Mitfords had been 'too consistently contradicted by events. The failure of the BU to make headway, for instance, ultimately spoke for itself, and did so even to Hitler's mind.' According to his aide, Wilfred von Oven, Goebbels judged that Unity, 'through her sledgehammer methods was more harmful to us than helpful'.

After attending Nuremberg, Diana turned her attention to the quest for a radio station in Heligoland. On 9 October Wiedemann reported to the Führer and informed Diana that 'apart from the consideration of the technical style and several things that the Ministry of Propaganda has raised – considerations, which under some circumstances could have been disregarded – the greatest objection was raised from the side of the military authorities. The Führer regrets that under these circumstances he is not able to agree to your proposal.' Diana learnt it was Goebbels, 'who, when things looked hopeful, always put a spoke in the wheel. As Propaganda Minister he wished to keep radio entirely in his own hands.'

Mosley was trying to put together a deal in Belgium, where his people 'had done a tremendous amount of work'. Oliver Hoare was his chief negotiator and Frederick Lawton visited Brussels to lay the legal groundwork. Mosley and Allen believed they had in their pocket a Belgian Cabinet Minister who could be bribed to give the necessary permission.

Mosley's Belgian associates were Joseph Hepburn-Ruston, who had divorced Baroness van Heemstra and was said to be working for the Bank of England, and his partner Dr Albert Tester. They were behind the creation of the controversial European Press Agency, which aimed to produce an anti-Communist and anti-Semitic newspaper. Tester admitted that he was acting for Mosley. Involved with the agency was Dr Richard Behn, a Hamburg barrister assisting the German Foreign Office and director of Tester's British Glycerine Co. Its Belgian directors included General Henri Maglinise, former Army Chief of Staff, and Baron Brugmann de Walzin, millionaire and Fascist sympathizer. Its backer was Sir Charles Allom, a contractor to the War Office for shells, who had known Mosley's grandfather as a member of the British Shorthorn Society. Rumours circulated in Belgium that the company was a Nazi 'front' for gathering commercial intelligence. In an interview in the *Telegraph* (5 April 1938), Belgian Rexist leader Léon Degrelle confirmed he had contact with Tester and had met Mosley.

L'Indépendance Belge was for sale and Dr Behn negotiated to buy it. In the Belgian Chamber of Deputies on 23 March 1938 a letter was read out, which indicated that in the previous year the agency had received £110,000 (£3,740,000) from German heads of industry who were working with Goebbels. Tester denied the allegation, though he had ties to Fritz Hesse, Ribbentrop's Press Attaché in the London embassy, who knew him as a 'propaganda leader with Mosley' and as an 'untrustworthy businessman with whom it was best doing no business'. The British Foreign Office judged Tester to be a first class crook who made his money through the formation of bogus companies. These were alleged to be 'fronts' that allowed German firms to overcome embargoes from European countries trying to avoid economic subordination to the Nazi regime. According to the *Express* (7 September 1940), Tester was considered by British Intelligence to be 'a shrewd agent of Himmler'. The Nazis were well aware of his 'strong anti-Jewish attitudes' which had 'made him many enemies'.

Mosley boasted he now ran 'a much more formidable and far sounder organisation conducted at a fraction of the cost'. He was, however, desperate for money and during November tried to persuade Mussolini to resume funding. Optimistic reports were sent to the Italian embassy, but to no avail. He was forced to put £700 (£23,800) into the coffers weekly to keep the BU afloat. From October to the following February £11,000 was deposited, with another £10,000 used to pay off an overdraft. 'I did not object to spending all my own fortune but I did object to failure. My immediate steps were to effect considerable economies.' He reduced his personal expenditure to about £5 (£170) a week. 'None of this mattered. All that mattered was that at our 1937 rate of expenditure I should exhaust my fortune before I achieved my objective.'

The Home Office feared Mosley might regroup the BU around the Duke of Windsor and it was resolved by MI5 that if he attempted to do so he would be arrested for sedition. Sir Robert Vansittart assembled a security file on the Windsors' dubious contacts and meetings with Fascists. They spent their honeymoon in Austria at an alpine castle owned by Count Paul Munster, a dual British and German citizen, who together with Fruity Metcalfe had joined Mosley's Windsor Club. Munster was under general observation due to his association with known backers of Mosley. Wallis's legal affairs were handled by the French lawyer and Nazi agent Armand Grégoire, who had dealt with Ernest Simpson's shipping contacts. French Sûreté reports note that he represented Mosley and may have channelled German funds to Mosley, who made a number of trips to Paris during 1937 with Diana, including representing Britain in the world fencing championships. US intelligence records suggest Mosley received funds from the Nazis via Belgium, France and Switzerland.

On 22 October the Windsors met Hitler in Berlin 'to express their gratitude for the moral support Germany had shown during the abdication crisis, and at the same time roundly annoy their opponents in Britain'. The transcript of their talk disappeared from Nazi files captured by the British at the end of the Second World War. The couple also dined with Hess and discussed the idea of a 'new world order'. Hess held out the prospect of the Duke's return to the throne. Goebbels suggested 'we could get an Anglo-German bloc with him'.

On 2 November the British ambassador, Sir Ronald Lindsay, told Sumner Welles, US Under Secretary of State, there was a 'very vehement feeling of indignation' against the Duke, which bordered on 'a state of hysteria'. This was because his supporters were 'known to have inclinations towards Fascist dictatorships'. His reception by Hitler could 'only be construed as a willingness to lend himself to these tendencies'. Lindsay said the Duke 'was trying to stage a come-back, and his friends and advisers were semi-Nazis'. During November one of the most influential men in Whitehall, Chief Industrial Adviser Horace Wilson, told Walter Monckton, Attorney-General to the Duchy of Cornwall, that the real worry was that if the Duke returned to England it would be exploited by extremist groups, by which he meant Mosley's Blackshirts. On 22 November Bruce Lockhart informed the Foreign Office that the Nazis were convinced Edward would 'come back as a social-equalizing King' and inaugurate an 'English form of Fascism and alliance with Germany'.

Outside of rallying around the former King, the Home Secretary considered the BU 'a troublesome nuisance rather than a political danger'. Cities such as Birmingham, Manchester and Liverpool no longer had an organization, while there were no more than a hundred active members in Lancashire. Chesterton, who had written a glowing biography of the Leader, blamed Mosley's inability 'to free himself from the influence of the party bureaucrats' led by Hawkins. By turning the movement into a conventional party, the BU was 'employing lies and political bribes in order to gain votes'. As Chesterton's biographer suggests, for the bureaucrats 'the party was fascism'. They gave Mosley 'their undivided support and thus bolstered his self-importance, something increasingly important to him as his crusade disintegrated in external indifference'.

The BU's low-key campaign in the November council elections was reflected in the poor results. Forty-eight candidates in five London boroughs polled an average of 560 votes. For the first time in its history the Communist Party won a seat, in Spitalfields East. The BU put up six candidates in Limehouse and lost them all. The thirty-eight candidates in Edinburgh, Sheffield and Southampton came bottom of the poll. In Leeds, with a large Jewish population, BU candidates polled 106 and 74 votes respectively, coming below even Social Credit.

Following his concussion at Liverpool, Mosley spent time with Diana recovering at Wootton. 'Solitude was what he craved, for a few days in the whirl of his crowded, busy life.' He used the time to write *Tomorrow We Live*, a 35,000-word update of his brand of Fascism. He decided not to spend Christmas with the children at Denham. There was 'not one word', recalled Irene. 'He is the utter limit.' Since no one knew they were married, this apparent flouting of the conventions was deemed scandalous.

At the beginning of 1938 diminishing finances forced another round of staff reductions. Prospects looked bleak. More than half of the active membership of 5,800 was concentrated in London. As the movement stagnated, the CP regarded Mosley as a spent force. Even the Nazis seemed to believe he was not worth supporting. In his report on British politics on 2 January, Ribbentrop placed no emphasis on the BU.

Rumours circulated that the Beaumonts of Sark were interested in operating a commercial radio station on the island. This surfaced on 13 January 1938 in the *Express*'s 'William Hickey' column, written by left-winger and MI5 informant Tom Driberg. Hickey said, 'The least pleasant feature of the scheme will be that some of its backers are wealthy businessmen known to be closely in touch with Fascist sympathisers.' The Post Office put paid to an agreement under a 1934 Act which forbade transmission from the island. Hickey's information probably came from MI5's Maxwell Knight, to whom Driberg had been introduced by Denis Wheatley. The three shared an interest in the occult and lunched at the Paternosters Club, where conversation often centred on British Fascism.

The Allens approached the Liechtenstein government and on 21 January Eckersley met its chief Minister Dr Hoop. At the same time Diana visited Berlin with proposals that she handed to Hitler. She 'assumed the famous Secret Service knew why I was there'. On her return she received a letter from Wiedemann, who said 'the Führer took the documents himself'. He advised her to return to Germany 'when things have settled down and then get your decision from the Führer himself'.

Eckersley met with Robert Boothby, who was a 'fixer' in Europe for the Jack Buchanan Radio Corporation of America and a director of the Allens' company, on 18 February at Mosley's London flat. Oliver Hoare of the 'Boothby Group' was employed in Belgium but his connections to Mosley became known to the authorities. On 12 March Dr Behn, the German barrister based in Brussels who had met Mosley in London through Dr Tester, was refused an entry permit to England. Behn suspected the 'English authorities' were aware of these contacts, having found a letter on him from Mosley. On 23 March the European Press Agency was 'exposed' in the Belgian Chamber of Commerce and three days later the British press picked up the story. The *Express* ran an interview with Tester in his capacity as 'legal adviser' to Hepburn-Ruston. He admitted his links to Mosley as his 'aide-de-camp' and proclaimed that the BU was best described as a National Socialist movement. The exposure of the agency was raised in the Commons on 7 April but the Home Secretary stated there was no evidence that it was financed by the Germans. The resultant publicity scuppered Mosley's ambitions. Perhaps the expected bribe was not big enough because the attempt to suborn the Belgian Minister failed and Hoare's deal collapsed.

Mosley's electoral ambitions to put up sixty candidates at a general election were also collapsing. After a year spent building up the St George's constituency, Westminster, Fuller decided to withdraw his name as a prospective candidate since 'the vast re-armament scheme, now in progress, has knocked the main props from under my feet. Since my name went forward I have been almost completely tabooed by the Press, with the result that journalism is practically debarred to me.' On 21 February Lady Downe, who intended to stand in Norfolk, told Collin Brooks that Mosley 'gets good meetings everywhere, and is really trying to eliminate the Fascist flavour from his movement'. She admitted that 'nobody about him has much brain and that he is often misled about the general public feeling' but was 'extremely anxious to get reports of his meetings into the Press – not support editorially but publicity'.

On 3 March Brooks saw Mosley, whose desk was dominated by a large autographed portrait of Hitler. Mosley said Communism was 'gaining ground in the North and that the Tories are deceived by a new Communist tactic. When Hitler triumphed in Germany, Communism saw that it was folly to divide the Leftist forces and allow Fascism to slip between them. They now work for a Popular Front, contemplate a kind of Kerensky Government, which they will overthrow, and so do not force forward their own candidates. The old Tories thus say – no candidates, no communism.' He added that it was better that Brooks was 'outside the movement than in it'.

Following Eden's resignation in February, Mosley remarked that his policy would have led to war but Neville Chamberlain's 'means humiliation'. He appeared to be proved right when Unity witnessed German troops cross the Austrian frontier and the country's incorporation into the Third Reich. On 22 January Austrian Chancellor Kurt von Schuschnigg learnt that Josef Leopold, leader of a faction of the warring Viennese Nazis, bragged to Robert Gordon-Canning that they were going to stage an armed uprising, aided by the German Reich. Three days later Leopold's headquarters were raided by von Schuschnigg's police who found documents relating to a *coup d'état*, coupled with an invasion by the German Army 'to prevent further bloodshed'. When a German agent told MI5 'orders had been issued to intensify arrangements for espionage against this country', at the end of March it was issued with a Home Office warrant to open Gordon-Canning's mail.

Von Schuschnigg announced a plebiscite to determine Austria's future, a decision which outraged Hitler. Having read his anti-Hitler speeches, Unity wrote to Churchill setting out her thoughts. He replied that 'a fair plebiscite would have shown that a large majority of the people of Austria would loathe the idea of coming under Nazi rule'. On 11 March 1938 German troops crossed the border and arrested the Chancellor. Unity believed Churchill was wrong, for on 14 March she witnessed scenes of wild jubilation as Hitler entered Vienna.

In Vienna, brothers of Baron Louis Rothschild, who owned Vitkowitz, Czechoslovakia's vast iron and steel works, begged him to leave Austria while there was still time. However, Louis did not believe disaster could overtake a Rothschild. The SS confiscated his passport and placed him under house arrest in the Hotel Metropole, in a room next door to von Schuschnigg. The Baron was interviewed by an intermediary of Goering, who told him he could have his freedom if he paid £40,000 and turned over Vitkowitz and banking assets in London to the German Reich. At which point 'internecine war' broke out in Berlin and Goering was forced to abandon the deal, which, curiously enough, was revived at the beginning of the next year through the intervention of Mosley.

Action described the advance of the Nazis as 'like a symphony; the Saar was the allegro, the Rhineland the andante. Austria the scherzo, there remained the finale to be played.' Following Hitler's takeover of Austria and the occupation of Prague on 15 March, Mosley launched a 'Stop the War' campaign. He wrote that Conservative foreign policy 'has been one of everlasting bluster, innumerable foreign commitments, followed inevitably by . . . abject humiliation'. With regard to the British government's guarantee to come to Poland's aid if attacked, he noted that 'any frontier incident which excites the light-headed Poles can set the world ablaze. British Government places the lives of a million Britons in the pocket of any drunken Polish corporal.' The BU plastered London with a new slogan: 'Who the heck cares for Beck'.

Churchill attacked the 'Heil Hitler Brigade in London Society', which included 'those like Mosley who are fascinated by the spectacle of brutal power. They would like to use it themselves. They grovel to Nazi dictatorship in order that they can make people in their turn grovel to them.' The 'Stop the War' campaign failed to achieve widespread support. Police reports indicated that Mosley's attempts to infuse life into the movement did not evoke a response outside the East End, where Micky Clarke was firmly entrenched. He was transferred to headquarters, leading to rumours that Mosley was 'jealous of him and wished to remove him from the limelight'. In fact, Mosley wished to downplay anti-Semitism, which was no longer a prominent part in BU propaganda and was dropped as a major issue from 1938 onwards, as policy on foreign affairs and the Empire took its place. In the spring Mosley was deprived of his foremost propagandist; another reason for the eclipse of anti-Semitism as the main propaganda plank. A. K. Chesterton resigned, disillusioned with Mosley's leadership.

Chesterton revealed his reasons in a pamphlet published by Joyce's National Socialist League. Mosley was associated with the intrigues that were 'part of the petty power politics within the Movement'. The 'ringmaster of the whole circus' was Hawkins but Mosley had been

the chief partner in this absurd little set which is a reflex of something real and large in his own mind. I have never known him give a decision against his favourites, or fail to come to their help when they have been embarrassed ... Clearly, they are very valuable to him: he finds them comfortable men, shielding him from the impact of every reality, subjecting him to no heartsearchings, no self-analysis, no stress or turmoil of intellectual conflict out of which great things might be born.

Mosley had been 'taken in far too many times by political con men', Chesterton added. The result was those who had access to his ear 'realised that he was gullible in relation to propaganda about the growth of the movement and that the best way to advancement was to tell him what he wanted to hear, whether it was true or not'. Flops were written up as triumphs and enormous efforts were made to 'give the impression of strength where there is weakness, of growth where there is declining influence'. Chesterton believed that, had not his enemies 'counter-demonstrated in thousands his marches would have been about as spectacular and exciting as the progress of a troop of bedraggled Boy Scouts on a rainy day'.

In April Mosley issued an apocalyptic warning, which hinted at megalomania: 'Facts will then be brought to light which are partly known to many already but are hidden from the people as a whole by the machinery of the system.' He referred to the 'politician who has served not his country but his personal gain, the traitor in a hundred ways to the people's cause'. He promised

clean courts of people's justice will be created to reveal all their foul transactions to the sterilizing light of day and to pass judgment upon them ... Let the rats of this putrescent system not think that any land will safely shelter them, nor any sewer of the world provide them with a refuge ... So to the jackals of putrescence we say today 'Beware!' ... The cleansing flame shall pursue you to the uttermost ends of the earth.

On 10 April Unity came across a Labour Party-organized rally in Hyde Park in support of Republican Spain, which was opposed by a small Fascist counter-demonstration. When Unity's swastika badge was spotted, the crowd turned on her, ripping off the badge. Back in Munich, the episode generated fan mail. On 28 April the Führer gave her two new swastika badges.

At the end of May Collin Brooks published a pamphlet, 'Can 1931 Come Again? An Examination of Britain's Present Financial Position', which argued that the economy was heading for a crisis. Brooks's pamphlet was praised by the anti-Semitic magazine *Truth*, whose editor, Henry Newnham, was a Mosley sympathizer and whose wife was a BU member. Throughout 1938 the BU made efforts to exploit the recession, which became quite severe. The rise in unemployment to 1,700,000 was, Mosley argued, 'a warning to all who believe that purely monetary measures can remedy a real economic crisis'. He avoided close association with the extreme right as 'spurious anti-Semitism gave way to the type of cogent economic analysis which had provided the *raison d'être* and the bedrock of Mosley's fascism'.

Eckersley made three more trips to Germany in pursuit of a radio contract, and Mosley gave Dudley Evans a special pass to see high-ranking Nazis. They were unsuccessful, the obstacle being the question of a wavelength in the medium band; to give any of these would be a sacrifice for the Germans. Despite the setbacks, Mosley told Frederick Lawton, he intended to concentrate on Germany. Lawton had been taken to see the Leader by Mosley's younger brother John. On the way, he informed him that Diana had married his brother: 'But it is secret and no one else must know.' Lawton was told he would work with Diana, whose appearance overwhelmed him: 'She was so strikingly beautiful.' Wiedemann wrote on 11 May suggesting she 'come here at the beginning of next week'. Lawton claimed his employment was 'strictly professional. I took no part in any negotiations.' Diana, however, admitted he was employed as a means of 'distancing Mosley from the project'. She dismissed him in that Mitford way as 'a Grammar school boy'.

Goebbels arranged for Diana to see the Minister of Posts and Telegraphs, Dr Wilhelm Ohnesorge, a short man with 'a ratlike face'. He was responsible for Hitler's personal income from the sale of stamps bearing the Führer's portrait. Most of the negotiations took place with Ohnesorge, who was sympathetic because he saw the advantage to Germany of a steady flow of hard currency. The Reich had a serious balance-of-payments deficit and Diana used this as a lever.

Following an exhausting meeting with officials, Lawton left Diana a note: 'Please sleep well tonight. No one could have used more skill and shown more courage.' Ohnesorge became her 'valuable ally' and approved the concession. Germany had taken over Austrian wavelengths and Goebbels decided they could authorize the leasing of one of them (the former Polish Katowitz frequency). 'You have your wavelength, and a very nice one, too,' Ohnesorge told Diana. Radio engineers roughed out a plan for the proposed German-based station. Diana and Lawton had a celebratory dinner, where, to his astonishment, she told him she had dined the previous night with Hitler, Goering and senior Nazis, and the topic of conversation had been what they would do when they took over Czechoslovakia.

Along with two Mosleyites working for Goebbels, Philip Spranklin and Bill

Rueff, Unity toured Czechoslovakia. They stopped at a German-speaking town, Eger, to contact local Nazis, and Karlsbad, where Spranklin knew the local MP, Senator Wollner. Goebbels reported she was 'being insulted and pulled to pieces in Czechoslovakia. There's quite a fuss about it. The Führer welcomes it. That Unity will have steeped herself in hatred.' Unity had taken no part in the radio negotiations but she now intervened at the highest level. She wrote to Diana on 4 June that Hitler 'thinks the whole thing is OK, he has spoken with the Minister and there will be no more [negotiation] necessary'. Hitler authorized a meeting with Bill Allen to discuss a joint venture based in Heligoland, in which Air Time would share the profits with the Germans.

A joint company, Gemona AG, was registered in Germany. The Reichspost owned 55 per cent of the equity and the remainder was Air Time's. A newly formed company set up by the Allens would sell advertising space, and from this income the British would pay for their share of construction and operating costs, and 5 per cent interest on the German capital. Mosley knew the Germans were keen on the arrangement because they would be repaid in foreign currency. 'What the German spends inside Germany he does not care about. What he minds, or did mind, was what he got in foreign exchange.' Once these charges were met, any profit would be divided 55 per cent to Germany, 45 per cent to the British. Programmes, recorded music and announcers would be provided by another company set up specifically for the purpose. The Germans agreed to finance construction of the station over a period of fourteen months and cover all operating expenses. Hitler authorized a meeting to exchange contracts. Diana and Mosley celebrated her success at Wootton on her birthday, 10 June. The Mosleys were in sight of an 'enormous fortune'.

The wartime Advisory Committee sought reasons for German willingness to make such an unusual concession. Mosley suggested it was partly personal: Hitler was granting a favour to Diana, whom he liked and admired. However, he added that the Germans 'had a certain knowledge of me by reputation which would lead them to the view that I should not swindle them in a business which was very liable to swindling'.

The British government was reconsidering its position in respect of radio advertising. Hoare and Boothby tried to persuade Lord Perth of the propaganda opportunities provided by commercial radio. On 7 June, in a secret Commons session on 'British Advertising Broadcasting', Boothby told MPs he was 'certain that if [they] knew that we were in a position to bring all the stations broadcasting in English (in Europe) . . . to cooperate with the authorities in cultural and propaganda work, that support would be practically unanimous'.

The Postmaster General, Major G. C. Tryon, said British firms had 'made strenuous effort to extend the scope of their operations'. He asked the Overseas Broadcasting Committee, chaired by Sir Thomas Inskip, Minister for the

Co-ordination of Defence, to examine radio advertising. It reported that 'use could very likely be made up of offers by any reputable British concerns, who, as in the case of Mr R. Boothby (director of Allens' group), wish to interest themselves in broadcasting from foreign stations and have offered to co-operate with HMG as regards the matter broadcast in foreign languages and who ask only that HMG should cease actively to oppose sponsored broadcasts in English from foreign stations'. Interestingly, this approach was not raised at Mosley's interrogation when Hoare's name was mentioned.

On 18 July 1938 the radio agreement drawn up by Lawton was finally settled with the Germans. Section B stated 'programmes shall contain no matter which can reasonably be construed as political propaganda or cause offence in Greater Germany or Great Britain'. Clause five prevented the Germans introducing anti-British material into the broadcasts. Mosley explained 'they knew it would immediately ruin their own business. They would not build a station at some expense and then interpolate propaganda which they could put over from other stations, ruin their business and cut off their whole revenue, leaving themselves with a station on their hands.' Educational talks on German life were allowed, conveying the impression of a cultured nation. Another clause forbade jokes about the Nazi regime by British comedians. To monitor content, a Nazi official would be present in the studio.

Once the agreement had been secured, Diana's role was over. With only a few months until the birth of her baby, she returned to Wootton. Because of the pregnancy, Diana's parents allowed her to visit their home, though Mosley was forbidden to set foot in the house. Diana was still regarded as 'the enemy' by her sister Decca.

Diana missed that year's Nuremberg festival; officially, the participation of British Fascists was prohibited. However, a distancing of the German government from the BU did not prevent the continuation of contact with individual members and invitations were sent to the BU through Lady Dyer, formerly Lucy Schroeder of the banking family and a distant Mosley relative. The German embassy in London warned against a relationship with the BU beyond a personal exchange of views. A reason for the coolness towards BU visits was, as Goebbels learnt, 'the British are placing spies in the Mosley Movement. Then they come to visit Germany as harmless fascists, in order to spy. So in future we're going to be more watchful.'

In July Mosley opened a 'British First' campaign. 'Czech behaviour today', Mosley declared, 'is threatening the peace of the world.' The BU stepped up its propaganda against German refugees who had settled in Britain for stealing work from Britons. The police reported sparsely attended meetings and the Jewish Board of Deputies said it had been a flop. A ban on marches through the East End and the fact that Mosley had spoken at only twenty-one meetings, which had all been trouble free, indicated a lack of enthusiasm and marked indifference by anti-Fascists, whose own meetings were more numerous than those of the Fascists.

As war loomed, part-time servicemen in the BU were called up. In addition some members, such as Major Yeats-Brown, resigned because Hitler's invasion of Czechoslovakia was 'a step too far'. However, according to Leonard Wise, a worker handling records, 'total membership did not fall – indeed it increased – because by now substantial numbers of anti-war recruits were coming in from the left.' The BU still needed Mosley's funds and on 27 July he gave the BU trusts £4,500 (£149,000).

In light of the European situation the Allens reduced their commitments. They relinquished the contract with Radio Toulouse and sold their Andorra holding to French partners. 'Radio had proved to be a bad experience,' Mrs Allen recalled. 'The Allen firm had lost a lot of money and wanted out.' Development costs and losses amounted to £65,000 (£2m). The Allens had been generous and now had to cut expenditure. Eckersley was the first casualty. He realized he was 'heading for bankruptcy'. Near to a nervous breakdown, he was 'not a pretty sight in those troubled times', Diana recalled.

Bill Allen needed to call in loans and on 28 August wrote to Mosley complaining the £3,000 (£102,000) given to the BU had not been repaid. The money was borrowed on the understanding 'that it was to be refunded in time for me to meet my obligation to the lender. The facts were made perfectly clear to your principal confidential representatives, and one of them signed a receipt on your behalf. If you are to repudiate, even theoretically, obligations entered into by one known to be your man of confidence, a situation is created in which it is difficult to have any but the most foul relations with you.' It was 'a matter of pain to me that I find myself forced to write this letter to one whom I had once believed – I will not say of friendship which one should probably never expect of a "Nietzschean" – but of normally honourable relations. I have really nothing but pity for a man who has to refer to a lawyer before being able to write an (unsigned) letter to his one surviving friend.' According to Allen's wife, Mosley 'refused to pay it back saying that the money was for the party and the party had no money to pay him back'.

Mosley later claimed Allen was 'very much involved with MI5, made no bones about it, that is why he wasn't imprisoned in the war, of course, because he had done so much for them'. He told Nicholas that Allen was 'probably reporting conversations with me which were probably largely fictitious: he was a tremendously boastful man . . . one of those men who simply lived in a dream world – a Walter Mitty world, as we could call it now'. Certainly, Allen liked dreaming up schemes but there is evidence that he was in some way being blackmailed by Mosley. Allen was not, in fact, an MI5 agent and did not talk to them until 1942 when he was confronted with evidence from telephone taps. He did then tell them that the radio project was a way for the

Germans to launder money to the BU through legitimate commercial concerns.

Allen probably reported to MI6, not MI5 as Mosley claimed. This places an interesting light on Allen's relationship with his friend Kim Philby, who was at the time operating in Fascist circles, in particular the Anglo-German Fellowship, as an undercover Soviet agent. Allen's falling out with Mosley was short-lived, partly because they still had business to conduct. There is a cryptic note from Allen in Mosley's papers that 'friend x' – a German connected to the radio project – is 'expected by us on 4/5 September in London'.

There were different interpretations within Nazi circles of the BU's effectiveness; most centred on 'how far advanced is the "judification" of Britain'. In 1938 Heinz Krieger published *Britain and the Jewish Question in History and the Present*, which refuted the official figure of 300,000 as the number of Jews in Britain. He believed, 'as the British fascists are more and more emphasising' a figure of two and a half to three million, which included those who have 'cleverly hidden themselves behind old English names' and 'the many half-breeds, especially among the aristocracy'. Krieger quoted with approval Mosley's campaign against Jewish control. 'In this country we are experiencing the same evil as was rampant in Germany until the rise of Hitler . . . Recently a prominent Jew declared that Britain could not possibly participate in a war, even when it is a question of self-defence, without the sanction of the Jews.' Krieger noted the presence of 'the jew Hore-Belisha' as War Minister in Chamberlain's Cabinet.

However, Krieger wrote, 'efforts to solve the Jewish Question which do not treat it as a racial question, as entirely fundamental, will always be unsuccessful'. Mosley's statement that he did not 'attack the Jews by reason of what they are, it resists them by reason of what they do', made 'no sense'. What they do 'can only be understood by what they are'. Even so, 'Germany will always find in the English Blackshirts friends full of understanding and fighters against the anti-German rabble-rousers.' In Britain was 'the beginnings of a popular awakening which is preparing the way for a general recognition of these questions and related matters'. He hoped one of Mosley's sayings would come true: 'After the victory of Fascism the power of the Jews in England will be broken for ever.' On 3 August 1938 Italy adopted anti-Jewish laws. Although anti-Semitism did not develop deep roots, between 8,500 and 15,000 Italian Jews died in the Holocaust.

One revealing aspect of Mosley's 18B interrogation was his reported willingness to expel Jews. Rather than keep them in ghettos, as 'an eternal irritant within the body politic', he would remove all foreigners. Asked if this included the Jews, Mosley replied, 'Quite right.' In 'Jews and Fascists' in *Query*, Mosley asked 'whether it is fair to regard the Jew as a foreigner. The simple answer is that he comes from the Orient, and physically, mentally, and spiritually is more alien to us than any Western nation.' His 'Final Solution' was to place all Jews in a new homeland (but not Palestine), where they 'may escape the curse of no nationality and may again acquire the status and opportunity of nationhood'. When Lord Birkett asked Mosley if he recognized 'a policy of hostility to the Jews at a time when Jews were being oppressed in Germany would not be very popular among humane people in this country', he replied that 'anti-semitism here has grown colossally in the last few years. When we began it hardly existed.' Krieger, it appeared, had grounds for optimism.

Strangely, as the true nature of the Nazi regime became more obvious, some aristocrats became even more enthusiastic about Hitler. A member of the Anglo-German Fellowship and the Link, the Mitfords' father David, second Lord Redesdale, had also become a firm Hitler admirer. 'Farve really does adore him in the same way we do,' wrote Unity to Diana on 12 September. 'He treasures every word and every expression.' When the crisis over Czecho-slovakia came to a head, the BU launched its 'National Campaign for Britain, Peace and People'. With reports of German troops massing on the border, Mosley told Irene, 'Hitler never strikes when he makes so much song and dance about it. He does his great moves silently.'

The Czech crisis was the impetus for three organizations: Joyce's National Socialist League, Lord Lymington's British Array and the League of Loyalists to create the British Council Against European Commitments. It was essentially a co-ordinating body for the Fascist fringe and part of a process that had been taking place since the spring. Mosley knew it was under surveillance by MI5 and avoided direct contact, preferring to maintain contact through intermediaries.

Maxwell Knight tracked these developments. He noted in September that Joyce, who renewed his passport on the 24th, had become more hysterical and militantly pro-German. MI5 obtained a Home Office warrant to intercept his mail. Knight had been aware for some time of contacts between Joyce, his brother Quentin, who worked in the Air Ministry, and a known Nazi agent, Christian Bauer. A Secret Intelligence Service report describes a meeting in Belgium between 'a casual MI6 informant', Joyce and former BU member John McNab, who was 'carrying secret messages to Bauer'. Knight said that if it came to war, Joyce's loyalty could not be relied on.

During the Czech crisis the PM's fixer Sir Joseph Ball wanted Radio Luxem-bourg to broadcast 'such messages as Mr Chamberlain's statement and Mr Roosevelt's appeal to Herr Hitler, of which he believed the German public were in complete ignorance'. Luxembourg's involvement in 'political warfare' was the result of private initiative and improvisation. It revealed a hidden area of Mosley's activities: the overlap between his own radio project and British attempts to construct a propaganda network. This crossing of wires had been made by the 'Boothby group', which pointed out the potential of commercial radio for propaganda, and advisers such as Eckersley, with their feet in both camps.

On 26 September Gerald Wellesley (soon to be the seventh Duke of Wellington) placed Luxembourg at Ball's disposal. How he was able to do this is a mystery. He served in the Foreign Office during the First World War with his 'oldest friend' Harold Nicolson, but his activities in the thirties remain obscure. His uncle, the fifth Duke, was a prominent anti-Semite and leading figure in the Anglo-German Fellowship, and later the Right Club. Gerald's son, the current Duke, knew the Mitford girls. 'I went with friends to Germany immediately before the war, and Unity was with us. I remember going out one night and we were furious because she joined a party of her friends who were Brownshirts. We were very angry.' Ball acted as Chamberlain's go-between with the Secret Services and conducted highly secret negotiations for an 'appeasement' of Hitler. In addition he pulled the strings behind *Truth*, which he used to attack opponents of Chamberlain and bolster those extremist groups against war with Germany.

Using Luxembourg for political warfare was a priority for MI6's Section D, which aimed to attack Germany by means other than military force. An off-shore company, Wireless Publicity, secretly took over from Captain Plugge's International Broadcasting Company and, flush with secret funds, installed its own presenter in Luxembourg, edited the scripts and, through the advertising agency J. Walter Thompson, built the most up-to-date studio in Europe, producing 'cultural propaganda'.

Efforts to co-ordinate propaganda activities culminated in the creation of a Joint Broadcasting Committee (JBC). In November Section D's Major Laurence Grand invited Hilda Matheson, BBC Director of Talks, to consider broadcasting propaganda to Germany. On the JBC were Mosley's friends Nicolson and Boothby. Matheson, who had been in MI5 during the First World War, was known to Mosley, having been secretary to Lady Astor. She had been secretary to Nicolson and lover of his wife Vita, and a companion of Dorothy, wife of Gerald Wellesley. Interestingly, she undertook a fact-finding tour of the very same European radio stations with which Mosley's group had been pursuing contracts. A clandestine 'Travel Association' was opened to sell British 'white' propaganda – which was couriered from London to Paris by Soviet agent Guy Burgess – for broadcast to Germany using British-leased commercial radio stations. Involved in this operation was Eckersley, who referred to his 'intelligence work'. Working for the Allens, he enquired of broadcasters as to their willingness to use 'special recordings' – the 'white' propaganda made by the JBC.

The signing on 30 September of the Munich Agreement proved to the Redesdales Hitler's good intentions. Chamberlain's return was watched by

Irene and the Mosley children, who stood in the rain as the PM's aeroplane touched down at Heston aerodrome. Diana and Mosley listened to the radio, hoping Munich was the prelude to a peace pact leading to the union of Europe.

'I don't care if 3½ million Germans from Czechoslovakia go back to Germany,' Mosley said in praising Chamberlain. 'I don't care if 10 million Germans go back to Germany, Britain will be strong enough, brave enough, to hold her own.' In a speech at Manchester he insisted Hitler could be trusted to keep to the agreement: 'Hitler no more wants the Czechs than we want the aliens in our midst.' He did, however, expect war. On 1 October German troops moved into Czechoslovakia. Mosley proclaimed the BU opposed 'root and branch a war which sacrifices British lives in an alien quarrel'. Diana admitted Munich was 'a watershed. Our slogan was Mind Britain's Business, the very last thing politicians of either party intended to do.'

The subsequent failure of Munich was not blamed on Hitler. Beaverbrook's claim that it was the fault of the Jews was not uncommon. 'They do not mean to do it. But unconsciously they are drawing us into war. Their political influence is moving us in that direction.' *Action* alleged they were buying country houses to let to evacuees at inflated rents. They had fled from London like 'a flowing river of grey slime'.

'Friend x' told Allen and Mosley the Germans were ready to sign the radio contract. Allen, who had patched up his quarrel with Mosley, had dealt with the signatories for the German-registered company Gemona AG, Dr Johannes Bernhardt, Director of Berlin-Grünewald and member of Goering's Four Year Plan team, and Kurt von Schroeder, President of the Cologne Chamber of Commerce. Mosley had to make his presence known for the signing of the contracts. 'We were always sure MI5 knew all about the wireless project,' Diana recalled, 'and it never seemed to Mosley to matter in the least. It was the Press that mattered, in connection with secrecy.' Taking Lawton with him, he met the German side in Paris.

Shortly before their first son was born, the Mosleys stayed at the Crillon – Diana's nurse went with them. For Lawton its luxury, 'as well as the excitement of Mosley's company, made it an exotic experience'. Accompanying Schroeder and Dr Bernhardt was Hitler's aide Wiedemann. A tour of Paris nightclubs began at the Sphynx, a high-class brothel where Lawton was stunned by the decor and the women's attire, and then the Scheherazade. On 9 November 1938 the two sides exchanged contracts.

That night the Nazis retaliated for the murder by a Jew of an embassy official in Paris. There was widespread smashing of Jewish shops and windows – *Kristallnacht* – and the burning of synagogues. The nature of the Nazi regime was apparent to all; except, it seemed, Mosley. His overriding quest for peace meant he was willing to excuse all their actions. 'Supposing that every allegation was true . . . that a minority in Germany were being treated as the papers allege, was that any reason for millions in Britain to lose their lives in war with Germany? Why was it only when Jews were the people affected that we had any demand for war with the country concerned?' By now he had succumbed to the conspiracy theory. 'Today Jewish finance controlled the press and political system of Britain. If you criticize a Jew at Home – then gaol threatens you. If others touch a Jew abroad – then war threatens them.'

With the news that the German station was 'on', Allen formed Wire Broadcasting, with offices in the Strand. Incorporated with capital of £15,000 (£510,000), the Allens agreed to pay Mosley £5,000 for their one-third share in the enterprise. As neither wanted the transaction to be traceable, Allen handed over used notes to the intermediary, Lawton, who channelled them to Mosley. Soon afterwards the company accountant, James Herd, met with his Nazi opposite number von Kaufmann, who travelled to London to discuss the proposed station. Herd was horrified when he was greeted with 'Heil Hitler!'.

Mosley returned to London with a signed agreement. 'Thus', he wrote, 'we had one Southern concession subject to a successful action before the Privy Council with fair prospects, the Eastern concession, and there was also some prospect of a Western concession too.' He intended 'to hold back the legal fight over the Sark concession until we were able to publicise the German concession . . . in order to make BBC and official resistance to the development of Sark appear more useless. Thus from at least two sides, and we hoped three, we should have bombarded the British advertising market. Our radio competitors would have had no chance against us . . .' Work began immediately to construct a transmitter on the island of Borkum in the North Sea. It seemed that the BU would soon be flush with funds.

21

The Darkening Clouds

Many observers poked fun at Mosley's pretensions. In P. G. Wodehouse's 1938 *The Code of the Woosters* he appeared as Sir Roderick Spode. At one point Wooster tells Sir Roderick,

The trouble with you, Spode, is that because you have succeeded in inducing a handful of halfwits to disfigure the London scene by going about in black shorts, you think you're someone. You hear them shouting 'Heil Spode!' and you imagine it is the Voice of the People. That is where you make your bloomer. What the Voice of the People is saying is: 'Look at that frightful ass Spode, swanking about in footer bags! Did you ever in your puff see such a perfect perisher!'

That was certainly the case in Lancashire where, in October, Mosley made yet another attempt to gain a foothold in the area. The Japanese ambassador, in replying to a request by his Foreign Minister for information on the BU, told Tokyo the BU was 'not powerful enough even to establish a branch office in Lancashire'. Intent on impressing the Germans, Diana wrote to Unity that Mosley 'had a wonderful campaign and huge crowds. Most of our class wanted to fight, but not the workers.'

The workers were benefiting from signs of economic recovery as the effects of rearmament took hold. Mosley recognized such spending 'could be regarded as a sort of public works programme'. Areas of deep unemployment such as Tyneside and the Clyde saw the benefits; as did Birmingham with its engineering base. Mosley's reception, on 28 October, at the city's Tony's Ballroom was marked up as a notable achievement by the BU press. Hundreds of Blackshirts marched down the Stratford Road and gave the Leader a rousing reception. A local bookseller, however, recalled seeing coaches arriving 'full of faces I'd never seen before'. Most had been imported to create the impression of vast local support.

The BU lost much of its working-class support. Special Branch reported that many supporters in the East End were 'imbued with a feeling of antagonism to Germany', which 'crystallised into open rebellion'. However, in west and north London the peace campaign drew in the middle and upper classes.

Mosley made contact with the pacifist fringe and it seemed he might emerge as leader of a 'peace front'. George Orwell wondered in a letter to Herbert Read whether 'Mosley will have the sense and the guts to stick out against war with Germany, he might decide to cash in on the patriotism business'.

Ties were cemented with the pro-Nazi groups, such as the Link, which had the support of Ribbentrop. Alison Oulthwaite, editor of *World Review*, told the *Express* that when the BU's Philip Spranklin, who was employed by Goebbels in Munich, spoke at the Link's Central London branch, he 'ranted against the freedom of the press, and extolled the German press and the German government'. He wondered what 'power' lay behind the press campaign against the Nazis. The one-hundred-strong middle-class audience 'appeared to agree with everything that was said'. Ms Oulthwaite was 'revolted' and resigned.

Mosley encouraged members to penetrate professional and trade bodies. Peter Heyward ran an 'Against Trust and Monopoly' column in *Action* and organized a British Traders Bureau to promote the BU. This paid off handsomely and Mosley received sympathetic coverage in the *Dairyman*, the *Green Badge* (cab drivers), the *Bakers Record*, the *National Newsagent*, *Bookseller and Stationer*. Four hundred taxi men attended a meeting where Mosley promised to eliminate private car-hire services who 'stole the cream from the hard-working British man who devoted his entire energies to the taxi-trade'. At the Memorial Hall, Farringdon Street, 1,000 shopkeepers attended a meeting and gave him a thundering ovation.

Towards the end of 1938 BU branches began to revive as 'vanguardist' activists adopted the Communist 'street-block-cell system' to build up popular grass-roots support. The cell system and immersion in local interests was in parallel with more sophisticated methods of propaganda. Local elite groups of ideological Fascists began to organize in London and Manchester. Stuart Rawnsley argues that the high turnover of membership of the early period – Chesterton said 100,000 had passed through the movement – was characterized by a lack of ideological commitment, but those who joined in the late 1930s were often imbued with steadfast beliefs in nationalist economics, anti-Semitism and Mosley's leadership. Membership increased by the end of 1938 to around 16,500.

Tempered by adversity, Blackshirts saw themselves engaged in a religious crusade. For Gordon-Canning the 'national socialist is a crusader – a warrior in the best sense; he does not fear Death. If necessary he runs to meet it . . . death for him is not something to be avoided, it is a fulfilment, it is a symbol, not of disintegration, but of Union.' They found in their support of Mosley, 'the sense of belonging, of finding meaning, of being involved in "greatness" just by having him at their head'. In turn, he claimed that 'in the local premises of over four hundred branches I was just one of them. This was the most complete companionship I have ever known, except in the old regular army in time of war.'

On 26 November 1938 Alexander Mosley was born at Grosvenor Road. His birth obliged the Mosleys to make public the fact that they were married. 'There was no more reason for secrecy,' recalled Diana. Rumours had surfaced in the *Mail* but the official disclosure made a splash, with the *Telegraph* and the *News Chronicle* breaking the story on 28 November – 'Hitler was Sir Oswald's Best Man'. Irene 'nearly fainted' when she read the truth: 'I felt that my brother-in-law's excuses of the need for secrecy and fear of his life were pretty sordid.' Opening her paper in Paris, Baba Metcalfe realized Mosley had been deceiving her on an epic scale. She could not forgive and for the rest of her life refused to speak of Diana.

Seventeen-year-old Vivien was at finishing school in Paris and refused to believe the papers – 'they've got it wrong.' It was months before she came to terms with the situation. Nicholas wrote to his father that he could not think why he had been kept in the dark. Mosley's mother was angry that she appeared as a liar to BU members who did not believe she did not know. When Irene finally met Diana at the end of December, her first impression was of Diana's affected voice: 'The Mitford drawl, with its up-and-down inflections, prolonged vowels ("orfficer" and "lorst") and idiosyncratic "exclamations" was at its most pronounced when Diana was nervous.'

On 21 December Gordon-Canning and Raven Thomson lunched with Collin Brooks and an unnamed MP to talk frankly about Brooks's pro-appeasement pamphlet, 'Can Chamberlain Save Britain'. Brooks said 'their Cromwell had emerged too soon. I gathered that the movement is short of money.'

In December John Beckett and Lord Lymington launched the Fascist and anti-Semitic *New Pioneer*, which championed non-involvement in European conflicts. Its pages featured former Mosleyite A. K. Chesterton, Major-General Fuller, Array members Anthony Ludovici and Rolf Gardiner, ILPer Ben Greene, H. T. V. ('Bertie') Mills and Nazi enthusiast and patriotic historian Sir Arthur Bryant. The journal enthusiastically reviewed *Mein Kampf* and devoted space to organic husbandry, whose supporters included BU agricultural expert Jorian Jenks.

MI5 no longer treated such bodies as merely eccentric lunatic-fringe organizations since they had close relations with German 'correspondents'. In general, their influence was 'negligible' but a small number were engaged in espionage, which MI5 found difficult to deal with since it was poorly funded and lacked manpower. There were only twenty-eight officers, backed by a surveillance section of six men, and an administrative and registry staff of eighty-six.

When, after the war, the *Abwehr*'s Nikolaus Ritter was quizzed on his spying operations against Britain, he did not divulge everything. A heavy-drinking electrical engineer, Arthur Owens (codenamed JOHNNY), supplied him with details of Admiralty contracts on which he worked. A Welsh nationalist, he was the linchpin of his operation but Ritter began to be suspicious when, in 1936, it became apparent that he was playing 'a double game'. He allowed Owens to continue to pass material to MI6 but he was abandoned by them and, though his file was passed on to MI5 under the codename SNOW, until the war he worked as a solely German agent. At some point Owens made an approach on the Germans' behalf to the BU, to whom he put forward 'a scheme for the establishment of four secret transmitters in England for the purpose of disseminating propaganda in time of war'. Owens told Ritter he had fifteen sub-agents in England. In his history of *The Double-Cross System*, J. C. Masterman wrote that 'it is probable, though not certain, that all these persons existed only in SNOW's imagination'.

The BU offered a source of spies but 'perhaps Ritter did not think of tapping it, or had no contacts with which to do so; perhaps he did not have the time'. In any event, suggests David Kahn, he did not recruit agents from the BU (this excludes propaganda agents recruited by other agencies). Scouts returned empty-handed from raids on the splintered Fascist groups. 'Deplorable as were the aid and comfort which members of these organisations gave the Nazis with their strident propaganda,' Kahn notes, 'none of them had any actual or direct connection either with the *Abwehr* or the *Sicherheitsdienst*.' Aside from Mosley's aide, Dr Tester, available Nazi records reveal no spies in BU ranks.

In December, following exposure in the British press, Tester talked with Hawkins and offered to quit the party so that it would not 'in any way be compromised'. Anthony Hepburn-Ruston went to Germany, where he continued his commitment to the Nazi Party. Hawkins, 'with his fair judgement, saw no infringement of Party discipline', and rejected Tester's offer. He attended a BU leaders' conference in Hastings where Mosley told them: 'Every single fascist must show initiative and not just wait for orders from central headquarters.' On 22 December Tester left Southampton in his yacht *Lucinda* for Lisbon, where he picked up Dr Richard Behn. The press asked 'what new crime of this English fascist of German extraction and supporter of Mosley had forced him to leave'. His secretary and BU member Horace Nadal was arrested in London and 'interrogated for days by the Secret Service'.

MI5's F2 branch controlled the monitoring of Nazi intelligence operations, while Knight's B5b M Section infiltrated its fourteen agents – even though six was regarded as the maximum number of agents to whom an officer could give sufficient attention – into 'subversive' groups such as the Link and the BU. MI5, Thurlow argues, was 'always in control in monitoring both suspect "aliens" and native fascists'.

Knight ran agents 'Q', a British subject of German parents, and 'X', Harald

Kurtz, aka Court, born in Stuttgart. His father, a publisher, was a Nazi supporter. His grandfather was Sir William Don Bt, of Yorkshire, which he visited on holiday while a student at Geneva University. Kurtz decided to stay and became private secretary to Lord Noel-Buxton. He was recruited in May 1938 as a salaried agent. A homosexual – which invited a risk of blackmail – he sought British citizenship, which gave Knight a hold over the spendthrift and alcoholic Kurtz. He had a flat in a boarding house in Ebury Street, along with agent Q. An actor, Ferdy Mayne, was a German Jew and son of a judge. He came to England in the early 1930s and had a cover job with the BBC.

By 1939 BU propaganda again stressed anti-Semitic conspiracy theories with the claim that Jews sought world domination. E. M. Forster noted that 'Jew-consciousness is in the air'. If you kept your ears open you would hear 'people who would not ill-treat Jews themselves, giggle when pogroms are instituted by someone else and synagogues defiled vicariously: "Serve them right really, Jews!"' The German ambassador, Herbert von Dirksen, reported that anti-Semitism was 'revealed more clearly by conversations with the man in the street than by press sources . . . one can speak of a widespread resentment against the Jews which, in some instances, has already assumed the form of hate. The view that the Jews want to drive Britain into war with Germany finds widespread belief.'

Von Dirksen's comments may have been wishful thinking but they were shared by many who sought peace. On 17 January Collin Brooks lunched with Sir George Buchanan MP, who thought Mosley 'may yet "pull it off"'. He was 'in despair at the Jewish influence over the English press'. An exception was *Truth*, which was stridently anti-Churchill, anti-American and anti-Semitic. *Action* warned: 'Jews Beware, for the whispers may very well become a great shout for the complete removal of his race from our shores.' This led to the use of the chilling expression 'The Final Solution'.

Former Mosleyite Wyndham Lewis completed his retreat from Fascism with publication of 'The Jews: are they human?', an attack on anti-Semitism. It was slated by Raven Thomson, who argued 'no one is going to deny that individual Jews can be both intelligent and interesting; but the problem convulsing the modern world is not that of the individual Jew, but of the collective Jew – the Jewish race'. Lewis was compared with Hilaire Belloc, who pointed out the folly of ignoring the Jews' 'racial peculiarity'. However, both were found wanting when compared with the BU leader: 'We prefer Belloc to Lewis, and Mosley to both, because he is prepared to take the lead in that inevitable segregation of the Jewish People, which Belloc had not the intellectual courage to advocate.'

Unable to reach a mass audience, Mosley sanctioned a campaign of disruption at meetings of mainstream politicians in east London. At Limehouse, Hackney, Shoreditch and Bethnal Green, prominent politicians were faced by organized interruption, including missiles and physical assault. Police officers were assured that if the disruption continued they would have 'the full support of the Commissioner if they err on the side of action rather than inaction' when dealing with disorder. Anti-Fascists, however, were worried by Home Office guidelines, which allowed police 'to assist stewards in dealing with concerted and obviously organized interruption . . . even though no breach of the peace has commenced'. In effect, they could act as anti-Fascist stewards.

On 16 January MI5's Brigadier 'Jaspar' Harker and his deputy, Guy Liddell, reported that relations between BU leaders and prominent Nazis were 'extremely close'. Based on Diana's numerous meetings with the Führer, Mosley told Irene that Hess was the supreme party technician, that his wife was greatly impressed by Himmler, that what Hitler enjoyed about Goebbels was his wit and that they all hated Streicher. MI5 had a list of fifty men and two women in whom they expressed interest, and received Home Office approval to intercept the mail of A. G. Findlay, one of Mosley's closest lieutenants with contacts in Germany. As BU relations with Germany became 'steadily warmer', those with Italy 'practically ceased'. Mosley still hoped to revive them; the Foreign Office reported that Dr Tester appeared 'to be negotiating with Mussolini'. The Foreign Office learnt on 1 March from a consul general that 'the yacht *Lucinda* visited Naples at the date which he does not specify but which was in any case before February . . . the owner or charterer of the yacht is a Mr Tester who, it is said, finances Sir Oswald Mosley's movement, and that he learns that the yacht remained for some time and that Tester had some conversations with Signor Mussolini'.

MI5 had no proof of German payments, despite 'a number of reliable reports that the movement does in fact obtain financial support from Germany'. Special Branch reported that BU spending was around £20,000 (£680,000) per year. Much of it came from Mosley who, at the beginning of January, paid £2,500 into the BU Trust and a similar amount to the BU districts. Two months later he handed over another £8,750.

After touring north-east Germany during March, Eckersley and German engineers planned to build their radio station at Osterlog, a remote site on the North Sea coast. His stepson James Clark retained a map on which Peter had pencilled in a beam station with a 100 kw medium-wave transmitter, which had London and the east coast of England in its arc. Its location became known to MI5 and Knight tasked his agent, naturalist Robert Blockey, to investigate fortifications in the area. Armed with powerful binoculars, Blockey reported seeing 'a new breed of bird, an array of aerials with wire wings'.

The source of the location may have been Eckersley, who was involved in government propaganda efforts. A report to the Cabinet stressed that it was important to broadcast to the German people 'to counter their leader's growing warlike tendencies'. When a Hamburg station began English broadcasts, the green light was given to MI6's Section D efforts to appeal to peace-supporting Germans. Eckersley was now deeply involved in this 'sinister business of radio'. He helped set up a station in Liechtenstein to challenge Luxembourg, one which had a secret agenda to carry British 'white' propaganda.

Appeasement of the dictators was a popular policy, at least until the dismemberment of Czechoslovakia in March 1938. Until then, BU policy with regard to Germany was little different from the government's. On 16 March Hitler tore up the Munich Agreement and occupied Prague. That night, Irene saw the British ambassador, Nevile Henderson, who was 'disillusioned and could see no daylight. He felt the out-and-out lefters, Goebbels, Streicher and Himmler, had rushed Hitler into this.'

The BU patriots questioned the wisdom of supporting Hitler's actions, given his failure to honour Munich. A Limehouse member said the Czech crisis provoked discussion by members who felt 'the Munich business seemed to be acceptable because Hitler was asking back for Sudeten Germans and there seemed to be a logic in this. The occupation of the rest of Czechoslovakia wasn't so acceptable because some said, "This is not Germany. He's really occupying another country."' An East Ham district treasurer bemoaned the fact that 'when we were getting people interested and joining us, ol' Hitler would start his nonsense again'. Mosley's failure to criticize Hitler led to the stagnation of the East End movement, though Special Branch overstated the 'crisis'.

Chamberlain's guarantee to Poland generated a resurgence of BU anti-war activity. On 25 March Mosley warned that 'the jackals of Jewish finance are again in full cry for war'. As the likelihood of war increased, the fear of being associated with a movement viewed as pro-German 'eased away' from the BU. By constantly attacking the Labour Party's 'war-mongering', Mosley appealed to a pacifist strain within Labour politics. Reports suggest support was coming from the middle and upper classes, with up to 30 per cent of Mosley's audiences being women and only 5 per cent under the age of thirty.

Membership began to rise. The number of active members in London and the rest of the country was 3,600 and 3,000 respectively. With an estimated one active to one and a half passive members, this suggests around 9,000 London members to 7,500 provincial members. Mosley's claim that his peace campaign produced a large increase in membership was probably accurate, but there was also a rapid turnover of members.

The military connections and impeccable anti-Communist credentials meant that prominent Fascists were not seen as security threats until the view of Nazism underwent a radical reappraisal following the occupation of Czechoslovakia. From spring 1939, MI5 viewed all Fascist activity with suspicion. Rumours spread within the BU that General Ironside, who had attended with

Unity a meeting of the Anglo-German Fellowship, was a secret member. This was reported by P. G. Taylor to Special Branch, where it caused consternation.

Ironside had appeared with Mosley on his first election platform but his son notes that Ironside 'was photographed so often in his role as C.-in-C. North Russia, there is always the possibility that Mosley could have been featured in any of the published prints to further his own ends in whatever business he was involved at the time'. Ironside had served, disguised as a German, with the German staff in the war in south-west Africa and was the model for Buchan's Richard Hannay. He met Hitler in 1937 but he made no impression on him. MI5 noted German attempts to capitalize on the pro-Nazi activities of Ironside's former colleague, Major-General Fuller. However, the German military attaché, von Scheppenburg, came to believe that Fuller's Fascism veiled his role as Rothermere's agent in Germany.

The threat of war increased MI5's influence as security became a dominating concern. This led to its expansion and increased monitoring of contacts between pro-Nazi groups and Germany. These contacts were co-ordinated by Gestapo agent Dr Roesel, the chief link between the BU and Goebbels's Ministry of Propaganda. Under pressure from MPs, the Anglo-German Fellowship closed down in the spring, which, Domvile claimed, made it 'all the more necessary for [the Link] to keep one life buoy on the stormy waters of Anglo-German relations'. In April MI5 argued for Roesel's deportation.

The Jewish Board of Deputies identified the main distributor of German propaganda as the Militant Christian Patriots, which acted under the aegis of the Nordic League, whose guiding spirit was Captain Archibald Maule Ramsay, MP for Peebles. Born in India into a distinguished Scottish family, he had been educated at Eton and Sandhurst. He was wounded in 1916 and awarded the MC. He had a London house in Onslow Square and owned Kellie Castle, Arbroath, where he indulged his passion for field sports. He was not a success at Westminster; the only highlight was his service on the Potato Marketing Board. When the Spanish Civil War broke out, Ramsay described the International Brigades as 'the Godless'. He chaired the United Christian Front, a group of pro-Franco supporters, including many prominent Tories. It was Spain and his wife's influence that made him a virulent anti-Semite. A powerful orator, he fulminated on the 'Judaeo-Bolshevik Plot' and was closely associated with pro-Nazi circles. As war drew nearer, Ramsay became convinced that Jews were orchestrating a confrontation between Britain and Germany. His first objective, however, 'was to clear the Conservative Party of Jewish influence'.

MI5 believed the League was directed from Berlin and was the centre of Nazi intrigue in Britain. Society ladies heard Fuller's talk on 'The Hebrew Mysteries' on 27 March, with men who 'bore the unmistakable stamp of the army officer in mufti'. Nina, Lady Douglas-Hamilton spoke of the PM as a traitor who had sold out to the Jews. While Ramsay's extreme anti-Semitism received a sympathetic hearing among upper-class Britons, his attempts to reach a wider audience at public meetings usually flopped.

Special Branch transcribed speeches at NL meetings, but the most important information was procured by an agent for the Jewish BoD. Neville Laski used his SB contacts to employ a retired Inspector Pavey to penetrate the NL and provide graphic accounts of the organization. Pavey's reports pointed to strong connections between the League and German and Japanese intelligence, and close liaison with the German embassy. Moreover, respectable groups such as the Liberty Restoration League, and prominent figures, were connected to it. Laski received information on the Link, too, from the BU's E. G. Mandeville-Roe, who also belonged to the Nordic League. Laski's intelligence was used to supplement information in the central card file of MI5's registry.

The Link was viewed by Goebbels as a vehicle for propaganda. MI5 was interested in its pro-Nazi Central London branch, founded in January 1939 and run by Bertie Mills and Richard Findlay. Its secretary Margaret Bothamley, a colonel's daughter, set its tone with her hatred of Jews and admiration of the Nazis. She gave cocktail parties at Cromwell Road, attended by IFL and Nordic League activists, including Lord Ronald Graham, son of the Duke of Montrose, Mary Allen and Aubrey Lees, who had worked in Palestine as a district commissioner for the Jaffa district. He disagreed with British policy over Zionist immigration and was very anti-Semitic. He returned to England in 1939 and lived with a governess who was in the BU, in which he himself was active. Other BU activists such as Claude Duvivier, the Eckersleys and Lady Pearson, described by Domvile as a 'mad Fascist', were attracted to the Link. In reply to a Commons question the Home Secretary, Sir Samuel Hoare, said on 30 March 1939 that the Link was 'mainly for the purpose of pro-Nazi and anti-Semite propaganda'.

Behind the façade of a campaign for peace, Link and NL leaders developed their extreme right-wing tendencies. The threat of Jewish Bolshevism led them to seek peace with Germany so that the Empire could be defended against both the 'enemy within' and the 'enemy without'. Domvile and Ramsay were convinced that Hitler would never attack the British Empire. Ramsay wrote in *The Nameless War* that 'totally suppressed as far as the British people were concerned was Hitler's repeated declaration of his willingness to defend the British Empire, if called upon to assist, by force of arms if necessary'.

Domvile considered Mosley 'a real leader and I like his policy and hope he will succeed'. On 20 March the two met to discuss a 'machiavellian plot' the BU leader was working on. Meetings were under way to co-ordinate Nordic League activities with the other groups. Most were without significance; however, an alliance of the far Right, with Mosley at its centre, would cause concern in official circles. MI5 reported that he had entered into negotiations with Commander Cole, with a view to putting informal co-operation on to a formal footing and 'to speaking from the League platform'. A key figure in these talks was Gordon-Canning, Mosley's former foreign affairs adviser, who married Australian film star Mary Maguire and publicly distanced himself from politics. It has been assumed that he had quarrelled with Mosley but Gordon-Canning continued to conduct business with the BU leader. It seems the publicized breach was a ploy, enabling him to act as a bridge to the other groups without being identified as a BU link.

Domvile recorded the meetings in his diary. Those who attended included, in addition to Mosley and Ramsay, Lord Tavistock (BCCSE), Gordon-Canning (BU and BCCSE), the BU's Commandant Allen, Hawkins, Fuller, Lady Dunn and Lady Pearson, Lieutenant-Colonel C. D. Roe (BU and Link), the Link's Aubrey Lees, Professor A. P. Laurie and R. F. Findlay, Bertie Mills (People's Campaign Against War and Usury), C. G. Grey (*The Aeroplane*), George Lane-Fox Pitt-Rivers Earl of Mar, Norman Hay, Viscount Lymington, Francis Yeats-Brown and Launcelot Lawton. The only exception to Ramsay's attempt to unify the Fascist fringe was Mosley's refusal to connect the BU directly to it.

At the end of March the government guaranteed Poland that if its independence was threatened 'His Majesty's Government and the French Government would at once lend them all the support in their power'. Mosley opposed the guarantee, believing it brought war closer. Germany's encirclement would infuriate Hitler, who would respond by an eastward push. On 15 April *Action* claimed 'the task of our generation: to find a new ideological basis of European union' so that a 'united Europe' could play its part in a world balance of powers. Britain and Germany alone, Mosley believed, could unite Europe.

In April Lymington's British Council Against European Commitments joined forces with Lord Tavistock's People's Campaign against War and Usury to form the British People's Party (BPP). Campaigning for peace, it rejected totalitarianism but, with ideas similar to those of the New Pioneer group, its programme was National Socialist and anti-Semitic. It worked closely at grass-roots level with the Link. MI5 took it seriously and Tavistock, who attended dinner parties held by the BU, had his letters intercepted, as were those of his 'confidential agent' Mrs Osborne Samuel.

The BPP provided an alternative focus for the peace movement to that given by Mosley. Tavistock was President, John Beckett Secretary and Ben Greene Treasurer. Greene, a huge man, six foot eight tall, was a cousin of the novelist Graham Greene. His successful campaign to change Labour's voting system to give more weight to ordinary party members made him a key player in Labour politics, earning him the dislike of party power-broker Ernest Bevin. He was a Quaker and a pacifist, and had undertaken famine relief work in the

Soviet Union and Germany. The BPP's National Council included Richard St Barbe Baker, a Dorset farmer and recent BU convert, Aubrey Lees and *Action* columnist John Scanlon. There was also a strong blood-and-soil element.

Tavistock recruited leading peers to the BPP's pro-German sentiment and activity, including Lords Darnley, Arnold and Brocket, the Duke of Buccleuch and the Earl of Mar, a leading Mosleyite. Another strong supporter was Lord Sempill, a famous aviator, who belonged to the Anglo-German Fellowship and the Link. Sempill knew Ribbentrop and was 'one of the hard core of German enthusiasts who argued publicly for peace with Germany from the Lords'. He believed the King and the government had been taken in by sinister forces consisting of Jews, Americans and the pro-war party in Britain.

On 20 April 1939 Brocket was accompanied to Hitler's fiftieth birthday celebrations in Berlin by the Duke of Buccleuch, Lord Steward of the Royal Household and the King's official channel to the House of Lords. King George VI sent congratulations to the German leader. Buccleuch believed Germany offered the potential of a bastion against Bolshevism. An 'imperial isolationist', his inclination to appeasement accorded with his conviction that it would aid Britain and her Empire.

Also invited by Ribbentrop to the army parade on 20 April was Fuller, whose presence caused a stir in the press. The night before he left for Germany he was called by a Foreign Office official: 'I thought it as well to tell you that Sir Ian Hamilton was also asked; but that we have warned him against going as it might prove dangerous.' Fuller replied, 'So far as I am concerned I rather enjoy a rough house.' In Berlin, Fuller learned that the Führer 'intended to have Danzig, war or no war, and that, if it came to war, Poland would be overrun in a minimum of three weeks or a maximum of six'.

Fuller watched 'a completely mechanized and motorized army roar past the Führer along the Charlottenburger Strasse. Never before or since have I watched such a formidable mass of moving metal.' It was a proud moment when he met Hitler, who shook his hand and said, 'I hope you were pleased with your children?' To which he answered, 'Your Excellency, they have grown up so quickly that I no longer recognize them.' Diana said Hitler admired Fuller's 'beautifully precise and logical mind', but thought he would be 'an awkward colleague', an observation which summed him up 'exactly, though to Mosley he was a loyal collaborator'.

Tavistock said 'adversity can make strange bedfellows' and the BPP co-operated with the extremes of left and right, including the pacifist Peace Pledge Union (PPU). With the threat of war growing, Greene was committed to pacifism, a strong current within the ILP. Former ILPer John Scanlon, like the writer Hugh Ross Williamson, regarded Fascism as heir to the isolationist tradition that rejected involvement in foreign affairs as a diversion from social reform. Director of the London General Press and a Labour candidate for West Dorset, Williamson contributed to *Action*. He argued in a speech at Parkstone in May that 'German control of Eastern Europe would be no menace to the people of England but it might be a menace to the great capitalist profiteers who rule England'. Scanlon put Greene in contact with 'Harry' Bohle who, in turn, introduced him to German Propaganda Ministry officials.

In May 1939 Ramsay founded a secret society, the Right Club. The shadowy John Carlton Cross was Secretary and the Duke of Wellington chaired its meetings. Ramsay hoped 'to avert war, which we considered to be mainly the work of Jewish intrigue'. He thus designed the club for 'infiltrating and influencing the Establishment'. The club attracted a wide range of support – a list of 235 members was drawn up by the summer – including the Eckersleys and a high proportion of female members, such as Mary ('Molly') Stanford, Mrs Christabel Nicholson and Anna Wolkoff. It forged connections with other extreme groups, and Ramsay, Cross and Mary Allen tried to steer the National Citizens Union into a more anti-Semitic and pro-Nazi line but were unsuccessful. Its London offices were, however, used as a cover for Ramsay's 'secret societies'.

Simultaneously, Ramsay formed a Co-ordinating Committee of Patriotic Societies to co-ordinate the activities of the British Empire Union, National Citizens Union, the British Democratic Party, Militant Christian Patriots, the Liberty Restoration League and the United Ratepayers Association. The Nordic League was represented but, significantly, the BU was not – perhaps because so many former members already belonged to the Right Club. Naturally, MI5 was interested in its meetings and from its inception the Right Club was infiltrated by agents – including Vincent Collier (Captain 'X') – working for the Jewish BoD and later MI5.

The BoD moles discovered members acting as pro-Nazi agents. Mandeville-Roe identified T. Victor Rowe, a BU member until 1936, and E. Munro as 'German agents'. Home Office reports state that Aubrey Lees, an associate of Richard Findlay, Lord Ronald Graham and Margaret Bothamley, made 'no secret of his great admiration for the Nazi regime and openly criticizes the British Government on account of "its failure to get rid of the Jewish menace"'. At the Nordic League, Lees met Captain J. Hughes, alias the BU's 'P. G. Taylor'. Although Lees knew he was an agent, Ramsay employed him as his personal representative at the secret co-ordinating meetings.

The *Jewish Chronicle* reported that at an NL public meeting at Caxton Hall on 23 May 'the wildest speech was made by A. K. Chesterton, who delighted the middle class audience by speaking of greasy little Jew-boy pornographers'. Mandeville-Roe heard among 'motor manufacturers, lawyers, boat-builders, other press agents and journalists . . . a growing view that "if only the ruddy Jews would keep quiet there wouldn't be all this bother. Who the hell wants to fight for Poland or any other Continental places? Let Hitler carve up Europe and we'll keep his colonies."' Mosley had recently declared that 'any Englishman who will not fight for Britain is a coward; any Englishman who wants to fight for Poland is a fool'. Mandeville-Roe said their views were those 'of men who haven't a good word for Mosley and have never even heard of the Nordic League'.

In May, Unity arrived at Hitler's alpine mountain-top retreat. At Berchtesgaden was Eva Braun, who was said to be wildly jealous of Miss Mitford. Hitler told Unity on 15 May, 'We will always keep up Anglo-German friendship, whatever the English Government may do.' MI5 concluded Unity was 'fundamentally a hysterical and unbalanced person who would probably be of no use to the Germans in a war. She could not bear a war because her loyalties were now at least half German, and would kill herself. If it had not been for her husband and children, Diana might have done the same.' Diana's depression, her son Jonathan Guinness notes, 'came from knowing that war meant ruin for Mosley'. It would certainly end the radio project. There was another round of staff reductions, with paid employees such as Olive Hawks and Anne Brock-Griggs being dismissed, although many stayed on as volunteer workers.

Mosley still hit the Germans with money-making schemes, including the successful extraction of 'The Austrian Rothschild' from the Gestapo. He used his wife's contacts with Heinrich Himmler to help the family. In Vienna, Himmler had told Baron Louis Rothschild that in order to secure his freedom he would have to pay £40,000 and assign to the Third Reich all his Austrian assets. After a few days' consideration, the Baron had accepted the conditions and was allowed to leave. The Mosleys acted as intermediaries, possibly through 'Kenmare', the agent involved with the Liechtenstein station concession employed by the Jewish publishers Roditi International. According to MI5's Guy Liddell, 'Mosley got some £40,000 for the part he played in getting some of the Rothschilds out.' The money was shared with the Rexists in Belgium. In May, Rothschild arrived safely in Paris and two months later the Reich undertook to buy the Vitkowitz iron and steel factory, but when war broke out the contract was never signed.

MI5's Director-General wrote to the Home Office on 16 May that there were 'a small number of British subjects whom I consider it essential should be put under lock and key immediately on the outbreak of hostilities'. Kell wanted orders signed in advance and held by MI5, but officials resisted asking the Home Secretary to sign orders 'under a power which does not at present exist'. On 2 June, however, it was agreed that MI5 would submit individual requests from which orders would be prepared in advance but not signed. The BU may have been aware of these moves. Mosley made contingency plans, which were explained by Donovan at a meeting of officials later in the month.

Mosley attracted a large audience at Manchester's Free Trade Hall but it was 'entirely ignored by the national press'. On 28 May Lady Downe was granted five minutes with Rothermere and requested a column in the *Mail* 'as a kind of open forum, with the idea of giving Mosley some publicity'. She also wanted him to advise Mosley. When Collin Brooks asked if he was susceptible to advice, Rothermere replied 'he wasn't. At the beginning of his campaign I gave him jolly good advice, and he wouldn't listen. I supported him very strongly, but I found he was on wrong lines. I fear he isn't the adroit leader that Hitler or Mussolini is.' He did, however, agree to meet him. At the Savoy on 12 June were the Imperial Policy Group's Lord Phillimore, publisher Ernest Benn and Lord Chaplin. Brooks had earlier met Philip Farrer and was told Chaplin was attempting to 'get some cohesion among the Right wing people'. Joining them to discuss starting a newspaper was the Chairman of Drummond's bank and BU supporter George Drummond. 'Mosley was very quiet,' Brooks recorded, 'but Cecil Harmsworth drew him out about how a national leader is found. Mosley was marvellous – very quiet, very expository, very modest, very impressive.' Brooks was asked to be 'the Head-quarter brains of the Right Wing movement', co-ordinating 'all the scattered efforts'. He hoped Mosley would fall into line.

Mosley argued that friendship with Germany was a necessity if 'the security of the Empire was to be maintained'. But he must have known Hitler's ambitions did not stop at Poland's borders. As Skidelsky suggests, 'a reputable public line . . . would have been to warn Hitler that, while there were powerful forces in England working for peace, the only chance they had to succeed was if Hitler moderated his methods . . . Such a warning would have served the cause of peace better than the policy of continued support for German actions.' Diana claimed that privately Mosley did this but it went against the grain to advise Hitler 'to respect the susceptibilities of opponents whom he regarded as second-rate'. Taking money from the Nazis and signing up to the radio project at a time when most people had judged this was a regime of terror was not the action of someone out to protect British interests.

Domvile wrote in his diary on 10 July, 'We are thinking up a plan to amalgamate all the parties who think the same on foreign policy.' Ramsay, too, talked of such collaboration, as Mosley tried to rally a peace front. The *Catholic Times*, *Catholic Herald* and Peace Pledge Union all came out against the government's war policy, and there was talk of an alliance with the ILP whose journal, *Forward*, attacked the 'Jewish control of British foreign policy'. Henry Williamson asked in *Action* on 15 July, 'Must the blood and sweat of his generation drip in agony, until the sun darken and fall down the sky, and rise no more upon his world?'

By now, large halls were closed to Mosley and he was not allowed on the radio, nor had he any access to the press. However, he managed to secure a booking at the Earls Court Exhibition Hall after a last-minute cancellation. Unity was in London to see political friends such as Fuller, and went along to Earls Court with Diana. Hitler had invited them to Bayreuth.

On 16 July over 20,000 people were inside Earls Court, for 'the largest indoor political meeting ever held anywhere in the world'. There were many middle-class and 'society' people from other pro-German groups. Domvile was delighted: 'We had lovely seats at 10/6 – met the Fullers, Drummond, Lady Redesdale, Streatfield and many other friends. The hall was laid out à la Nuremberg.' Irene and Baba came with Mosley's children and his mother Lady Mosley, and his friend Mike Wardell. Diana's brother and new BU member Tom, who had joined the Queen's Westminster Territorials, was present with Lord Hinchingbrooke MP, and Randolph Churchill. The *Evening Standard* spotted Tom with a raised arm and complained to his colonel. The Italian embassy asked for twenty-four passes for correspondents. Domvile recalled 'masses of the Press, all giving Fascist salute'. Goebbels insisted German reporting of the meeting should be light 'so that the democratic press has no locus to depict him as being in Germany's pay'.

The rally opened with a fanfare of trumpets, followed by 'the pageantry of the BU Drum Corps leading the massed flags and honour standards of hundreds of branches'. The anti-war audience, even if they were not pro-Mosley, cheered as the cry 'MOSLEY' echoed around the hall. There was 'a roll of drums and a searchlight drawn down the centre of the hall', the BU's John Charnley recalled, 'and in the distance you could see the figure in black. There stood Mosley in a dark suit, black shirt and tie.' He marched down the centre aisle, 'as he did so the cheers began to rise, developing and expanding until I thought the roof would come down! This was the man upon whom we had pinned our hopes, the man who could save our country and Empire.' At the plinth Mosley raised his hand, and then began his last appeal. Charnley thought it 'the finest speech he ever delivered. At many points he had to stop speaking because of the wave of applause.'

'We say to the parties tonight . . . if any country in the world attacks Britain, then every single member of this great audience of British Union would fight for Britain . . . but a million Britons shall never die in your Jews' quarrel. Why is it a moral duty to go to war if a German kicks a Jew across the Polish frontier but no moral duty to lift a finger if a Briton is kicked in Tsientsin?' He thundered that 'the Empire is sold . . . My friends, can we conceive of a policy of greater insanity, heading more straight for suicide, than this: to be prepared to fight a world war over a few acres which do not belong to us, but to make a present to the whole of mankind of the land which was won by the sweat, blood and heroism of our forefathers?' At this point Randolph Churchill walked out.

'I am told that Hitler wants the whole world. In other words,' Mosley went on, 'Hitler is mad. What evidence have they got . . . to show that he has gone suddenly mad? Any man who wants to run the whole of the modern world with all its polyglot population and diverse peoples and interests – such a man is undoubtedly mad, and I challenge my opponents to produce one shred of such evidence about that singularly shrewd and lucid intellect whom they venture so glibly to criticise.'

Express reporter Frank Waters noted how 'the audience howled, hugging itself. He knew exactly when to make it laugh, when to cheer, when to jeer and sneer. A top-line variety star could hardly have shown greater versatility.' After two hours came the climax. Mosley asked whether 'we are going, if the power lies within us . . . to say that our generation and our children shall not die like rats in Polish holes'. He dedicated himself to the memory of those who had gone before. 'To the dead heroes of Britain in sacred union we say – Like you we give ourselves to England: across the ages that divide us – across the glories of Britain that unite us – we gaze into your eyes and we give to you this holy vow: We will be true – today, tomorrow and for ever – England Lives!'

Domvile thought the rally 'perfectly splendid'. Francis Yeats-Brown, who had joined the Right Club, had his doubts. He wrote to Lord Elton that Mosley was 'as good as Goebbels as a speaker. His references to Jews and Baldwin were greeted with prolonged booing. Personally I agreed with three-quarters of what he said, but the other quarter is a stumbling block . . . I listened in vain for any word that would have shown that if a crisis came suddenly he would be behind the government.' He would use the opportunity for political ends, making it impossible to rally the peace forces under his banner.

In its coverage the German press had few illusions about the mood for peace in Britain. Helmut Sundermann, Otto Dietrich's right-hand man, warned 'war hysteria' was spreading in Britain and that the people, 'chloroformed by mass propaganda', were asking when war against Germany would start. An anti-war BPP candidate at the Hythe by-election failed miserably. BU members helped Harry St John Philby, who received only 578 votes. On 18 July Hitler hailed Mosley's speech, in which he called for an abandonment of the armaments race, the return of German colonies and the preservation of the Empire, as a plea for peace. 'The meeting showed that Mosley had arrived at a clear programme: this is directed against the agitation for war and against the influence of Jewry.'

On 19 July German Ambassador Dirksen forwarded to Berlin a report on the growth of anti-Semitism in Britain, following the arrival of 60,000 refugees. He said, 'Opportunities for disseminating anti-Jewish ideas are very limited. This fact is already reflected by the suppression of all reports of Mosley's Fascist meetings, which are sometimes very well attended, as well as of the antisemitic clashes that occur almost daily in East London.' He noted that 'the very well-connected Capt. Ramsay is beginning to play a definite role', as was Lady Alexandra Hardinge's organization, which was 'showing an anti-semitic film in which, among other things, Jewish ritual slaughter is depicted. A further increase of the anti-Jewish feeling in Britain can be expected.'

Close ties developed between the Link, Nordic League, Right Club and the BU, with respectable societies used as 'cover' for meetings, including the premises of a society of Druids. A *Daily Worker* reporter graphically described a League meeting, where guests were scrutinized by BU stewards, 'held in a large room decorated with imitation dolmens. The platform stands under a kind of papier mâché Stonehenge. Torch-like fittings give out a dim light. The wildest accusations are made against the Jews . . . The audience works itself up into a frenzy of anti-semitism with cries of "Down with the Jews". At the end of the meeting all rise, cry "The King", and shoot out their hands in the Nazi salute.'

The 'Nazi connection' implicated a number of Mosley's inner circle. Domvile's visit to Salzburg during the summer to found a German branch of the Link attracted press criticism. MI5 discovered that Commandant Allen, whose 'connection to the BU was a closely guarded secret', made clandestine flights from a Kent airport to hold secret talks with Goering, Himmler and Hitler. The Right Club's violently anti-Semitic and pro-Nazi Anna Wolkoff visited Czechoslovakia. Though the Wolkoff family was down on its luck, Anna's background meant she was used to the company of diplomats and people such as Rudolf Hess. On 17 July she met General Hans Frank, right-hand man of Konrad Henlein, the Sudeten German leader: 'Frank and I talked for two and a half hours, and it was then that I heard of the forthcoming German–Soviet pact and all it would imply.'

Like Wolkoff, Allen went to secret meetings of the extreme Right at the Cromwell Road home of Miss Margaret Bothamley, wife of Lieutenant-Colonel Charles Strong, a prominent BU member. They were attended by Germans. At the end of July Bothamley, who had tried to found a German branch of the Link, left by plane from Croydon for Germany. She returned, but made her way back to Berlin where, like Frances Eckersley, she joined the English section of the German broadcasting service working alongside William Joyce. MI5 discovered letters Joyce had written on 20 July to German agent Christian Bauer to tell him that his brother, Quentin, would travel to Berlin in early September. Joyce told Beckett that if war broke out he would go to Germany and offer his services to Hitler. Beckett turned down his offer to go with him. MI5 recommended that in the event of a war Joyce be detained.

Mosley was pursuing the radio project and set up a new company, Radio Variety, to sell advertising and develop programmes for the German station.

He provided the capital of £5,000 (£170,000) for the front directors, Eckersley and accountant James Herd. Eckersley had recruited announcers to introduce the broadcasts of live concerts, operas and sporting events. Details were sent to von Kaufman in Berlin and construction of the station, due to open on 1 October, went ahead.

It became apparent, however, that the understanding between Mosley and Bill Allen had broken down, and the latter withdrew from the project. Without Allen, Radio Variety stood little chance of success. It would be, as Herd put it, 'a flop'. An agreement was made for Mosley to pay Allen £10,000 in return for control of the Museum Trust and Air Time. Despite the setback, Mosley believed he was about to make 'an immense fortune', which would be 'clean money, made by our own abilities'. He still sought the sanction of the British government and on 23 July Oliver Hoare asked Lord Perth whether the Foreign Office was interested in the commercial broadcasting station they were 'shortly to set up'. Perth said the Joint Broadcasting Committee 'deals with this sort of thing. They have all the information required.'

On 26 July the Mosleys gave a dinner party for sympathetic MPs, pro-Nazi journalists and prominent figures connected with the Anglo-German Fellowship, the Link and the Nordic League. Guests of honour were Tory MPs Lieutenant-Colonel Moore-Brabazon, Captain Ramsay and Sir Jocelyn Lucas, newly elected and assistant to Sir Henry Page Croft. A prominent A-GF member, Special Branch noted that Lucas was also involved with the National Socialist League and the British Council Against European Commitments. The *Standard*'s 'Londoner's Diary' said other guests included Mosley's mother, Sir Barry and Lady Domvile, Professor Laurie, Fuller, and journalists G. Ward Price and James Wentworth Day, formerly of Lady Houston's *Saturday Review*.

Also present was Philip Farrer, recently private secretary to Lord Salisbury, Leader of the Lords, and member of a subversive group set up by Nazi journalist Thost. Farrer and Mosley had taken part in talks with Lord Clive and Lord Queenborough, President of the Royal Society of St George, Collin Brooks and others, about creating a new right-wing newspaper.

Thost returned to Germany and published a book on England, warning that Nazi propaganda which stressed the British only wanted peace and lacked the will to fight would not succeed. Communist demonstrations against the BU 'gave the English towns a very small taste of what Germany had to go through', but he was not optimistic about Mosley's prospects because he stuck 'too closely to the Italian and German models to have the slightest chance of success. Fascism is such a typically Italian movement, and National Socialism such a typically German movement, that the British fascists have succeeded so little in building something typically British.'

*

The day after hosting the dinner party, Diana left for Germany as Hitler's guest at the Bayreuth Festival. She flew to Munich where Unity had a flat found with Hitler's help – 'it had belonged to a Jewish couple who had decided to leave'.

A young John F. Kennedy wrote from Munich to his father that Unity was 'not at all pretty' but had 'a certain fine Aryan look'. She was 'in a state of high nervous tension and thinks only of the Führer', who had 'a tremendous admiration for the British and would do them no harm unless they forced his hand . . . the situation in England was due mainly to Jewish propaganda and the only way to clear it up was to throw them out . . . Even though England got beaten in battle the Germans would give England its empire for they could not run the world by themselves.' She added, 'It would be much better if the English got defeated.' Kennedy thought her 'the most fervent Nazi imaginable, and is probably in love with Hitler'.

On 28 August Major Gerhard Engel, an army adjutant on Hitler's staff, attended a dinner party at Frau Wagner's where 'the possibility of fascism in Britain was thoroughly discussed'. Diana 'painted a very optimistic picture. She emphasised that anti-Semitism is constantly on the increase in Britain.' This undermines her claim that she never talked about the subject with her Nazi hosts. Hitler said that 'fascism did not lie in the English character, and although Mosley might be a fine person and had grasped the weakness of English politics, he could not seduce a whole nation'. When Unity disparaged Italy and was ticked off by one of his staff, Hitler came to her defence. Subsequently, even the slightest discussion of Italy would cause him to catch her eye and giggle.

Engel found Unity 'to be an excellent authority on the British arms situation. This was music to the Führer's ears. Should her statements be correct, then the German Military Attaché's reports are wrong. She said frankly that Britain cannot wage a war. For the whole of London there are just eight anti-aircraft batteries. The army has only ageing weaponry and there are tanks for only two divisions.' Her information came from a cousin (possibly Randolph Churchill). Engel worried whether she was 'a spy, a poseur or is she really the fanatical admirer of the Führer that she always makes herself out to be? One thing is clear, she has an excellent intelligence network at her disposal. She always knows where the Führer is.' The inner circle 'sought information about her. She had a shadow on her but nothing else, and Hitler did not even want that much.' Hitler told her 'a lot of political and military secrets because he thought he could rely on having them passed on to the right people by that means. He was sure she would hand on to the English, especially Churchill, whatever information he pre-selected.'

The account of the dinner was confirmed by Hitler himself in the Bormann-preserved 'Table Talk'. Hitler claimed

Churchill and his friends decided on war against us some years before 1939. I had this information from Lady Mitford; she and her sisters were very much in the know. One day she suddenly exclaimed that in the whole of London there were only three anti-aircraft guns! Her sister, who was present, stared at her stonily and then said slowly: 'I do not know whether Mosley is the right man, or even if he is in a position to prevent a war between Britain and Germany.'

On the last day at Bayreuth, 2 August, Diana found Hitler in a state of depression. He believed Britain was determined upon war. Unity's diary quotes him as saying: 'If there is no miracle I see the outlook as very black. And I do not believe in miracles.' Diana said her husband would 'continue his campaign for peace for as long as such a campaign was legal'. Hitler appreciated 'that he has been opposed to war but I want to warn him that if he does, he may be assassinated like Jaurès in 1914'. Jean Jaurès, editor of the socialist newspaper *L'Humanité*, had been assassinated by a French nationalist for advocating arbitration with Germany rather than violence. Mosley recalled that Hitler had 'a strong historic sense and my position of political opposition to the war seemed to him similar to that of the French statesman'. Diana gave Hitler a report on her husband's speeches, about which he showed great interest. After they left, Unity told Diana that she would kill herself if there was war.

That evening's performance was of Wagner's *Götterdämmerung*. 'Never had the glorious music seemed so doom-laden,' Diana wrote. 'I had a strong feeling that I should never see Hitler again, that a whole world was crumbling, that the future held only tragedy and war.' As for Unity's fate, 'there was nothing to be done. She and I had talked it over and over; I dreaded her iron resolve.' When the sisters were alone, Unity said again that she would not live to see the tragedy of war between Britain and Germany. 'I knew well what Unity, sitting beside me, was thinking. Next day I left for England with death in my heart.' Diana took the train to Derby where she met Mosley. 'As we drove through the summer night to Wootton I told him Hitler's words, and what Unity had said.'

On 3 August the Home Secretary was asked in the Commons if the Link was 'an instrument of the German propaganda service financed by Germany'. Domvile and Carroll had visited the German chemical firm Bayer, which promised 'to help the Link'. Its journal was subsidized by predominantly German advertisers and A. P. Laurie received £150 (£5,000) for a work of undisguised propaganda, *The Case for Germany* (Berlin, 1939). Although reluctant to act unless the law was broken, Sir Samuel Hoare said the Link was 'being used as an instrument of the German propaganda service and that money has been received from Germany by one of the active organisers'.

Mosley's radio project was a clandestine affair. On 15 August Herd travelled to Dover to meet a senior German official, von Kaufman. They travelled to the Radio Variety offices, where the German told Eckersley that because of the international situation the radio deal was off. That night, Eckersley went with von Kaufman to Plymouth to meet a German colleague on the SS *Carribea*, in an endeavour to persuade him to come to London for further discussions. The official refused and the two Germans left on the *Carribea*. Eckersley, Herd later told Special Branch, 'came back alone, very disappointed'. Quizzed about Eckersley's loyalty, Herd said he was 'so pro-Hitler' that he 'would not put him in control of anything which would bring him in contact with propaganda'. He was anti-Semitic and a member of the Link: 'Anyway, he's a bloody Nazi.'

The Germans gave Mosley money as recompense and returned the capital sum for Gemona. Allen 'heard about it and, in a fury, threatened to expose where Mosley had obtained funds for the BU if he did not immediately return the money to the rightful owners'. He did return the money, accusing Allen of blackmail. Allen said this was a compliment, coming from 'such an accomplished blackmailer'. Mosley's radio gamble accounts for the tone of his peace campaign, with its refusal to criticize Hitler. It was impossible for him to head a broader based peace movement: 'his hands', suggests Skidelsky, 'were tied by his own negotiations with Berlin. He was still juggling; still sacrificing public causes for private considerations.'

Mosley wrote that at the outbreak of war, 'One thing at least is certain, that but for the accident of war we should have made an immense fortune. I should have achieved my ambition to be the first revolutionary in history to conduct a revolution and at the same time to make the fortune which assured its success ... It was a great labour. It went down by an accident.' Diana believed the station in Germany, which was the furthest advanced of the concessions in terms of planning, was completed and went on air as Bremen I, broadcasting propaganda to Britain during the war.

Despite the rapidly deteriorating situation in Europe and fears within the British government that Hitler would strike out within weeks, Diana wrote to Ribbentrop on 21 August, with 'best regards' from her husband, and accepted an invitation to the Reichsparteitag at Nuremberg for herself and Unity. 'Tickets were like gold' and Diana requested they be accompanied by Lady Downe. 'She is a very good National Socialist. I am sure the Führer would like her very much. She is an old friend of Queen Mary's, and she does a great deal of good in a small way, trying to get people to see our point of view.' The guest list largely contained figures unconnected with Mosley who the Nazis hoped would raise the respectable image of the Third Reich in Britain.

That Nuremberg would go ahead was always unlikely, even more so when it was revealed that the Germans and the Soviet Union had signed a pact on 23 August 1939. It also meant that hopes of a European crusade against Bolshevism had been dashed. 'War for Poland was always a crime,' Mosley wrote, 'now it is madness.' The news led to talk on the Right of a Mosley *coup d'état*; an idea which seemed to intrigue Collin Brooks.

On 22 August MI5 submitted to the Home Office the names of twenty-three people they wished to detain. Nineteen were suspected spies or 'of hostile origin', and three (one being Joyce) simply pro-Nazi. Joyce's friend Angus McNab returned from Germany, where he had stayed with Bauer, claiming he would never help Britain's enemies. MI5, however, intercepted a letter to Bauer, disclosing Joyce's intention to go to Germany. 'He has identified himself unreservedly with the Nazi cause, maintains close contact with Nazi officials and has shown he would be quite willing to take action inimical to this country.' Vernon Kell fed fears of German spies and invasion to his lifelong friend Churchill, who believed – against all the evidence – that 20,000 Nazi agents were in Britain, ready to stimulate an outbreak of sabotage.

On 24 August Sir Samuel Hoare presented the Emergency Powers (Defence) Bill in the Commons. He warned that he was seeking 'very wide, very drastic, and very comprehensive powers', which would not be introduced 'until the country is actually involved in hostilities'. It was passed by an Order in Council, which did not require parliamentary assent. During the day, Joyce renewed his British passport (at his post-war trial it emerged that the passport officer became distressed in answering simple questions about this remarkable action, for Joyce was on the arrest list).

Joyce's sister Joan said that in the evening he received a telephone call from an MI5 officer warning he was to be interned. Joyce was telephoned by his old British Fascist friend Maxwell Knight, who said Defence Regulations would become effective in two more days and that his detention order had already been signed. Joyce had been giving Knight information on Communists; the hope, implausibly, was that he would continue to do so from Germany. On 26 August Mosley's former chief propagandist left for Berlin, accompanied by his second wife, Margaret, destined to become 'Lord Haw Haw', the most notorious broadcaster in Germany. When the order for his detention was issued, Special Branch's Inspector Keeble went to arrest him, but he had already caught the boat train to Ostend. Joyce was accompanied by a second person making his way to Berlin whose identity remains unknown.

Novelist Henry Williamson was distraught by the worsening news. He could not believe Hitler intended to wage war and, in desperation, wrote to Mosley suggesting that he, Williamson, fly to Germany in a last-ditch attempt to persuade the Führer not to proceed. 'If I could see Hitler, as the common soldier of 1914 who fought the common soldier of his Linz battalion at Ypres,' thinks Williamson's autobiographical hero Philip Maddison, 'might I not be able to give him, the German common soldier, that amity he so desired from England – to beg him to halt his troops, and to save the two white giants of Europe . . . from bleeding to death, while Oriental Bolshevism waits on, to bring Asia to the chalk cliffs of Normandy?'

On 26 August Williamson went to see Mosley, 'a man in whose ability and realistic vision I believed. With his invariable courtesy he rose to greet me, but the calm and aloof strength of his usual self was withdrawn, as though for the moment he had expended all his life, and was poor. He held my letter half-crumpled in his hand, as though it had been thrust hastily into his pocket.' Mosley considered it a futile gesture: 'I'm afraid it is too late – the curtain is down.' Williamson asked, 'What will you do?' He repeated what Hitler had told his wife: 'They might shoot me as Jaurès was shot in Paris in 1914.' Then he said, 'I shall keep on, while I can, to give a platform for peace should our people want it. I cannot see my country sink.' When he left, he noticed the newsbills read NAZIS SEIZE DANZIG. Heeding Mosley's advice, he returned to his Norfolk farm, appalled by the approach of a 'two-sided brothers' war'.

With the approach of war, Special Branch noted 'the Nordic League has ceased' but leading members, together with more active IFL members, met regularly at the house of Oliver Gilbert. At the same time the Duke of Westminster, on the advice of *Truth* editor Henry Newnham, joined the Link. Diana Cooper recalled that on leaving the Savoy Grill on 1 September 1939, in the blackout, she and Duff were given a lift in the Duke's car. He began 'abusing the Jewish race', praising the Germans and 'rejoicing that we were not yet at war'. When he added that 'Hitler knew after all that we were his best friends', her husband spat 'that by to-morrow he will know that we are his most implacable and remorseless enemies'.

Mosley expected air raids to begin the moment war broke out. He suggested that Irene and the children leave Denham for the safety of Staffordshire. On 27 August Irene, the children and Micky's nanny arrived at Wootton, where she removed the photograph of Hitler by Diana's bed and one of Goering from the mantelpiece. That evening Mosley addressed a large crowd at Hackney, accusing the government of creating a situation in which 'if Poland whistles, a million Englishmen have got to die'. Blackshirts carried placards with slogans such as 'The Jews Want War – We Want Peace' and 'We Won't Fight for Poland'. *Action* warned that 'the warmongers have still to reckon with the will to peace of the British people finding expression through the inspired voice of Oswald Mosley! Hail Mosley! Hail Peace!' It said thousands of Londoners had shouted these slogans, arms raised in the Nazi salute.

Mosley genuinely believed he was getting somewhere: 'Our British movement achieved so much in face of steadily declining unemployment figures that it cannot be doubted we should have won in Britain if the crisis had deepened.' This was an example of his willingness to deceive himself but even respected journalist Hannen Swaffer took the view that but for the war, Britain would have been a Fascist country: 'Would British fascism, one wonders, have done so disastrously at a general election in 1940 fought in the trough of a new depression?' John Warburton, who joined the BU in 1933 aged fourteen, said that there was in the run-up to the war, 'a realisation that it would have to be in a moment of crisis and that we could not achieve power'. He later believed 'that we could have achieved seats but deep down I didn't think we could achieve power but would make a breakthrough'.

'The question is,' Mosley suggested to Peter Liddle near the end of his life,

had I stayed in the old parties, had I possibly become Prime Minister, could I have prevented the only thing that mattered, the Second World War. I am perfectly satisfied I could not have got anything serious done on unemployment, poverty, suffering, the questions of the age, in the old Parties, but I might conceivably, having, if you like, this obsession against war, I might have prevented a second world war, if I had been in that position. However, the drive for war was so tremendous that no individual in any position could have stopped it.

22

The Phoney War

On 1 September 1939 German troops crossed into Poland. Mosley issued a message to British Union members to 'stand fast . . . you have lit a flame in Britain which all the corrupt Jewish money-power cannot extinguish'. He said 'Britain intervenes in an alien quarrel' but asked members 'to do nothing to injure our country, or to help the other Power. Our members should do what the law requires of them; and, if they are members of any of the Forces or Services of the Crown, they should obey their orders and, in every particular, obey the rules of the Service.' He asked them 'to take every opportunity within your power to awaken the people and to demand peace'.

Neville Laski brought the message to Scotland Yard's attention but Mosley had cleared it with the Ministry of Information, which asked it not be published but only distributed via BU notice boards. The authorities concluded that his policy of opposing the war while asking his followers not to take any action which would hinder its prosecution was the product of a very clever mind determined to keep the BU within the law. Thereafter, BU publications were monitored for signs of propaganda prejudicial to the defence of the realm.

Chamberlain announced on the radio on 3 September that Britain and Germany were at war. Diana remembered 'a hot and cloudless morning; a minute or two later the sirens blew an air raid warning. We went on to our river balcony but nothing appeared in the serene blue sky.' Unity was 'shattered by the outbreak of war between the countries she loved'. She attempted suicide by shooting herself in the head. She did not succeed and lay unconscious in a Munich hospital. On 4 September two Blackshirts in the RAF, Kenneth Day and George Brocking, were killed in action in a daylight bomber raid over Brunsbüttel.

Mosley imagined the authorities would close the BU down and forbid him to speak. 'If he had been,' wrote Diana, 'he would have obeyed absolutely. His whole record shows that; he never disobeyed the police.' The Nazi–Soviet pact immobilized local Communist anti-Fascism, but claims that peace meetings were 'larger and more enthusiastic than any in the BU's history' are not borne out by the facts. The general absence of public interest in the BU contributed to a decline in the numbers attending its open-air meetings, though those in north-east London attracted 'fair crowds' of stalwarts. Large halls in Manchester and Leeds were closed to it and during September the only BU meetings took place in London.

Claims that membership had recovered to the peak level of support of 1934 are probably exaggerated; Special Branch estimated sales of *Action* to be 14,000. Local branches were paralysed with many of the male speakers conscripted into the armed forces. Women and young Mosleyites filled the leadership vacuum and supported the ongoing peace campaign. For many the BU was their first initiation into politics and their ties to it were tenuous. Mosley was aware the movement might just disintegrate and ordered tightened discipline.

To protect the BU in the event of his arrest, Mosley made contingency plans, which had been outlined by Brian Donovan to officials during the summer. Deputies for all posts were appointed and, besides Donovan and Francis Hawkins, six officials were sanctioned to oversee the movement: J. H. Hone, national inspector for the North; Commander C. E. Hudson, member of the Anglo-German Friendship society and election candidate; K. E. Marsden, northern propaganda officer; Rafe Temple-Cotton, regional inspector and candidate for Exeter; E. Dudley Elam, BU receptionist; and Hector McKechnie, meetings organizer and senior London administrator. The eight received a signed document stating that each of them had Mosley's 'complete confidence and is entitled to do what he thinks fit in the interests of the Movement on his own responsibility'. MI5 suspected others – Jorian Jenks, BU Agricultural Adviser – had been authorized. Documents had been sent to regional inspectors and area organizers, including Charles Hammond and Ralph Gladwyn Jebb, a candidate for West Dorset.

These were not leaders of an underground organization since their BU role was public knowledge and they were likely to be interned. There was another covert layer, including district organizer Lawrence Harding, a former Royal Navy officer. MI5 did not appreciate Harding's importance, an unknown figure close to Mosley. Bitterly anti-Communist, ultra patriotic, he spoke German and had contacts with Germany, where he received 'training' and acted as BU liaison with the Nazis. Harding kept his secrets and burnt all his diaries for the period.

Mosley had transferred funds to Mrs Norah Elam, a former suffragette who ran the London and Provincial Anti-Vivisection Society, a BU front organization. Her husband was one of the anointed eight. Mosley explained that he feared Headquarters might be bombed and that he might be assassinated, so decided Mrs Elam should take 'charge of part of our funds for a short period before and after the declaration of war. There was nothing illegal or improper about this.' The Elams were among those members who regularly attended the secret meetings to organize collaboration between the 'patriotic societies'.

The Home Office considered Mosley's peace campaign to be subversive. He hoped that 'out of the misery and hardships of a long war he may eventually be able to establish a Fascist State with himself as Dictator'. However, officials remained wary of arresting a former Minister who threatened to sue those who impugned his patriotism.

When Diana told Irene that Mosley intended to carry on the BU, she despaired at their attitude. Anthony Eden's address on 11 September on Hitler's crimes drew protests from Diana. An angry Irene left the house but she did later speak to her brother-in-law, who predicted Germany and Russia winning but was 'by no means so sure we would. Hence his mission to get a peace while the Empire was still intact.' She thought he saw himself as 'a potential smasher-up of all our capitalist system when the disruption of communism creeps over Europe and towards us, and with anti-Semitism as his pillar of hate he will arise from the ashes of conservatism and profitmaking'. He talked 'earnestly on the curious thing that great fanatical faith has to have hate to work on'.

During the following day's lunch he was 'so wild with rage he tore up and down the room in a filthy blasphemous state'. He said he would 'at once make peace with Hitler, letting him have his huge bloc to the Mediterranean if Hitler leaves us and our empire alone, but if he touches it we fight'. Irene argued that Hitler 'must touch us somewhere' but noted that Mosley did 'not mind the Poles being sacrificed'. He attacked Chamberlain for saying Hitlerism must be wiped out – 'cannot 80 million Germans choose their Government and would we stomach Hitler butting in here and condemning our Government and telling them he would fight to exterminate them?' Irene found the tirade 'horrendous'.

Irene rebelled against using her money for the children's upkeep even when they were at Wootton. She had 'crashed their castle and the funds they wanted to give to fascism cannot now be safe unless they live in a cottage'. Mosley said he was through with Irene.

The government was obsessed with information leaking to the enemy and the possibility that Mosley's supporters might make use of foreign embassy diplomatic bags. Risk of leakage increased with the creation on 3 September of the unwieldly Anglo-French Supreme War Council. The appointment of Sir Edmund Ironside as Chief of the Imperial General Staff worried MI5. The Minister for War, Leslie Hore-Belisha, told Ironside he was suspected of being indiscreet and having dubious connections (rumours he was a secret BU member were not raised). On 13 September the King asked Ironside to make room for the Duke of Windsor as a liaison officer on the Military Mission to the French. Ironside argued this would mean the Duke having access to secret plans, which would inevitably be made known to the Duchess, who was not to be trusted. The King did not dispute Ironside's assessment but suggested top secret information be kept from the Duke.

A role had been sought for the Duke so that pro-German forces did not coalesce around him as a 'Peace Party'. David Cannadine suggests his views on Germany were similar to Mosley's – 'and no one would suggest that Mosley should be regarded as a non-risk man in the Second World War'. Diana shared their view that the First World War had been 'a total failure, that the Versailles Treaty was grossly unfair, and that Germany should never have been encircled in the 1930s'. Hitler should have been allowed to deport the Jews. 'The Jews behaved abominably in Germany and all he wanted to do was be rid of them . . . anti-Semitism was endemic everywhere in Central Europe . . . if the right people had been in power in England, particularly Lloyd George, there could have been a negotiated peace.'

A Peace Party seemed to be forming on 11 September at the house of Britain's richest man, the Duke of Westminster, President of the Link. At the conclave were the Duke of Buccleuch and Lords Rushcliffe, Arnold and Mottistone (J. E. B. Seely, a member of the Anglo-German Fellowship); war correspondent Sir Philip Gibbs; and Collin Brooks, about to edit *Truth*. The pro-German Buccleuch said war would 'play into the hands of Soviet Russia, Jews and Americans'. He was already under surveillance by MI5. Westminster read his guests a paper by former MP and BU funder Henry Drummond Wolff, who argued that the war could be 'set aside by deflecting Hitler's aggressive intentions from the external to the internal; in other words by fomenting a revolution within Germany itself'. Mottistone told Foreign Secretary Halifax about the meeting, which was described by Lord Hankey as 'somewhat defeatist and pacifist'.

A second meeting included Lord Noel-Buxton (whose secretary was MI5 agent Harald Kurtz) and Lord Harmsworth. Westminster lamented that London – much of which he owned – was 'the best aerial target on the face of the earth'. Churchill later warned his friend that 'when a country is fighting a war, very hard experiences lie before those who preach defeatism and set themselves against the main will of the Nation'.

On 16 September Mosley urged the government to 'leave the foreigners on the continent to fight out their own quarrels'. He wanted Britain turned into an isolated fortress and its energy converted into developing the Empire. 'If Germany does not blame us for any breach of the rules of war by our Polish allies, no more should we blame them for such measures of retaliation as they have undertaken in the East.' War would lead to 'the disaster of defeat, the triumph of communism and the loss of the British Empire despite victory'. Britain was the only country which could not benefit from war.

MI5 reported that Mosley and the Right Club's Captain Ramsay met at the

London and Provincial Anti-Vivisection Society, where Fascists and anti-Semites discussed the threat posed by the promulgation of Defence Regulation 18D on 1 September 1939 and the internment of four Fascists. They agreed to continue a peace campaign while avoiding activity which could be construed as treasonable. On 11 September Nordic League members joined the BU in support of Mosley's prediction that a revolutionary situation would develop against the 'Jewish War'. Special Branch believed they would 'continue to work underground' by working with the Peace Pledge Union, even though they were 'no more pacifist than Hitler'.

In *Action* on 16 September Mosley was portrayed as the unifying leader of the anti-Semitic and Fascist groups campaigning for a negotiated peace. On 11 September his former foreign affairs adviser Robert Gordon-Canning who, he later admitted, had not left the BU and was probably still working on his behalf, saw Admiral Domvile as part of the agreement process with Ramsay. Eight days later Domvile, John Beckett and ILP activist Ben Greene met at Gordon-Canning's flat, where they were joined by prominent members of the Link, the Nordic League and the Right Club. The aim was to forge ties between the Link and the British People's Party, in a new joint organization, the British Council for a Christian Settlement in Europe (BCCSE), which would work for a negotiated peace. It was chaired by Lord Tavistock, with Gordon-Canning as Treasurer and Beckett as Secretary.

Francis Hawkins, as BU's chief negotiator, met Tavistock about co-ordinating the activities of those groups that held similar views to the BU. Special Branch noted that more than one senior BU official had 'gone so far as to state this country would be better off under German rule'. It feared members were being encouraged to join civil defence units in order to spread defeatist propaganda and to register falsely as conscientious objectors. It claimed a BU 'pack' sent to teachers called upon 'students of the revolution' to prepare themselves for 'the day of the British Union's final advance'. It emphasized Mosley's belief that a revolutionary situation could be created which Fascists could either exploit for themselves, or use their armed service contacts to defeat the Communists. This might provide an opportunity for a 'march to power'.

On 22 September two leading NL and former BU members on MI5's Suspect List, Oliver Gilbert and Victor Rowe, were interned for their pro-Nazi connections. They were alleged to be part of a group 'prepared to go further'. 'Hoffman' of Munich had provided Gilbert with anti-Jewish propaganda for distribution at NL meetings. The two were deemed to be in association with other disloyal British citizens, 'who were hostile to the true interests of the country'.

Captain Luttman-Johnson, Secretary of the Windsor Club and a visitor to Germany, was on MI5's list but was not detained. Mosley was alarmed by the arrest (along with the IFL's Quentin Joyce) of BU members E. Fawcett and William F. Craven, active in the Liverpool docks, and Eric Thomas, a candidate for Wood Green, who visited Germany with Gilbert during the spring and was suspected of being a Gestapo agent.

German files reveal Thomas's attendance at the German embassy as 'propaganda director of the English National Socialists'. He was 'a dangerous dreamer, about whom one should be warned'. Living in Berlin, marketing washing-machine motors, Putzi Hanfstaengl introduced him to leading Nazis. He edited the anti-Semitic *Investigator*, and in 1938 went to Nuremberg and made contact with the Auslands Organization. Thomas served until July 1939 as Limehouse district leader and was Mosley's contact with Hans Keller, President of the Institute for the Rights of Nations, who allegedly introduced him to a Nazi intelligence officer. When arrested, Thomas was asked whether he represented the BU in Berlin, if it received Nazi funding and whether he had met Mosley in Germany. He was warned not to mention the matter 'or you will come back inside again'.

Under 18B the authorities could detain without trial people they believed capable of prejudicial acts against the State. Reasons for detention did not have to be revealed either to the detainee or to the Advisory Committee dealing with appeals. Herbert Morrison attacked the 'extraordinary sweeping powers' under which 'anybody whom the Home Secretary did not like could be hanged, drawn or quartered almost without any reasonable or proper means of defending himself'. The idea of a legally managed 'day in court' in which evidence could be challenged was, notes Professor Brian Simpson, 'wholly incompatible with the world of MI5, where unchecked assertions and reports from agents and informers built up a file, where suspicion served as a substitute for proof of guilt, and where the object of suspicion was normally never even interviewed before the case against him was acted upon'.

Worried by Thomas's Nazi connections, Mosley was in the dark as to what exactly MI5 knew. His solicitor obtained a copy of Thomas's Detention Order in which he was accused of 'close association with prominent members of the Nazi Party'; 'sympathy with the Nazi Regime' and of having been in relations with a Nazi Party member 'suspected of being hostile to a person or persons currently residing in the United Kingdom'. He was held in solitary for twenty-five days without charge under special watch orders. He was not allowed a solicitor and no visitors except his wife. His 'filthy' cell was artificially lit for twenty-four hours a day with the small windows sandbagged.

Mosley protested in *Action* and Ramsay raised in the Commons the manner in which the regulations were being implemented. Domvile's diary and the testimony of Francis Hawkins and Lees to the Advisory Committee confirm that secret meetings discussed the Thomas case, mutual collaboration and setting up a newspaper advocating peace. The participants were recorded in the Domvile diary (about which MI5 had no knowledge) and included Mosley, Ramsay, Lymington and Domvile; prominent BU members such as Hawkins, Fuller, Commandant Allen and Lady Pearson; members of the Right Club, the BPP and the Nordic League, including Tavistock and Gordon-Canning (BCCSE), Bertie Mills, Yeats-Brown, Professor A. P. Laurie and Richard Findlay (RC), C. D. Roe (RC and Link); and maverick figures such as George Lane-Fox Pitt-Rivers Earl of Mar, Lady Dunn and C. G. Grey (editor of *The Aeroplane*). Home Office reports on civilian morale suggested there was considerable support for a negotiated peace and the appearance of a general alliance of the far Right caused concern in official circles.

In October plans for a gathering of the patriotic societies took shape. Domvile was the co-ordinator and was aided by Richard Findlay, his channel between Ramsay and Mosley. On 1 October a meeting at the National Citizens Union was attended by Ramsay and other RC/NL members, NCU representatives, including the pro-Nazi Leigh Vaughan-Henry and Charles Featherstone-Hammond, and BU members such as Mrs Newnham, whose husband was editor of *Truth*. They accepted Ramsay as leader. Two days later Domvile saw Mosley but there was no Ramsay 'which was a pity'. He was in Scotland to meet Findlay and Luttman-Johnson (both in contact with Mosley).

MI5 viewed the Right Club as a 'Fifth Column' organization which 'under the cloak of anti-Jewish propaganda conducts pro-German activities'. Special Branch reported that it was 'centred principally upon the contacting of sympathisers especially among officers in the Armed Forces' and talk had 'reached the stage that a military *coup d'état* is feasible'. Members welcomed a German invasion and contemplated actions to bring this about. Churchill helped feed such ideas, warning the Cabinet that 20,000 German parachutists were ready to land on the east coast. Given his wish to cleanse Britain of Jews, it was not unreasonable for MI5 to suspect Ramsay of being willing to co-operate with the Germans, though the evidence suggests he was an eccentric patriot, to whom the concept of treason was anathema. Most Blackshirts were unwilling to assist the enemy, though some contemplated overthrowing the government and instigating peace terms with the Nazis. Ramsay fell into this latter category and so did Mosley.

Marjorie Amor (aka Mrs Marjorie Mackie) had joined the Right Club in August at the instigation of MI5's Maxwell Knight. Assistant secretary of the Christian Defence Movement, she had already met the Ramsays during their crusade to rescue Christendom in Soviet Russia. She asked Ramsay if, in the event of a revolution, she should follow Mosley. He said, 'Certainly not. Before such a situation arises I shall be in touch with all the members and you will then be told who is to be your leader.' Mrs Ramsay said Mosley had tried 'to get Jock to join in with him' and 'he had promised him Scotland'. Special Branch said members felt that 'if a leader should step forward the movement would make rapid headway. Naturally, the name of the Duke of Windsor is mooted by some ... but little hope is felt that he would lend himself to such an intrigue.' When Amor asked what she could do to help, Ramsay suggested she get a job in censorship because he wanted a contact there. Twelve days later Knight found her a job in censorship.

Ramsay considered Mosley 'a near Bolshevik' and Mosley considered him to be 'mentally unbalanced about the Jews'. Ramsay oscillated between a wild extremism, which sanctioned the use of force against Jews, and a rigid constitutionalism with warnings to followers not to use illegal methods. Brian Donovan said he would not think much of any conspiracy in which Ramsay was a prime mover since he was just a Jew hater and disliked Donovan because he had once been a Mason.

Knight claimed the Club had contacts in foreign embassies, which were used to communicate with Germany by means of diplomatic bags. Mrs Amor gathered from Wolkoff that Molly Stanford was in coded correspondence with Margaret Bothamley in Germany, via an IFL member living in Brussels. They had contacts via Belgian embassy diplomats Jean Nieuwenhus and Comte Antoine de Laubespin, who became Minister for Foreign Affairs, and Guy Niermans, the Club's agent in Belgium. Wolkoff sent 'letters that she did not want to be seen' through the Belgian diplomatic bag. Special Branch claimed an NL meeting on 8 October discussed 'communicating with Germany' by way of Ireland, the nearest neutral country.

MI5 informed the Home Secretary that the NL advocated violence and that at a meeting with the BU T. St Barbe made a 'wild speech' that the King should abdicate and a ruling council be set up by the Duke of Windsor and General Ironside. Mosley welcomed its support, but feared its extremism.

Domvile introduced other right-wing activists to the Mosley/Ramsay efforts at collaboration. On 10 October he met Mosley, who encouraged the idea of co-operation. In the evening, he received a telephone call from Ramsay who wanted the BU, NL–Right Club, the Link and Information and Policy to come together. The idea was discussed at a productive meeting of Mosley, Hawkins and Domvile. Significantly Ramsay, though expected, failed to turn up but the group now included Lords Tavistock and Lymington, who were close to Peace Party circles, which included the historian Arthur Bryant.

The British Council for Christian Settlement in Europe held its first public meeting at Conway Hall. The *Dispatch* reported that 150 Britons met 'to bring peace to the world'. They 'praised Hitler. They reviled the British Government and ended by sending a resolution to Mr Chamberlain calling on him to start peace negotiations.' Beckett 'liked Hitler' and as an ex-serviceman was 'now a conscientious objector' who 'could not take part in this preposterous lunacy'. Ben Greene, whose Peace and Progressive Information Service was described as 'National Socialist Propaganda of a remarkably noxious kind', described British policy 'as one of bluff and treachery' and declared that Hitler 'had been justified in all he had done'. MI5 said Greene 'doesn't even think we shall win the war ... But he does think that our Government has taken the opportunity of the war to kill the trade union movement.' On 10 October Greene met Labour MP Richard Stokes, who expressed interest in the BCCSE and whose Peace Aims Group had its first meeting on 26 October.

There was 'almost universal anti-semitic feeling' in London and a widespread view in patriotic circles of Jews as a Fifth Column endangering the war effort. George Ward Price wrote in the *Mail* on 9 October that 'many enemy agents came here as refugees' and many of them 'are Jews ... Many of the German Jews, often themselves recent immigrants from Eastern Europe, were the worst of their kind. In this country the national character is strong enough to absorb the better Hebrew type; in Germany, the Jewish aliens formed a class-conscious, self-interested community, and the misdeeds of some brought down reprisals on the rest.'

Mosley's peace campaign did begin to find an audience. At the Stoll Theatre on 15 October, in front of 2,700 people, he condemned 'Jewish capitalists for starting a war in which Britons had no real interest'. Diana was 'astonished by the reception he got from the crowds who went to hear him'. At the end of his speech Mosley asked them 'to lift up their arms "for peace". A forest of arms goes up. All this was very different from what we had expected.' At the New Hippodrome, 2,000 people – three-quarters of whom gave him the Fascist salute – heard him attack War Minister Hore-Belisha as a 'Jewish warmonger'. Hecklers who shouted 'Down with Hitlerism' were ejected by stewards. *Der Stürmer* praised Mosley's efforts 'to save England from war. Until the very last day he fought against the catastrophic Jewish policy of the British Government. Mosley did not give up his struggle, even when Chamberlain and Churchill had already decided on war.'

Despite successful meetings MI5 believed Mosley had failed to capitalize on the public's weak support of government policy. Ministers were told he was 'not likely to take action at present which would expose himself to a prosecution'. Since his anti-war propaganda was harmless, they decided prosecution of peace campaigners would do more harm than good.

Following the success of German tanks in Poland, Ironside wanted Major-General Fuller as his deputy. When Hore-Belisha put the case for his employment to the Cabinet on 19 October he referred to his 'particular qualifications for work in connection with mechanised formations'. He also acknowledged the objections to employing Fuller – his antagonistic character and BU membership. Ironside hoped an undertaking to keep him firmly under his command would overcome any objections but Ministers said his political views outweighed his professional qualities and rejected his appointment.

There were continuous meetings of the Fascist fringe. On 18 October

Domvile, Beckett and Finlay met Gordon-Canning at the Lansdowne Club to discuss the BCCSE. Three days later Domvile discussed with Fuller creating a newspaper. On the 26th Domvile attended 'Mosley's meeting'. Nine people were present, representing five constituencies: Mosley and Hawkins (BU), Ramsay (NL/RC), Domvile and Laurie (Link), Hay and Lawton (Information and Policy), Tavistock and Lymington (New Pioneer and BPP). The BU, Link and NL were enthusiastic but the antipathy of BCCSE activists to Mosley was an obstacle.

There was relief when Eric Thomas was released on 26 October for lack of evidence. Detainees could appeal to the Advisory Committee, chaired by barrister Norman Birkett. MI5 controlled what the detainee was told and, although the Chairman could complain if the information was inadequate, he had no authority over its officers. From 'personal files', MI5 produced the 'Statement of the Case' for detention but, ignorant of the procedures, detainees had no warning of questions and were 'reduced to general denials, protests or grovelling'. Often the Committee based its assessment on the question: is the detainee a sound, reliable chap? Simpson suggests there was something 'appallingly British' about this. It was ironic that BU members were victims of a system which Mosley would have introduced to decide whether Jews were patriotic Englishmen or not.

Thomas was released after an appeal to the Home Secretary (he was detained again on 24 May 1940). Richard Bellamy claimed 'this proved to be of great significance, for it led to the BU's modest collaboration with other anti-war groups'. In fact, it had begun three weeks before his arrest. It did show Mosley, however, that collaboration required greater secrecy, particularly with regard to his own participation.

Berlin was kept informed about the Peace Party through Baron de Ropp, an agent for both MI6 and the Nazis. He told Alfred Rosenberg that certain 'English circles' wanted 'an early peace because of their concern for the Empire'. De Ropp suggested it 'would be necessary now to strengthen further these circles which had meanwhile increased in power'. On 23 October the German Minister at The Hague informed Berlin that 'around Lloyd George, the opposition to a war is even greater than elsewhere in England'. It would, however, 'be a mistake to believe that in spite of all his talk Lloyd George would support a peace that would leave the solution of the questions in the East and Southeast to Russia and us alone'. De Ropp wrote on 31 October that he 'agreed with Mosley on many points. Unfortunately, however, Mosley was of no consequence and therefore of no use to the "English party". He was not a personality and had moreover made too many mistakes in his personal life, also in respect to capitalism, to make it likely for him to acquire any significant following among the English people.'

On 1 November Rosenberg suggested to Hitler there was 'a strong England which is an important security factor and of cultural value, and a second unscrupulous one led by Jews. We had hoped to work with the first, but it wasn't our fault if the second had won.' He added that 'a strong personality could not stand in the way of Churchill even if Mosley also thought himself brave'. Hitler said 'that Mosley has shown himself to be brave. Something like a sense of blood has come to life in this Briton.' Rosenberg was employing one of Mosley's collaborators in Frankfurt. 'It's good to keep hold of all the threads.' The identity of this agent is not known.

In the *Spectator* on 3 November author Peter Fleming (brother of Ian) attacked 'the thin yellow line of pacificism' which had manifested itself among Bloomsbury intellectuals. He abused Mosley as leader of the right wing of the 'Stop-the-War Front': 'His shoddy claque is weak and too discredited to get or deserve a hearing.' It was led by politicians, 'either dim or formerly distinguished; by people who habitually court those politicians, by some rich women; by bores'. It had been the Russian occupation of Poland 'which swung Bloomsbury into the Stop-the-War Front like a great wave of used bathwater'.

Mosley found time to see Baba, who was still in thrall to him but considered his attitude 'quite dreadful; you can't make him admit Germany is to blame'. Fruity focused on Mosley as the cause of their marriage problems. 'I sincerely hope and trust that you are not seeing anything [underlined eight times] of Tom Mosley.' In fact, she was seeing more of Lord Halifax, who often stayed at her Jacobean house in Little Compton, close to the PM's weekend residence of Chequers.

During November BU meetings continued but only Mosley had big audiences. There were 2,000 at Bethnal Green, though all but a few hundred were BU members. Mosley claimed in conspiratorial tones that war had not been declared on the Soviet Union because 'Russian communism had long been controlled by the same force that controlled British capitalism – namely International Jewish Finance'. Resurrecting the Jewish–Bolshevik bogey helped to bring in recruits from traditional constituencies.

On 8 November Mosley and Domvile presided over a third secret meeting. Mosley read out a long statement relating to the BU internee Eric Thomas. There was a shift in emphasis, with the presence of Lord Lymington and the introduction of associates of Ramsay, including Aubrey Lees. Domvile said Lees, who talked about alleged Jewish atrocities in Palestine, was on extended leave because 'he knows too much'. Home Office reports state that Lees made 'no secret of his great admiration for the Nazi regime' and criticized the government for 'its failure to get rid of the Jewish menace'. Because he attended these meetings, Lees was accused of being a BU member and was interned.

Much of the information on these Mosley–Ramsay discussions was derived from Special Branch and Knight's agents, who were identified in the internment files of Lees and John Beckett. Lees was told by the Advisory Committee that

James Hughes ('P. G. Taylor') was 'an intelligence agent'. He knew Hughes, who was employed by Ramsay as his representative, to be an agent and asked him, 'By the way, aren't you a Home Office agent, or expert, or something?' Hughes replied, 'I was.' As a leading BU official, Hughes had access to meetings which Special Branch alleged were dominated by revolutionary rhetoric. He was not, however, according to Beckett, a reliable witness. 'Taylor' 'came to see me and told me a long story about his own illegal activities, of which I did not believe a word, and he then told me a long story about Mosley's illegal activities, of which I did not believe a word either, and then he leaned forward to me and said: "I hope you are doing something of the sort, what are you doing?" He is a man I have suspected for a long time of being some kind of agent.'

Mosley complained in *Action* about the harsh treatment to which Thomas had been subjected. In response to threats of legal action, on 18 November MI5 informed the Home Secretary that he could 'rest assured that all interrogations undertaken by the department are conducted in a manner to which no possible exception can be taken'. In fact, MI5 used techniques to break down an internee's resolve. A pamphlet, 'It Might Have Happened to You!', claimed they had been housed in windowless cells, made to observe total silence and kept in solitary confinement. In early December internees at Latchmere House were isolated and subjected to 'continuous third-degree questioning'. The authors referred to the case of a suspected agent, Peter Whinfield, son of Muriel Whinfield (herself later detained) and Lieutenant-Colonel H. C. Whinfield, friends of Mosley and BU members. Peter travelled extensively in Europe and was in Austria at the time of the *Anschluss*. MI5 said he had been in contact with espionage agents Peter and Lisa Kruger, and was described as 'a strictly pro-German man who was working directly for the Nazis'. He was arrested and described in a list supplied to Churchill, as one who 'tried to emulate Lord Haw Haw'.

Domvile was busy on Mosley's behalf seeing associates in an attempt to create a peace front. On 12 November he saw Fuller, who told him 'Ironside is with us'. As Thurlow notes, 'It is not surprising that MI5 viewed Ironside's possible connections with some alarm.' Fuller's diary reveals his regular meetings with the Duke of Alba, the Spanish ambassador, later denounced by Churchill as a suspect person. MI5 was tapping Fuller's telephone and keeping track of his visits to the Mosleys.

Meetings of the Mosley–Ramsay–Domvile group on 22 November and 6 December were concerned with the 'Menace to Freedom'. Ramsay announced on 23 November that he had had 'personal evidence only yesterday of the methods whereby people in responsible positions may be supplied with bogus information purporting to be evidence'. At the second meeting he said the internment procedure – with 'no judge, no jury, no witnesses – was like the Star Chamber'. The meeting was expanded with the presence of Right Club members and, for the first time, Lady Redesdale. Tavistock and Lymington accompanied the Earl of Mar, Scotland's leading earl, who donated money to Mosley's peace campaign in appreciation of 'your ceaseless and strenuous work to protect Britain from the chaos and destruction that threaten to develop from various forces and to rage with utterly uncontrollable force if the flames of European War are not stamped out'. Mosley was described as 'the greatest political leader in the world', which Domvile felt was 'going a bit far!' P. G. Taylor sent a report on the meeting to Special Branch.

On 1 December Mosley had been seen by Richard Stokes, who had brought together a group of fellow Labour MPs to oppose the war, providing a link with the ILPers James Maxton, George Buchanan and John McGovern. McGovern was an ally and co-ordinated his efforts with Scanlon and Beckett, who knew he was being followed and used techniques to escape detection.

The meetings were increasingly dominated by Mosley, which may explain Ramsay's decision to withdraw. When Mrs Amor met Mrs Ramsay and was introduced to Anna Wolkoff, she reported that Anna 'had a superstitious nature and an interest in spiritualism, clairvoyance, astrology and anything to do with the occult'. MI5 played on this and the fact that she was 'very poor'. Mrs Amor became a leading figure within the Right Club, whose activities were run by a ten-strong mainly female inner circle, which included Molly Stanford, Christabel Nicholson, Wolkoff and a new member, racing driver and BU member Fay Taylour. Wolkoff acted as organizing secretary and Ramsay's aide-de-camp, a role increasingly assumed by Mrs Amor.

Taylour was interned in Holloway, along with Mrs Amor, who claimed to be the RC's 'Secretary, Founder and Organiser'. She was at some level an agent provocateur. She told Taylour of 'top secret' plans to take over radio stations, newspapers and the government. Taylour laughed 'at the thought of fat, well-heeled, coffee drinking women marching on government positions'. According to MI5, Wolkoff told Mrs Amor she looked forward to the Germans' triumphal march through London and promised her a seat of honour next to Himmler. She boasted that when they controlled the country she would be its 'Julius Streicher'. Mrs Nicholson cautioned the Advisory Committee that Anna 'was always full of wild statements and one did not really believe more than 25 per cent of anything she said'.

Wolkoff's hatred of the Jews found an outlet in a 'sticky-back' campaign to 'educate the public sufficiently to maintain the atmosphere in which the "phoney war" might be converted into an honourable negotiated peace'. By publicizing German radio stations, the sticky-backs were considered 'prejudicial to the efficient prosecution of the war'. BU chalk squads were active, targeting 'refu-Jews', who 'excited anti-Semitic feeling where, prior to their getting asylum in this country, it did not exist at all'. Britain would 'shortly have British Tommies at the front while alien Jews take their jobs at home'. The Soviet attack on Finland on 30 November made possible the converting of the anti-war crusade into an anti-Stalin crusade.

On 8 December 1939 Bill Allen was briefly interned at Brixton, a worrying moment for Mosley, given their quarrel. In fact, Allen was contemptuous of the security officials and told them little. He was allowed to join his regiment in East Africa, though colleagues were aware he had been interviewed by security. David Smiley knew Allen as a member of Mission 101 in Khartoum, specializing in guerrilla operations. 'Extremely intelligent, well travelled, an expert in a number of strange languages, he had a dry sense of humour and was a most entertaining companion.' Allen later took part in cloak-and-dagger operations with the Special Operations Executive, serving as an Information Officer in Beirut and Iraq.

A lunch held at Commandant Mary Allen's Club, the Ladies' Carlton, on 11 December endorsed Mosley as leader of the Fascist fringe. Lady Mosley, Mrs Elam and Mrs Huth Jackson (whose Ladbroke Grove home was the venue for future meetings) were among those present. Allen openly called for a negotiated peace. At the end of lunch the audience 'drank a toast to the Leader' which, said Domvile, 'made the eyes of all the old bitches round the room stick out like prawns'.

Seven days later, as part of the investigation of Peter Whinfield, Special Branch raided Mrs Elam's flat and the London and Provincial Anti-Vivisection Society. They found the list of officials to assume control in the event of Mosley's arrest, together with a letter stating Mrs Elam 'had his full confidence, and was entitled to do what she thought fit in the interest of the movement on her own responsibility'. This was considered sinister by MI5, who were 'not worried so much about the propaganda, but were looking for an underground organisation which they thought existed'. They were also concerned about potential leaks.

On 19 December Goebbels recorded that he had received a 'long report on the secret session of the English Parliament. I shall have this broadcast by the clandestine radio stations.' There had been a secret session of the Commons six days before and Ramsay was suspected of reporting it to the enemy, an action which constituted treason. The authorities believed he had assisted the 'Loch Lomond Wireless', a German station.

MI5's conspiratorial view gained the upper hand in Whitehall, where officials doubted they could restrain a Service which put security above justice. Communist Jenifer Hart was private secretary to Sir Alexander Maxwell, the Home Office Permanent Under-Secretary of State, and oversaw the issuing of telephone and mail interception warrants. Maxwell did not want to 'restrict freedom of thought however unpleasant the thought, or generally freedom of speech, unless this resulted in obnoxious actions or disorder'. Hart said it was 'not always easy to make these distinctions, particularly when deciding what to do about the activities of fascists', but Maxwell and the Home Secretary were 'the personification of the [then] Home Office tradition that civil liberties should be restricted as little as possible and only then as a result of urgent administrative necessity'. Sir John Anderson resisted interning Fascists 'until the pressure of events forced him to accept their necessity'.

At Christmas the Advisory Committee Chairman, Sir Norman Birkett, was weary of resuming his 'thankless task. I say thankless because MI5 want everybody interned, whilst I cannot bring myself to send some simple German girl for years of detention, when I am quite satisfied that she has been in the country in some household for years and is not the slightest danger to anybody . . . I want to keep some small element of Justice alive in a world in which we are supposed to be fighting for it.'

The Mosleys spent Christmas at Wootton. Irene was appalled by Diana's 'pro-German attitude'. On Boxing Day they listened to Lord Haw Haw attacking the British government. Irene told the children he was William Joyce, until recently their father's chief propagandist. There were rows over money. The Official Solicitor now objected to the children's trust money being used for Wootton, thus freeing Mosley's income for the BU. Mosley wanted Irene to bear the cost but she declined and with no one willing to pay, Wootton had to be given up. Mosley moved to Dolphin Square and took two adjacent flats on the seventh floor of Hood House – almost next door to MI5's Maxwell Knight.

With a bullet lodged in her head, Hitler arranged for Unity to be moved to neutral Switzerland, where her mother and sister Deboarah (Duchess of Devonshire) travelled in January 1940 to fetch her home. Hitler deeply regretted her fate: 'She lost her nerve, just when, for the first time, I could really have used her.' Her sister found her desperately ill: 'She could not walk, talked with difficulty and was a changed personality . . . she was a stranger.' MI5's Guy Liddell insisted Unity and her entourage – 'known Nazi supporters' – be searched on arrival, since 'we had no evidence to support the press allegations that she was in a serious state of health and it might well be that she was brought in on a stretcher in order to avoid publicity and unpleasantness to her family'. He was furious when the Home Secretary stopped the search. On 8 January he received a report that 'there were no signs of a bullet wound' and warned that failure to imprison Unity would suggest she was receiving preferential treatment because she was a peer's daughter. She was placed under the care of Professor Cairns, neurosurgeon at the Nuffield Hospital in Oxford. She learnt to walk again but never fully recovered and was reduced to a childlike state. Her mother devoted herself to Unity and looked after her until, in 1948, the bullet moved position and she died aged thirty-four.

*

On 5 January 1940 anti-Semites successfully dislodged Leslie Hore-Belisha, the Minister for War, who advocated an aggressive campaign against Germany. On the previous day Lord Halifax told the PM Hore-Belisha 'would have a bad effect on the neutrals both because HB was a Jew and because his methods would let down British prestige'. Chamberlain asked for the Minister's resignation because 'there was a prejudice against him'. The PM had been under pressure from Buckingham Palace and the military, particularly General Ironside, who had referred to 'Horeb Elisha'. Duff Cooper had warned the Minister the military 'might try to make it hard for him as a Jew'. His criticisms of the BEF in France angered the War Office, even though they proved to be correct. Reports suggested rumours about him originated with Ironside's friend Fuller.

Newnham's editorial in *Truth*, 'Belisha is No Loss', was openly anti-Semitic. Using information collated by the BU, it listed his bankrupt business ventures, with particular stress on his Jewish colleagues. This was distributed by Ramsay to the MPs who heard Hore-Belisha's resignation speech. *Action* celebrated the resignation of 'this little Jew'. Mosley later wrote 'it was a personal sorrow to me' that the BU 'played a part in that assault, as years before I had much liked him, but it would have been a denial of public duty to prevent it'. Perhaps as a result of this campaign, Mrs Amor reported on 17 January that Ramsay was 'being urged by the leading members of the Right Club to get in touch with General Ironside'.

On 17 January Mosley and Domvile met at Hawkins's flat with Link and NL members for negotiations. Under Mosley's spell and, despite denials that he was connected to the BU, six days later Domvile was admitted into its inner circle. His articles in *Action* (between December 1939 and March 1940), under the pen-name 'Canute', show him to be anti-Semitic, pro-Mosley and pro-Nazi. He wrote on 18 January that 'Hitler did not want war, there was no reason why he should take the initiative in starting the mass murder of his young people, by hurling them against a wall of steel and concrete'.

Domvile was aware of MI5 interest but had no inkling that the 'nice young man called Court' visiting him was Knight's agent, Harald Kurtz. Aware that informers were active, Mosley concealed the links between himself, Ramsay and others. A decision was made to confuse MI5 by having Mosley and Ramsay not meet together, but instead use go-betweens such as Aubrey Lees.

Mosley made it known that Gordon-Canning, now Lord Tavistock's assistant, had not, in fact, left the BU. He was with his ailing wife, MI5 discovered, on the French Riviera, where he met James Strachey Barnes, who was behind peace movements in Italy. In *Action* Tavistock said the government was responsible for the war. He came to prominence after obtaining peace proposals from Henning Thomson, Secretary to the German Legation in Dublin. These 'official' terms (previously stated by Hitler in a Reichstag speech) offered an independent Poland and Czechoslovakia, a plebiscite in Austria, a new League of Nations and general disarmament, in return for Germany regaining former colonies and the Jews being given a national home. Tavistock conveyed the proposals to Lord Darnley, who took them to Foreign Secretary Halifax on 19 January. When Tavistock was interviewed the Foreign Office's Alex Cadogan described the proposals as 'absolute bilge – fraudulent propaganda' from pacifists and halfwits. 'If the Germans want to say anything to us, they won't use this drain for their communication.'

At Allied War Committee headquarters the Duke of Windsor compiled reports for Ironside on the poor state of French defences. He was prohibited from going near the front, because General Alan Brooke feared he might 'stage a kind of "come back" with the troops out here'. Without advising the Palace, the Duke flew secretly to London and on 18 January reported to Ironside, met Churchill and persuaded the military to lift the ban on visiting the front. He also tried to influence the government into opening up communications with the Nazis to discuss a swift end to the war. The Duke had a meeting with Ironside's friend Fuller, who recorded the event in his diary but not the purpose of the discussion.

Edward also met Beaverbrook at the home of the Duke's go-between to the Palace, Walter Monckton, who realized Edward's 'idea of himself as the leader of an international "Peace Movement"' and 'rival leader to his brother, had never left his mind'. Monckton was disturbed by what he heard and disclosed to the Foreign Office's Charles Peake that Beaverbrook and the Duke had been 'in agreement that the war should be ended at once by a peace offer to Germany'. Peake told Harold Nicolson that Edward had spoken about 'the inevitable collapse of France' and that 'he would return to England and conduct a movement for peace with Germany'. Beaverbrook had replied, 'Go ahead, Sir, and I shall back you.' Monckton warned the Duke 'he had been speaking high treason' and reminded him that if he returned to Britain 'he would be liable to UK income tax'. This, apparently, 'made the little man blench and he declared with great determination that the whole thing was off'.

Ironside's son claims his father 'determined that the Duke was a serious security leak. He was giving the Duchess a great deal of information that was classified in the matter of the defences of France and Belgium. She in turn was passing this information on to extremely dangerous enemy-connected people over dinner tables in Paris. As a result, the information made its way into German hands.' On 26 January Cadogan reported that 'secret documents were communicated . . . to the German Government! I can trust no-one.' On the following day the German ambassador to Holland, Count von Zech-Burkersroda, reported to Berlin information gleaned from his meeting with the Duke's adviser Charles Bedaux. There was 'something like the beginning of a Fronde forming around W'. MI5 feared this peace front might include Mosley.

There was little direct evidence of illegal activity by the BU at this time. Hinsley and Simkins list ten minor infringements of the Defence Regulations by members of the BU during the war. However, on 8 January a naturalized Belgian farmer and BU officer in Exmouth, Claude Duvivier, was arrested (there was no suggestion of espionage). In a letter to a colleague, William Crowle, he wrote that his heart went 'out to those men on the *Graf Spee* – heroes fighting for the cause, every one of them'. A former dockyard worker, Crowle supplied information on naval shipping to Duvivier, who planned to send it to *Action* to reveal 'facts about Churchill and British ships which had been kept from the public'. MI5 learnt that before the trial, Duvivier wrote a letter to BU Assistant Director Donovan, complaining about his arrest and the confiscation of his documents.

Fascists had not been harassed by the authorities, however, with the Crowle/Duvivier case and detention of Peter Whinfield, and on 24 January SB officers, accompanied by MI5 officer Francis Aikin-Sneath, raided BU headquarters to obtain the letter to Donovan. Responsible for monitoring the BU, Aikin-Sneath was 'appalled by the rise of Nazism, and progressively adopted the view that Christianity was the riposte to it'. He believed Mosley had been financed by Mussolini and Hitler but the intelligence was 'vague and sketchy'.

Mosley was not surprised by the raid and assumed they were investigating Whinfield's 'gadding about the Continent'. With 'an attitude of disarming frankness', he explained that he had been 'awaiting the opportunity of talking to the authorities'. He had met Whinfield at the Elams' with others including Lord Cottenham (an MI5 officer) and Dr Kruger, an anti-Semitic author. After the letter (which was not significant) had been dealt with, Aikin-Sneath suggested some BU members had 'an almost unbalanced admiration of everything German. Did he approve of this?' Mosley offered a list of those expelled on those grounds and added that he had forbidden his wife to contact Unity, to forestall accusations of pro-Nazi sympathies. Did he think the Germans might use pro-Nazi members for their own purposes? He thought no but admitted 'an enemy agent would find the BU a good cover'. He added, 'I do not want the Germans to win. I want peace now ... After the politicians reduce England and the Empire to a dung heap, they are not going to get me to take over. I shall retire from politics.'

When asked about the BPP, Mosley gave an unflattering portrait of its leading figures – Tavistock was 'woolly headed'; Beckett was 'a crook'; and Ben Greene was 'not very intelligent'. MI5 reported that Mosley was 'immensely vain, a bad judge of men, extremely urbane and cunning, and entirely lacking in sincerity. His chief handicap is probably his excessive vanity, which must make it difficult for him to take an objective view of any situation. It also makes it impossible for him to tolerate any other outstanding personality in his entour-age.' Hawkins was 'a complete nonentity . . . lacking in intelligence'; Thomson was less stupid but dim.

There was no evidence that either Cowle or Duvivier, who was sentenced by Exeter magistrates on 29 January to six months' imprisonment, were acting on Mosley's orders. However, an agent's report of a closed meeting of officials on 30 January shook MI5. Donovan urged the need for 'militancy in London' with the aim of connecting in the public's mind 'Mosley and Peace', and Jewry with 'war and suffering'. Donovan stressed the BU was a revolutionary movement and revolution was on the way, at which point Mosley entered and claimed 'our time is approaching . . . reward and victory are in sight'. It was decided to contest by-elections for the publicity. More women would be involved in the peace campaign, which would be concentrated in the East End. 'They knew what they wanted and knew what would happen but they must not talk – everyone present would know what he meant. They must bring in new members – not necessarily a large number but a moderate number of reliable men and women who would take their place in the ranks when the time came for the sweep forward, which the movement would make, as their brother parties in other countries had made when their hour of destiny struck.' Underlying the speech, the agent reported, was a strong hint of a march to power by armed force.

'Mosley is making his presence felt,' Goebbels recorded on 25 January. 'If he goes ahead skilfully he will have several opportunities.' The BU was now seen as the English branch of the NSDAP by MI5 and 'not merely a party advocating an anti-war and anti-government policy'. It would 'assist the enemy in every way it can' and possessed 'a core of fanatics who would be prepared to take active steps to this end if the opportunity occurred'. MI5 may have had in mind Dr Tester, but he had escaped their net and was now working on behalf of German interests in the Mediterranean. He kept one step ahead of the authorities but still sent Mosley 'the documentary [proof] for my work and asked him to send me his instructions'.

MI5's assessment led to serious disagreements with a cautious Home Secre-tary. When Anderson recalled this period he said MI5 'had for months pressed him to deal with the fascists' but he had resisted the pressure. In a rebuff to MI5, between January and May he signed only twenty-eight detention orders.

On 7 February Mosley convened a meeting at 48 Ladbroke Grove, home of Mrs Huth Jackson and the office of the London and Southern Counties Anti-Vivisection Society. An SB mole said 'the proceedings were dominated by Mosley' and agreement was reached for the BU to contest by-elections at Silvertown and North-East Leeds. The group consisted entirely of Mosley enthusiasts (Ramsay did not attend) and was less of a coming together of the patriotic societies than a BU 'think-tank'.

Two days later *Truth* published a letter from Tavistock claiming peace was negotiable. On 13 February he invited the BCCSE and Mosley's circle to discuss the peace proposals and dealings with the PM. Domvile left with 'more hope than I had anticipated'. This was down to the Duke of Buccleuch, who was trying to persuade Downing Street officials of the advantages of a negotiated peace. He argued Britain would eventually have to sue for peace, so 'why not do so now, when comparatively little damage has been done and when there is still time to avert economic ruin?' As was the pattern, Domvile briefed the absent Mosley, who showed great interest in the meeting.

In February a new element entered the circle around Ramsay, which had a dramatic effect on the Right Club and, indirectly, Mosley. Barbara Allen, the American-born wife of Bill Allen's brother Sam, ran the American Club, where she met a young diplomat at the US embassy. The right-wing and anti-Semitic Tyler Kent had reported for duty in London the previous October after serving in Moscow. Kent was born in China. His father had been posted there as a member of the American Consular Service and Kent emulated him by joining the Diplomatic Service in 1934. Intelligence officer Malcolm Muggeridge described Kent, who was lionized by society ladies, as 'one of these intensely gentlemanly Americans who wear well-cut tailor-made suits, with waistcoat and watch-chain, drink wine instead of high-balls, and easily become furiously indignant'. As an isolationist, he attacked Roosevelt's foreign policy. US diplomats were 'taking part in the formation of hostile coalitions in Europe . . . which they had no mandate to do'.

Kent was illegally copying and storing at his flat hundreds of US embassy documents, dealing with 'Germany', 'Czechoslovakia', 'British Cabinet' and 'Halifax'. Others were requests from MI5 for US assistance in tracking down Nazi and Soviet agents, which disclosed the identities of operatives in Britain and America. The remainder were US Military and Naval Attaché reports on British forces, but the most interesting were copies of cables between President Roosevelt and the First Sea Lord, Churchill. Recently released files show that MI5 was in the dark about the diplomat's identity and displayed little interest in his activities.

On 21 February Barbara Allen introduced Kent to Anna Wolkoff. On the following day Wolkoff told Mrs Amor she had a contact at the Belgian embassy who could send letters to William Joyce through the diplomatic bag. Who suggested doing this is open to question, since Mrs Amor admitted she herself wanted to send a letter. Wolkoff was aware her friend had been associated (in fact, in an undercover role for Knight) with a Communist group and suspected she might be a Communist spy. A new MI5 agent recruit to the RC was Helene de Munck, who made periodic visits to her family in Belgium, still a neutral country. Described as a 'drug fiend' and an anti-Semite, she was asked by Wolkoff to carry a message to an RC agent in Brussels, enquiring about the progress of 'our work in Belgium'.

A curious aspect of the whole Kent/Wolkoff case is that Wolkoff met MI5's director-general at a dinner during the winter given by MI5 officer Mark Cottenham. Another odd aspect is that on 24 February Kent applied to the US Chargé d'Affaires in Germany for a transfer from London to Berlin but was turned down. Did he intend to take his documents with him? With this route closed, did he now seek an alternative channel?

Wolkoff visited Kent, who allowed her to see the copied cables, including those between Churchill and Roosevelt. MI5 was aware via MI8, the signals-gathering unit picking up radio traffic between Hans Georg von Mackensen, German ambassador in Rome, and Berlin, that the Churchill–Roosevelt correspondence was being leaked. When cryptanalysts decoded one message, it turned out to be a paraphrase of one such cable. MI5 agents in the RC, led by case officer Philip Brocklehurst, believed they had stumbled across a breach of national security.

The by-election at Silvertown, East London, was regarded as a fruitful area for the BU, even though it was a Labour stronghold. Mosley declared it would be 'the only chance the people have of expressing their will. British Union owes to the people the duty of giving them that chance.' On 23 February former boxing champion Tommy Moran received 151 votes against Labour's 14,343. With less than one-sixth of Harry Pollitt's vote for the Communists, it was proof that the BU had derisory support. Despite the setback, Mosley planned a 'monster' women's peace campaign. On 28 February at Holborn, his chief women's officer Anne Brock-Griggs, along with Commandant Allen and Olive Hawks, addressed the first large-scale BU indoor meeting organized entirely by women. The *Jewish Chronicle* noted the women 'adopted a more hysterical anti-Jewish attitude than did their men-folk'. A March Home Intelligence memo commented that Fascist propaganda was generally unsuccessful, but not so anti-Semitism, which was 'their only popular appeal'.

On 1 March Mosley addressed 500 people packed into the Criterion for a BU luncheon. It received wide publicity and was deemed a great success. Present were prominent 'fellow-travellers' of the extreme Right, including Lord Ronald Graham and Anna Wolkoff from the Right Club; the Domviles, Elams and the Fullers, Viscountess Downe, Lady Pearson, Commandant Allen and Mrs Huth Jackson, Aubrey Lees and Henry Williamson from the BU; the Link's Pitt-Rivers; Ben Greene from the BCCSE and SB's P. G. Taylor. Many respectable society figures were not worried about attending a public event at which Mosley said 'the real reason why the British Government had declared war on Germany and now refused to fight Russia [over Finland] was because

Britain was controlled by Jews and they desired to see the end of the present German Government so that they could resume their exploitation of the German people'. Goebbels, increasingly positive in his assessment of the BU leader, noted on 3 March, 'Mosley is doing fabulously again. If he keeps on like this he will get somewhere.'

Tavistock pursued his peace proposals and asked an emissary, Gerald Hamilton, to 'go to Ireland to continue negotiations which had begun quite favourably'. He tried to make the journey with a party of Irish nuns but 'thanks to the venality of a decoding clerk in the neutral Embassy which had been so helpful to me, my plan was betrayed and so never reached Ireland on that occasion'. However, he later admitted that 'a neutral embassy was kind enough to allow me to use their bag'. The subsequent arrest in Dublin of an IRA man, Stephen Held, uncovered a spy ring which led to an Englishman named Brandy, who had 'collaborated with the provocateur Hamilton'.

The bright young thing Brian Howard asked Hamilton, 'Why do you persist in remaining so "Right" when all your friends are "Left"?' Section D records reveal the 'dangerous' Hamilton was in touch with Guy Burgess, who was attached to MI6 as part of the radio propaganda war. Burgess, who reported his findings to Moscow, was a member of an anti-Fascist private spy network run by Lord Rothschild, who had just joined MI5. Burgess used his homosexual and Comintern contacts to penetrate Fascist groups and keep surveillance on the BU. Edmund Warburton met Burgess at a mecca for left-wing intellectuals in Bloomsbury, The Book. He realized he 'was being run by some government agency, and not Special Branch'.

Hitler had stated that 'we shall have friends who will help us in all the enemy countries'. MI5 claimed 'if there were any party designed to play this part in the United Kingdom it was Mosley's BU'. It began compiling a 'Suspect List' of pro-Fascists who might assist the Nazis in the event of invasion. To penetrate the groups it used 'a well-tried pre-war agent who had for many years given good inside information about the British Union and was in touch with a number of people of British and German origin who held Fascist views'.

It was for Knight's agent to be 'placed at the disposal of Lord Rothschild in order to attempt to penetrate "fifth column" circles in this country'. The enquiry gradually spread until 'the agent was directly or indirectly in contact with some *five hundred Fascist-minded people* – not all of British origin – through a number of unconscious sub-agents'. 'Roberts' acted as an agent of the Gestapo, whose 'business is to check up on the reliability of certain people who the Germans think might be ready to assist them in time of invasion'.

Brian Howard was party to the invasion list operation as an outside 'contact' in 'strictest mufti'. His biographer notes 'it was not surprising that [MI5] wished to make use of Brian's extensive knowledge of pro-Nazi personalities'. Also 'seeking out traitors' was John Bingham, who had been disgusted by the events at Olympia. On 18 April he enlisted Collin Brooks, who thought 'it was rather like a cheap detective novel'. The use of agent provocateur methods against Mosleyites drew Home Office criticism. MI5 retorted that 'if these methods cannot be employed to investigate the Fifth Column field we cannot be responsible for its investigation at all'.

On 29 February a meeting of the BCCSE, Link, Lords Mar, Arnold, Lymington and Darnley, and Richard Stokes of the Peace Aims Group, discussed Tavistock's peace proposals, which were published in the *Telegraph* on 1 March. Goebbels noted that 'London is putting peace feelers out but we are responding strongly against them. These decaying plutocrats are as stupid as they are insolent.' They had Beaverbrook's support who, a Foreign Office official noted on 11 March, was 'under the impression that there is a widespread feeling in this country in favour of a negotiated peace provided there were some change of government in Germany'. He was said to be 'acting in conjunction with certain other big money interests'.

The sense of panic over the war was reported to Washington by the State Department's Sumner Welles. When at Buckingham Palace on 11 March Welles mentioned the Soviet Ivan Maisky, the King misheard the name as Mosley. Wrongly assuming he was privy to certain transatlantic arrangements, the King reminded Welles – much to his puzzlement – of 'our agreement that the United States could do something – if the Mosleys don't take over'. This is the first indication that the threat of Mosley was used as a bargaining chip – principally by Churchill – in negotiations with President Roosevelt.

Mosley was tied up with the Leeds by-election and could not attend all the meetings, though he was at Ladbroke Grove on 13 March. Developing a new theme which worried MI5, he stated Lloyd George would have to take over and head a 'peace' government. When questioned about the meetings, Aubrey Lees refused to discuss their object. Two days later an SB agent reported on a private meeting addressed by Mosley. 'His expressed determination to defeat "the enemy" [the Jew] if not by the ballot box then by "other and more drastic means"' was cheered to the echo. He added that 'if we had ideas, which we no doubt all had, about the ultimate future, it did not do to tell our enemies about the more unpleasant things which were liable to happen to them'. Implicit was 'the suggestion of armed revolution and pogroms'. Special Branch claimed it had reliable reports of a closed Right Club meeting where Ramsay ended his anti-Semitic diatribe with the assertion that 'the British people should rid themselves of this menace [the Jews], and if one method did not work, another should be tried . . . any means, whatever they were, would be used if necessary'.

Mosley claimed in March that BU membership was 'greater than that of the corresponding month in any year since the movement's inception'. Home Office figures put it at 9,000, which undermines Mosley's assertion. Certainly it had no electoral support. In North-East Leeds the BU only polled 722 votes against the Conservatives' 23,882. The disastrous result may have been why Mosley resorted to wild rhetoric.

MI5 had no evidence of contacts with Germany 'of a kind that justified alarm' but with the military situation deteriorating, the secret meetings were now seen in a sinister light. Mosley and Ramsay used them to discuss forming 'a vast revolutionary organisation, in which they would all collaborate' and to 'make preparations for a fascist *coup d'état*'. Collaboration was hindered by the failure to agree on a leader.

That the Right Club was viewed as a threat by MI5 was known to Anna Wolkoff, who wrote to Vernon Kell, protesting about the accusation. She found it difficult to believe her anti-Jewish propaganda could be construed as anti-government and asked Kell for advice. The Club had shrunk to a small group that was, as Thurlow put it, 'farcical rather than sinister'. It consisted of 'Ramsay, Kent, five women with eccentric views and three MI5 "moles"'. Kell suggested Wolkoff meet Maxwell Knight at the War Office. On 19 March she admitted using sticky-backs but asked if it was an offence to hold anti-Jewish views. Mrs Amor reported that Wolkoff was spending 'a great deal of time with this man from the American embassy'. Wolkoff said he was 'pro-German' and, from what Amor had gleaned, was engaged in 'disseminating defeatist and anti-Allied propaganda'. It was not until 29 March that he was identified as Tyler Kent.

Mosley finally fell out with Gordon-Canning – who, Special Branch reported on 27 March, was suing him for £9,000 – for reasons not known. Mosley no longer had a conduit at the heart of the BCCSE, which on 3 April held a large public meeting at the Kingsway Hall on the 'Tavistock Peace Plan'. Chaired by John Beckett, Hugh Ross Williamson gave 'an extraordinary tirade' against Churchill, while John McGovern delivered 'a fulsome speech in praise of Hitler and what he had done for the working-classes'. This ILP faction had lost Beaverbrook's backing, who ten days before had told Monckton that he was giving up the peace campaign. Of the 1,500 people present half were said to belong to the Peace Pledge Union. MI5 reported that the BU was trying to infiltrate it.

On the day (9 April 1940) Hitler's forces invaded Scandinavia Knight moved against Wolkoff in an agent provocateur operation. Norway's collapse led to a belief that it had been brought about by 'quislings'. Journalists picked up on the Norwegian name of Quisling, which became a byword for traitor, as the press stoked up the Fifth Column scare. The concept had been invented during the Spanish Civil War. Nationalists argued that Catholics, trapped by Republican-controlled Madrid, had provoked internal disorder behind the lines, leading to the collapse of defences. The Madrid Fifth Column, however, was just as much a myth as the alleged role of Vidkun Quisling. It was a decade before it was established that he had not played an active role in Hitler's attack on Scandinavia. The fear whipped up by the press, however, put pressure on MI5 to block off potential allies for the Nazis in the event of an invasion.

MI5 thought most Fascists were 'true patriots', who believed Britain was 'controlled by Jewish financiers who had plunged half the world into war for their private gain'. They were convinced 'the best interests of their country required its liberation by any means . . . from its Jew masters'. If helping the Nazis was the 'best method of establishing National Socialism in Britain, then it was the duty of every patriot to collaborate with the Nazis who would free Britain from her alien chains'. There were concerns about the broadcasts of Lord Haw Haw and attempts to orchestrate a Fifth Column, but the crude propaganda and Joyce-inspired rumours made little impact and became the object of ridicule. Attention turned to the spate of leaks of classified information.

Ironside noted that knowledge of plans for an Allied force to land at Narvik in Norway was widespread among military attachés. 'You cannot keep anything secret with so many people with a finger in the pie.' MI5, however, believed the Nazis learnt of the operation's plans through Wolkoff's Belgian contact. In fact, the source was B-Dienst, the cryptanalytic agency, which deciphered British naval messages outlining a plan to mine the entrance to Narvik. Using the information for deception, a German decoy force put out to sea and was spotted on 7 April by the British, who ordered their fleet to head for Narvik. 'As they raced away from where the action was, the German transports completed their voyage undisturbed and landed their occupation troops without a hitch.' Churchill's admission that the navy had been 'completely outwitted' led to paranoid fears that a Fifth Column had leaked the plans.

On 9 April Wolkoff was asked by a naval officer in the Right Club, Lord Ronald Graham, to meet a friend. He introduced her to 'James Hughes', who asked if she would be 'prepared to do something that would really help in the cause of anti-semitism'. When she replied she would, Hughes enquired if she had 'ever sent anything to the Continent through a diplomatic bag'. Wolkoff said she could if it was important. Hughes handed her an envelope addressed to 'Herr W. B. Joyce, Rundfunkhaus, Berlin', containing 'some good anti-Jewish stuff'. Wolkoff believed the letter writer [probably Knight] was a friend of Joyce. She learnt during the afternoon from Ramsay that Hughes had three aliases, one of which was 'Cunningham', and that he was not to be trusted. Cunningham was working for MI2, a unit about which she was ignorant but whose remit was of significance. It was responsible for 'interpreting reports received from Scandinavia about German intentions' and and was 'privy to plans for British intervention in Norway'.

That evening Knight added to his roster of agents within the Club Joan Miller, a former employee of Elizabeth Arden, who was secretary to Lord Cottenham in MI5's transport section. Wolkoff happened to have a crush on the sixth Earl. Miller's account of her activities in the operation is fictitious. Wolkoff had sought a contact for the Club within MI5 and hoped a young secretary could be educated into 'our way of thinking', and Knight had responded. Wolkoff told her she had a letter she wanted to send to Joyce, about the line he should take in his broadcasts, but her normal channels were unavailable.

Miller passed Wolkoff on to de Munck, who falsely said she had 'a friend in the Romanian Legation', who could pass on the letter. Wolkoff had now done enough to be categorized as an 'enemy agent' within the provisions of the Official Secrets Act. On 11 April, using de Munck's typewriter, Wolkoff added a postscript (in German): 'It is now very important that we hear more about the Jews and Free Masons.' She specified Joyce acknowledge the letter's receipt by broadcasting a reference to 'Carlyle', Joyce's favourite writer.

Around 12 April Ramsay was introduced to Kent and browsed the Churchill–Roosevelt cables at his flat. He said they 'might be useful in his political activities'. Kent lent Wolkoff two telegrams, which revealed Churchill had arranged for the navy to give American shipping preferential treatment over the blockade. MI5 discovered that the German ambassador in Rome had access to this correspondence which, note Bearse and Read, 'was so secret that even when the messages reached the Foreign Office they were regarded as forgeries, until one of the tiny group of people in the know spotted them, recognized them as genuine, and raised the alarm'.

On 13 April MI5 watchers trailed Wolkoff to a White Russian émigré photographer, Eugene Smirnoff, a friend of her father's, who worked in the Censorship Department and collaborated closely with MI5. He photographed two Churchill–Roosevelt telegrams. The same day marked the establishment of the Right Club's new meeting place. The Parlour in Manson Mews, conveniently close to the Russian Tea Rooms. The flat had been rented by MI5 and was occupied by Mrs Amor. A Knight agent reported on 16 April that Wolkoff had obtained 'a great deal of information through Tyler Kent'. She told her RC colleagues – all MI5 agents – about a conversation on the Norwegian campaign between the US ambassador, Joseph Kennedy, and Lord Halifax.

While Diana celebrated the birth of her fourth son, Max, on 13 April 1940, Mosley was busy with BU affairs. Commandant Allen agreed to head the BU's Women's Section, after Anne Brock-Griggs was dismissed for 'inefficiency'. Allen wrote a weekly column in *Action*, which was unmistakably anti-Semitic and pro-German. With Diana resting at a Sutton nursing home, Mosley attended a Women's Peace meeting at Friends House, during which Allen delivered a ranting speech against a 'wrong and unjust' war. At the end of the month a second private luncheon at the Criterion restaurant was supported by a rich Mosleyite, Percy Thomas Lovely. The guests heard Mosley outline plans to build on the success of the women's peace campaign.

On 15 April Mosley held a conference of district officials at the Denison Hall, Vauxhall Bridge Road, to prepare for a May Day demonstration. Mosley, Special Branch reported, spoke about 'our brother parties' on the Continent and praised the success of the BU's copy of the Nazi street leadership plan. The agent observed that 'underlying all his remarks about the scheme was the hint that the BU was preparing without delay for any opportunity that might arise of a "march to power" by armed force'. A Home Office official wrote on the report that it seemed Mosley 'had abandoned constitutional methods of making progress, although he confined himself to dark hints'.

Two days later, in Ladbroke Grove, Mosley attended a meeting of the 'Mosley group'. Special Branch claimed the discussion centred on the formation of 'a vast secret revolutionary organisation', in which all would collaborate. A Home Office file on Commandant Allen refers to meetings in March, April and May, whose purpose was to plan collaboration and a coup.

On 19 April Conservative MPs met to consider the Fifth Column, increasing pressure on the government. Three days later Anderson submitted a report to the Cabinet recognizing the strong desire for action against those impeding the war effort. Rothermere told Collin Brooks 'there is a move to "get out" Ironside as being no good'. As fear grew within the Fascist fringe that they were going to be arrested, Mosley met with Fuller, even though he knew he was being monitored.

With the BU facing increased public hostility and in danger of being dismembered by the Defence Regulations, Mosley turned on its former allies. Raven Thomson 'proposed the audacious plan of launching a propaganda attack on the Nordic League people, accusing them of being Nazi traitors, and emphasising the movement's absolute loyalty to Britain and the Empire'. Attacks began on Aubrey Lees, in whose possession Special Branch found invitations to secret meetings. Mosley said Lees was 'certifiable' and accused the NL of being parasites who 'made the whole principled stand of the peace campaign look foolish'.

The climax of the peace campaign came at a May Day meeting at Victoria Park. Mosley's anti-Semitic outburst that the war would create 'a land fit for Hebrews to live in' was cheered by the 4,000-strong crowd. He said Britain could defend itself against a dominant Continental power but could not impose its will on one. If France held the Maginot Line, Germany would be forced to fight a defensive war and Britain could afford to sit across the Channel and allow the war to peter out. 'Behind minefields, navy and air force', Mosley wrote in *Action* on 9 May, 'would rest a people entirely united at the disposal of their nation. Therefore it is extremely unlikely that any such attack will be delivered.' In the event of invasion, every BU member 'would resist the foreign invader with all that is in us. However rotten the existing government, and however much we detested its policies, we would throw ourselves into the effort of a united nation until the foreigner was driven from our soil.' Victory could only be won by America or Russia intervening, but this would destroy the Empire.

The situation, wrote the Duke of Windsor, 'can't possibly go any better until we have purged ourselves of many of the old lot of politicians and much of our out-of-date system of government'. Goebbels noted on 4 May that 'even Lloyd George is being named as a successor'. Three days later, on the eve of the Commons debate on Norway, Lloyd George was asked by Nancy Astor to take a leading role, but he 'preferred to await his country's summons a little longer', as he 'expected to receive it as the peril grew'. Hitler described the English leaders as criminals. 'They could have had peace on the most agreeable of terms.' However, 'there are some people whom you can talk sense into only after you've knocked out their front teeth'.

On 3 May one of Knight's agents revealed that Ramsay – recently recorded as saying he would 'welcome a Civil War with shots in the streets' – had been told by P. G. Taylor that he, Wolkoff and Lord Ronald Graham were being investigated by MI5. On 8 May de Munck informed Knight that Wolkoff had heard from an RC member that Joyce had acknowledged receipt of her letter. It is unclear, however, whether he actually did so.

The military's Field Security Police reported that Ironside's car had been seen outside a house in Holland Park which, investigating officer Malcolm Muggeridge noted, belonged to persons of 'dubious political association'. This was possibly 17 Stanley Gardens, home of Dr Leigh Vaughan-Henry, who worked for the BBC. He was married to a German wife and mixed in anti-Semitic and pro-Nazi circles. There was a 'whispering campaign' against Ironside because of his rumoured Fascist associations, though Muggeridge thought the visits were 'personal rather than political'. Ironside's friend Fuller, who maintained his close ties to Mosley, lunched with the US military attaché General Lee, who reported to MI5 that Fuller was 'a very little, old, wizened-up man, who is bitter and outspoken against the War Office, the British Government, and the way the war is being conducted . . . but a lot of his ideas are all mixed up. He kept saying that the war need never have occurred.'

On 9 May Neville Chamberlain realized he might have to resign as PM. Approaches were made to Labour's Clement Attlee and Arthur Greenwood about whether they would serve in a coalition government. They consulted the national executive at the annual conference at Bournemouth, where Hugh Ross Williamson recalled talk was dominated by 'whether or not the Labour

Leaders had made the arrest and imprisonment of Mosley a condition of their entering Government. The general feeling was that they had – or at least, that they ought to.' That evening Hitler boarded his train, bound for the Western Front. On the following morning Operation Yellow began, with German tanks and airborne troops invading the Low Countries and France.

Ramsay claimed he had been about to see Chamberlain and show him the 'improper' correspondence between Churchill and Roosevelt he had seen at Tyler Kent's flat. However, he had failed to see him because on 10 May – at a time when Hitler had invaded the Low Countries and France was disintegrating – he went on a fortnight's holiday to Scotland before he had time to make copies. Back in London, according to Robert Bruce Lockhart, in seeking Labour support Churchill promised Attlee and Greenwood 'the Government will deal ruthlessly with the Fifth Column', which was equated with the BU. Not long before he had appeared as the champion of civil liberties. On 10 May Churchill replaced Chamberlain as Prime Minister.

On 10 May, too, the Chiefs of Staff accepted the Joint Intelligence Committee's view that the Nazis had a Fifth Column in place in the event of an invasion. In deferring to the military, the Home Secretary authorized the internment of all male enemy aliens in southern coastal areas. This draconian action had been influenced by Quisling's alleged activities in Norway and an anonymous letter from a German refugee (who turned out to be a crank), 'who warned of an imminent airborne invasion and sabotage attacks in the south-east'. During the day Churchill discreetly warned the Duke of Westminster not to take part in appeasement efforts. He left for Ireland. The Duke of Buccleuch, a friend of the Windsors and brother-in-law of the Duke of Gloucester, was removed from the post of Steward of the Royal Household for his part in the appeasement faction.

Beginning on 11 May, enemy aliens were interned. In agreement with the JIC, MI5 recommended the detention of 500 BU members, a move resisted by the Home Office, which was angry at attempts to bypass it. Another reason was that MI5's records were in a mess. Only recently had Cecil Liddell written to Chief Constables requesting additions to the list of BU officials which was accurate 'up to the end of last year'. The Home Secretary, Sir John Anderson, interviewed Irene Ravensdale and asked her if she had evidence that Mosley might betray his country. She had none but feared that if he felt a version of National Socialism was desirable for Britain 'he might do anything'.

On 12 May Mrs Amor ascertained that Kent, Wolkoff, her friend Enid Riddell and an Italian, 'Mr Macaroni', had dined together. MI5's suspicions of Kent were increased by a series of monitored telephone calls to the American embassy, which suggested he was Wolkoff's contact. Knight learnt that she had 'diplomatic material of a confidential nature'. On 16 May Mrs Amor reported that Wolkoff passed documents to Mr Macaroni. At the subsequent trial, MI5's de Muncke testified that she delivered an envelope – containing 'plans for the invasion of Norway' or 'an innocuous US press release' – from Wolkoff to his address at Cadogan Square. MI5 believed Wolkoff was a German agent, passing on sensitive information gathered from her contacts through the Right Club and the Russian Tea Rooms. However, there was no direct evidence for this assertion.

On 16 May Roosevelt received a telegram from his ambassador in Paris, William C. Bullitt, that France was about to be crushed. 'You should have in mind the hypothesis that, in order to escape from the ultimate consequences of absolute defeat, the British may install a government of Oswald Mosley . . . which would cooperate fully with Hitler. That would mean that the British navy would be against us.' He urged the President to ensure that the British fleet be moved to Canada. That day, Roosevelt cabled Churchill declining his request for the 'loan of forty or fifty of our older destroyers'. Tyler Kent showed the telegram (No. 872) to Wolkoff and a copy was later found in the possession of fellow RC member Christabel Nicholson. The matter was considered 'so secret' that her prosecution was 'out of the question'. She was detained but was acquitted when brought to trial in 1941, because the State Department would not allow the telegram to be used as evidence. A word-for-word translation, found among captured Berlin Foreign Ministry documents, had been forwarded by the Italians 'from an unimpeachable source' on 23 May 1940.

What is intriguing about telegram 872 is that MI5's Guy Liddell revealed in his diary that Roosevelt 'was proposing to give us 100 destroyers . . . He also proposed to give us a portion of his first-line aircraft . . . There is little room for doubt that Roosevelt would bring the whole country into the war now, if he possibly could.' Was the Roosevelt–Churchill correspondence a deception? The telegrams had been sent in 'Gray', a low-grade code which had been compromised. Roosevelt knew this and during the Abyssinian crisis had deliberately used it in a message to Rome, knowing it would be intercepted and passed on to Mussolini. Churchill and Roosevelt wanted the Axis powers to read their correspondence. The 'unimpeachable source' was not Wolkoff but Italian signals intelligence.

With the Low Countries overrun, there was a Fifth Column panic, as Mass Observation reported public morale at a low ebb. On 16 May MI5's Director-General saw Police Commissioner Sir Philip Game to plan for an operation against the Fascists. The US State Department's Harvey Klemmer discussed the threat with MI5 officers and produced estimates of the Fifth Column's size, which varied from 1,000 to 10,000. The JIC said Fifth Column activities 'might well play a dangerous part at the appropriate moment selected by the enemy. Indeed, the absence of sabotage up to date reinforces the view that such activities will only take place as part of a prearranged military plan.' The case against the BU was being 'worked up'. Mosley's safe had been 'rifled and a document has been obtained showing the whole scheme for setting up wireless masts in Germany'. Liddell was telephoned by the Home Office's Sir Ernest Holderness, who was preparing a memo on the BU. He was sympathetic to MI5 and Liddell offered the use of its officers to help him.

MI5 claimed the BU had been 'in the closest touch with the German Nazi leaders. Mosley, Raven Thomson, W. E. D. Allen, Major General Fuller, Gordon-Canning and other leaders were frequently in Germany'. BU members working abroad for the Germans included Edward Whitfield, who was in touch with two German espionage agents, Clement Brunning, Phillip Spranklin, and William Joyce. However, there was no evidence of contact since the war began. The Home Secretary was still against internment and repulsed demands to intern Fascist leaders.

MI5 wanted Mosley interned and used the Tyler Kent affair to increase the pressure. It began after midnight on 18 May with a telephone call to Herschel V. Johnson at the American embassy, requesting a meeting to discuss 'a delicate matter'. Maxwell Knight explained surveillance of the Right Club led them to Kent, who had been visited by a suspected Gestapo agent in October 1939, though he gave no reason why the embassy had not been informed. Nor could he explain why, having carried out their sting on 9 April, MI5 waited until now before making a move. The reality was that the evidence that Knight later gave the Americans was a concoction, a carefully contrived record which portrayed MI5 in the best possible light but which ignored the truth that its operation had been a litany of fantasy, incompetence and wish-fulfilment. Knight said the authorities would arrest Wolkoff on 20 May. Johnson approved ending Kent's diplomatic immunity and a search of his flat.

The Kent affair tipped the balance in MI5's favour and, against a backdrop of the military disaster in France, led inexorably to the internment of the Fascists. Mosley's liberty was a luxury the government could no longer afford and restrictions against him would be 'popular and a unifying force'. On 18 May Churchill ordered the internment of 'very considerable numbers' of Fascists. He based his decision on the argument he used with Roosevelt: 'If the Germans broke through, and Mosley became Prime Minister, a pro-German government might obtain easier terms from Germany by surrendering the fleet.'

On 19 May Mosley was in Middleton, Lancashire, to support his by-election candidate, who polled just 418 votes against the Conservatives' 32,036. It was his last BU public appearance and it ended with him being escorted under police guard to the local branch, where several thousand people gathered, 'hurling stones until every window was smashed'. The BU faced a hostile public; even the Cimmie Mosley Day Nursery in Kensington was vandalized. The police had to close meetings, even in the stronghold of Dalston because of anti-Fascist violence.

The British Army was retreating towards Dunkirk and it looked as though the invasion of Britain was imminent. There was no evidence that Mosley intended any treacherous activities by helping a German invasion but there was evidence, suggests Tony Kushner, that with Ramsay he was willing to reach 'a negotiated settlement by means that were unacceptable to a country on the verge of being invaded'. On 20 May the Foreign Office's Sir Alexander Cadogan wrote in his diary that 'the quicker we get [the Hoares] out of the country the better. But I'd sooner send them to a penal settlement. He'll be the Quisling of England when Germany conquers us and I am dead.'

On 20 May 1940 Knight raided Wolkoff's flat and then Tyler Kent's. The search uncovered 1,500 diplomatic documents and the 'Red Book', the Right Club's membership list, which Ramsay had given him in the belief it would be protected by diplomatic immunity. 'It is appalling,' the US embassy cabled Washington, 'it means not only that our codes are cracked a dozen ways but that our every diplomatic manoeuvre was exposed to Germany and Russia ... No doubt the Germans will publish another White Book during our political campaign which will have as its purpose the defeat of Roosevelt.'

MI5 believed the raid demolished Anderson's objections. It had the evidence to implicate Ramsay and Wolkoff as dangerous Fifth Columnists. It succeeded in condemning all the extreme groups by linking them with the RC's 'pro-German and subversive activities'. On 21 May Churchill received a 'grave document' on the treasonable activities of Wolkoff, Kent and Ramsay. The Home Secretary was told that 'dangerous elements should be interned without further delay'. Attlee and Greenwood agreed, and further pressure from the military led to another meeting between Anderson and MI5.

Anderson needed to be convinced the BU might assist the enemy but without such evidence 'it would be a mistake to imprison Mosley and his supporters who would be extremely bitter after the war when democracy would be going through its severest trials'. Knight described the 'underground activities' of the 25 to 30 per cent of BU members who would go to any lengths if so ordered by Mosley. His order at the start of the war was 'merely an example of how insincere Mosley really was and how many of his supporters simply regarded utterances of that kind as a figure of speech'. MI5, however, lacked evidence of 'acts prejudicial' or 'hostile associations' to arrest Mosley. Anderson agreed the case against Ramsay was 'rather serious' but it did not involve the BU. Knight claimed the two were in 'constant touch with one another' and that RC members were also members of the BU, some of whom were 'collecting arms'. Frank Newsam, the real power in the Home Office, thought MI5 improperly wanted detention first and evidence later.

Anderson recalled that, although there was no evidence to justify the prosecution of Fascists, it appeared they were preparing secret plans in the event of an invasion, to range themselves on the side of the enemy, or to seize power by a *coup d'état* and make terms with Hitler. Mosley and Ramsay were obsessed with a 'march to power' with the BU leader made Prime Minister and the Duke of Windsor back on the throne. Even so, the calm and cool-headed Anderson never really believed in MI5's alarmist theories. He seemed to think, wrote Liddell, that the possibility of invasion was 'no more than a vague suggestion'. MI5's view was that 'if somebody didn't get a move on there would be no democracy, no England, no Empire, and that this was almost a matter of days'. The Home Secretary said Mosley was 'too clever to put himself in the wrong by giving treasonable orders. He realised the War Cabinet might take the view that, notwithstanding the absence of such evidence, we should not run any risk in this matter, however small.'

On 22 May Sir Robert Vansittart, the Foreign Secretary's adviser, talked with Violet Bonham-Carter about the 'English Quislings'. Ramsay was 'one of them – and had given at meetings lists of people he would have shot – including Van himself'. Vansittart wanted to strike at them because of the attempts to unify the Fascist, anti-Semitic and peace groups in search of a negotiated peace. That day Richard Stokes saw Lloyd George, hoping to persuade him to join the search. However, he thought 'the idea that we could sign a humiliating peace was ridiculous . . . If there were a general agreement on disarmament, there might be an understanding about the Navy in order to get world peace. Otherwise we should fight to the bitter end.'

After the raid on his flat, Kent was arrested and stripped of diplomatic immunity. It was this case that moved Churchill and led to the 'witch-finding' atmosphere which triggered the security revolution initiated by the PM, who 'rolled up Magna Carta, suspended habeas corpus, incarcerated the bigoted, the cranky, the extremist and the influential'. The BU was harried out of existence, or, in the words of Herschel Johnson who studied MI5's methods, 'squelched'.

In the absence of Churchill, who was in France, Chamberlain raised the case at the War Cabinet meeting on 22 May. The PM would 'agree to whatever the Cabinet thinks best'. MI5 said Ramsay had been engaged in 'treasonable practices' in conjunction with Kent and the Right Club was 'carrying on pro-German activities, and secret subversive work, with the object of disorganizing the Home Front and hindering the prosecution of the war'. Anderson explained that Wolkoff, who had been interned two days previously, had been in relations with Kent and had means of communicating with the enemy. Ramsay had been in relations with Wolkoff, and also with Mosley, 'though, as regards the latter, not in connection with this woman'.

MI5 had no evidence the BU was involved in Fifth Column activities so action was impossible under the existing regulation. Anderson said new powers were required since he did not want the party, in reaction to a few arrests, to rebuild itself as an underground organization. He envisaged arresting a small number of officials. The decision was taken by Chamberlain, Halifax, Attlee and Greenwood to authorize whatever was needed 'to cripple the organisation'; military personnel observing included Ironside. Defence Regulation 18B was amended to allow the State to intern those who had sympathy towards enemy powers. Fearing a possible right-wing coup, the Cabinet wanted action taken as quickly as possible 'against persons known to be members of this organisation'. Orders were given for the arrest of Mosley and thirty-three BU members. Afterwards Halifax, who had suffered the barbs of Mosley's oratory, noted with satisfaction that 'we succeeded in getting a good deal done about fascists, aliens and other doubtfuls, Tom Mosley being among those picked up'.

Bizarrely, it was only on 22 May that 'Mr Macaroni', the Italian contacted by Wolkoff, was identified by MI5 as Military Attaché Duke Antonio del Monte, the intelligence liaison with the BU. He was suspected of passing secret information to Italy, using the diplomatic pouch. Knight was ecstatic at the news: 'It is therefore reasonably certain that the known confidential information extracted from the Embassy records by Kent is now in the hands of the Italians.' The breakthrough, however, came late in the day and Knight brooded on the case for the rest of the war, aware there were 'various loose ends which are still untied'. In a report dated 12 March 1945, Knight made enquiries of the Italian government about the Duke and what happened to the information he received from Wolkoff. The reply has been weeded from the files. Two months later he visited Kent in prison to talk about del Monte. Kent said the pseudonym was 'a rather silly' alias but maintained he had no idea that Anna was going to transmit information via del Monte or anyone else. Knight reported that he felt 'forced to record that I am now prepared to believe Kent'.

On the evening of 22 May the Privy Council passed a regulation covering those active in the furtherance of the objects of an organization which the Secretary of State was satisfied was 'subject to foreign influence or control', or persons controlling the organization 'have or have had associations with persons concerned in the government of, or sympathies with the system of government of, any power with which His Majesty is at war'. It was loosely drawn – because MI5 did not have the evidence that the BU was under foreign control – but was not used against the Right Club, the Communists, or other groups. Mosley was one of thirty-three set out in an 'omnibus' detention order signed that evening.

Next morning in *Action* Mosley refuted the charge that 'I desire to assist the enemy'. He had for years 'warned the country to be armed and prepared against any attack'. If any invading parachutists arrived, they should be treated as what they were, enemy soldiers. Mosley emphasized that he would fight an invader, but doubted whether Britain could be successfully invaded.

The arrests began on 23 May. Diana arrived at their flat and spotted four men 'aimlessly staring into space'. She said, 'Look, Coppers.' Inspector Jones stepped forward and said he had a warrant for Mosley's arrest. Mosley cheerfully assured him 'he had been expecting arrest and that naturally he had made some precautions for the safe custody of such of the British Union records as he did not wish to fall into the hands of the authorities'. Some were buried under railway arches in south London. Mosley made a bonfire of his papers. By chance 'one or two floated over a wall and came into the hands of the police'. On one was written 'Gerald Brenan, Bell Court, Aldbourne'. The police had considered interning Brenan until they discovered it was 'a letter to the *Telegraph* urging that Sir Oswald be arrested, and was therefore an enemy of the Fascist Party and his name and address noted as such'. Among documents in Mosley's custody was a forty-four-page typed list of officers, agents, contacts and speakers, corrected up to 25 January 1940. The police also took away three handguns and two rifles. The officers took him to Brixton prison.

Cadogan confided in his diary: 'Ramsay and Mosley arrested! Quite right. But there are 1,000's of others who ought to be.' Ramsay told Richard Stokes that he had been arrested because he believed in the Protocols of the Learned Elders of Zion and knew of the Churchill–Roosevelt cables. When Mosley's arrest was announced Hugh Dalton's wife said, 'We had to lose Norway to get rid of Chamberlain, and to lose Boulogne to get rid of Mosley.' In Berlin, Goebbels noted 'a wave of arrests of fascists. Mosley imprisoned as well. The fat plutocrats are protecting their hides.'

John Beckett, Secretary of the Duke of Bedford's (formerly Lord Tavistock) British People's Party, was arrested despite having left the BU. He received a letter from Fuller who had taken up an unspecified War Office appointment and could not proceed with their ex-servicemen's campaign to ensure 'young men who are fighting should not have the empire pawned behind their backs, as was the case last time'. BPP membership lists and contact files had been put in a safe place. Also interned was Norah Elam, who in 1918 had called for the imprisonment of 'every man and woman of enemy blood, high and low, rich and poor'. All headquarters staff were arrested and remained in detention until 1944. They included Director-General Neil Francis Hawkins and his assistant who had volunteered for war service, Brian Donovan; *Action* editor Alexander Raven Thomson; propaganda officer Mick Clarke; London administrator Hector G. McKechnie and Mosley's secretary, George Sutton. Some officials were left at large in the hope that they would reveal their part in plans for going underground. Mosley's secretary, Miss E. M. Monk, was not detained. MI5's E. B. Stamp told the Home Office she was being kept under surveillance.

When Diana told eight-year-old Desmond what had happened he was perfectly calm. She decided, however, to go back to Denham. As she drove through London, posters announced 'MP arrested'. She telephoned Nicholas's Eton housemaster to tell him of the arrest, worried Nicholas might be persecuted because of it. Mr Butterwick said, 'He's got his friends and that's that.' At Summer Fields, Jonathan was protected because his surname was Guinness. However, he was 'well aware of Mosley's anti-war stance, especially in contrast to the fervent schoolboy patriotism around him'. He thought 'it was no wonder the government regarded him as an enemy'. That evening, Diana was having dinner when police streamed through the gate. She ran upstairs and slipped a photograph of Hitler, with an affectionate inscription, under Max's cot mattress.

Fascists claimed internment was carried out indiscriminately. Individuals were detained on 'unsubstantiated allegations, local gossip, the use of agents provocateurs, and whatever dubious insinuations could be hastily cobbled together'. The arrests, Leonard Wise wrote, 'were carried out in such a haphazard way that I have never had any faith in the Intelligence Services since'. Non-active members were arrested, while the most active were not. Birmingham schoolteacher Louise Irvine was aware that headquarters had a list of 'those 9,000 or so members who were currently active' but individual branches 'also had a secret membership consisting of people who could not afford to be publicly associated with us – senior police officers, local government officials, businessmen and civil servants. Records of these secret members were kept neither at Headquarters nor on the branch premises.'

The immunity of prominent Fascists Viscountess Downe, former Lady-in-waiting to Queen Mary, and her friend Lady Pearson was suspicious. Pearson was arrested but soon released after her brother, Sir Henry Page Croft MP, Churchill's Under-Secretary for War and Vice-President of the Army Council, approached Anderson. Her agent, secretary and minor Canterbury Fascists were detained. Lady Dunn, who attended the secret meetings, escaped detention, though Howard Hall, butler-secretary to Sir James Hamet Dunn Bt, was arrested. He was suspected of organizing an undercover group, the Home Defence Movement, which distributed sticky-backs.

Leonard Wise was puzzled by the choice of targets: 'It all depended on whether or not one's name had appeared in one of our publications.' Neither John Warburton nor any other member of his branch was ever detained, 'though many members of neighbouring branches were. It is another example of the apparently random and indiscriminate way in which the Emergency Powers were applied.' Blackshirts agreed 'the Government was right, in a desperate military situation, to act against anyone whose loyalties it regarded as doubtful', but many against whom 'nothing incriminating had been discovered', became 'useful scapegoats, and stayed in prison for years'. Over 700 British Union members were detained and found themselves 'suddenly branded as traitors in a way that seemed likely to scar the rest of their lives'.

On the day after Mosley's arrest Mass Observation took a snap poll. Very seldom had observers found such a high degree of approval for anything, with most people saying that 'it should have been done a long time ago'. However, some people did object to a person being arrested for what he might do rather than what he had done. Nancy Mitford wrote to Mark Ogilvie-Grant on 24 May that she was 'thankful Sir Oswald Quisling has been jugged aren't you but think it quite useless if Lady Qs still at large . . .'

23

Prisoner Number 2202

When the commander of the British forces was ordered on 27 May to evacuate troops from Dunkirk, the hand of those who wanted a negotiated peace was strengthened. The Cabinet considered a grim military paper questioning whether Britain could continue the war if France fell. Rumours swept the country that the royal family had left for Canada and that a shadow government had been formed. The idea that Mosley might head a puppet government was widespread. President Roosevelt saw Canadian Prime Minister Mackenzie-King's emissary and told him Britain was doomed and that Hitler was going to demand its fleet. He wanted Churchill to send it across the Atlantic.

Churchill told the Cabinet 'it was idle to think that, if we tried to make peace now, we should get better terms from Germany than if we went on and fought it out. The Germans would demand our fleet . . . We should become a slave state,' though a British government which would be Hitler's puppet would be set up – 'under Mosley or some such person. And where should we be at the end of all that?' As long as morale held they should carry on and deal with the Fifth Column.

Vernon Kell was dismissed as Head of MI5, partly because of a personality clash with Churchill. The creation of executive security committees and the higher profile of the military and MI5 in policy created increased tension between politicians and the security authorities. Problems arose over the PM's wish to appoint Lord Trenchard as Commander-in-Chief (Home Forces). There was dismay at the dictatorial powers he wanted. Instead, General Ironside was 'volunteered' for the post.

From 28 May, in the light of a 'certain eventuality', a German invasion, national security was overseen by the (Security) Executive, chaired by Lord Swinton. Its principal object was 'to consider questions relating to defence against the Fifth Column and to ensure action'. A report by Lord Hankey accepted the Fifth Column's existence and urged 'the fullest possible weight' be given to MI5 efforts to counter it.

Swinton's committee was a curious affair since its deputy was Sir Joseph Ball, the man behind *Truth*, which campaigned from a hawkish position on behalf of 18B detainees, in particular Admiral Domvile. It wanted martial law under Ironside and argued detainees should be tried and, if convicted, shot, if not, released. It wanted to protect 'fellow-travellers of the right' from detention. Links between the committee and *Truth* were strengthened by the recruitment of a solicitor close to the magazine, William Crocker, who was chosen to reorganize MI5. Also appointed was Dr Dearden, a psychiatrist who devised MI5's interrogation techniques. Richard Stokes referred to 'this rather odd secret Gestapo . . . with a couple of toughs named Crocker and Ball'. Alfred Wall, General Secretary of the London Society of Compositors and a former Communist, was selected by the PM and Herbert Morrison, fellow members of the anti-Nazi council, Focus. The PM's representative was Desmond Morton, his adviser on intelligence matters.

On 30 May the Home Secretary decided Diana Mosley was not to be interned immediately because 'there would be advantages in having her carefully watched as it is possible she may be a channel through which we can get further information'. Diana paid the wages of remaining BU officials such as Tommy Moran, who took over the leadership. Anonymous information that she was a liaison between interned BU leaders and the movement outside persuaded Sir John Anderson to issue warrants to monitor her correspondence and telephone calls. 'My wife,' Mosley recalled, 'too, experienced the results of a bugged telephone or room microphone after my arrest.'

Action editor E. D. Hart was detained but not before he put out on 30 May an issue with the headline FREE MOSLEY – SAVE BRITAIN. BU members had been arrested but 'not a shred of evidence had been found to support any allegation that BU was, or ever had been under foreign influence'. It acknowledged 'more of us will see the inside of a prison, but where Mosley goes we gladly follow'. Members were urged to 'prepare the minds of the people for the greatness that will be theirs when Mosley leads as Mosley most surely will'. The slogan 'We Carry On' appeared in the final issue of 6 June, which exhorted women to keep alive the movement, whose activities continued with the production of leaflets and sticky-backs. An order comprising 345 BU members was signed on 30 May. Compiled by Scotland Yard in collaboration with MI5, it was based on information supplied by chief constables on prominent or active BU members. Some BU members were arrested as they came back from the beaches at Dunkirk; one was detained after returning from a bombing mission over Germany.

Few Right Club members were interned. The Home Office said it would be wrong to publish the names of these 'simple-minded' people, which included MPs and peers, who were unaware of their leaders' activities. BU members, none of whose leaders was ever charged with an offence, were not given the benefit of such doubt. 'As to the scum, quite rightly', Swinton wrote, 'we put lots of them inside at the critical time, but a good many of them did not matter very much.' Anderson told Irene Ravensdale he had been in a cleft stick. The order had been to hurl all suspects in prison but he soon had to 'let many out who had needlessly got caught up in the vortex. Much suffering was thereby caused to many by the heavy-handed methods that were adopted in handling the alleged quislings.'

In the Commons on 4 June, Churchill spoke of the necessity of taking measures of 'increasing stringency ... against British subjects who may become a danger or a nuisance should the war be transported to the United Kingdom'. Many were enemies of Nazi Germany but 'we cannot under the present stress, draw all the distinctions which we should like to do'. There were Fifth Columnists, for whom he felt 'not the slightest sympathy'. He would use the necessary powers to put down their activities until he was satisfied that 'this malignancy in our midst has been effectively stamped out'. Overnight British Fascists were transformed from a political irrelevance to potential allies of a Nazi invasion. Even Mosley's firmest supporters wavered. Henry Williamson told Diana he thought of writing to *The Times* to enquire 'if it had been discovered that funds had been received from any foreign country, for if so, thousands of people like myself would then immediately disclaim all connection with such a party'.

Acting Director-General and Ball's friend Alan Harker laid out MI5's assessment of the BU in a memorandum. 'Doubtless a situation was envisaged in which the country would be forced to ask for terms of peace, and should this situation arise Hitler would only make peace with an England led by Mosley. It was therefore Mosley's aim to make it difficult for the government to carry on the war.' MI5 expected BU members to assist the Nazis in the event of invasion. Material collected for the Suspects List by Rothschild's agent 'left no room for doubt that this danger was a real one'.

The Minister for Home Security, Herbert Morrison, admitted Harald Kurtz had provided false information against John Beckett and Ben Greene. Kurtz acted as a pro-Nazi, self-confessed member of the Fifth Column, who was trying to make contacts in the services and was in touch with German agents, supplying them with lists of reliable supporters. He claimed Beckett offered to join the anti-parachute corps and would harbour escaping pro-Germans who had been in contact with the Nazis. MI5 concluded there were many people who 'supplied information of military value to our agent in the belief that he was in a position to communicate it to the German Secret Service'.

At the end of May Norah Briscoe, a typist in the Ministry of Supply, and 'Mollie' Hiscox, a BU member in the Right Club and Link, were found guilty of communicating secret information to a German agent (in fact, MI5's Kurtz). Therefore it seemed plausible that the misconduct of Tyler Kent, Anna Wolkoff and Captain Ramsay was the tip of an iceberg. The military certainly thought so. On 31 May Ironside reported a mass of Fifth-Column activity. 'Telegraph poles marked, suspicious men moving at night all over the country . . . Perhaps we shall catch some swine.' He remained puzzled, though, that 'we have never been able to get anything worth having. And yet there is signalling going on all over the place and we cannot get any evidence. A German wife of an RAF man who has been in domestic service in the Admiral's house at Portsmouth was run in for trying to get hold of some blueprints.'

Marie Ingram worshipped Hitler and joined the BU. She said the war had been started by 'Jews, Communists and Freemasons', and that Britain would be better off with a Fascist victory. She was employed by a naval officer who oversaw mine design, and told BU members she had obtained some information and had sent it out of the country. She was convicted of espionage with a dockyard worker, William Swift, and sentenced to ten years, but acquitted of stealing blueprints. Swift received fourteen years. Mrs Ingram's espionage was believed to be part of wider treachery. There was talk of armed conspirators helping German invaders and members joining the Local Defence Volunteers to obtain arms. It all lent reality to MI5's view that there were BU members who were willing 'to go to any lengths'. Swift claimed that 'when the Germans gained power in Britain Sir Oswald would become head of state'. Mrs Ingram looked forward to seeing the swastika flying over London.

Special Branch claimed that information from P. G. Taylor, who attended the 'secret meetings', revealed evidence of planning for a *coup d'état*. A sceptical Home Office requested more details about the 'vast secret revolutionary organisation'. On 8 June the branch conceded that, while 'a certain amount of collaboration' had taken place, 'no concrete plans were made, principally because those present could not agree on a leader'. There was evidence Mosley believed there was a chance of seizing power. There was certainly a fear that a coup might replace George VI with the Duke of Windsor, leading to the establishment of a peace government with Lloyd George or Sir Samuel Hoare. Another scenario envisaged Hitler, after a successful invasion, inviting Windsor to take back the throne and appoint Lloyd George or Mosley as his Prime Minister. Ramsay said at his Advisory Committee hearing that Mosley had offered him Scotland 'in certain circumstances'.

US Ambassador William Bullitt reported to Roosevelt on 4 June about a 'dismaying luncheon' with Marshal Pétain, who accused Britain of intending 'to permit the French to fight without help until the last drop of French blood should have been shed' and then, under a Fascist leader, to make a compromise peace with Hitler. Bullitt advised that if the British refused to commit fighters to France, it suggested they planned 'to conserve their fleet and air force and their army, and either before a German attack on England or shortly afterwards, to install eight fascists trained under Oswald Mosley and accept vassalage to Hitler'. Churchill would not contemplate peace talks but a compromise government would. He met calls for the prosecution of 'appeasement party' members with the riposte that it would be 'foolish as there are too many in it'.

On 9 June Churchill briefed Ambassador Lord Lothian, who was going to meet the US President, that 'if Britain broke under invasion, a pro-German Government might surrender the British Fleet . . . if Mosley were Prime Minister or some other Quisling Government set up, it is exactly what they would do'. At the last moment Churchill struck out the phrase 'if Mosley were Prime Minister'. On the following day, Italy entered the war on the side of the Axis powers. Again Churchill sought to stir fears about what a Mosley government might do to save the country from destruction.

Four days later Hitler talked about Mosley with the Nazi hierarchy. His adjutant, Major Engel, recalled that he 'did not think much of him as a personality' but he was the 'only Englishman who has understood the German-European idea'. If Churchill and Bernard Shaw were 'afraid of him and also respect' such 'a vain man, who usually just womanises', then there 'must be something behind it'. He added it was 'a shame that he's more an intellectual than a tribune of the people' but the Labour Party 'did a very stupid thing when it dropped him'. Hitler still thought that 'perhaps he can stop this war' and was 'convinced his role has not run its course yet'. That was the view within the German Foreign Office. After Dunkirk, the anti-Nazi Adam von Trott was 'genuinely worried that the victorious German advance might well take in Britain and that he would need to do the maximum to protect his friends there in the event of a German puppet government – most probably under Mosley – being set up'.

Mosley told the Advisory Committee it was 'an extraordinary idea' to suggest he would 'act as an agent of a foreign power . . . am I in my whole life that sort of man?' Diana said he expected the war to be a long drawn-out affair without an invasion of Britain, as he never imagined the French Army would collapse. But how would he have reacted if the Germans had invaded? Would he have done the same as Harold Nicolson, who intended to take poison in the event of an invasion, rather than come to an accommodation with the Nazis?

The Germans might have tried to set up a government under Mosley, though he believed that before this could happen he would have been assassinated by MI5. Romantically, he said he had planned to escape from prison to become a resistance fighter against the invader. 'I would have put on my old Army uniform and fought to a finish and no doubt have been killed, which would have settled the problem.' Ultimately, he told Norman Longate, he would have been recognized as 'an uncompromising opponent, so that he might have found himself back in Brixton, with German gaolers instead of British ones'. There was no question of being a quisling in charge of a puppet Nazi regime.

Once opposition had been crushed – the stay-behind British Resistance

Organization was expected to hold out for a few weeks – Mosley believed the Nazis would rule with a military governor until, 'like a victim continually injected with some poisonous drug, they set up a collection of old gentlemen', or failing that 'a weak local leader like Pétain in France'. In conversation with Churchill on 18 June, Chamberlain wondered whether Lloyd George was 'waiting to be the Marshal Pétain of Britain'. The PM said, 'Yes, he might, but there won't be any opportunity.' In Hitler's grand design, Lloyd George would have been the leading candidate for the role of 'national saviour whose statesmanship alone could save his country further humiliation'.

Major-General Fuller was considered by MI5 'an obvious leader (in the absence of Mosley) of the fascist element in this country. We think he may covet a position not dissimilar to that of Marshal Pétain.' Fuller would have been arrested by Special Branch at the onset of an invasion. He was identified as a military strongman willing to take part in a British Vichy, though Mosley told Kenneth Macksey, author of *The German Invasion of Britain*, he could not conceive him playing such a role. He was 'so perverse and incapable of doing what he was told that he could never have become a Nazi puppet', even though he called for 'a *coup d'état* by Mosley'.

In June, Mosley's former aide-de-camp, Dr Tester, left Athens. Before his departure he talked with the British Consul General, Mr Sebastian. 'I explained that it was my conviction that in the short or long term a fascist government would take power in England . . . that the English people would sweep away the Churchill government and that Mosley was the only person who, through a peaceful settlement with Hitler, could end this war.' He added that 'the defeat of England was not to be stopped and had become for me an absolute certainty'. Sebastian had one word for Tester: 'Quisling'.

It has been suggested that Hitler would have preferred an anti-Semitic puppet leader such as Ramsay or Domvile, rather than Mosley. They were on the 'White List' of collaborators. Mosley was not included precisely because Hitler intended him to play a key role. Macksey 'took Mosley's protestations with a pinch of salt'. Maurice Cowling believed Mosley toyed with the idea, because 'his only hope was a German occupation'. A prison officer overheard Mosley, during a meeting with his solicitor, admit that 'Hitler had, in fact, appointed him to be a sort of co-leader in England'. In Brixton a member of Mosley's entourage accosted Beckett. 'Hail Mosley. The Leader says that at this time of danger for our nation, past disagreements should be put to one side. He offers you a place in his provisional government.' Beckett simply laughed. The gossip in BU circles was that Mosley would appoint Fuller Minister of War.

Mosley was not a potential traitor in the sense of either welcoming a Nazi invasion or contemplating actions that would bring it about. However, he had considered the overthrow of the government with the aim of negotiating peace terms. But would he have collaborated in, if not a puppet regime, then a pro-German government? Everything we know about Mosley, with his idea of the 'great men' of history making their mark at the time of crisis, suggests he would not have passed over the opportunity to be Britain's saviour. Hitler and Mosley might have come to an agreement that saved the Empire and allowed Germany to pursue its objectives in Eastern Europe and Russia. In such circumstances a publicly reluctant Mosley would not have been seen as a traitor – at least in his eyes – but as the man of destiny who had saved Britain from the horror of war.

Mosley hinted at the possibility of heading a pro-German government in the BBC programme *If Britain Had Fallen*. 'If and when' the Germans withdrew, 'leaving British people, British soil and the British Commonwealth intact, then, and not before, by commission of the crown and by election of the people, I will, if I am asked to, form a government.' That depended, of course, on which king and what constitution. An official in the embassy in Lisbon, Marcus Cheke, reported that the Duke of Windsor had predicted the fall of Churchill and his replacement by a government which would negotiate peace terms. The King would abdicate, there would be a revolution, and the Duke would be recalled. Britain would then lead a coalition of France, Spain and Portugal, with Germany left free to march on Russia. When Primo de Rivera suggested he might return to the throne, the Duke said constitutionally it would be impossible. But if Britain lost the war, de Rivera argued, even the constitution would not be inviolate. At this 'the Duchess in particular became very thoughtful'.

It is not difficult to envisage a situation in which Edward, back as King of an intact Empire, asks Mosley to take part in an election of a pro-German one-party state, where the navy has been scuttled and Fascist squads round up Jews and Communists. Faced with no alternative, the prospects of guaranteed security and no war might well have made a Lloyd George–Mosley National government a winning proposition.

Having seen its files, the Advisory Committee noted MI5 had no evidence that BU leaders 'desire a German victory, or have any other concern than to take the fullest advantage of the present situation in order to bring BU to power with Mosley as its leader'. This caused consternation and MI5 arranged to brief Committee Chairman Sir Norman Birkett. The outcome was a 'Reasons for Order', dated 19 June, of the case against the BU, which was 'subject to foreign control or influence by Italian or German political or national organisations'. It had received funds from Italy and Mosley had associations with German officials with regard to the radio project and on visits to Germany had received 'signs of honour from Herr Hitler'. There was an 'affinity' between the NSDAP and the BU, and Mosley extolled the German system of government with the object of introducing National Socialism to Britain. There was nothing about an underground BU, plans for a *coup d'état*, or Mosley being 'in relations' with Ramsay, but the BU could be used 'for purposes prejudicial to the defence of the Realm' and 'the efficient prosecution of the war'.

Mosley was held at Brixton prison in 'F' wing, condemned as unfit for use. The unhygienic facilities shocked middle-class BU detainees but, 'after Winchester', Mosley wrote, 'prison was nothing'. His next-door companion was a black musician who had played in the Berlin Philharmonic Orchestra. On the other side was John Beckett, resentful that Mosley had been allowed a radio and he had not. Close by was Ramsay, who talked about the Tyler Kent affair. He thought he was on to 'something of world-shaking importance' but Mosley could see nothing improper in Churchill's actions. He 'had nothing to attack Churchill about . . . the whole thing was a mare's nest'. He had 'a perfect right to correspond with the President'. The interned Gerald Hamilton remembered Lady Mosley coming to see her son. 'The warder called out to the landing, "Mosley, come down, there's a visitor for you." Many of the interned people shouted out at the wretched warder, "Call him Sir Oswald, you bastard!"' Viewing the scene, Beckett caustically remarked, 'There goes Mosley with his kosher fascists.'

During June Irene applied for guardianship of Mosley's three elder children. He was brought from prison to the Chancery Court. She argued she had been responsible for financing the upkeep of their home (Savehay had been requisitioned by the Ministry of Supply as a centre for research into Chemical Warfare) and thought they might share guardianship. The father role 'did not come easily to him', agreed Diana, but he was incensed by the proposal, which seemed 'as unnecessary as it was insulting'. The judge decided Mosley should be guardian in name only and 'have no direction in their education or anything else'. He declined responsibility without authority and Irene was made guardian. Vivien, nineteen, and Nicholas, seventeen, did not object to the arrangement, since they did not know their father had objected. He was fond of them, noted Diana, 'but he felt no more responsibility for them; they had been taken from him against his forcibly expressed will'. Nicholas stayed on at school until he was called up.

On 17 June Diana met Fuller, who said 'the French are asking for an armistice'. She was astonished: 'The most powerful army in Europe, beaten in a matter of weeks.' When she asked about his own position, his wife said 'they'll never arrest Boney. He knows too much.' Fuller wrote, 'Although the masses of people, secure behind a sea wall, were not greatly perturbed by the German advance, the Government lost its head, and at the very moment when in order to maintain internal calm, contempt of danger was imperative . . . hundreds of loyal people whose only crime was that they considered the war a blunder, were arrested and held in custody for years on end.'

With Ironside discredited, Fuller's protector was General Sir Alan Brooke, Chief of the General Staff, who decided, after an Army Security briefing, he had no 'unpatriotic intentions', though he continued to be monitored by MI5. His non-internment puzzled Mosley, who believed he was not arrested because 'they' toyed with using him, which indeed seems to have been the case. His biographer notes that Fuller was the only senior BU member not destroyed by his association with Mosley.

With the fall of France and fear of invasion growing, even Churchill wobbled. He told 'Pug' Ismay on 12 June, 'You and I will be dead in three months' time.' As yet, no US arms or planes had arrived at British ports. On 24 June he warned the Canadian PM he would 'never enter into any peace negotiations with Hitler' but could not 'bind a future government, which, if we were deserted by the United States and beaten down here, might easily be a kind of Quisling affair ready to accept German overlordship and protection'. On the following day he repeated the warning to his ambassador in Washington: 'In this case the British Fleet would be the solid contribution with which this Peace Government would buy terms.' Goebbels recorded that Hitler had 'not yet decided whether he wants to go at England. He wants a settlement. There are already indirect negotiations about that.'

On 27 June the Germans, who expected help from the Duke of Windsor in semi-exile in Lisbon, had been negotiating to form an anti-Russian alliance, with an opposition government under Edward. They believed King George 'will abdicate during attack on London'. Keeping an eye on the Windsors, David Eccles reported that they were 'very nearly fifth column'.

The Security Executive assumed the power to proscribe the BU, though it was not closed down until 10 July. The delay enabled MI5 to identify its 'second line' of leaders who continued its activities. Believing the threat of internment had passed, Commandant Allen told a journalist of 'her admiration for the Gestapo and Himmler' and 'more or less said that she would help the Germans if they came here' – a message which alarmed security. At her 18B hearing she proved to be 'an untruthful witness', who lied about attending secret meetings. However, Anderson 'found it difficult to accept on the basis of his personal knowledge that she could be really dangerous'. She was only prevented from travelling to specified areas.

MI5 hoped Diana would lead them to Fifth Columnists, since she had been the principal channel of communication between Mosley and Hitler. On 20 June Nancy Mitford revealed that she had told Gladwyn Jebb at the Ministry of Economic Warfare 'what I know (very little actually) of Diana's visits to Germany'. She thought 'something should be done to restrain her activities'. Diana was 'far cleverer and more dangerous than her husband, and will stick at nothing to achieve her ambitions – she is wildly ambitious, a ruthless and shrewd egotist, a devoted Fascist and admirer of Hitler'. She 'desires the downfall of England and democracy'. Baba Metcalfe said 'it was Diana we were all scared of coming to power, not him'.

On 25 June Diana's former father-in-law, Lord Moyne, who had asked her son's governess, Jean Gillies, to spy on her, warned Swinton that failure to intern her would lead many 'to draw the conclusion that there is one law for the influential rich and another for the friendless poor'. He enclosed a summary of Miss Gillies's conversations with Diana and a list of dates of visits to Germany, which he believed involved 'bringing over funds from the Nazi government'. There was 'little doubt that she acted as a courier between her husband and the Nazi government'. According to the governess, Diana had said, 'We are revolutionaries and we would kill.' She believed 'England would never fight and told Hitler so' and triumphantly said that if Belgium was overrun, it would not be possible to extract the British Army, which 'would be caught by a pincer movement'. She made 'no secret of her delight in what was happening'. Diana predicted the Germans would break through in France, cut off the British Army and take the Channel ports. Moyne believed the strategic outline came from Hitler.

The Home Secretary thought it advantageous to leave Diana at liberty under surveillance, but her detention order had been dispatched by MI5 barrister Jim Hale, who felt 'very strongly that this extremely dangerous and sinister young woman should be detained at the earliest possible moment'. On 28 June Churchill showed MI5's list of 150 prominent people to be arrested to his aide John Colville. It remains secret but included two distant relatives of Clementine Churchill: Diana and George Pitt-Rivers. Their presence 'piqued Winston and caused much merriment among his children'.

On 29 June Diana was arrested. Given the option of taking ten-week-old Max with her she declined, since London might be bombed. At Holloway she was locked in 'a dark, airless and very dirty cell. The tiny window was entirely blocked by sandbags.' There was a straw mattress on the wet floor, with some dirty blankets and grubby sheets. Ten-year-old Jonathan was at his prep school Summer Fields, where the headmaster told him, 'They've shut your mother up.'

There was one filthy toilet for the thirty inmates. Diana was told the red cross on its door indicated it was for those with venereal disease. A prison wardress said Diana felt tortured by living in such close confinement and disliked eating with the BU women: 'As soon as I decently could I abandoned the communal style of living – upstairs and downstairs had to be kept apart!' She was welcomed by the dedicated Fascists, who showed their devotion by cleaning her cell. 'It is probably difficult for someone who has not experienced it', she recalled, 'to imagine how demoralizing it is to be imprisoned without trial. It is like being kidnapped – you cannot see the end.' Jonathan visited and thought she looked 'funny' because she was thin and white-faced, and wore no make-up.

Mosley prepared a reply to the 'Reasons for Order' for his appeal. 'The police have raided my flat, my wife's flat, the London house we used to occupy, my children's house in the country. They have also raided the offices of British Union. At the end of this process what shred of evidence can they produce to support the allegation that I would play the traitor to my country?' Advisory Committee Chairman Birkett needed to construct as good a case as possible to justify his internment, even though 18B (1A) had been specially drafted to apply to him. Committee procedures combined 'the inquisitorial questioning of a court martial with the atmosphere of a vicarage tea-party'. In an Orwellian touch, officially it had only three members, even though four sat in, but since MI5 did not legally exist, its case officer was not counted. Evidence was accepted without valuation of the reliability of MI5's sources, legal representation was not permitted and internment was often recommended even though there was no evidence that a crime had been committed. Files depended on unsubstantiated allegations and use of agents provocateurs. Nellie Driver's explanation that the people who visited her at night for alleged secret meetings were, respectively, an insurance agent, her landlord and an uncle was not untypical.

There were scraps of information from agent reports and the tapping of telephones. 'Every little man', Mosley wrote, 'with a "hush-hush" job could flatulate his innuendos over the cocktails . . . provided by the tax-payer. What a chance for every mediocrity and dunce on the fringe of politics; for every little "Tadpole" and "Taper" to strut his little hour!' It underlined for Mosley 'the necessity for cross-examination in open court of all narks, spies, informers, keyhole peepers, and the rest of the pestilential tribe who seek to pay off old scores when fate gives them the chance'.

Birkett worried that Mosley might turn the appeal into a legal nightmare. He had been the losing prosecuter in his libel case against the *Star* and had been made to look foolish during his cross-examination of the Fascist leader. The first hearings on 2 and 3 July were 'little short of a disaster'. Birkett was not impressive, despite knowing in advance Mosley's defence. MI5 had supplied him with information 'derived from a very secret and delicate source'. During his sixteen-hour interrogation, Mosley insisted his politics were motivated by patriotism.

'For the last seven years', Mosley claimed, 'I have spent much of my time demanding that Britain should properly be armed to resist attack, and have violently attacked the old parties . . . for neglecting our defences. In particular I have demanded air parity with the strongest other country – which was Germany.' He did not think Britain 'should go to war for the sake of Poland or any Eastern European question' and was 'opposed to intervention in a foreign war when Britain was not properly armed for war'. He wanted to know that if he was accused of treachery, what was his motive? 'Some overweening, inordinate, or insane ambition? Is it really suggested that my ambition is to be the ruler of a country which is totally dependent upon a foreign power? ... I have always admitted that I hold the high ambition to make a great country even greater. It is not compatible with such ambitions to be the lackey of a foreign power.' He added, 'If it was wrong openly to advocate Peace, why were we not told to shut up?' The Home Secretary had powers to warn publications such as *Action* and institute heavy penalties but 'a warning was never given'. Birkett made the point that BU policy was the 'immediate making of peace', which Mosley did not deny. He did not oppose German occupation of Czechoslovakia, Poland, Belgium and France, because European politics were not Britain's vital interest.

He had attacked the Jews because they attacked him. The BU's anti-Semitism was 'an old English growth'. Mosley added that in the Fascist state Jews would have to prove their loyalty before a state tribunal (he saw no irony in that he was appearing before one) and that those found not working for the national interest would be 'humanely' expelled. He described Joyce as 'an offensive little beast' and conceded the BU had attracted a pro-Nazi fringe – including Claude Duvivier, H. W. Luttman-Johnson, Richard Findlay and H. P. Puller. Asked about the Right Club, Mosley said he had known nothing of the 'American business' but was evasive about relations with Ramsay and the secret meetings.

Mosley denied that the BU was under foreign influence; its emblem had been invented by Piercy and the use of spectacle was suggested by the Durham Miners Gala. He admitted some members had become 'Germanised', including Unity. 'In strict confidence, it was one of the small reasons why I did not want [my marriage] published, because this girl was going on this way, and my wretched wife, a much more intelligent woman, has struggled with it for years.' Birkett asked about opposition in a Fascist Britain. Mosley said 'party politics fade out ... so that the microbe of party politics cannot live'.

After admitting intelligence that the BU was under foreign influence was 'scanty', Birkett adjourned the hearing until 15 July in order to give MI5 a chance to produce evidence of co-operation with the Germans through agents or organizations such as the Link. 'If "The Link" can be connected directly with Germany, and the BU can be connected directly with "The Link", that would be some kind of evidence which at the moment is absent from these papers.'

Admiral Sir Barry Domvile was interned at Brixton on 7 July. The evidence against him depended on the testimony of an unnamed agent (Kurtz). Lord Tavistock (twelfth Duke of Bedford) was placed on the Suspect List, because he was expected to be appointed a Nazi regional governor or used as a puppet prime minister. Although he was known as a 'sexual pervert, physical coward and a rebel against all authority', he was not detained because MI5 did not want to provide the pacifist cause with a high-profile martyr. The Swinton Committee wanted to deport overseas the BU leaders. It reasoned that because Mosley was so fearful of such action, there must be 'some plot on hand to liberate them from jail for the purpose of starting serious trouble'. The 400 Fascists held at Ascot and York should be kept under military care or removed from the country. They are 'nasty gangsters who will stick at nothing'.

In early July Rothermere's nephew Cecil King recorded that 'the country is already reconciling itself to the idea of a Nazi conquest'. The German officer responsible for compiling 'White Lists' of potential allies was Major Walter zu Christian, chief of espionage in Spain and Portugal, who switched to Berlin to study British institutions. In 1936 he travelled to Britain, where he had worked for a German export house, to create intelligence dossiers. In 1939 he took charge of a Reich Security Ministry department in Hamburg devoted to Britain and ordered to draw up the Sonderfahndungsliste GB (Special Search List GB). The 'Black Book' of 2,700 enemies of the Reich was compiled hurriedly during May 1940 for Walter Schellenberg, Chief of the Reichs-Sicherheitshanptamt – Reich Security Head Office. On the list were 'Captain King' (aka Maxwell Knight) of 308 Hood House, Dolphin Square, where 'MI5 briefs and debriefs its contacts', and James Mogurk [sic] Hughes, a British captain of 144 Sloane Street. It is likely their names were provided by their friend William Joyce.

Ben Greene alleged the names of the Fifth Column, among whom he ranked himself, 'are recorded in Germany for use when the Germans arrive'. A White List of thirty-nine single women students who had visited Germany shortly before 1939 had been compiled in the Gestapo's Munich office. Post-invasion, the Nazis intended to rely on 'Englishmen detained since the beginning of the war on the ground of "friendship with Germany"'. After checking these 'political prisoners' against Home Office files, Mosley's men would be attached to Search Commissions, with internment camps set up to screen suspects. Nazi officials would collaborate with 'anti-Churchill groups' and search for 'people prepared to co-operate with us'. It was realized there would be few traitors but, zu Christian noted, 'very conveniently you had lodged all your political prisoners, or those you thought dangerous, together in the Isle of Man'. Just as Swinton feared, special airborne Einsatzgruppen Kommando groups were to seize those camps and free Mosley's men.

On 2 July Hitler ordered pre-planning for Operation Lion, the invasion of southern Britain at some point in September 1940. Two days later Churchill proposed sending the Duke of Windsor to the Bahamas as Governor because the Duke was 'well-known to be pro-Nazi' and might 'become a centre of intrigue'. When Foreign Office Permanent Under-Secretary Alexander Cadogan dined at Buckingham Palace on 10 July, he talked to the King, who was 'amused' at the Chief of MI6's 'report of the Quisling activities of "my brother!"'. On the following day Ribbentrop told colleagues he wanted to keep the Duke in Spain, where he would 'hold himself in readiness for further developments. Germany is determined to force England to peace by every means ... and would be prepared to accommodate any desire expressed by the Duke, especially with a view to the assumption of the throne by the Duke.' On 15 July Hitler talked with *Abwehr* chief Admiral Wilhelm Canaris about the Duke, who he regretted 'had not been more fully signed up when it was still time'. He then considered 'the matter of Mosley. If and how he could be got hold of.' Major Engel had the impression Hitler was 'still undecided and he does not know what and how he must do'.

On the following day Hitler agreed to Sealion – 'Preparation of a Landing Operation Against England'. On 19 July he made known his willingness to end the war if the British asked for terms. Labour's Richard Stokes wanted Churchill to consider the proposal but the PM said it would be 'detrimental to National Defence at a most grave moment. Even the steps which you have thought it right to take, if they become generally known, will be a powerful stimulus to Fifth Column activities.'

Newspapers on 19 July carried the headline 'IRONSIDE SACKED'. The Commander-in-Chief Home Forces had been removed after a whispering campaign against him but, 'in order that the matter should be placed on a good footing', was promoted Field Marshal. His obsession with security led him to suggest strange conspiracies concerning a German invasion. Malcolm Muggeridge was responsible at Kneller Hall for protecting Home Forces headquarters against subversion by enemy agents. Colonel Ross-Atkinson gave him a report that Ironside's car had been spotted outside a house in Holland Park occupied by known Fascists. After consulting a colleague, Bobby Barclay, they informed his stepfather Lord Vansittart. Next day it was revealed that Sir Alan Brooke had replaced Ironside. Fuller was warned to be politically inactive on pain of instant arrest.

On 22 July Italy's *Gazetta del Popolo* claimed the Duke of Windsor wanted a government under Lloyd George and Ribbentrop received information from London that he had urged the King to appoint a pro-appeasement Cabinet. 'There are now rumours', wrote George Orwell, 'that Lloyd George is the potential Pétain of England.' When Churchill rejected Hitler's offer, Goebbels told the foreign press, 'Gentlemen, there will be war.'

By the time Birkett returned to the fray, MI5 uncovered the BU's secret bank account but not the source of the funds paid into it. Major Tabor admitted being given 'large packs of foreign notes by Allen to pay into the account, but he never had any idea where the money came from'. It was 'unlikely that we shall ever be able to drag the truth from him' and those in a position to know refused to help. Mosley's cell had been bugged and a former secretary was being monitored; suggesting close links between the prosecution and judicial process. Aikin-Sneath was present on the final day when Mosley was pressed on funding and was made to look evasive. He denied Italian subsidies, insisting he had not enquired into the source of funds. But 'even if it were true. I ask why it should be a reason for holding me or my colleagues in gaol?' With regard to the radio project, he emphasized the deal had been purely commercial. His answer that the German directors were 'businessmen and are not in the government of Germany' was accurate but one was Goering's personal representative and the other a major funder of the Nazis.

Birkett concluded the BU was under German influence. Mosley's statement asking his followers 'to do nothing to injure our country or to help any other power' was 'the strangest message to give the supporters of an intensely patriotic organisation'. The need to make it showed that the BU was not patriotic at all. The Committee concluded Mosley had been frank with it when it suited his purpose and evasive when he wished to cover up his actions. Even so, the hearing was more ritualistic than judicial; it had no intention of setting Mosley free. Committee secretary Jenifer Williams was anti-Fascist and delighted at Mosley's detention but came to feel 'it had not been necessary, even considering the desperate situation of Britain'. She had seen at first hand the violence at Mosley's meetings but believed that as many detainees had fought in the first war, they had been attracted to the BU in a simple-minded way in order to prevent another war.

Mosley claimed Birkett withdrew the allegation of treachery. He had, however, been responding to Mosley's reference to his time in the Foreign Office. 'I do not think that anybody in their wildest statements said that you were anything approaching a traitor in those days.' Mosley replied, 'Thank you very much.' But Birkett added that he did not have to be a traitor to be detained, and so an order did not imply the detainee was one. He was willing to concede he had been interned for having 'advocated a negotiated peace'.

The ultra secret Security Executive was exposed by the *Herald* as 'our secret weapon against the fifth column'. The 'mystery committee' was hard at work in a big 'hush-hush' job but would be 'discriminating in their snooping'. The revelation provoked a parliamentary storm but further information was 'refused in the Public Interest'. The Committee's William Crocker wrote in his autobiography, 'Like the Ghost in *Hamlet*, I also "am forbid to tell the secrets of my prison-house".'

The Committee recommended sending BU leaders to Latchmere House, Ham Common, to obtain information about links to the Fifth Column. A former mental hospital, Camp 002 was opened as an interrogation centre under pressure from Swinton, Ball and Crocker. Its head was Colonel 'Tin-Eye' Stephens, an authoritarian oddball. On his return from India to England in 1933, he was attached to the courts at Lincoln's Inn, where he met Crocker. He undertook a mysterious role during the Italian–Abyssinian crisis and in

1939 joined MI5. Twenty-seven BU 'subversives' arrived at Ham on 27 July and were subjected to interrogations devised by Dr Harold Dearden, another friend of Crocker, who belonged to the Bath Club, popular with intelligence officers. In his history of Ham, Stephens skates over this period, except to mention a few 'treacherous . . . shabby nonentities'.

Detainees were placed on starvation rations and kept isolated with little sleep in cells that were lit twenty-four hours a day. They were moved around and either told of their impending release or of firing parties and hangings. Guards intimidated internees and committed them to punishment cells for minor offences. Portrayed as kindly, Stephens was also considered 'an extremely unpleasant and sadist interrogator'. Domvile's son Compton said his memory 'began to deteriorate. Certain periods of my life completely disappeared from my mind.' The resident doctor told Compton the treatment was 'intended to produce a state of "mental atrophy and unreserved loquacity"'. Little was learnt from the interrogations.

The authorities did not subject Mosley to Latchmere, which in fact was not an official place of detention, though a list of detainees was kept by the Home Office's Jenifer Williams, one of the few officials allowed to know anything about it. When Mosley heard what was going on, he began legal proceedings and 'the whole grisly charade quickly came to an end'. Dearden's techniques were refined and used during Britain's post-war counter-insurgency campaigns, and were the basis of the illegal methods used in Northern Ireland in the early seventies.

Mosley was involved in a libel case concerning his own prison conditions. The *Sunday Pictorial* claimed on 4 August that Brixton's 'Number One Guest' was living a life of luxury. 'Every morning his paid batman delivers three newspapers at the door of his master's cell. After his midday meal he fortifies himself with alternative bottles of red and white wine . . . He calls occasionally for a bottle of champagne. He selects a different smartly cut lounge suit every week. His shirts and silk underwear are laundered in Mayfair.' It was untrue but the authorities decided the detainees should be treated as remand prisoners. Gerald Hamilton admitted they were generally 'well treated. We weren't locked up in cells or anything. The cells were unlocked in the morning and they weren't locked up until you went to bed at night.' But 'all everybody thought about', recalled Hamilton, 'was when on earth could they get out'. Diana spent the libel damages on a fur coat. When she saw her husband in court, she was shocked by his appearance. He had grown a beard and his phlebitis was recurring.

It became clear to the Security Executive there was no Fifth Column. German radio propaganda claims that parachutists and enemy agents were fomenting such activity were a myth. Even MI5 was 'very much inclined to doubt' whether it existed. Swinton suggested as much to the US State Department's

Harvey Klemmer, who was studying Britain's handling of the problem. Swinton put his colleague in contact with MI5's recently retired deputy Sir Eric Holt-Wilson. Mowrer's report to Washington on 1 August claimed 'there is now no organized effort to assist the Germans here. He believes that most of the disloyal elements have been pretty well squelched. He does feel, however, that, were the Germans to come in, some thousands of people . . . would rediscover their Fascist sympathies and team up with the invaders.' MI5 were convinced the BU received funds from Germany. 'Investigators maintain that the BU spent money at a rate that could not possibly be accounted for by the Party's meagre contributions (members paid but a few pennies a week). It is claimed that the money spent by the BU fell off to practically nothing the moment war was declared and it was not possible to communicate with Germany.'

On 15 August Churchill told the Commons he had always thought the Fifth Column danger was 'exaggerated' and was satisfied it had been 'reduced to its proper proportions'. MI5's 'Black Book of British Fascism' conceded there was no evidence the BU was engaged in 'sabotage or espionage on behalf of the enemy'. Aikin-Sneath concluded that some members 'had joined without any realization that its policy involved disloyalty', but 'most were imbued with the leadership conception and were prepared to follow the leader blindly'. In September Hitler postponed his invasion plan until the spring of 1941.

The occupant of cell number 23 of F3 wing of Holloway, prisoner number 5433, presented a problem to the authorities since she had never been a BU member. On 2 October Diana appeared before the Advisory Committee, regretting she had not prepared 'a devastating indictment of the unprincipled politicians and their disgraceful behaviour'. She felt helpless in the face of 'rumour, gossip, spite and lying tongues'. MI5 claimed she acted as 'a channel of communication' between Mosley and the German leaders; that she had carried on with BU activities; and that she had 'publicly and privately given expression to pro-fascist and pro-German sentiments'. She was classed an 'extremely dangerous and sinister young woman'.

When they broke for lunch one member sent Diana a bottle of claret. She returned in 'a belligerent and unrepentant mood', admitting to Fascist sympathies, friendship with Hitler, liking Himmler and admiring the Nazi regime. She denied her governess's claims but agreed 'up to a point' with Hitler's treatment of the Jews: 'I am not fond of Jews.' Birkett was interested in the marriage in Germany attended by Hitler as it illustrated in the clearest terms the intimacy which existed between the Mosleys and the Nazi leaders. Diana considered his questions silly. 'This friend of yours is now bombing London!' She replied that 'since Britain had declared war on Germany and we had bombed Berlin it was rather obvious that the Germans would bomb London'. Britain had been 'dying for a war'. She accused Birkett of being hostile but she, in turn, was hostile towards him. When he asked if she 'would displace the present form of government with a fascist regime', she replied, 'Yes.'

Birkett informed the Home Office's Sir Alexander Maxwell on 4 October that 'it would be quite impossible, having regard to her expressed attitude and her past activities with the leaders of Nazi Germany, to allow her to remain at liberty in these critical days'. The Committee felt 'the views of Hitler on the British statesmen have been to some extent coloured by the views put forward by Lady Mosley'. There was no problem in Diana's children being allowed to see their mother in Holloway but a meeting with Mosley would set a precedent.

The decision to prosecute Tyler Kent had been delayed to allow Knight to complete his investigation of the Right Club, which he believed was 'not only a secret society but a revolutionary society'. Ramsay would 'welcome a civil war with shots in the streets and Mrs Ramsay is talking of getting her husband out of prison with bombs when the revolution starts. She is deriving keen pleasure from the anticipation of seeing the staff of the Home Office swinging from the lamp posts.' She expected Hitler 'would leave Great Britain as a protectorate with Ramsay as a ruler'. He sued the *New York Times* on 25 August for claiming he 'sent to the German legation in Dublin treasonable information given him by Tyler Kent'. Justice Atkinson awarded damages of one farthing but declared 'he was disloyal in heart and soul to our King, our Government, and our people . . . the expression "Fifth Columnist" applied to Captain Ramsay beyond question.' A charge of conspiracy was dropped for being 'too complicated'. Kent went for trial because the Americans wanted him muzzled and a secret trial provided the mechanism.

On 23 October the trials of Kent and Anna Wolkoff began at the Central Criminal Court. She was charged with intending to assist the enemy by attempting to send a coded letter to William Joyce. 'At one point', Field Security Police Officer Malcolm Muggeridge observed, 'a whole contingent of internees were summoned from the Isle of Man . . . distraught women in battered fur coats, blond hair whitening and dishevelled, make-up running; men in tweed jackets to their knees, leather-patched, frayed club ties, suede shoes'. A bearded Mosley spoke 'with the vibrant voice of a wronged man who asked only to be allowed to join his regiment in the battle line to fight for King and Country'. Wolkoff claimed the letter had been planted on her to incriminate her, and that, in turn, she had given it to Helene de Munck in order to incriminate her. Wolkoff was pro-Nazi and would have assisted the Germans in the interests of anti-Semitism, but she was the victim of entrapment; her conviction rested largely on technical issues.

The prosecution admitted no conspiracy existed between Kent and Wolkoff but it convinced the court she was a foreign agent – in a limited sense of the term

– and that he broke the Official Secrets Act. It had no evidence that she passed on secret information. In the end, she was convicted as a result of an agent provocateur, who provided the means of communicating with Germany. Kent was found guilty and sentenced to seven years, and remained incommunicado for the remainder of the war.

Morrison, who took over as Home Secretary in October, was sympathetic to MI5's hardline approach. On 12 October the PM told his private secretary John Colville how 'much he disliked locking people up and the suspension of Habeas Corpus'. In any case, 'those filthy Communists' were 'really more dangerous than the fascists'. During November the Security Executive decided detentions should only continue where there were reasons other than office in, or membership of, the BU. Morrison admitted to the Cabinet that 'we could now afford to take a rather less stringent line'. In the Commons Stokes demanded the release of people imprisoned through 'tittle-tattle'. He said 'it was quite insufferable that people should be locked up for an indefinite period and not be allowed to have even an open trial'. Mosley should either be tried or released. Morrison dismissed such arguments as those of 'classic Liberalism', which were inappropriate in wartime.

Over 60 per cent of the 18B internees were released by the end of 1940. Churchill asked Morrison on 22 December to improve the conditions of those detained, including allowing husbands and wives to visit each other. Public danger had justified an action 'so utterly at variance with all the fundamental principles of British liberty', but 'that danger is now receding'. Arrangements were made for Mosley to visit Holloway once a month to see Diana.

Old friends such as Robert Boothby, James Maxton and Harold Nicolson, 'in another courageous act of friendship', visited Mosley. When Boothby's visit became known, 'his enemies were abusive; others were impressed'. Mosley spent the time railing against the unfairness of his incarceration. It turned into a public meeting with Mosley 'as the speaker – no, the orator – and Mr Boothby the audience'. On a pre-arranged signal Boothby blew his nose and the governor ended the ordeal. Maxton's visit led to a row on the ILP national council. 'God's truth, Jimmy, how could you lower yourself – especially to visit that bastard Mosley?' said one member. 'No other person in the party', wrote John McGovern, 'would have got away with it so easily, but his personal popularity allowed him to ride the storm.'

Mosley refused to see Nicolson because of a broadcast he made, which Diana said was 'silly and dishonest'. She blamed it on the 'Communist spy' and BBC producer Guy Burgess, with whom he shared a flat. It did not bother Mosley that as a junior Minister working on propaganda in the Ministry of Information, Nicolson displayed 'great moral courage in acknowledging the tie of friendship with a man assumed by many to be a traitor'. Also visiting was Burgess's fellow spy Anthony Blunt, employed by Rothschild in MI5.

The reason for the visit by Blunt, whose mother was related to the Mosleys, is unknown. During spring 1941 Mosley visited Diana, accompanied by the 'delightful and clever' Domvile, who saw his own wife. Mosley was experiencing symptoms of phlebitis but it had not yet spread.

This was the time of Churchill's worst political peril with military disasters in North Africa, the Balkans and the Middle East. There was much criticism of him, which Oliver Harvey, Secretary to the Foreign Secretary, noted on 18 April was led by 'remnants of the Chamberlainites', who used the failures as a 'dishonest cloak of defeatism – at the end of that road lies Lloyd George, who would readily be a Pétain to us, with the support of the Press Barons and City Magnates'.

Spywriter 'Richard Deacon' (aka Patrick McCormick), who worked with Ian Fleming in Naval Intelligence, claimed MI6 infiltrated groups proposing peace negotiations with the aim of using them for deception purposes. 'Even former sympathisers with Germany among the ranks of ex-fascists and right-wingers who had now come to see the menace of Hitlerism allowed their names to be lent to this kind of false encouragement to the Nazis.' Was Fuller one? Does this explain why Fuller was not arrested?

Fuller refused to commit himself as to the result of the war and believed 'it would have been better for Europe and ourselves had we come to terms with Hitler'. The war 'is just a vast Bedlam with Churchill as its glamour boy: a kind of mad hatter, who one day appears as a cow puncher and the next as an Air Commodore ... to many the war is a Hollywood show'. He did, however, keep his intelligence ties. In early 1941 he met with MI6 Chief Menzies and had lunch with 'Blunt'.

In April 1941, in response to a letter to the Duke of Hamilton from Albrecht Haushofer, who was acting on behalf of Hess in requesting a meeting for talks 'somewhere on the outskirts of Europe', MI5 approached the successor to the Duke of Buccleuch as Steward to the King, with a view to using him in a deception operation. According to MI5's 'Tar' Robinson, head of the double-cross section, the 'slow-witted' Hamilton belonged to the peace party but now believed 'the only thing the country can do is to fight to the finish'. He helped with an MI6 'sting' operation to extract information from Haushofer. Deacon claimed Fleming established an 'underground' Link with cells in Lisbon, Tangier and Berne and agents posing as pro-Nazis. It had 'influential members which could pave the way to a negotiated peace and the overthrow of the Churchill government'.

MI6 was also busy in Madrid tracking down a former BU member spying for the Germans. Counter-espionage head Kenneth Benton knew of an intercepted radio message sent from Ast Hamburg to *Abwehr* Madrid, 'giving details of a new agent, being trained and equipped for his spying mission in England'. The BU member 'had been in danger of arrest and had fled, early in the war, to Germany, hoping to get work in anti-British propaganda'. He may be the unidentifed man who accompanied Joyce to Berlin shortly before war was declared. Hamburg decided it was 'too risky to let him use his British passport, even with false personal details and photograph, and he had been given a "false-false" passport with a real but altered photograph and a new name'. The agent, ready for dispatch to Spain en route for England, had been trained to construct a radio transmitter and possessed a list of British Fascist contacts. Benton learnt that he was booked on a flight from Lisbon to England. What happened to this BU man is unknown – was he turned and used for deception purposes like the other spies?

On the day of Hess's arrival on 10 May, the 'suspect' Duke of Bedford wrote to a friend suggesting Lloyd George should make a stand for a negotiated peace, as 'the one man who could save the country'. The situation changed with Operation Barbarossa on 22 June 1941 when Hitler aimed to 'crush Soviet Russia in a swift campaign'. Churchill proclaimed that 'any man or state who fights on against Nazism will have our aid . . . It follows, therefore, that we shall give whatever help we can to Russia and the Russian people.' In private he assumed 'Russia will assuredly be defeated'. Hitler expected Britain would then sue for peace. Deception schemes continued. On 22 October Fuller met with Brendan Bracken of the Ministry of Information and the War Office's 'Colonel Drew', a deception specialist.

At the Peel Camp on the Isle of Man, detainees were allowed political meetings, elections and newspapers. Initially, those at the Ascot Camp were demoralized and blamed Mosley for their arrest. Others blamed the public and 'hoped Germany would give them a good hiding. Some said they would only see British Union put into power by Hitler; could only visualize being ultimately released by the men in grey green uniforms.' Most 'would resist such a step with their lives'. Discipline was reimposed by Charlie Watts, who formed the 'Hail Mosley' and 'F 'em all Association'. As Simpson notes, 'There is absolutely nothing to equal persecution for consolidating ideological belief.'

Churchill was approached via his wife, Clementine, on behalf of Diana, to see if the Mosleys could be imprisoned together. On 23 September 1941 Baba dined with the PM, David Margesson and Halifax. Churchill 'saw no disadvantages in putting the couples together but Herbert Morrison will be the stumbling block. He is hard, narrow-minded and far from human about a matter like this, and in this case he has a special dislike of Tom.' When Baba said it was awful to see Mosley in prison, the PM agreed but warned 'it may be for years and years'. On 15 November he told Morrison he would 'not be prepared to support the regulation indefinitely if it is administered in such an onerous manner'. The Home Secretary was reluctant to do anything on 'security and political grounds', but was willing to release Lady Domvile and transfer the others, except the Mosleys, to married accommodation on the Isle of Man.

Morrison had not wanted to transfer Mosley in case it hardened Fascist attitudes. Celebrations of almost a religious character took place on Mosley's birthday on 16 November. Clement Hill recalled 200 BU members toasting the Leader. 'As the cans were raised, a rustle of curtains turned our gaze in the direction of the stage and a portrait of the Leader came into view . . . No picture, sketch or photograph has ever brought a more spontaneous burst of cheering than that which echoed and re-echoed throughout the building that night.'

Watts channelled the enthusiasm into reconstituting the BU under his leadership with the aim of keeping alive 'the Spirit of BRITAIN FIRST'. MI5 was increasingly concerned that Fascism appeared to be reviving. In October 1941 the British Union of Freemen was caught producing anti-Semitic leaflets advertising the New British Broadcasting Station. The Constitutional Research Association and the People's Common Law Parliament acted as stalking horses for Fascists. The former's leading spirit was Major Harry Edmonds, formerly of the British People's Party and the National Socialist League. Involved with the German Zeppelin company, he founded the Wagner Society after meeting the Wagner family. He was, John Beckett recalled, 'always concerned with much more than musical appreciation'. Edmonds knew Major-General Fuller and was on the Suspect List. On 20 November General Sir Alan Brooke, C.-in-C. Home Forces, talked with the Director of Security about Fuller's Nazi activities but dismissed the idea that he had 'unpatriotic intentions'. However, the blots on his copybook were, as his biographer suggests, 'more than faint smudges'.

MI5's F3 section monitored Fascist, pacifist and nationalist groups, pro-Germans and defeatists. It found the new groups used anti-Semitism and even opposition to an extension of bureaucracy to attract recruits. They were weak financially and numerically, but George Orwell noted the many pockets of anti-Semitism, which was 'not violent but pronounced enough to be disquieting. The Jews are supposed to dodge military service, to be the worst offenders on the Black Market etc. I have heard this kind of talk even from country people who had probably never seen a Jew in their lives.' Hitler claimed in his 'Secret Book' that the struggle between Aryans and Jews in Britain was 'undecided' and in November told confidants he expected an outbreak of anti-Semitism on an 'unparalleled' scale.

On 24 November Morrison agreed to the transfer of couples to married quarters. A medical report persuaded him Mosley might catch pneumonia if he spent the winter in Brixton and the last thing he wanted was to turn him into a martyr. It was announced that the Mosleys would be housed in Holloway. On 21 December they were given a flat in the detention wing and permitted to employ prisoners as servants. Alexander and Max were allowed to stay for two nights. For Diana, 'one of the happiest days of my life was spent in prison'.

They had a floor consisting of a dining room, double bedroom and a communal kitchen. It was referred to as 'Lady Mosley's Suite'. Their neighbour Major de Laessoe was, Diana recalled, an 'admirable person who had won the MC and the DSO in the first war – brave, intelligent and very kind'. She had been suffering from diarrhoea, when the Major 'fished in the trunk which contained all their worldly possessions and gave me an opium pill, which he said always did the trick. I passed into a deep coma for four or five days. One would have felt so awful for the poor major if one had died – he'd have felt such guilt. But it cured me.'

Confinement tested the Mosley marriage but it had an unexpected outcome. It was, Anne de Courcy notes, 'the first time Diana had been the sole focus of Mosley's attention, with neither his political work nor other women to distract him'. They were both 'so personally fastidious that they had until then never so much as shared a bathroom'. Diana overcame the irritations and found Mosley was 'a superb companion, amusing, appreciative of the smallest pleasures, laughing at the absurdities which abound in all institutions, brilliant, loving, even-tempered and unselfish'. Prison welded them together.

Hitler believed in early 1942 that Germany's position in this 'racial war' was stronger. Policy on Britain was co-ordinated by the England Komitee, whose chief, Fritz Hesse, was Ribbentrop's personal liaison to Hitler. The committee included Franz Six, earmarked to oversee Britain in the event of an invasion, Hitler's interpreter Paul Schmidt, Karl von Loesch and Dr Roderich Dietze of the Reich radio service and a friend of William Joyce. Erich Hetzler worked at the Bureau Concordia on radio propaganda and had liaised in London with Dr Roesel, compiling 'White Lists' of potential collaborators.

On 13 January Hitler predicted to Bormann that Churchill would fall but 'they have in reserve men like Mosley. When I think that Mosley and more than 9,000 of his supporters – including some belonging to the best families – are in prison because they didn't want this war!' He suggested to Himmler that 'if Samuel Hoare were to come to power . . . all he'd have to do would be to set free the Fascists. The English have to settle certain social problems which are ripe to be settled . . . Mosley would have had no difficulty in solving the problem, by finding a compromise between Conservatism and Socialism, by opening the road to the masses but without depriving the elite of their rights.' On 26 February he reiterated his belief that if the masses made 'a bloody revolution', the only thing left to the Conservatives 'would be to make an alliance with the 9,000 supporters of Mosley. They'd need a Cromwell to save them, a Premier who would take everything into his own hands.'

The England Committee believed the Mosleyites were in a strong position 'because many of the English are turning away from [Sir Stafford] Cripps and fear Bolshevism'. There was a good opportunity for them to develop

propaganda, which could be 'spread among the English who live in Switzerland, France, Spain and Portugal'. They intended to use Mosley's former
aide-de-camp Dr Tester. With a Gestapo agent, he had set up a myriad of
front companies in Italy, the Balkans, Turkey and Egypt, whose purpose, the
British Foreign Office discovered, was to eliminate Britain's economic interests
in those areas. In Athens at the time of the German occupation in 1941, Tester
worked for *Abwehr* Counter-Intelligence in Bucharest, dealing with allied
intelligence. He was later assigned to 'work' on the case of Major Chastelain,
a US officer parachuted into Romania to offer peace terms to the Romanian
government. When the Iron Guard attempted its putsch in 1941, the SD forces
sent to assist were housed in Tester's estate in Deva.

The *Abwehr*'s von Rohrschiedt considered Tester 'a solid man, who spoke
openly, didn't lie, highly intelligent, a convinced national-socialist, who
believed in the final victory'. He was 'one of those unfortunate men caught
between their two nationalities'. He made money by providing visas for rich
Romanian Jews. Tester was skilled in propaganda operations and during April
1941 suggested broadcasting talks based around Mosley's 'English Revolution' and the British defeats in Europe and Africa. 'It was necessary to put
the plutocrats on trial, Mosley should be freed and named as Prime Minister.'

Tester's articles outlining his relationship with Mosley and the BU's view
of National Socialism and anti-Semitism were collated into a book, *Quo Vadis
England*, which the Nazis considered 'excellent propaganda material'. It was
read by Mussolini who tried to recruit him as a propagandist. German
ambassador von Killinger was against it since it was Tester who had turned
Mosley away from Italian Fascism towards National Socialism. In June 1942
he arrived in Berlin, where, to the *Abwehr*'s fury, the Gestapo arrested him
for fraud. Joyce was wary of a rival and claimed Tester, whom he knew in the
BU, was a 'British agent'. The *Abwehr* insisted the accusations were 'pure
invention' and the Foreign Ministry stepped in and announced Tester was
'under our protection'.

Tester told Paul Schmidt of plans for broadcasts from a transmitter in
Bucharest, designed 'to win over foreign peoples to the new order under
German orientation'. Tester wanted to create an alternative British government, the 'Revolutionary Committee of the British Union'. The project would
be run from Berlin under Foreign Office and the English Committee control.
He proposed the Revolutionary Committee 'declare that it take over the
running of the fascist party for as long as the leaders are imprisoned in
England'. Mosleyites could be 'found amongst British prisoners-of-war and
they will be prepared to take part in propaganda against the British government and to work with the Revolutionary Committee'. Tester hoped it would
lead to 'the formation of cells in various parts of the Empire, especially in
South Africa. This could lead to the formation of revolutionary committees

even in England.' Schmidt believed Tester was 'the man to lead this propaganda action'.

On 18 June 1942 it was agreed in principle to recognize the Revolutionary Committee and to seek BU members in PoW camps. Berlin would compile a list of members and broadcasts would start of 'Mosley's Revolutionary Committee Calling Britain'. It would seek the downfall of Churchill and his replacement by Mosley who would negotiate peace with Germany. The programmes would be 'in a fight directed not against the English people but against the Churchill government and the plutocrats, slaves of the Jews'. They would be repeated from Rome and leaflets would be distributed among PoWs and released over Egypt, in Libya to Montgomery's troops and even in England.

Hesse was cautious and said that if he had been informed Tester was in Berlin he 'could have got somewhere with him. Now too late.' Ribbentrop vetted the proposals but after 'higher consultation' (i.e. Hitler) it was 'decided Mosley must not be endangered. Must save him for later.' Therefore, Tester's 'proposals cannot be carried out' in Romania 'where we have no control over the activities of this dark and not quite reliable man', though there was the possibility of forming a Revolutionary Committee 'in areas under our control'. The idea was sidelined and revived in a different form at the end of the year.

The potential fate of traitors was vividly illustrated by the Special Operations Executive's uncovering of an infiltrator in France during 1942. Agent 'Blanchet' claimed to have penetrated SOE on behalf of Mosley's BU. French agent Marie-Madeleine Fourcade was ordered by MI6's *éminence grise*, Claude Dansey, to kill 'Blanchet' after he admitted betraying a Paris cell and operating a 'double-cross' radio source for the *Abwehr*. The assassination turned into an ordeal. Fourcade ordered her people to administer a lethal cyanide pill but when the poison failed to kill, she told them 'to get him on to a boat and drown him'. The moon, however, proved to be too bright and in the end he was taken out and shot. 'We offered to bring a priest to him,' Fourcade recalled, 'but he refused.'

Mosley pressed for the right to defend himself in court and wrote to Churchill that it was 'wrong that our fellow-countrymen should be given any occasion to think that we have done something disloyal to our country'. He wanted to be able to defend himself 'before the whole nation from any such suggestion.' The Cabinet refused him the opportunity.

Increasing numbers of detainees were released – 150 were still interned – and many were eager to renew political activity. Through visits from supporters such as the Elams and via smuggled-out letters, Mosley retained control over BU members, who wanted to set up an organization which, besides collecting funds to aid released detainees, would fight by-elections on a negotiated peace line with a 'dummy' leader, who could be replaced by Mosley at a suitable moment. As a tactic, Mosley insisted it be non-political and as widely based as possible. Of particular importance in these plans was the *Patriot*, whose circulation was less than 5,000 but 'it reached a wide audience in social clubs and among the forces'. Its offices were a meeting point for anti-Semites and ex-18B detainees.

Set up in August 1942 with funds from the Duke of Bedford, Edward Godfrey's British National Party (BNP), which demanded a negotiated settlement with Hitler, was seen as a revival of the BU. Godfrey, who had served under Domvile in the navy, was a former BU member but denied being a Fascist, preferring the title 'English nationalist'. He was supported by Captain Bernard Acworth of *Truth* and the *Patriot*, and the League of Ex-Servicemen, which helped the BU candidate at Leeds in 1940 and was at the forefront of the Fascist revival.

The *Patriot* helped form in September a charity, the 18B Detainees Aid Fund, and the 18B Publicity Council, run by George Dunlop, a BU speaker in Limehouse. Hoped-for support from Osbert Sitwell, Henry Williamson and Hugh Ross Williamson failed to materialize and, apart from Francis Yeats-Brown, was limited to ex-18Bs and the *Patriot*, though Nora Elam was able 'to re-apply the tactics she had used during suffragette days when she had agitated for the release of her fellow dissidents'. Mosley's solicitor, Oswald Hickson, warned that these groups were 'spending a tremendous amount of money'. Mosley had contributed £1,000 (£20,000) and Bedford £1,500.

The 18B groups were used, as Morrison feared, 'as a nucleus for a political party until the ban on the BU is raised'. Yeats-Brown wrote on 1 December to Henry Williamson, 'So we aren't all sheep, and we still want to hear of British Union!' The first public meeting organized by Acworth on 6 December at Holborn Hall was a reunion for ex-detainees. Mosley hoped new leaders would emerge who would pave the way for his return. After his release, Charlie Watts created a network of ex-BU internees and circulated an underground newspaper, the *Flame*. There were plans for a secret organization based on a cell system. Out of the 'ostracism, ridicule, hate, persecution and punishment', Blackshirts would fight so that 'the new Greater Britain may arise, a new Phoenix, under our children's hands'. Fascist slogans reappeared in London, including the painting by Watts's colleague Arthur Beavan of 'P. J.' on the Lenin memorial.

It was, Morrison told MPs in early 1943, a mistake to believe Mosley's Fascism was a 'weak and pallid affair compared with the European variety'. He was 'not sure there would have been anything soft or gentle if Sir Oswald Mosley had become the Hitler of Great Britain'. He reported there had been attempts to revive the BU. At an 18B meeting in Westminster on 17 March, 500 people heard opposition to Churchill, Russia and the war effort. This was mingled with cries of 'Mosley a hero' and 'filthy Jews'. The popular outcry against such public meetings led to the closure of the BNP. It reappeared in April 1943 as the English National Association and acted as a clearing house for those wanting to revive the BU. However, within the revived groups many were suspicious of those not interned, who were seen as suspect agents provocateurs or MI5 agents. Even the 18B Aid Fund was viewed with suspicion and Special Branch reported on petty jealousies between rivals bidding to attract the Leader's eye. Their mutual dislike of each other and fear of MI5 produced few problems for the authorities.

The England Committee's Paul Schmidt befriended the traitor, John Amery, wayward son of the Secretary of State for India Leo Amery. Captured in France, he joined the circle around the Front Generation socialist turned Fascist Jacques Doriot, and collaborationist leader Marcel Déat. Schmidt saw Amery as an ideal vehicle for propaganda but was unaware of his Jewish background. His father, author of the Balfour Declaration proclaiming British support for a Jewish homeland, hid the fact that his own mother, Elisabeth Leitner, was Jewish.

When Amery arrived in Berlin in September 1942 he met Joyce, who resolved, as he had with Tester, to sabotage his position with the Nazis. In turn, Amery thought Joyce's broadcasts were counter-productive. He told Hesse it was 'insane to carry on as they did calling the British "the enemy" and so forth'. The feud dated back to the time when Amery had been a visitor to the Black House. Anti-Bolshevik, he told Hesse he was 'not interested in a German victory as such' but wanted 'a just peace where we could all get together against the real enemies of civilisation'. Amery was run by Hesse's assistant Ziegveld, a student in England at the outbreak of the last war who had been interned and was a founder member of the Link.

The war was now turning in the Allies' favour and Hitler needed an accommodation with them before a second front was opened in the west, and gave his consent to use Amery as a conduit for peace moves. On 19 November 1942 he repeated on the Reichsrundfunk's English-language service the deal offered two years previously: British acceptance of Germany's position in Europe in return for German non-interference in the Empire. 'Between you and peace stands only the Jew and his tool, namely the Bolshevik and American Governments. I am saying that not as a defeatist but as a patriot whose primary concern is the preservation of the British Empire.' Hitler described Amery as 'by far the best propagandist to England that we have'.

On 28 December Hitler approved an Amery plan to recruit British PoWs for 'an English legion'. 'The only personnel who should come into the framework should be former members of the English Fascist party or those with similar ideology – also quality, not quantity.' The SS Legion of St George would need a platoon strength of thirty men before going into action. An anti-Bolshevik legion 'would have great propaganda value on the Eastern Front' and a

57. Women clash with police in riots at a Fascist Rally, Bermondsey, 1937. Violence erupted as 15,000 anti-fascists tried to stop the 4,000 fascists lead by Mosley

58. The BUF's chief philosopher and propagandist, Alexander Raven Thomson

59. A BUF pamphlet 'Defenders of democracy' with photographs of 'typical specimens snapped at Red demonstrations in London'

60. Diana photographed by Mosley, 1937

61. Diana Mosley was the main channel of communication between her husband and Hitler

62. The former chief engineer of the BBC, Peter Eckersley, was employed by Mosley to front his radio project

63. In 1936 the Mosleys rented Wootton Lodge in Staffordshire. It was convenient for Mosley who held many meetings in the Midlands and North of England

64. Diana, seen here relaxing with her husband, step-daughter Vivien and sister Deborah (the Duchess of Devonshire) at Wootton

(Right) 65. Mosley returned to recuperate at Wootton after a violent meeting in Liverpool on 10 October 1937 where he was hit on the head by a metal object

66. With the looming threat of war, Mosley's peace campaign began to attract large crowds of pro-fascist supporters. A British Union meeting in Bermondsey, south-east London, May Day 1938

67. On the eve of the war, Mosley held at Earls Court his last major meeting, reputedly the largest ever political indoor meeting. It was the epitome of Fascist spectacle with marching bands and banners in the Nazi-style

68. No photograph was believed to exist of the mysterious James McGuirk Hughes (aka P.G. Taylor) but one finally surfaced in 2005 courtesy of his daughter

69. Escaping the clutches of the British authorities was Mosley's adviser, Dr Albert Tester

70. Mosley's military adviser Major-General J.F.C. Fuller was one of the few foreigners to be invited to Hitler's birthday celebrations in 1939

71. Fuller was protected by Field Marshal Ironside, Chief of the Imperial General Staff (1939-40) seen here with Churchill

72. Mosley was reluctantly released in November 1943 by Home Secretary Herbert Morrison because of illness

73. Mosley and Diana lived under near house arrest at the Shaven Crown hotel in Oxfordshire

74. In 1946 Mosley bought a house and farm with 1,000 acres at Crowood, near Ramsbury, Wiltshire. Diana and Mosley seen here with their two sons, Alexander and Max

'devastating effect' on British domestic opinion. The operation was set in train without the unpredictable Amery. When Rheinhardt Spitzy saw him at the Foreign Press Club, he was 'absolutely paralytic and incapable of conducting a conversation'. He was 'plagued by increasingly dark depressions and saw no way out for himself'.

John Brown was one PoW the England Committee hoped to attract. A Royal Artillery sergeant captured on the way to Dunkirk, he had been a manager at Truman's Brewery in Surrey and was the most senior BU member to fall into German hands. BU colleagues said he had been 'fond of a rough-house on the streets of Whitechapel and Bethnal Green against the hated Reds and of course their Jewish co-conspirators'. In fact, he was a 'self-made spy', who learnt the codes to communicate with London from an agent of MI6's escape and evasion organization MI9. British Intelligence learnt from him in February 1943 – the remnants of the German 6th Army had just surrendered in Stalingrad – of plans for a 'British anti-Bolshevik Legion'.

In April, Amery launched his book *England Faces Europe*. In a poor mental state and drunk, on the 8th he mistakenly gave his wife, who requested a headache pill, a poison ampoule which he carried with him to ensure a quick death in the event of being abducted. When the following morning he tried to rouse her she was dead. On 21 April he entered St Denis PoW camp on behalf of a 'committee in England' and appealed to Britons 'to answer this call to arms in defence of our homes . . . against Asiatic and Jewish bestiality. Within the limits of military possibilities, the Legion of St George will fight at the junction of the German and Finnish troops.' He found no support but in Paris told Antonia Hunt, a Briton detained by the SS, that 'when the Germans win the war, we will have the Duke of Windsor as King of occupied England'. An alternative government would be used to enhance peace elements within England.

The England Committee did recruit twenty pro-Germans (PGs) who refused to be imprisoned alongside Jews and regarded Windsor as their king and Mosley as their Leader. They were led by Thomas Cooper, whose mother was German. Working for a firm of oil importers in the East End, he joined the BU's Hammersmith branch in 1938. John Brown became Cooper's assistant and sent the information he collected via coded Red Cross letters to London. Also recruited was Roy Courlander of New Zealand's 2771 Intelligence Section, who had seen at first hand the defeat on Crete and believed the Germans would win the war.

Arrested at the end of the war, Courlander made a statement detailing the Nazi blueprint for Britain presented to them. Hitler had told the England Committee that if the British legion achieved 5,000 recruits, he would countenance the formation of a 'provisional British Government' based on British territory – the German-held Channel Islands. The Duke of Windsor would be held in reserve for when the provisional government moved to London. In autumn 1943 Hitler said that 'after final victory, we must effect a reconciliation. Only the King must go – in his place the Duke of Windsor. With him we will make a permanent treaty of friendship instead of a peace treaty.' The designated SD commander of Britain would be Franz Six, with Mosley acting as PM. Lost in this fantasy world, Amery saw himself as the future foreign minister.

Amery told Courlander an anti-Jewish committee in England had offered £300,000 to fund the Legion. He cited Domvile, Fuller, the Duke of Hamilton and persons associated with the Link, the Anglo-German Fellowship, the Right Club, the 'Cliveden set' and other pre-war pro-German groups. Few picked up on Courlander's fantastical revelations. What is interesting is the similarity of the committee to Haushofer's view of the 'peace party'. Was Amery a victim of the British deception operation sprung in 1941?

Following a German Foreign Office directive, in September 1943 the British Legion was placed in the hands of Waffen-SS recruiter Gottlob Berger. He had 'no great belief in this unit' but within three months the SS possessed a British Free Corps (BFC), largely made up of former BU personnel. 'In our barracks', wrote Alfred Minchin, 'we had a photograph of the Duke of Windsor, whom we all admired as he was also a rebel. We all recognised him as the King of England.' The BFC never fought on the Eastern Front, though Cooper boasted 'he had taken part in atrocities against the Jews'. After the war these renegades were tried and imprisoned.

Excluded from the BFC, Amery travelled to Vichy France and met with BU member Mariette Smart. Daughter of a German mother, she worked as an interpreter in interrogations and accompanied the Gestapo on arrests of Jews, whose deportation she directed. She delighted in betraying her French neighbours and after the war was arrested and sentenced to death by a Court in Cannes. Smart had been recruited as an *Abwehr* agent for missions in Switzerland and Italy, where she met Theodore Schurch, the BU member working for the Italians. When Mussolini was ousted and Italy changed sides in September 1943, Schurch was handed over to the *Abwehr* as a 'going concern' for operations in southern France and northern Italy. Captured in Rome in April 1945 while on a mission to report on Vatican attitudes towards the Allies, he claimed to be Swiss and his defence lawyer pleaded he had been misled by Fascists at home. 'Many more illustrious people than himself held these views,' said Schurch. The court, however, was unmoved and condemned him to be hanged.

During the hot summer of 1943 Diana recalled that she and Mosley stripped off to sunbathe in the prison yard. A priest told a warden it was 'like the Garden of Eden out there – Lady Mosley in her little knickers'. Mosley could

80. Exiling himself to Europe and Ireland for much of the fifties, Mosley returned to the fray following the outbreak of the Notting Hill riots

81. The Mosleys visited Venice with their sons in 1954

(Right) 82. Max seen here with his mother in August 1962, leaving Old Street Magistrates Court, after a hearing held into disturbances in Dalston

75 and 76. Mosley returned to street politics in May 1948 with the formation of the Union Movement

77. Mosley seen here with his main officials and supporters in the UM, Jeffrey Hamm, Commandant Mary Allen, Raven Thomson, Victor Burgess and Tommy Moran

78. A key collaborator was former South African Defence Minister, Oswald Pirow, with whom he constructed the apartheid-minded Euro-Africa policy

79. Mosley's rival in influencing the post-war neo-Nazi networks was a young and deranged American lawyer at the Nuremberg War trials, Francis Parker Yockey